● **End-of-Chapter Cases** are based on
actual organizations and include questions
that ask you to apply chapter concepts to
real situations.

EFFECTIVE
HUMAN RELATIONS:

PERSONAL AND ORGANIZATIONAL APPLICATIONS

EFFECTIVE HUMAN RELATIONS:

PERSONAL AND ORGANIZATIONAL APPLICATIONS

NINTH EDITION

BARRY L. REECE
Virginia Polytechnic Institute and State University

RHONDA BRANDT
Ozarks Technical Community College

HOUGHTON MIFFLIN COMPANY
Boston   New York

12-13-05

EDITOR-IN-CHIEF: George T. Hoffman

ASSOCIATE SPONSORING EDITOR: Joanne Dauksewicz

EDITORIAL ASSISTANT: Kira Robinson-Keates

SENIOR PROJECT EDITOR: Rachel D'Angelo Wimberly

EDITORIAL ASSISTANT: Sarah Cleary

SENIOR PRODUCTION/DESIGN COORDINATOR: Jill Haber

MANUFACTURING MANAGER: Florence Cadran

MARKETING MANAGER: Steven W. Mikels

MARKETING ASSOCIATE: Lisa E. Boden

Cover Image: © Weinberg/Clark/Getty Images

Copyright © 2005 by Houghton Mifflin Company. All rights reserved.

No part of this work may be reproduced or transmitted in any form or by any means, electronic or mechanical, including photocopying and recording, or by any information storage or retrieval system without the prior written permission of Houghton Mifflin Company unless such copying is expressly permitted by federal copyright law. Address inquiries to College Permissions, Houghton Mifflin Company, 222 Berkeley Street, Boston, MA 02116-3764.

Printed in the U.S.A.

Library of Congress Control Number: 2003109900

ISBN: 0-618-34587-6

1 2 3 4 5 6 7 8 9 -- DOW -- 08 07 06 05 04

In memory of my daughter Colleen, 1964-2003

BARRY L. REECE

Patrick, Matthew, Manda, Arabella, and Bairon

RHONDA BRANDT

BRIEF CONTENTS

CO NTENTS

ABOUT THE AUTHORS

Effective Human Relations: Personal and Organizational Applications, ninth edition, represents a compilation of more than twenty-five years of research by authors Barry Reece and Rhonda Brandt. Their combined years of post-secondary teaching experience and on-site consulting with business, industry, and educational institutions provide the basis for their real world approach to human relations skill building. With their diverse backgrounds, they work together to consistently offer their readers up-to-date information and advice in this best-selling text.

Barry L. Reece is a professor at Virginia Polytechnic Institute and State University. He received his Ed.D. from the University of Nebraska. Dr. Reece has been actively involved in teaching, research, consulting, and designing training programs throughout the past three decades. He has conducted more than 500 workshops and seminars devoted to leadership, human relations, communications, sales, customer service, and small business operations. He has received the Excellence in Teaching Award for classroom teaching at Virginia Tech and the Trainer of the Year Award presented by the Valleys of Virginia Chapter of the American Society for Training and Development. Dr. Reece has contributed to numerous journals and is author or co-author of thirty books. He has served as a consultant to Lowe's Companies, Inc., Wachovia Corporation, WLR Foods, Kinney Shoe Corporation, and numerous other profit and not-for-profit organizations.

Rhonda Brandt teaches interpersonal and business communications, human resources management, and various related courses in the Business and Marketing Division of Ozarks Technical Community College in Springfield, Missouri. She received her bachelor's degree in business education with vocational certification from the University of Northern Iowa and a master's degree in Practical Arts and Vocational/Technical Education from the University of Missouri. She has served as a faculty member at Hawkeye Community College and Administrative Support Department Chair at Springfield College. Because of the tremendous demand for Internet-based educational resources, Rhonda is currently planning two new online courses and hopes to be able to teach the Human Relations course online in the near future. Rhonda continues to conduct workshops and seminars for teachers, small businesses, and large corporations throughout the nation, just as she has done for more than twenty-five years.

PREFACE

The importance of human relations can be summarized in one concise law of personal and organizational success: All work is done through relationships. Leaders achieve success when they put people first and strategy second. Employees are more productive when they have the ability to develop effective relationships with their boss, fellow workers, customers, and clients. Organizations are increasingly using relationship-building strategies to develop customer loyalty. The new economy is not just about exchanging information, it is about building relationships.

The goal of each revision of *Effective Human Relations: Personal and Organizational Applications* is to develop the most practical and applied text available. The revision process begins with a thorough review of several hundred articles, books, and research reports. This is followed by numerous reviews by current adopters. We continue to present the timeless fundamentals that apply to a wide range of work settings while searching for new trends and developments that keep the book on the cutting edge. One of the major outcomes of the literature review is the discovery of real world examples that help clarify various human relations concepts and develop student interest.

● Building on Traditional Strengths

Effective Human Relations: Personal and Organizational Applications is one of the most widely adopted human relations texts available today. This book has been successful because the authors continue to build on strengths that have been enthusiastically praised by instructors and students.

■ The **"total person" approach** to human relations has been expanded and enriched in this edition. We continue to believe that human behavior at work and in our private lives is influenced by many interdependent traits such as emotional balance, self-awareness, integrity, self-esteem, physical fitness, and healthy spirituality. This approach focuses on those human relations skills needed to be well-rounded and thoroughly prepared to handle a wide range of human relations problems and issues.

■ This edition, like all previous editions, provides the reader with an in-depth presentation of the **seven major themes of effective human relations:** Communication, Self-Awareness, Self-Acceptance, Motivation, Trust, Self-Disclosure, and Conflict Resolution. These broad themes serve as the foundation for contemporary human relations courses and training programs.

■ Some of the most important human relations concepts are covered in more than one chapter. The various dimensions of the **communication** theme, for example, are discussed in Chapters 2, 3, and 8. Some of the additional chapters focus on specific communication issues and problems. For example,

Chapter 13 discusses ways to communicate fundamentals used in the conflict resolution process. The authors believe that some themes are so multifaceted that they cannot be covered in a single chapter. This text has been successful because it provides complete content coverage.

■ **Self-development opportunities** are strategically placed throughout the entire text. One of the few certainties in today's rapidly changing workplace is the realization that we must assume greater responsibility for developing and upgrading our skills and competencies. In many cases, self-development begins with self-awareness. The text provides multiple opportunities to complete self-assessment activities and then reflect on the results. Each chapter includes thinking/learning starters, end of chapter questions, application exercises, and case problems. Every effort has been made to encourage self-assessment, reflection, planning, and goal setting.

■ A hallmark of this edition, and all previous editions, is the use of many **real world examples** of human relations issues and practices. These examples build the reader's interest and promote understanding of major topics and concepts. Many of the organizations cited in the ninth edition have been recognized by the authors of *The 100 Best Companies to Work for, The 100 Best Corporate Citizens, 100 Best Companies for Working Mothers,* and *America's 50 Best Companies for Minorities.* The ninth edition also includes many examples from successful smaller companies featured in *Inc.* and *Fast Company* magazines and from America's trading partners within the international community.

● Staying on the Cutting Edge

The ninth edition of *Effective Human Relations: Personal and Organizational Applications* has been updated to reflect the growing importance of the human element in our service-oriented, information-saturated, global economy. It is a practical text designed to help students achieve insight, knowledge, and relationship skills needed to deal with a wide range of people-related problems. The most significant changes include:

■ The new edition is a more concise, **tightly focused textbook.** Information not essential to coverage of the topic or concept has been removed. The finished product is very "reader friendly" because the text is focused on important "must know" information. Real world examples that enhance student interest and clarify important concepts are provided in every chapter.

■ In response to suggestions from current adopters and reviewers, and a thorough review of the current literature, **many new topics** are included in this edition. Some examples include a new series of goal-setting principles; root causes of negative attitudes; introduction of the Reiss Profile instrument used to classify our basic desires; the use of "branding" to achieve greater visibility in a crowded job market; discrimination based on a person's religious preference; new ways to classify various forms of technostress; and new support for the importance of emotional intelligence.

■ Several new **Human Relations in Action boxed inserts** have been included in the text. These inserts are a mix of "how to" tips and real world examples that advance our understanding of human relations problems and issues. These inserts also encourage reflection and self-assessment.

■ The ninth edition provides greater **emphasis on diversity.** Coverage of diversity issues and developments is not limited to a single chapter. The challenge of valuing diversity, working across cultures, and learning to work effectively with persons who differ in terms of national origin, race, communication style, religion, gender, and other dimensions of diversity requires support information found in several chapters.

■ The Internet has had a major impact on the workplace. A major effort has been made to integrate **Internet-related content** in appropriate chapters. For example, Chapter 2 provides guidelines for effective use of e-mail correspondence. Chapter 14 provides information on how computer use can result in technostress. In this chapter students learn how to cope with computers and related technologies in a healthy manner.

Every chapter includes an **Internet application exercise.** These exercises include websites complete with reliable URLs. However, because URLs and specific website content can change over time, these exercises are repeated on the text's website, and will be updated as necessary.

■ This edition includes new information on strategies that can be used to **resolve work/life tensions.** Throughout the past few years we have seen an explosion of books, articles, and reports on how to achieve work/life balance. We provide comprehensive coverage of this important area of human relations.

■ Many of the teaching/learning aids featured throughout the text have been updated. Most of the chapter opening vignettes are new to this edition. These real world examples introduce chapter topics and build reader interest in the material. Over half of the case problems have been replaced or rewritten. Many of these focus on an employee issue or problem within the context of a specific organization. Several of the Thinking/Learning Starters within each chapter have been rewritten or replaced, and many new Total Person Insights appear throughout the text.

● Chapter Organization

This book is divided into six parts. **Part I, "Human Relations: The Key to Personal Growth and Career Success,"** provides a strong rationale for the study of human relations and reviews the historical development of this field. One important highlight of Chapter 1 is a detailed discussion of the major developments influencing behavior at work. This material helps students develop a new appreciation for the complex nature of human behavior in a work setting. The communication process, the basis for effective human relations, is explained from both an individual and organizational level in Chapter 2.

Part II, "Career Success Begins with Knowing Yourself," reflects the basic fact that our effectiveness in dealing with others depends in large measure on our self-awareness and self-acceptance. We believe that by building high self-esteem and by learning to explore inner attitudes, motivations, and values, the reader will learn to be more sensitive to the way others think, feel, and act. Complete chapters are devoted to such topics as communication styles, building high self-esteem, personal values and ethical choices, attitude formation, and motivation.

Part III, "Personal Strategies for Improving Human Relations," comprises four chapters that feature a variety of practical strategies that can be used to develop and maintain good relationships with coworkers, supervisors, and managers. Chapters on constructive self-disclosure, learning to achieve emotional control, positive energy, and developing a professional presence are featured in this part of the text.

In **Part IV, "If We All Work Together . . . ,"** the concepts of team building and conflict resolution are given detailed coverage. Because employers are increasingly organizing employees into teams, the chapter on team-building leadership strategies (Chapter 12) takes on new importance. The chapter on conflict resolution (Chapter 13) describes several basic conflict resolution strategies, discusses ways to deal with difficult people, and provides an introduction to the role of labor unions in today's work force.

Part V, "Special Challenges in Human Relations," is designed to help the reader deal with some unique problem areas—coping with personal and work-related stress, working effectively in a diverse work force, and understanding the changing roles of men and women. The reader is offered many suggestions on ways to deal effectively with these modern-day challenges.

Part VI, "You Can Plan for Success," features the final chapter which serves as a capstone for the entire text. This chapter offers suggestions on how to develop a life plan for effective human relations. Students will be introduced to a new definition of success and learn how to better cope with life's uncertainties and disappointments. This chapter also describes the nonfinancial resources that truly enrich a person's life.

Tools That Enhance the Teaching/Learning Process

The extensive supplements package accompanying the ninth edition of *Effective Human Relations: Personal and Organizational Applications* includes a variety of new and traditional tools that will aid both teaching and learning. The supplements emphasize learning by doing.

Classroom Activities Manual   This workbook is much more than just a study guide; it is a manual for independent work as well as in-class participation. Each chapter begins with twenty cognitive study guide questions, as well as a list of chapter objectives in question format. An outline of each chapter is provided for those students who are visual learners. They will be able to see how each segment of the chapter relates to other segments. Every chapter includes a variety of questionnaires, self-assessment instruments, role-playing situations, and small group discussion exercises that will help students improve and internalize the human relations skills presented in that chapter. Each chapter also includes an exercise that deals specifically with valuing diversity, a critical skill that permeates all chapter topics. To access cutting edge information, three Internet searches are suggested for each chapter's specific topic. An opportunity to write a journal entry concludes each chapter.

Student and Instructor Websites   The student website includes a **resource center** with links of general interest to anyone studying human relations, links to the specific companies highlighted in the textbook's boxes and cases, and **ACE self-test questions** to help students prepare for exams.

The instructor website includes downloadable Word files from the **Instructor's Resource Manual** so that instructors can edit the outlines and other teaching materials to suit their own course needs. The site also includes downloadable **PowerPoint® slides,** which provide complete lecture outlines illustrated with figures from the text.

Instructor's Resource Manual with Test Bank   The Instructor's Resource Manual is a complete teaching guide. The opening material provides a review of the most important **teaching and learning principles** that facilitate human relations training, a review of several **teaching methods,** and a description of suggested **term projects.**

Part I, **Chapter Teaching Resources,** provides a chapter preview; chapter purpose and perspective; a presentation outline; and suggested responses to the Thinking/Learning Starters, review questions, and case problem questions for every chapter in the text. Answers, when applicable, are also provided for the text's application exercises.

Additional application exercises are included. Between the material in the textbook and the Instructor's Resource Manual, the instructor can now choose from over 100 application exercises.

Part II contains the **test items** and answers. True/false, multiple-choice, completion, short answer, essay, and mini-case questions are provided.

Part III includes two **instructional games** entitled "Ethical Decision Making" and "Coping with Organizational Politics." The ethics game stimulates in-depth thinking about the ethical consequences of certain decisions and actions. Politics surface in every organization and the politics game prepares the student to cope effectively with common political situations. Each game simulates a realistic business environment where employees must make difficult decisions. Students play these games to learn without having to play for keeps. This section of the Instructor's Resource Manual includes complete instructions on how to administer these learning activities in the classroom.

Part IV of this manual includes the answers to the cognitive study questions in the **Classroom Activities Manual,** as well as suggestions for effective implementation of each of the activities.

Part V provides a list of **instructional videos** and a corresponding list of video vendors. Instructors who wish to supplement their course with videos beyond what is provided in the video program may use this list for reference.

HM Testing   This electronic version of the printed test items allows instructors to generate and change tests easily. The program includes an online testing feature by which instructors can administer tests via their local area network or over the Web. It also has a gradebook feature that lets users set up classes, record and track grades from tests or assignments, analyze grades, and produce class and individual statistics.

Call-in Test Service   This service lets instructors select items from the Test Bank and call our toll-free faculty services number (800–733–1717) to order printed tests.

Video Program   The video package that accompanies the text includes several segments that illustrate important concepts from the text. The videos focus on topics that include ethics, motivation, diversity, leadership, and organizational culture. These videos provide examples from real world organizations and bring chapter content to life. The accompanying **Video Guide** provides a description of each video, suggested uses, and issues for discussion.

Transparency Package   Seventy-five color transparencies are available for use by adopters of the ninth edition of *Effective Human Relations: Personal and Organizational Applications.* The transparency program includes figures, graphs, and key concepts featured in the text, as well as pieces that are exclusive to the transparency program.

Online/Distance Learning Support   Instructors can create and customize online course materials to use in distance learning, distributed learning, or as a supplement to traditional classes. The **Blackboard Course Cartridge** and **WebCT e-Pack** that accompany the text include a variety of study aids for students, as well as course management tools for instructors.

● The Search For Wisdom

The search for what is true, right, or lasting has become more difficult because we live in the midst of an information explosion. The Internet is an excellent source of mass information, but it is seldom the source of wisdom. Television often reduces complicated ideas to a sound bite. Books continue to be one of the best sources of knowledge. Many new books, and several classics, were used as references for the ninth edition of *Effective Human Relations: Personal and Organizational Applications.* A sample of the books we used to prepare this edition follows:

Anger, Rage, and Resentment by Kimes Gustin
The Art of Happiness by the Dalai Lama and Howard C. Culter
Be Your Own Brand by David McNally and Karl D. Speak
Civility—Manners, Morals, and the Etiquette of Democracy by Stephen L. Carter
Complete Business Etiquette Handbook by Barbara Pachter and Majorie Brody
Creative Visualization by Shakti Gawain
Do What You Love . . . The Money Will Follow by Marsha Sinetar

Emotional Intelligence by Daniel Goleman
Empires of the Mind by Denis Waitley
The Four Agreements by Don Miquel Ruiz
Getting to Yes by Roger Fisher and William Ury
How to Control Your Anxiety Before It Controls You by Albert Ellis
How to Win Friends and Influence People by Dale Carnegie
The Human Side of Enterprise by Douglas McGregor
I'm OK—You're OK by Thomas Harris
Minding the Body, Mending the Mind by Joan Borysenko
Multiculture Manners—New Rules of Etiquette For a Changing Society by Norine Dresser
The 100 Absolutely Unbreakable Laws of Business Success by Brian Tracy
1001 Ways to Reward Employees by Bob Nelson
The Power of 5 by Harold H. Bloomfield and Robert K. Cooper
Psycho-Cybernetics by Maxwell Maltz
Re-Engineering the Corporation by Michael Hammer and James Champy
Self-Matters: Creating Your Life from the Inside Out by Phillip C. McGraw
The 7 Habits of Highly Effective People by Stephen Covey
The 17 Essential Qualities of a Team Player by John C. Maxwell
The Situational Leader by Paul Hersey
The Six Pillars of Self-Esteem by Nathaniel Branden
Spectacular Teamwork by Robert R. Blake, Jane Srygley Mouton, and Robert L. Allen
The 10 Natural Laws of Successful Time and Life Management by Hyrum W. Smith
When Talking Makes Things Worse by David Stiebel
Working with Emotional Intelligence by Daniel Goleman
You Just Don't Understand: Women and Men in Conversation by Deborah Tannen

● Acknowledgments

Many people have made contributions to *Effective Human Relations: Personal and Organizational Applications*. Throughout the years the text has been strengthened as a result of numerous helpful comments and recommendations. We extend special appreciation to the following reviewers and advisors who have provided valuable input for this and prior editions:

James Aldrich, *North Dakota State School of Science*
Thom Amnotte, *Eastern Maine Technical College*
Garland Ashbacker, *Kirkwood Community College*
Sue Avila, *South Hills Business School*
Shirley Banks, *Marshall University*
Rhonda Barry, *American Institute of Commerce*
C. Winston Borgen, *Sacramento Community College*
Jayne P. Bowers, *Central Carolina Technical College*
Charles Capps, *Sam Houston State University*
Lawrence Carter, *Jamestown Community College*

Cathy Chew, *Northampton Community College*

John P. Cicero, *Shasta College*

Anne C. Cowden, *California State University Sacramento*

Michael Dzik, *North Dakota State School of Science*

John Elias, *Consultant*

Mike Fernsted, *Bryant & Stratton Business Institute*

Dave Fewins, *Neosho County Community College*

Dean Flowers, *Waukesha County Technical College*

Jill P. Gann, *Ann Arundel Community College*

M. Camille Garrett, *Tarrant County Junior College*

Roberta Greene, *Central Piedmont Community College*

Ralph Hall, *Community College of Southern Nevada*

Sally Hanna-Jones, *Hocking Technical College*

Daryl Hansen, *Metropolitan Community College*

Carolyn K. Hayes, *Polk Community College*

John J. Heinsius, *Modesto Junior College*

Stephen Hiatt, *Catawba College*

Larry Hill, *San Jacinto College—Central*

Bill Hurd, *Lowe's Companies, Inc.*

Dorothy Jeanis, *Fresno City College*

Marlene Katz, *Canada College*

Robert Kegel, Jr., *Cypress College*

Karl N. Kelley, *North Central College*

Vance A. Kennedy, *College of Mateo*

Deborah Lineweaver, *New River Community College*

Thomas W. Lloyd, *Westmoreland County Community College*

Jerry Loomis, *Fox Valley Technical College*

Roger Lynch, *Inver Hills Community College*

Edward C. Mann, *The University of Southern Mississippi*

Paul Martin, *Aims Community College*

James K. McReynolds, *South Dakota School of Mines and Technology*

Russ Moorhead, *Des Moines Area Community College*

Marilyn Mueller, *Simpson College*

Erv J. Napier, *Kent State University*

Barbara Ollhoff, *Waukesha County Technical College*

Leonard L. Palumbo, *Northern Virginia Community College*

James Patton, *Mississippi State University*

C. Richard Paulson, *Mankato State University*

Naomi W. Peralta, *The Institute of Financial Education*

William Price, *Virginia Polytechnic Institute and State University*

Shirley Pritchett, *Northeast Texas Community College*

Linda Pulliam, *Pulliam Associates Chapel Hill, N.C.*

Lynne Reece, *Alternative Services*

Jack C. Reed, *University of Northern Iowa*

Robert Schaden, *Schoolcraft College*

Mary R. Shannon, *Wenatchie Valley College*

J. Douglas Shatto, *Muskingum Area Technical College*

Marilee Smith, *Kirkwood Community College*

Cindy Stewart, *Des Moines Area Community College*
Rahmat O. Tavallali, *Wooster Business College*
V. S. Thakur, *Community College of Rhode Island*
Linda Truesdale, *Midlands Technical College*
Wendy Bletz Turner, *New River Community College*
Marc Wayner, *Hocking Technical College*
Tom West, *Des Moines Area Community College*
Steven Whipple, *St. Cloud Technical College*
Burl Worley, *Allan Hancock College*

We would also like to thank Amy E. Anderson of the University of Dayton for her assistance in revising the test items and preparing ACE questions for the student website; and Lynn Bradman of Metropolitan Community College for preparing the PowerPoint slides.

Over 200 business organizations, government agencies, and nonprofit institutions provided us with the real world examples that appear throughout the text. We are grateful to organizations that allowed us to conduct interviews, observe workplace environments, and use special photographs and materials.

The partnership with Houghton Mifflin, which has spanned nearly three decades, has been very rewarding. Several members of the Houghton Mifflin College Division staff have made important contributions to this project. Sincere appreciation is extended to Joanne Dauksewicz who has worked conscientiously on the text from the planning stage to completion of the book. We also offer sincere thanks to other key contributors: George Hoffman, Rachel D'Angelo Wimberly, Sarah Cleary, Jill Haber, Florence Cadran, Steven Mikels, and Lisa Boden.

BARRY L. REECE
RHONDA BRANDT

EFFECTIVE
HUMAN RELATIONS:

PERSONAL AND ORGANIZATIONAL APPLICATIONS

PART I

HUMAN RELATIONS: THE KEY TO PERSONAL GROWTH AND CAREER SUCCESS

1 INTRODUCTION TO HUMAN RELATIONS

2 IMPROVING PERSONAL AND ORGANIZATIONAL COMMUNICATIONS

1

1

INTRODUCTION TO HUMAN RELATIONS

Chapter Preview

After studying this chapter, you will be able to

- Understand how the study of human relations will help you achieve career success and increased work/life balance.

- Explain the nature, purpose, and importance of human relations in an organizational setting.

- Identify major developments in the workplace that have given new importance to human relations.

- Identify major forces influencing human behavior at work.

- Review the historical development of the human relations movement.

- Identify seven basic themes that serve as the foundation for effective human relations.

Each year *Fortune* magazine publishes a list of the 100 best companies to work for in America. Job seekers study the list carefully because these are the companies where morale is high and relationships are characterized by a high level of trust and camaraderie. The list changes each year because more companies are discovering ways to attract talented new employees and to keep current employees who have helped make the company successful. Companies, in fact, compete for a place on the list.

Some companies rank near the top of the list year after year. One such example is SAS Institute, a software developer based in Cary, North Carolina. The company offers a state-of-the-art fitness center, an on-site health center, flexible work schedules, and day care for children. Its forty-six hundred U.S. employees have a rewarding work life and a life outside of work.

The Container Store, a chain of retail stores that sell high-quality storage and organizational products for home or office, ranked number one on the 2000 list and number two on the 2001 and 2002 lists. Visit a Container Store and you notice that employees are honestly happy and that they delight in providing outstanding service to customers. Employees also display a fierce sense of ownership in the company. The owners share everything with employees, including financial information. This emphasis on communication helps nurture intense employee loyalty. In an industry where employee turnover ranges from 80 to 130 percent, it is 15 percent at The Container Store.[1]

Both of these companies emphasize open communication, employee loyalty, and meaningful work. Like other top companies on the *Fortune* list, they put people first and believe that cutting jobs should be the last thing a company does rather than the first thing.

The SAS Institute is the world's largest software company in private hands. Year after year it ranks near the top of *Fortune* magazine's list of 100 best companies to work for in America. The 200-acre SAS campus offers employees a gym, cafeteria (with pianist), childcare, and a health clinic.

The Nature, Purpose, and Importance of Human Relations

Many of America's best-managed organizations are not simply being "nice to people"; they are genuinely helping employees come alive through their work. We have learned that the goals of worker and workplace need not be in conflict. America's best companies also realize that all work is done through relationships. This chapter focuses on the nature of human relations, its development, and its importance to the achievement of individual and organizational goals.

● Human Relations Defined

The term **human relations** in its broadest sense covers all types of interactions among people—their conflicts, cooperative efforts, and group relationships. It is the study of *why* our beliefs, attitudes, and behaviors sometimes cause relationship problems in our personal lives and in work-related situations. The study of human relations emphasizes the analysis of human behavior, prevention strategies, and resolution of behavioral problems.

● Human Relations in the Age of Information

The restructuring of America from an industrial economy to an information economy has had a profound impact on interpersonal relationships. Living in an age in which the effective exchange of information is the *foundation* of most economic transactions means making major life adjustments. Many people feel a sense of frustration because they must cope with a glut of information that arrives faster than they can process it. The age of information has spawned the information technology revolution, and many workers experience stress as they try to keep up with ever changing technology.

Fast Company magazine asked its superbusy readers to reflect on this question: Does the new economy leave you feeling tested, bested, toasted, and roasted? Most readers probably answered with a resounding yes! Increased reliance on information technology often comes at a price—less human contact. Sources of connection away from work are also being trimmed way back. Unfortunately, a human-contact deficiency weakens the spirit, the mind, and the body.[2] To thrive, indeed to just survive, we need warm-hearted contact with other people.

The authors of *The Social Life of Information* describe another price we pay for living in the age of information. A great number of people are focusing on information so intently that they miss the very things that provide valuable balance and perspective. Neglecting the cues and clues that lie outside the tight focus on information can limit our effectiveness. Think about written proposals negotiated on the Internet and signed by electronic signature. Such transactions lack the essence of a face-to-face meeting: a firm handshake and a straight look in the eye. Today's knowledge worker needs to take more account of people and a little less of information.[3]

The Importance of Human Relations

One of the most significant developments in the age of information has been the increased importance of interpersonal skills in almost every type of work setting. Technical ability is often not enough to achieve career success. Studies indicate that many of the people who have difficulty in obtaining or holding a job, or advancing to positions of greater responsibility, possess the needed technical competence but lack interpersonal competence.

Several important developments in the workplace have given new importance to human relations. Each of the following developments provides support for human relations in the workplace.

- *The labor market has become a place of churning dislocation caused by the heavy volume of mergers, acquisitions, business closings, bankruptcies, and downsizings.* Layoffs in America, which often exceed 200,000 workers per month, have many negative consequences. Large numbers of companies are attempting to deal with serious problems of low morale and mistrust of management caused by years of upheaval and restructuring. Employees who remain after a company reduces its ranks also suffer; they often feel demoralized, overworked, and fearful that in the next round of cuts they will be targeted.[4]

- *Changing work patterns create new opportunities and new challenges.* Massive downsizing has resulted in the large-scale use of temporary workers. Strong demand for temps has surfaced in such diverse fields as medical services, banking, heavy manufacturing, and computers. During tough economic times we have seen the creation of a phenomenon called "Free

Agent Nation," the growth of self-employed workers who are engaged in consulting and contract work. About 16 million people are now "soloists." Telecommuting, another significant workplace trend, now involves nearly 20 million workers.[5] Finally, you can expect to work for many different employers. The U.S. Department of Labor reports that workers hold an average of nine jobs before turning 32. These and other trends will continue to change where, when, and how we work.

■ *Organizations are increasingly oriented toward service to clients, patients, and customers.* We live in a service economy where relationships are often more important than products. Restaurants, hospitals, banks, public utilities, colleges, airlines, and retail stores all must now gain and retain the patronage of their clients and customers. In any service-type firm, there are thousands of "moments of truth," those critical incidents in which customers come into contact with the organization and form their impressions of its quality and service.

In the new economy almost every source of organizational success—technology, financial structure, and competitive strategy—can be copied in an amazingly short period of time.[6] To illustrate, let's revisit The Container Store. The layout of these stores, store policies, and inventory could be duplicated by a competitor in a short period of time. However, making customers the center of the company culture takes years.

We live in a service economy where relationships are often more important than products.

TOTAL PERSON INSIGHT	**HARRY E. CHAMBERS** AUTHOR, *THE BAD ATTITUDE SURVIVAL GUIDE* "No matter what we do, we do it with people. People create the technology. People implement the technology. People make it all happen. People ultimately use whatever it is we create. No matter how small your organization or how technical its process, it takes people to be successful."

■ *Workplace incivility is increasingly a threat to employee relationships.* A popular business magazine featured a cover story entitled "The Death of Civility."[7] The author describes an epidemic of coarse and obnoxious behavior that weakens worker relationships. At a team meeting, a member's cell phone rings several times and is finally answered. As the person talks loudly on the phone, the rest of the team members wait. An employee routinely brushes his teeth at the drinking fountain, and the boss takes three phone calls during an important meeting with an employee. Stephen L. Carter, author of *Civility,* believes that rudeness, insensitivity, and disrespect are the result of people believing in "me" rather than "we." He says civility is the sum of many sacrifices we are called on to make for the sake of living and working together.[8]

■ *Many companies are organizing their workers into teams in which each employee plays a part.* Organizations eager to improve quality, improve job satisfaction, increase worker participation in decision making and problem solving, and improve customer service are turning to teams.

Many organizations are structured around teams. Team-based structures have become popular because they encourage greater employee involvement. Team members need skills in group decision making, leadership, conflict resolution, and communication.

Although some organizations have successfully harnessed the power of teams, others have encountered problems. One barrier to productivity is the employee who lacks the skills needed to be a team member. In making the transition to a team environment, team members need skills in group decision making, leadership, conflict resolution, and communications.[9]

■ *Diversity has become a prominent characteristic of today's work force.* A number of trends have contributed to greater work force diversity. Throughout the past two decades, participation in the labor force by Asians, African Americans, and Hispanics has increased; labor force participation by adult women has risen to a record 60 percent; the employment door for people with physical or mental impairments has opened wider; and larger numbers of young workers are working with members of the expanding 50-plus age group. Within this heterogeneous work force we will find a multitude of values, expectations, and work habits. There is a need to develop increased tolerance for persons who differ in age, gender, race, physical traits, and sexual orientation. The major aspects of work force diversity are discussed in Chapters 15 and 16.

■ *Growing income inequality has generated a climate of resentment and distrust.* Most measures of income and wage distribution indicate that the wage gap continues to exist. The top 20 percent of American families on average earn about $10 for every dollar earned by the bottom 20 percent. About 31 million people live in poverty, and over 40 million do not have health insurance. Scientists are finding that socioeconomic status—our relative status influenced by income, job, education, and other factors—impacts our physical and mental health. Most agree that psychological factors such as pessimism, stress, and shame are burdens of low social class.[10]

HUMAN RELATIONS IN ACTION

Civility Under Siege

Rude, obnoxious behavior is not illegal, according to a recent court ruling. The U.S. Court of Appeals in Chicago upheld a lower court dismissal of a lawsuit in which a black female employee of S. C. Johnson & Company charged a male coworker with sexual and racial harassment. The man had berated her with obscenities (some with racial overtones), let a door slam in her face, and cut her off in the parking lot. The court found that the man treated all his coworkers with disrespect and concluded that "equal opportunity harassers" are not guilty of discrimination.

These developments represent trends that will no doubt continue for many years. Many other developments have also had an unsettling impact on the U.S. work force in recent years. In 2001 the economy was jarred by the collapse of several hundred dot.com companies. The World Trade Center terrorist attack on September 11, 2001, crippled the airline and aerospace industries. Soon after this tragic event, Boeing Company cut thirty thousand jobs and over one hundred thousand airline employees were fired or furloughed. In 2002 public trust in the corporate establishment was shaken by a wave of corporate scandals that involved Enron, Tyco, Merrill Lynch, Arthur Anderson, WorldCom, and many other companies.

It is safe to say that no line of work, organization, or industry will enjoy immunity from these developments. Today's employee must be adaptable and flexible to achieve success within a climate of change and uncertainty.

● The Challenge of Human Relations

To develop and apply the wide range of interpersonal skills needed in today's workplace can be extremely challenging. You will be working with clients, customers, patients, and other workers who vary greatly in age, work background, communications style, values, cultural background, gender, and work ethic. Because every person you come in contact with is unique, each encounter offers a new challenge.

Human relations is further complicated by the fact that we must manage three types of relationships (see Figure 1.1). The first relationship is the one with ourselves. Many people carry around a set of ideas and feelings about themselves that are quite negative and in most cases quite inaccurate. People who have negative feelings about their abilities and accomplishments and who engage in constant self-criticism must struggle to maintain a good relationship with themselves. The importance of high self-esteem is addressed in Chapter 4.

The second type of relationship we must learn to manage is the one-to-one relationships we face in our personal and work lives. People in the health care field, sales, food service, and a host of other occupations face this challenge many times each day. In some cases, racial, age, or gender bias serves as a barrier to good human relations. Communication style bias, a topic that is dis-

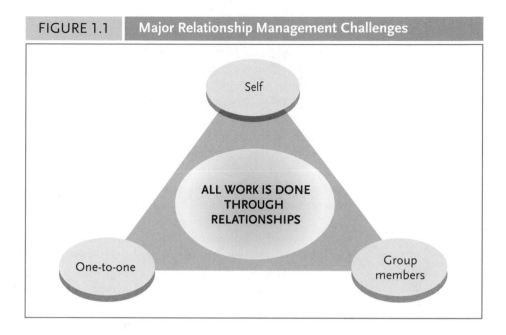

FIGURE 1.1 | **Major Relationship Management Challenges**

Self

ALL WORK IS DONE
THROUGH
RELATIONSHIPS

One-to-one

Group
members

cussed in Chapter 3, is another common barrier to effective one-to-one relationships.

The third challenge we face is the management of relationships with members of a group. As already noted, many workers are assigned to a team on either a full-time or a part-time basis. Lack of cooperation among team members can result in quality problems or a slowdown in production.

● The Influence of the Behavioral Sciences

The field of human relations draws on the behavioral sciences—psychology, sociology, and anthropology. Basically, these sciences focus on the *why* of human behavior. Psychology attempts to find out why *individuals* act as they do, and sociology and anthropology concentrate primarily on *group* dynamics and social interaction. Human relations differs from the behavioral sciences in one important respect. Although also interested in the why of human behavior, human relations goes further and looks at what can be done to anticipate problems, resolve them, or even prevent them from happening. In other words, this field emphasizes knowledge that can be *applied* in practical ways to problems of interpersonal relations at work or in our personal life.

● Human Relations and the "Total Person"

The material in this book focuses on human relations as the study of *how people satisfy both personal and work-related needs.* We believe, as do most authors in the field of human relations, that such human traits as physical fitness, emotional control, self-awareness, self-esteem, and values orientation are interdependent. Although some organizations may occasionally wish they could employ only a person's physical strength or creative powers, all that can be employed is the **total person.** A person's separate characteristics are part of a single system making up that whole person. Work life is not totally separate from home life, and emotional conditions are not separate from physical conditions. The quality of one's work, for example, is often related to physical fitness or one's ability to cope with the stress created by family problems.

Many organizations are beginning to recognize that when the whole person is improved, significant benefits accrue to the firm. These organizations are establishing employee development programs that address the total person, not just the employee skills needed to perform the job. At 3M Corporation employees attend lunchtime seminars on financial planning, parenting, and other topics that help them achieve work/life balance. Intuit, maker of Quicken software, provides workers with on-site dental services, yoga classes, and home loan assistance. The wellness center at Tires Plus corporate headquarters offers classes on nutrition and healthy cooking, weight loss, and smoking cessation.[11]

Synovus Service Corporation, ranked near the top of *Fortune's* list of the 100 best companies to work for, strongly supports the total person concept. Genie Mize, director of the Center for People Development of Synovus, says, "We make sure we look at the whole person, and in doing so, we truly believe that they are going to be producing at a level that benefits not only themselves, but also the business."[12]

TOTAL PERSON INSIGHT	**DANIEL GOLEMAN**
	AUTHOR, *WORKING WITH EMOTIONAL INTELLIGENCE*
	"The rules for work are changing, and we're all being judged, whether we know it or not, by a new yardstick—not just how smart we are and what technical skills we have, which employers see as givens, but increasingly by how well we handle ourselves and one another."

● The Need for a Supportive Environment

Lee Iacocca, the man who was credited with helping Chrysler Corporation avoid bankruptcy, said that all business operations can be reduced to *people, product,* and *profit.* He believed that people come first. Iacocca understood that people are at the heart of every form of quality improvement.

Some managers do not believe that total person development, job enrichment, motivation techniques, or career development strategies help increase productivity or strengthen worker commitment to the job. It is true that when such practices are tried without full commitment or without full management support, there is a good chance they will fail. Such failures often have a demoralizing effect on employees and management alike.

A basic assumption of this book is that human relations, when applied in a positive and supportive environment, can help individuals achieve greater personal satisfaction from their careers and help increase an organization's productivity and efficiency.

The Forces Influencing Behavior at Work

A major purpose of this text is to increase your knowledge of factors that influence human behavior in a variety of work settings. An understanding of human behavior at work begins with a review of the six major forces that affect every employee, regardless of the size of the organization. As Figure 1.2 indicates, these are organizational culture, supervisory-management influence, work group influence, job influence, personal characteristics of the worker, and family influence.

FIGURE 1.2 | Major Forces Influencing Worker Behavior

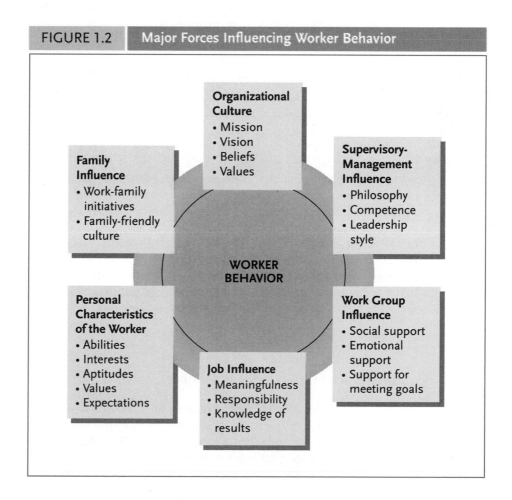

● Organizational Culture

Every organization, whether a manufacturing plant, retail store, hospital, or government agency, has its own unique culture. The **organizational culture** is the collection of shared values, beliefs, rituals, stories, and myths that foster a feeling of community among organizational members.[13] The culture of an organization is, in most cases, the reflection of the deeply held values and behaviors of a small group of individuals. In a large organization, the chief executive officer (CEO) and a handful of senior executives will shape the culture. In a small company, the culture may flow from the values held by the founder.[14]

Enron Corporation, the second-largest company in U.S. history to file for bankruptcy, maintained a corporate culture that pushed everything to the limits: business practices, laws, and personal behavior. This culture drove Enron to dizzying growth, but it eventually collapsed under the weight of greed, deception, and corruption.[15]

By contrast, eBay, the auction website company, has developed a culture that emphasizes customer service and a loyal work force. The culture is based on two principles: "We believe people are basically good" and "We believe everyone has something to contribute."[16]

Many employees are fired or choose to quit their jobs because they are a poor fit with the corporate culture. It's a good idea to carefully study the organization culture of a company before accepting employment there.

HUMAN RELATIONS IN ACTION | **Timberland Culture in the Age of Information**

At a recent conference, Jeffrey Swartz, CEO of Timberland Company, described the evolution of his company. He explained that his grandfather had started the company, making boots by hand. Everything about the process was personal: "When he sold you a pair of boots and promised that the boots would last a lifetime, it wasn't a customer-service program. It was my grandfather looking you in the eye and making a personal promise that if anything went wrong, you could bring the boots back and he himself would make

you another pair." Later Jeffrey Swartz's father took over Timberland and made it a national company. Today, the third-generation CEO says his challenge is to make the business personal all over again. He says, "These days, when people buy something from you, they want to know who you are, what you believe in."

Swartz also believes in giving something back to the community. Every employee gets paid for 40 hours a year of volunteer work.

● Supervisory-Management Influence

Supervisory-management personnel are in a key position to influence employee behavior. It is no exaggeration to say that supervisors and managers are the spokespersons for the organization. Their philosophy, competence, and leadership style establish the organization's image in the eyes of employees. Each employee develops certain perceptions about the organization's concern for his or her welfare. These perceptions, in turn, influence such important factors as productivity, customer relations, safety consciousness, and loyalty to the firm.

Supervisory-management personnel hold the key to both outlook and performance. They are in a unique position to unlock the internal forces of motivation and help employees channel their energies toward achieving the goals of the organization.[17]

TOTAL	**WILLIAM RASPBERRY**
PERSON	SYNDICATED COLUMNIST
INSIGHT	"Jobs do a lot more than merely provide income. They provide the opportunity to learn and enhance skills, to have some control over one's fate and, perhaps most important, to gain a sense of self-worth, a sense of carrying one's own weight."

● Work Group Influence

In recent years, behavioral scientists have devoted considerable research to determining the influence of group affiliation on the individual worker. This research has identified three functions of group membership. First, it can satisfy *social needs*. Several studies have found that having a best friend at work is one of the employee circumstances most likely to signal a highly productive workplace. When employees feel more connected to their colleagues at work, they are generally more productive.[18] Many people find the hours spent at work enjoyable because coworkers provide needed social support. Second, the work group can provide the *emotional support* needed to deal with pressures and problems on or off the job. Finally, the group provides *assistance in solving problems and meeting goals*. A cohesive work group lends support and provides the resources we need to be productive workers.

These considerations are especially important in light of today's mergers and acquisitions, which can have a disruptive influence on a network of friends. Workplace ties are often torn apart as a result of layoffs and restructuring. A major shift to a contingent (temporary) work force can also hasten the decline in workplace intimacy.

● Job Influence

Work in modern societies does more than fulfill economic needs. When we find meaning and fulfillment in our jobs, we become more complete as human beings.[19] As one organizational consultant noted, work has taken center stage in the lives of most people: "We spend most of our waking hours doing our jobs, thinking about work, and getting to and from our workplaces. When we feel good about our work, we tend to feel good about our lives. When we find our work unsatisfying and unrewarding, we don't feel good."[20] Unfortunately, many people hold jobs that do not make them feel good. Many workers perceive their jobs to be meaningless and boring. Some workers experience frustration because they are powerless to influence their working conditions.

"We spend most of our waking hours doing our jobs, thinking about work, and getting to and from our workplaces."

● Personal Characteristics of the Worker

Every worker brings to the job a combination of abilities, interests, aptitudes, values, and expectations. Worker behavior on the job is most frequently a reflection of how well the work environment accommodates the unique characteristics of each worker. For more than half a century, work researchers and theorists have attempted to define the ideal working conditions that would maximize worker productivity. These efforts have met with some success, but unanswered questions remain.

Identifying the ideal work environment for today's work force is difficult. A single parent may greatly value a flexible work schedule and child care. The recipient of a new business degree may seek a position with a new high-tech firm, hoping to make a lot of money in a hurry. Other workers may desire more leisure time.

Coming into the workplace today is a new generation of workers with value systems and expectations about work that differ from those of the previous generation. Today's better-educated and better-informed workers value identity and achievement. They also have a heightened sense of their rights.

● Family Influence

A majority of undergraduates name balancing work and personal life as their top career goal.[21] Most people want time for family, friends, and leisure pursuits. However, finding employers who truly support work/life balance can be difficult, especially during a slowing economy.

The New Economy is a 24/7 economy. When businesses operate twenty-four hours a day, seven days a week, the result is often a culture of relentless overwork. In many cases workers must live with on-call-all-the-time work schedules. In the service industry, the 24/7 schedule is usually driven by consumer demand. In manufacturing, it is more likely driven by economics. Every hour a costly plant sits idle is a drain on the bottom line.

The number of dual-income families has doubled since 1950. Both parents have jobs in 63 percent of married-couple homes. When both partners are working long hours, it's difficult to stay committed to a good life together. A study conducted by Howard Markman, University of Denver psychology professor, found that marital distress costs companies over $6 billion in lost productivity. He encourages companies to invest in relationship-building programs that help employees maintain healthy marriages.[22]

Many organizations have found that family problems are often linked to employee problems such as tardiness, absenteeism, and turnover. The discovery has led many companies to develop work-family programs and policies that help employees juggle the demands of children, spouses, and elderly parents.[23]

The Development of the Human Relations Movement

The early attempts to improve productivity in manufacturing focused mainly on trying to improve such things as plant layout and mechanical processes. But over time, there was more interest in redefining the nature of work and perceiving workers as complex human beings. This change reflected a shift in values from a concern with *things* to a greater concern for *people*. In this section we briefly examine a few major developments that influenced the human relations movement.

The Impact of the Industrial Revolution

The Industrial Revolution marked a shift from home-based, handcrafted processes to large-scale factory production. Prior to the Industrial Revolution, most work was performed by individual craftworkers or members of craft guilds. Generally, each worker saw a project through from start to finish. Skills such as tailoring, carpentry, and shoemaking took a long time to perfect and were often a source of pride to an individual or a community. Under this system, however, output was limited.

The Industrial Revolution had a profound effect on the nature of work and the role of the worker. Previously, an individual tailor could make only a few items of clothing in a week's time; factories could now make hundreds. However, the early industrial plants were not very efficient because there was very little uniformity in the way tasks were performed. It was this problem that set the stage for research by a man who changed work forever.

Taylor's Scientific Management

In 1874 Frederick W. Taylor obtained a job as an apprentice in a machine shop. He rose to the position of foreman, and in this role he became aware of the inefficiency and waste throughout the plant. In most cases workers were left on their own to determine how to do their jobs. Taylor began to systematically study each job and break it down into its smallest movements. He discovered ways to reduce the number of motions and get rid of time-wasting efforts. Workers willing to follow Taylor's instruction found that their productivity soared.[24]

Frederick W. Taylor started the **scientific management** movement, and his ideas continue to influence the workplace today. Critics of Taylor's approach say that the specialized tasks workers perform often require manual skills but very little or no thinking. It's fair to say that Taylor's ideas gave workers the means to work more efficiently, but they left decisions about how the work should be done to foremen and supervisors.[25]

TOTAL	**JAMES BAUGHMAN**
PERSON	DIRECTOR OF MANAGEMENT DEVELOPMENT, GENERAL ELECTRIC CO.
INSIGHT	"You can only get so much more productivity out of reorganization and automation. Where you really get productivity leaps is in the minds and hearts of people."

Mayo's Hawthorne Studies

Elton Mayo and his colleagues accidentally discovered part of the answer to variations in worker performance while conducting research in the mid-1920s at the Hawthorne Western Electric plant, located near Chicago. Their original goal was to study the effect of illumination, ventilation, and fatigue on production workers in the plant. Their research, known as the **Hawthorne studies,** became a sweeping investigation into the role of human relations in group and individual productivity. These studies also gave rise to the profession of industrial psychology by legitimizing the human factor as an element in business operations.[26]

After three years of experimenting with lighting and other physical aspects of work, Mayo made two important discoveries. First, all the attention focused on workers who participated in the research made them feel more important. For the first time, they were getting feedback on their job performance. In addition, test conditions allowed them greater freedom from supervisory control. Under these circumstances, morale and motivation increased and productivity rose.

Second, Mayo found that the interaction of workers on the job created a network of relationships called an **informal organization.** This organization exerted considerable influence on workers' performance.

Although some observers have criticized the Hawthorne studies for flawed research methodology,[27] this research can be credited with helping change the way management viewed workers.

● From the Great Depression to the New Millennium

During the Great Depression, interest in human relations research waned as other ways of humanizing the workplace gained momentum. During that period, unions increased their militant campaigns to organize workers and force employers to pay attention to such issues as working conditions, higher pay, shorter hours, and protection for child laborers.

After World War II and during the years of postwar economic expansion, interest in the human relations field increased. Countless papers and research studies on worker efficiency, group dynamics, organization, and motivational methods were published. Douglas McGregor, in his classic book *The Human Side of Enterprise,* argued that how well an organization performs is directly proportional to its ability to tap human potential.[28] Abraham Maslow, a noted psychologist, devised a "hierarchy of needs," stating that people satisfied their needs in a particular order. Later Frederick Herzberg proposed an important theory of employee motivation based on satisfaction. Each theory had considerable influence on the study of motivation and is explored in detail in Chapter 7.

Since the 1950s, theories and concepts regarding human behavior have focused more and more on an understanding of human interaction. Eric Berne in the 1960s revolutionized the way people think about interpersonal communication when he introduced transactional analysis, with its "Parent-Adult-Child" model. At about the same time, Carl Rogers published his work on personality development, interpersonal communication, and group dynamics. In the early 1980s, William Ouchi introduced the Theory Z style of management, which is based on the belief that worker involvement is the key to increased productivity.

There is no doubt that management consultants Tom Peters and Robert Waterman also influenced management thinking regarding the importance of people in organizations. Their best-selling book *In Search of Excellence,* published in 1982, describes eight attributes of excellence found in America's best-run companies. One of these attributes, "productivity through people," emphasizes that excellent companies treat the worker as the root source of quality and productivity. The editors of *Fast Company* magazine say that *In Search of Excellence* "fired the starting gun in the race to the New Economy."[29]

We have provided you with no more than a brief glimpse of selected developments in the human relations movement. Space does not permit a review of the hundreds of theorists and practitioners who have influenced human relations in the workplace. However, in the remaining chapters, we do introduce the views of other influential thinkers and authors.

THINKING / LEARNING STARTERS

1. What do you personally find to be the basic rewards of work?

2. The book *In Search of Excellence* cites "productivity through people" as an attribute of excellent companies. Do you agree or disagree with this view?

3. What degree of worker involvement have you experienced in places where you have worked or volunteered?

Major Themes in Human Relations

Seven broad themes emerge from the study of human relations. They are communication, self-awareness, self-acceptance, motivation, trust, self-disclosure, and conflict resolution. These themes reflect the current concern in human relations with the twin goals of (1) personal growth and development and (2) the achievement of organizational objectives. To some degree, these themes are interrelated (see Figure 1.3), and most are discussed in more than one chapter of this book.

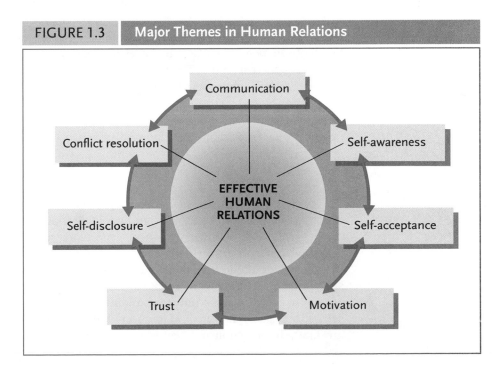

FIGURE 1.3 Major Themes in Human Relations

● **Communication**

> *It is not an exaggeration to describe communication as the "heart and soul" of human relations.*

It is not an exaggeration to describe communication as the "heart and soul" of human relations. **Communication** is the means by which we come to an understanding of ourselves and others. To grow and develop as persons, we must develop the awareness and the skills necessary to communicate effectively. John Diekman, author of *Human Connections,* says that "if we are going to do anything constructive and helping with one another, it must be through our communication."[30] Communication is the *human* connection. That is why the subject is covered in more than one section of this book. In Chapter 2 we explore the fundamentals of both personal and organizational communication. It is these fundamentals that provide the foundation for all efforts to improve communication. Chapter 3 provides an introduction to communications styles and outlines several practical tips on how you can cope with communication style bias. Chapter 8 explains how constructive self-disclosure, an important form of personal communication, can be used to improve human relationships.

● **Self-Awareness**

One of the most important ways to develop improved relationships with others is to develop a better understanding of ourselves. With increased **self-awareness** comes a greater understanding of how our behavior influences others. Stephen Covey, author of *The Seven Habits of Highly Effective People,* says that self-awareness enables us to stand apart and examine the way we "see" ourselves, as well as to see other people.[31]

The importance of self-awareness is being recognized by an increasing number of authors, trainers, and educators. Daniel Goleman, author of the best-selling book *Emotional Intelligence,* has given us new insights into the importance of self-awareness. Goleman says IQ accounts for only about 20 percent of a person's success in life. The rest, he says, you can credit to "emotional intelligence." Of all the elements that make up emotional intelligence, Goleman asserts, self-awareness is the most important. He notes that a deficit in self-awareness can be damaging to one's personal relationships and career.[32] Self-awareness is discussed in greater detail in the chapters that are featured in Part II.

● **Self-Acceptance**

The degree to which you like and accept yourself is the degree to which you can genuinely like and accept other people. **Self-acceptance** is the foundation of successful interaction with others. In a work setting, people with positive self-concepts tend to cope better with change, accept responsibility more readily, tolerate differences, and generally work well as team members. A negative self-concept, however, can create barriers to good interpersonal relations. Self-acceptance is crucial not only for building relationships with others but also for setting and achieving goals. The more you believe you can do, the more you are likely to accomplish. Chapter 4 explains why high self-esteem (complete self-acceptance) is essential for effective human relations. That chapter also helps you identify ways to achieve greater self-acceptance.

● Motivation

Most people who engage in the study of **motivation** seek answers to two questions: "How do I motivate myself?" and "How do I motivate others?" If you are really committed to achieving peak performance, you must motivate yourself from within.[33] Inner drives for excellence can be very powerful. To motivate others, you need to understand time-proven, well-researched theories and well-established motivation strategies. Chapter 5 will help you identify the priorities and values that motivate you. Chapter 7 explores the complex nature of motivation, particularly of self and others, and examines various motivation strategies. In Chapter 10 you will learn how incentives and various positive reinforcement methods serve as external motivators.

● Trust

Trust is the building block of all successful relationships with coworkers, customers, family members, and friends. There is compelling evidence that low levels of trust in a work force can lead to reduced productivity, stifled innovation, high stress, and slow decision making.[34] When a lack of trust exists in an organization, a decline in the flow of information almost always results. Employees communicate less information to their supervisors, express opinions reluctantly, and avoid discussions. Cooperation, so necessary in a modern work setting, deteriorates. When a climate of trust is present, frank discussion of problems and a free exchange of ideas and information are encouraged. The concept of trust is discussed in Chapters 8 and 12.

HUMAN RELATIONS IN ACTION

A Well-Managed Work Force Impacts the Bottom Line

Companies that do a good job of recruiting and rewarding workers, and provide them with a flexible, collegial workplace, offer a larger return to shareholders. This is the finding of research conducted by Watson Wyat Worldwide, a human resources consulting firm in Bethesda, Maryland. A well-managed workplace can increase a corporation's market value by as much as 30 percent. Personal satisfaction of the work force results in higher productivity and lower employee turnover. Low employee turnover can have a positive impact on profits. The per-person cost of replacing an entry-level employee will range from $5,000 to $10,000. The cost of replacing an executive can be $50,000 to $100,000.

● Self-Disclosure

Self-disclosure and trust are two halves of a whole. The more open you are with people, the more trust you build up. The more trust there is in a relationship, the safer you feel to disclose who you are. Self-disclosure is also part of good communication and helps eliminate unnecessary guessing games.

Managers who let their subordinates know what is expected of them help those employees fulfill their responsibilities. Chapter 8 emphasizes the need of individuals to verbalize the thoughts and feelings they carry within them and provides many practical suggestions on how to use constructive self-disclosure.

● Conflict Resolution

Conflict in one form or another surfaces almost daily in the lives of many workers. You may experience conflict during a commute to work when a careless driver cuts you off at a freeway exit ramp. If your job includes supervisory-management responsibilities, you will spend a great deal of time in **conflict resolution,** attempting to resolve conflicts among members of your staff. As a team member, you may assume the role of mediator when other team members clash. Resolving conflict with coworkers can require a great deal of energy. Conflict also surfaces when working parents attempt to balance the demands of both work and family. Stressful conditions at home often interfere with work performance, and on-the-job pressures create or magnify problems at home.[35]

Conflict can obstruct cooperative action, create suspicion and distrust, and decrease productivity. The ability to anticipate or resolve conflict can be an invaluable skill. Although Chapter 13 deals specifically with the topic of conflict

The amount of time and money invested in conflict resolution is surprisingly high. Learning how to resolve conflict at work and in our personal lives is an important human relations skill.

resolution, the chapters devoted to communication, achievement of emotional control, and team building provide many valuable suggestions on how conflict can be handled constructively.

THINKING / LEARNING STARTER

Now that you have had an opportunity to read about the seven themes of human relations, what do you consider your strongest areas? In which areas do you feel you need improvement? Why?

Human Relations: Benefits to You

As previously noted, the work force is currently characterized by downsizing, mergers, buyouts, business closings, and other disruptive forces. We are seeing more emphasis on quality products and quality services. In addition, diversity has become a more prominent characteristic of today's work force. These conditions will very likely continue in the new millennium. One of the best ways to cope with these changes is to develop and apply the interpersonal skills needed for success in today's working world.

A basic course in human relations cannot give you a foolproof set of techniques for solving every people-related problem that might arise. It can, however, give you a better understanding of human behavior in groups, help you become more sensitive to yourself and others, and enable you to act more wisely when problems occur. You may even be able to anticipate conflicts or prevent small problems from escalating into major ones.

Many leaders feel that courses in human relations are important because very few workers are responsible to themselves alone. These leaders point out that most jobs today are interdependent. If people in these jobs cannot work effectively as a team, the efficiency of the organization will suffer.

■ Summary

The study of human relations helps us understand how people fulfill both personal growth needs and organizational goals in their careers. Many organizations are beginning to realize that an employee's life outside the job can have a significant impact on work performance, and some are developing training and education programs that address the total person. Increasingly, organizations are discovering that many forces influence the behavior of people at work.

Human relations is not a set of foolproof techniques for solving people-related problems. Rather, it gives people an understanding of basic behavior concepts that may enable them to make wiser choices when problems arise, to anticipate or prevent conflicts, and to keep minor problems from escalating into major ones. Several important developments in the workplace have given new importance to human relations.

The forces influencing work behavior are the organizational culture, the actions of supervisors and managers, the behavior of the work group, the characteristics of the job, the worker's personal characteristics, and the worker's family.

The development of the human relations movement involved a redefinition of the nature of work and the gradual perception of managers and workers as complex human beings. Two landmarks in the study of motivation and worker needs are Frederick Taylor's work in scientific management and Elton Mayo's Hawthorne studies. Many industry leaders predict an increased emphasis on human relations research and application. The reasons for this trend include greater awareness that human relations problems serve as a major barrier to the efficient operation of an organization, the employment of workers who expect more from their jobs, and worker organizations and government agencies pressing for attention to employee concerns.

Seven major themes emerge from a study of human relations: communication, self-awareness, self-acceptance, motivation, trust, self-disclosure, and conflict resolution. These themes reflect the current concern in human relations with personal growth and satisfaction of organizational objectives.

■ Career Corner

Q: The daily newspapers and television news shows are constantly reporting on mergers, business closings, and downsizing efforts. With so much uncertainty in the job market, how can I best prepare for a career?

A: You are already doing one thing that is very important—keeping an eye on labor market trends. During a period of rapid change and less job security, you must continuously study workplace trends and assess your career preparation. Louis S. Richman, in a *Fortune* magazine article entitled "How to Get Ahead in America," said, "Climbing in your career calls for being clear about your personal goals, learning how to add value, and developing skills you can take anywhere." After you clarify the type of work that would be rewarding for you, be sure you have the skills necessary to be competitive in that employment area. Keep in mind that today's employers demand more, so be prepared to add value to the company from day one. Search for your employer's toughest problems and make yourself part of the solutions.

The skills you can take anywhere are those transferable skills required by a wide range of employers. These are important because there are no jobs for life. Be prepared to work for several organizations, and anticipate changing careers.

■ Key Terms

human relations	self-awareness
total person	self-acceptance
organizational culture	motivation
scientific management	trust
Hawthorne studies	self-disclosure
informal organization	conflict resolution
communication	

■ Review Questions

1. Given the information provided in this chapter, define *human relations*.

2. List and briefly describe the major developments that have given new importance to human relations.

3. Describe the total person approach to human relations. Why is this approach becoming more popular?

4. List and describe the six major forces influencing human behavior at work.

5. Do you agree or disagree with the view that all work is done through relationships? Explain.

6. How did Taylor's work help usher in the modern assembly line? What are some possible negative outcomes of the assembly-line approach?

7. Mayo's research indicated that workers could influence the rate of production in an organization. What discoveries did Mayo make that led to this conclusion?

8. 3M Corporation offers employees seminars on financial planning and parenting, and Tires Plus offers classes on nutrition and healthy cooking, work/life balance, weight loss, and smoking cessation. Do these programs represent a good use of company funds? Explain your answer.

9. What seven themes emerge from a study of human relations? Describe each one briefly.

10. Reread the Total Person Insight that quotes Daniel Goleman, and then indicate what you feel is the meaning of this quotation.

■ Application Exercises

1. Throughout this book you will be given many opportunities to engage in self-assessment activities. Self-assessment involves taking a careful look at the human relations skills you need to be well rounded and thoroughly prepared for success in your work life and fulfillment in your personal life. To assess your human relations skills, complete the Human Relations Abilities Assessment Form in the appendix of this text. This assessment form will provide you with increased awareness of your strengths and a better understanding of the abilities you may want to improve. Each item offers an opportunity for goal setting to achieve personal development. Goal setting guidelines are described in Chapter 4.

2. The seven broad themes that emerge from the study of human relations were discussed in this chapter. Although these themes are interrelated, there is value in examining each one separately before reading the rest of the book. Review the description of each theme and then answer these questions:

   a. When you take into consideration the human relations problems that you have observed or experienced at work, school, and home, which themes represent the most important areas of study? Explain your answer.

   b. In which of these areas do you feel the greatest need for improvement? Why?

Internet Exercise

Companies featured in *Fortune's* list of the 100 best companies to work for in America are characterized by openness, fairness, camaraderie among employees, job security, opportunities for advancement, and sensitivity to work/family issues. These companies are concerned about the total person, not just the skills that help the company earn a profit. Here are some of the companies that have made the "best companies" list:

Company	Location	Type of Business
Southwest Airlines	Dallas, TX	Airline
SAS Institute	Carey, NC	Computer software
MBNA	Wilmington, DE	Issuer of credit cards
Harley-Davidson	Milwaukee, WI	Manufacturing
Nordstrom	Seattle, WA	Retailing

Develop a profile of two of these companies by visiting their websites and reviewing the available information. Also, visit Hoover's Online, a resource that provides access to profiles of about 2,800 companies. Additional information on each of these companies may be found in *Business Week, Forbes, Fortune,* and other business publications.

Case 1.1   Challenges in the New Economy

At the beginning of the new millennium, a growing number of social researchers, economists, and consultants tried to predict what the world of work would be like in the years ahead. We pay close attention to these and to even more recent forecasts because work is a central part of our identities. As one writer has noted, our working life—in a few short decades—adds up to life itself. Work can also be one of the major fulfillments in life. What will the New Economy be like from a worker's viewpoint? Here are three predictions:

■ *In the New Economy, everyone is an entrepreneur.* This is the view expressed by Thomas Petzinger, Jr., author and former columnist for the *Wall Street Journal.* He reports on factories where shop floor employees handle customer service calls and create new ways to solve customer problems. The employees who deliver freight for Western Kansas Xpress carry business cards and search out potential customers. Tellers at First National Bank in Montevideo, Minnesota, are actively involved in sales and service activities. They complete training courses designed to help them solve customer service problems and sell products and services offered by the bank. To become an entrepreneur in a corporate setting often means using your creativity more often, taking some risks, and moving beyond your job description. The new economy will give many workers an opportunity to take more responsibility for their work.

■ *The New Economy features the art of the relaunch.* How often will you change jobs during your lifetime? Five times? Ten? Fifteen? The New Economy offers more career options, more challenges, and more uncertainty. Chances are, you will need to relaunch your career several times. Molly Higgins held a career track job in the human resources department of a large company. When she discovered that in the entire department there wasn't a single position she aspired to, it was time to relaunch her career. In recent years, thousands of people joined the ranks of new dot.com companies, only to lose their jobs in a matter of weeks or months. One analyst says that changing jobs will require using your learning skills and applying the skills you have already learned.[36]

■ *In the New Economy, getting a job may be easier than getting a life.* We have, in recent years, seen an increase in the standard of living. The price we pay for a bigger home, a nicer automobile, or a vacation in Italy is often a more demanding work life. Some people choose to work harder in order to acquire more "things." In some cases, corporate downsizing has left fewer people to do the same amount of work. Working more hours and working harder during those hours can result in greater stress, a breakdown in family life, and a decrease in leisure time.[37]

■ Questions

1. Would you feel comfortable assuming the duties of an entrepreneur within an existing company, or would you rather start your own business?

2. You are likely to relaunch yourself several times during the years ahead. Does the prospect of several relaunches seem frightening to you, or do you look forward to the challenge?

3. What steps would you take to achieve better work/life balance?

Case 1.2   In Search of Work/Life Balance

A growing number of workers do not feel there's a healthy balance between work and personal life. Some are tired of working 10- to 12-hour days and weekends. Many want a better balance between work and family. These employees search for companies that offer family-friendly features such as flexible scheduling, telecommuting, and child care. Each year *Working Mother* magazine publishes a list of the 100 best companies for working mothers. Let's look at two of the companies that made the list.

■ Arnold & Porter is a large law firm with almost seven hundred lawyers practicing in its U.S. and international operations. New mothers get a combined eight-week maternity and eight-week parental leave at full pay. New fathers get an eight-week parental leave, also at full pay. Special programs are also available to parents who are adopting.

■ DuPont Company is a science company that employs seventy-nine thousand employees. About half work outside of the United States. Employees can use job sharing, part-time scheduling, and telecommuting. About twelve thousand data lines have been installed in employees' homes for telecommuting, and roughly 30 percent of DuPont's work force are telecommuters.

Managers can encourage or discourage the use of family-friendly services by mothers and fathers. At Citigroup Corporation, managers attend seminars on various work/life issues and are encouraged to support programs developed for employees.[38]

▪ Questions

1. A majority of today's workers do not think there is a healthy balance between work and personal life. How do you feel?

2. Some companies develop work/life programs that focus primarily on mothers and fathers who have children. What are the advantages and disadvantages of this approach?

2

IMPROVING PERSONAL AND ORGANIZATIONAL COMMUNICATIONS

Chapter Preview

After studying this chapter, you will be able to

- Understand the impact advanced technology has had on today's communications.

- Differentiate impersonal from interpersonal communication.

- Understand the communication process and the filters that affect communication.

- Identify ways to improve personal communication, including developing listening skills.

- Understand how communications flow throughout an organization and how to improve the flow when necessary.

- Learn how to communicate effectively through technology, including voice mail and e-mail.

When the managers at GE Capital Services were asked to define communication, they described specific, relatively infrequent things such as newsletters and meetings. GE Capital employees, however, viewed communication as an everyday electronic, verbal, and visual process that provided information needed in their jobs.[1] This particular definition gap is common. Yet both managers and employees have an accurate view of communication in an organization, and their views are not mutually exclusive. Organizations that use multiple communication techniques will thrive in the information age as they learn that the key to effective communication is variety.

To enhance communication at Advanced Cardiovascular Systems, each executive is assigned a coach from the rank-and-file employees. These coaches are trained to gather very specific information from all the employees about their executive's openness and honesty. As a result of her coach's insights, Ginger Graham, president and CEO, added weekly walk-arounds to her schedule, ate in the cafeteria rather than at her desk, and began holding brown bag lunches with small groups of employees throughout the year so they could voice their views directly to her.[2]

In Arizona, Eric Schechter, president of Great American Events, provides his employees with e-mail, Internet access, and PalmPilots, all of which enable them to share project management files and to facilitate group scheduling. He discovered, however, that many times information would be lost in an electronic folder—and the average employee wouldn't have time to search or know where to find it. So when information of a time-sensitive nature needed to be shared immediately, Schechter simply wrote a note on the whiteboard in the company conference room where employees ate lunch. Federal Express, headquartered in Tennessee, has an internal private business television network (FXTV) that provides live telecasts to all employees in the United States, Canada, and Europe. Air time often includes phone-in question-and-answer sessions between corporate officers and employees.[3]

In today's fast-paced communications environment, progressive organizations cannot depend on one medium to send a message. They must use a combination of face-to-face, print, and electronic methods to meet the needs and interests of all those involved.

Advanced Technology's Impact on Communication

The new millennium has ushered in the age of information, led by rapid advances in technology-based communication. But technology without the involvement of people can be very inefficient. We must not lose the human touch that keeps customers coming back. The global business boom presents workers with the additional challenge of learning how to communicate across language and cultural barriers, often without seeing one another.

Not everyone is in the communication business, but everyone is in the business of communicating. Today many workers are consumed by over 200 messages a day through various options such as the telephone, voice mail, telephone message slips, Post-it Notes,

Not everyone is in the communication business, but everyone is in the business of communicating.

interoffice mail, e-mail (electronic mail), postal mail, instant messaging, overnight couriers, faxes, pagers, and personal digital appliances with wireless connections to the Internet.[4] Some of these options enhance the communication process; others can create barriers to effective communication. Often individuals must wade through useless data to find the information they are seeking—and this data glut has become a serious issue in the workplace. Although the speed and volume of information have increased, the average person cannot process it any faster. As the number of messages increases, workers often find themselves distracted and unable to concentrate because of the constant interruptions and volume of information. This often leads to a breakdown in communications between individuals and organizations. The breakdown can result in human relations problems that may be hard to fix once the damage is done.

The Communication Process

Most people take communication for granted. When they write, speak, or listen to others, they assume that the message given or received is being understood. In reality, messages are often misunderstood because they are incomplete or because different people interpret messages in different ways. The diversity of today's work force calls for a greater understanding of how to communicate effectively, through technology or face to face, with people from different cultures, countries, and lifestyles. Yet even though people and communication methods may be diverse, the basic communication process remains the same.

● Impersonal Versus Interpersonal Communication

In a typical organization the types of communication used to exchange information can be placed on a continuum ranging from "impersonal" on one end to "interpersonal" on the other.[5] When we use such words as *transmit* or *transfer*, we are talking about a one-way information-giving process. This impersonal, one-way communication process can be used to give basic information such as company policies, instructions, or facts. Generally, organizations use memos, letters, e-mail, computer printouts, voice mail, manuals, and/or bulletin boards as quick, easy ways to "get the word out." The major limitation of these forms of **impersonal communication** is that people receiving the information usually have little opportunity to ask the sender to clarify vague or confusing wording. Even e-mail has its limitations, because the person sending the information cannot be sure when the person receiving the information will retrieve it. If the message is retrieved hours—or even days—later, the sender may not be available to clarify any misunderstandings.

Interpersonal communication is the verbal exchange of thoughts or information between two or more people. Such words as *share, discuss, argue,* and *interact* refer to this form of two-way communication. Interpersonal communication can take place in meetings, over the phone, in face-to-face interviews, or even during classroom discussions between instructors and students. If interpersonal communication is to be effective, some type of **feedback,** or response, from the person receiving the information is necessary. When this verbal

TOTAL PERSON INSIGHT	**ERIC MAISEL**
	AUTHOR, *20 COMMUNICATION TIPS @ WORK*
	"Many skills are valuable at work, but one skill is essential: the ability to communicate. Whether you are presenting your ideas at a commitee meeting, dashing off fifteen e-mails in a row, chatting with a coworker at a copy machine, evaluating an employee, or closing a deal over the phone, what you are doing is communicating. These exchanges are the backbone and the life blood of every organization and every relationship."

exchange happens, the person sending the information can determine whether or not the message has been understood in the way he or she intended. This is one of the reasons that some managers still prefer person-to-person meetings and telephone calls instead of e-mail.

But interpersonal communication takes time, and because it does, many companies use the faster, impersonal means of conveying information. Indeed, the speed of disseminating information has increased dramatically through the use of new technology. Yet many workers say they are out of touch. A young narrator in a television commercial for Volkswagen expressed the feelings of many people:

> I've got gigabytes. I've got megabytes. I'm voice-mailed. I'm e-mailed. I surf the net. I'm on the Web. I am Cyber-Man. So how come I feel so out of touch?[6]

Technology can be invaluable when it comes to impersonal information giving, but it cannot replace the two-way, interpersonal communication process when feedback and discussion are necessary.

● Sender—Message—Receiver

Effective communication, in its most basic form, is composed of three elements: a sender, a receiver, and an understood message.[7] To illustrate, suppose your friend phones from your neighborhood convenience store and asks for directions to your home. You give your friend the appropriate street names, intersections, and compass directions so that he can drive to your door without getting lost. When your friend repeats his understanding of your directions, you clarify any misunderstandings, and he drives directly to your home. A simplified diagram of this communication process would look like Figure 2.1.

Now suppose you are late for an appointment, and the plumber you had requested three days ago calls you from her cellular phone and asks directions to your house. She explains that she has gotten lost in this neighborhood before, and it is obvious that English is her second language. The communication process becomes much more complicated, as shown in Figure 2.2. As your message travels from you to your plumber, it must pass through several "filters," each of which can alter the way your message is understood. Most communications flow through this complex process.

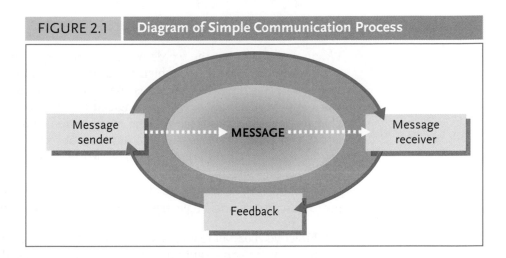

FIGURE 2.1 | **Diagram of Simple Communication Process**

Communication Filters

Messages are sent—and feedback is received—through a variety of filters that can distort the intended message. (See Figure 2.2.) When people are influenced by one or more of these filters, their perception of the message may be totally different from what the sender was attempting to communicate. Since the message received *is* the message, both sender and receiver must be keenly aware of these possible distortions so that they can intercept any miscommunication.

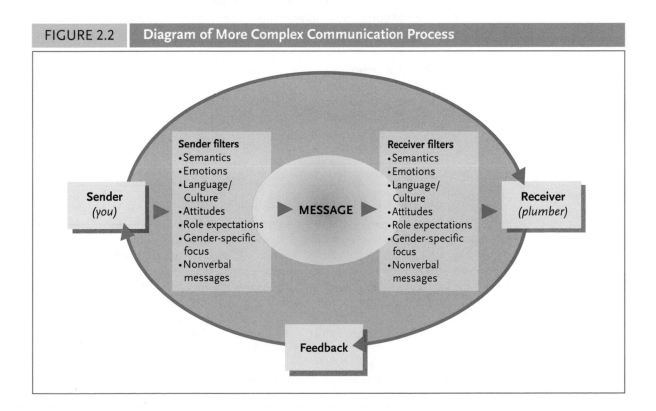

FIGURE 2.2 | **Diagram of More Complex Communication Process**

● Semantics

We often assume that the words we use mean the same things to others, but this assumption can create problems. Words are not things; they are labels that stand for something. **Semantics** is the study of the relationship between a word and its meaning(s). We have agreed that particular words have associated meanings and usages. We can easily understand what words like *typewriter, computer,* or *envelope* mean. But more abstract terms, such as *job satisfaction, downsizing, internal customers,* or *word processing,* have less precise meanings and will be interpreted by different people in different ways. The more abstract the term, the less likely it is that people will agree on its meaning. Some professionals have been strongly criticized for using abstract words:

- Effective 2002, all federal agencies are required to communicate in writing that is clear and easy to understand. For example, OSHA has replaced the phrase "ways of exit access" with "exit door" on all its documents.[8]

- When Enron wanted to cover up questionable business practices, employees developed some creative accounting jargon. One report included the following sentence: "Enron entered into share settled costless collar arrangements. . . . The transactions resulted in noncash increases to noncurrent assets and equity."[9]

- Corporate employees often use important-sounding jargon that is almost incomprehensible. Better Communications, a firm that teaches writing skills to employers, clipped this statement from a memo circulated at a *Fortune* 500 company: "Added value is the keystone to exponentially accelerating profit curves."[10]

● Language and Cultural Barriers

If your organization is connected to the Internet, it has automatically entered the global marketplace. English has been the dominant language throughout the free world for several decades. However, as more and more developing coun-

---

HUMAN RELATIONS IN ACTION

Jargon Predates Bubble Burst at WorldCom

Long before massive fraud was uncovered at WorldCom Incorporated, critics said its employees were using strange new words to describe services and to close deals. Some of the jargon used sounded like language from another world. Promotional software was "seedware." WorldCom technologists didn't troubleshoot; they "blamestormed." An embarrassing bug in a sales pitch was a "blevit." Members of the sales force often invented words that were designed to impress the customer. Although some customers were thoroughly perplexed, they were too intimidated to ask questions. Soon after WorldCom filed for bankruptcy, there was a backlash against invented words. In an effort to pacify stockholders, creditors, and other injured parties, a WorldCom spokesperson said, "We're making a really concerted effort to call things what they are."

tries connect with the Internet and as transnational organizations (companies conducting business with more than one country) expand their global markets, multilingual transactions have become a serious communications issue. People who speak English fluently must remember to speak slowly and avoid slang when communicating with those whose first language is not English.

Culture, which is an accumulation of values, forms of expression, beliefs, language, and the like, shapes one's interpretations of what events mean. Communication problems can be caused by conflicting cultural assumptions. For example, people living in the United States, Canada, Europe, Israel, or Australia usually prefer direct-approach communication; they tend to say more or less exactly what they mean. Their cultures value clarity, fluency, and brevity in communication. People from the Orient, the Arab world, and much of Africa prefer a more indirect style of communication and therefore value harmony, subtlety, sensitivity, and tact more than clarity. They try hard to connect with their listeners.[11]

Cultures have different standards for how fast you should talk, how much you should talk, how long you should pause between ideas, and how long you should wait after someone finishes talking before you say something.[12] Navajo people, for example, consider it impolite to begin talking immediately after another person finishes.

Today, culture is getting more attention because of globalization, rapid increases in immigrant groups, and growing support for cultural diversity by employers. As you communicate with people from other cultures, keep in mind how

Many companies are doing business in the global marketplace, so culture is getting more attention. When you have contact with people from other cultures, keep in mind how your words and gestures may influence how the other person is interpreting your message.

your words and gestures may influence how the other person is interpreting your message. At the same time, avoid making potentially incorrect judgments about others' messages if they are coming from a culture different from your own.

● Emotions

Emotions can be a powerful communication filter. Strong emotions can either prevent people from hearing what a speaker has to say or make them too susceptible to the speaker's point of view. If they become angry or allow themselves to be carried away by the speaker's eloquence, they may "think" with their emotions and make decisions or take action they regret later. They have shifted their attention from the content of the message to their feelings about it.

You may have had the experience of your spouse or parent angrily demanding to know why you forgot to run an errand. If you allow someone else's anger to trigger your own, the conversation quickly deteriorates into an argument. The real issue—what happened and what is to be done about it—is lost in the shouting match. Detaching yourself from another's feelings and responding to the content of the message is often difficult. It is hard to realize that another person's emotional response is more likely about fear or frustration than it is about you as an individual. Yet many jobs require that employees remain calm and courteous regardless of a customer's emotional state. Emotional control is discussed in Chapter 9.

● Attitudes

Attitudes can be a barrier to communication in much the same way emotions can—by altering the way people hear a message. The listener may not like the speaker's voice, accent, gestures, mannerisms, dress, or delivery. Perhaps the listener has preconceived ideas about the speaker's topic. For instance, a person who is strongly opposed to abortion will most likely find it difficult to listen with objectivity to a pro-choice speaker. Negative attitudes create resistance to the message and can lead to a breakdown in communication. Overly positive attitudes can also be a barrier to communication. Biased in favor of the message, the listener may fail to evaluate it effectively. More is said about forming attitudes in Chapter 6.

● Role Expectations

Role expectations influence how people expect themselves, and others, to act on the basis of the roles they play, such as boss, customer, or subordinate. These expectations can distort communication in two ways. First, if people identify others too closely with their roles, they may discount what the other person has to say: "It's just the boss again, saying the same old thing." A variation of this distortion occurs when we do not allow others to change their roles and take on new ones. This often happens to employees who are promoted from within the ranks of an organization to management positions. Others may still see the new manager as a secretary instead of a supervisor, as "old Chuck" from accounting rather than as the new department head.

Second, role expectations can affect good communication when people use their roles to alter the way they relate to others. This is often referred to as "position power." For example, managers may expect employees to accept what they say simply because of the authority invested in the position. Employees are not allowed to question the manager's decisions or make suggestions of their own, and communication becomes one-way information giving.

● Gender-Specific Focus

Research in gender communication conducted in the early 1990s supported the belief that there are major differences between the communication styles of men and women. Some of these early studies have been redone, and the communication scholars now present more moderate findings, contending that men and women are far more alike than different.[13]

Nevertheless, gender roles learned throughout childhood can influence the way men and women communicate. After all, boys and girls do grow up in different worlds, and they are conditioned to approach communication in different ways. Boys have been socialized to "take charge" and be more directive. Girls have been conditioned to be more facilitative and cooperative. Therefore, women are more likely to be supportive conversationalists.[14] Chapter 16, "The Changing Roles of Men and Women," discusses specific strategies you can use to communicate more effectively with those whose gender differs from your own.

● Nonverbal Messages

When we attempt to communicate with another person, we use both verbal and nonverbal communication. **Nonverbal messages** are "messages without words" or "silent messages." These are the messages (other than spoken or written words) we communicate through facial expressions, voice tone, gestures, appearance, posture, and other nonverbal means. Research indicates that our nonverbal messages have much more impact than verbal messages. Peter Drucker, author of numerous management books, said, "The important thing in communication is to hear what isn't being said."[15] He recognized that when someone else is speaking, your understanding of what is said depends very heavily on what you see (facial expression, gestures, eye contact, physical appearance) and what you hear (tone of voice, verbal expressiveness). This chapter limits its discussion to the form of nonverbal communication commonly referred to as "body language." Physical appearance is discussed in detail in Chapter 11.

"The important thing in communication is to hear what isn't being said."

Many of us could communicate more clearly, more accurately, and more credibly if we became more conscious of our body language. We can learn to strengthen our communications by making sure our words and our body language are consistent. When our verbal and nonverbal messages match, we give the impression that we can be trusted and that what we are saying reflects what we truly believe. But when our body language contradicts our words, we are often unknowingly changing the message we are sending. If a manager says to an employee, "I am very interested in your problem," but then begins to look at his watch and fidget with objects on his desk, the employee will most likely believe the nonverbal rather than the verbal message.

You can improve your communication by monitoring the nonverbal messages you send through your eye contact, facial expressions, gestures, and personal space.

Eye Contact   Eyes transmit more information than any other part of the body. Because eye contact is so revealing, people generally observe some unwritten rules about looking at others. People who hold direct eye contact for only a few seconds, or avoid eye contact altogether, risk communicating indifference. However, a direct, prolonged stare between strangers is usually considered impolite, even potentially aggressive or hostile.

As a general rule, when you are communicating in a business setting, your eyes should meet the other person's about 60 to 70 percent of the time. This timing is an effective alternative to continuous eye contact.

Facial Expressions   If you want to identify the inner feelings of another person, watch facial expressions closely. A frown or a smile will communicate a great deal. We have all encountered a "look of surprise" or a "look that could kill." Most of our observations are very accurate. If we are able to assess the inner emotions of the other person, we can be sure that person is doing the same to us, drawing conclusions based on our facial expressions.

Gestures   Gestures send messages to people about how you are reacting to them and to the situation in which you find yourself. Some people will walk into a business meeting with their shoulders slumped forward and head down. They will slouch into their chair, lean their chin on the palm of their hand, play with a pencil or paperclip on the table, or clutch their arms across their chest. Others will walk into the room with chin held high and shoulders back, sit straight in their chairs and lean slightly forward, and take notes with both arms "open" to whoever is speaking during the meeting. Experts agree that the words you say during a meeting with others, no matter how powerful, are often forgotten or disregarded unless your gestures command respect.[16]

In light of our expanding global marketplace, be aware that some gestures that may be common in the American culture may have dramatically different meanings to people from outside the United States. Although nodding your head up and down means "yes" in most countries, it means "no" in Greece and Bulgaria.[17] To use your fingers to call someone forward in a crowd is insulting to most Middle and Far Easterners.[18] And that common American gesture of folding your arms in front of you shows disrespect in Fiji.[19]

Personal Space   Research conducted by Edward Hall provides evidence that people use the space around them to define relationships. It is possible to make others uncomfortable by standing too close to them or too far away from them. A customer may feel uncomfortable if a salesperson stands too close. A job applicant may feel uncomfortable if the interviewer maintains a distance of several feet. Hall identified four "zones" of comfortable distances that help us understand this nonverbal effect on others:[20]

1. *Intimate distance* includes touching to approximately 18 inches from another person. Most people will respond with defensiveness when strangers intrude into this territory.

2. *Personal distance* ranges from 18 inches to 4 feet. This distance is usually reserved for people we feel close to, such as spouses or close friends.

3. *Social distance* is 4 to 12 feet and is used for most business meetings and impersonal social gatherings. Business can be conducted with a minimum of emotional involvement.

4. *Public distance,* which usually involves one-way communication from a speaker to an audience, is 12 to 15 feet.

It is important to keep in mind that these distances vary from one culture to another. For example, Asians are accustomed to close contact, but Americans want more space around them.

● Who Is Responsible for Effective Communication?

The sender and the receiver share *equal* responsibility for effective communication. The communication loop, as shown in Figure 2.2, is not complete if the message the receiver hears, and acts upon, differs from the one the sender intended. When the sender accepts 100 percent of the responsibility for sending a clear, concise message, the communication process begins. But the receiver must also accept 100 percent of the responsibility for receiving the message as the sender intended. Receivers must provide senders with enough feedback to ensure that an accurate message has passed through all the filters that might alter it. In other words, rather than assuming that everyone understands what you are saying, take the time to make sure everyone really hears it.

THINKING / LEARNING STARTERS

1. Are you aware of the messages you send through body language? Recall your nonverbal behavior during a difficult meeting with a supervisor or a job interview. Was your behavior consistent with your words? Explain.

2. Acute sensitivity to nonverbal messages is an important skill for people to develop. In general, do you feel that nonverbal messages are more trustworthy than verbal ones? Describe specific nonverbal messages that you have learned to trust in your friends or coworkers.

How to Improve Personal Communication

Now that you understand the communication process and the various filters messages must pass through, you can begin to take the necessary steps to improve your own personal communication skills.

● Send Clear Messages

Become a responsible sender by always sending clear, concise messages with as little influence from filters as possible. A general rule of thumb is to give clear instructions and ask clear questions so you won't be misunderstood. A new employee stood before the paper shredder in her new office. An administrative assistant noticed her confused look and asked if she needed some help. "Yes, thank you. How does this thing work?" "It's simple," said the assistant and took the thick report from the new employee and fed it through the shredder. "I see," she said, "but how many copies will it make?" This kind of miscommunication could easily have been avoided if both parties had followed these simple rules:

- *Use simple, clear, and concise words.* As noted previously, abstract words, whether spoken or written, often become barriers to effective communication. Avoid slang, jargon, or complex, official language. Tailoring the message to the receiver by using words the listener understands will help ensure that your message is understood.

- *Use repetition.* When possible, use parallel channels of communication. For example, by sending an e-mail and making a phone call, you not only gain the receiver's attention through dialogue but also make sure there is a written record in case specific details need to be recalled.

- *Use appropriate timing.* Keep in mind that most employees, particularly at the managerial level, are flooded with messages every day. An important memo or e-mail may get no attention simply because it is competing with more pressing problems facing the receiver. When you need someone's cooperation, be acutely aware of his or her schedule and workload so that you can avoid causing any inconvenience or frustration. Timing the delivery of your message will help ensure that it is accepted and acted on.

- *Consider the receiver's preferences.* Some people prefer to receive information via e-mail, and others prefer telephone calls or face-to-face contact. Monitor and discover the preferences of those you communicate with on a regular basis, and adjust your communications with them accordingly.

● Develop Active Listening Skills

We may be born with the ability to hear, but we have to learn how to listen. We may think we are good listeners, but the truth is that most people don't listen at all. They simply speak and then think about what they are going to say next, rather than concentrating on what the other person is trying to say. Studies show that most people listen at a 25 percent efficiency rate in typical situations and therefore miss about 75 percent of the messages.[21] Many of the misunderstandings in life that interrupt effective human relations are due to poor listening habits.

Many people believe that listening is passive, something that does not require any response. Actually, **active listening** requires an intense involvement as you concentrate on what you are hearing, exhibit your listening attitude

Career Advice

A recent college graduate wrote to Anne Fisher, career advice columnist for *Fortune* magazine, and asked: "I just graduated from Yale and am about to start my first real job, and I'm curious about something. If you had to pass along just one piece of advice on which to build a career, what would it be?"

Anne answered, "I've always liked Albert Einstein's dictum: 'If A equals success, then the formula is $A = X + Y + Z$. X is work. Y is play. And Z is, Keep your mouth shut.' Or as my dad used to say, 'Nobody ever learns anything while they're talking.' If you make it a habit to listen more than you speak, you can't go too far wrong."

Good listening is fueled by curiosity.

through your body language, and feed back to the speaker what you think he or she meant. When you learn how to become an active listener—sometimes referred to as a "generous" listener—you have the opportunity to:

■ *Gain stronger relationships.* One of the highest compliments you can pay anyone is to really listen. This communicates respect, and people will be more likely to listen receptively to you in return.[22]

■ *Learn new information.* "Nobody ever learns anything while they're talking." Good listening is fueled by curiosity.

■ *Make fewer mistakes.* You are acting on more accurate information.

This attorney listens carefully to her client. She will ask questions and use her active listening skills to acquire the information she needs to be an effective legal representative. Active listening is a skill that can be learned.

TABLE 2.1	Active Listening Skills

1. *Develop a listening attitude.* Regard the speaker as worthy of your respect and attention. Drop your expectations as to what you are going to hear or would like to hear. Maintain good eye contact and lean slightly forward. Don't rush the speaker. Be patient and refrain from planning what to say in response until the speaker has finished talking.

2. *Give the speaker your full attention.* This is not easy because the messages you hear are often spoken at a much slower rate than you are able to absorb them. This allows your mind to roam. Your senses are constantly receiving extraneous information that may divert your attention. To stay focused, you may want to take notes, if it is appropriate to do so.

3. *Clarify by asking questions.* If something is not clear because the speaker has referred to a person or an event that you are not familiar with, ask him or her to back up and explain. If you want the speaker to expand on a particular point, ask open-ended questions such as "How do you feel about that?" or "Can you tell us some ways to improve?"

4. *Feed back your understanding of the speaker's message.* Paraphrase, in your own words, your understanding of what the speaker has just said: for example, *"Do you mean . . . ?" "Am I right in assuming that we should . . . ?" "What I hear you saying is . . ."* or *"In other words, we . . . ."*

Carefully examine Table 2.1, Active Listening Skills, and implement these ideas the next time you want to improve a relationship. You may be surprised by the impact you can make.

To add depth and dimension to your active listening skills, consider honing your *critical* and *empathic* listening skills.

TOTAL	**HARRIET LERNER**
PERSON	AUTHOR, *THE DANCE OF CONNECTION*
INSIGHT	"Listening well is at the heart of intimacy and connection. When we are able to listen to another person with attention and care, that person feels validated and enhanced."

Critical Listening **Critical listening** is the organized, cognitive process you use to carefully examine the thinking of others in order to clarify and improve your understanding.[23] It is the attempt to see the topic of discussion from the *speaker's* point of view, and to consider how the speaker's perception of the situation may be different from your own. To improve your ability to critically view the new information, be sure to listen for evidence that challenges as well as confirms your own point of view.

It is especially important to implement your critical listening skills when emotions are involved. The active listening skills you use when trying to learn something new (giving your full attention, asking questions, repeating your understanding of the new idea) and those you use in arguing with another person *should* be similar. However, emotions tend to distort your ability and/or willingness to listen. To activate your critical listening skills, ask yourself, Does the speaker's reasoning make sense? What evidence is being offered as part of each reason? Do I know each reason to be true, valid, or from my own experience? Is each reason based on a source that can be trusted?[24]

Critical listening is vitally important during interpersonal communication, but it is just as important during impersonal communication. When there is no opportunity for feedback, you must be careful to analyze the source of the information and determine its validity and credibility. Realize, for example, that viewing "tabloid" television and Internet or network television news requires all of your critical listening skills.

Empathic Listening   Many workers today face serious personal problems and feel the need to talk about them with someone. They do not expect specific advice or guidance; they just want to spend some time with an empathic listener. Stephen Covey, the noted author and consultant, described **empathic listening** as listening with the intent to understand how the person feels. Empathic listening, according to Covey, requires listening with your ears, your eyes, and your heart.[25] If you want to practice empathic listening, adopt the following practices:

■ *Avoid being judgmental.* Objectivity is the heart and soul of empathic listening. The person is communicating for emotional release and does not seek a specific response.

■ *Accept what is said.* You do not have to agree with what is being said, but you should let the person know you are able to understand his or her viewpoint.

■ *Be patient.* If you are unable or unwilling to take the time to hear what the person has to say, say so immediately. Signs of impatience send a negative message to the person needing to talk.[26]

At this point you may be thinking, "This information sounds good, but I don't know very many empathic listeners." The truth is, we live in a culture where empathic listening is quite rare. Interrupting has become all too common as people rush to fill every gap in the conversation. Nevertheless, empathic listening is greatly valued by those with personal or work-related problems—people who want to spend time with a good listener.[27]

THINKING / LEARNING STARTERS

1. Think of some people you know who are active listeners. How can you tell? Describe an instance when their active listening improved their relations with you or another person.
2. Have you recently been approached by someone who wanted to talk to an empathic listener? Were you able to respond in the manner recommended? Explain.

Communications in Organizations

The healthy functioning of any organization, large or small, depends on teamwork. Good communication helps build teamwork by permitting a two-way exchange of information and by unifying group behavior. Poor communication can create an atmosphere of mistrust. Therefore, it is important that workers know the appropriate channels through which communication flows.

Organizations usually establish formal channels or structures through which communication travels. In most organizations, however, an informal channel, commonly referred to as the grapevine, offers a major communications link. For an organization to function smoothly, everyone needs to know how to use both formal and informal channels of communication.

● Formal Channels

Official information in an organization generally moves along **formal channels.** Vertical channels carry messages between the top executive levels and the lowest level in the organization. Horizontal channels carry messages between departments, divisions, managers, or employees on the same organizational level.

Vertical Channels   Communications moving through vertical channels from top management reach a great many people and carry considerable force. In general, if the level of trust between management and employees is fairly high, these messages will usually pass down through the organization effectively. Messages will be understood, believed, accepted, and acted on. If the level of trust is low, however, workers will tend to put more faith in rumors, even if such information conflicts with the formal message.

Communication traveling through vertical channels may be delivered in writing, face to face, or electronically. Many managers find that making brief phone calls to their staffs is more effective than sending memos or e-mail messages because phone calls allow for immediate feedback. Sensitive matters, however, are best handled face to face. Communicating down vertical channels is fairly routine. Communicating back up can be more difficult because top managers sometimes have the mistaken impression that their subordinates have nothing important to say.

Horizontal Channels   People on the same level of authority communicate across horizontal channels. This communication may take place during structured meetings or informal conversations. In some situations, horizontal channels may intersect with vertical authority lines. Project teams, for example, often bring to-

gether people from different departments and with different levels of authority. Boeing has used project teams to accelerate the product development process. The Boeing 777 jetliner project involved teams made up of representatives from several different departments.[28]

● Informal Channels

Messages passed through the vertical and horizontal channels are easily tracked through linear paths, but the pathway of gossip may look more like a cobweb interwoven throughout the organizational chart. Many executives believe that if official information moved through an organization as fast as gossip does, most organizations would be much better off. The **grapevine,** the informal communications channel, exists in every organization and can have either a positive or a negative effect. Many times the grapevine will clarify orders sent through the formal channels. At times, however, messages that move through the grapevine may be exaggerated, distorted, or completely inaccurate. So much of what ends up on the grapevine is based on interpretations of body language and nonverbal signals. For example, when two people meet behind closed doors, those who gossip are often more interested in the fact that the door is closed than in what is actually being discussed in the meeting.[29]

Learning to make effective use of the grapevine can be a powerful human relations skill. Career coach Marilyn Moats Kennedy says, "You cannot affect what people do unless you influence what they hear." She suggests *working the grapevine* by identifying the organization's information leaders.[30] These leaders may not be identified by their title or position in the organization. Instead, ask those who are trusted and respected to clarify information you receive through the grapevine.

Once you are identified as a gossip, others will not trust you again.

Unless you know for sure that the information is fact, never participate in gossip. Once you are identified as a gossip, others will not trust you again. This can destroy all your efforts to build solid future relationships within that organization. You will discover that others will not share confidential information with you—information that might be important to your career.

● How to Improve Organizational Communication

SUPERVISOR: "We've really got to get closer to our employees, communicate with them better."

TRAINER: "Yes, we have a big problem there."

SUPERVISOR: "They don't understand the new changes, even though they have all the details."

TRAINER: "We just need to spend time with them."

SUPERVISOR: "Yes, you're right. We've got to educate them."

In this dialogue, notice the quick deterioration from "get closer" and "communicate" to "they don't understand" and "educate them." Note how quickly the concept of two-way communication was transformed into one-way instruction.

This "talking down" style of communication is common in many organizations. Individuals can learn how to effectively communicate with each other, but until the organization itself develops an effective "listening environment," the benefits it reaps from that communication will be limited.

Encourage Upward Communication   **Upward communication,** the process of encouraging employees to share their feelings and ideas with their managers, is one of the most effective ways to improve organizational communication and is common among the best companies to work for in America. Employees with limited power are naturally very cautious about discussing mistakes, complaints, and failings with a more powerful person. However, when managers demonstrate the desire to listen to their subordinates, ideas, suggestions, and complaints begin to flow upward. To facilitate this upward communication, companies often establish suggestion systems, schedule informal meetings, establish intranet (Internet connections among company employees only) chat rooms, and conduct exit interviews with employees leaving the organization.[31] Here are a few examples of leaders who have taken steps to improve upward communication:

■ "Ask Al" is an area on the Born Information Services Inc. intranet where employees can anonymously ask president Alan Bauman questions. He willingly posts his responses for everyone to see and encourages debate.[32]

Carly Fiorina, CEO of Hewlett-Packard, realizes the importance of upward communication. Successful leaders create a non-threatening environment where employees can communicate upward through the organization without endangering their career.

- The "Individual Dignity Entitlement" program at Motorola allows all employees (145,000) and their managers one-to-one conversations every quarter. The intent is to create a new form of partnership between managers and employees in which people can ask and answer questions.[33]

- Peter Brabeck, CEO of Nestlé, meets with twelve to fourteen employees each month over lunch. Their bosses are not in attendance. He encourages the employees to talk frankly about their work and to ask questions.[34]

These organizations actively pursue ways to remove barriers that prevent open communication. They recognize that improving communications will inevitably help build trust among all employees, regardless of their position in the organization.

Communicating via Technology

The traditional memos, letters, phone calls, and face-to-face conversations seem to be the exception rather than the rule in today's high-tech communications environment. Many organizations now maintain **virtual offices,** networks of workers connected by the latest technology. These workers can "set up shop" wherever they are—at home, on an airplane, in a motel room—and communicate with coworkers via e-mail, cellular phone, fax modem, or some other method. **Telecommuting,** an arrangement that allows employees to work from their homes, enables people scattered all over the world to work as one office staff. The Labor Department estimates that up to 19 million Americans now work online from home or from other locations outside the office.[35]

Today information can be shared by **voice mail;** recorded telephone messages can be sent or retrieved from anywhere in the world. **Scanners** take pictures of documents and transmit them electronically. Documents can be sent via **fax modems** (transmission of information directly from a computer screen) to a fax machine or photocopier in another office, building, state, or country. Of course e-mail has become part of every computer owner's daily life. Many cell phones now allow users to retrieve their e-mail from remote locations.

The advantages of using these technology-based communication alternatives are obvious. Time efficiency is unsurpassed because people can transmit simple or detailed information across all time zones, and receivers can retrieve the information at their convenience. Cost effectiveness is unsurpassed because fiber-optic and satellite transmissions cost the consumer virtually pennies compared to traditional transworld phone calls.

In all the frantic speed with which communication now flows, many people forget that communication still must be carefully created before it is transmitted. Voice mail can be frustrating and time-consuming if it is not handled properly, and poorly written e-mails can leave the impression that the sender is either uneducated or not very intelligent.

● Voice Mail

Now that everyone is adjusting to the opportunities that immediate communication systems offer, nothing is more dismaying than playing voice mail tag (the exchange of several voice mails without successful transmission of the message). Whether you are on the sending or the receiving end, though, there are ways to avoid this counterproductive exercise in frustration.

For incoming calls, be sure you keep your recorded message updated; daily, if necessary. It is a good idea to practice your greeting before recording it, so that you will sound more natural. Include your first and last names, the date, and when you will be retrieving your messages. If you are going on an extended business trip or vacation, your retrieval date will prevent repeat calls from colleagues or customers who might get angrier with each unanswered message. Forward your calls to another person's extension, if possible. Always explain how the caller can reach a live person if the call is urgent.

When retrieving your voice mail, keep a notepad beside your phone. Write down the essential information you need for calls you want to return; then delete them. And even in our high-tech environment, the Golden Rule still applies: "Do unto others as you would have them do unto you." Return calls promptly!

When you are leaving someone a voice mail message, be courteous. For example, give your name at the beginning of the message and leave your phone number at the end. Speak clearly and slowly, and do not smoke, drink, or eat while talking. Avoid rambling and repeating; keep your message short and simple. If possible, let the receiver know when you will be available or set a time when you will call again.[36] One of the best ways to avoid voice mail tag is to state *why* you are calling. Then, if the receiver reaches *your* voice mail when calling back, he or she can simply give you the information you wanted and get back to business.

● E-mail

Sending information electronically has become the standard operating procedure for most business and personal communications because it offers many advantages over the traditional face-to-face meeting, phone call, letter, or memo process. Not only is e-mail often faster, but it also provides a wonderful alternative for those painfully shy individuals who find it difficult to express themselves face to face. It has become the great equalizer: Lower-level employees can now send messages to executives without anyone in between misinterpreting, sabotaging, or blocking the message.

In some cases, however, e-mail may be slower than a phone call or face-to-face meeting because it may take longer to compose an efficient and accurate message. Researchers at the E-Collaboration Research Center at Temple University's Fox School of Business and Management asked ten groups of people who worked in the same organization to analyze a business process—such as how the company markets a particular product—and attempt to improve it by interacting face to face. Another ten groups were asked to accomplish the same task using e-mail. The study measured the time it took to communicate by e-mail compared to talking face to face. They discovered it took about 10 minutes to contribute a 600-word idea during a face-to-face meeting, but it took over an hour to communicate the same idea electronically. While this might be construed as a negative aspect of e-mail, Ned Kock, director of the study, noted

HUMAN RELATIONS IN ACTION

E-mail Tips

- Do not send e-mail when you are angry or exhausted.
- When a face-to-face meeting is necessary, do not use e-mail as a substitute.
- When receiving large amounts of e-mail, you may selectively choose which ones you want to read by scanning the subject lines and deleting those that do not need a response.
- Make every attempt to create e-mail messages that are error-free. Messages that

contain errors may misrepresent your competence and give the wrong impression.
- Do not use e-mail to share rumors or innuendos or to say anything sensitive or critical that touches on someone's job competence.
- Avoid using unprofessional abbreviations such as BCNU for "Be seeing you," GG for "Got to go," or J/K for "Just kidding."

that "despite the increase in effort, . . . most participants perceived that they performed the task better by e-mail."[37] The study cited two explanations for this feeling: (1) Individual contributions by the group members were better constructed; and (2) there was not as much counterproductive interruption with electronic communication as within a group meeting. In addition, group members could respond to e-mails at a time that was most convenient for them. The study indicates that while e-mail may take more time and effort, it may be more effective in the long run.[38]

E-mail takes careful planning and new writing skills. Those who read your e-mail will make judgments about your intelligence and competence, whether you want them to or not. Therefore, you need to carefully monitor not only what you write about but also how you word your messages. Here are some guidelines to follow:

Know your company's e-mail policies Most organizations monitor their employees' e-mail carefully. Keep in mind that even deleted messages live on indefinitely in the company's hard drives and may resurface. E-mail that might be sexually offensive could be considered sexual harassment and have serious ramifications. (See Case 2.1, Cybersurveillance, at the end of this chapter.)

Keep work-related messages professional and avoid sending personal e-mail messages on company time. A young analyst working in the Carlyle Group's Seoul office sent friends an e-mail in which he described his glamorous life that included a "harem of chickies," bankers catering to his "every whim," and other comments. Several people receiving the e-mail forwarded it to others in the financial community. Excerpts of it even appeared in the *New York Times*. The analyst was promptly fired.[39]

Create an appropriate e-mail address Carefully design your e-mail address to give the impression you want to convey. Addresses such as Crazylady@_____.com or Buddyboy@_____.com may be acceptable for personal e-mail but should never be used in a business setting. If you are the only person in your organization with your last name, that name could be your address. However, if there are, for instance, several Smiths, the appropriate alternative could be psmith@_____.com. If there is more than one P. Smith, perhaps psmith2@_____.com or Patrick_Smith@_____.com would work.

Although this may seem obvious, *always* make sure you are sending an e-mail to the correct address. This quick double-check will prevent delays and embarrassment for everyone involved if your message contains negative or potentially libelous comments about colleagues, or semiprivate information.

Use the *Subject:* line One of the best ways to set the stage for effective communications is to learn how to appropriately use the *Subject:* line available on all e-mail messages. It usually appears next to the sender's name on the receiver's screen. This brief introduction to your message will cue the receiver as to the probable content of your message. If your message is time-critical, use *Urgent* on the subject line. If you merely want to share information and don't expect a response, insert *FYI* ("For Your Information") on the subject line. If you are placing an order, announcing a baby's birth, or responding to an e-mail, give the receiver an abbreviated clue as to your intent.

Watch your language The biggest clue to your competence will be the words you use. Be sure they are all spelled correctly and that there are no typographical errors. (E-mails filled with typing errors convey an attitude of disrespect toward the reader, which may come right back at the sender.) Be sure that you have selected the appropriate word—when choosing, for example, from *there/their/they're; sight/site/cite; then/than; which/witch,* and so on. Do your verbs agree with their subjects? If your writing skills are limited, use software that includes grammar- and spelling-checkers.

Keep your messages brief by summarizing your main points, indicate the action or response you are seeking, and be sure you provide all the details the receiver needs. Be very careful about the *tone* of your messages. Remove any potentially offending words and phrasing from your documents. Some people feel that they have to use stronger language to get a message across because the receiver cannot "hear" them. If you use solid capital letters in your e-mail, though, readers may think you are shouting at them.[40]

Warning: E-mail does not easily convey emotions, because you cannot hear voice inflections or see body language. Neither the sender not the receiver can assume anything about the correspondent's frame of mind. Readers will not be able to tell if you are serious or being sarcastic, prying or simply curious, angry or merely frustrated. After creating your message, reread it as a stranger might. If words or phrases might be misconstrued, rewrite it so as to make clear *exactly* what you mean to say.

Avoid forwarding junk mail Advertisements, jokes, funny photographs, and so forth should be left for personal e-mail opportunities and sent from your private home computer only. Do *not* send them through your organization's system. Many such attachments include viruses that can shut down an entire operating system when someone views the contents. Often the people receiving

HUMAN RELATIONS IN ACTION	Selected Telephone Tips

- Identify yourself and the company you represent.
- Set yourself apart from others by using a friendly tone and impeccable phone manners.
- Never smoke, drink, eat, click a retractable pen, or tap on the desk while talking on the phone.
- Keep brief customer profiles near your phone. Details might include personal details (hobbies, birthday, family members' names), contact dates, and business history.

- Smile when you speak; your telephone listener can hear it in your voice.
- When completing the call, briefly summarize whatever action that will be taken and thank the caller for his or her time.
- If you are using a speakerphone, let the caller know it. Don't use a speakerphone if you share space with other people.
- Never talk on a cellular phone while you are in a meeting or at a restaurant. If you receive a call, excuse yourself and talk with the caller only when you reach a private area.

your "junk" classify you as a "junky" and will merely delete future messages from you.

If your organization has been kind enough to provide you with Internet access and e-mail capabilities, respect the gift and use your account properly. In the information age, e-mail etiquette is just as important as other forms of business etiquette.[41]

■ Summary

business.college.hmco.com/students

The age of information has generated rapid advances in communications technology. But technology needs people to make it work. No longer is there a need to communicate more; instead, we need to sort through the mounds of information that bombard us daily and learn to communicate more effectively. This becomes possible when we understand the communication process.

Impersonal, one-way communication methods can be effectively used to share basic facts, policies, instructions, and other such information that requires no feedback from the receiver. Interpersonal communication involves a two-way exchange in which the receiver understands the message in the same way the sender intended it.

Communication is often filtered through semantics, language and cultural barriers, emotions, attitudes, role expectations, and nonverbal messages. Often, too, men and women view conversations through their gender-specific focus. Body language conveys information about a person's thoughts and feelings through eye contact, facial expressions, gestures, and use of personal space.

Individuals can make their messages clearer by choosing words carefully, using repetition, and timing the message so that the receiver can focus on what is being said. They can also learn active, critical, and empathic listening skills.

Communication in organizations unifies group behavior and helps build teamwork. Formal communication channels follow the structure of the organization and can be vertical or horizontal. Informal channels, such as the grapevine, often transmit information more rapidly than formal channels but can also have an extremely negative effect on the organization if the rumors are untrue. Organizations can improve their internal communications by creating a climate that encourages upward communication.

The virtual office concept has expanded companies' use of telecommuters, working in "offices without walls" and relying on communication technologies such as cell phones, voice mail, and e-mail, all of which require new skills and appropriate business etiquette.

■ Career Corner

Q: I have just been "released" from the job I held for twelve years because my company was bought out by our competitor. I am highly skilled, competent, and dependable, but it's been a long time since I went on a job interview, and I'm scared to death. How should I communicate my strengths and commitment to a prospective employer? What happens if I blow it?

A: Fear is your greatest enemy, so be confident that many employers are currently experiencing a shortage of highly skilled job candidates. They are seeking capable employees, so make your best appearance and see what's out there. Remember that no one wants to hire a "victim," so do not refer to your "release" or your employer in a negative way. Memorize an exit statement that explains why you are looking for a new opportunity. It should focus on your strengths rather than on why you were released: for example, "My computer skills far exceeded the needs of my company's new owner." Be aware that your degree, references, wardrobe, and handshake get you in the door, but that interviews today often include probing questions that test your ability to react and respond quickly. Most interviewers expect applicants to ask their own series of questions, such as: How does this position fit into the organizational structure? Why is the position vacant? What are the opportunities for advancement? If you want the job at the conclusion of the interview, ask for it! Be sure to send a follow-up note to the interviewer that reemphasizes your strengths. If you feel you blew it, contact the interviewer by phone or letter to correct misleading or misinterpreted information. This type of persistence will show that you sincerely want the job. If you don't get the job, consider the interview a great practice session and enter the next one with renewed confidence!

■ Key Terms

impersonal communication	formal channels
interpersonal communication	grapevine
feedback	upward communication
semantics	virtual offices
nonverbal messages	telecommuting
active listening	voice mail
critical listening	scanners
empathic listening	fax modems

■ Review Questions

1. Describe the difference between impersonal and interpersonal communication. Explain the communication process in your own words.

2. Why is feedback essential to good communication?

3. Compare the responsibilities of both sender and receiver in the communication process.

4. Identify five communication filters. How can they be stumbling blocks to effective communication?

5. What techniques can be used to send clear messages? How can you know if you have been successful?

6. Describe what happens when a sender's nonverbal cues do not agree with the verbal message being sent.

7. Why do organizations have formal communication channels? When are they most effective?

8. Describe the strengths and weaknesses of informal communication channels in an organization.

9. What steps can you take to avoid voice mail tag?

10. Compare the advantages and disadvantages of using e-mail.

■ Application Exercises

1. Carefully examine Table 2.1, Active Listening Skills. Select a partner from your class and explain your favorite hobbies to each other. As your partner is speaking, follow the four guidelines in the table. When both have completed this exercise, discuss whether or not each felt the partner was really listening. Did either of you find that the other person was distracted and not really paying attention? Be prepared to share your insights with your instructor and other class members.

2. Print out the most recent e-mails (if you have an account) that you have sent and received and bring them to class. Analyze their effectiveness in terms of the e-mail tips in this chapter. Did the messages violate any of the tips? If so, which ones? How could these messages be improved?

 ## Internet Exercise

As noted in this chapter, we spend more time listening than we spend speaking, reading, or writing. However, most of us are not good listeners. To learn more about listening and how to improve your listening skills, access Amazon.com and search for "active listening" and "empathic listening." Examine the information available on these topics. Could this information be useful as you attempt to improve your listening skills? Explain.

Case 2.1 Cybersurveillance: Big Brother Is Watching!

One of the most combustible issues in today's organizations is cybersurveillance, the electronic eavesdropping employers can do when organizations' computers are connected to the Internet. Nearly 80 percent of U.S. companies say they actively monitor their workers' communications. Computer programs such as LittleBrother and MIMEsweeper alert employers when individual employees are ordering a new wardrobe, planning a vacation, participating in cyberaffairs, or day-trading stocks. Software like Investigator tracks every keystroke and mouseclick, churning out reports as specific as desired.

Companies use cybersurveillance to root out wasted time, stop sexual harassment, and catch employees who are disloyal or dishonest. In many cases, the companies had good cause to crack down.

- UPS caught an employee running a personal business during working hours.

- Wolverton & Associates, a civil engineering company, discovered that 4 percent of its Internet capacity was being consumed by employees downloading music.

- A Chevron Corp. intranet e-mail posting that listed "25 reasons why beer is better than women" cost that company $2.2 million to compensate employees who were offended.

- According to a Vault.com survey, about 70 percent of the traffic on Internet porn sites occurs during regular business hours.

- Twenty-five percent of those surveyed in a recent American Management Association study reported that they have fired employees for viewing porn sites, trading stocks, gambling on line, or posting to chat rooms.

The courts have consistently ruled that communications written on company-provided computers and e-mail systems belong to the company and are not private. Privacy proponents argue that Internet transmissions—largely accessed via phone lines—should fall under the federal laws about listening to phone conversations. (It takes a court order and tight supervision to listen legally over a telephone link.) In an attempt to control potential invasion of privacy, some states have passed legislation that allows companies to monitor but requires them to notify employees when their computer-based communications are being monitored.

Human resource professionals are attempting to measure the tradeoff between monitoring employees' online activities and the potential for offending their employees and creating a climate of mistrust. As this issue becomes more volatile, some organizations have made adjustments. Boeing Co. allows employees to use faxes, e-mail, and the Internet for personal reasons, but sets guidelines for such use. The policy contains phrases like "reasonable duration and frequency" and "embarrassment to the company." The National Labor Relations Board recently ordered Pratt & Whitney to back off on a blanket policy barring employees' use of e-mail for nonbusiness purposes. Some workers have successfully argued that they deserve to take care of personal business during work hours, since "personal" hours are severely limited because of the virtual office trend and the resultant blurring of lines between work life and personal life.[42]

■ **Questions**

1. Do you believe that computers at work should be used only to provide service to customers and for other business purposes? Explain.

2. Opponents of cybersurveillance feel these practices represent a violation of employee privacy. They also suggest that employers have the capability to "set up" or "entrap" employees already targeted for dismissal. Proponents of cybersurveillance believe these practices result in better customer service and they help identify employees who are violating company policies. Do you agree with the proponents or the opponents? Explain your reasoning.

3. When Microsoft was being investigated for violation of antitrust laws, prosecutors unveiled a rich trail of electronic communications among Microsoft employees that indicated that there was collaboration to create a business monopoly. The defendants spent countless hours, and lost face with the public, in attempting to explain these electronic messages.[43] Do you agree or disagree that the courts should allow this type of information to be introduced as evidence? Explain your opinion.

Case 2.2   Reading Nonverbal Cues

Gestures, body movements, tone of voice, and facial expressions are to speech what periods, commas, and exclamation points are to written language. They can make your message meaningful or confusing. They can confirm or contradict what you are trying to say. Without a word, seemingly insignificant changes in your body language can communicate confidence or fear, trust or mistrust, curiosity or boredom. In a typical interaction with another person, hundreds of nonverbal cues stream past us defining what that person means or feels, while at the same time we react to their message with our own set of nonverbal cues. Research shows that over half of human communication takes place at this level.

Because of this powerful, often subconscious communication process, law enforcement officials across the world are stepping up the use of "behavior profiling." Rather than selecting people to be interrogated based on what they look like (often referred to as "racial profiling"), they are being trained to look for telltale body language. When they identify suspicious individuals, they ask them pointed questions to increase their stress levels. In addition to listening for inconsistencies in what is said, law enforcement officials then look for minute physical reactions on the faces of people being questioned.

The science of spotting nervous or threatening behaviors is gaining newfound respect following the terrorists' attacks on September 11, 2001. The FBI has started teaching nonverbal behavior analysis to all new recruits. Officials at Logan Airport in Boston have trained more than 200 Massachusetts state troopers to watch for travelers who exhibit nonverbal signals such as darting eyes and hand tremors. Systems are under development to enhance security cameras so that they can monitor certain nonverbal behaviors, and computer software with voice-stress sensors are being installed at various airport check-in desks.

All U.S. customs agents are required to watch videos teaching them techniques for studying body language. One international traveler caught the attention of a customs inspector at John F. Kennedy Airport in New York because his lips were dry and chapped to the point of being almost white. His carotid artery was visibly throbbing. After questioning the man, inspectors discovered he had paid cash for a business-class ticket, even though he was a low-paid service worker from South America. When they x-rayed him, they found he had swallowed several bags of heroin pellets.[44]

■ Questions

1. Do you believe "behavior profiling" is a viable method of interpreting a person's actions? Why or why not?

2. There is no simple codebook of nonverbal cues that is accepted across all the cultures of the world. How would you enhance the training programs discussed in this case so that they compensate for cultural diversity?

3. How do you feel about hidden security devices that monitor your nonverbal signals yet protect you from those who might cause you harm?

PART II

CAREER SUCCESS BEGINS WITH KNOWING YOURSELF

3

UNDERSTANDING YOUR COMMUNICATION STYLE

Chapter Preview

After studying this chapter, you will be able to

- Understand the concept of communication style bias and its effect on interpersonal relations.

- Realize the personal benefits that can be derived from an understanding of communication styles.

- Discuss the major elements of the communication style model.

- Identify your preferred communication style.

- Improve communications with others through style flexing.

Let's face it, some of those business articles that focus on inventory control, return on investment, and product distribution can be a little boring. However, articles that focus on the human side of the organization, such as leader profiles, can be quite interesting. Early profiles of Al "Chainsaw" Dunlap described a man who was aggressive, frank, opinionated, and impatient. He earned his nickname by ordering huge layoffs when he was the CEO responsible for restructuring companies such as Scott Paper and Sunbeam Corporation. Deborah Hopkins earned the nickname "Hurricane Debby" for the way she conducted business while holding executive positions at Unisys, GM Europe, Boeing, and Lucent Technologies. Her demanding, ambitious, and sometimes emotional style often created personality clashes.[1] Jeff Bezos, founder and CEO of Amazon.com, seems to be a happy extrovert. A reporter for *Fast Company* magazine recorded forty-three belly laughs during a 40-minute interview with Bezos. Jim Parker, the low-profile CEO of Southwest Airlines, describes himself as "fairly boring."[2]

We draw conclusions about people by observing their behavior. The thoughts, feelings, and actions that characterize someone are generally viewed as their **personality.**[3] Communication style is one important aspect of our personality.

Jeff Bezos, founder and CEO of Amazon.com, is definitely an extrovert. He frequently laughs at himself and seems to like an informal relationship with others.

Communication Styles: An Introduction

Have you ever wondered why it seems so difficult to talk with some people and so easy to talk with others? Can you recall a situation where you met someone for the first time and immediately liked that person? Something about the individual made you feel comfortable. You may have had this experience when you started a new job or began classes at a new school. A major goal of this chapter is to help you understand the impact your communication style has on the impression others form of you. This chapter also provides you with the information you will need to cope effectively in today's workplace, which is characterized by greater diversity and teamwork.

● Communication Style Defined

The impressions that others form about us are based on what they observe us saying and doing. They have no way of knowing our innermost thoughts and feelings, so they make decisions about us based on what they see and hear.[4] The patterns of behavior that others can observe can be called **communication style.**

Each person has a unique communication style. By getting to know your style, you can achieve greater self-awareness and learn how to develop more effective interpersonal relations with coworkers. Accurate self-knowledge is truly the starting point for effectiveness at work. It is also essential for managing the three key relationships described in Chapter 1: relationships with self, with another person, and with members of a group. If your career objective is to become a supervisor or manager, you will benefit by being more aware of your employees' communication styles. Job satisfaction and productivity increase when employees feel that their leaders understand their personal needs and take these into consideration.

It is sometimes difficult for us to realize that people can differ from us and yet not be inferior.

It is sometimes difficult for us to realize that people can differ from us and yet not be inferior. Understanding other people's communication styles improves working relationships by increasing our acceptance of other people and their way of doing things. Knowledge of the various communication styles helps us communicate more effectively with people who differ from us.

In recent years, thousands of people have sought to improve their interpersonal relationship skills through the study of communication styles. They seek not only greater awareness of their own style, but also greater sensitivity to and tolerance for other persons' styles. And they learn how to use the strengths of their styles in organizational settings.

● Fundamental Concepts Supporting Communication Styles

This may be your first introduction to communication styles. Therefore, let's begin by reviewing a few basic concepts that support the study of this dimension of human behavior.

1. *Individual differences exist and are important.* Length of eye contact, use of gestures, speech patterns, facial expressions, and the degree of assertiveness people project to others are some of the characteristics of a personal communication style. We can identify a person's unique communication style by carefully observing these patterns of behavior.[5]

2. *Individual style differences tend to be stable.* The basics of communication style theory were established by Swiss psychiatrist Carl Jung. In his classic book *Psychological Types,* he states that every individual develops a primary communication style that remains quite stable throughout life. Each person has a relatively distinctive way of responding to people and events.[6] Many psychologists now believe that people are born with a predisposition to prefer some behaviors (actions) over others. Because these preferred behaviors are easily and naturally used, they are exercised and developed further over least preferred preferences. For example, a gregarious child—one who enjoys the company of others—will seek ways to experience a wealth of relationships. This personality trait (often described as extroversion) will be nurtured and strengthened over the years.[7]

3. *There is a limited number of styles.* Jung observes that people tend to fall into one of several behavior patterns when relating to the world around them. He describes four behavior styles: intuitor, thinker, feeler, and sensor.[8] Those in the same behavior category tend to display similar traits. The thinker, for example, places a high value on facts, figures, and reason.

4. *A communication style is a way of thinking and behaving.* It is not an ability but instead a preferred way of using the abilities one has. This distinction is very important. An *ability* refers to how well someone can do something. A *style* refers to how someone likes to do something.[9]

5. *To create the most productive working relationships, it is necessary to get in sync with the behavior patterns (communication style) of the people you work with.*[10] Differences between people can be a source of friction unless you develop the ability to recognize and respond to the other person's style. The ability to identify another person's communication style, and to know how and when to adapt your own preferred style to it, can give you an important advantage in dealing with people. Learning to adapt your style to fit the needs of another person is called "style flexing," a topic that is discussed later in this chapter.

● **Learning to Cope with Communication Style Bias**

Several forms of bias exist in our society. People over 40 sometimes complain that they are victims of age discrimination. Gender bias problems have made headlines for years. And people of color—blacks, Hispanics, Asians, Native Americans—say that racial and ethnic bias is still a serious problem today. Communication style bias represents another common form of prejudice.

Almost everyone experiences **communication style bias** from time to time. The bias is likely to surface when you meet someone who displays a style distinctly different from your own. For example, a quiet, reflective person may feel uncomfortable in the presence of someone who displays a dynamic, outgoing style. If, however, the person you encounter has the same communication style as yours, communication style bias is less likely to occur. We could say, using the analogy of radio, that you are both on the same wavelength.

TOTAL	**PAUL MOK AND DUDLEY LYNCH**
PERSON	HUMAN RESOURCE DEVELOPMENT CONSULTANTS
INSIGHT	"By knowing our own communicating style, we get to know ourselves better. And we get along with others better as we develop the ability to recognize—and respond to—their styles."

At this point, you may be saying to yourself, "But in the world of work, I don't have a choice—I have to get my message across to all kinds of people, no matter what their communication style is." You are right. Office receptionists must deal with a variety of people throughout each day. Bank loan officers cannot predict who will walk into their offices at any given time.

How can you learn to cope with communication style bias? First, you must develop awareness of your own unique style.[11] Recall from Chapter 1 that self-awareness is one of the major themes of this text. Accurate self-knowledge is essential for developing strong interpersonal relationships. Knowledge of your communication style gives you a fresh perspective and sets the stage for improved relations with others. The second step in coping with communication style bias is learning to assess the communication style of those people with whom you have contact. The ability to identify another person's communication style, and to know how and when to adapt your own preferred style to it, can afford you a crucial advantage in dealing with people. The ability to "speak the other person's language" is an important relationship-management skill that can be learned.

The Communication Style Model

This section introduces a model that encompasses four basic communication styles. This simple model is based on research studies conducted over the past seventy years and features two important dimensions of human behavior: dominance and sociability. As you study the communication style model, keep in mind that it describes your *preferences,* not your *skills* or *abilities.*

● The Dominance Continuum

In study after study, those "differences that make a difference" in interpersonal relationships point to dominance as an important dimension of style. **Dominance** can be defined as the tendency to display a "take-charge" attitude.

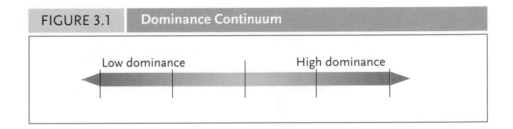

FIGURE 3.1   Dominance Continuum

Low dominance   High dominance

Every person falls somewhere on the **dominance continuum,** illustrated in Figure 3.1. David W. Johnson in his book *Reaching Out—Interpersonal Effectiveness and Self-Actualization* states that people tend to fall into two dominance categories: low or high.[12]

1. *Low dominance.* These people are characterized by a tendency to be cooperative and eager to assist others. They tend to be low in assertiveness and are more willing to be controlled by others.

2. *High dominance.* These people give advice freely and frequently initiate demands. They are more assertive and tend to seek control over others.

The first step in determining your most preferred communication style is to identify where you fall on the dominance continuum. Do you tend to be low or high on this scale? To answer this question, complete the dominance indicator form in Figure 3.2 (on the next page). Rate yourself on each scale by placing a checkmark at a point along the continuum that represents how you perceive yourself. If most of your checkmarks fall to the right of center, you rank high in dominance. If most fall to the left of center, you are low in dominance.

Another way to assess the dominance dimension is to ask four or five people who know you well to complete the dominance indicator form for you. Their assessment may provide a more accurate indication of where you fall on the continuum. Self-assessment alone is sometimes inaccurate because we often lack self-insight.[13] Once you have received the forms completed by others, try to determine if a consistent pattern exists. (Note: It is best not to involve parents, spouses, or close relatives. Seek feedback from coworkers or classmates.)

● Where Should You Be on the Dominance Continuum?

People who are high in dominance must sometimes curb their desire to express strong opinions and initiate demands.

Is there any best place to be on the dominance continuum? Not really. Successful people can be found at all points along the continuum. Nevertheless, there are times when people need to act decisively to influence the adoption of their ideas and communicate their expectations clearly. This means that someone low in dominance may need to become more assertive temporarily to achieve an objective. New managers who are low in dominance must learn to influence others without being viewed as aggressive or insensitive. The American Management Association offers a course entitled "Assertiveness Training for Managers," which is designed for managers who want to

| FIGURE 3.2 | Dominance Indicator Form |

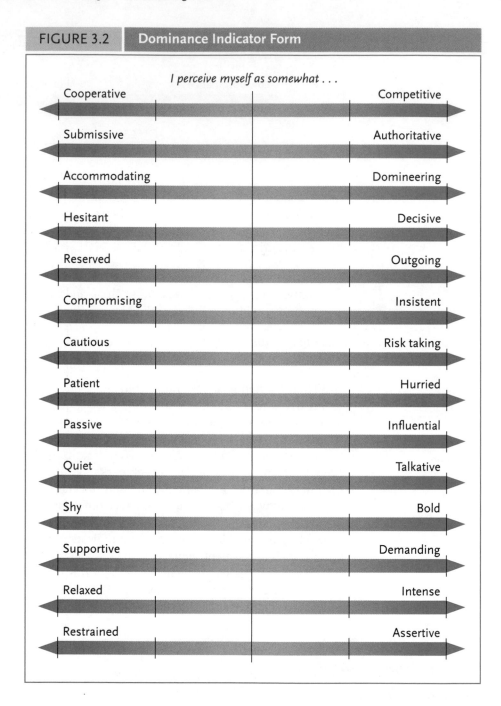

I perceive myself as somewhat . . .

Cooperative				Competitive
Submissive				Authoritative
Accommodating				Domineering
Hesitant				Decisive
Reserved				Outgoing
Compromising				Insistent
Cautious				Risk taking
Patient				Hurried
Passive				Influential
Quiet				Talkative
Shy				Bold
Supportive				Demanding
Relaxed				Intense
Restrained				Assertive

exercise a greater influence on others, get their proposals across more effectively, and resolve conflict situations decisively yet diplomatically.[14]

People who are high in dominance must sometimes curb their desire to express strong opinions and initiate demands. A person who is perceived as being extremely strong-willed and inflexible will have difficulty establishing a cooperative relationship with others.

THINKING / LEARNING STARTERS

1. After you have determined your own place on the dominance scale, think about your closest coworkers and friends. Who is most dominant in your circle? Who is least dominant? Under what circumstances have they displayed high dominance? Under what circumstances have they displayed low dominance?

2. Complete the dominance indicator form shown in Figure 3.2 for one of the people you have just listed.

● **The Sociability Continuum**

Have you ever met someone who was open and talkative and who seemed easy to get to know? An individual who is friendly and expresses feelings openly can be placed near the top of the **sociability continuum**.[15] The continuum is illustrated in Figure 3.3. **Sociability** can be defined as the tendency to seek and enjoy social relationships.

Sociability can also be thought of as a measure of whether you tend to control or express your feelings. Those high in sociability usually express their feelings freely, whereas people low on the continuum tend to control their feelings. The person who is classified as being high in sociability is open and talkative and likes personal associations. The person who is low in sociability is more reserved and formal in social relationships.

The second step in determining your most preferred communication style is to identify where you fall on the sociability continuum. To answer this question, complete the sociability indicator form shown in Figure 3.4. Rate yourself

FIGURE 3.3	Sociability Continuum

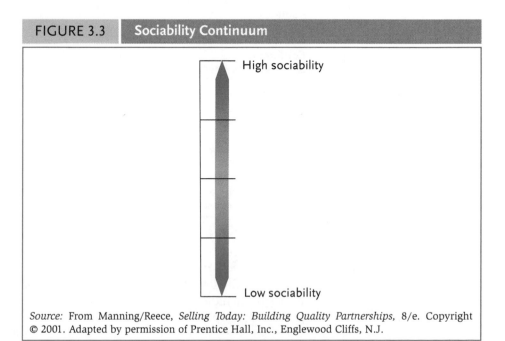

Source: From Manning/Reece, *Selling Today: Building Quality Partnerships*, 8/e. Copyright © 2001. Adapted by permission of Prentice Hall, Inc., Englewood Cliffs, N.J.

FIGURE 3.4	Sociability Indicator Form

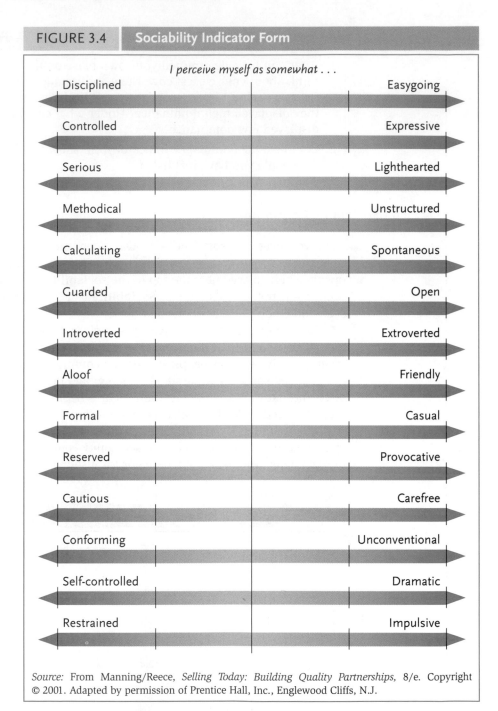

I perceive myself as somewhat . . .

Disciplined	Easygoing
Controlled	Expressive
Serious	Lighthearted
Methodical	Unstructured
Calculating	Spontaneous
Guarded	Open
Introverted	Extroverted
Aloof	Friendly
Formal	Casual
Reserved	Provocative
Cautious	Carefree
Conforming	Unconventional
Self-controlled	Dramatic
Restrained	Impulsive

Source: From Manning/Reece, *Selling Today: Building Quality Partnerships,* 8/e. Copyright © 2001. Adapted by permission of Prentice Hall, Inc., Englewood Cliffs, N.J.

on each scale by placing a checkmark at a point along the continuum that represents the degree to which you feel you exhibit each of the characteristics. If most of your checkmarks fall to the right of center, you are high in sociability. If most fall to the left of center, you are low in sociability.

The sociability indicator form is not meant to be a precise instrument, but it will provide you with a general indication of where you fall on each of the scales. You may also want to make copies of the form and distribute them to friends or coworkers for completion. (Remember, it is advisable not to involve parents, spouses, or close relatives in this feedback exercise.)

● **Where Should You Be on the Sociability Continuum?**

Where are successful people on the sociability continuum? Everywhere. There is no best place to be. People at all points along the continuum can achieve success in an organizational setting. Nevertheless, there are some common-sense guidelines that persons who fall at either end of the continuum are wise to follow.

A person who is low in sociability is more likely to display a no-nonsense attitude when dealing with other people. This person may be seen as impersonal and businesslike. Behavior that is too guarded and too reserved can be a barrier to effective communication. Such persons may be perceived as unconcerned about the feelings of others and interested only in getting the job done. Perceptions are critical in the business world, especially among customers. Even a hint of indifference can create a customer relations problem.

People who are high in sociability openly express their feelings, emotions, and impressions. They are perceived as being concerned with relationships and therefore are easy to get to know. At times, emotionally expressive people need to curb their natural exuberance. Too much informality can be a problem in some work relationships. The importance of adapting your style to accommodate the needs of others is discussed later in this chapter.

THINKING / LEARNING STARTERS

1. After you have determined your own place on the sociability scale, think about your closest coworkers and friends. Who is most sociable in your circle? Who is least sociable? Under what circumstances have they displayed high sociability? Under what circumstances have they displayed low sociability?

2. Complete the sociability indicator form shown in Figure 3.4 for one of the people you have just listed.

● **Four Basic Communication Styles**

The dominance and sociability continua can be combined to form a rather simple model that will tell you more about your communication style (see Figure 3.5 on the next page). The **communication style model** will help you identify your most preferred style. Dominance is represented by the horizontal axis and sociability by the vertical axis. The model is divided into quadrants, each representing one of four communication styles: emotive, director, reflective, or supportive. As you review the descriptions of these styles, you will likely find one that is "most like you" and one or more that are "least like you."

Emotive Style The upper-right-hand quadrant combines high sociability and high dominance. This is characteristic of the **emotive style** of communication (Figure 3.6 on page 67).

FIGURE 3.5	When the dominance and sociability dimensions are combined, the framework for communication style classification is established.

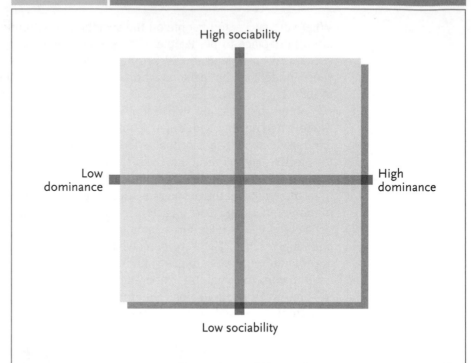

Source: From Manning/Reece, *Selling Today: Building Quality Partnerships*, 8/e. Copyright © 2001. Adapted by permission of Prentice Hall, Inc., Englewood Cliffs, N.J.

Rosie O'Donnell, popular TV personality, frequently displays spontaneous, uninhibited behavior. Like other emotives, she expresses her views with enthusiasm and uses vigorous hand gestures.

FIGURE 3.6	The emotive style combines high sociability and high dominance.

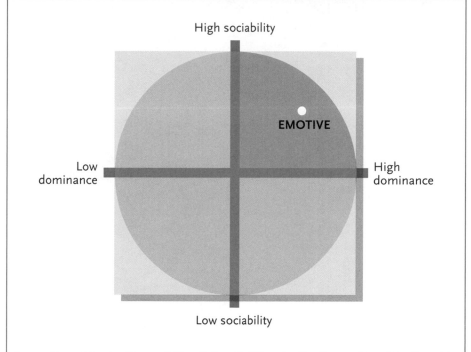

Source: From Manning/Reece, *Selling Today: Building Quality Partnerships,* 8/e. Copyright © 2001. Adapted by permission of Prentice Hall, Inc., Englewood Cliffs, N.J.

You can easily form a mental picture of the emotive type by thinking about the phrases used earlier to describe high dominance and high sociability. A good example of the emotive type of person is comedian Jay Leno. Rosie O'Donnell also projects an outspoken, enthusiastic, and stimulating style. Richard Branson, founder of Virgin Atlantic Airways, displays the emotive style. He is animated, frequently laughs at himself, and seems to like an informal atmosphere. Larry King, popular talk-show host, and Jeff Bezos also project the emotive communication style. Here is a list of verbal and nonverbal clues that identify the emotive person:

1. *Displays spontaneous, uninhibited behavior.* The emotive person is more apt to talk rapidly, express views with enthusiasm, and use vigorous hand gestures. David Letterman and Jim Carrey fit this description.

2. *Displays the personality dimension described as extroversion.* Extroverts typically enjoy being with other people and tend to be active and upbeat. The emotive person likes informality and usually prefers to operate on a first-name basis.

3. *Possesses a natural persuasiveness.* Combining high dominance and high sociability, this person finds it easy to express his or her point of view dramatically and forcefully.

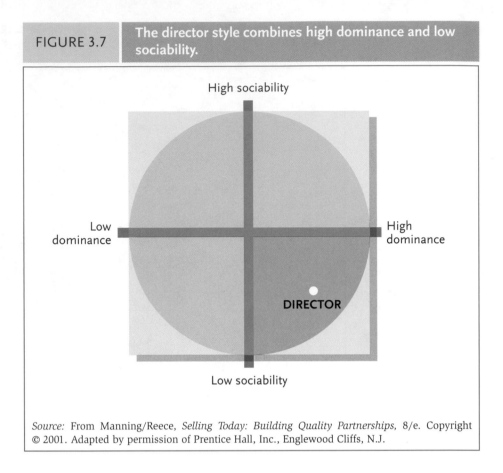

| FIGURE 3.7 | The director style combines high dominance and low sociability. |

Source: From Manning/Reece, *Selling Today: Building Quality Partnerships,* 8/e. Copyright © 2001. Adapted by permission of Prentice Hall, Inc., Englewood Cliffs, N.J.

Director Style The lower-right-hand quadrant represents a communication style that combines high dominance and low sociability—the **director style** (Figure 3.7). Martha Stewart and Jesse Ventura, former governor of Minnesota, project the director style. So does Greta Van Susteren (television personality). Bob Dole, former presidential candidate, easily fits the description of this communication style. All these people have been described as frank, assertive, and very determined. Some behaviors displayed by directors include the following:

1. *Projects a serious attitude.* Mike Wallace, one of the reporters on the popular television show *60 Minutes,* usually communicates a no-nonsense attitude. Directors often give the impression that they cannot have fun.

2. *Expresses strong opinions.* With firm gestures and a tone of voice that communicates determination, the director projects the image of someone who wants to take control. Judge Judith Sheindlin of the *Judge Judy* television show displays this behavior.

3. *May project indifference.* It is not easy for the director to communicate a warm, caring attitude. He or she does not find it easy to abandon the

FIGURE 3.8	The reflective style combines low dominance and low sociability.

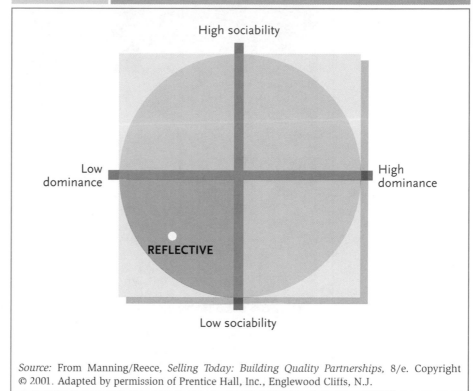

Source: From Manning/Reece, *Selling Today: Building Quality Partnerships,* 8/e. Copyright © 2001. Adapted by permission of Prentice Hall, Inc., Englewood Cliffs, N.J.

formal approach in dealing with people. Vice President Dick Cheney faces this challenge.

Reflective Style   The lower-left-hand quadrant of the communication style model features a combination of low dominance and low sociability. This is the **reflective style** of communication (Figure 3.8).

The reflective person is usually quiet, enjoys spending time alone, and does not make decisions quickly. The late physicist Albert Einstein fits this description. He once commented on how he liked to spend idle hours: "When I have no special problem to occupy my mind, I love to reconstruct proofs of mathematical and physical theorems that have long been known to me. There is no goal in this, merely an opportunity to indulge in the pleasant occupation of thinking."[16] Alan Greenspan, chairman of the Federal Reserve, former president Jimmy Carter, and Dr. Joyce Brothers (psychologist) also display the characteristics of the reflective communication style. Some of the behaviors characteristic of this style are as follows:

1. *Expresses opinions in a disciplined, deliberate manner.* The reflective person does not seem to be in a hurry. He or she expresses measured opinions. Emotional control is a common trait of this style.

When you meet Bill Gates for the first time he appears to be preoccupied with other matters. He expresses measured opinions and displays a high degree of emotional control. Persons with the reflective style tend to be somewhat formal in social relationships.

2. *Seems to be preoccupied.* The reflective person is rather quiet and may often appear preoccupied with other matters. As a result, he or she may seem aloof and difficult to get to know. Bill Gates displays this personality trait.

3. *Prefers orderliness.* The reflective person prefers an orderly work environment. At a meeting, this person appreciates an agenda. A reflective person enjoys reviewing details and making decisions slowly.

Supportive Style The upper-left-hand quadrant combines low dominance and high sociability—the **supportive style** of communication (Figure 3.9). People who possess this style tend to be cooperative, patient, and attentive.

The supportive person is reserved and usually avoids attention-seeking behavior. Additional behaviors that commonly characterize the supportive style include the following:

1. *Listens attentively.* Good listeners have a unique advantage in many occupational settings. This is especially true of loan officers, sales personnel, and supervisors. The talent comes more naturally to the supportive person.

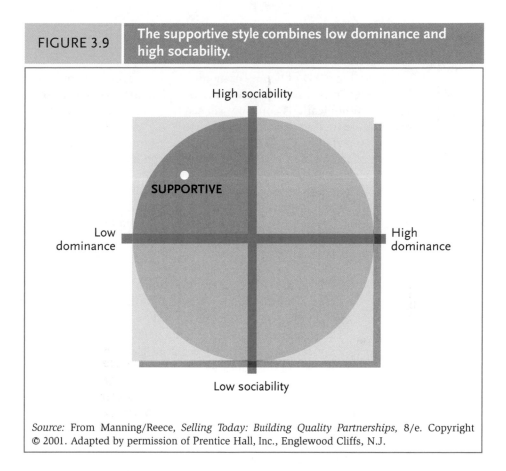

| FIGURE 3.9 | The supportive style combines low dominance and high sociability. |

Source: From Manning/Reece, *Selling Today: Building Quality Partnerships,* 8/e. Copyright © 2001. Adapted by permission of Prentice Hall, Inc., Englewood Cliffs, N.J.

2. *Avoids the use of power.* Supportive persons are more likely to rely on friendly persuasion than power when dealing with people. They like to display warmth in their speech and written correspondence. The late Charles Kuralt, CBS News journalist, and Neil Armstrong, Apollo 11 crew member, fit this description.

3. *Makes and expresses decisions in a thoughtful, deliberate manner.* Supportive persons appear low-key in a decision-making role. Meryl Streep, Paul Simon, Meg Ryan, Kevin Costner, the late Princess Di, and Mary Tyler Moore all display characteristics of this style.

Did you find one particular communication style that is most like yours? If your first attempt to identify your most preferred style was not successful, do not be discouraged. No one conforms completely to one style. You share some traits with other styles. Also, keep in mind that communication style is just one dimension of personality. As noted previously, your personality is made up of a broad array of psychological and behavioral characteristics. It is this unique pattern of characteristics that makes each person an individual. *Communication style* refers only to those behaviors that others can observe.

HUMAN RELATIONS IN ACTION

Closing the Sale

Rich Goldberg, CEO of Warm Thoughts Communications, a New Jersey–based marketing communications company, sensed he was about to lose an important client. He met with his staff, and together they created a profile based on their knowledge of the client's communication style. It soon became apparent that there was a mismatch between the client and the salesperson who called on that person. The customer was low in sociability but high in dominance. The customer was also described as someone who needed facts and figures. The salesperson was spending too much time on relationship building, and this approach was agitating the client. Goldberg counseled his staff to keep conversations with this customer brief, use facts and figures frequently, and clearly spell out the company's commitment to the client.

Did you discover a communication style that is least like yours? In many cases, we feel a sense of tension or discomfort when we have contact with persons who speak or act in ways that are at odds with our communication style. For example, the person with a need for orderliness and structure in daily work may feel tension when working closely with someone who is more spontaneous and unstructured.

● Variation Within Your Communication Style

Communication styles also vary in intensity. For example, a person may be either moderately or strongly dominant. Note that the communication style model features zones that radiate outward from the center, as illustrated in Figure 3.10. These dimensions might be thought of as **intensity zones.**

Zone 1 People who fall within Zone 1 will display their unique behavioral characteristics with less intensity than people in Zone 2. This means that it may be more difficult to identify the preferred communication style of people in Zone 1. They will not be as obvious in their gestures, tone of voice, speech patterns, or emotional expressions. You may have trouble picking up the right clues to identify their communication style.

Zone 2 People who fall within Zone 2 will display their behavioral characteristics with greater intensity than those in Zone 1. For example, on the following dominance continuum, Sue, Mike, Harold, and Deborah each fall within a different zone.

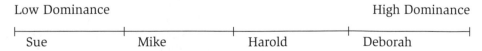

Low Dominance   High Dominance

Sue   Mike   Harold   Deborah

In terms of communication style identification, it is probably easier to distinguish between Sue and Deborah (who are in Zone 2) than between Mike and Harold (who are in Zone 1). Of course, the boundary line that separates Zone 1

| FIGURE 3.10 | Communication Style Intensity Zones |

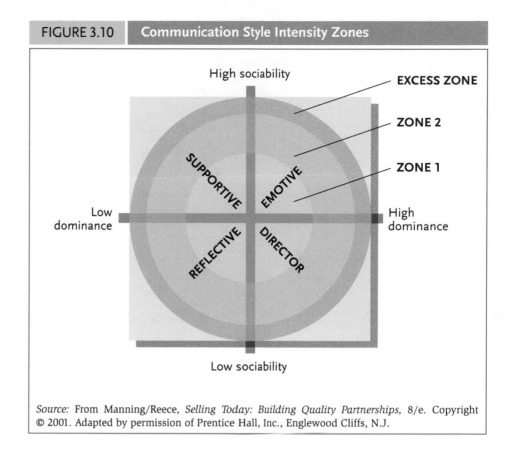

Source: From Manning/Reece, *Selling Today: Building Quality Partnerships,* 8/e. Copyright © 2001. Adapted by permission of Prentice Hall, Inc., Englewood Cliffs, N.J.

from Zone 2 should not be viewed as a permanent barrier. Under certain conditions, people will abandon their preferred style temporarily.

You can sometimes observe this behavior change when a person is upset or angry. For example, Sue is a strong supporter of equal rights for women. At school she hears a male student say, "I think a woman's place is in the home." At that point, she may express her own views in the strongest possible terms. This forcefulness will require temporarily abandoning the comfort of her low dominance style to display assertive behavior.

Inflexible and rigid communication styles are likely to lead to a breakdown in human relations.

Excess Zone The **excess zone** is characterized by a high degree of intensity and rigidity. It can also be labeled the "danger" zone. When people occupy this zone, they become inflexible and display a lack of versatility (see Table 3.1 on the next page). Extreme intensity in any quadrant is bound to interfere with good human relations.

People often move into the excess zone when they are under stress or not feeling well. A person who feels threatened or insecure may also move into the excess zone. Even a temporary excursion into the excess zone should be avoided if at all possible. Inflexible and rigid communication styles are likely to lead to a breakdown in human relations.

TABLE 3.1	Behaviors Displayed in the Excess Zone
Supportive Style	Attempts to win approval by agreeing with everyone Constantly seeks reassurance Refuses to take a strong stand Tends to apologize a great deal
Director Style	Is determined to come out on top Will not admit to being wrong Appears cold and unfeeling when dealing with others Tends to use dogmatic phrases such as "always," "never," or "you can't"
Emotive Style	Tends to express highly emotional opinions Is outspoken to the point of being offensive Seems unwilling to listen to the views of others Uses exaggerated gestures and facial expressions
Reflective Style	Tends to avoid making a decision Seems overly interested in detail Is very stiff and formal when dealing with others Seeks to achieve perfection

● Tips on Style Identification

To identify a person's communication style, focus your full attention on observable behavior. The best clues for identifying styles are nonverbal. Learn to be observant of people's gestures, posture, and facial expressions, and the rapidity and loudness of their speech.[17] Animated facial expressions and high-volume, rapid speech are characteristic of the emotive communication style. Infrequent use of gestures, speaking in a steady monotone, and few facial expressions are characteristic of the reflective style. Of course verbal messages will also be helpful. If a person tends to be blunt and to the point and makes strong statements, you are likely observing a director.

We have noted that communication style is determined by where a person falls on the sociability continuum and the dominance continuum. Once you have identified as many verbal and nonverbal clues as possible, use this information to place the person on each continuum. Let's assume that the clues indicate that the person is low in dominance. This means you can automatically eliminate the emotive and director styles because both are characterized by high dominance. The next step is to place the person on the sociability continuum. If the clues indicate that the person is low in sociability, you automatically eliminate the supportive style. By the process of elimination, you conclude that this person is probably reflective. The authors of *People Styles at Work,* however, warn that your initial perception of another person's style should not be carved in stone. You should continue to collect new information and reassess your initial observations.[18]

Keep in mind that different situations bring out different behaviors. If you observe someone participating in a classroom discussion, then later observe the same person relaxing with friends at a local restaurant, you may witness two different behavioral patterns. Getting to know someone is hard work, and it's best not to look for shortcuts.[19]

Versatility: The Third Dimension

Earlier in this chapter we described two important dimensions of the communication style model: dominance and sociability. You will recall that these dimensions of human behavior are independent of each other. Now we are ready to discuss versatility, an important third dimension of human behavior.

Persons who can create and maintain interpersonal relations with others, regardless of their communication styles, are displaying versatility. **Versatility** can be defined as acting in ways that earn a social endorsement. Endorsement means simply other people's approval of our behavior. People give us their endorsement when they feel comfortable and nondefensive with us.[20]

The dimension of versatility is independent of style. This means that the emotive style is no more or less likely to be versatile than is the reflective style. Communication style remains relatively stable throughout life, whereas versatility is changeable.

Versatility is a trait we exhibit ourselves rather than elicit from others. Versatile people recognize that they can control their half of relationships and that it is easier to modify themselves than it is to modify others. The versatile person asks, "What can I do to make it easier for the other person to relate to me?"[21]

● Achieving Versatility Through Style Flexing

Getting classified according to communication style doesn't mean you are "typecast" for life. You can always learn to strengthen areas of your most preferred communication style in order to get along better with others.[22] One way

Versatility, the third dimension of the communication style model, is very important in any job that requires regular contact with the public. This salesperson must frequently use style flexing in order to meet the needs of his customers.

to broaden your personality is to engage in **style flexing,** which is the deliberate attempt to change or alter your style to meet the needs of another person. It is a temporary effort to act in harmony with the behavior of another person's communication style. Style flexing is communicating in a way that is more agreeable to persons of other styles. As noted earlier in this chapter, you can learn to adapt your style to accommodate others.

Style flexing has proven to be an important skill needed in many occupations. In personal selling, for example, research indicates that salespeople with high versatility scores were likely to outperform salespeople with low versatility.[23]

Style Flexing at Work To illustrate how style flexing can be used in an organizational setting, let's take a look at a communication problem faced by Jeff Walker, buyer of sporting goods for a small chain of sporting goods stores. Jeff has a strong emotive communication style and usually gets along well with other emotive communicators. His immediate supervisor is Rhonda Greenbaum, a reflective person who tends to approach her work in an orderly, systematic manner. Jeff finds it difficult to curb his stimulating, promotional style and therefore is sometimes viewed as "unstable" by Ms. Greenbaum.

What might Jeff do to improve communication with his supervisor? Jeff is naturally an open, impulsive communicator. During meetings with a reflective person, he should appear less spontaneous, slow his rate of speech, and avoid the use of dramatic gestures. He should try to appear more reserved.

The reflective person admires orderliness, so Jeff should be sure he is well prepared. Prior to each meeting, he should develop a mental agenda of items that he wants to cover. At the beginning of the meeting he might say, "Ms. Greenbaum, there are three things I want to discuss." He would then describe each item concisely and present information slowly and systematically. This disciplined approach will be appreciated by the reflective supervisor.

How could Jeff's boss use style flexing to foster better communication? She could avoid appearing too stiff and formal. During meetings, the reflective person should try to avoid being "all business." (The emotive person does not object to small talk during meetings.) The reflective communicator might also be more informal about starting and ending meetings exactly on time, might allow the emotive person to depart from the agenda now and then, or might bring up an item spontaneously. The reflective person should try to share feelings and concerns more openly in the presence of an emotive person.

● Strategies for Adapting Your Style

Once you have identified the dominant style of the other person, begin thinking of ways to flex your style to gain a social endorsement. Remember, you can control your half of the relationship. What can be done to meet the interpersonal needs of the other person? Here are a few general style adaptation strategies:

Flexing to the Emotive Style

■ Take time to build a social as well as a business relationship. Leave time for relating and socializing.

■ Display interest in the person's ideas, interests, and experiences.

■ Do not place too much emphasis on details. Emotive people like fast-moving, inspirational verbal exchanges.

■ Maintain a pace that is fast and spontaneous.

Flexing to the Director Style

■ Be specific, brief, and to the point. Use time efficiently.

■ Present the facts logically, and be prepared to provide answers to specific questions.

■ Maintain a pace that is fast and decisive; project an image of strength and confidence.

■ Messages (written or oral) should be short and to the point.

Flexing to the Reflective Style

■ Appeal to the person's orderly, systematic approach to life. Be well organized.

■ Approach this person in a straightforward, direct manner. Get down to business quickly.

■ Be as accurate and realistic as possible when presenting information.

■ Messages (written or oral) should be detailed and precise. The pace of verbal messages should be slow and systematic.

Flexing to the Supportive Style

■ Show a sincere interest in the person. Take time to identify areas of common interest.

■ Patiently draw out personal views and goals. Listen and be responsive to the person's needs.

■ Present your views in a quiet, nonthreatening manner. Do not be pushy.

■ Put a priority on relationship building and communication.

In those situations where you are attempting to win the support or cooperation of another person, try to avoid saying or doing things that might cause tension to arise. Tony Alessandra and Michael O'Connor, authors of *People Smart,* state that if we don't think first of the other person, we run the risk of unintentionally creating a tension-filled relationship.[24]

HUMAN RELATIONS IN ACTION

Al "Chainsaw" Dunlap Seemed Comfortable in the Excess Zone

Patricia Sellers, a reporter for *Fortune* magazine, has vivid memories of her last telephone conversation with Al "Chainsaw" Dunlap. The embattled CEO of Sunbeam Corporation was about to be fired by the board of directors. Dunlap, famous for his booming voice, abruptness, and strong opinions, wasn't pleased to learn from Sellers that *Fortune* planned to report that several large Sunbeam investors wanted him out: "Geez, this idea that Dunlap's in jeopardy. That's bull!" he raved. Soon after that conversation Dunlap was tossed out by the board. The man who rose to prominence by taking over large corporations and then firing tens of thousands of people was fired for using unorthodox accounting practices. Sellers says, "My ears are still ringing from the shrill sound of Al Dunlap fighting to hold on to his job." Dunlap always seemed comfortable in the excess zone.

● Style Flexing: Pitfalls and Possibilities

Is style flexing just another way to manipulate others? The answer is yes if your approach is insincere and your only objective is to get something for yourself. The choice is yours. If your objective is to build an honest, constructive relationship, then style flexing can be a valuable and productive communication skill.

In an organizational setting, style flexing is especially critical when something important is at stake. Let's assume that you are head of a major department in a large hospital. Tomorrow you will meet with the hospital administrator and propose the purchase of new x-ray equipment that will cost a large amount of money. This is a good time to think about the administrator's communication style and consider your style-flexing strategies. Every decision is influenced by both reason and emotion, but the weight given to each of these elements during the decision-making process can vary from one person to another. Often we make the mistake of focusing too much attention on the content of our message and not enough on how to deliver that message.[25]

A Final Word of Caution

It is tempting to put a label on someone and then assume the label tells you everything you need to know about that person.

A discussion of communication styles would not be complete without a few words of caution. It is tempting to put a label on someone and then assume the label tells you everything you need to know about that person. In *The Name of Your Game,* Stuart Atkins says we should be careful not to use labels that make people feel boxed in, typecast, or judged. He says we should not classify *people;* we should classify their *strengths* and *preferences* to act one way or another under certain circumstances.[26] As noted in Chapter 1, the "total person" is made up of such interdependent traits as emotional control, values orientation, self-esteem, and self-awareness. To get acquainted with the whole person takes time and effort. Atkins makes this observation: "It requires much more effort to look beyond the label, to experience the person as a dynamic process, to look at the fine print on the box and carefully study the ingredients inside the package. We have been conditioned to trust the label 'and look no further."[27]

You must also be careful not to let the label you place on yourself become the justification for your own inflexible behavior. If you discover that your most preferred communication style is reflective and take the position that "others will simply have to get used to my need for careful analysis of data before making a decision," then you are not displaying the characteristics of a versatile person. Try not to let the label justify or reinforce why you are unable to communicate effectively with others.[28]

● Strength/Weakness Paradox

As noted previously in this chapter, there is no "best" communication style. Each style has its unique strong points. Supportive people are admired for their easygoing, responsive style. Directors are respected for the thoroughness and determination they display. The stimulating, personable style of emotive persons can be very refreshing. And the emotional control and disciplined nature of reflective persons are almost universally admired.

Problems arise when people overextend or rely too much on the strengths of their style. The director who is too demanding may be viewed by others as "pushy." The supportive person may try too hard to please others and risk being viewed as "wishy-washy." An emotive person may be viewed as too excitable or not serious enough in a business setting. The reflective person who cannot seem to make a decision without mountains of information may be viewed as too cautious and inflexible. Some people rely too heavily on established strengths and fail to develop new skills that will increase their versatility.

To get along with people at all levels of an organization, you must be able to build rapport with those who are different from you. Customizing your communication style often requires learning *how to overcome your strengths.*[29]

■ Summary

ACE

business.college.hmco.com/students

Self-tests

Communication styles are the patterns of behaviors that are observable to others. Communication style tends to be somewhat stable throughout a person's lifetime. Each person has a distinctive way of responding to people and events. Communication style bias is a common problem in organizations and should be viewed as a major barrier to good human relations.

The communication style model is formed by combining two important dimensions of human behavior: dominance and sociability. Combinations of these two aspects create four communication styles—emotive, director, reflective, and supportive. With practice you can learn to identify other people's communication styles. A third dimension of human behavior—versatility—is important in dealing with varying communication styles. You can adjust your own style to meet the needs of others—a process called style flexing.

We must keep an open mind about people and be careful not to use labels that make them feel typecast or judged. Keeping an open mind requires more thought than pigeonholing.

■ Career Corner

Q: The company I work for discourages personal phone calls during working hours. I am a single parent with two young children. How can I convince my supervisor that some personal calls are very important?

A: Placing personal phone calls during working hours is an issue that often divides employers and employees. From the employer's point of view, an employee who spends time on nonwork calls is wasting time, a valuable resource. Also, many organizations want to keep telephone lines clear for business calls. From your point of view, you need to know about changes in childcare arrangements, serious health concerns of family members, and similar problems. In fact, you will probably perform better knowing that family members are secure. Explain to your supervisor that some personal calls will be inevitable. It is very important that you and your supervisor reach an agreement regarding this issue. When possible, make most of your personal calls during your lunch hour or during work breaks. Encourage friends to call you at home.

To improve communications with your supervisor, get acquainted with his or her communication style. Once you have identified this person's dominant style, use appropriate style flexing strategies to gain a social endorsement.

■ Key Terms

personality	emotive style
communication style	director style
communication style bias	reflective style
dominance	supportive style
dominance continuum	intensity zones
sociability continuum	excess zone
sociability	versatility
communication style model	style flexing

■ Review Questions

1. How would you define *communication style bias?*

2. What are the five basic concepts that establish a foundation for understanding communication styles?

3. How will someone employed in an organization benefit from an understanding of communication styles?

4. Explain the difference between the dominance continuum and the sociability continuum.

5. What are the four communication styles? Provide a brief description of each.

6. What are some nonverbal clues that might help you identify a person's most preferred communication style?

7. Explain why there is no "best" communication style. Feel free to use examples from your personal life to support your answer.

8. Explain the strength/weakness paradox.

9. Define the term *versatility*. Explain the meaning of *style flexing*.

10. The Total Person Insight by David Merrill and Roger Reid suggests that we should try to control what we say and do to make others more comfortable. Would it be easy or difficult for people to follow this advice? Explain your answer.

■ Application Exercises

1. Oprah Winfrey has become one of America's most popular talk-show hosts. Consider the behaviors she displays on her show, and then complete the following exercises:

   a. On the dominance continuum, place a mark where you feel she belongs.

   b. On the sociability continuum, place a mark where you feel she belongs.

   c. On the basis of these two continua, determine Oprah Winfrey's communication style.

   d. In your opinion, does Oprah Winfrey display style flexibility?

2. To get some practice in identifying communication styles, watch two or three television shows and attempt to identify the style of individuals portrayed on the screen. To fully develop your skills of listening and observing, try this three-step approach:

   a. Cover the screen with a towel or newspaper and try to identify the style of one or two persons, using voice only.

   b. Turn down the volume, uncover the screen, and attempt to identify the style of the same persons, using visual messages only.

   c. Turn up the volume and make another attempt to identify the communication style of the persons portrayed on the screen. This time the identification process should be easier because you will be using sight and sound.

   These practice sessions will help you learn how to interpret the nonverbal messages that are helpful in identifying another person's communication style. When you select TV shows, avoid situation comedies that often feature persons displaying exaggerated styles. You may want to watch a talk show or a news program that features interviews.

Internet Exercise

The primary purpose of this chapter is to provide you with an introduction to communication styles and prepare you to apply at work and in your personal life the concepts presented here. You now have the foundation you need to continue your study. A great deal of information related to communication styles can be found on the Internet. Using your search engine, type in the following keywords, and then review the resources available:

communication styles
personality types
personality profiles
psychological types
Jungian personality types

Examine the resources (such as books, articles, and training programs), and then prepare a brief summary of your findings. Pay special attention to new information that was not covered in your textbook.

Case 3.1   Steve Ballmer Keeps the Good Times Rolling at Microsoft

Bill Gates, chairman of Microsoft Corporation, and Steve Ballmer, CEO of Microsoft, met as undergraduates at Harvard University. Both were math whizzes. Gates eventually dropped out of Harvard to form Microsoft, and Ballmer ended up teaching at the Stanford Business School. When Gates needed a tough-minded manager at his fledgling company, he gave Ballmer the assignment. Ballmer built a sales organization to compete with IBM in large corporate accounts.

Gates and Ballmer have different communication styles. Gates displays the reflective style; he is impressed by proposals that are supported by data. Ballmer displays the director style; he is a take-charge person who can be quite demanding.

During the early years at Microsoft, Ballmer was known as a very aggressive executive with little patience. His explosive temper was legendary, and he often terrified his staff members. He once needed throat surgery because he yelled so much. He had a domineering management style and was unwilling to delegate decision making; still, he accomplished a great deal. Ballmer was promoted to president in 1998 and then to chief executive officer in January of 2000. As CEO, he has managed to fortify Microsoft's position as an industry leader.

Today Ballmer's leadership style is more diplomatic, and he's more likely to delegate decision-making authority. One of his goals is to do a better job of developing managers and leaders. Many people at Microsoft say Steve Ballmer has mellowed. In 2003 *Business Week* named him one of the nation's best managers.[30]

■ Questions

1. If Steve Ballmer and Bill Gates met for the first time, would any form of communication style bias surface? Explain.

2. What are Steve Ballmer's primary communication needs?

3. If you made a sales call on Steve Ballmer and you wanted to develop an effective business relationship, how would you speak and act during the meeting?

| **Case 3.2** | **Communication Style Training Builds Teamwork** |

Many organizations interested in improving customer service, promoting greater teamwork among employees, and increasing quality have developed training programs that emphasize an understanding of communication styles. These programs help employees understand the four communication styles one is likely to encounter on the job.

When General Electric Co.'s Business Information Center (GEBIC) was instructed to reduce the layers of management and create a self-directed work force, the staff members weren't sure how to carry out the downsizing effort. They did realize that with fewer supervisory-management personnel, employees would have to contribute more to solving problems and making decisions. With the assistance of a consultant, a decision was made to help employees develop the interpersonal skills needed to become effective team members. The newly formed GEBIC team completed the LIFO workshop offered by Stuart Atkins Incorporated, a California-based training company.

LIFO training invites self-examination and promotes self-development in a comfortable, nonthreatening environment. Workshop participants complete the LIFO Survey, a self-scoring instrument that helps them identify their most preferred communication style. During the workshop, GEBIC employees also spent time learning how to identify the most preferred style of others. LIFO scores for all team members were posted and discussed at the workshop. This information contributed to an understanding of the team members' communication style preferences. Upon completion of the LIFO training, employees reported that they felt greater confidence in their ability to communicate effectively with other team members and with the customers served by GEBIC. One person described her experience this way:

> LIFO not only empowers me as an individual in terms of my interaction with other people, but enables me to empower the other people I am dealing with. When you understand their strong points and blind sides, you both interact more effectively. For example, if I know my boss likes a lot of detail and nitty gritty, I'm going to be prepared when I present a new idea to him.

How has LIFO training influenced productivity at GEBIC? The major responsibility of this division is to handle outside calls from industrial customers or prospects who need assistance. Thus, one way to measure productivity is to examine call volume (customers served per employee) and cost per customer served. During the first two years of the self-directed work-team approach, call volume rose 53 percent, and during the same period the cost per call dropped

34 percent. Team members take pride in the fact that they can usually identify the caller's communication style and then quickly adjust their own style to communicate effectively with the customer.[31]

■ Questions

1. Each GEBIC team member was given the LIFO scores of other team members. What are the advantages of this practice? Are there any disadvantages? Explain.

2. GEBIC team members reported that LIFO training gave them the skills needed to identify the communication style of most callers. If your contact with another person is a telephone call, what factors (clues) would influence your decision regarding the caller's communication style?

3. Would you recommend LIFO training, or a similar program that focuses on communication style theory, to an organization that is attempting to increase the level of teamwork among its employees? Explain.

4

BUILDING HIGH SELF-ESTEEM

Chapter Preview

After studying this chapter, you will be able to

- Define self-esteem and discuss how it is developed.

- Explain how self-esteem influences human relations and success at work.

- Identify the characteristics of people with low and high self-esteem.

- Explain the roles mentors can play in your professional life.

- Identify ways to raise your self-esteem.

- Understand the conditions organizations can create that will help workers raise their self-esteem.

Gene Keluche, a Native American from the Wintun tribe, was raised in a foster home and did not know he was an Indian until age 12. At that young age, he began to explore his Indian heritage by spending time alone in the woods. Over time, he discovered that nature offers opportunities to understand oneself: "I discovered that we have little control over most things around us except our own selves. Out in the woods, I reinvented myself."[1] Later he earned a degree at Harvard Business School and used his curiosity to discover ways to help business firms succeed. Today he is CEO of International Conference Resorts Incorporated.

At the age of 22, Delores Kesler was divorced, the mother of a small child, and struggling to survive with a series of dead-end jobs. With the help of a $10,000 loan and the advice of her father, who told her she could accomplish anything she wanted in life, she founded a temporary-staffing agency in Jacksonville, Florida. When she retired twenty years later, her company, AccuStaff, had projected revenues of $2 billion.[2]

Gene Keluche and Delores Kesler understood that you can control only one thing in this world—the way you think. When you take control over your thinking, you can take control over other aspects of your life. They were able to free themselves from self-limiting beliefs and visualize career success.

To change or improve anything in your life, you must begin by changing the inner aspects of your mind. Many people think that other people or external events cause the problems in their lives, but this is not the case. Your outer world is a reflection of your inner world.[3]

The Power of Self-Esteem

Nathaniel Branden, author of *The Six Pillars of Self-Esteem* and *Self-Esteem at Work,* has spent the past three decades studying the psychology of self-esteem. In countless speeches, articles, and books, he has attempted to describe the connection between self-esteem and many of the human problems common to our society today. He notes that high self-esteem enhances our ability to build effective relationships with others:

> The healthier our self-esteem, the more inclined we are to treat others with respect, benevolence, goodwill, and fairness—since we do not tend to perceive them as a threat, and since self-respect is the foundation of respect for others.[4]

The importance of self-esteem as a guiding force in our lives cannot be overstated.

The importance of self-esteem as a guiding force in our lives cannot be overstated. It is very difficult for people to act beyond their deepest vision of who and what they believe themselves to be.[5] Many business owners, managers, and team leaders recognize the importance of self-esteem. During orientation new employees at Starbucks are introduced to guidelines for on-the-job interpersonal relations. The first guideline is to maintain and enhance self-esteem. Starbucks and many other successful companies have discovered that when employees feel respected, they are less likely to leave the company.[6]

The Power of Strong Self-Efficacy

Over the years many people we now know to be extremely intelligent and talented have had to develop a strong belief in themselves. If they had relied on others' opinions of their capabilities and potential, who knows where this world would be!

Walt Disney was fired by a newspaper editor for lack of ideas. He went bankrupt several times before he built Disneyland.

Thomas Edison's teacher said he was "too stupid to learn anything."

Charles Darwin, father of the theory of evolution, wrote in his autobiography, "I was considered by all my masters and my father, a very ordinary boy, rather below the common standard of intellect."

Fred Astaire recalls the 1933 memo from the MGM casting director that stated, "Can't act. Can't sing. Slightly bald. Can dance a little."

Vince Lombardi, successful football coach and motivational speaker and writer, recalls an expert's description of his talents: "He possesses minimal football knowledge and lacks motivation."

Albert Einstein did not speak until he was 4 years old and did not read until he was 7. His teacher described him as "mentally slow, unsociable, and adrift forever in foolish dreams."

● Self-Esteem = Self-Efficacy + Self-Respect

Nathaniel Branden states that the ultimate source of **self-esteem** can only be internal: It is the relationship between a person's self-efficacy and self-respect. **Self-efficacy** is the belief that you can achieve what you set out to do.[7] When your self-efficacy is high, you believe you have the ability to act appropriately. When your self-efficacy is low, you worry that you might not be able to do the task, that it is beyond your abilities. Your perception of your self-efficacy can influence which tasks you take on and which ones you avoid. Albert Bandura, a professor at Stanford University and one of the foremost self-efficacy researchers, views this component of self-esteem as a resilient belief in your own abilities. According to Bandura, a major source of self-efficacy is the experience of mastery, in which success in one area builds your confidence to succeed in other areas.[8] For example, an administrative assistant who masters a sophisticated computerized accounting system is more likely to master future complicated computer programs than is a person who feels computer illiterate and may not even try to figure out the new program, regardless of how well he or she *could* do it.

Self-respect, the second component of self-esteem, is what you think and feel about yourself. Your judgment of your own value is a primary factor in achieving personal and career success. People who respect themselves tend to act in ways that confirm and reinforce this respect. People who lack self-respect may put up with verbal or physical abuse from others because they feel they are unworthy of praise and deserve the abuse.[9] When you respect yourself, you are more likely to earn the respect of others.

Walt Disney, successful animator and motion picture studio founder, was not an overnight success. He was once fired by a newspaper editor for lack of ideas and he went bankrupt several times before he built Disneyland. Fortunately, throughout a variety of disappoints he continued to believe in himself.

Self-efficacy and self-respect are central themes of the definition of self-esteem adopted by the National Association for Self-Esteem. NASE defines self-esteem as "The experience of being capable of meeting life's challenges and being worthy of happiness."[10] A sense of competence is having the conviction that one is able to make appropriate choices and decisions, and to be effective in the many roles we play in life, such as that of friend, daughter or son, husband or wife, employee or employer, leader, and so on. Our sense of competence is strengthened through meaningful accomplishments, overcoming adversities, and bouncing back from failure.

The NASE definition of self-esteem helps us make the distinction between authentic or healthy self-esteem and false or unhealthy self-esteem. Authentic self-esteem is not expressed by self-glorification at the expense of others or by the attempt to diminish others so as to elevate oneself. Arrogance, boastfulness, and overestimation of your abilities (egocentrism) are more likely to reflect inadequate self-esteem rather than, as it might appear, too much self-esteem.

● How Self-Esteem Develops

To understand the development of self-esteem, it is helpful to examine how you formed your self-concept. Your **self-concept** is the bundle of facts, opinions, beliefs, and perceptions about yourself that are present in your life every moment of every day.[11] The self-concept you have today reflects information you have received from others and life events that occurred throughout childhood, adolescence, and adulthood. You are consciously aware of some of the things you have been conditioned to believe about yourself. But many comments and events that have shaped your self-concept are processed at the unconscious level and continue to influence your judgments, feelings, and behaviors whether you are aware of them or not.[12]

Childhood   Researchers have discovered that a child's potential is greatly influenced during the early years. The neurons of the brain—those long wiry cells that carry electrical messages through the nervous system and the brain—literally make their connections during the birth-to-preschool period. If these connections are not made, the child may suffer later in life. For example, emotional stability, which directly affects how individuals feel about themselves, is greatly affected by how the brain develops in the first two years of life. Too much television viewing can have a negative influence on brain development during this period.

Because childhood events are retained in your brain, poor performance in school, abusive or uncaring parents, or a serious childhood accident can be defining experiences in your life. Messages from siblings, teachers, and various authority figures can have a lasting impact on your self-concept. Consider the father who repeatedly says, "Real men don't cry" or places undue emphasis on successful performance during contact sports. These childhood experiences can form the foundation for your level of self-esteem that emerges later in life.

TOTAL	**OPRAH WINFREY**
PERSON	FOUNDER AND EDITORIAL DIRECTOR, *O, THE OPRAH MAGAZINE*
INSIGHT	"Feeling good about who you are and what you're here on earth to do—that is the real work of your life. And it's ongoing. Each of us arrives with all we need to feel valued and unique, but slowly that gets chipped away."

Adolescence   The years from age 12 to age 18 are among the most crucial in developing and consolidating your feelings about yourself. During these years, you are moving away from the close bond between parent and child and are attempting to establish ideals of independence and achievement.[13] You fluctuate between determination to reach your goals and self-doubt about whether or not you are capable. You must also deal with physical changes, relationships with your peers, the loss of a carefree childhood, and the assumption of some adult responsibilities.

Hugs are great at any age, but they are critical during the early years. As adults our daily thoughts and feelings are filtered through the events and feelings of child-hood. This eight-year-old girl needs reminders of her mother's love.

Teens often feel vulnerable as the media and real life expose them to more violence in the form of schoolroom and drive-by shootings, date rape, sexual abuse, and drug-induced behaviors. To compensate, they frequently adopt an attitude of not caring.[14] When you do not care about anything or anyone, you do not care about yourself, and the result is low self-esteem.

Teens with low self-esteem are sometimes vulnerable to peer pressure, measuring their worth as compared to their friends. They look at movies, music videos, and magazines and attempt to emulate the unrealistic body images and fashions their peers deem worthwhile.

Parents and teachers can have a powerful effect on their teenagers' self-esteem. When they offer encouragement, support, enthusiasm, and commendation for achievements, they enable teens to learn how to take healthy risks, tolerate frustration, and feel proud of their accomplishments. They deserve good relationships and positive experiences. As they learn to recognize and appreciate the impact of their choices and behaviors, teens will be more likely to view themselves as competent people rather than as victims of circumstance and fate.

Adulthood   When you reach adulthood, you are greatly influenced by a time-reinforced self-concept that has been molded by people and events from all your past experiences. You have been bombarded over the years with positive and negative messages from your family, friends, teachers, strangers, and the media. You may compare yourself to others, as was so common in adolescence, or you may focus on your own inner sense of self-worth. Emmett Miller, a noted authority on self-esteem, says that as adults we tend to define ourselves in terms of:[15]

1. *The things we possess.* Miller says this is the most primitive source of self-worth. If we define ourselves in terms of what we have, the result may be an effort to accumulate more and more material things to achieve a greater feeling of self-worth. The idea that we can compensate for self-doubt and insecurity with our checkbook is widely accepted in America.[16] People who define themselves in terms of what they have may have difficulty deciding "what is enough" and may spend their life in search of more material possessions.

2. *What we do for a living.* Miller points out that too often our self-worth and identity depend on something as arbitrary as a job title. Amy Saltzman, author of *Downshifting,* a book on ways to reinvent (or redefine) success, says, "We have allowed our professional identities to define us and control us."[17] She points out that we have looked to outside forces such as the corporation, the university, or the media to provide us with a script for leading a satisfying, worthwhile life.

3. *Our internal value system and emotional makeup.* Miller says this is the healthiest way for people to identify themselves:

© Lynn Johnston Productions, Inc/Distributed by United Feature Syndicate, Inc.

If you don't give yourself credit for excellence in other areas of life, besides your job and material possessions, you've got nothing to keep your identity afloat in emotionally troubled waters. People who are in touch with their real identity weather the storm better because they have a more varied and richer sense of themselves, owing to the importance they attach to their personal lives and activities.[18]

As an adult, you will be constantly adjusting the level of your self-esteem as you cope with events at work and in your personal life. The loss of a job or being passed over for a promotion may trigger feelings of insecurity or depression. A messy divorce can leave you with feelings of self-doubt. An unexpected award may raise your spirits and make you feel better about yourself.

The Past Programs the Future Phillip McGraw, better known as "Dr. Phil," has developed a one-sentence guide to understanding the importance of your self-concept: *The past reaches into the present, and programs the future, by your recollections and your internal rhetoric about what you perceived to have happened in your life.*[19] Past experiences and events, which McGraw describes as "defining moments," can influence your thinking for a lifetime and program your future. They get incorporated into your deepest understanding of who you are because they are often the focus of your internal dialogue—a process we call "self-talk." Later in this chapter, we will discuss how to avoid the influence of negative self-talk and build upon positive messages.

TOTAL PERSON INSIGHT	**DON MIGUEL RUIZ**
	AUTHOR, *THE FOUR AGREEMENTS*
	"How many times do we pay for one mistake? The answer is thousands of times. The human is the only animal on earth that pays a thousand times for the same mistake. The rest of the animals pay once for every mistake they make. But not us. We have a powerful memory. We make a mistake, we judge ourselves, we find ourselves guilty, and punish ourselves. . . . Every time we remember, we judge ourselves again, we are guilty again, and we punish ourselves again, and again, and again."

THINKING / LEARNING STARTERS

1. Can you recall two or three people from your childhood or adolescence who had a positive effect on your self-esteem? What did these people say or do? Were there any who had a negative effect on you? What did they say or do?

2. Identify at least two people who exhibit the characteristics of people with high self-esteem. What behaviors helped you identify them?

Self-Esteem Influences Your Behavior

Your level of self-esteem can have a powerful impact on your behavior. Your sense of competence and resulting self-respect, the two components of self-esteem, stem from the belief that you are generally capable of producing the results in life that you want by making appropriate, constructive choices. This confidence makes you less vulnerable to the negative views of others, which then enables you to be more tolerant and respectful of others. People with authentic or healthy self-esteem tend to have a sense of personal worth that has been strengthened through various achievements and through accurate self-appraisal.[20]

● Characteristics of People with Low Self-Esteem

1. *They tend to maintain an external locus of control.* People who believe they are largely responsible for what happens to them maintain an **internal locus of control**—that is, they make decisions for their own reasons based on their standards of what is right and wrong. People who maintain an **external locus of control** believe that their life is almost totally controlled by outside forces and that they bear little personal responsibility for what happens to them.[21] Even when they succeed, they tend to attribute their success to luck rather than to their own expertise and hard work. This often results in reliance on the approval of others. When we rely too heavily on validation from external sources, we can lose control over our lives.[22]

> *When we rely too heavily on validation from external sources, we can lose control over our lives.*

2. *They are more likely to participate in self-destructive behaviors.* If you do not like yourself, there is no apparent reason to take care of yourself. Therefore, people with low self-esteem are more likely to drink too much, smoke too much, and eat too much. Some may develop an eating disorder such as bulimia or anorexia, often with devastating results.

3. *They tend to exhibit poor human relations skills.* Individuals with low self-esteem are more likely to be unfriendly, and show a lack of respect for themselves and others. Workers with low self-esteem may reduce the efficiency and productivity of a group: They tend to exercise less initiative,

hesitate to accept responsibility or make independent decisions, and are less likely to speak up in a group and criticize the group's approach.

4. *They may experience the failure syndrome.* If your subconscious mind has been saturated with thoughts of past failures, as noted previously in this chapter, these thoughts will continue to undermine your efforts to achieve your goals. If you see yourself as a failure, you will usually find some way to fail. William Glasser, author of *Reality Therapy* and other books on human behavior, calls this the **failure syndrome.** Individuals with a failure syndrome think, "I always fail. . . . Why try?" High self-esteem, on the other hand, tends to facilitate persistence after failure.[23]

● Characteristics of People with High Self-Esteem

1. *They are future oriented and not overly concerned with past mistakes or failures.* They learn from their errors but are not immobilized by them. They believe every experience has something to teach—if they are willing to learn. A mistake can show you what does not work, what not to do. One consultant, when asked whether he had obtained any results in trying to solve a difficult problem, replied, "Results? Why, I've had lots of results. I know a hundred things that won't work!" The same principle applies to your own progress. Falling down does not mean failure. Staying down does.

2. *They are better able to cope with life's problems and disappointments.* Successful people have come to realize that problems need not depress them or make them anxious. It is their attitude toward problems that makes all the difference. In his book *They All Laughed: From Lightbulbs to Lasers,* Ira Flatow examines the lives of successful, innovative people who had to overcome major obstacles to achieve their goals. He discovered that the common thread among these creative people was their ability to overcome disappointing events and press on toward their goals.

3. *They are able to feel all dimensions of emotion without letting those emotions affect their behavior in a negative way.* They realize emotions cannot be handled either by repressing them or by giving them free rein. Although you may not be able to stop feeling the emotions of anger, envy, and jealousy, you can control your thoughts and actions when you are under the influence of these strong emotions. Say to yourself, "I may not be able to control the way I feel right now, but I can control the way I behave."

4. *They are less likely to take things personally.* Don Miguel Ruiz, author of the best-selling book *The Four Agreements,* cautions us to avoid taking others' comments personally: "When you make it a strong habit not to take anything personally, you avoid many upsets in your life." He says that when you react strongly to gossip or strongly worded criticism ("You're so fat!"), you suffer for nothing. Ruiz notes that many of these messages come from people who are unable to respect you because they do not respect themselves.[24]

5. ***They are able to accept other people as unique, talented individuals.*** They learn to accept others for who they are and what they can do. Our multicultural work force makes this attitude especially important. Individuals who cannot tolerate other people who are "different" may find themselves out of a job. (See Chapter 15, "Valuing Workforce Diversity.") People with high self-esteem build mutual trust based on each individual's uniqueness. These trusting relationships do not limit or confine either person because of group attributes such as skin color, religion, gender, lifestyle, or sexual orientation. Accepting others is a good indication that you accept yourself.

6. ***They exhibit a variety of self-confident behaviors.*** They accept compliments or gifts by saying, "Thank you," without making self-critical excuses and without feeling obligated to return the favor. They can laugh at their situation without self-ridicule. They let others be right or wrong without attempting to correct or ridicule them. They feel free to express opinions even if their ideas differ from those of their peers or parents.

THINKING / LEARNING STARTERS

1. Have you ever felt envious of another person's possessions, relationships, or lifestyle? How did this feeling affect your relationship with that person?
2. When you make decisions in your personal life, do you operate from an internal or external locus of control? Give an example.

How to Build Self-Esteem

"The level of our self-esteem is not set once and for all in childhood," says Nathaniel Branden. It can grow throughout our lives or it can deteriorate.[25] Examining your present self-concept is the first step in understanding who you are, what you can do, and where you are going.

The person you will be tomorrow has yet to be created. Many people continue to shape that future person in the image of the past, repeating the old limitations and negative patterns without realizing what they are doing. The development of a new level of self-esteem will not happen overnight, but it can happen. Such a change is the result of a slow evolution that begins with the desire to overcome low self-esteem.

● Search for the Source of Low Self-Esteem

Many people live with deep personal doubts about themselves but have difficulty determining the source of those feelings. They even have difficulty finding the right words to describe those negative feelings. People with low self-esteem are less likely to see themselves with great clarity. The self-image they possess is like a reflection in a warped funhouse mirror; the image magnifies their weaknesses and minimizes their strengths. To raise your self-esteem requires achieving a higher level of self-awareness and learning to accurately perceive your particular balance of strengths and weaknesses.[26]

To start this process, take time to list and carefully examine the defining moments in your life. Pay special attention to those that were decidedly negative, and try to determine how these moments have shaped your current self-concept. Next, make a list of the labels that others have used to describe you. Study the list carefully, and try to determine which ones you have internalized and accepted. Have these labels had a positive or negative influence on your concept of yourself? Phillip McGraw says, "If you are living to a label, you have molded for yourself a fictional self-concept with artificial boundaries."[27]

● Identify and Accept Your Limitations

Become realistic about who you are and what you can and cannot do. Demanding perfection of yourself is unrealistic because no one is perfect. The past cannot be changed: Acknowledge your mistakes; learn from them; then move on.

Acting as an observer and detaching yourself from negative thoughts and actions can help you break the habit of rating yourself according to some scale of perfection and can enable you to substitute more positive and helpful thoughts. A good first step is learning to dislike a behavior you may indulge in, rather than condemning yourself. Criticizing yourself tends to make the behavior worse. If you condemn yourself for being weak, for example, how can you muster the strength to change? But if you become an "observer" and view the activity as separate from yourself, you leave your self-esteem intact, while you work on changing the behavior.

● Take Responsibility for Your Decisions

Psychologists have found that children who were encouraged to make their own decisions early in their lives have higher self-esteem than those who were kept dependent on their parents for a longer period of time. Making decisions helps you develop confidence in your own judgment and enables you to explore options. Take every opportunity you can to make decisions both in setting your goals and in devising ways to achieve them. As you make your decisions, be willing to accept the consequences of your actions, positive or negative. It's okay to have anxious, scared, or depressed feelings—as long as you don't let them stop you from doing what you have to do.[28]

TOTAL	**FRAN COX AND LOUIS COX**
PERSON	AUTHORS, *A CONSCIOUS LIFE*
INSIGHT	"There is little understanding in our culture that being an adult is an ongoing process of learning and self-correcting: Life is always changing, revealing what was previously unknown and unplanned for."

Know Your Stuff

Esther Dyson, chair of EDventure Holdings, a New York City–based venture capital firm, urges the new employees to learn everything about the new job: "Your best guarantee of credibility is to know your stuff, even if it means staying up all night reading trade jour- nals, product manuals, anything you can get your hands on." Dyson also encourages new employees to take chances. She says, "A fail- ure can be the best learning experience you'll ever have."

The attitude that you must be right all the time is a barrier to personal growth. With this attitude you will avoid doing things that might result in mistakes. Much unhappiness comes from the widespread and regrettable belief that it is important to avoid making mistakes at all costs.[29] Taking risks that reach beyond what you already know how to do can often be fun and extremely rewarding.

Develop Expertise in Some Area

Developing "expert power" not only builds your self-esteem but also increases the value of your contribution to an organization. Identify and cultivate a skill or talent you have, whether it is a knack for interviewing people, a facility with math, or good verbal skills. Developing expertise may involve continuing your studies after completing your formal education. Some institutions offer professional courses to enable people to advance in their careers. For example, the Institute of Financial Education conducts courses for persons employed by financial institutions, and the Certified Medical Representatives Institute offers a series of professional development courses for pharmaceutical representatives.

Seek the Support and Guidance of Mentors

Chip Bell, author of *Managers as Mentors: Building Partnerships for Learning,* defines a **mentor** as "someone who helps someone else learn something the learner would otherwise have learned less well, more slowly, or not at all."[30] In most organizations mentoring is carried out informally, but formal programs that systematically match mentors and protégés are common.

General Electric has traditionally used mentoring programs pairing veteran employees with new workers who need to learn how things are done at GE. When the company decided to aggressively pursue e-commerce to reduce costs and open new markets, the CEO turned the tables. He ordered his top 600 managers to search their rank-and-file employees for Internet-savvy "youngsters" who could serve as their mentors and teach them how to surf the Internet.[31]

Although many mentoring programs match a new employee with a senior person, Intel Corporation created a different approach. Since the chip-making

This mentor relationship is setting the stage for the new employee's success. Most people who have had a mentoring experience say it was an important development tool.

industry changes with stunning speed, Intel needed a program that would help thousands of employees quickly acquire the knowledge and skills needed to do their jobs. The human resources department created a system that matches mentors with protégés who need specific assistance. Thus the system depends less on seniority and more on area of expertise. Because Intel is a far-flung organization,[32] these mentoring relationships often stretch across state lines and national boundaries.

Most people who have had a mentoring experience say it was an effective development tool. However, many surveys indicate that only a small percentage of employees say they have had a mentor. In today's fast-paced work environment, where most people have a heavy workload, you must be willing to take the initiative and build a mentor relationship. Here are some tips to keep in mind.

1. ***Use multiple mentors.*** Some people feel the need for both internal and external mentors. An internal mentor, an experienced associate or supervisor, can provide guidance as you navigate the organizational bumps and potholes. An external mentor, someone who does not work for your company, can provide an objective, independent view of your skills and talents.[33] Many people benefit from short-term "learning partners" who will coach them on specific skills.

2. ***Search for a mentor who has the qualities of a good coach.*** Mentors need to be accomplished in their own right, but success alone does not make

someone a good mentor. Look for someone whom you would like to emulate, both in business savvy and in operating style. Be sure it is someone you trust enough to talk about touchy issues.[34] A good mentor is someone who will give you feedback in a straightforward manner.

3. *Market yourself to a prospective mentor.* The best mentor for you may be someone who is very busy. Sell the benefits of a mentoring partnership. For example, point out that mentoring can be a mutually rewarding experience. Describe specific steps you will take to avoid wasting the time of a busy person. You might suggest that meetings be held during lunch.

Although mentors are not mandatory for success, they certainly help. Indeed, there will always be days when you feel nothing you do is right. Your mentor can help repair damaged self-esteem and encourage you to go on. With the power of another person's positive expectations reinforcing your own native abilities, it is hard to fail.

● Set Goals

Research points to a direct link between self-esteem and the achievement of personal and professional goals. People who set goals and successfully achieve them are able to maintain high self-esteem. Why? Because setting goals enables you to take ownership of the future. Once you realize that just about every behavior is controllable, the possibilities for improving your self-esteem are endless. Self-change may be difficult, but it's not impossible. Some people lack self-esteem because they haven't achieved enough goals and experienced the good feelings that come from success.[35]

The major principles that encompass goal setting are outlined in Table 4.1 (on the next page). Goal setting should be an integral part of your efforts to break old habits or form new ones. Before you attempt to set goals, engage in serious reflection. Make a list of the things you want to achieve, and then ask yourself this question: What goals are truly important to me? If you set goals that really excite you, desire will fuel your will to achieve them.[36]

● Practice Visualization

To **visualize** means to form a mental image of something. The power to visualize (sometimes called guided imagery) is in a very real sense the power to create. If you really want to succeed at something, picture yourself doing it successfully. Once you have formed a clear mental picture of what you want to accomplish, identify the steps needed to get there and then mentally rehearse them. The visualization process needs to be repeated over and over again.[37]

Many athletes choreograph their performance in their imagination before competitions. Studies by the U.S. Olympic Training Center show that 94 percent of the coaches use mental rehearsal for training and competitions. Kathy Ann Colin, the number one U.S. kayaker in 2000, describes her mental rehearsal: "I focus on the feel of the boat and on my paddling. I am in the race. I get nervous energy. My muscles are triggered as I simulate a stroke in my mind." During warm-ups on the water, Colin again uses visualization: "I'll

TABLE 4.1	Goal-Setting Principles

Goal setting gives you the power to take control of the present and the future. Goals can help you break old habits or form new ones. You will need an assortment of goals that address the different needs of your life. The following goal-setting principles should be helpful.

1. *Spend time reflecting on the things you want to change in your life.* Take time to clarify your motivation and purpose. Set goals that are specific, measurable, and realistic. Unrealistic goals increase fear, and fear increases the probability of failure.

2. *Develop a goal-setting plan that includes the steps necessary to achieve the goal.* Put the goal and the steps in writing. Change requires structure. Identify all activities and materials you will need to achieve your goal. Review your plan daily—repetition increases the probability of success.

3. *Modify your environment by changing the stimuli around you.* If your goal is to lose five pounds during a one-month period, make a weight chart so you can monitor your progress. You may need to give up desserts and avoid restaurants that serve huge portions. Gather new information on effective weight loss techniques, and seek advice from others. This may involve finding a mentor or joining a support group.

4. *Monitor your behavior, and reward your progress.* Focus on small successes, because each little success builds your reservoir of self-esteem. Reinforcement from yourself and/or others is necessary for change. If the passion for change begins to subside, remind yourself why you want to achieve your goal. Be patient—it takes time to change your lifestyle.

hold a stop watch and imagine the start. My strategy is to figure out the number of strokes I need to win. I tell myself I want to get 152—and then I make the plan. I know exactly where I'll be when I stop, and I'll be within a second of my goal."[38]

Visualization can be used in many work settings, too. Let's assume your team members have asked you to present a cost-saving plan to management. The entire team is counting on you. The visualization process should begin with identifying the steps you will take to get approval of the plan. What information will you present? What clothing will you wear? Will you use Power-Point or some other visual presentation method? Will you use any printed documents? Once you have identified all important contingencies and strategies for success, visualize the actual presentation. See yourself walking into the room with your chin up, your shoulders straight, and your voice strong and confident. Picture yourself making appropriate eye contact with people in the room. The focus of your preparation should be on things within your control.

● **Use Positive Self-Talk**

Self-talk takes place silently in the privacy of your mind.

Throughout all of your waking moments, you never stop talking to yourself. **Self-talk** takes place in the privacy of your mind. It can be rational and productive, or it can be irrational and disruptive. When the focus of this internal conversation is on negative thoughts, you are usually less productive.[39] Some psychologists refer to these negative thoughts as your **inner critic.** The critic keeps a record of your failures but never reminds you of your strengths and accomplishments. A major step toward improving your self-esteem is to understand how to respond to the negative influence of your inner critic.[40]

| FIGURE 4.1 | Self-Esteem Cycles |

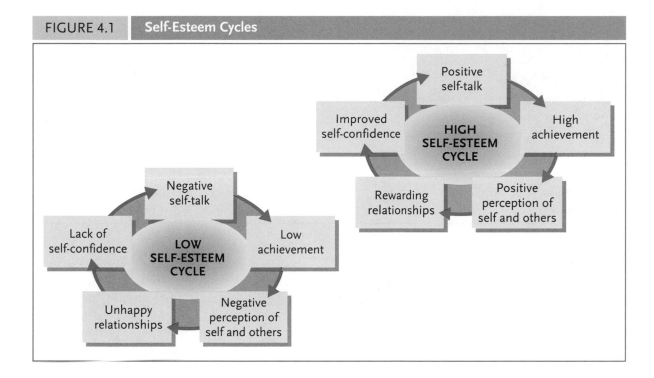

It helps to refute and reject these negative messages with *positive* self-talk. Talking back to your inner critic may take the form of words and phrases that are designed to disarm the critic. If you are preparing for a job interview and the messages you hear are "You don't measure up" or "You are incompetent," respond with the message "These are lies" or "Stop this garbage."[41] Figure 4.1 indicates how self-talk is part of the cycle of self-esteem, whether that talk is negative or positive.

If you want to develop and achieve a specific goal, positive self-talk can help. Create self-talk statements for each of your goals by using the following guidelines:

1. Be *specific* about the behavior you want to change. What do you want to do to increase your effectiveness? You should firmly believe that what you want is truly possible.

2. Begin each self-talk statement with a first-person pronoun, such as *I or my.* Use a present-tense verb, such as *am, have, feel, create, approve, do,* or *choose.* Don't say "My ability to remember the names of other people *will* improve." Instead, focus on the present: "I *have* an excellent memory for the names of other people."

3. Describe the results you want to achieve. Be sure to phrase the statement as though you have already achieved what you want. Table 4.2 (on the next page) offers several general self-talk statements that might help you improve your self-esteem.[42]

TABLE 4.2	Creating Semantically Correct Self-Talk
Wrong	**Right**
I can quit smoking.	I am in control of my habits.
I will lose twenty pounds.	I weigh a trim _____ pounds.
I won't worry anymore.	I am confident and optimistic.
Next time I won't be late.	I am prompt and efficient.
I will avoid negative self-talk.	I talk to myself, with all due respect.
I will not procrastinate.	I do it now.
I'm not going to let people walk all over me anymore.	I care enough to assert myself when necessary.

This last step is critical. Because your brain is merely a computer filled with various data from all your past experiences, you need to use, literally, the correct words. When you think of the words *spider, tornado,* or *blue,* your brain develops an automatic understanding of each word and a response or image based on years of conditioning and training. If you are attempting to quit smoking, don't mention the word *smoke* in your self-talk because your brain will react to the word. "I will not smoke after dinner" conjures an image in your subconscious mind, and your behavior follows accordingly. Say instead, "I am in control of my habits" or "My lungs are clean."

One warning: If your self-talk statements use the word *not,* you are probably sending the wrong message to your brain. Consider the following statement: "I will not eat chocolate for dessert." Now remove the word *not* from the statement, and the remaining words represent the message being sent to your brain. Does the remaining statement represent your goal? Be careful to semantically design your self-talk statements so that they take you in the direction you want to go; otherwise, they will take you straight toward what you don't want.

Keep in mind that positive self-talk that is truly effective consists of thoughts and messages that are realistic and truthful. It is rationally optimistic self-talk, not unfounded rah-rah hype. Positive internal dialogue should not be a litany of "feel good" mantras; it should be wholly consistent with your authentic self.[43]

Organizations Can Help

Even though each of us ultimately is responsible for raising or lowering our own self-esteem, we can make that task easier or more difficult for others. We can either support or damage the self-efficacy and self-respect of the people we work with, just as they have that option in their interactions with us. Organizations are beginning to include self-esteem modules in their employee- and management-training programs.

When employees do not feel good about themselves, the result will often be poor job performance. This view is shared by many human resource profes-

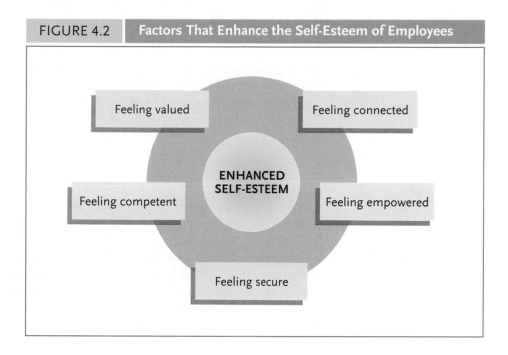

FIGURE 4.2 Factors That Enhance the Self-Esteem of Employees

sionals and managers. Many organizations realize that low self-esteem affects their workers' ability to learn new skills, to be effective team members, and to be productive. Research has identified five factors that can enhance the self-esteem of employees in any organization[44] (see Figure 4.2).

■ *Workers need to feel valuable.* A major source of worker satisfaction is the feeling that one is valued as a unique person. Self-esteem grows when an organization makes an effort to accommodate individual differences and to recognize individual accomplishments.

■ *Workers need to feel competent.* Earlier in this chapter we noted that self-efficacy grows when people feel confident in their ability to perform job-related tasks. One of the best ways organizations can build employee confidence is to involve employees in well-designed training programs. Effective training programs give employees plenty of opportunities to practice newly acquired job skills.

■ *Workers need to feel secure.* Employees are more likely to feel secure when they are well informed and know what is expected of them. Managers need to clarify their expectations and provide employees with frequent feedback regarding their performance.

■ *Workers need to feel empowered.* Progressive organizations such as Corning Incorporated and Federal Express Corporation are demonstrating to employees that their opinions and views matter and that their ideas are being implemented in significant ways. These companies make sure that each person has a voice in helping the organization achieve its goals. This topic is discussed in more detail in Chapter 12, "Team Building: A Leadership Strategy."

■ *Workers need to feel connected.* People are likely to achieve high self-esteem when they feel their coworkers accept, appreciate, and respect them. Many companies are fostering these feelings by placing greater emphasis on mentoring and teamwork. Team-building efforts help promote acceptance and cooperation.

■ Summary

ACE

business.college.hmco.com/students

Self-tests

Self-esteem is a combination of self-respect and self-efficacy. If you have high self-esteem, you are more likely to feel competent and worthy. If you have low self-esteem, you are more likely to feel incompetent, unworthy, and insecure. Self-esteem reflects your feelings of adequacy about the roles you play, your personality traits, your physical appearance, your skills, and your abilities. High self-esteem is the foundation for a successful personal life and professional life.

A person starts acquiring and building self-esteem from birth. Parents, friends, associates, the media, and professional colleagues all influence the development of that person's self-esteem. As an adult, a person often defines herself or himself in terms of possessions, jobs, and/or internal values. People with high self-esteem tend to be future oriented, cope with problems creatively, handle their emotions, and do not take things personally. They also accept others as unique, talented individuals and exhibit self-confident behaviors.

To build high self-esteem, individuals must accept the past and build for the future. They have to accept their limitations and develop expertise in some area. Making decisions and living with the consequences, positive or negative, can also help build self-esteem. Individuals need to set goals by visualizing the person they want to be and monitoring their self-talk.

Many organizations now realize that they need to help build employees' self-esteem and are doing so through training sessions, clear statements of expectations and feedback, giving greater respect to individuals in the workplace, and fostering teamwork.

■ Career Corner

Q: As a teenager, I was involved in a major car accident in which several bones in my face were broken. I was left with a large scar on my chin. Although I have had several operations to correct the visible damage, I still feel self-conscious whenever I meet new people. It is affecting my career opportunities. What can I do to gain more confidence?

A: In his book *Psycho-Cybernetics,* plastic surgeon Maxwell Maltz demonstrates that what your mind has been conditioned to believe about yourself can override or undermine what you actually see in the mirror. Throughout his twenty-five-year practice, Maltz operated on wounded soldiers, accident victims, and children with birth defects. Many of these individuals saw only their defects and doubted that they could ever be successful. Even after their corrective surgery, these patients' deformities continued to exist in their minds. Their inner self-images had not been changed.

You can learn to use the creative power of your subconscious mind. Even though your external image has been improved, you still need to change the inner self-image you carry within your mind. When you are successful in changing your mental image of yourself, your self-confidence will increase.

■ Key Terms

self-esteem   failure syndrome
self-efficacy   mentor
self-respect   visualize
self-concept   self-talk
internal locus of control   inner critic
external locus of control

■ Review Questions

1. What is self-esteem? Why is the development of high self-esteem important in a person's life?

2. What influences help shape a person's self-esteem?

3. What characteristics do people with high self-esteem exhibit?

4. Describe the behaviors of people with low self-esteem.

5. List the steps you can take to build high self-esteem. Which two do you feel are the most important? Why?

6. Explain how a person with an internal locus of control differs from a person with an external locus of control. Which of these two people is more likely to have high self-esteem and therefore greater human relations skills?

7. What influence does self-talk have on a person's self-esteem? How can this influence be controlled?

8. In your own words, explain the two cycles portrayed in Figure 4.1.

9. List the three elements necessary for the construction of positive self-talk statements. Give three examples of such statements.

10. How can organizations help raise the self-esteem of workers? How might organizations benefit if they are able to successfully implement these strategies?

■ Application Exercises

1. Review Table 4.1, Goal-Setting Principles, on page 100. Work through each of the four principles in light of something you would like to change in

your world. It could be a physical characteristic such as weight control or beginning an exercise regimen. It might be a component of your personality such as becoming more confident or assertive. Perhaps you would like to reexamine your career goals. Whatever your choice, write out your plan for change; then follow it through.

2. Think about people you know at school, at work, or in your social environment who seem to exhibit low self-esteem. Describe the qualities that give you this impression. Now think about people you know who exhibit high self-esteem. List their qualities. Often these two lists will reflect direct opposites, such as "has a sloppy appearance/keeps a neat appearance," "slumps down the hall/walks tall," or "avoids eye contact during conversations with others/makes eye contact." What steps might the people you identified as having low self-esteem take to enhance their images? How might these steps improve their self-esteem? Could you take any similar steps to improve your own self-esteem? Explain.

3. Identify a quality that you would like to experience more frequently in your life. Examples might be the ability to develop rapport quickly with new acquaintances, the patience to enjoy leisure time, or the perseverance to maintain a daily exercise program. Once you select a specific quality, create in your mind a very detailed mental picture of this behavior. Now develop positive self-talk statements that will guide you toward the desired change in behavior. Use the guidelines on page 101 to ensure that you achieve your goal.

Internet Exercise

As noted in this chapter, self-esteem has two interrelated components: self-respect and self-efficacy. Self-efficacy can be thought of as the confidence you have in your ability to do specific things. Your confidence level can influence which tasks you take on and which ones you avoid. To learn more about self-efficacy and how it can influence your career, visit the Internet and determine what types of resources (such as books, articles, and training programs) are available on this topic. Using your search engine, type in "self-efficacy" and "self-esteem," and then study the available information. Pay special attention to information on how one achieves high self-efficacy. Prepare a written report of your findings.

Case 4.1   "Popeye" Lives On

Dave Longaberger's grandfather and father were master craftsmen and worked in the Dresden Basket Company until it closed during the Depression. Even then, Dave's father hand-made baskets at home after working all day in the paper mill. In his autobiography, completed just before his death, Dave attributed his strong work ethic to his father's powerful influence. "Although I never gave it much thought as a kid, our parents and the environment where we grow up have a strong influence on who we become as adults. We grew up knowing we had to work hard, be honest, and help others."[45] Dave's eleven brothers and sisters provided peer pressure of a different kind from that usually encountered today. Neither he nor his siblings wanted to do anything that might hurt or embarrass their parents because they had so much love and respect for them.

Although his home life was loving and stable, Dave's early years were not easy. His grandfather nicknamed him "Popeye" at birth, he spent two years in first grade and three years in fifth grade because of a learning disorder, and he stuttered so badly that few people could understand anything he said. But his family's strong work ethic gave him the desire to work. Throughout his childhood, he stocked shelves for a local grocer, shoveled snow, delivered papers, mowed grass, and hauled trash. His father gave him a new label: "the 25-cent millionaire." After Dave finally graduated from high school at age 21, he sold Fuller Brushes door to door to improve his speech. Following a stint in the army, he bought a small restaurant and subsequently a grocery store of his own. His lack of a college education never deterred him.

During the 1970s, Dave noticed a growing interest in baskets and asked his father to make a dozen, which sold immediately. In 1973, his bankers were shocked when Dave sold his profitable restaurant and grocery store, hired five weavers, and started The Longaberger Company. In 1978, this business maverick veered away from traditional retail sales and moved into the then fledgling marketing concept of selling directly to the customer through independent distributors conducting in-home product shows. He led his employees and distributors with consistent positive attitudes, a constant emphasis on teamwork, an environment that made everyone feel valued, and a strong sense of humor—which included starting food fights at company events and building a basket-shaped headquarters building. When he died of cancer in 1999, Dave Longaberger's company employed more than seven hundred people, supported over fifty thousand independent sales associates, and topped $1 billion in sales. His daughter, Tami, took over the company following Dave's death. When she was asked what she learned from her father, she said: "You can't inherit respect. You have to earn it. . . . If you respect people around you, whether it's employees, customers, sales associates, or vendors, they will respond positively and constructively."[46]

■ **Questions**

1. What role did Dave Longaberger's self-esteem play in the success of his businesses?

2. Explain what dynamics were present in Dave Longaberger's life that helped him maintain his self-esteem and motivation, even though he faced seemingly insurmountable obstacles as a child.

3. Another generation has now taken control of this family business. Explain how Dave's obvious self-respect and self-confidence might still be evident in his company, even though he has passed on.

Case 4.2   Find Your Yoda

Just as young Luke Skywalker listened to the advice of his mentor, Yoda, when he needed help in his battle between good and evil in *Star Wars,* so do aspiring young people in today's marketplace. Surveys show that most workers are concerned with gaining experiences and opportunities for growth by using effective formal and informal mentoring opportunities. Larry Daloz, author of *Effective Teaching and Mentoring,* declares, "I think what people are finding is that in times of change and turmoil, we reach out for stability and guidance. Mentors give us a sense of continuity. They have been there before. They have advice for us. They have experience to pass on."[47] Mack Tilling, CEO of Instill Corporation, says, "Being able to talk about your work with an experienced executive can help anyone—even a CEO—make better decisions. Mentors help you see things in a way that you might not have thought about."[48]

Many organizations today realize the value of developing mentoring relationships among their employees. They know these relationships are critically important when it is time to pass knowledge along to the next generation of workers. Lee Ballew, a human resources development manager at Intel, was frustrated when top managers were moved out of Intel's New Mexico factory to run new factories opening around the world. That left the New Mexico facility with few experienced people and a steep learning curve for fresh trainees. "We'd been tapped out. . . . We'd sent off our experts and we needed to grow new ones."[49] The resolution at Intel was to develop a new mentoring program that formally matches individual employees and then provides specific guidelines for maximizing the potential for these relationships.

Results from an Emerging Workforce study show that 35 percent of employees who do not receive regular mentoring intend to look for another job within twelve months. When the economy is strong, talented employees can easily jump from job to job. Those interviewing for new positions often ask, before they accept a job, if their new employer has a mentoring program. To help obtain and retain valuable employees, the human resources division of Deloitte & Touche created the guidebook *Supporting Success,* which describes the organization's guiding principles for their 90,000 employees, who conduct business in more than 130 countries. The guidebook deals with such tactical issues as performance management, goal setting, evaluation, and career planning, but the first chapter addresses mentoring.

Mentoring programs can be far less formal than the programs at Deloitte & Touche and Intel, but just as effective. If the organization you work for does not have a formal mentoring program, realize that a mentoring relationship can often develop in a very casual, comfortable way. There is likely to be someone at work that you respect and turn to for answers to your questions. When you have an idea, you can bounce it off this person to learn the most appropriate way of proceeding within the organization. Ronna Lichtenberg, author of *It's Not Business, It's Personal,* remembers when coworkers who cared took her aside and said, "No, Ronna, you may not do that. . . . This is how we get things done."[50] Trusted Yodas who get to know and respect you may speak up on your behalf when you are being considered for a promotion or special assignment. An Ohio

State University study revealed that individuals who were being mentored were much more likely to be promoted than those who were not.[51]

■ **Questions**

1. Mentoring programs help bring new employees up to speed with what is going on in the organization and they often help employees advance in the organization. What elements of a mentoring program contribute to building an employee's self-esteem?

2. A well-developed mentoring program can make a major contribution to the success of an organization, yet many companies do not have such programs. What are some reasons why some organizations do not support mentoring programs?

3. Would you prefer the formal approach to mentoring programs within organizations, or would you prefer the informal approach? Explain your reasoning.

5

PERSONAL VALUES INFLUENCE ETHICAL CHOICES

Chapter Preview

After studying this chapter, you will be able to

- Explain the personal benefits of developing a strong sense of character.

- Understand how personal values are formed.

- Understand values conflicts and how to resolve them.

- Learn how to make the right ethical decisions based on your personal value system.

- Understand the danger of corporate crime and the steps being taken to eliminate it.

Louis Bloomfield, physics professor at the University of Virginia, heard rumors that some of his students were plagiarizing material for a term paper that was required in his class. He developed a computer program that would detect similar words or consecutive phrases in papers submitted electronically. After a careful review of all his students' papers, he charged 156 students with honor code violations. Many of them were found guilty and expelled from the university; others left the university after admitting guilt.[1]

This highly publicized cheating scandal, as well as similar disclosures on other campuses, ignited a national debate over the question "Does honor have a future?" Cheating is also a problem in high schools. In a survey conducted by *Who's Who Among American High School Students,* 80 percent of high-achieving high school students admitted to having cheated at least once. Nearly all of those who responded said they had never been caught, and half said they did not believe cheating was necessarily wrong.[2] A much publicized incident at Piper High School in Kansas helps illustrate the prevalence of academic cheating as well as our inclination to forgive it. Christine Pelton, a tenth-grade biology teacher, used an online database designed to detect plagiarism to review 118 student papers. She found that 28 students had plagiarized material for their papers. Pelton issued failing grades to these students, but angry parents petitioned the Piper school board, and she was forced to change her grading. This change allowed all but one of the students to pass rather than fail the course. Pelton resigned in protest the same day.[3]

Students on the University of Virginia Honor Committee spent countless hours determining the fate of 156 students who were involved in the largest cheating scandal in memory. Honor code violations are a serious matter at this university.

Is lying and cheating in high school and college really such a big deal? It certainly is when these behaviors continue after graduation. Michael Josephson, president of the Josephson Institute of Ethics, said, "The evidence is that a willingness to cheat has become the norm. . . . The scary thing is that so many kids are entering the workforce to become corporate executives, politicians, airplane mechanics, and nuclear inspectors with the dispositions and skills of cheaters and thieves."[4]

The new generation of workers are occupationally and educationally ambitious. They are coming of age at a time when our culture is placing a great deal of emphasis on self-gratification, the crossing of many moral boundaries, and the breaking of many social taboos. This chapter will help you understand how to make the right ethical decisions based on a value system that embraces honor and integrity. It will help you understand how your values are formed, how to clarify which values are important to you, and how to resolve human relations problems that result when your personal values conflict with others.

Character, Integrity, and Moral Development

If you have character, that's all that matters; and if you don't have character, that's all that matters, too.

Former United States senator Al Simpson said, "If you have character, that's all that matters; and if you don't have character, that's all that matters, too."[5] **Character** is composed of personal standards of behavior, including honesty, integrity, and moral strength. It is the main ingredient we seek in our leaders and the quality that earns us respect in the workplace. In *The Corrosion of Character*, author Richard Sennett says that we have seen a decline of character which can be traced to conditions that have grown out of our fast-paced, high-stress, information-driven economy.[6] He notes that many people are no longer connected to their past, to their neighbors, and to themselves.

Integrity is the basic ingredient of character that is exhibited when you achieve congruence between what you know, what you say, and what you do.[7] When your behavior is in tune with your professed standards and values—when you practice what you believe in—you have integrity. When you say one thing but do something else, you *lack* integrity.

How important is it to be viewed as a person with integrity and a strong sense of character in the eyes of your friends, family members, fellow workers, and leaders? When you look closely at the factors that contribute to warm friendships, strong marriages, successful careers, and successful organizations, you quickly come to the conclusion that character and integrity are critical.

You are not born with these qualities, so what can a person do to build his or her character? One approach, recommended by author Stephen Covey, is to keep your commitments. "As we make and keep commitments, even small commitments, we begin to establish an inner integrity that gives us the awareness of self-control and courage and strength to accept more of the responsibility for our own lives."[8] Covey says that when we make and keep promises to ourselves and others, we are developing an important habit. We cannot expect to maintain our integrity if we consistently fail to keep our commitments.

The Josephson Institute of Ethics acknowledged the lack of character training by forming the Character Counts Coalition. The coalition is an alliance of organizations such as the American Federation of Teachers, the American Association of State Boards of Education, and the American Association of Community Colleges. Their mission is to address the issue of character development in educational institutions and organizations throughout the country. They have developed a variety of grassroots training activities involving what they refer to as the "six pillars of character": trustworthiness, respect, responsibility, fairness, caring, and citizenship.[9] Other organizations involved in this movement include the Center for the Advancement of Ethics and Character at Boston University; the Character Education Partnership in Washington, D.C.; the Center for the 4th and 5th Rs at the State University of New York at Cortland; and the Jefferson Center for Character Education in Pasadena, California. They all offer conferences, workshops, and publications to help individuals and organizations learn more about building character and integrity.[10]

TOTAL PERSON INSIGHT	**PETER SENGE**
	AUTHOR, *THE FIFTH DISCIPLINE*
	"People working together with integrity and authenticity and collective intelligence are profoundly more effective as a business than people living together based on politics, game playing, and narrow self-interest."

How Personal Values Are Formed

Once you are aware of your value priorities and consistently behave accordingly, your character and integrity are enhanced, and life in general is much more satisfying and rewarding.

Hyrum Smith, author of *The 10 Natural Laws of Successful Time and Life Management,* says that certain natural laws govern personal productivity and fulfillment. One of these laws focuses on personal beliefs: Your behavior is a reflection of what you truly believe.[11] **Values** are the personal beliefs and preferences that influence your behavior. They are deep-seated in your personality. To discover what really motivates you, carefully examine what it is you value.

Table 5.1 details the values clarification process. These five steps can help you determine whether or not you truly value something. Many times you are not consciously aware of what is really driving your behavior because values exist at different levels of awareness.[12] Unless you clarify your values, life events are likely to unfold in a haphazard manner. Once you are aware of your value priorities and consistently behave accordingly, your character and integrity are enhanced, and life in general is much more satisfying and rewarding.

TABLE 5.1	A Five-Part Valuing Process to Clarify and Develop Values

Thinking

We live in a confusing world where making choices about how to live our lives can be difficult. Of major importance is developing critical thinking skills that help distinguish fact from opinion and supported from unsupported arguments. Learn to think for yourself. Question what you are told. Engage in higher-level thinking that involves analysis, synthesis, and evaluation.

Feeling

This dimension of the valuing process involves being open to your "gut level" feelings. If it doesn't "feel right," it probably isn't. Examine your distressful feelings such as anger, fear, or emotional hurt. Discover what you prize and cherish in life.

Communicating

Values are clarified through an ongoing process of interaction with others. Be an active listener and hear what others are really saying. Be constantly alert to communication filters such as emotions, body language, and positive and negative attitudes. Learn to send clear messages regarding your own beliefs.

Choosing

Your values must be freely selected with no outside pressure. In some situations, telling right from wrong is difficult. Therefore, you need to be well informed about alternatives and the consequences of various courses of action. Each choice you make reflects some aspect of your values system.

Acting

Act repeatedly and consistently on your beliefs. One way to test whether or not something is of value to you is to ask yourself, "Do I find that this value is persistent throughout all aspects of my life?"

Source: Howard Kirschenbaum, *Advanced Values Clarification* (La Jolla, Calif.: University Associates, 1977).

● Identifying Your Core Values

Hyrum Smith says that everything starts with your **core values,** those values that you consistently rank higher than others. When you are able to identify your core values, you have a definite picture of the kind of person you want to be. Anne Mulcahy, an executive at Xerox Corporation and mother of two sons, says she and her husband make decisions at home and work based on their core values: "Our kids are absolutely the center of our lives—and we never mess with that."[13] Maura FitzGerald, CFO of FitzGerald Communications, Inc., a public relations firm, asks all her employees to adhere to the "FitzGerald Family Values" before accepting a job with her company. All her workers carry with them a wallet-size card listing the organization's basic operating principles, one of which is "Never compromise our integrity—this is our hallmark."[14]

We often need to reexamine our core values when searching for a job. Joanne Ciulla, author of *The Working Life*, says taking a job today is a matter of choosing among four core values: high salary, security, meaningful work, and lots of time off.[15] Needless to say, most jobs would require putting at least one of these values on the back burner.

TABLE 5.2	People and events have influenced the formation of values for three groups of Americans: Matures, Baby Boomers, and Generation X. These three generations were recently joined by the Millennial generation, whose life events are still happening. This means that today's work force represents the broadest range of ages and values in American history.		
Matures (born 1928–1945)	**Baby Boomers (born 1946–1961)**	**Generation X (born 1962–1972)**	
Eisenhower	Television	AIDS	
MacArthur	The Cold War	The Wellness movement	
The A-bomb	The space race	Watergate	
Dr. Spock	The Civil Rights Act	War with Iraq	
John Wayne	The pill	Glasnost	
Mickey Mantle	The drug culture	The Oklahoma City bombing	
The Great Depression	Gloria Steinem	MTV	
World War II	The Vietnam War	The World Wide Web	
The New Deal	John Travolta	Health care reform	
Andy and Opie Taylor	JFK and MLK assassinations	Work/life balance concerns	

● Influences That Shape Your Values

As you engage in the values clarification process, it helps to reflect on those things that have influenced your values, such as people and events of your generation, your family, religious groups, schools, the media, and people you admire.

People and Events Table 5.2 provides a summary of some of the key events and people that have shaped the values of three generations: the Matures, the Baby Boomers, and Generation X. These three major generations have recently been joined by a new generation labeled by Haynes Johnson, the noted historian, as Millennials—those born after 1977 and entering adulthood in the year 2000.[16] People and events that may have an impact on this generation's values include the September 11, 2001, terrorist attacks and the resulting war on terrorism, the war with Iraq, corporate scandals, Oprah, and "Dr. Phil."

Millennials are only now defining themselves in the workplace, but the early reports on this group are quite positive. They think inclusively and collaboratively, so being a "team player" comes naturally. They are also more accepting of multiculturalism than previous generations. They want to be involved in work that really matters and expect increasing responsibility as a reward for accomplishments.[17]

Your Family Katherine Paterson, author of books for children, says being a parent these days is like riding a bicycle on a bumpy road—learning to keep your balance while zooming full speed ahead, veering around as many potholes as possible.[18] Parents must assume many roles, none more important than moral teacher. In many families in contemporary society, one parent must assume full responsibility for shaping children's values. Some single parents—those overwhelmed with responsibility for career, family, and rebuilding their own

On the morning of the first anniversary of the World Trade Center terrorist attacks, people gathered at the site to pay respect to the victims. In the wake of this tragedy, many Americans began to rethink their priorities. Values that were pre-eminent for many people—career advancement, personal fulfillment, money, and status—are taking a back seat to more fundamental needs: family, community and connectedness with others.

personal lives—may lack the stability necessary for the formation of the six pillars of character. And in two-parent families, both parents may work outside the home and at the end of the day may lack the time or energy to intentionally direct the development of their children's values. The same may be true for families experiencing financial pressures or the strains associated with caring for elderly parents.

Religious Groups Many people learn their value priorities through religious training. This may be achieved through the accepted teachings of a church, through religious literature such as the Koran and the Bible, or through individuals in churches or synagogues who are positive role models. Some of the most powerful spiritual leaders do not have formal ties to a particular religion. John Templeton is one example. He is a successful investor and one of the greatest philanthropists of the modern age. Templeton says the only real wealth in our lives is spiritual wealth. Over the years, he has given over $800 million to fund forgiveness, conflict resolution, and character-building projects.[19]

Religious groups that want to define, instill, and perpetuate values may find an eager audience. Stephen Covey and other social observers say that many people are determinedly seeking spiritual and moral anchors in their lives and in their work. People who live in uncertain times seem to attach more importance to spirituality.[20] Healthy spirituality is discussed in Chapter 17.

Schools Many parents, concerned that their children are not learning enough about moral values and ethical behavior, want character education added to the curriculum.[21] William J. Bennett, author of *The Book of Virtues,* sees moral education as a fundamental purpose of education. In support of this practice, Thomas Lickona, professor of education at the State University of New York, says children have very little sense of right and wrong, so schools must help out. Educators are concerned about the constant barrage of messages children are getting about behavior in corporate America. Twenty grade schools, middle schools, and high schools in New York and Chicago are currently testing an ethics curriculum created by Junior Achievement, whose mission is to teach youngsters about the free-enterprise system.[22]

In the 1970s, many schools included values clarification in their curriculum. As various factions of society objected, fearing that values would be "imposed" on children, schools eliminated these classes, and teachers learned to be "value neutral." Today, however, there is a nationwide resurgence of the movement to teach moral values and ethics in the classrooms. Sanford McDonnell, chairman of the Character Education Partnership, says the schools have the greatest potential for overcoming what he describes as "the national crisis of character." The Character Education Partnership defines "good character" as understanding, caring about, and acting on core ethical values. McDonnell says our nation will not be strong if we graduate young people who are brilliant but dishonest or have great intellectual knowledge but do not care about others.[23]

The Media　Some social critics say that if you are searching for signs of civilization gone rotten, you can simply tune into the loud and often amoral voices of mass entertainment on television, radio, and the Internet. They point out that viewers too often see people abusing and degrading other people without any significant consequences. Mainstream television, seen by a large number of young viewers, continues to feature a great deal of violence and antisocial behavior.

Is there a connection between violence in the media and violence in real life? The American Academy of Pediatrics and the American Psychiatric

"I swear I wasn't looking at smut—I was just stealing music."

Association report that repeated exposure to violent imagery desensitizes children and increases the risk of violent behavior.[24] Research has also found a connection between heavy television viewing and depressed children. More research is needed to help us fully understand the extent of the influence of media on our culture's values.

People You Admire   In addition to being influenced by the media, you have probably also done some **modeling**—you have shaped your behavior to resemble that of people you admire and embraced the qualities those people demonstrate. The heroes and heroines you discover in childhood and adolescence help you form a "dominant value direction."[25] The influence of modeling is no less important in our adult life. Most employees look to their leaders for moral guidance. Unfortunately, there is a shortage of leaders who have a positive impact on ethical decision making. A recent survey found that less than half of employees in large organizations think their senior leadership is highly ethical.[26] In addition to role models at work, you may be influenced by religious leaders, sports figures, educators, and others whom you admire.

● Avoiding Values Drift

Once you have examined the various influences on your values and have clarified what is important to you now that you are an adult (see Table 5.1), you also need to be aware of **values drift,** the slow erosion of your core values over time—those tiny changes that can steer you off course. When you observe lying, abuse, theft, or other forms of misconduct at work, or feel pressure to make ethical compromises, carefully and intentionally reflect on the values you hold dear and choose the appropriate ethical behavior that maintains your character and integrity. Monitor your commitment to your values and make adjustments when necessary to get your life back on track. In his book *Conversations with God,* Neal Donald Walsch discusses the process of building a strong foundation for your daily decisions as they lead you toward your life's goals. He suggests: "Do not dismantle the house, but look at each brick, and replace those which appear broken, which no longer support the structure."[27] This careful examination of each of your values in light of each day's decisions will help keep you on track throughout your life.

THINKING / LEARNING STARTERS

1. Identify the events and individuals that have been influential in forming your value system. Are those of your childhood and adolescence still important to you?

2. Based on the media's influence and the concept of modeling, what do you predict the next generation's values will be? The children of today will be your coworkers in the future. Will their attitudes and values be a potential problem for you?

Values Conflicts

One of the major causes of conflict within an organization is the clash between the personal values of different people. There is no doubt about it, people are different. They have different family backgrounds, religious experiences, education, role models, and media exposure. These differences can pop out anywhere and anytime people get together. Many observers suggest that organizations look for **values conflicts** when addressing such problems as declining quality, absenteeism, and poor customer service. The trouble may lie not so much in work schedules or production routines as in the mutual distrust and misunderstanding brought about by clashes in workers' and managers' value systems.

Soon after the World Trade Center was attacked by terrorists, many people began to rethink their priorities and reexamine their values. Some decided to spend more time with family and friends, thinking that although overtime may be an opportunity to make more income, it was also an obstacle to maintaining a commitment to their family. Of course, this priority often clashed with a recession-induced speedup at work. Some workers also decided that their "work and spend" lifestyle no longer made sense. Before the terrorist attacks, a 28-year-old market research manager described herself as "very driven" and motivated to acquire things. Following September 11 she said, "Maybe I don't need all this stuff."[28]

TOTAL	**WILLIAM J. BENNETT**
PERSON	AUTHOR, *THE BOOK OF VIRTUES*
INSIGHT	"If you want young people to take notions like right and wrong seriously, there is an indispensable condition: they must be in the presence of adults who take right and wrong seriously."

● Internal Values Conflicts

A person who is forced to choose between two or more strongly held values is experiencing an **internal values conflict.** As a manager, you may be torn between loyalty to your workers and loyalty to upper management. As an employee, you may find yourself in conflict between fulfilling family obligations and devoting the time and energy required to succeed at work. A recent study of Generation Xers by Catalyst, a group that seeks to advance women in business, found that professionals ages 26 to 37 are seeking a well-rounded life. They are not frenetic job hoppers as some social commentators maintain, but traditionalists at heart. They value company loyalty and are inclined to stay with their current company. Earning a great deal of money is not nearly as important to these Xers as having the opportunity to share companionship with family and friends. They are able to prioritize their values and make their decisions accordingly.[29]

How you resolve internal values conflicts depends on your willingness to rank your core values in the order of their importance to you. This ranking process will help you make decisions when life gets complicated and you have to make difficult choices. If one of your values is to be an outstanding parent and another is to maintain a healthy body, you should anticipate an internal values conflict when a busy schedule requires a choice between attending your daughter's soccer game and your weekly workout at the fitness center. However, when you rank which value is most important, the decision will be much easier.

● Values Conflicts with Others

As we have noted, four distinct generations have come together in the workplace. Employees from each generation bring with them different experiences and expectations. Values conflicts are more likely in this environment. Workers may clash over different interpretations of the work ethic, or work assignments. Unless such conflicts are handled skillfully, confrontation can make the situation worse, not better.

How will you handle a tense situation where it is obvious your values conflict with those of a colleague? You may discover your supervisor is a racist and you strongly support the civil rights of all people. One option is to become indignant and take steps to reduce contact with your supervisor. The problem with being indignant is that it burns your bridges with someone who can influence your growth and development within the organization. The opposite extreme would be to do nothing. But when we ignore unethical or immoral behavior, we compromise our integrity, and the problem is likely to continue and grow.[30] With a little reflection, you may be able to find a response somewhere between these two extremes. If your supervisor tells a joke that is demeaning to members of a minority group, consider meeting with her and explaining how uncomfortable these comments make you feel. When we confront others' lapses in character, we are strengthening our own integrity.

HUMAN RELATIONS IN ACTION

Values Clarification at Levi Strauss

At Levi Strauss & Co., values are considered a living element, an evolving foundation needed to guide employees in the decision-making process. In a meeting of 200 managers, each person was instructed to select key personal values from a deck of 50 "value cards." Each person arranged the cards according to his or her most important and least important values, then placed his or her name card on the piles. Next, everyone was encouraged to walk around the room and look at each array. Managers were surprised at the diversity of values and the range of values people selected as most important. Each table of participants then discussed how their values influenced the way they performed their duties at work.

Personal Values and Ethical Choices

Ethics refers to principles that define behavior as right, good, and proper. Your ethics, or the code of ethics of your organization, does not always dictate a single moral course of action, but it does provide a means of evaluating and deciding among several options.[31] Ethics determine where you draw the line between right and wrong.

As competition in the global marketplace increases, moral and ethical issues can become cloudy. Although most organizations have adopted the point of view that "good ethics is good business," exceptions do exist. Some organizations encourage, or at least condone, unethical behaviors. Surveys show that many workers feel pressure to violate their ethical standards in order to meet business objectives.[32] Thus, you must develop your own personal code of ethics.

Every job you hold will present you with new ethical and moral dilemmas. And many of the ethical issues you encounter will be very difficult. Instead of selecting from two clear-cut options—one right, one wrong—you often face multiple options.[33]

● How to Make the Right Ethical Choices

According to the Association of Certified Fraud Examiners, unethical acts by workers cost U.S. businesses more than $600 billion a year.[34] The following guidelines may help you avoid being part of this growing statistic.

Learn to distinguish between right and wrong. Although selecting the right path can be difficult, a great deal of help is available through books, magazine articles, and a multitude of online resources. Support may be as close as your employer's code of ethics, guidelines published by your professional organization, or advice provided by an experienced and trusted colleague at work. In some cases, you can determine the right path by *restraining* yourself from choosing the *wrong* path. For example:

- Just because you have the power to do something does not mean it is the proper thing to do.

- Just because you have the right to do something does not mean it is right to do.

- Just because you want to do something does not mean you should do it. Choose to do more than the law requires and less than the law allows.[35]

Make certain your values are in harmony with those of your employer. You may find it easier to make the right ethical choices if your values are compatible with those of your employer. Many organizations have adopted a set of beliefs, customs, values, and practices that attract a certain type of employee (see Figure 5.1 on page 122). Harmony between personal and organizational values usually leads to success for the individual as well as the organization. These shared values provide a strong bond among all members of the work force.

FIGURE 5.1	GEAR for Sports' Vision and Value Statements

GEAR For Sports® Vision

Guided by our GEAR values, we strive to be the leader in quality and delivery of our customer's image through marketing innovative sportswear, accessories and services.

GEAR Values

GEAR For Sports' business is predicated on respect for, and attention to, all of our customers, business partners, employees, government and community. We value:

Customers
by exceeding their expectations.

Excellence
by taking pride and responsibility in everything we do.

Employees
by demonstrating respect and consideration for each other.

Teamwork
by fostering trust and recognition among all stakeholders.

Professionalism
by exhibiting integrity and proficiency.

Innovation
by embracing creativity and change.

Social Responsibility
by caring for and sharing with each other and our community.

Source: "GEAR For Sports® Vision and Values Statement". Reprinted by permission of Chamberlain Marketing Group. GEAR For Sports is an apparel manufacturer of decorated products to Bookstore, Resort and Corporate markets.

BMS Software in Houston, Texas, provides a work environment where you can find sustenance for the whole self—mind, body, and spirit. Employees can pump iron in the gym, enjoy a gourmet meal, or participate in massage therapy. The self-contained community offers an array of services (banking, dry cleaning, hair salon, etc.), and there is a large kitchen with free fruit, popcorn, soda, and coffee on each floor of the company's two glass towers. You live comfortably at BMS, but you also work long hours. Many employees work 10- to 12-hour days.[36] Some people would feel comfortable working for this company, but others would be unhappy about the long hours.

If you are active in an environmental group that is committed to reducing global-warming emissions, then working for General Motors Corporation or Ford Motor Company might create a values conflict. Both of these companies have fought calls from the government for tougher emission standards. They take the position that these standards would threaten their sales of profitable sport-utility vehicles and pickup trucks.[37]

TOTAL	**DAN RICE AND CRAIG DREILINGER**
PERSON	MANAGEMENT CONSULTANTS; AUTHORS, "RIGHTS AND WRONGS OF ETHICS
INSIGHT	TRAINING"

"Nothing is more powerful for employees than seeing their managers behave according to their expressed values and standards; nothing is more devastating to the development of an ethical environment than a manager who violates the organization's ethical standards."

Don't let your life be driven by the desire for immediate gratification. Progress and prosperity have almost identical meanings to many people. They equate progress with the acquisition of material things. One explanation is that young business leaders entering the corporate world are under a great deal of pressure to show the trappings of success. This is the view expressed by John Delaney, who is a professor at the University of Iowa and has done extensive research on ethics. He says, "You're expected to have the requisite car and summer house to show you're a contributor to society, and many people do whatever it takes to get them."[38] Many people are trapped in a vicious cycle: They work more so that they can buy more consumer goods; then, as they buy more, they must work more. They fail to realize that the road to happiness is not paved with Rolex watches, Brooks Brothers suits, and a Lexus. Chapter 17 offers support for finding satisfaction through nonfinancial resources that make the biggest contribution to a fulfilling life.

The "get-the-deal-done-today" mentality seems to leave little time for ethical deliberation.

To achieve immediate gratification often means taking short-cuts. It involves pushing hard, cutting corners, and emphasizing short-term gains over the achievement of long-term goals. Greed has motivated many high-tech companies to promise investors, customers, and employees things they cannot deliver. Some companies have discovered clever ways to recycle their balance sheets in ways that mislead current and potential investors. The "get-the-deal-done-today" mentality seems to leave little time for ethical deliberation.[39]

THINKING / LEARNING STARTERS

1. Think about the last time you felt guilty about something you did. Did you hurt someone's feelings? Did you take credit for something someone else accomplished? Which of your basic values did your actions violate?

2. When was the last time you broke off a friendship or relationship with another person in your personal or professional life? Does the reason for the breakup reflect back to a values conflict between the two of you? Explain.

Corporate Values and Ethical Choices

When organizations consistently make ethical decisions that are in the best interest of their stakeholders—employees, customers, stockholders, and the community—they are considered good corporate citizens because they are socially responsible. The list "The 100 Best Corporate Citizens" published by *Business Ethics* magazine reminds us that a company can be socially responsible and still achieve excellent earnings. In her *Business Week* article "A Conscience Doesn't Have to Make You Poor," Susan Scherreik interviewed stockholders who invest only in companies that are good corporate citizens. One stated, "I see the damage that many companies do to people's health and the environment by polluting or creating dangerous products. Investing in them makes no sense because these companies won't flourish in the long run."[40]

● Corporate Crime

Many organizations have gotten into serious trouble by ignoring ethical principles. In recent years, the media have carried headlines concerning organizations involved in corporate crime.

■ Archer Daniels Midland Company, maker of various food products, paid a $100 million fine to the U.S. government for price fixing.[41]

■ Xerox Corporation paid a $10 million civil penalty for financial reporting violations. The Securities and Exchange Commission filed the charges against Xerox.[42]

■ A unit of Exide Technologies, the maker of automotive batteries, agreed to plead guilty to fraud and pay criminal fines of $27.5 million. Exide admitted to supplying inferior batteries to Sears, Roebuck & Company, trying to cover up the defects, and spending $80,000 to bribe a Sears battery buyer.[43]

Those items represent only a small fraction of the corporate crime that goes on today. Many offenders are not caught or brought to trial. But, on the positive side, recent surveys indicate that a large majority of America's major corporations are actively trying to build ethics into their organizations.

■ Minnesota Life Insurance Company has been able to steer clear of scandal for more than one hundred years by adopting a values-based management philosophy that rewards integrity and honesty.[44]

■ At Harley-Davidson the soul of the "Hog" can be traced to values that emphasize strong working relationships. The company's idea of a healthy working relationship is embedded in five formal values that constitute a code of behavior for everyone:[45] tell the truth; be fair; keep your promises; respect the individual; and encourage intellectual curiosity.

■ Honesty tops the list of employee expectations at Swanson Russell Associates, a marketing communications firm in Lincoln, Nebraska. The mandate is carefully reviewed during new employee orientation and it's posted in every employee's work area.[46]

Many say they have difficulty determining the right course of action in difficult "gray-area" situations. And even when the right ethical course of action is clear, competitive pressures sometimes lead well-intentioned managers astray.[47] Tom Chappell, author of *The Soul of a Business* and founder of Tom's of Maine, explains why organizations often have difficulty doing what is morally right and socially responsible: "It's harder to manage for ethical pursuits than it is to simply manage for profits."[48]

● How to Prevent Corporate Crime

Establish and support a strong code of ethics. We have recently seen an increase in ethical initiatives that make ethics a part of core organizational values. **Codes of ethics,** written statements of what an organization expects in the way of ethical behavior, can give employees a clear indication of what behaviors are acceptable or improper.[49] An ethics code can be a powerful force in building a culture of honesty, but only if it is enforced without exception. The list of corporate values at Enron Corporation included respect, integrity, communication, and excellence. As events have shown, these values did not prevent unethical conduct at the highest levels of the company. Empty values statements create cynical and dispirited employees and undermine managerial credibility.[50]

Hire with care. Thomas Melohn, president of North American Tool & Die Inc., located in San Leandro, California, says the key to operating a successful company is to first identify a guiding set of values and then "make sure you find people who have those values and can work together."[51] He says the hiring process should be given a very high priority. Melohn never hires any employee without checking references and conducting a lengthy job interview.

Some companies use integrity tests (also called honesty tests) to screen out dishonest people and drug users. The first honesty test was developed more than forty years ago by Reid Psychological Systems. Many people question the accuracy of these tests and the fairness of using them to hire or turn away applicants. Some states have made it illegal to deny someone a job on the basis of low integrity-test scores. Testing companies admit that these tests are not foolproof.

Provide ethics training. Many ethical issues are complex and cannot be considered in black-and-white moral terms. It is for this and other reasons that ethics training has become quite common. In some cases, the training involves little more than a careful study of the company ethics code and its implications for day-to-day decision making. In other cases, employees participate in in-depth discussions of ethical decisions.

Sears, Roebuck and Company provides its employees with a booklet entitled *Code of Business Conduct*. It outlines the company's position on a wide range of issues, such as receiving gifts, employee discounts, care of company

"Welcome stockholders, I'd love to be there in person, but as you may have read, I am under house arrest."

assets, and foreign business dealings. It also includes guidelines for making ethical decisions (see Table 5.3).

Develop support for whistleblowing.   When you discover that your employer or a colleague is behaving illegally or unethically, you have three choices. You can keep quiet and keep working. You can decide you can't be party to the situation and leave. Or you can report the situation in the hope of putting a stop to it. When you reveal wrongdoing within an organization to the public or to those in positions of authority, you are a **whistleblower.**

TOTAL	**EDMUND BURKE**
PERSON	NINETEENTH-CENTURY ENGLISH POLITICAL PHILOSOPHER
INSIGHT	"All that is necessary for evil to triumph is for good men to do nothing."

FBI attorney Coleen Rowley wrote a memo to FBI director Robert Mueller claiming that the department ignored the pleas of the Minneapolis field office to investigate Zacarias Moussaoui, who was subsequently indicted as a September 11 co-conspirator. Cynthia Cooper informed WorldCom's board of directors that illegal accounting procedures covered up $3.8 billion in corporate losses. Enron's vice president Sherron Watkins wrote a letter to Enron's chairman Kenneth Lay alerting him to the illegal accounting procedures that misled stockholders about Enron's financial picture. All three of these women tried to keep their concerns "in house" by speaking the truth to executives in a position of power, not to the public. As details exploded in the media, these women

TABLE 5.3	Sears's Guidelines for Ethical Decision Making

Guidelines for Making Ethical Decisions:

1. Is it legal?
2. Is it within Sears's shared beliefs and policies?
3. Is it right/fair/appropriate?
4. Would I want everyone to know about this?
5. How will I feel about myself?

Source: Guidelines for Making Ethical Decisions from the *Code of Business Conduct,* Sears, Roebuck and Co. Reprinted by permission of Sears, Roebuck and Co.

were plunged into the public eye. *Time* magazine proclaimed them "Persons of the Year for 2002" and made them national celebrities, but their personal and professional lives were permanently altered, as their jobs, their health, and their privacy were threatened.[52]

Because of these women—and a multitude of other whistleblowers—organizations now have a legal responsibility to support whistleblowing. The landmark Sarbanes-Oxley Act of 2002 makes it illegal for employers to retaliate against whistleblowers who work for publicly held corporations. (Privately held organizations are exempt.) Their executives can be held criminally liable and imprisoned for up to ten years. The Occupational Safety and Health Administration (OSHA) fields the complaints of individuals who make a disclosure—to a supervisor, law enforcement agency, or congressional investigator—that

Sherron Watkins is sworn in before a special U.S. Senate hearing on Enron Corporation. She discovered illegal accounting procedures that misled stockholders and reported the unethical practices.

could have a "material impact" on the value of the company's shares. If the company attempts to retaliate, the whistleblower has ninety days to report the incident to the Department of Labor, which can order the organization to rehire the whistleblower without going to court. The employee can file suit against the employer in federal court if the Department of Labor fails to act on those charges within six months.[53]

Because of this new legislation and media coverage of high-profile whistle-blowers, a new culture seems to have emerged that emphasizes "doing the right thing," despite potentially high personal costs.[54] Hollywood has made movies and heroes of those who step forward to expose environmental contamination, accounting fraud, harmful pharmaceuticals, or manipulated business deals. In reality, however, you can expect your employer to *attempt* to retaliate in some way if you choose to become a whistleblower. Even your fellow colleagues may resent the disruption your revelations cause in their lives. They may be impressed with your integrity, but not everyone will be on your side in your struggle to do what is right and ethical. Your efforts may result in months or even years of emotional and financial turmoil. A survey conducted by the National Whistleblower Center in Washington, D.C., showed that half of the respondents were fired because of their actions. Most reported being unable to acquire new jobs because prospective employers perceived them as troublemakers. Others faced demotions or were placed in jobs with little impact or importance.[55]

Each individual must make his or her own decision as to whether the disturbing unethical offense is worth the personal cost. Table 5.4 lists four questions potential whistleblowers should ask themselves before taking action.

TABLE 5.4	Whistleblower Checklist

Experts say that people who are thinking about tattling on their company should ask themselves four important questions before doing so.

1. Is this the only way?

Do not blow the whistle unless you have tried to correct the problem by reporting up the normal chain of command and gotten no results. Make sure your allegations are not minor complaints.

2. Do I have the goods?

Gather documentary evidence that proves your case, and keep it in a safe place. Keep good notes, perhaps even a daily diary. Make sure you are seeing fraud, not merely incompetence or sloppiness.

3. Why am I doing this?

Examine your motives. Do not act out of frustration or because you feel underappreciated or mistreated. Do not embellish your case, and do not violate any confidentiality agreements you may have.

4. Am I ready?

Think through the impact on your family. Be prepared for unemployment and the possibility of being blacklisted in your profession. Last but not least, consult a lawyer.

Source: Paula Swyer and Dan Carney, with Amy Brrus and Lorraine Woellert in Washington and Christopher Palmeri in Los Angeles, "Year of the Whistleblower," *Business Week,* December 16, 2002, pp. 107–108.

Wanted: Employer with Ethics

The recent wave of corporate scandals has motivated job seekers to go to greater lengths to gauge the ethical standards and practices of would-be employers. They are asking prospective employers as well as current and former employees probing questions, such as:

■ Do you have a formal code of ethics? Is it widely distributed and enforced?

■ Do employees feel pressure to make ethical compromises?

■ Is ethical misconduct disciplined swiftly and justly?

■ Do employees have formal channels available to make their concerns known confidentially?

■ Is integrity considered a core value by top management?

Values and Ethics in International Business

If the situation is complex on the domestic scene, values and ethical issues become even more complicated at the international level. The subject is too broad to treat in detail in this chapter, but we can provide an overview of some problem areas that exist in international business. Here are some examples.

1. *Bribery used to secure foreign contracts.* Most industrial nations have signed a multinational treaty outlawing corporate bribery. Nevertheless, many corporate employees and government officials still seek payments for favors. In 1977 the U.S. Congress passed the Foreign Corrupt Practices Act, which bars companies from bribing government officials.

2. *Human rights violations.* American business firms are under great pressure to avoid doing business with overseas contractors that permit human rights violations in their factories. Starbucks Coffee, Levi Strauss, and many other companies have developed codes of conduct that focus on such problem areas as child labor, low wages, and long hours.

3. *Lack of sensitivity to foreign customs.* Being aware of foreign business etiquette is very important if you are conducting international business; otherwise, you may unwittingly offend people from foreign countries. If you are doing business in Central or South America, don't be alarmed if the person you are meeting is late for an appointment. However, in Germany there is a strong emphasis on punctuality. In Israel it is not impolite to discuss business during the evening meal, whereas in England it would be poor manners to talk about business after the end of the workday.[56]

As we take steps to strengthen trade relations with countries such as Vietnam, South Africa, and China, it is important for all parties to recognize value differences and to spend time and effort building mutual respect and understanding.

■ Summary

A strong sense of character grows out of your personal standards of behavior. When you consistently behave in accordance with your values, you maintain your integrity. Your values are the personal importance you give to an object or idea. People's values serve as the foundation for their attitudes, preferences, opinions, and behaviors. Your core values are largely formed early in life and are influenced by people and events in your life, your family, religious groups, schools, the media, and people you admire.

Internal values conflicts arise when you must choose between strongly held personal values. Values conflicts with others, often based on age, racial, religious, gender, or ethnic differences, require skilled intervention before they can be resolved.

Once you have clarified your personal values, your ethical decisions will be easier. You must learn to distinguish right from wrong, choose an employer whose values you share, and avoid the pursuit of immediate gratification. Shared values unify employees in an organization by providing guidelines for behavior and decisions.

Corporate values and ethics on both the domestic and the international levels are receiving increasing attention because of the devastating effect and expense of corporate crime. Many organizations are developing ethics codes to help guide employees' behaviors, hiring only those individuals who share their corporate values, offering ethics training opportunities to all employees, and supporting whistleblowing. As transnational organizations increase in number, the individuals involved will need to consciously examine their values and ethical standards to deal effectively with differing value structures in each country.

■ Career Corner

Q: I will soon graduate from college and would like to begin my career with an organization that shares my values. I have carefully examined what is most important to me and believe I know the type of organizational culture in which I can thrive. But how do I discover the "real" values of an organization when my interviews are permeated with buzzwords such as *family-friendly* and *teamwork-oriented*? How can I determine whether or not they truly mean what they seem to say?

A: Direct questions about an organization's values often result in well-rehearsed answers from the interviewer. Try using *critical incident* questions such as "How did your organization handle the September 11 crisis?" or "Tell me about the heroes in your organization." And don't depend solely on the interviewer's answers. Seek out an honest current or former employee who will tell you the unvarnished truth about the organization. Listen carefully to the language used during your interviews. Do you hear a lot of talk about "love," "caring," and "intuition," or do you hear statements like "We had to send in the SWAT team," "They beat their brains out," and "We really nailed them!" If possible, sit in on a team meeting with your potential coworkers. Be forthright about work/life values, and make them a standard part of your interview process. A perfect match between your values and your potential employers' values is hard to find, so be patient. You may need to compromise.

■ Key Terms

character	values conflict
integrity	internal values conflict
values	ethics
core values	codes of ethics
modeling	whistleblower
values drift	

■ Review Questions

1. How do values differ from attitudes, opinions, or behavior?

2. How are core values formed? How have values changed in recent years?

3. Differentiate between internal values conflicts and values conflicts with others.

4. Explain the five dimensions of Kirschenbaum's valuing process (see Table 5.1).

5. Describe the advantages and disadvantages of employees sharing the same values as their organization.

6. Explain the negative effects of the pursuit of immediate gratification.

7. How do top management values affect the purpose and direction of an organization?

8. List some of the steps corporations are taking to eliminate crime in their organizations.

9. How might an ethics code help organizations be more productive?

10. How do seemingly accepted unethical business practices in foreign countries affect Americans' ability to compete for business contracts in those countries?

■ Application Exercises

1. Guilt and loss of self-respect can result when you say or do things that conflict with what you believe. One way to feel better about yourself is to "clean up" your integrity. Make a list of what you are doing that you think is wrong. Once the list is complete, look it over and determine if you can stop these behaviors. Consider making amends for things you have done in the past that you feel guilty about.[57]

2. In groups of four, discuss how you would react if your manager asked you to participate in some sort of corporate crime. For example, the manager could ask you to help launder money from the company, give a customer misleading information, or cover up a budget inaccuracy and keep this information from reaching upper management. You might want to role-play the situation with your group. Follow up with class discussion.

3. One of the great challenges in life is the clarification of our values. The five-part valuing process described in Table 5.1 can be very helpful as you attempt to identify your core values. Select one personal or professional value from the following list, and clarify this value by applying the five-step process.

a. Respect the rights and privileges of people who may be in the minority because of race, gender, ethnicity, age, physical or mental abilities, or sexual orientation.

b. Conserve the assets of my employer.

c. Utilize leisure time to add balance to my life.

d. Maintain a healthy lifestyle.

e. Balance the demands of my work and personal life.

Internet Exercise

Visit the website of the Josephson Institute: *www.josephsoninstitute.org*. Navigate through the various icons available. Take notes on those items you consider relevant to your life at work, home, or school. Report your discoveries to your class members.

Case 5.1 Character Counts as Much as Credentials

The revelations of the deceit at Enron, WorldCom, Global Crossing, Tyco, and other companies make it appear that lying has become standard operating procedure in today's world. The media are filled with stories of powerful individuals who climb to the top of their career ladder and are then exposed as liars. But what about you personally? How often do you tell a little white lie, put inaccurate information in your resumé, change the dates or figures on seemingly minor documents, or agree to participate in a colleague's plan of deception? Compared to the great scheme of things, your random acts of deceit may seem minor, but tallied together, they can lead to larger breaches in ethics so gradually that you might not realize how bad things are getting.

Psychologists attribute this subtle honesty erosion to the preponderance of "useful myths"—the stories we tell ourselves, not necessarily the facts of what happened. Joseph Ellis, Pulitzer Prize–winning biographer and professor at Mount Holyoke College, spiced up his lectures with stories of his experiences as a paratrooper in Vietnam when in fact he was an instructor at West Point and was never in Vietnam. Newly hired Notre Dame football coach George O'Leary resigned when the media exposed that he had falsified his academic and athletic credentials for decades. Some experts say that people who inflate their resumés are more likely to be men, who typically add fictitious academic, athletic, or military achievements to their list of credentials. This represents a recurring problem for employers.

HireRight, a firm that investigates job candidates, found that 85 percent of *Fortune* 500 companies do background checks on applicants. Their advice: "Be honest and up-front about your record. Character counts as much as credentials."[58] Apparently some job applicants have not gotten the message. Jude M. Werra & Associates, a Wisconsin executive search firm, publishes the semiannual "Liars Index," which measures the percentage of applicants who fudge data about their majors, their graduation and attendance dates, or their degrees or licenses. In 2001, the Index was 20.4 percent and climbing. Werra says, "It's hard to believe in this day and age when people can verify information on you in seconds that people still do it."[59] Firms like Credentials Inc., EdVerify, and *www.degreechk.com* offer almost instant verification of prospective employees' credentials for organizations across the nation.

So why do job seekers continue to lie about their qualifications? Psychologists say we learn this technique as children when we attempt to avoid trouble and take control of the future by saying such things as "Yes, Daddy, I washed my hands" or "No, Mommy, I didn't hit him" This coping mechanism is an important developmental stage for kids as they attempt to separate from their parents and become independent. While most parents struggle to stop their children from lying—a seemingly hopeless effort—perhaps they should try to teach them how to have the courage to tell the truth.[60]

■ Questions

1. What did your parents teach you about telling the truth? Remember not only what they said to you, but also how they acted.

2. If the job you really want requires a college degree different from the one you earned, will you present the false academic major on your resumé so that you will be considered for an interview? Why or why not?

3. What liability do you think a company has if it hires someone who has presented false credentials?

4. What would you do if you discovered that your boss lied on his resumé?

Case 5.2   To Get to the Bottom of the Scandal, Go to the Top

Hosting the Olympic games is big business. The chosen city typically wins millions of dollars in infrastructure improvements and receives millions more as athletes, media personnel, and spectators spend their tourist dollars once the games begin. Multinational companies pay big money to help sponsor the Olympic games. As a result, the competition to be selected as a host city is fierce, as evidenced by the scandal that surrounded the 2002 Winter Olympics in Salt Lake City, Utah.

The scandal started with the revelation that some members of the International Olympic Committee (IOC) accepted over $1 million worth of bribes from members of the Salt Lake Olympic Committee (SLOC) to ensure Salt Lake City's successful bid as the host for the 2002 Winter Olympics. In addition to cash, bribes included medical benefits, college tuition payments, first-class air tickets, hotel accommodations, and thousands of dollars in shopping sprees. The scheme worked: Salt Lake City hosted the event, it enjoyed a major economic surge, and its Olympic Committee made a $101 million profit (which will be used to finance U.S. sports programs and keep the venues in Salt Lake City in shape for training and competition).[61] While it is unlikely that any actual criminal activity took place, the decision by the SLOC to offer—and the IOC to accept—the bribes was certainly unethical. Those investigating the scandal blamed the mess on a "long-standing culture of corruption" and recommended widespread reform throughout the Olympics. SLOC members maintained that they "did not invent this culture. They joined one that was already flourishing."[62]

The process to select the Olympic sites will never be the same. Athens, Greece, was awarded the 2004 Summer Games before the Salt Lake City scandal broke. However, before Turin, Italy, was awarded the 2006 Winter Games and Beijing, China, the 2008 Summer Games, strict rules were implemented in accordance with the IOC's new Code of Conduct and ethics panel. This panel approved over fifty proposals, including one that bars voters from visiting any of the bidding cities. IOC officials believe that the new rules "fireproof" the system against any form of corruption or improper influence in the future.[63]

■ Questions

1. The Olympic games, a worldwide event, have traditionally been a force for positive political and social change. How do you feel the scandal affected the way business is conducted in countries directly or indirectly involved in the Olympic games?

2. Do you believe the IOC's ethics panel will be effective against the "culture of corruption" surrounding the Olympic events?

3. Are there any recent discoveries of cheating by Olympic athletes or judges? Explain. What impact do you believe the top Olympic officials' standards of behavior have on this activity?

6

ATTITUDES CAN SHAPE YOUR LIFE

Chapter Preview

After studying this chapter, you will be able to

- Understand the impact of employee attitudes on the success of individuals as well as organizations.

- List and explain the ways people acquire attitudes.

- Describe attitudes that employers value.

- Learn how to change your attitudes.

- Learn how to help others change their attitudes.

- Understand what adjustments organizations are making to develop positive employee attitudes.

Workers at Seattle's famous Pike Place Fish Market have a cold, wet job. Fish guts, blood, and scales produce a strong stench during their 12-hour shifts. However, when you visit the fish market, you will find that the workers are not downtrodden about their environment.[1] They laugh and joke as they toss fish to each other and over the heads of those who are standing at the counter waiting to pay for their purchases. Some customers even participate in the fish-tossing antics and make spectacular "catches" themselves. Pike Place employees' attitudes, expressed through their energetic clowning, seem contagious.

Not all organizations encourage this type of atmosphere at work. In companies where managers are very controlling, *play* is a four-letter word that means activities that disrupt efforts to be efficient. That's one of the reasons John Christensen, CEO of ChartHouse Learning, coauthored the training books *Fish!, Fish! Tales,* and *Fish! Sticks* and created video and management training programs based on the workplace atmosphere at Pike Place. He wanted to provide an opportunity for managers to learn how to instill a positive, productive atmosphere at work. He knew that a playful corporate culture can be created but cannot be mandated. Customers can tell the difference between employees who truly enjoy their jobs and those who are following a company mandate to have a positive attitude. Even Pike Place's owner, John Yokoyama, admits that he was once a grouchy and difficult boss. Then he "got some training" and realized that change was possible.[2] Yokoyama and millions of others have discovered that joyful, lighthearted attitudes occur naturally when people enjoy what they are doing.

Aly Wagner, U.S. women's soccer team midfielder, holds aloft a salmon she caught during a fish tossing demonstration at Seattle's famous Pike Place Fish Market. This business is known for its playful company culture that creates a high energy, fun atmosphere.

Those who embrace what has become known as the "Fish Movement" believe in two basic ideas. First, they believe that a positive attitude is a good thing. Second, they believe that in most situations one can learn to adapt and accept one's current circumstances even if at first they seem undesirable.[3] It's all a matter of attitude.

Attitudes Can Be Learned

Attitudes are not tangible items that you can wrap up in a box and give as a gift. **Attitudes** are merely thoughts that you have accepted as true and that lead you to think, feel, or act positively or negatively toward a person, idea, or event. They represent an *emotional readiness* to behave in a particular manner.[4] You are not born with these thoughts; you learn them. Therefore, it is reasonable to conclude that you can learn new attitudes and/or change old ones.

Your values, those beliefs and preferences you feel are important, serve as a foundation for your attitudes. For example, if you believe your religion is important, you may form negative attitudes toward those people and activities that restrict your religious privileges and positive attitudes toward those who support your convictions. Your attitudes, in turn, serve as a motivation for your behavior (see Figure 6.1). So, when someone attempts to interfere with your right to practice your religion, you might become angry and retaliate. But you also have the freedom to choose another response. Perhaps another value comes into play—peace—and it seems more important than "defending" yourself. So, instead of retaliating, you decide to just ignore the interference. In a similar fashion, the fish people *chose* to accept their smelly environment. The most amazing things can happen once you realize that you can always choose which attitude you will act upon.

As you grow, you form attitudes toward political movements, national leaders, various occupations, government programs, laws, and other aspects of your daily life. They may seem "ingrained" in your personality. You tend to have a positive attitude toward things you like or enjoy and a negative attitude toward things that you are against or that make you unhappy. Some attitudes

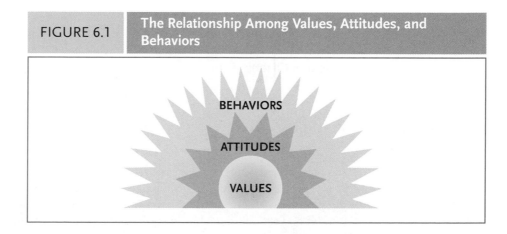

FIGURE 6.1 — The Relationship Among Values, Attitudes, and Behaviors

may be so strong that you encourage others to adopt your views and copy your behaviors. But if others hold strong contrasting attitudes based on *their* values and past experiences, a potential human relations challenge exists unless both parties remember that they have a choice.

● Root Causes of Negative Attitudes

Some people are positive thinkers and see daily obstacles as opportunities rather than roadblocks. Others tend to dwell on things that can go wrong. Generally speaking, positive attitudes generate positive results and negative attitudes generate negative results. If attitudes are a choice (we can choose our thoughts), why would anyone *choose* to think negatively? There are several factors that exist individually or blend together to produce negative attitudes. We will briefly describe some common root causes of negative attitudes.[5]

Low Self-Esteem   In Chapter 4 we described self-esteem as a blend of self-efficacy and self-respect. People with low self-esteem often lack a sense of personal worth and tend to embrace negative thoughts about the future. This negative outlook influences their ability to get along with others.

Unresolved Conflict   We have seen an increase in conflict in recent years. Unresolved conflict can be very costly in terms of lost productivity at work, broken marriages and lost friendships. Chapter 13 is devoted to conflict resolution strategies.

Work that Is Not Satisfying   Negative attitudes can often be traced to work. Many workers rebel against the monotony of repetitive job functions or working for a boss who fails to recognize work well done. In Chapter 7, "Motivating Yourself and Others," we will discuss job designs that provide a sense of achievement, challenge, variety, and personal growth.

Fear or Uncertainty   Negative attitudes can sometimes be traced to feelings of fear or uncertainty. This can happen when someone takes a sliver of fact, rumor, or observation and expands it into something dramatically negative. Fear and other emotions will be discussed in Chapter 9, "Achieving Emotional Balance in a Chaotic World."

TOTAL PERSON INSIGHT	**PRICE PRITCHETT** CHAIRMAN, *EPS SOLUTIONS* "The biggest career challenges these days are *perceptual . . . psychological*. Not technical. Not even skills-based. The major adjustments we need to make are mental. For example, how we frame things at work. The way we process events in our head. Our attitudes and outlook about how our jobs and organizations now have to operate."

● The Powerful Influence of Attitudes

One of the most significant differences between high and low achievers is choice of attitude. People who go through life with a positive attitude are more likely to achieve their personal and professional goals. People who filter their daily experiences through a negative attitude find it difficult to achieve contentment or satisfaction in any aspect of their lives.

When Bellagio, a Las Vegas luxury resort, needed to hire 9,600 workers, 84,000 applied. A team of managers conducted 27,000 interviews. The hiring managers asked a series of questions that helped them assess the candidates' attitudes toward various aspects of work in the service industry. Bellagio, like most other employers, searches for employees who display initiative, collegiality, openness to change, and other positive attitudes.[6]

Attitudes represent a powerful force in any organization. An attitude of trust, for example, can pave the way for improved communication and greater cooperation between an employee and a supervisor. But an attitude of cynicism can make a manager's sincere attempts to improve something useless. These same actions by management, filtered through attitudes of trust and hope, may result in improved worker morale.

● The Age of Information Mandates Attitude Changes

The age of information is characterized by a rapidly changing economic, social, and cultural environment that often requires us to take a look at our attitudes toward the traditional way of doing things. Employees who resist change or see

During the weeks that preceded the opening of Bellagio, 84,000 workers applied for jobs. This Las Vegas luxury resort was searching for employees who display such qualities as initiative, collegiality, openness to change, and other positive attitudes.

it as a threat can become a liability to an organization that is trying to adapt to changing economic conditions. Since change permeates every successful organization, it is helpful to remember that one *can* change one's attitude.

One major attitude adjustment that some long-time employees are facing is the focus on teams in the workplace, rather than the traditional boss/subordinates hierarchy. As a team member, you can expect occasional conflict between what is best for the team and your own self-interests. The temptation to take credit for success or place the blame for mistakes on others will be present in most team situations. Perhaps you will have to make personal sacrifice part of the price you pay for winning your team's support.

In the industrial economy, people gave their loyalty and commitment to their employer in exchange for a lifetime of job security. The shift from an economy based on industrial production to an economy based on information and customer service has displaced millions of workers. Many of them are now working in service-related jobs in which work is done through relationships with customers. This is a difficult transition for many production-oriented workers. If they cannot make the adjustment, they are often replaced with workers who have developed strong interpersonal skills.

How Attitudes Are Formed

Throughout life you are constantly making decisions and judgments that help formulate your attitudes. These attitude decisions are often based on behaviors your childhood authority figures told you were right or wrong, childhood and adult behaviors for which you were rewarded or punished, role models you selected, and the various environmental and corporate cultures you chose to embrace.

● Socialization

The process through which people are integrated into a society by exposure to the actions and opinions of others is called **socialization.**[7] As a child, you interacted with your parents, family, teachers, and friends. Children often feel that statements made by these authority figures are the "proper" things to believe. For example, if a parent declares, "People who live in big, expensive houses either are born rich or are crooked," the child may hold this attitude for many years. In some cases, the influence is quite subtle. Children who observe their parents recycling, using public transportation instead of a car to get to work, and turning off the lights to save electricity may develop a strong concern for protection of the environment.

● Peer and Reference Groups

As children reach adolescence and begin to break away psychologically from their parents, the **peer group** (people their own age) can have a powerful influence on attitude formation. In fact, peer-group influence can sometimes be stronger than the influence of parents, teachers, and other adult figures. With the passing of years, reference groups replace peer groups as sources of attitude formation in young adults. A **reference group** consists of several people who share a common interest and tend to influence one another's attitudes and behaviors. The reference group may act as a point of comparison and a source of information for the individual member. In the business community, a chapter of the American Society for Training and Development or of Sales & Marketing Executives International may provide a reference group for its members.

● Rewards and Punishment

Attitude formation is often related to rewards and punishment. People in authority generally encourage certain attitudes and discourage others. Naturally, individuals tend to develop attitudes that minimize punishments and maximize rewards. A child who is praised for sharing toys with playmates is more likely to develop positive attitudes toward caring about other people's needs. Likewise, a child who receives a weekly allowance in exchange for performing basic housekeeping tasks learns an attitude of responsibility.

As an adult, you will discover that your employers will continue to attempt to shape your attitudes through rewards and punishment at work. Many organizations are rewarding employees who take steps to stay healthy, avoid accidents, increase sales, or reduce expenses.

● Role Model Identification

Most young people would like to have more influence, status, and popularity. These goals are often achieved through identification with an authority figure or a role model. A **role model** is that person you most admire or are likely to

---

HUMAN RELATIONS IN ACTION

Attitude Is Everything

Keith Harrell was captain of the Seattle University basketball team for three years in a row. He fully expected to be drafted by the National Basketball Association after graduation, but the call never came. Harrell walked away from that dream and later spent fourteen years with IBM. When he made presentations as a trainer for IBM, audiences were always receptive to his comments because he had the ability to combine humor and wisdom. Soon he started dreaming of a new career as a professional speaker. He developed a presentation entitled "Attitude Is Everything" and started knocking on doors. Before long, he was presenting his thoughts on attitudes to audiences across the United States. He always tells his listeners that "the only difference between a bad day and a good day is attitude." Today he receives $10,000 each time he reminds an audience that "Attitude Is Everything."

> *Role models can exert considerable influence—for better or for worse—on developing attitudes.*

emulate. As you might expect, role models can exert considerable influence—for better or for worse—on developing attitudes.

The media have a tremendous influence on people's selection of role models. Many of the television programs people watch are dominated by crime, violence, and stereotyped or deviant characters and life situations. At the other extreme, other programs present positive superheroes with superhuman abilities. With this constant reinforcement from fictional negative and positive role models, young people sometimes have difficulty sorting out which behaviors and attitudes are acceptable in the real world.

In most organizations, supervisory and management personnel have the greatest impact on employee attitudes. The new dental hygienist and the recently hired auto mechanic want help adjusting to their jobs. They watch their supervisors' attitudes toward safety, cost control, accuracy, grooming, and customer relations and tend to emulate the behavior of these role models. Employees pay more attention to what their supervisors *do* than to what they *say*.

● Cultural Influences

Our attitudes are influenced by the culture that surrounds us. **Culture** is the sum total of knowledge, beliefs, values, objects, and ethnic customs that we use to adapt to our environment. It includes tangible items, such as foods, clothing, and furniture, as well as intangible concepts, such as education and laws.[8]

Today's organizations are striving to create corporate cultures that attract and keep productive workers in these volatile times. When employees feel comfortable in their work environment, they tend to stay.

HUMAN RELATIONS IN ACTION

Avoiding the Things That Annoy

Harry Griendling, creator of the Staffing Solutions Group, called together his team of recruiting consultants, who work from their home offices helping corporate clients find employees, and asked them to create the kind of company benefits they'd always wanted but could not find in any other organization. They started by creating a list of all the practices that had irked them in previous jobs. Using the list as a "Don't go there" guideline, the team developed the following plan.

■ An open book policy allows all employees to access any financial information about the company they need in order to do their job.

■ All employees and spouses (not just the sales staff) attend yearly training seminars in exotic vacation locations.
■ Employees submit their own annual assessment of their strengths, weaknesses, and goals in place of the traditional performance review conducted by a supervisor.
■ Salary guidelines were created according to a mutually agreed upon formula for assessing overhead and splitting profits.

In turn, the happy employees made the company number 251 on *Inc.* magazine's list of 500 top performers and increased annual sales from $255,000 to more than $3 million in five years.

■ When it comes to providing a strong, "fun," corporate culture, Icarian Inc., a provider of online software that helps companies hire and manage their work forces, is a prime example of going the extra mile. Balloons and roller-hockey gear are everywhere, and pet dogs frolic in the hallways. Employees work hard, and at break time they play hard with chess, Ping-Pong, and other games in the lunchroom. Employees are encouraged to work at home, and community volunteerism is rewarded with time off to participate. After-hours events include wine tasting and barbecues. Happy workers, CEO Doug Merritt believes, are bound to be productive.[9]

■ Executives at MBNA, the highly successful credit card company, understand that satisfied employees are more likely to provide excellent customer service. Every day the 23,000 MBNA employees are given a gentle reminder that the customer comes first. The words THINK OF YOURSELF AS A CUSTOMER are printed over every doorway of every office. Each year this Delaware-based company makes *Fortune* magazine's list of the 100 best companies to work for.[10]

■ The U.S. Marines have developed an eleven-week basic training program that has a dramatic impact on those who complete it. Recruits emerge as self-disciplined Marines who are physically fit, courteous to their elders, and drug-free. Many have had to overcome deep differences of class and race and have learned to live and work as a team. They live in an organizational culture where a hint of racism can end a career and the use of illegal drugs is minimized by a "zero tolerance" policy.[11]

THINKING / LEARNING STARTERS

1. Identify at least one matter you feel strongly about. Do you know how you acquired this attitude? Is it shared by any particular group of people? Do you spend time with these people?

2. Think of an attitude that a friend or coworker holds but that you strongly disagree with. What factors do you believe contributed to the formation of this person's attitude?

Attitudes Valued by Employers

Many organizations have discovered the link between workers' attitudes and their profits. During recent periods of economic decline that began early in 2001, employers began paying more attention to job candidates' personalities.[12] Whether you are looking for your first career position, anticipating a career change, or being retrained for new opportunities, you may find the following discussion helpful concerning what attitudes employers want in their employees.

Basic training in the United States Marine Corps focuses on development of the mind as well as the body. Those who complete the eleven-week program are physically fit and prepared to live and work as a team.

People who are self-motivated are inclined to set their own goals and monitor their own progress toward those goals. They do not need a supervisor hovering around them making sure they are on task. . . .

● Self-Motivation

People who are self-motivated are inclined to set their own goals and monitor their own progress toward those goals. Their attitude is "I am responsible for this job." They do not need a supervisor hovering around them making sure they are on task and accomplishing what they are supposed to be doing. Many find ways to administer their own rewards after they achieve their goals. Employers often retain and promote those employees who are capable of making their own decisions and following through. They want their employees to feel driven to find better ways of doing old jobs and curious about learning new ones. They are happy when workers read professional publications, become active in professional organizations, and monitor news reports for advances in research and technology.

● Openness to Change

In the age of information, the biggest challenge for many workers is adjusting to the rapidly accelerating rate of change. Some resistance to change is normal merely because it may alter your daily routine. However, you will get into trouble if you choose the following three attitudes:[13]

1. *Stubbornness* Some workers refuse to be influenced by someone else's point of view. They also find fault with every new change.

2. *Arrogance* Employees who reject advice or who give the impression that they do not want retraining or other forms of assistance send the wrong message to their employer.

3. *Inflexibility* Displaying a closed mind to new ideas and practices can only undermine your career advancement opportunities.

● Team Spirit

In sports, the person who is a "team player" receives a great deal of praise and recognition. A team player is someone who is willing to step out of the spotlight, give up a little personal glory, and help the team achieve a victory. Team players are no less important in organizations. Employers are increasingly organizing employees into teams (health teams, sales teams, product development teams) that build products, solve problems, and make decisions. Chapter 12 contains some tips on how to become a respected team member.

● Health Consciousness

The ever growing cost of health care is one of the most serious problems facing companies today. Many organizations are promoting wellness programs for all employees as a way to keep costs in line. These programs include tips on healthy eating, physical-fitness exercises, stress management practices, and other forms of assistance that contribute to a healthy lifestyle. Employees who actively participate in these programs frequently take fewer sick days, file fewer medical claims, and bring a higher level of energy to work. Some companies even give cash awards to employees who lose weight, quit smoking, or lower their cholesterol levels. Chapters 14 and 17 discuss health and wellness in greater detail.

● Appreciation of Coworker Diversity

To value diversity in the work setting means to make full use of the ideas, talents, experiences, and perspectives of all employees at all levels within the organization. People who differ from each other often add richness to the organization. An old adage states: If we both think alike, one of us is not necessary.

Development and utilization of a talented, diverse work force can be the key to success in a period of fierce global competition. Women and people of color make up a large majority of the new multicultural, global work force. Many people, however, carry prejudiced attitudes against those who differ from them. They tend to "prejudge" others' value based on the color of their

"Where am I going? Straight to the top, Sir, and nothing's going to stop me!"

skin, gender, age, religious preference, lifestyle, political affiliation, or economic status. Although deeply held prejudices that have developed over a long time are difficult to change, employers are demanding these changes. Chapter 15 contains specific guidance on how to develop positive attitudes toward joining a diverse work force.

● Honesty

Honesty and truthfulness are qualities all employers are searching for in their employees. This is because relationships depend on trust. An honest employee's attitude is "I owe my coworkers the truth." If you cannot be honest with your employer, customers, fellow workers, and friends, they cannot trust you, and strong relationships will be impossible.

How to Change Attitudes

If you are having difficulty working with other team members, if you feel you were overlooked for a promotion you should have had, or if you go home from work depressed and a little angry at the world, you can almost always be sure you need an attitude adjustment. Unfortunately, people do not easily adopt new attitudes or discard old ones. It is difficult to break the attachment to emotionally laden beliefs. Yet attitudes *can* be changed. There may be times when you absolutely hate a job, but you can still develop a positive attitude toward it as a steppingstone to another job you actually do want. There will be times as well when you will need to help colleagues change their attitudes so that you

It is often said that life is 10 percent what happens to you and 90 percent how you react to it.

can work with them more effectively. And, of course, when events, such as a layoff, are beyond your control, you can accept this fact and move on. It is often said that life is 10 percent what happens to you and 90 percent how you react to it. Knowing how to change attitudes in yourself and others can be essential to effective human relations—and your success—in life.

● Changing Your Own Attitude

You are constantly placed in new situations with people from different backgrounds and cultures. Each time you go to a new school, take a new job, get a promotion, or move to a different neighborhood, you may need to alter your attitudes to cope effectively with the change. Some events are beyond your control, but you do have the power to shape your attitudes. The following attitudes will help you achieve positive results in today's world.

Choose Happiness In his best-selling book *The Art of Happiness*, the Dalai Lama presents happiness as the foundation of all other attitudes. He suggests that the pursuit of happiness is the purpose of our existence. Survey after survey has shown that unhappy people tend to be self-focused, socially withdrawn, and even antagonistic. Happy people, in contrast, are generally found to be more sociable, flexible, and creative and are able to tolerate life's daily frustrations more easily than unhappy people.[14]

Michael Crom, executive vice president of Dale Carnegie Training, believes that happiness is the state of mind that permits us to live life enthusiastically. He views enthusiasm as an energy builder and as the key to overcoming adversity and achieving goals.[15] But how can you become happy and enthusiastic when the world around you is filled with family, career, and financial crises on a daily basis? Most psychologists, in general, agree that happiness or unhappiness at any given moment has very little to do with the conditions around us, but rather with how we perceive our situation, how satisfied we are with what we have.[16] For example, if you are constantly comparing yourself to people who seem smarter, more attractive, or wealthier, you are likely to

HUMAN RELATIONS IN ACTION

Doing Business in Russia

In Russia, 3M encourages managers to respect the country's traditions and leverage its positive cultural traits. For example, 3M Russia has capitalized on a long-standing Russian tradition of making charitable contributions to the community. By adopting a policy of good corporate citizenship, it has made itself more "Russian," thus winning the respect of average Russian citizens and government authorities.

Bribes and requests for protection money are common in Russia. Rather than simply banning these practices, 3M Russia actively promotes ethical behavior and takes steps to secure the personal security of its employees. The company has enhanced its reputation as an attractive employer by working with its employees to avoid illegal acts and personal harm. It also offers training courses in business ethics for its customers.

develop feelings of envy and frustration. By the same token, you can achieve a higher level of happiness by reflecting on the good things you have received in life.[17]

Embrace Optimism   Optimistic thoughts give rise to positive attitudes and effective human relationships. When you are an optimist, your coworkers, managers, and—perhaps most important—your customers feel your energy and vitality and tend to mirror your behavior.

It does not take long to identify people with an optimistic outlook. Optimists are more likely to bounce back after a demotion, layoff, or some other disappointment. According to Martin Seligman, professor of psychology at the University of Pennsylvania and author of *Learned Optimism,* optimists are more likely to view problems as merely temporary setbacks on their road to achieving their goals. They focus on their potential success rather than on their failures.[18]

TOTAL	**HIS HOLINESS THE DALAI LAMA AND HOWARD C. CUTLER**
PERSON	COAUTHORS, *THE ART OF HAPPINESS*
INSIGHT	"We don't need more money, we don't need greater success or fame, we don't need the perfect body or even the perfect mate—right now, at this very moment, we have a mind, which is all the basic equipment we need to achieve complete happiness."

Pessimists, in contrast, tend to believe bad events will last a long time, will undermine everything they do, and are their own fault. A pessimistic pattern of thinking can have unfortunate consequences. Pessimists give up more easily when faced with a challenge, are less likely to take personal control of their life, and are more likely to take personal blame for their misfortune.[19] Often pessimism leads to **cynicism,** which is a mistrusting attitude regarding the motives of people. When you are cynical, you are constantly on guard against the "misbehavior" of others.[20] If you begin to think that everyone is screwing up, acting inconsiderately, or otherwise behaving inappropriately, cynicism has taken control of your thought process, and it is time to change.

If you feel the need to become a more optimistic person, you can spend more time visualizing yourself succeeding, a process that is discussed in Chapter 4. Monitor your self-talk, and discover whether or not you are focusing on the negative aspects of the problems and disappointments in your life or are looking at them as learning experiences that will eventually lead you toward your personal and professional goals. Try to avoid having too much contact with pessimists, and refuse to be drawn into a group of negative thinkers who see only problems, not solutions. Attitudes can be contagious.

Think for yourself   One of the major deterrents to controlling your own attitude is the power of "group think," which surfaces when everyone shares the same opinion. Individuals can lose their desire and ability to think for themselves as they strive to be accepted by a group. You are less likely to be drawn into group think if you understand that there are two overlapping relationships among coworkers. *Personal relationships* develop as you bond with your coworkers. When you share common interests and feel comfortable talking with someone, the bonds of friendship may grow very strong. You form small, intense groups. But there still exists the larger group—the organization. Within this setting, *professional relationships* exist for just one purpose: to get the job done.[21] Having two kinds of relationships with the same people can be confusing.

Let's assume you are a member of a project team working on a software application. The deadline for completion is rapidly approaching, yet the team still needs to conduct one more reliability test. At a team meeting, one person suggests that the final test is not needed because the new product has passed all previous tests, and it's time to turn the product over to marketing. Another member of the team, a close friend of yours, enthusiastically supports this recommendation. You have serious concerns about taking this shortcut but hesitate to take a position that conflicts with that of your friend. What should you do? In a professional relationship, your commitment to the organization takes precedence—unless, of course, it is asking you to do something morally wrong.[22]

Keep an open mind   We often make decisions and then refuse to consider any other point of view that might lead us to question our beliefs. Many times our attitudes persist even in the presence of overwhelming evidence to the contrary. If you have been raised in a family or community that supports racist views, it may seem foreign to you when your colleagues at work openly accept and enjoy healthy relationships with people whose skin color is different from your own. You may need to consider that this attitude is realistic, even though you are "conditioned" to reject it. You can always expose yourself to new information and experiences beyond what you have been socialized to believe.

In his book, *The 100 Absolutely Unbreakable Laws of Business Success,* Brian Tracy suggests reflecting on the "Law of Flexibility." He said "You are only as free in life as the number of well-developed options you have available to you." The more thoroughly you open your mind to the options available to you, the more freedom you have.[23] This flexibility to see beyond what you thought was true and examine others' perspectives could be one of the most powerful tools you have to inspire the rest of your life.

● Helping Others Change Their Attitudes

As the Serenity Prayer (Figure 6.2) expresses, you have a choice whether to accept circumstances or try to change them. Sometimes we *can* do more than just change our attitude—perhaps we can change a condition over which we have no absolute control but which we might be able to influence. For example, at some point you may want to help another person change his or her attitude about something. In such a situation, you will get nowhere if you try to beg, plead, intimidate, or even threaten him or her into thinking differently. Rather, the process is similar to attempting to push a piece of yarn across the top of a table. When you *push* the yarn in the direction you want it to go, it gets all bent out of shape. When you gently *pull* the yarn with your fingertips, it follows you

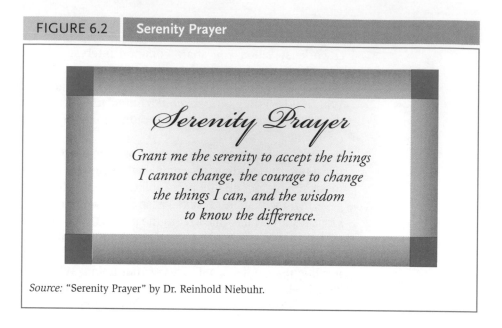

FIGURE 6.2 | **Serenity Prayer**

Serenity Prayer

Grant me the serenity to accept the things
I cannot change, the courage to change
the things I can, and the wisdom
to know the difference.

Source: "Serenity Prayer" by Dr. Reinhold Niebuhr.

wherever you want it to go. Two powerful techniques can help you pull people in the direction you want them to go:

1. Change the *conditions* that precede the behavior.

2. Change the *consequences* that follow the behavior.

Change the Conditions   If you want people to change their attitudes, identify the behaviors that represent the poor attitudes and alter the conditions that precede the behavior. Consider the following situation.

A new employee in a retail store is having a problem adjusting to her job. The manager needed her on the sales floor as soon as possible, so he rushed through her job training procedures without taking time to answer her questions. Now she finds there are many customers' questions she cannot answer, and she has trouble operating the computerized cash register. She wants to quit, and her negative attitudes are affecting her job performance and the way she handles her customers.

The manager could easily have prevented this employee's negative attitudes by answering all her questions *before* she was placed on the sales floor. Perhaps he could have asked an experienced salesperson to stay with her as she helped her first few customers. Above all, he could have displayed a caring attitude toward her.

Change the Consequences   Another way to help other people change their attitudes is to alter what happens *after* they exhibit the behavior you are attempting to change. A simple rule applies: When an experience is followed by positive consequences, the person is likely to repeat the behavior. When an experience is followed by negative consequences, the person will likely stop the behavior. For example, if you are a supervisor, and several of your employees are consistently late for work, you might provide some form of negative consequence each time they are tardy, such as a verbal reprimand or reduced pay. Keep in mind, however, that we tend to focus attention on the people who exhibit disruptive attitudes and to ignore the employees exhibiting the attitudes we want to encourage. Saying: "Thank you for being here on time. I really appreciate your commitment" can be an extremely effective reward for those who arrive at work on time. Behaviors rewarded will be repeated.

An attitude is nothing more than a personal thought process. We cannot control the thinking that takes place in someone else's mind, but we can sometimes influence it. And sometimes we can't do that either, so we have to set certain rules of behavior. Some organizations have come to the conclusion that behavior that offends or threatens others must stop. It may be impossible to stop someone from thinking prejudicial thoughts, but you can establish a zero tolerance policy regarding acts that demean or threaten others.[24]

THINKING / LEARNING STARTERS

An important first step in changing your attitude is reflecting on your current thought patterns. How do you view your personal life today? What is your outlook on work? Do you tend to be an optimist or a pessimist? Sentence-completion exercises can be powerful vehicles for self-understanding and personal growth, so take a few minutes and complete the sentences that follow. To get the most out of this activity, add four or five different endings to each sentence. Work as rapidly as possible, and don't worry about whether the ending is reasonable or significant; the object is to identify your state of mind. In the process of completing each sentence, you will achieve greater insight and pave the way for behavioral change.[25]

I am very thankful for . . .

I am glad I'm not . . .

When I wake up in the morning, my first thoughts are . . .

My most common reaction to an annoying situation is . . .

Personal happiness to me means . . .

I often compare myself to . . .

Organizations' Efforts Toward Improving Employees' Attitudes

Most companies realize that an employee's attitude and performance cannot be separated. When employees have negative attitudes about their work, their job performance and productivity suffer. When they have positive attitudes, job performance and productivity are likely to improve. One CEO of a software company has stated, "The way you get superior performance is to get people's passionate loyalty and belief. That means being flexible and giving your people what they need to do a great job."[26] For generations, employers and labor unions focused on salaries and fringe benefits as the rewards that would keep workers producing at top efficiency. But gradually, both labor and management discovered that money was not always the primary reward for a satisfying job.

People who are asked what they most want from their job typically cite mutual respect among coworkers, interesting work, recognition for work well done, the chance to develop skills, and so forth. If employers want to maintain or improve the positive attitudes of their workers, and thereby maintain or improve productivity, they need to provide the benefits workers consider important. Of course, workers expect the pay to be competitive, but they want so much more. As author and management consultant Peter Drucker says, "To make a living is not enough. Work also has to make a life."[27] Organizations are finding creative ways to influence worker attitudes. The following companies made *Fortune* magazine's list of the 100 best companies to work for.[28]

- Plante & Moran is an accounting firm with a human touch and a sense of humor. The company describes itself as "relatively jerk-free." Full-time employees get at least four weeks of paid vacation.

- Baptist Health Care is a hospital that the competition tries to imitate. Top management maintains close contact with all employees, and employee-led initiatives have resulted in low turnover among registered nurses.

- Adobe Systems, a successful Silicon Valley firm, strives to generate camaraderie among its employees. It schedules frequent all-hands meetings, job rotations, and Friday night parties.

What do these organizations have in common? Each has given thought to the attitudes that are important for a healthy work environment and has taken steps to shape these attitudes. Many organizations are attempting to improve employee attitudes and productivity by enhancing the quality of their employees' work life.

This nurse can take pride in knowing her employer, Baptist Health Care, is one of the 100 best companies to work for in America. The company's "No-secrets" policy means she is privy to the same financial information as the chief financial officer. Recently every employee received a $100 check as thanks for the hospital's high scores in patient satisfaction.

A Final Word

Viktor Frankl, a survivor of the Auschwitz concentration camp and author of *Man's Search for Meaning*, said, "The last of the human freedoms is to choose one's attitude in any given set of circumstances." Changing an attitude can be a challenge, but the process can also be an important step toward your continued growth and success.

■ Summary

business.college.hmco.com/students

An attitude is any strong belief toward people and situations. It is a state of mind supported by feelings. People possess hundreds of attitudes about work, family life, friends, coworkers, and the like.

Attitudes represent a powerful force in every organization. If the employees of a service firm display a caring attitude toward customers, the business is likely to enjoy a high degree of customer loyalty and repeat business. If the employees of a manufacturing firm display a serious attitude toward safety rules and regulations, fewer accidents are likely to occur.

People acquire attitudes through early childhood socialization, peer and reference groups, rewards and punishment, role model identification, and cultural influences. However, these are not set in stone. You always have the power to *choose* your attitude toward any situation.

Employers hire and attempt to retain employees who are self-motivated, accept change, are team players, are concerned about their health, value coworker diversity, and are honest.

You can decide to change your attitude by choosing to be happy; becoming an optimist; thinking for yourself without undue pressure from others; and keeping an open mind. You can help others change their attitudes by altering the consequences and conditions that surround the situation. Positive consequences and conditions produce positive attitudes. Organizations are taking steps to improve employee attitudes by enhancing the quality of their work life.

■ Career Corner

Q: Two years ago I left a job I loved when the executives of an exciting new company offered me a position that seemed to have tremendous potential. I gave my two weeks' notice and jumped to the new employer. I worked day and night to help the new company be successful and enhance my climb to the top of it. Last week I was informed that it is declaring bankruptcy next month. I am choosing how I react to this devastating news and am trying not to panic, but I need advice on how to approach my former employer about returning to my old position. I still see some of my former colleagues socially, and they believe that there might be an opportunity to return to my old job. What can I do to enhance my chances at reentry?

A: You are not alone! Many workers grab new job opportunities when they believe the grass might be greener on the other side, only to discover they were better off in the first location. You were smart when you offered two weeks' notice before leaving your position. This considerate attitude toward your colleagues and customers will speak well for you during your reentry attempt. Determine what new skills you learned with the new organization and how those skills might be transferred to your former employer. Did you learn to effectively handle multiple priorities simultaneously, work faster, or take more risks? Point out why this new knowledge makes you even more valuable to your former employer. Who knows, they may reinstate you in a higher position than before! However, keep an open mind about the form and fashion in which you return. Be willing to eat a little humble pie, and be prepared to accept a pay cut.

■ Key Terms

attitudes	role model
socialization	culture
peer group	cynicism
reference group	

■ Review Questions

1. It has been said that "attitudes represent a powerful force in any organization." What examples can you give to support this statement?

2. List five ways in which we form our attitudes.

3. Describe how rewards and punishment can shape the attitudes of employees in an organization. Give at least one example of each.

4. Why is happiness considered the foundation of all attitudes?

5. Describe the attitudes employers are looking for in their employees.

6. Explain how consequences can influence the shaping of attitudes in an organization.

7. Robert Mager says that the conditions that surround a subject can play an important role in shaping attitudes. Provide at least one example to support Mager's statement.

8. Identify the difference between a person with an optimistic attitude and one with a pessimistic viewpoint.

9. What are organizations doing to help improve the attitudes of their workers? Why do they bother to keep their workers happy?

10. Describe the impact your attitude has on your professional and personal relationships. Give an example.

■ **Application Exercises**

1. Describe your attitudes concerning

   a. a teamwork environment

   b. health and wellness

   c. life and work

   d. learning new skills

   How do these attitudes affect you on a daily basis? Do you feel you have a positive attitude in most situations? Can you think of someone you have frequent contact with who displays negative attitudes toward these items? Do you find ways to avoid spending time with this person?

2. Identify an attitude held by a friend, coworker, or spouse that you would like to see changed. Do any conditions that precede this person's behavior fall under your control? If so, how could you change those conditions so the person might change his or her attitude? What positive consequences might you offer when the person behaves the way you want? What negative consequences might you impose when the person participates in the behavior you are attempting to stop?

3. For a period of one week, keep a diary or log of positive and negative events. Positive events might include the successful completion of a project, a compliment from a coworker, or just finding time for some leisure activities. Negative events might include forgetting an appointment, criticism from your boss, or simply looking in the mirror and seeing something you don't like. An unpleasant news story might also qualify as a negative event. At the end of one week, review your entries and determine what type of pattern exists. Also, reflect on the impact of these events. Did you quickly bounce back from the negative events, or did you dwell on them all week? Did the positive events enhance your optimism? Review the root causes of negative attitudes, and try to determine if any of these factors influence your reaction to negative or positive events.

■ **Internet Exercise**

Every Friday, ABC News posts a new article called "Working Wounded," by Bob Rosner, author of the book with the same title. Each article discusses some aspect of the challenges people face in their life at work. Visit the website at *www.ABCNEWS.go.com* and access this week's "Working Wounded" article. Write a brief paper explaining your reaction to the comments. If time allows, go to *www.WorkingWounded.com* and read articles with titles that pique your interest. Report your findings to your classmates.

Case 6.1   Where Is My Stability?

Lewis Jenkle has worked for the past fourteen years as an accountant for Quest Electronics. He has always been happy and satisfied with his work environment, knowing exactly what was expected of him. During the past year, however, his entire department has been dismantled and all his accounting buddies are now assigned to various project teams. When a team's work is completed, the team members are assigned to another project. Sometimes Lewis is asked to participate in several team assignments at one time. He feels he is in constant chaos, with no one telling him what to do next because teams rarely have a designated boss; everyone just digs in and gets the job done. This autonomy and sense of responsibility make him nervous. His coworkers seem to enjoy the challenge and excitement of starting new projects and seeing their completion. However, Lewis misses the former stability of his once-traditional workplace. He has thought about changing jobs but has discovered that this project management approach is being used everywhere. Each day at work, his frustration and anger build. He is not a happy camper!

Many workers are experiencing this kind of trauma, and it is affecting their attitudes and productivity as well as their personal and professional relationships. It appears that the concept of project management is here to stay, but not everyone wants this kind of accountability. It seems obvious that if the unhappy workers want to have a satisfying life in this new atmosphere, they are going to have to change their attitudes.

In her book *Career Intelligence,* Dr. Barbara Moses offers support to those individuals who want or need to find satisfaction in their short-term work assignments and relationships. She suggests that they learn to connect with coworkers quickly through creative use of e-mails, faxes, videoconferences, phone calls, and one-to-one meetings. When handling more than one project at a time, developing a stable system that helps track various deadlines and individual team members' strengths and weaknesses may help prevent the feeling of chaos. She recommends that individuals conduct a personal strengths assessment by asking friends and colleagues to appraise specific talents the individual brings to specific projects. After receiving these appraisals, these individuals can try to position themselves to be assigned the projects of their choice. This will help strengthen their attitude that they *are* in control of *something.*[29]

■ Questions

1. Dr. Jean Claude Kaufmann, a French sociologist, studied homemakers and their attitudes toward housework. While half of his subjects found the repetitive work drudgery, the other half described their tasks as pleasurable—even erotic! If the tasks were the same, what made the difference between drudgery and pleasure? What could Lewis Jenkle learn from this study?

2. What changes do you anticipate will happen in your career field over the next five to ten years? Will you have to adjust your attitude as time progresses? If so, why?

3. What steps identified in this chapter will you take to keep your personal and professional relationships productive as inevitable changes occur in your life?

Case 6.2   Life Is Good at the Pike Place Fish Market

The popular books *Fish!*, *Fish! Tales*, and *Fish! Sticks* mentioned at the beginning of this chapter, present a business philosophy that focuses on building employees' commitment to their employers and organizations. This philosophy is applicable to almost every organization because it is based on the idea that most people like working in happy places, so they are more likely to stay on the job and do a better job. While some people might argue that these "feel-good" attitudes are "soft skills" and do not affect the bottom line, a spokesperson for a very large organization said that the savings they experienced as a result of implementing the *Fish!* philosophy was in the millions of dollars because of employee retention.

The philosophy emphasizes four ways that companies can help employees and workers can help themselves.

- *Play*. A sense of playfulness makes a huge difference between those who perceive their jobs as no fun and those who have fun doing their jobs. When employees are having as much fun as they can at whatever they are doing, they generate a spirit of innovation and creativity.

- *Be there*. Don't daydream about what you could be doing and things you do not have. Make the most of where you are. Listen in depth to customers' and colleagues' concerns or ideas. When you really focus on a conversation and postpone other activities such as answering phone calls or processing paperwork, you avoid communicating indifference to the other person.

- *Make someone's day*. Delight customers instead of grudgingly doing the bare minimum. Do favors for others, even those who make you uncomfortable, and your job will become much more rewarding.

- *Choose your attitude*. People often add unnecessary stress to their lives because they stay upset with certain aspects of their job that they cannot control, rather than focusing on how they can make things better.

The employees of Rochester Ford Toyota in Minnesota adopted the *Fish!* philosophy, and soon profits and morale went up dramatically. The sales and service personnel went out of their way to make their customers happy. On one cold night, a woman from out of town who was staying in Rochester temporarily because her husband was a patient at the Mayo Clinic called the shop to check on the status of her car's repairs. When she expressed frustration with her car's constant repairs and the desire to simply buy a new car, the sales staff sent a taxi to bring her to the dealership. They warmed up a car and drove her around the lot until she found a car she wanted. At the same time, the service staff took the initiative to appraise her old car. Once the deal was completed, employees prepared the new car for delivery, moved her personal belongings into it, and drew her a map back to her hotel. The next day she returned with her husband, who wanted to thank the group of employees for taking such good care of his wife.

Southwest Airlines has also established a lighthearted and playful "Fish" corporate culture that results in effective customer service. Peter Nelson, manager of creative development for Southwest, explains that a customer-friendly attitude is "excruciatingly hard to instill in people."[30] The reason is that people tend to limit their fun because they worry too much how others will judge them and think others may not take them seriously if they are enjoying their work. But when you can convince employees that it is OK to enjoy their jobs, they begin to display attitudes such as courtesy and respect for internal employees as well as for external customers. You see a lot more authentic service rather than people saying at every workstation, "Have a nice day." Instead of a disinterested "Hello," they look people in the eye and say "Good Morning!"

First Essex Bank chairman and CEO Leonard Wilson admits that "*Fish!* isn't going to make horrible, inexperienced employees into good employees. . . . But most workers can give an extra 10 to 40 percent. . . . *Fish!* is a way to get at an employee's 'pool of discretionary effort.'"[31]

■ Questions

1. Which of the four *Fish* principles do you believe can have the most dramatic effect on employees' productivity? Explain your answer.

2. What would you say to someone who sincerely believed that the *Fish* principles were ridiculous and frivolous?

3. Would you like to work for a *Fish* organization? Why or why not?

4. Identify workers and/or organizations that you believe have caught on to the powerful impact of this "attitude adjustment" program. How can you tell? What effect has it had on the individuals' and/or the organizations' success?

7

MOTIVATING YOURSELF AND OTHERS

Chapter Preview

After studying this chapter, you will be able to

- Differentiate between internal and external motivators in the workplace.

- Explain the five characteristics of motives.

- Describe Maslow's hierarchy of needs and Herzberg's motivation-maintenance theory.

- Compare and contrast Theory X and Theory Y leadership styles.

- Describe how expectations influence motivation.

- List and describe contemporary motivation strategies.

- Describe selected self-motivation strategies.

About ninety years ago, explorer Ernest Shackleton prepared to set sail for Antarctica. He hoped to lead the first expedition to travel across that dangerous continent by way of the South Pole. The tale of Shackleton's journey has been resurrected in books, photo exhibitions, an IMAX movie, and case studies used in college business courses.

How do you recruit people for such a perilous trek? Shackleton placed the following ad in the personal column of the *London Times*:

> Men wanted for hazardous journey. Small wages, bitter cold, long months of complete darkness, constant danger, safe return doubtful. Honour and recognition in case of success.

About five thousand men applied, and twenty-seven were selected. Before they reached landfall, his ship became frozen in a sea of ice, stranding him and his crew for twenty-two months. The quest to return home turned out to be one of the greatest survival sagas of all time. Every member of the party returned alive.[1]

Fast-forward to the year 2000, and meet Ellen MacArthur. She became the youngest sailor, and only the second woman, to finish the Vendee Globe sailing race. The race involves sailing nonstop alone around the world—a distance of about twenty-eight thousand miles. After the second-place finish she asserted, "If you really have a dream, you can make it happen."[2]

What motivated Ellen MacArthur to prepare for and enter the Vendee Globe sailing race, a race that involves sailing nonstop alone around the world? We may never know the complete answer. Human motivation is very complex.

Questions about what motivates people like Shackleton and MacArthur to risk their lives are difficult to answer. Questions about what motivates anyone are not easily answered because each individual differs so much in values, attitudes, and needs.

Knowing what motivates other people is basic to establishing and maintaining effective relationships with them.

Learning what motivates you can be an essential part of knowing yourself. This process is possible once you understand your value priorities (Chapter 5) and have a clear understanding of how your attitudes affect your behavior (Chapter 6). The information on motivation presented in this chapter will help you gain some useful insights into your personal needs.

The material in this chapter also contributes to the development of your human relations skills. Knowing what motivates other people is basic to establishing and maintaining effective relationships with them.[3] This chapter also examines why management is so concerned with understanding the factors that motivate employees. Because productivity and profitability are crucial to the success of any organization, employees must be motivated to do their very best.

The Complex Nature of Motivation

People are motivated by many different kinds of needs. They have basic needs for food, clothing, and shelter, but they also need acceptance, recognition, and self-esteem. Each individual experiences these needs in different ways and to varying degrees. To complicate matters more, people are motivated by different needs at different times in their lives. Adults, like children and adolescents, continue to develop and change in significant ways throughout life. Patterns of adult development have been described in such important books as *Passages* and *Pathfinders,* by Gail Sheehy, and *Seasons of a Man's Life*, by Daniel Levinson. No one approach to motivation works for all people or for the same person all the time.

● Motivation Defined

People interact with each other in a variety of ways because they are driven by a variety of forces. **Motivation,** derived from the Latin word *movere,* meaning "to move," can be defined as the influences that account for the initiation, direction, intensity, and persistence of behavior. The study of motivation is complicated by the fact that the number of possible motives for human behavior seem endless. *Emotional* factors such as fear, anger, and love are some sources of motivation. Others may stem from *social* factors that are influenced by parents, teachers, friends, and television. And then there are the basic *biological* factors such as our need for food, water, or sleep.[4]

TOTAL	**STEPHEN R. COVEY**
PERSON	AUTHOR, *THE 7 HABITS OF HIGHLY EFFECTIVE PEOPLE*
INSIGHT	"Dependent people need others to get what they want. Independent people can get what they want through their own efforts. Interdependent people combine their own efforts with the efforts of others to achieve their greatest success."

Although the major focus of this chapter will be motivation in a work setting, it is important to realize that some people find meaning through the obsessions that consume their leisure time. To earn a living, Henry Sakaida helps operate a wholesale nursery in Rosemead, California, but his passion is World War II aviation history. For the past twenty years he has arranged healing meetings between Japanese and American pilots who once shot at each other over the Pacific.[5] Tatsuo and Yukiko Ono operate a small business in Japan, but they get their greatest satisfaction from following the band The Rolling Stones. They have attended about three hundred Stones concerts held at major cities around the world.[6]

In a work setting, it is motivated employees who get the work done. Without them, most organizations would falter. Motivation is two dimensional; it can be internal or external.

Internal motivation comes from the satisfaction that occurs when work is meaningful and gives us a sense of purpose. Organizations that are truly people-centered recognize the value of rewards that are self-granted and internally experienced. Psychologist Frederick Herzberg has said that motivation comes from an internal stimulus resulting from job content, not job environment. He has suggested that jobs be enriched to provide challenge, opportunity for achievement, and individual growth.[7] These intrinsic rewards motivate some people more than money, trophies for outstanding performance, or other similar external rewards.

> *External rewards are rarely enough to motivate people on a continuing basis.*

External motivation is an action taken by another person. It usually involves the anticipation of a reward of some kind. Typical external rewards in a work setting include money, feedback regarding performance, and awards. Some organizations are using **incentives** to encourage workers to develop good work habits and to repeat behavior that is beneficial to themselves and the organization. An incentive can take the form of additional money, time off from work, or some other type of reward.

External rewards are rarely enough to motivate people on a continuing basis. Ideally, an organization will provide an appropriate number of external rewards while permitting employees to experience the ongoing, internal satisfaction that comes from meaningful work.

● **The Motivation to Satisfy Basic Desires**

Steven Reiss, professor of psychology and psychiatry at Ohio State University, conducted a major study to determine what *really* drives human behavior. He asked six thousand people from many stations in life which values were most

FIGURE 7.1	The Sixteen Basic Desires in the Reiss Profile (Order of Presentation Not Significant)

DESIRE	DEFINITION
CURIOSITY	The desire for knowledge
ACCEPTANCE	The desire for inclusion
ORDER	The desire for organization
PHYSICAL ACTIVITY	The desire for exercise of muscles
HONOR	The desire to be loyal to one's parents and heritage
POWER	The desire to influence others
INDEPENDENCE	The desire for self-reliance
SOCIAL CONTACT	The desire for companionship
FAMILY	The desire to raise one's own children
STATUS	The desire for social standing
IDEALISM	The desire for social justice
VENGEANCE	The desire to get even
ROMANCE	The desire for sex and beauty
EATING	The desire to consume food
SAVING	The desire to collect things
TRANQUILITY	The desire for emotional calm

Source: Steven Reiss, *Who Am I?* (New York: Berkley Books, 2000), pp. 17–18.

significant in motivating their behavior and in contributing to their sense of happiness.[8] The results of his research showed that nearly everything we experience as meaningful can be traced to one of sixteen basic desires or to some combination of these desires (see Figure 7.1). The challenge is to determine which ones (the fundamental values) are most important and then live your life accordingly. You do not need to satisfy all sixteen desires, only the five or six that are most important to you.

Reiss and his research team found that most people cannot find *enduring* happiness by aiming to have more fun or pleasure. People who focus primarily on "feel-good" happiness (partying, drinking, etc.) discover that this source of satisfaction rarely lasts more than a few hours. It is "value-based" happiness that gives life meaning over the long run.[9] In Chapter 5 you were encouraged to identify and reflect on the values that are important in your life. Now would be a good time to revisit the values clarification process. After studying the sixteen basic desires and identifying the five or six that seem most important to you, return to Table 5.1. The five-part valuing process will help you confirm your earlier efforts to clarify and develop your values.

● Characteristics of Motives

Motives have been described as the "why" of human behavior. An understanding of the following five characteristics of motives can be helpful as you seek to understand the complex nature of motivation.[10]

Motives Are Individualistic   People have different needs. What satisfies one person's needs, therefore, may not satisfy anyone else's. This variation in individual motives often leads to a breakdown in human relationships unless individuals take the time to understand the motives of others.

Motives Change   As noted at the beginning of this chapter, motives change throughout our lives. What motivates us early in our careers may not motivate us later on. Many employees at new Internet-based companies work long hours during the critical start-up period; 100-hour workweeks are not uncommon. Later they become more interested in leisure time, which enhances creativity and helps them look at things in a different way.

Motives May Be Unconscious   In many cases, we are not fully aware of the inner needs and drives that influence our behavior. The desire to win the "Employee of the Month" award may be triggered by unconscious feelings of inadequacy or the desire for increased recognition.

HUMAN RELATIONS IN ACTION	Greatest Comeback in Sports History

In 1998 Lance Armstrong returned to cycling after almost losing his life to testicular cancer. His goal at that point was to dominate the Tour de France, the world's most grueling biking competition. To fully appreciate the challenge facing Armstrong, you need to understand the immense physical endurance the Tour demands. Cyclists compete in the 2,000 mile race for over three weeks and spend nearly 90 hours on the bike. The Tour de France has been described as the equivalent of running 20 marathons in 20 days. Armstrong has won this event five times in a row. He joins only four others as five time winners of the Tour.

Tour de France winner Lance Armstrong waves as he rides down the Champs-Élysées after the final stage. He has won this grueling three-week event five times in a row.

Motives Are Often Inferred   We can observe the behavior of another person, but we can only infer (draw conclusions about) what motives caused that behavior. The motives underlying our own behavior and others' behavior are often difficult to understand.

Motives Are Hierarchical   Motives for behavior vary in levels of importance. When contradictory motives exist, the more important motive usually guides behavior. Workers often leave jobs that are secure to satisfy the need for work that is more challenging and rewarding.

Influential Motivational Theories

The work of various psychologists and social scientists has added greatly to the knowledge of what motivates people and how motivation works. The basic problem, as many leaders admit, is knowing how to apply that knowledge in the workplace. Although many theories of motivation have emerged over the years, we will discuss four of the most influential.

● Maslow's Hierarchy of Needs

According to Abraham Maslow, a noted psychologist, people tend to satisfy their needs in a particular order—a theory he calls the **hierarchy of needs.** Maslow's theory rests on three assumptions: (1) People have a number of needs that require some measure of satisfaction. (2) Only unsatisfied needs motivate behavior. (3) The needs of people are arranged in a hierarchy of pre-potency, which means that as each lower-level need is satisfied, the need at the next level demands attention.[11] Basically, human beings are motivated to satisfy physiological needs first (food, clothing, shelter); then the need for safety and security; then social needs; then esteem needs; and, finally, self-actualization needs, or the need to realize their potential. Maslow's theory is illustrated in Figure 7.2.

Physiological Needs   The needs for food, clothing, sleep, and shelter, or physiological needs, were described by Maslow as survival or lower-order needs. When the economy is strong and most people have jobs, these basic needs rarely dominate because they are reasonably well satisfied. But, needless

FIGURE 7.2 | Maslow's Hierarchy of Needs

Self-actualization

Esteem

Social or Belongingness

Safety and Security

Physiological

to say, people who cannot ensure their own and their family's survival, or are homeless, place this basic need at the top of their priority list.

Safety and Security Needs   People's desire for order, predictability, and freedom from threats is reflected in safety and security needs. Safety needs often focus on protection from physical harm. On the job, this means a guarantee of safe working conditions. Unions or employee groups can make sure employers maintain safety standards and reduce the risk of accidents or injuries resulting from work hazards. But a person's need for safety and security is not limited to freedom from violence or injury. People have to know that they can provide for their families and that they will have enough money and resources to take care of themselves in sickness or old age.

Social or Belongingness Needs   Whereas the first two types of needs deal with aspects of physical safety and survival, social or belongingness needs deal with emotional and mental well-being. Research has shown that needs for affection, for a sense of belonging, and for identification with a group are powerful. There are two major aspects of the need to belong: frequent, positive interactions with the same people and a framework of stable, long-term caring and concern.[12]

Esteem Needs   *Self-esteem* is a term that describes how you feel about yourself. Esteem needs relate to a person's self-respect and to the recognition and respect he or she receives from others. Several esteem-building initiatives are discussed in Chapter 4.

Self-Actualization Needs   The four needs just described motivate people by their *absence*—that is, when people feel a lack of food and shelter, security, social relationships, or esteem. Self-actualization needs, however, represent the need for growth, and they motivate people by their *presence.* Self-actualization is people fulfilling their potential or realizing their fullest capacities as human beings.

Maslow used *self-actualization* in a very specialized sense to describe a rarely attained state of human achievement. Because of the uniqueness of each person, the way of achieving self-actualization is an individual matter.[13] Table 7.1 (on p. 168) summarizes some ways of satisfying self-actualization and other needs at work.

● Maslow's Theory Reconsidered

Although Maslow's theory has helped us understand human behavior, his hierarchical arrangement of needs has been questioned by several behavioral scientists who tested his theory. Their findings point to a two-level rather than a five-level hierarchy. Physiological and safety needs are arranged in hierarchical fashion; but beyond that point, any one of a number of needs may emerge as most important, depending on the individual. The behavioral scientists' research shows that human beings may be motivated at any one time by a complex array of needs.[14]

TABLE 7.1	Ways of Satisfying Individual Needs in the Work Situation
Need	**Organizational Conditions**
Physiological	Pay Breakfast or lunch programs Company services
Safety and security	Company benefits plans Pensions Seniority Pay
Social or belongingness	Coffee breaks Sports teams Company picnics and social events Work teams
Esteem	Recognition of work well done Responsibility Pay (as symbol of status) Prestigious office location and furnishings
Self-actualization	Challenge Autonomy

Source: Adapted from Judith Gordon, *A Diagnostic Approach to Organizational Behavior,* 3d ed. (Boston: Allyn & Bacon, 1991), p. 144.

It is also worth noting that Maslow's list of higher-level needs does not take into consideration the needs of the new generation of workers, such as the need for learning, leisure, and family relationships.[15] Although Maslow's theory has not stood up well under real-life testing, it teaches us one important lesson: A need that is satisfied will not motivate an individual.[16] If you have food and shelter, you will not be motivated when someone offers you those same items. It is important to remember that Maslow's theory has made major contributions to our understanding of human behavior at work. His original works have been republished in a new book, *Maslow on Management.* It is considered a classic in the field of management theory.[17]

● Herzberg's Motivation-Maintenance (Two-Factor) Theory

Psychologist Frederick Herzberg proposes another motivation theory called the **motivation-maintenance theory.**[18] **Maintenance factors** represent the basic things people consider essential to any job, such as salaries, fringe benefits, working conditions, social relationships, supervision, and organizational policies and administration. We often take such things for granted as part of the job. These basic maintenance factors do not act as motivators, according to Herzberg; but if any of them is absent, the organizational climate that results can hurt employee morale and lower worker productivity. Health insurance, for example, generally does not motivate employees to be more productive, but

We humans are social beings and enjoy spending time with others. The need for belongingness may have motivated some of these workers to join friends for a casual lunch.

the loss of it can cause workers to look for employment in another organization that provides the desired coverage.

Motivational factors are those elements that go above and beyond the basic maintenance factors. They include opportunities for recognition, advancement, or more responsibility. When these are present, they tend to motivate employees to improve their productivity. The workers may seek out new and creative ways to accomplish their organizations' goals as well as their personal goals. Herzberg's list of motivational factors parallels, to some degree, Maslow's hierarchy of needs (see Table 7.2).

Herzberg theorizes that if employees' motivational factors are not met, they may begin to ask for more maintenance factors, such as increased salaries

TABLE 7.2	Comparison of the Maslow and Herzberg Theories	
	Maslow	**Herzberg**
Motivational factors	Self-actualization	Work itself Achievement Responsibility
	Esteem needs	Recognition Advancement Status
Maintenance factors	Social or belongingness needs	Social network Supervision
	Safety and security needs	Company policy and administration
	Physiological needs	Job security Working conditions Salary

and fringe benefits, better working conditions, or more liberal company policies regarding sick leave or vacation time. Critics of Herzberg's theory have pointed out that he assumes that most, if not all, individuals are motivated only by higher-order needs such as recognition or increased responsibility, and that they seek jobs that are challenging and meaningful. His theory does not acknowledge that some people may prefer more routine, predictable work and may be motivated more by the security of a regular paycheck (a maintenance factor) than by the prospect of advancement. Nonetheless, Herzberg made an important contribution to motivation theory by emphasizing the importance of enriched work.

● The Expectancy Theory

The **expectancy theory** is based on the assumption that motivational strength is determined by whether or not you *believe* you can be successful at a task. (This theory is an expansion of the self-efficacy concept detailed in Chapter 4.) If you really want something and believe that the probability of your success is high, then your motivation increases. *Perception* is an important element of this theory. Research conducted at the University of Kansas found a link between expectations and achievement in college. Students who wanted to complete college and believed they were capable of doing so earned higher grades and were less likely to drop out. In fact, aspirations combined with expectations predicted achievement better than standardized test scores.[19] This somewhat mysterious connection between what you expect in life and what you actually achieve is sometimes referred to as the **self-fulfilling prophecy:** If you can conceive it and believe it, you can achieve it.

● The Goal-Setting Theory

Successful people and successful organizations have one thing in common: They share the power of purpose. The more you focus on achieving a desired outcome, the greater your likelihood of success.[20] Your goals play a key role in bringing purpose to your life.

> *Your goals play a key role in bringing purpose to your life.*

Motivation researchers indicate that goals tend to motivate people in four ways (see Figure 7.3). First, goals provide the power of purpose by directing your attention to a specific target. Second, they encourage you to make the effort to achieve something difficult. Third, reaching a goal requires sustained effort and therefore encourages persistence. Fourth, having a goal forces you to bridge the gap between the dream and the reality; it fosters your creating a plan of action filled with strategies that will get you where you want to go.[21]

Applying the goal-setting theory requires an understanding of the criteria for developing realistic goals. Establishing goals in a sales career is very common and provides a good example of the goal-setting process. Suppose, for instance, the goal is to increase sales over the next year—a nice goal, but not good enough to really motivate the average person. Goals need to be specific: Increase this year's sales by 12 percent over last year's figures. That goal may

| FIGURE 7.3 | A Model of How Goals Can Improve Performance |

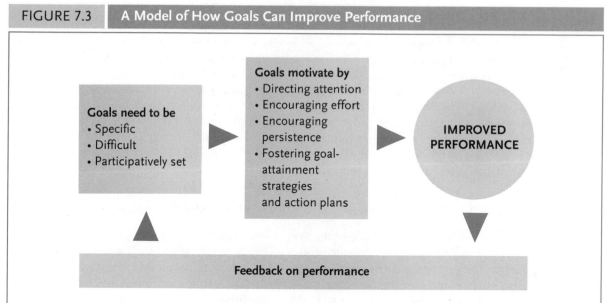

Source: "A Model of How Goals Can Improve Performance," from Robert Kreitner, *Management* (Boston: Houghton Mifflin, 2000). Reprinted by permission of Houghton Mifflin Company. All rights reserved.

be a stretch, but it is possible. If something is easy to achieve and requires little effort, the goal does not serve as a motivator. Remember, though, that goals need to be difficult enough to challenge you but not impossible to reach. Goal setting is an excellent self-motivation strategy. Take a moment and review the goal-setting principles listed in Table 4.1.

Contemporary Employee Motivation Strategies

A healthy, mutually supportive relationship based on trust, openness, and respect can create a work climate in which employees want to give more of themselves. However, creating this type of organizational culture in the age of information may not be easy. How do you motivate employees who work from virtual offices? How do organizations experiencing major upheavals keep their employees' trust? The answers may have been provided by Jeffrey Pfeffer, a Stanford professor who has reported a strong connection between people-centered practices and an organization's higher profits and lower employee turnover. Organizations that recognize human wants, needs, passions, and aspirations and put people first understand that many of the following motivation strategies have merit even during times of great uncertainty.[22]

● Motivation Through Job Design

We have noted that today's workers place a high value on jobs that provide rewards such as a sense of achievement, challenge, variety, and personal growth. It is possible to redesign existing jobs so they will have characteristics or

HUMAN RELATIONS IN ACTION

McGregor's Theory X / Theory Y

Adrian Wooldridge, a journalist with *The Economist,* says management theorists are essentially divided into two groups. One group thinks that workers are basically stupid and have to be goaded into doing things. The other group holds the opposite set of assumptions: that workers are basically creative, innovative people who want to please and do their best. Over forty years ago Douglas McGregor, author of the classic book *The Human Side of Enterprise,* presented similar points of view. He outlined a set of highly optimistic assumptions about human nature and labeled them Theory Y. He described traditional thinking about workers as Theory X. A brief description of each follows.

Theory X: The Pessimistic View

People do not really want to work—they have to be pushed, closely supervised, and prodded into doing things, either with incentives such as pay or with punishments for not working. Because they have little or no ambition, workers prefer to avoid responsibility and do only as much work as they have to in order to keep their jobs.

Theory Y: The Optimistic View

Work is as natural to people as play or rest. People are capable of self-direction and can learn to both accept and seek responsibility if they are committed to the objectives of the organization. The assumption is that people will become committed to organizational objectives if they are rewarded for doing so.

outcomes that are intrinsically satisfying to employees. There are at least three design options.[23]

Job Rotation **Job rotation** involves allowing employees to move through a variety of jobs, departments, or functions. Employees are encouraged to alternate tasks—two, three, or more—in a predefined way over a period of time. For example, a worker might attach a wheel assembly one week, inspect it the next, and organize the parts for assembly during the third week. Job rotation facilitates career advancement by cross-training workers, and it also allows management a hedge against absenteeism. Apex Precision Technologies Inc., a customer-machine shop in Camby, Indiana, continually trains workers on all of its equipment so that they can move around depending on what sort of orders come in from customers.[24]

Job Enlargement **Job enlargement** means expanding an employee's duties or responsibilities. When a job becomes stale, motivation can often be increased by encouraging employees to learn new skills or take on new responsibilities. Lands' End, the mail order company, has developed a job enlargement arrangement in which telephone sales representatives take one-day leaves to work in another area of the company. One person leaves the sales desk each Thursday to work in the returns department. Another employee works one day a week setting up product shots in the catalog photo shop. Employees enjoy the new challenges, and the company benefits by having employees who are trained in several facets of work. During busy periods these employees can fill strategic gaps.[25]

Job Enrichment   **Job enrichment** is an attempt to make jobs more desirable or satisfying, thereby triggering internal motivation. One approach assigns new and more difficult tasks to employees; another grants them additional authority. The Ritz-Carlton Hotel Co. has used this job-enrichment strategy to improve customer service. When a customer has a problem, employees are encouraged to find a solution immediately. They have the discretion to spend up to $2,000 to fix a problem.[26]

Job rotation, job enlargement, and job enrichment appeal to Generation Y workers, who often do not value work for only external rewards. These workers are more apt to view work as a valuable learning experience that leads to something better.[27]

Motivation Through Incentives

Incentives are often used to improve quality, reduce accidents, increase sales, improve attendance, and speed up production. They often focus on improving behaviors that will cut expenses and improve customer satisfaction. At Sysco Corporation, the Houston-based marketer of food service products, incentive pay for managers, drivers, and loaders depends on whether the right products get delivered at the right time, with no torn bags or dented cans.[28] Organizations are searching for innovative compensation programs that will improve productivity but will not sabotage employee morale. We are seeing new incentive plans that erase the idea that everyone is motivated by the same thing, a "one-size-fits-all" approach. Incentives and rewards are discussed in more detail in Chapter 10.

Many companies are experimenting with programs that reward the development of new ideas. These programs, known as **intrapreneurship,** encourage employees to pursue their ideas at work, with the company providing the money, equipment, and time to do so. For example, 3M Company permits employees to spend 15 percent of company time experimenting with their own ideas. This practice resulted in the development of Post-it Notes. The 3M approach can be considered an incentive and a form of job enrichment.

Motivation Through Learning Opportunities

Learning opportunities, both on and off the job, can be a strong motivational force. Employees realize that education and training are critical to individual growth and opportunity. Rosabeth Moss Kanter says, "The chance to learn new skills or apply them in new arenas is an important motivator in a turbulent environment because it's oriented toward securing the future."[29] Of course, employees will be more motivated to participate in training programs if they perceive that such participation will lead to salary increases, advancement, or more meaningful work.

Many companies are using advanced communications technology to deliver instruction. Digital Equipment Corporation maintains its training curriculum catalog on the Internet, which enables employees to access self-paced courses from their personal computers.[30] Many other organizations provide tuition reimbursement for online courses offered by colleges and universities across the country.

● Motivation Through Empowerment

Throughout the industrial age, employees were often expected to surrender their opinions, creativity, and outside interests when starting a job. Many workers were confronted with rigid work rules and policies. Today, we are witnessing the emergence of a new work force made up of people who want to take more responsibility for their work. They want more opportunity for self-expression and opportunities to make decisions that really matter.[31]

We are witnessing the emergence of a new work force made up of people who want to take more responsibility for their work. They want more opportunity for self-expression and opportunities to make decisions that really matter.

Empowerment refers to those policies that share information, authority, and responsibility with the lowest ranks of the organization. It is a crucial aspect of the new economy. When employees are empowered to make decisions for the good of the organization, they experience feelings of pride, self-expression, and ownership.

Empowerment as a motivation strategy is based on the premise that workers want challenge and personal meaning from their jobs. It also acknowledges that lower-level employees often possess critical information about how to improve products and processes and better meet customer needs.

■ At a Xerox site in Dallas, 320 employees were allowed to arrange their own work schedules. Through group decisions, the flextime arrangement worked so well that absenteeism dropped by 30 percent and creativity increased.[32]

■ The Royal Dutch/Shell Group of companies is considered one of the largest organizations in the world, with 101,000 employees in 130 countries. Steve Miller's job is to manage Shell's "grassroots" program that allows frontline employees in this massive transnational organization to participate in corporate decisions. He believes that this helps management get an unfiltered picture of what is going on in the organization and that the frontline workers inspire people in middle and upper management who may have become jaded.[33]

Although empowerment efforts are growing in popularity, this motivational strategy should not be viewed as a quick fix. Empowerment requires a long-term commitment of human and financial resources from top management down.

● Motivation Through Others' Expectations

Earlier in this chapter you were introduced to the power of your own self-fulfilling prophecy: You will probably get whatever it is you expect. But there is another aspect of the expectancy theory: the power *others'* expectations can have on your motivation.

Research has confirmed that people tend to act in ways that are consistent with what others expect of them. In the classic study *Pygmalion in the Classroom,* Harvard University professors Robert Rosenthal and J. Sterling Livingston described the significant effect of teachers' expectations on students. They discovered that when teachers had high expectations for certain students who they believed had excellent intellectual ability and learning capacity, those students learned at a faster rate than others in the same group—even though the teachers did not consciously treat the higher-achieving students differently. These teachers had unintentionally communicated their high expectations to the students they *thought* possessed strong intellectual abilities.

Teachers, parents, and supervisors are in a position to communicate high or low expectations. MTW Corporation, a provider of software and Internet applications to the financial services industry, effectively uses this power by writing expectation agreements to help achieve corporate objectives. Each agreement establishes a set of mutually agreed on objectives between an individual and his or her boss.[34] Sometimes well-intentioned bosses can inadvertently reduce the performance of subordinates by communicating messages that create employees' self-doubt. Let's say an employee makes an important but poorly prepared presentation to a client. Later, the boss begins watching this person very closely and checking to see that his projects are completed. The employee senses a loss of the supervisor's trust and begins to doubt his own judgment; he takes less initiative and offers fewer suggestions. This confirms the boss's suspicions. The boss then engages in even closer supervision of the employee. At this point, both are caught in a destructive relationship that benefits no one.[35]

THINKING / LEARNING STARTERS

1. In places where you have worked, would you say the managers believed in Theory X or Theory Y? (See Human Relations in Action on p. 172.) Give specific examples to support your answer.

2. What types of incentives and rewards will motivate you? Money in the form of a year-end bonus? Recognition in front of your peers? A prize, such as a new car or trip? Do you believe the factors that motivate you will change as you grow older? Explain.

Self-Motivation Strategies

The material presented in this chapter explains how, why, when, and where motivation strategies work, and we have identified many organizations that do all they can to motivate their employees to stay on the job and to improve their productivity. But let's face it; some organizations just don't care if you are motivated or not, as long as you get your job done. If you are satisfied with your life and work, that's great! If you are yearning for a more exciting professional and/or personal life, guess what? It's up to you! The following self-motivation strategies can help you achieve your potential.

Go outside your comfort zone.   Many people do not achieve their full potential because they are afraid to venture outside their "comfort zone." These individuals often earn less than they deserve, exert little effort to win a promotion to a more challenging position, and refuse assignments that might enhance their career. Some people stay in their comfort zone because they fear success.

A good starting point for avoiding the fear of success is to reflect on messages you received from family and friends while growing up. Did they resent people who experienced career success or were wealthy? Did they tell you to let other children win at games or various contests, because otherwise no one would like you? Do you see how a "fear of success" pattern might develop? Learn to showcase your abilities. This might involve volunteering to work on a new project that will allow you to demonstrate your skills. Sell yourself to people who make decisions about your earnings and your advancement. Don't be afraid to toot your own horn.[36]

Build immunity to cynicism.   Employees often mistrust the motives of employers who are not open and honest. Unfortunately, this cynical attitude toward management tends to color employees' beliefs about all aspects of the company. To build immunity to cynicism, you must first maintain an open mind and avoid the temptation to blame management for every real or perceived problem. Take time to learn about the reasons for changes being made, and try to separate fact from fiction. Remember, the grapevine can be a source

"Nothing serious. I just hate my job."

of accurate *and* inaccurate information. In most cases, bad news gets more attention than good news.

Strive for balance. Motivation often decreases when we no longer have a sense of balance in our life. The fine line between a person's work and personal life is often blurred. To achieve balance, take time to reflect on what is most important in your life, and then try to make the necessary adjustments. Employees at Miller & Associates, a Dallas wholesaler of kitchen equipment, complete annual "life-purpose" statements. Each person records the ten most satisfying experiences in his or her life, making note of those that carry special meaning. When David Rogers, a salesperson, finished his "life-purpose" statements, he realized that he wasn't taking time to do some of the things he most valued. He said, "I was so weighted toward work that it was getting in the way of work." Once he cut back on his hours, freeing up time for his social life, his sales actually increased.[37]

> *Motivation often decreases when we no longer have a sense of balance in our life.*

TOTAL	**JOAN BORYSENKO**
PERSON	AUTHOR, *MINDING THE BODY, MENDING THE MIND*
INSIGHT	"People who feel in control of life can withstand on enormous amount of change and thrive on it. People who feel helpless can hardly cope at all."

Take action. If you are feeling bored or trapped in a dead-end job, you can enhance your self-motivation by taking responsibility for the situation you are in, and then taking action to improve it. Taking personal responsibility for your current situation is not easy because it is sometimes easier to blame others. Maybe "they" won't or can't do anything about your situation, but you can. Don't just wait and hope that things get better. Do something!

- Instead of waiting to see what will happen, volunteer for a project or make a request.
- Have lunch with the person in your organization who is doing work that you find intriguing.
- Talk to your boss about the things you want to do.
- Follow up on an idea you have had for a long time.
- Read a book, attend a conference, or do something else that will help you grow and learn.[38]

■ Summary

Motivation is a major component of human relations training because it provides a framework for understanding why people do the things they do. Internal motivation occurs when the task or duty performed is in itself a reward. External motivation is initiated by another person and usually is based on rewards or other forms of reinforcement for a job well done.

People are motivated by different things. Motives are individualistic and can change over the years. Because there is no valid measure of a person's motives, motives can only be inferred. Motives vary in strength and importance and are therefore hierarchical. Maslow's hierarchy of needs theory states that physiological needs will come first, followed by safety and security, social, esteem, and then self-actualization needs. According to Maslow, although any need can be a motivator, only higher-order needs will motivate people over the long run. Herzberg's motivation-maintenance theory contends that when motivational factors such as responsibility, recognition, and opportunity for advancement are not present, employees will demand improvement in maintenance factors, such as higher salaries, more benefits, and better working conditions.

Personal expectations, as well as the expectations of others, have a powerful influence on a person's motivation. These expectations can become self-fulfilling prophecies. Managers can motivate employees by expressing belief in their abilities and talents. McGregor's Theory X and Theory Y reflect a pessimistic and an optimistic view of human behavior, respectively.

Managers must reach their goals through and with other people, and they are primarily responsible for motivating their subordinates. The goal-setting motivation theory suggests that people become more focused and persistent if they establish specific, realistic goals in cooperation with their supervisors. Contemporary organizations attempt to motivate their employees through positive expectations and job-design modifications such as job rotation, job enlargement, and job enrichment. They are also discovering the effects of various incentives, intrapreneurship opportunities, additional training, and empowerment.

People must make their own plan to keep themselves motivated. They need to strive to go beyond their comfort zone regardless of past failures, avoid cynicism, strive for a balance between their professional and personal lives, take responsibility for their current situation, and take action to improve it.

■ Career Corner

Q: I love what I do, but I hate where I work. My workplace is very old, has no windows, and is very depressing. Besides, the two-hour commute is killing me! I've been with the company almost 6 months and hate to leave because the money and benefits are great, but I believe I can do my work from my home. When I asked my supervisor if she would consider allowing me to telecommute, she said her company tried that several years ago and it just didn't work.

A: For decades, managers have relied on the ability to walk past an employee's work area and *see* that the job is being done. Happily, that tradition has changed in the past few years. Technology has made major advances, and many managers have discovered that telecommuters are no more difficult to manage than in-house workers. Conduct your own research on the success of other organizations' telecommuting programs and succinctly present your findings to your supervisor. We believe you will find that the research supports the idea that good employees make good telecommuters. Therefore, it is important that you establish your credibility with your supervisor and work team. Employers know how difficult it can be to find and keep good workers, so they may be more willing to allow you to telecommute once you've proven your worth to them. Suggest a 90-day trial period. If your employers are not satisfied with the arrangement, they can discontinue it. If you like the telecommuting arrangement and disagree with their decision, take your skills elsewhere where employers are more flexible.

■ Key Terms

motivation	expectancy theory
internal motivation	self-fulfilling prophecy
external motivation	job rotation
incentives	job enlargement
hierarchy of needs	job enrichment
motivation-maintenance theory	intrapreneurship
maintenance factors	empowerment
motivational factors	

■ Review Questions

1. Given what you have read in this chapter, how would you define *motivation?*

2. Describe the difference between external and internal motivations and give examples.

3. Describe the needs present in Maslow's hierarchy. How can organizations attempt to meet these needs so that employees are motivated to produce more work?

4. Who is the best judge of what is and what is not a motivating factor for employees? Explain.

5. Explain Herzberg's motivation-maintenance theory.

6. Why and how should people set goals?

7. Describe the likely motivational strategies of a Theory X manager as opposed to a Theory Y manager.

8. Identify the various ways a job can be redesigned to motivate an employee.

9. How might empowering employees with authority and responsibility affect their job performance? In what ways will this empowerment affect their human relations skills?

10. Identify five ways you can motivate yourself.

■ **Application Exercises**

1. This chapter describes the following contemporary employee motivational strategies:

   a. job rotation
   b. job enlargement
   c. job enrichment
   d. intrapreneurial incentives

   e. training and education
   f. incentives
   g. intrapreneurship
   h. empowerment

   To gain practice in identifying what motivates other people, select two people you think you know well, and write their names on a piece of paper. From the list above, choose three factors you believe would motivate each of these people at work. Then ask the same two people what really would motivate them to do their best. Did you accurately judge their motives? Explain. How might developing this skill of identifying others' motivating factors help you improve your human relations on the job?

2. Prepare a list of all the things you need to accomplish in the coming week: your "to do" list. Identify those activities and/or responsibilities that you will avoid completing, even though you know you have to do them. What self-motivating strategies identified in this chapter can you implement to improve your chances of completing those tasks successfully?

3. Are you frustrated with any aspect of your personal or professional life right now? Write a major frustration on a piece of paper but do not put your name on it. Form a group of four or five class members who have completed the same task. Pass each other's papers randomly from group member to group member until your instructor says stop. One at a time, each group member can describe his or her ideas on how to overcome the frustration identified on the paper he or she is holding. At the conclusion of this exercise, describe how this "outsider's" viewpoint of your situation has influenced your thinking.

 Internet Exercise

Examine *Fortune* magazine's 100 best companies to work for (*www.fortune.com*). Access the webpage of the company that seems most appealing to you, and link onto its employment area. Which of its job opportunities would you like to pursue? What do you need to do to become qualified for this job? Are you willing to do what is necessary to meet those requirements? Why or why not?

Case 7.1   Motivating Employees During Tough Times

In the economic downturn following September 11 and the subsequent war on terrorism, many workers felt depressed and insecure. Frequent news of mergers, downsizing, and business closings added more layers of insecurity. Stephen

Lundin, coauthor of *Fish!,* said, "It's dark out there. Most workplaces are toxic energy dumps: places that are just so dead you wonder how people could drag themselves back there every day."[39] Whether you agree with this statement or not, it is obvious that a depressing work environment can reduce overall productivity and get in the way of teamwork and creative problem solving.

To survive—let alone thrive—during difficult times, progressive organizations focus on finding ways to give employees hope for the future. They strive to provide a "complete employment experience," knowing that a happy worker is a loyal worker. But what makes and keeps employees happy? When the economy is suffering, many organizations cannot afford to offer prospective employees huge salaries, so they attempt to entice them with their benefits packages. If organizations do not offer a reasonable benefits program—vacation pay, health insurance, and a 401-K retirement plan—the world's brightest and finest job seekers may not give them a second look. Most employees aren't too particular about the enhancements of one benefits package over another as long as these basics exist. Hiring bonuses, stock options, and flexible hours work for some but not for all. A single millennial worker gauges a satisfying employment experience differently than an older working mother of three. An organization that addresses each employee's individual preferences is more likely to win the most talented workers.

For some workers, a fat paycheck, stock options, and profit sharing are the factors that keep them motivated. However, what really motivates many of today's workers are those unique opportunities that help them get excited about going to work each day. They include the following:

- A trusting climate unencumbered with bureaucracy, a hands-off management style, and a comfortable, flexible work environment. Most talented employees will leave when they feel they are treated in a controlling, disrespectful, or negative manner.

- A feeling they are doing something with a purpose, even if it is outside the workplace. When an employer participates in fundraising for local charities, many workers jump on board and express appreciation that their employer is encouraging these types of activities. They want to be affiliated with an organization that is perceived as ethical and actively involved in the community. The opportunity to make a difference will often keep today's workers from moving on to greener pastures.

- A balance in work/life issues. Many employees want flexibility in working hours to handle child-rearing tasks, to give them the opportunity to travel, to enjoy leisure time, and in some cases to continue their education.

Some incentive programs are designed to keep people at work, such as overtime pay or accelerated sales commissions based on new business rather than repeat customers. John Metzger, the innovative leader of Boulder, Colorado's, Metzger Associates Inc., allowed his employees to design the company's "Live Long and Prosper" incentive and benefit plan. This resulted in employees being reimbursed for those activities that take them *out* of the office: $600 for physical fitness activities (gym memberships, a stationary bicycle), $500 for outdoor living activities (ski passes, sailing classes), $600 for relaxation activities (guitar instruction, vacations), and $1,000 for education. Employee turnover dropped from 15 percent to 2 percent after this program was started. When Metzger was asked why he budgets these creative motivational incentives, he said, "We want people to be passionate about life and hobbies and outside pursuits, because we want passionate people."⁴⁰

■ **Questions**

1. Which of the motivational factors identified in this case appeal to you? Explain.

2. Should Herzberg's motivation-maintenance theory be considered when designing a basic benefits plan? Explain your reasoning.

3. It can be said that some employees may rely too heavily on their organization to manage their happiness. If they are not happy, they quit and move on to the next opportunity. How can people determine for themselves what motivates them and find happiness in and outside the workplace? What would be the benefits of discovering these self-motivational factors?

Case 7.2   Let the People Have the Power

The greatest challenge in most organizations is to create employee excitement and anticipation and to keep all employees involved in their own as well as the organization's progress on a daily basis. When you study those organizations that are successful in building this type of employee motivation, you discover that each one encourages its employees to stay involved in the day-to-day search for ways to improve business practices and increase profits.

When organizations provide employees with information relevant to various business decisions and allow them to identify and fix problem areas along the way, everyone wins. This open-book management style gives employees the opportunity to be an important part of the organization's future. When they are empowered to make the necessary decisions to correct problems, they feel in control of their own future as well.

Jack Stack, president of Springfield Remanufacturing Company, literally wrote the book on employee empowerment through open-book management.⁴¹ Each year, his employees study the numbers and determine what the greatest threat to SRC's success is. They then develop a plan to overcome the threat. If they achieve the desired results, each employee receives a share of the resulting profit through a year-end bonus that can exceed 18 percent of his or her pay. Employees meet weekly to review numbers and decide how to improve operations. Everyone understands that part of his or her job is to help prevent losses and increase productivity. "If we don't achieve a goal, we find out very quickly why we missed it. Everybody is looking through the numbers to see what the problem is."⁴² If a department is having trouble, another department will send in reinforcements, and everybody understands why. They spontaneously help each other out, sometimes at great inconvenience. Even in tough times, SRC has never had a layoff. When it slightly missed its sales goal one year, 60 percent of the employees said they did not want their bonus. Obviously, money was *not* their only motivating factor.

Logical Net Corporation, an Internet service provider, discovered it was losing $130,000 a month and heading for imminent bankruptcy. Instead of hiding the information to save face and avert employee panic, the CEO distributed financial information to all managers and asked: What are we doing wrong, and what can we do to correct it? The sales staff researched which products and services produced the highest profit and increased their efforts accordingly. They discovered six-digit, past-due accounts receivable and nudged their customers to pay their bills. A field employee discovered that the company was maintaining two service cables with identical functions. When one was shut down, the company saved thousands of dollars each month. Engineers discovered they could use a remote-access server in storage rather than spending $25,000 for a new one. Six months later, when the company was thriving—not bankrupt—it was obvious that miracles can happen when employees consider the financial ramifications of their decisions.[43]

■ Questions

1. What are the motivating factors at SRC and Logic Net? Where do they fit on Maslow's hierarchy of needs pyramid?

2. If you were an employee at either company, would these factors motivate you to hunt for another job or stay put? Explain.

3. In the months before the fall of the Enron Corporation, employees were led to believe that "all was well" with the company and were encouraged to continue to invest their time and money in its future. If Enron executives had implemented the motivational strategies exemplified at SRC and Logic Net, how might Enron's story have been altered? Explain your reasoning.

PART III

PERSONAL STRATEGIES FOR IMPROVING HUMAN RELATIONS

8

IMPROVING INTERPERSONAL RELATIONS WITH CONSTRUCTIVE SELF-DISCLOSURE

Chapter Preview

After studying this chapter, you will be able to

- Explain how constructive self-disclosure contributes to improved interpersonal relationships and teamwork.

- Understand the specific benefits you can gain from self-disclosure.

- Identify and explain the major elements of the Johari Window model.

- Explain the criteria for appropriate self-disclosure.

- Understand the barriers to constructive self-disclosure.

- Apply your knowledge and practice constructive self-disclosure.

What do you say to people after you've been laid off? Jeffrey Zaslow had to answer this question after he was laid off as a columnist at the *Chicago Sun-Times*. Friends, colleagues, and readers were very supportive, but talking to them about the loss of a job he had held for fourteen years was difficult. When he told his children, they asked some hard questions: "Will we have to sell our house?" "Are you sad, daddy?"[1]

William Brams, a financial planner, often paused when people asked, "How's the family?" He was uncertain how they might react if he told them about his struggles with his rebellious teenage sons. When he did tell the truth, some clients reacted with sympathy. Brams says that talking about his kids eased the isolation he feels. Some clients told him about their own troubled teens.[2]

Throughout life you will need to prepare for a variety of difficult conversations. What do you say to a boss who delegates tasks and then second-guesses every decision you make? What do you say to a customer who is constantly badmouthing your company with inaccurate statements? How do you talk to a grieving coworker who lost her spouse in an auto accident? Expressing personal thoughts and feelings to supervisors, coworkers, friends, and family members can be very difficult.

Talking to people after you have been laid off is not easy. Syndicated columnist Jeffrey Zaslow worked at the *Chicago Sun-Times* for fourteen years and then, very suddenly, he was out of work. Throughout life we need to be prepared for a variety of difficult conversations.

Self-Disclosure: An Introduction

As a general rule, relationships grow stronger when people are willing to reveal more about themselves and their work experiences. It is a surprising but true fact of life that two people can work together for many years and never really get to know each other. In many organizations, people are encouraged to hide their true feelings. The result is often a weakening of the communication process. Self-disclosure can lead to a more open and supportive environment in the workplace.

Self-disclosure in the workplace can take many forms. At a recent staff meeting, for instance, your boss praised the work of two coworkers but said nothing about an important project you completed ahead of schedule. You feel that your accomplishments have been ignored in the past and decide that now it's time to meet with your boss and tell her how you feel.

In some cases self-disclosure takes the form of an apology or of granting forgiveness to someone who apologizes to you. If you are a supervisor or manager, self-disclosure may take the form of constructive criticism of an employee whose performance is unsatisfactory. This chapter focuses on constructive self-disclosure and on conditions that encourage appropriate self-disclosure in a work setting.

● Self-Disclosure Defined

Self-disclosure is the process of letting another person know what you think, feel, or want. It is one of the important ways you let yourself be known by others. Self-disclosure can improve interpersonal communication, resolve conflict, and strengthen interpersonal relationships.

It is important to note the difference between self-disclosure and self-description. **Self-description** involves disclosure of nonthreatening information, such as your age, your favorite food, or where you went to school. This is information that others could acquire in some way other than by your telling them. Self-disclosure, by contrast, usually involves some degree of risk. When you practice self-disclosure, you reveal private, personal information that cannot be acquired from another source. Examples include your feelings about being a member of a minority group, job satisfaction, and new policies and procedures.

The importance of self-disclosure, in contrast to self-description, is shown by the following situation. You work at a distribution center and are extremely conscious of safety. You take every precaution to avoid work-related accidents. But another employee has a much more casual attitude toward safety rules and often "forgets" to observe the proper procedures, endangering you and other workers. You can choose to disclose your feelings to this person or stay silent. Either way, your decision has consequences.

● Benefits Gained from Self-Disclosure

Before we discuss self-disclosure in more detail, let us examine four basic benefits you gain from openly sharing what you think, feel, or want.

TOTAL
PERSON
INSIGHT

ALBERT J. BERNSTEIN AND
SYDNEY CRAFT ROZEN

AUTHORS, *SACRED BULL: THE INNER OBSTACLES THAT HOLD YOU BACK AT WORK AND HOW TO OVERCOME THEM*

"It's great when employees can read the subtle nuances of your behavior and figure out exactly what you require of them. But let's face it: Most people aren't mind readers. Even if they're smart, they may be oblivious to what's important to you—unless you spell it out for them."

1. *Increased accuracy in communication.* Self-disclosure often takes the guesswork out of the communication process. No one is a mind reader; if people conceal how they really feel, it is difficult for others to know how to respond to them appropriately. People who are frustrated by a heavy workload but mask their true feelings may never see the problem resolved. The person who is in a position to solve this problem may be oblivious to what's important to you—unless you spell it out.

> *Self-disclosure often takes the guesswork out of the communication process.*

The accuracy of communication can often be improved if you report both facts and feelings. The other person then receives not only information but also an indication of how strongly you feel about the matter. For example, a department head might voice her concern about an increase in accidents this

"I wouldn't mind talking to you about information sharing, but right now I'm trying to keep too many things from you."

way: "Our accident rate is up 20 percent over last year, and to be honest, I feel terrible! Everyone must pay more attention to our safety procedures."

2. *Reduction of stress.* Sidney Jourard, a noted psychologist who wrote extensively about self-disclosure, states that too much emphasis on privacy and concealment of feelings creates stress within an individual. Too many people keep their thoughts and feelings bottled up inside, which can result in considerable inner tension. When stress indicators like blood pressure, perspiration, and breathing increase, our immune function declines. The amount of stress that builds within us depends on what aspects of ourselves we choose to conceal. If you compulsively think about a painful human relations problem but conceal your thoughts and feelings, the consequence will likely be more stress in your life.[3]

3. *Increased self-awareness.* Chapter 1 stated that self-awareness is one of the major components of emotional intelligence at work. Daniel Goleman, author of *Working with Emotional Intelligence,* defines **self-awareness** as the ability to recognize and understand your moods, emotions, and drives, as well as their effect on others.[4] Self-awareness is the foundation on which self-development is built. To plan an effective change in yourself, you must be in touch with how you behave, the factors that influence your behavior, and how your behavior affects others. A young Asian associate at a financial services firm learned from her supervisor that she was perceived as not being assertive enough in her dealings with clients. As she reflected on this feedback and listened to views expressed by her female peers, the associate became aware of how her cultural background influenced her communication with clients. This feedback motivated her to modify her communication style.[5]

The quality of feedback from others depends to a large degree on how much you practice self-disclosure. The sharing of thoughts and feelings with others often sets the stage for meaningful feedback (see Figure 8.1).

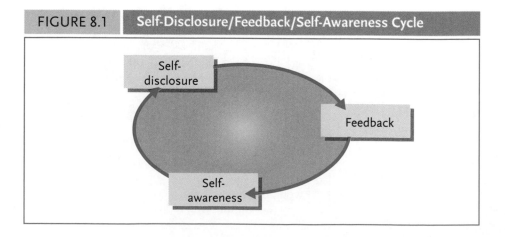

FIGURE 8.1   Self-Disclosure/Feedback/Self-Awareness Cycle

4. *Stronger relationships.* Another reward from self-disclosure is the strengthening of interpersonal relationships. When two people engage in an open, authentic dialogue, they often develop a high regard for each other's views. Often they discover they share common interests and concerns, and these serve as a foundation for a deeper relationship. John Powell, author of *Why Am I Afraid to Tell You Who I Am?* says this about the importance of openness: "Anyone who builds a relationship on less than openness and honesty is building on sand. Such a relationship will never stand the test of time, and neither party to the relationship will draw from it any noticeable benefits."[6] Of course, relationships can also be damaged by inappropriate self-disclosure. We discuss appropriate self-disclosure practices later in this chapter.

THINKING/LEARNING STARTER

Mentally review your previous work or volunteer experience. Identify at least one occasion when you felt great frustration over some incident but avoided disclosing your feelings to the person who could have solved the problem. What factors motivated you not to self-disclose? In retrospect, do you now perceive any benefits you might have gained by choosing to self-disclose?

The Johari Window: A Model for Self-Understanding

A first step in understanding the process of self-disclosure is to look at the **Johari Window,** illustrated in Figure 8.2 (on p. 192). The word *Johari* is a combination of the first names of the model's originators: Joseph Luft and Harry Ingham. This communication model takes into consideration that there is some information you know about yourself and other information you are not yet aware of. In addition, there is some information that others know about you and some they are not aware of. Your willingness or unwillingness to engage in self-disclosure, as well as to listen to feedback from others, has a great deal to do with your understanding of yourself and with others' understanding of you.[7]

● The Four Panes of the Johari Window

The Johari Window identifies four kinds of information about you that affect your communication with others. Think of the entire model as representing your total self as you relate to others. The Johari Window is divided into four panes, or areas, labeled (1) open, (2) blind, (3) hidden, and (4) unknown.[8]

Open Area The **open area** of the Johari Window represents your "public" or "awareness" area. This section contains information about you that both you and others know and includes information that you do not mind admitting about yourself. As your relationship with another person matures, the open pane gets bigger, reflecting your desire to be known.

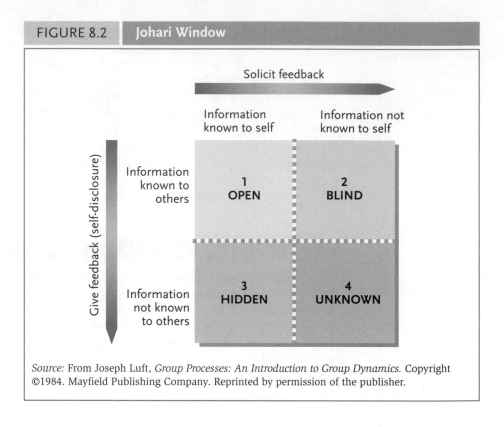

FIGURE 8.2   Johari Window

Source: From Joseph Luft, *Group Processes: An Introduction to Group Dynamics.* Copyright ©1984. Mayfield Publishing Company. Reprinted by permission of the publisher.

The open pane is generally viewed as the part of the relationship that influences interpersonal productivity. Therefore, a productive interpersonal relationship is related to the amount of mutually held information. Building a relationship with another person involves working to enlarge the open area. As self-awareness and sharing of information and feelings increase, the open pane becomes larger.

Blind Area   The **blind area** consists of information about yourself that others know, but you are not aware of. Others may see you as aloof and stuffy, whereas you view yourself as open and friendly. Or you may view your performance at work as mediocre, and others see it as above average. You may consider your dress and grooming practices appropriate for work, but others feel your appearance is not suitable for such a setting. Information in the blind area is acquired when you learn about people's perceptions of you.

Building a relationship and improving interpersonal effectiveness often involve working to enlarge the open pane and reduce the size of the blind pane. This can be achieved as you become more self-disclosing and thereby encourage others to disclose more of their thoughts and feelings to you (see Figure 8.1). People are more likely to give feedback to a person who is open and willing to share appropriate personal information with them.

Hidden Area   The **hidden area** contains information about you that you know but others do not. This pane is made up of all those private feelings, needs, and past experiences that you prefer to keep to yourself. These could be incidents that occurred early in life or past work-related experiences you would rather not share.

Sometimes people spend too much effort building a wall of separation between their inner and outer lives. They conceal too much private information, leading others to ask, "Is this person the same on the inside as he presents himself on the outside?" If we perceive in others—or they in us—a lack of authenticity, human relations problems are more likely to occur. It's very difficult to mask who we are because the people we work with are usually adept at discerning our thoughts, values, and beliefs.[9]

Unknown Area   The **unknown area** of the Johari Window is made up of things unknown to you and others. Because you, and others, can never be known completely, this area never completely disappears. The unknown may represent such factors as unrecognized talents, unconscious motives, or early childhood memories that influence your behavior but are not fully understood. Many people have abilities that remain unexplored throughout their lives. A person capable of rising to the position of department manager may remain a receptionist throughout his or her career because the potential for advancement is unrecognized. You may possess the talent to become an artist or musician but never discover it. Elizabeth Layton did not discover her talent for drawing until she was 68. This artist, who spent most of her life as a homemaker in the small prairie town of Wellsville, Kansas,

Throughout life some people conceal too much private information. On the other hand, some tend to overwhelm others with highly emotional or intimate information. Both of these problems can create a barrier to building a close relationship.

thereafter exhibited her works of art in galleries and museums throughout the United States.[10]

Some of the unknown information that is below the surface of awareness can be made public with the aid of open communication. Input from others (teacher, mentor, or supervisor) can reduce the size of the unknown pane and increase the size of the open area.

The four panes of the Johari Window are interrelated. As you change the size of one pane, others are affected. At the beginning of a relationship, the open area is likely to be somewhat small. When you start a new job, for example, your relationship with your supervisor and other workers may involve a minimum of open communication. As time passes and you develop a more open relationship with coworkers, the open area should grow larger.

● Self-Disclosure/Feedback Styles

Our relationship with others is influenced by two communication processes over which we have control. We can consciously make an effort to self-disclose our thoughts, ideas, and feelings when such action would improve the relationship. And we can also act to increase the amount of feedback from others. Figure 8.3a represents a self-disclosure/feedback style that reflects minimum use of self-disclosure and feedback processes. This style represents an impersonal approach to interpersonal relations, one that involves minimal sharing of information. Figure 8.3b represents a self-disclosure/feedback style that reflects considerable use of self-disclosure and feedback. Candor, openness, and mutual respect are characteristics of this style.

You can take positive steps to develop a larger open window (Figure 8.3b) by displaying a receptive attitude when others attempt to give you feed-

FIGURE 8.3 | **Johari Window at the Beginning of a Relationship (left) and After a Closer Relationship Has Developed (right)**

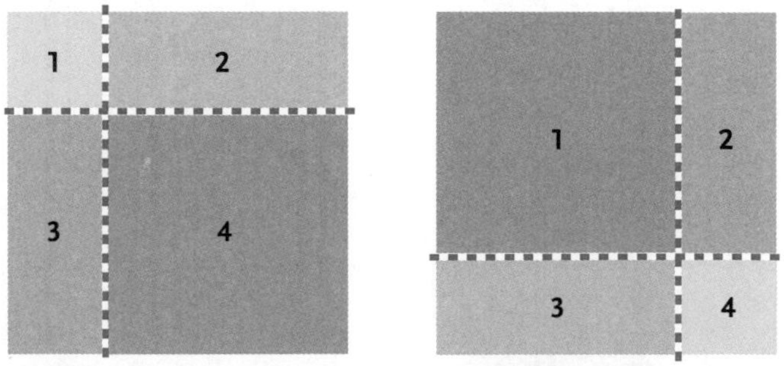

(a) Beginning of relationship   (b) A closer relationship

Source: From Joseph Luft, *Group Processes: An Introduction to Group Dynamics.* Copyright ©1984. Mayfield Publishing Company. Reprinted by permission of the publisher.

back. Openness to feedback from supervisors and coworkers, as opposed to defensiveness, is an important key to success in the workplace. If you become defensive, this behavior is likely to cut off the flow of information you need to be more effective in your job. You can also actively solicit feedback from your supervisor and coworkers so that they will feel comfortable in giving it to you.

360-Degree Feedback   Many organizations are using an assessment strategy known as **360-degree feedback.** With this approach, employees are rated not just by their immediate boss but also by their peers, team members, subordinates, and, in some cases, even customers. Feedback often comes in the form of a completed questionnaire or inventory, is generally anonymous, and usually provides valuable insights regarding a worker's talents and shortcomings.

Although 360-degree feedback programs have been successful at many companies, this type of appraisal can create problems. When multisource feedback programs are poorly planned and implemented, the result may be heightened political tensions and low morale. Using 360-degree feedback in the context of performance management involves some risks.[11]

THINKING / LEARNING STARTERS

To test your understanding of the Johari Window, write the term *open, blind, hidden,* or *unknown* in each appropriate space.

1. _____ Gary, a data entry clerk with a large insurance company, has the potential to become a proficient computer programmer. Neither he nor his coworkers are aware of this latent talent.

2. _____ Three years ago, Sara was fired from a job without any explanation from her employer. She has never shared this information with anyone.

3. _____ At a recent meeting with her sales manager, Jean expressed doubts about her ability to close sales. The sales manager indicated that he had experienced the same feelings early in his career.

4. _____ Jerry sees himself as humorous and entertaining. Coworkers view his type of humor as vulgar and offensive.

Appropriate Self-Disclosure

At the beginning of this chapter, we stated that the primary goal of self-disclosure should be to build stronger relations. Self-disclosure is also a condition for emotional health, according to Sidney Jourard. These goals (strong relationships and good emotional health) can be achieved if you learn how to disclose in constructive ways. Appropriate self-disclosure is a skill that anyone can learn. However, developing this skill often means changing attitudes and behaviors that have taken shape over a lifetime.

Many workers personalize their work area with art, family pictures, awards and other items. These things often tell us what is important to that person. Deborah Forte, executive vice president of Scholastic, a children's book publisher, displays fun stuff in her office. She likes to be around things that delight children.

In the search for criteria for developing appropriate self-disclosure, many factors must be considered. How much information should be disclosed? How intimate should the information be? Who is the most appropriate person with whom to share information? Under what conditions should the disclosures be made? In this section we examine several criteria that will help you develop your self-disclosure skills.

● Use Self-Disclosure to Repair Damaged Relationships

Many relationships at work and in our personal life are unnecessarily strained. The strain often exists because people refuse to talk about real or imagined problems. Self-disclosure can be an excellent method of repairing a damaged relationship. The business manager for a large hospital and the physician in charge of the emergency room maintained a feud for three months because neither person was willing to sit down and openly discuss the problem. The problem began when a member of the physician's staff sent some incomplete medical records to the business office for processing. The business manager called the doctor and accused her staff of incompetence. As soon as he spoke

HUMAN RELATIONS IN ACTION

Are You Really Sorry?

When is an apology not really an apology? You have to ask the person who receives the message. When Bobby Knight apologized for his explosive temper in the spring of 2000, some people said the former University of Indiana basketball coach was not sincere enough. When former president Bill Clinton said in a national television address, "I am profoundly sorry for all I have done wrong in words and deeds," some people said he didn't act like someone who was *truly* contrite. Knight and Clinton failed to make amends because they didn't seem to truly regret their actions. Critics felt they didn't act or sound like persons who were genuinely sorry for their mistakes.

the words, he was sorry. He had overreacted. The doctor in charge of the emergency room, anxious to defend her department, responded angrily with very strong language. She later regretted her lack of self-control. After several weeks, the business manager visited the emergency room and said, "Look, I'm sorry for what I said to you. You and your staff provide outstanding service to our patients, and I should not have reacted to the problem with such anger. Please accept my apology." The business manager and the doctor shook hands, and each returned to work feeling relieved that the problem was solved.

> *Even in cases where your intention was not to upset or hurt someone, the apology must come from your heart.*

The Art of Apologizing If your actions have caused hurt feelings, anger, or deep-seated ill will, an apology is in order. A sincere apology can have a tremendous amount of healing power for both the receiver and the giver. In addition, it may set the stage for improved communications in the future. Many people avoid apologizing because they feel awkward about admitting they were wrong. If you decide to apologize to someone, the best approach is to meet with the injured party in private and own up to the wrongdoing. In a private setting, feelings can be exchanged with relative comfort. An effective apology will communicate the three Rs: Regret, Responsibility, and Remedy.[12]

- *Regret*. The regret that you feel must be communicated sincerely. Even in cases where your intention was not to upset or hurt someone, the apology must come from your heart.

- *Responsibility*. Do not make excuses or blame others for what you did. Don't say, "I'm sorry about what happened, but you shouldn't have . . ." You must accept total responsibility for your actions.

- *Remedy*. A meaningful apology should include a commitment that you will not repeat the behavior. It might also include an offer of restitution.

The Art of Forgiveness If someone you work with, a friend, or a family member offers a sincere apology, be quick to forgive. Forgiveness is almost never easy, especially when you feel you have been wronged. But forgiveness is the only way to break the bonds of blame and bitterness. To forgive means

TOTAL	**BEVERLY ENGEL**
PERSON	AUTHOR, *THE POWER OF APOLOGY*
INSIGHT	"Almost like magic, apology has the power to repair harm, mend relationships, soothe wounds and heal broken hearts."

to give up resentment and anger. D. Patrick Miller, author of *A Little Book of Forgiveness,* says: "To carry an anger against anyone is to poison your own heart, administering more toxin every time you replay in your mind the injury done to you." He also says forgiveness provides healing and liberates your energy and your creativity.[13]

When you convey an apology to someone or forgive another person, remember that you reveal a great deal through nonverbal messages. The emotion in your voice, as well as your eye contact, gestures, and body posture, will communicate a great deal about your inner thoughts.

● Present Constructive Criticism with Care

Constructive criticism is a form of self-disclosure that helps another person look at his or her own behavior without putting that individual on the defensive. Constructive criticism is not the same as blaming. Blaming people for mistakes will seldom improve the situation.

Many people are very sensitive and are easily upset when they receive criticism. However, giving criticism effectively is a skill that can be mastered through learning and practice. Here are two effective methods for giving constructive criticism. First, avoid starting your message with "You," such as "You didn't complete your monthly inventory report" or "You never take our customer service policies seriously." For better results, replace "You-statements" with "I-statements." Say, "I am concerned that you have not completed your monthly inventory report." Another way to avoid defensiveness is to request a specific change in the future instead of pointing out something negative in the past. Instead of saying, "You did not have authorization to order office supplies," try saying, "In the future, please obtain authorization before ordering office supplies."[14]

● Discuss Disturbing Situations As They Happen

You should share reactions to a work-related problem or issue as soon after the incident as possible. It is often difficult to recapture a feeling once it has passed, and you may distort the incident if you let too much time go by. Your memory is not infallible. The person who erred is also likely to forget details about the situation.

If something really bothers you, express your feelings. Clear the air as soon as possible so you can enjoy greater peace of mind. Some people maintain the burden of hurt feelings and resentment for days, weeks, even years. The avoidance of self-disclosure usually has a negative effect on a person's mental and physical health as well as on job performance.

● Accurately Describe Your Feelings and Emotions

It has been said that one of the most important outcomes of self-disclosure is the possibility for others to become acquainted with the "real" you. When you accurately describe your feelings and emotions, others get to know you better. This kind of honesty takes courage because of the risk involved. When you tell another person how you feel, you are putting a great amount of faith in that person. You are trusting the other person not to ridicule or embarrass you for the feelings you express.[15]

Experiencing feelings and emotions is a part of being human.

Too often, people view verbalizing feelings and emotions in a work setting as inappropriate. But emotions are an integral part of human behavior. People should not be expected to turn off their feelings the moment they arrive at work. Experiencing feelings and emotions is a part of being human. If we don't know each other, we can't be close to each other.[16]

What is the best way to report emotions and feelings? Some examples may be helpful. Let's suppose you expected to be chosen to supervise an important project, but the assignment was given to another worker. At a meeting with your boss, you might make the following statement: "For several weeks I've been looking forward to heading up this project. I guess I didn't realize that anyone else was being considered. Now I feel not only disappointed but also embarrassed."

Or suppose a coworker constantly borrows equipment and supplies but usually fails to return them. You might say: "Thanks for taking a few minutes to meet with me. I'm the type of person who likes to keep busy, but lately I've spent a lot of time retrieving tools and supplies you've borrowed. I've experienced a great deal of frustration and decided I should tell you how I feel."

As you report your feelings, be sure the other person realizes that your feelings are temporary and capable of change. You might say, "At this point I feel very frustrated, but I am sure we can solve the problem." Expressing anger can be especially difficult. This special challenge is discussed in Chapter 9.

● Select the Right Time and Place

Remarks that otherwise might be offered and accepted in a positive way can be rendered ineffective not because of what we say but because of when and where we say it.[17] When possible, select a time when you feel the other person is not preoccupied and will be able to give you his or her full attention. Also, select a setting free of distractions. Telephone calls or unannounced visitors can ruin an opportunity for meaningful dialogue. If there is no suitable place at work to hold the discussion, consider meeting the person for lunch away from work or talking with the person after work at some appropriate location. If necessary, make an appointment with the person to ensure that time is reserved for your meeting.

● Avoid Overwhelming Others with Your Self-Disclosure

Although you should be open, do not go too far too fast. Many strong relationships are built slowly. The abrupt disclosure of highly emotional or intimate information may actually distance you from the other person, who may find your

Sharing Secrets in the Workplace Can Be Treacherous

Monica Lewinsky decided to share a secret with her friend Linda Tripp. Within a few weeks, millions of people would learn about her relationship with the president of the United States. In recent years, keeping secrets seems to be losing favor as openness becomes the mantra of modern America. More and more people are willing to talk about their love life, mental health problems, or rocky marriages. Information that was once exchanged only between the very closest of friends and lovers is sometimes shared with complete strangers. William Rawlins, professor of communication at Purdue University, says there is a new kind of workplace friendship that can be treacherous. People thrown together in the same department sometimes begin to share intimacies as if they have had a long, trusting relationship. Rawlins notes, "We want those work friendships to live up to the ideals we associate with other friendships, but sometimes they don't."

behavior threatening. Unrestricted "truth" can create a great deal of anxiety, particularly in an organization where people must work closely together. Dr. Joyce Brothers says we must balance the inclination to be open and honest with the need to be protective of each other's feelings.[18] Disclosure of areas of privacy, in some cases, can create a barrier to building a close relationship.

Buddha gave some good advice about what to say and not say to others. The founder of Buddhism recommended that a person ask three vital questions before saying anything to another person: (1) Is the statement *true?* (2) Is the statement *necessary?* (3) Is the statement *kind?* If a statement falls short on any of these counts, Buddha advised that we say nothing.[19] His recommendations establish a high standard for anyone who engages in self-disclosure.

THINKING / LEARNING STARTER

Review the criteria in the text for appropriate self-disclosure. On a sheet of paper, describe at least two situations in which another person violated one or more of these criteria while self-disclosing information to you. Describe your feelings at the time these experiences occurred. What impact did the person's behavior have on your relationship?

Barriers to Self-Disclosure in an Organizational Setting

At this point you might be thinking, "If self-disclosure is such a positive force in building stronger human relationships, why do people avoid it so often? Why do so many people conceal their thoughts and feelings? Why are candor and openness so uncommon in many organizations?" To answer these questions, let's examine some of the barriers that prevent people from self-disclosing.

● Lack of Trust

Trust exists when we firmly rely on the integrity, ability, or character of a person or organization. Although trust is intangible, it is at the core of all meaningful relationships.[20]

Lack of trust is the most common—and the most serious—barrier to self-disclosure.

Trust is a complex emotion that combines three components: caring, competency, and commitment. Consider the relationship between a doctor and her patient. Trust builds when the patient decides that the doctor is competent (capable of diagnosing the health problem), caring (concerned about the patient's health) and committed (willing to find a solution to the medical problem).[21] Trust between a salesperson and a customer is built upon the same three components. Customers want to do business with a salesperson who can accurately diagnose their needs, prescribe the right product, and provide excellent service after the sale.

When the trust level in an organization is low, the consequences are a culture of insecurity, high turnover, marginal loyalty, and often damaged customer relations.[22] Unfortunately, in a work environment characterized by rapid change and uncertainty caused by frequent layoffs, trust has greatly declined in many organizations. The recent wave of business scandals has also undermined employee trust at many companies.

Lack of trust is the most common—and the most serious—barrier to self-disclosure. Without trust, people usually fear revealing their thoughts and feelings because the perceived risks of self-disclosure are too high. When trust is present, people no longer feel as vulnerable in the presence of another person, and communication flows more freely.[23]

TOTAL PERSON INSIGHT	**TERRY MIZRAHI**
	PRESIDENT, NATIONAL ASSOCIATION OF SOCIAL WORKERS
	"Trust is the core of all meaningful relationships. Without trust there can be no giving, no bonding, no risk taking."

Jack Gibb, in his book *Trust: A New View of Personal and Organizational Development,* points out that the trust level is the thermometer of individual and group health. When trust is present, people function naturally and openly. Without it, they devote their energies to masking their true feelings, hiding thoughts, and avoiding opportunities for personal growth.[24]

THINKING / LEARNING STARTERS

1. Recall a situation in which a friend or coworker created the impression that he or she did not trust you. What did the person do or say to create this impression? How did you react to this behavior?
2. If you have a manager in your work setting, do you trust him or her? Why or why not?

Many people spend part of their time building trust and part of their time destroying trust. Table 8.1 (on p. 202) compares behaviors that build trust with behaviors that destroy it. Essentially, the way to build trust is to be trustworthy all the time.

TABLE 8.1	How Trust Can Be Built and Destroyed	
Building Trust		**Destroying Trust**
■ Openly share information.		■ Withhold information.
■ Admit your mistakes.		■ Cover up mistakes.
■ Network with coworkers.		■ Keep your distance from coworkers.
■ Display competence.		■ Display incompetence.
■ Be honest all the time.		■ Be honest only some of the time.
■ Be clear in your convictions.		■ Avoid commitment.
■ Be true to your values.		■ Ignore your values.

Fear/Distrust Cycle Jack Gibb states that the normal fears people bring to a new job are magnified when they encounter tight controls, veiled threats, and impersonal behavior. This climate sets the stage for what he describes as the "fear/distrust cycle" (see Figure 8.4).[25] The cycle begins with the management philosophy that people are basically lacking in motivation and cannot be trusted (discussed in Chapter 7 as Theory X). To bring about maximum production, management tries to maintain tight control over employees by initiating a series of strict rules and regulations. As management increases the controls, workers often become more defensive and resentful. The spirit of teamwork diminishes, and everyone in the organization begins talking in terms of "we" versus "they."

● Role Relationships Versus Interpersonal Relationships

Self-disclosure is more likely to take place within an organization when people feel comfortable stepping outside their assigned roles and displaying openness and tolerance for the feelings of others. In our society, role expectations are often clearly specified for people engaged in various occupations. For example, some

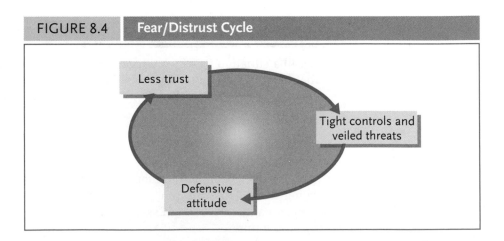

FIGURE 8.4	Fear/Distrust Cycle

Less trust

Tight controls and veiled threats

Defensive attitude

people see the supervisor's role as an impersonal one. Supervisors are supposed to enforce policies, maintain high production, and avoid getting too close to the people they supervise. The advice given to some new supervisors is "Don't try to be a nice guy, or people will take advantage of you." Yet often the most effective supervisors are those who are approachable, display a sense of humor, and take time to listen to employee problems.

Some newly appointed supervisors may deliberately try to build barriers between themselves and subordinates. They draw a sharp distinction between **role relationships** and **interpersonal relationships.** They are too impersonal and aloof, thinking that this is appropriate "role" behavior. Employees usually respond to these actions by becoming defensive or less trusting.

Roles are inescapable, but they need not contribute to the depersonalization of relationships. Each role is played by a person. Others should be able to get to know that person regardless of the role the individual has been assigned.

Practice Self-Disclosure

Many people carry around an assortment of hurt feelings, angry thoughts, and frustration that drains them of the energy they need to cope with life's daily struggles. Although self-disclosure provides a way to get rid of this burden, some people continue through life imprisoned by negative thoughts and feelings. If you avoid disclosing your thoughts and feelings, you make it harder for others to know the real you. You will recall from the beginning of this chapter that self-disclosure involves revealing personal information that cannot be acquired from other sources. This type of information can often improve the quality of your relationships with others.

Could you benefit by telling others more about your thoughts, wants, feelings, and beliefs? To answer this question, complete Figure 8.5 (on p. 204), which will give you an indication of your self-disclosure style. If you tend to agree with most of these items, consider making a conscientious effort to do more self-disclosing.

Becoming a more open person is not difficult if you are willing to practice.

Becoming a more open person is not difficult if you are willing to practice. If you want to improve in this area, begin by taking small steps. You might want to start with a nonthreatening confrontation with a friend or neighbor. Pick someone with whom you have had a recent minor problem. Tell this person as honestly as possible how you feel about the issue or problem. Keep in mind that your objective is not simply to relate something that is bothering you but also to develop a stronger relationship with this person.

As you gain confidence, move to more challenging encounters. Maybe you feel your work is not appreciated by your employer. Why not tell this person how you feel? If you are a supervisor and one of the people you supervise seems to be taking advantage of you, why not talk to this person openly about your thoughts? With practice you will begin to feel comfortable with self-disclosure, and you will find it rewarding to get your feelings out in the open. As you become a more open person, the people you contact will be more likely to open up and share more thoughts, ideas, and feelings with you. Everyone wins!

FIGURE 8.5	Self-Disclosure Indicator

Instructions: Read each statement and then place a checkmark (✔) in the appropriate space.

	YES	NO
1. In most cases I avoid sharing personal thoughts and feelings with others.		
2. My relationships with others tend to be quite formal.		
3. I would not be comfortable discussing personal problems at work.		
4. I tend to avoid discussing my concerns even when feelings of frustration build inside me.		
5. I tend to avoid giving praise or criticism to others.		
6. I tend to believe that familiarity breeds contempt.		
7. I find it difficult to apologize.		
8. I find it difficult to forgive the wrongdoer.		

■ Summary

business.college.hmco.com/students

ACE

Self-tests

Open communication is an important key to personal growth and job satisfaction. Self-disclosure—the process of letting another person know what you think, feel, or want—improves communication. It differs from self-description in that it usually involves some risk. Most people want and need accurate feedback from coworkers and the person who supervises their work.

Constructive self-disclosure can result in many rewards to people and organizations. It can pave the way for increased accuracy in communication, reduction of stress, increased self-awareness, and stronger interpersonal relationships.

The Johari Window helps conceptualize four kinds of information areas involved in communication: the open area, what you and others know about you; the blind area, what others know about you that you don't know about yourself; the hidden area, what you know but others do not; and the unknown area, what neither you nor others know. Most people gradually increase the open area as they learn to communicate with others.

Everyone can learn how to use self-disclosure in a constructive way. Your goal should always be to approach self-disclosure with the desire to improve your relationship with the other person. Describe your feelings and emotions accurately, and avoid making judgments about the other person. Use self-disclosure to repair damaged relationships. It is helpful to understand the art of apologizing and the art of forgiveness. Disturbing situations should be discussed as they happen; it is difficult to recapture feelings once they have passed. Select the right time and place to share your thoughts, and avoid inappropriate disclosure of highly emotional or very intimate information.

A climate of trust serves as a foundation for self-disclosure. In the absence of trust, people usually avoid revealing their thoughts and feelings to others. Self-disclosure is also more likely to take place within an organization when people feel comfortable stepping outside their assigned roles and displaying sensitivity to the feelings of others.

As with learning any new skill, you can improve your ability to disclose your thoughts and feelings by starting with less threatening disclosures and proceeding slowly to more challenging situations.

■ Career Corner

Q: The company I work for recently adopted the assessment approach known as 360-degree feedback. Every department head completed a three-day workshop on this feedback strategy. When my boss returned from the workshop, she held a staff meeting and said she wants to know what we think of her performance. We have been instructed to schedule a meeting with her and be prepared to "tell it like it is." I think she sincerely wants feedback regarding her strengths and areas needing improvement. Should I share with her the "good" and the "bad"?

A: Although your boss may be seeking assessment feedback, she could be turned off by your complaints or by criticism of the way she manages the department. Most managers respond poorly to direct criticism—even when they seek feedback. Criticism of her leadership may damage your career. Of course it would be a mistake to bottle up a major source of frustration inside you. If you are upset about a particular policy or practice, find the right time and place to disclose your feelings. Before the meeting, try to think of a good solution to the problem. Most bosses are turned off by employees who complain about something but fail to offer an alternative way of doing things.

■ Key Terms

self-disclosure	unknown area
self-description	360-degree feedback
self-awareness	constructive criticism
Johari Window	trust
open area	role relationships
blind area	interpersonal relationships
hidden area	

■ Review Questions

1. What is the major difference between self-disclosure and self-description?

2. How can self-disclosure contribute to improved teamwork within an organization?

3. List four major benefits to be gained from self-disclosure.

4. Describe how self-disclosure can contribute to increased self-awareness.

5. What is the major difference between the blind area and the hidden area of the Johari Window?

6. What types of interpersonal relationship problems are overdisclosers and underdisclosers likely to encounter?

7. List the guidelines to follow when making appropriate self-disclosure.

8. In the absence of trust, what major problems can surface in an organization?

9. What are some of the major factors that have contributed to the decline of trust at some companies?

10. What are the major factors that contribute to an effective apology?

■ Application Exercises

1. To learn more about your approach to self-disclosure, complete each of the sentences below. Once you have completed them all, reflect on your written responses. Can you identify any changes in your approach to self-disclosure that would improve communications with others? Are there any self-disclosure skills that you need to practice?

    a. "For me, the major barrier to self-disclosure is . . ."

    b. "To establish a more mutually trusting relationship with others, I need to . . ."

    c. "In order to receive more feedback from others, I need to . . ."

    d. "In situations where I should apologize for something or voice forgiveness, I tend to . . ."

2. On Friday afternoon a coworker visits your office and requests a favor. She wants you to review a proposal she will give to her boss on Monday morning at 10:00 A.M. You agree to study the proposal sometime over the weekend and give her feedback on Monday before her meeting. You put a photocopy of the proposal in your briefcase and take it home. Over the weekend you get busy and forget to review the proposal. In fact, you are so busy that you never open your briefcase. On Monday morning you make a call on a customer before reporting to the office. While sitting in the customer's office, you open your briefcase and see the report. It is too late to study the report and give feedback to your coworker. Which of the following actions would you take?

    a. Try to forget the incident and avoid feeling guilty. After all, you did not intentionally avoid your obligation.

    b. Call the person's boss and explain the circumstances. Confess that you simply forgot to read the report.

    c. Meet with your coworker as soon as possible and offer a sincere apology for failing to read the report and provide the feedback.

Provide a rationale for your choice.

3. Constructive self-disclosure is based on a foundation of trust. When the trust level is low, open and honest communication is unlikely to occur. We inspire trust by what we say and what we do. Some behaviors that inspire trust are listed below. Rate yourself with this scale: U = Usually; S = Sometimes; I = Infrequently. After you finish the self-assessment, reflect on your ability to inspire trust, and think about ways to improve yourself in this area.

	U	S	I
I disclose my thoughts and feelings when appropriate.	☐	☐	☐
I admit my mistakes.	☐	☐	☐
Others know that I keep confidences.	☐	☐	☐
I keep my promises and commitments.	☐	☐	☐
I avoid distortion of information when communicating with others.	☐	☐	☐

Internet Exercise

A careful study of the Johari Window communication model can provide helpful information about constructive self-disclosure. The Internet provides additional information about this model. Using your search engine, type in "Johari Window," and then review the available resources (such as books, articles, and training programs). Provide a brief summary of your findings. Pay special attention to new information that was not covered in your textbook.

Case 8.1   The Art of Giving Criticism

Large numbers of employees feel uncomfortable giving negative feedback to people they work with. Robert A. Baron, chair of the management department at Rensselaer Polytechnic Institute in Troy, New York, says, "Everybody is reluctant to give negative feedback, so all they do is bite their tongue until they can't stand it anymore." If someone is doing something that interferes with your work, causes you discomfort, or puts you in danger, do not remain silent. When you allow someone to do something you do not want, you become part of the problem. By remaining quiet, you allow the behavior to continue.

We live in a culture that encourages outspokenness, but the disclosure of thoughts and feelings must be handled with care. How something is said can be more important than what was said. Robert Genua, author of *Managing Your Mouth*, says that the most important thing is to pause before you speak and think about what you are going to say. If you are highly critical of someone's suggestion and express your views with strong sarcasm, the people who work with you may not remember that you happen to be right. However, they will remember your insensitive behavior. Genua says, "People who choose their words carefully come across as well-mannered, polished and refined."

Although some people are too direct in giving feedback and may actually be perceived as threatening, others make passive statements and fail to solve the problem. When giving negative feedback, you should look the person in the eye and be straightforward in expressing your thoughts and feelings. If someone is taking credit for your suggestions and ideas and has ignored your protests, you might say, "I want you to stop taking credit for my ideas. If you do not stop, I will ask our department head to schedule a meeting for the three of us so we can discuss the problem." To leave some things unchallenged can have negative results. Your reputation is formed not only by what you stand for but by what you won't stand for.

If you are a supervisor, the major reason you give negative feedback is to improve performance. Robert Baron has researched how bosses criticize employees and says some criticize too much and others criticize too little. Some give negative feedback for the wrong reasons, such as to reinforce their sense of power or to get revenge. To improve performance, you want to avoid comments that will make the other person angry or defensive. When it comes to giving criticism, do it with sensitivity.[26] Avoid the temptation to blame or condemn the person for mistakes made.

■ Questions

1. Do you agree that speaking out at work is generally beneficial to you and your employer? Explain your answer.

2. Why are many people reluctant to give negative feedback to another person? What are some of the reasons some people are afraid to speak out?

3. If a coworker openly criticizes your work in a meeting and says things that are not true, what should your immediate response be? Should you make contact with this person after the meeting and try to resolve the problem? Explain your answer.

Case 8.2 360-Degree Feedback Uncovers Blind Spots

One of the more controversial employee-development practices has been the introduction of an assessment approach known as 360-degree feedback. As noted earlier in this chapter, organizations that have adopted this assessment strategy believe employees will benefit from feedback collected from several different sources. This means an employee may be evaluated by peers, subordinates, a supervisor, and sometimes even customers. Each review typically enlists the opinions of eight to twelve people.

Feedback usually comes in the form of a completed questionnaire or inventory. This feedback—generally anonymous—usually provides valuable insights regarding one's talents and shortcomings. An executive at Ameritech Corp. learned that his habit of making points by stabbing at a person with his index finger, thumb upright, was threatening to some subordinates. A written anonymous comment from an employee said, "Don't make your hand into a gun and point at people. . . . It's very intimidating." The executive's reaction: "I wish someone had told me this thirty years ago."

A major goal of 360-degree feedback is to increase self-awareness. Some people simply do not know themselves well enough. In companies that incorporate peer reviews in their 360-degree feedback effort, coworkers deliver performance reviews of one another. Tenneco Automotive Inc. uses peer reviews to reduce injury rates at its seventy-four plants. Hourly workers share twice-a-week peer evaluations, and the findings are used for solving safety problems.

Peer appraisals have become quite common at companies that maintain a leaner, less hierarchical organization structure and rely more on teams. Although some employees pull their punches to avoid hurting a coworker's feelings, others deliver criticism with candor. One goal of peer reviews is to give members an opportunity to disclose feelings of frustration and to comment on others' behaviors that bother them. Another goal is to give group members a chance to boost one another's self-esteem by praising good performance.[27]

■ Questions

1. Today 360-degree feedback has been introduced into most *Fortune* 100 companies, and it continues to spread among smaller companies. Do you feel that multisource feedback is superior to feedback from a single source such as your supervisor? Explain.

2. Would you feel comfortable giving anonymous performance reviews to coworkers? To your supervisor?

3. Multisource feedback evolved over the past two decades as a development tool—a way to help people develop new skills and overcome weaknesses. Today, a few companies use feedback data to make decisions regarding pay raises and promotions. Do you see any risks involved in using the feedback data for major human resource decisions?

9

ACHIEVING EMOTIONAL BALANCE IN A CHAOTIC WORLD

Chapter Preview

After studying this chapter, you will be able to

- Describe how emotions influence our thinking and behavior.

- Understand the factors that contribute to emotional balance.

- Explain the critical role of emotions in the workplace.

- Describe the major factors that influence our emotional development.

- Learn how to deal with your anger and the anger of others.

- Understand the factors that contribute to workplace violence.

- Identify and explain the most common emotional styles.

- Describe strategies for achieving emotional control.

Jimmy Nobles, veteran oil rig worker employed by Transocean Sedco Forex, says, "We care about other people's feelings." This is not a comment you would expect to hear from someone who vividly remembers numerous shouting matches and occasional fights in the cramped living space of an oil rig. Today, says Nobles, "It's a different deal." The company enrolled all employees in a workshop that gave them an opportunity to assess their behavioral style. After completing the workshop, employees place two colored dots on their hard hats to tell coworkers how best to communicate with them. A yellow dot, for example, indicates that someone is emotional and talkative; a green dot indicates that the person is cautious and serious. "Behavior styles" charts explaining the various colors are posted on the oil rig bulkhead.[1]

Ai, a Washington-based architectural and interior design firm, discovered that too much communication was creating friction among the workers because they spent their days in cubicles. In cubicles there are no doors to shut when you're busy, so a coworker might walk right in and start talking. How do you tell the person in the neighboring cubicle he is talking too loud on the telephone? Well, the creative minds at Ai developed Protoblocs. Protoblocs are three foam shapes—a green pyramid, a yellow sphere, and a red cube—that communicate a specific message. The red cube means no interruptions under any circumstances. The yellow sphere tells coworkers to proceed with caution when entering your cubicle, and the green pyramid means you are available for a chat.[2] America Online, World Bank, and American Express are just a few of the many companies that are using Protoblocs to improve productivity and reduce tension.

Anger, fear, love, joy, jealousy, grief, and other emotions can influence our behavior at work and in our personal world. To the extent that we can become more aware of our emotions and assess their influence on our daily lives, we have the opportunity to achieve a new level of self-understanding. That greater awareness can help us avoid inappropriate behavior.

Emotions—An Introduction

An **emotion** is a strong, temporary feeling that is positive or negative. Emotional experiences tend to alter the thought processes by directing attention toward some things and away from others. Emotions energize our thoughts and behaviors.[3]

Throughout each day our feelings are activated by a variety of events (see Figure 9.1 on p. 212). You might feel a sense of joy after learning that a coworker has just given birth to a new baby. You might feel overpowering grief after learning that your supervisor was killed in an auto accident. Angry feelings may surface when you discover that someone borrowed a tool without your permission. Once your feelings have been activated, your mind interprets the event. In some cases, the feelings trigger irrational thinking: "No one who works here can be trusted!" In other cases, you may engage in a rational thinking process: "Perhaps the person who borrowed the tool needed it to help a customer with an emergency repair." The important point to remember is that we can choose how we behave. We can gain control over our emotions.

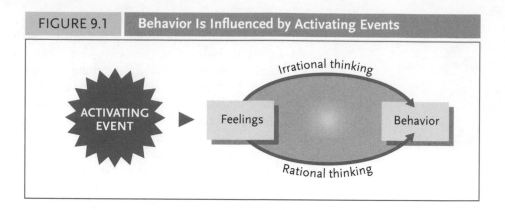

FIGURE 9.1 Behavior Is Influenced by Activating Events

Achieving Emotional Balance—A Daily Challenge

The need to discover ways to achieve emotional balance has never been greater. To be successful in these complex times, we need to be able to think and feel simultaneously. People make choices dictated primarily by either their heads (reason) or their hearts (feelings). The thinking function helps us see issues logically; the feeling function helps us be caring and human.[4] Many organizations are spawning fear, confusion, anger, and sadness because the leaders lack emotional balance.

The basic emotions that drive us—such as fear, love, greed, joy, and anger—have scarcely changed over the years. However, we are now seeing enormous differences in the expression of emotions. Today, people are much more likely to engage in aggressive driving, misbehave during commercial airline flights, or become abusive when they are unhappy with service. In the workplace many people experience emotional pain because of disagreeable bosses.

Emotional Intelligence

Daniel Goleman, author of two popular books on emotional intelligence, challenges the traditional view of the relationship between IQ and success. He says there are widespread exceptions to the rule that IQ predicts success: "At best, IQ contributes about 20 percent to the factors that determine life success, which leaves 80 percent to other forces."[5] The focus of Goleman's research is the human characteristics that make up what he describes as *emotional competence*. The emotional competence framework is made up of two dimensions:[6]

Personal Competence This term refers to the competencies that determine how we manage ourselves. Recognizing one's emotions and their effects, keeping disruptive emotions and impulses in check, and maintaining standards of honesty and integrity represent a few of the competencies in this category.

Social Competence This refers to the competencies that determine how we handle relationships. Sensing others' feelings and perspectives, listening

Game officials and players run off the field as debris thrown by fans rains down on them. The football game between the Cleveland Browns and the Jacksonville Jaguars was stopped for about 30 minutes because of violence that erupted after an unpopular call by officials. Anger is one of many emotions that can influence our behavior.

openly and sending convincing messages, and negotiating and resolving disagreements represent some of the competencies in this category.

Although IQ tends to be stable throughout life, emotional competence is learnable and tends to increase throughout our life span. The emotional competencies that really matter for work can be learned.

Research in the area of emotional intelligence continues. Toronto-based Multi-Health Systems Incorporated has developed the BarOn EQ-i, an assessment instrument designed to measure key emotional and social competencies. Many of the people involved in EQ training programs are persons with high IQs and advanced technical knowledge but little people awareness and business sense.[7]

● Emotional Expression

We sometimes suffer from a lack of emotional balance because we learn to inhibit the expression of certain emotions and to overemphasize the expression of others. Some families, for example, discourage the expression of love and affection. Some people are taught from an early age to avoid expressing anger. Others learn that a public display of grief (crying, for example) is a sign of weakness. If as a child you were strongly encouraged to avoid the expression of anger, fear, love, or some other emotion, you may repress or block these feelings as an adult.[8]

Emotional imbalance also develops if we become fixated on a single emotion. The high incidence of violent crime in America has motivated some people to become almost totally infused with the emotion of fear. One writer noted that people who are preoccupied with fear may be intensifying the problem:

HUMAN RELATIONS IN ACTION

Savvy Thinking on Super Bowl Sunday

It was Super Bowl Sunday and the departing flight from New York to Detroit was delayed two hours. Tension among the passengers—mostly businessmen—was increasing. When the plane finally arrived in Detroit, a glitch with the boarding ramp required the plane to stop about a hundred feet from the gate. Frantic passengers, concerned about being late, leaped to their feet. At that point the flight attendant needed to get everyone to sit down so that the plane could finish taxiing to the gate. She could have gone to the intercom and announced in a stern voice, "Federal regulations require that you be seated before we can move to the gate." Instead, she warbled in a singsong tone reminiscent of a playful warning to an adorable child who has done something naughty, "You're staaan-ding!" The passengers laughed and sat back down until the plane reached the gate.

"We have a habit of keeping ourselves overwhelmed, through the news media, with bad and scary things that have happened all over the world each day; and the chronic pattern of worrying about which of these bad things might happen to us in the future."[9] To focus on one emotion to the exclusion of others creates a serious imbalance within us.

● The Emotional Factor at Work

Emotions play a critical role in the success of every organization, yet many people in key decision-making positions—leaders with outstanding technical skills—fail to understand the important role emotions play in a work setting. In part, the problem can be traced to leadership training that emphasizes that "doing business" is a purely rational or logical process. Some leaders learn to value only those things that can be arranged, analyzed, and defined. One consultant put the problem into proper perspective when he said, "We are still trying to do business as if it requires only a meeting of the minds instead of a meeting of the hearts."[10]

Tim Sanders, chief solutions officer at Yahoo! says, "How we are perceived as human beings is becoming increasingly important in the new economy." He notes that compassion is an important key to long-term personal success. This is the human ability to reach out with warmth through eye contact, physical touch, or words. It is a quality machines can never possess.[11]

TOTAL	**JAMES C. GEORGES**
PERSON	CHIEF EXECUTIVE OFFICER, THE PAR GROUP
INSIGHT	"All of our technology is underutilized and will remain so until we put the emotion of doing business onto parity with the logical and rational aspects of performance improvement."

A customer service associate talks with a customer during the opening day at the People's Bank branch. Frontline employees are responsible for delivering quality service and building long-term relationships with customers.

Relationship Strategy   Emotional undercurrents are present in almost every area of every organization. Most banks, hospitals, retail firms, hotels, and restaurants realize that they need a relationship strategy—a plan for establishing, building, and maintaining quality relationships with customers. Cosco Systems, for example, measures itself by the quality of its relationships with customers. Salespeople achieve their bonuses based in large part on customer satisfaction instead of on gross sales or profit.[12]

> Emotional labor, *which taxes the mind, is often more difficult to handle than physical labor, which strains the body.*

Frontline employees, those persons responsible for delivering quality service and building relationships, engage in "emotional labor," and those who have frequent contact with the public often find the work very stressful.[13] *Emotional labor,* which taxes the mind, is often more difficult to handle than physical labor, which strains the body. For this reason, frontline employees need the support of leaders who are both caring and competent.

THINKING / LEARNING STARTERS

1. Recall a situation at work or at school where the leadership displayed emotional blindness. What are some of the reasons the important role of emotions was not taken into consideration?

2. Do you agree that emotional undercurrents are present in almost every area of the typical organization? Can you think of any exceptions?

Factors That Influence Our Emotions

The starting point in achieving greater emotional control is to determine the source of emotional difficulties. Why do we sometimes display indifference when the expression of compassion would be more appropriate? Why is it so easy to put down a friend or coworker and so hard to recognize that person's accomplishments? Why do we sometimes worry about events that will never happen? To answer these and other questions, it is necessary to study the factors that influence our emotional development.

● Temperament

Temperament refers to a person's individual style of expressing needs and emotions; it is biological and genetically based. It reflects a contribution by nature to the beginning of an individual's personality.[14] Researchers have found that certain temperamental characteristics are apparent in children at birth and remain somewhat stable over time. For example, the traits associated with extroversion and introversion can be observed when a baby is born. Of course, many events take place between infancy and adulthood to alter or shape a person's temperament. Personality at every age reflects the interplay of temperament and of environmental influences, such as parenting.[15]

● Unconscious Influences

The **unconscious mind** is a vast storehouse of forgotten memories, desires, ideas, and frustrations, according to William Menninger, founder of the famed Menninger Foundation.[16] He noted that the unconscious mind can have a great influence on behavior. It contains memories of past experiences as well as memories of feelings associated with past experiences. The unconscious is active, continuously influencing conscious decision-making processes.

Although people cannot remember many of the important events of the early years of their lives, these incidents do influence their behavior as adults. Joan Borysenko offers this example:

> Inside me there is a seven-year-old who is still hurting from her humiliation at summer camp. Her anguish is reawakened every time I find myself in the presence of an authority figure who acts in a controlling manner. At those moments, my intellect is prone to desert me, and I am liable to break down and cry with the same desolation and helplessness I felt when I was seven.[17]

This example reminds us that childhood wounds can cause us to experience emotions out of proportion to a current situation. Also, we often relive the experience in a context very different from the one we experienced as a child. A worker who is strongly reprimanded by an angry supervisor may experience the same feelings that surfaced when he was scolded by his mother for breaking an expensive vase.

Transactional Analysis A promising breakthrough in understanding the influence of the unconscious came many years ago with the development of the

Transactional Analysis (TA) theory by Eric Berne. After years of study, Berne concluded that, from the day of birth, the brain acts like a two-track stereo tape recorder. One track records events, and the other records the feelings associated with those events.

To illustrate how feelings associated with early childhood experiences can surface later in life, picture in your mind's eye a 3-year-old walking around his mother's sewing room. He picks up a pair of sharp scissors and begins walking toward the staircase. The mother spots the child and cries, "Tommy, drop those scissors! Do you want to kill yourself?" Tommy's tape recorder records both the event (walking with scissors) and the emotions (fear and guilt). Ten years later, Tommy is taking an art class and his teacher says, "Tommy, bring me a pair of scissors." As he begins to walk across the room, his mind is flooded by the feelings of fear and guilt attached to that earlier childhood event.

The practical applications of Transactional Analysis were discussed in such books as *I'm OK—You're OK,* written by Thomas Harris; *Staying OK,* by Amy Bjork Harris and Thomas Harris; and *Born to Win,* by Muriel James and Dorothy Jongeward. TA concepts have been incorporated into many corporate training programs.

● Cultural Conditioning

A professor at Dartmouth College said, "Culture is what we see and hear so often that we call it reality. Out of culture comes behavior."[18] Culture helps shape just about every aspect of our behavior and our mental processes. Culture is frequently associated with a particular country; but actually, most countries are multicultural. African Americans, Hispanic Americans, Asian Americans, and American Indians represent a few of the subcultures within the United States.[19]

The rate of interpersonal violence in the United States is higher than in other industrialized countries. Domestic abuse is the leading cause of injury to women in this country. The United States Justice Department estimates that one in four women have been involved in abusive relationships. Many people, both men and women, are victims of verbal abuse, which may take the form of insults or swearing.[20]

Too much violence makes it difficult for us to achieve emotional balance. People who have experienced violence, or the threat of violence, express high levels of fear and distress. As life becomes a constant state of tension and anxiety, their ability to build and maintain good relationships with others decreases.

Thus far we have established two important points regarding the role of emotions in our life:

1. *It is important that we remain open to the full range of emotions that influence our thinking and behavior.* To deny our feelings or attempt to repress them is not a healthy way to handle emotions. Shakti Gawain, a pioneer in the field of personal growth, says, "Our feelings are an important part of the life force that is constantly moving through us. If we don't allow ourselves to fully experience our emotions, we stop the natural flow of that life force."[21]

2. *Emotional undercurrents are present in every aspect of our work, and separating our mental and emotional energies at work is very difficult because*

they are so closely intertwined.[22] We live in a society where many people are openly suspicious of emotions, so it is not surprising that in many work settings employees are encouraged to express their thoughts but not their feelings.

Coping with Your Anger and the Anger of Others

Anger may be defined as the thoughts, feelings, physical reactions, and actions that result from unacceptable behavior by others.[23] The negative emotion of anger often triggers hostility. Learning to deal effectively with anger is a key to a healthy relationship and to your physical and mental health. The authors of *Anger Kills* say that about 20 percent of the general population has levels of hostility high enough to be dangerous to health, another 20 percent has very low levels, and the rest of the population falls somewhere in between.[24]

● Managing Your Anger

> *Learning to deal with your anger and the anger of other people is one of the most sophisticated and mature skills people are ever required to learn.*

Learning to deal with your anger and the anger of other people is one of the most sophisticated and mature skills people are ever required to learn. Intense anger takes control of people and distorts their perceptions, which is why angry people often make poor decisions.[25]

Dr. Art Ulene, author of *Really Fit Really Fast,* says the first step in anger management is to monitor your anger. How often do you get angry each day? What are the causes of irritation in your life? How upsetting is each episode of anger? How well do you manage each episode? Ulene suggests using a diary or journal to record this information. This self-monitoring activity will help you determine the impact of anger in your life. Record not only the source of the irritation, but the feelings that surfaced when you

HUMAN RELATIONS IN ACTION

Stick Swinging, Choking, and Trash Talk

Marty McSorley, a member of the Boston Bruins hockey team, was suspended for knocking out Donald Brashear, a player for the Vancouver Canucks. Near the end of a tension-filled game, McSorley skated up—out of Brashear's view—and swung his stick with both hands against Brashear's head. Later McSorley said, "I have to come to terms with what I did. There's no excuse. It was so stupid, I can't believe I did it."

In some cases, the coach is the victim of violence. Latrell Sprewell was suspended from the Golden State Warriors basketball team for choking his coach, P. J. Carlesimo. Sprewell had been the target of several of Carlesimo's tirades that involved screaming and profanity.

Trash talk, the practice of boasting and insulting one's foe, sometimes results in physical violence. Commercials from athletic companies such as Nike often glorify trash talking, implying that bad manners are essential to good basketball. Critics of professional sports say there are too few good role models and too many negative messages.

became angry. Also record the behaviors you displayed when angry. Ulene says that people who monitor their behavior carefully see positive results: "Without even trying, their behavior begins to change in ways that are usually desirable."[26]

Intense anger often takes the form of rage.

What makes you angry? The anger journal will help you identify your most common anger triggers. You may find that irritations and annoyances such as traffic delays, interruptions, or loud noise are very irritating. You may discover that your anger is frequently connected to disappointment in someone or to some annoying event. Tony Stewart, the 2002 NASCAR Winston Cup champion, was fined $10,000 and put on probation after punching a photographer following a race. He was also fined $50,000 by Home Depot, his sponsor. He admits that anger control is a challenge when members of the press become pushy and invade his privacy.[27] Anger is a common problem in many areas of athletic competition.

Intense anger often takes the form of rage. In addition to road rage, air rage, and customer rage, we are witnessing more incidents of "workplace rage." Workplace rage can take the form of yelling, verbal abuse, and physical violence. It is more likely to occur when workers are stressed by long hours, unrealistic deadlines, cramped quarters, excessive e-mail, lack of recognition, or bullying incidents.

Anger control has been a challenge for Tony Stewart, winner of the 2002 NASCAR Winston Cup championship. On one occasion he voiced negative comments about the fans who attend the races at Talladega race track. After his comments were quoted in several local newspapers, he decided it was time to laugh at himself.

● Effective Ways to Express Your Anger

Buddha said, "You will not be punished for your anger, you will be punished by your anger." Intense anger that is suppressed will linger and become a disruptive force in your life unless you can find a positive way to get rid of it. Expressing feelings of anger can be therapeutic, but many people are unsure about the best way to self-disclose this emotion. To express anger in ways that will improve the chances that the other person will receive and respond to your message, consider these suggestions:

1. *Avoid reacting in a manner that could be seen as emotionally unstable.* If others see you as reacting irrationally, you will lose your ability to influence them.[28] Failure to maintain your emotional control can damage your image.

2. *Do not make accusations or attempt to fix blame.* It would be acceptable to begin the conversation by saying, "I felt humiliated at the staff meeting this morning." It would not be appropriate to say, "Your comments at the morning staff meeting were mean spirited and made me feel humiliated." The latter statement invites a defensive response.[29]

3. *Express your feelings in a timely manner.* The intensity of anger can actually increase with time. Also, important information needed by you or the person who provoked your anger may be forgotten or distorted with the passing of time.

4. *Be specific as you describe the factors that triggered your anger, and be clear about the resolution you are seeking.* The direct approach, in most cases, works best.

In some cases the person who triggers your anger may be someone you cannot confront without placing your job in jeopardy. For example, one of your best customers may constantly complain about the service he receives. You know he receives outstanding service, and you feel anger building inside you each time he complains. But any display of anger may result in loss of his business. In this situation you rely on your rational thinking power and say to yourself, "This part of my work is very distasteful, but I can stay calm each time he complains."

Research conducted by the Yale School of Management found that nearly one out of four working men and women were "chronically" angry at work. The most common reason for their anger was believing that their employers had violated basic promises and had not fulfilled the "expected psychological

TOTAL	**ROBERT ROSELL**
PERSON	PRESIDENT, QUALITY MEDIA RESOURCES, INC.
INSIGHT	"Learning to develop respectful relationships at work is perhaps the most important work-related skill we can develop."

contract with their workers." This problem, according to the authors of the study, remains mostly "underground" because workers tend not to express their anger openly.[30]

● How to Handle Other People's Anger

Dealing with other people's anger may be the most difficult human relations challenge we face. The following skills can be learned and applied to any situation where anger threatens to damage a relationship.

1. *Recognize and accept the other person's anger.* The simple recognition of the intense feelings of someone who is angry does a lot to defuse the situation.[31] In a calm voice you might say, "I can see that you are very angry," or "It's obvious that you are angry."

2. *Encourage the angry person to vent his or her feelings.* By asking questions and listening carefully to the response, you can encourage the person to discuss the cause of the anger openly. Try using an open-ended question to encourage self-disclosure: "What have I done to upset you?" or "Can you tell me why you are so angry?"

3. *Do not respond to an angry person with your own anger.* To express your own anger or become defensive will only create another barrier to emotional healing. When you respond to the angry person, keep your voice tone soft. Keep in mind the old biblical injunction, "A soft answer turns away wrath."[32]

4. *Give the angry person feedback.* After venting feelings and discussing specific details, the angry person will expect a response. Briefly paraphrase what seems to be the major concern of the angry person, and express a desire to find ways to solve the problem. If you are at fault, accept the blame for your actions and express a sincere apology.

Violence in the Workplace

A former Navistar International Corporation employee forced his way into a suburban Chicago factory and fired nearly thirty shots from an AK-47. Four workers were killed. Workplace murder is the second leading cause of death on the job and has afflicted numerous companies.[33]

Although workplace homicides have not increased in recent years, workplace violence is ranked as the number one security concern by security officials who participated in a study conducted by Pinkerton, a security-services firm.[34] And many workers are less productive because they fear workplace violence.

Violence in the workplace is often triggered by loss of a job, conflict between the employee and management, or a personal tragedy, such as divorce or separation. Abusive behavior by supervisors and managers is widespread, according to Columbia University psychologist Harvey Hornstein. In his book

Brutal Bosses and Their Prey, Hornstein says the abusive behavior takes the form of verbal and physical threats, lying, deviousness, and sexual harassment.[35] A rigid, autocratic, impersonal work environment also appears to foster violence.

Although homicides get the most attention, they do not represent the most common form of workplace violence. Workplace violence encompasses a wide range of behaviors, including hostile remarks, intimidation of another employee by stalking, physical assaults, and threatening phone calls.

● Employee Sabotage

Employee sabotage is a problem that is causing nightmares throughout corporate America. It is often described as employee misconduct tinged with an edge of revenge. Employee sabotage may involve deliberate nonperformance, financial fraud, slander, destruction of equipment, arson, or some other act that damages the organization or the careers of people within the organization. Computer crimes have become a common form of sabotage. Computer sabotage by ex-workers is rising.[36]

Sabotage is committed most often by employees who have unresolved grievances, want to advance by making others look less qualified, or want to get even for real or imagined mistreatment. Today, many employees are acting out their anger, rather than discussing it.[37]

● Preventing Workplace Violence

The National Safe Workplace Institute estimates that incidents of workplace violence cost employers and others several billion dollars each year. This figure does not, of course, reflect the human suffering caused by acts of violence. Although violence cannot be eliminated, some steps can help curb violent behavior in the workplace.

1. *Use hiring procedures that screen out unstable persons.* In-depth interviews, drug testing, and background checks can help identify signs of a troubled past.

2. *Develop a strategy for responding to incidents* **before** *they actually occur.* Adopt a zero-tolerance policy that makes it clear that violent incidents will not be tolerated.[38]

3. *If someone must be demoted, fired, or laid off, do it in a way that does not demoralize the employee.* Some rigid, authoritarian companies handle such personnel actions in a very dehumanizing manner.

4. *Provide out-placement services for laid-off or terminated employees.* These services may include development of job-search skills, retraining, or, in cases where the employee is displaying signs of aggression, counseling.

5. *Establish a systematic way to deal with disgruntled employees.* Federal Express Corp. developed the Guaranteed Fair Treatment program to pro-

> *As the workplace gets leaner, it need not become meaner.*

vide a forum for employees who feel they have been treated unfairly. (Chapter 13 covers conflict resolution programs in more detail.)

6. ***Provide supervisors and managers with training that will help them prevent workplace violence and deal effectively with violence if it does occur.*** Workplace violence is a growing problem in America, but it is not a problem without solutions. As the workplace gets leaner, it need not become meaner.

Emotional Styles

A good starting point for achieving emotional control is to examine your current emotional style. How do you deal with emotions? Your style started taking shape before birth and evolved over a period of many years. As an adult, you are likely to favor one of four different emotional styles when confronted with events that trigger your emotions.

● Suppressing Your Emotions

Some people have learned to suppress their feelings as much as possible. They have developed intellectual strategies that enable them to avoid dealing directly with emotional reactions to a situation. In response to the loss of a loved one, a person may avoid the experience of grief and mourning by taking on new responsibilities at work. This is not, of course, a healthy way to deal with grief. Some people become upset but keep their anger bottled up inside. Controlling your anger does not mean you have to run and hide from your feelings.

To continually suppress feelings, hide fears, swallow annoyances, and avoid displaying anger is not healthy. If suppressing your feelings becomes a habit, you create opportunities for mental and physical health problems to develop. Research indicates that headaches, asthma, back pain, and cardiovascular difficulties can sometimes be traced to suppressed emotions.[39]

HUMAN RELATIONS IN ACTION

Should You Hold Back the Tears?

Dan Reeves, coach of the Atlanta Falcons, knows the rules: Football coaches are not supposed to cry. Sometimes, however, his fiery temper is joined by a softer side. "I start crying at Road Runner cartoons," he once said, only half jokingly.

Chris Brayton also has difficulty holding back tears. He reflects on the time he cried at work and thinks it may have damaged his career. His supervisor asked him to work on a new project. He accepted the new assignment only after explaining that he wanted to keep his daytime work schedule. A father of four, he wanted to be with his children in the evening. After he completed a four-week training program, his bosses placed him on the night shift and turned down his request to return to his previous assignment. At a meeting with his bosses, he started getting choked up and tears came to his eyes. After that meeting Brayton suspected that his bosses viewed him differently.

Brayton may have good reason to be concerned. Crying is often taboo in a workplace that values intellect over emotion.

● Capitulating to Your Emotions

People who display this emotional style see themselves as the helpless victims of feelings over which they have no control. By responding to emotion in this manner, one can assign responsibility for the "problem" to external causes, such as other people or unavoidable events. For example, Paula, a busy office manager, is frustrated because her brother-in-law and his wife frequently show up unannounced on weekends and expect a big meal. Paula has a tight schedule during the week, and she looks forward to quiet weekends with her family. She is aware of the anger that builds within her, but tends to blame others (family members) for these feelings. Paula would rather endure feelings of helplessness than find a positive solution to this problem. People who capitulate to their emotions are often overly concerned about the attitudes and opinions of others.[40]

● Overexpressing Your Emotions

In a work setting, we need to be seen as responsible and predictable. One of the quickest ways to lose the respect and confidence of the people you work with is to frequently display a lack of emotional control. Frequent use of foul and vulgar language, flared tempers, raised voices, and teary eyes are still regarded as unacceptable behavior by most coworkers and supervisors.

One acceptable way to cope with fear, anger, grief, or jealousy is to sit down with pen and paper and write a letter to the person who triggered these emotions. Don't worry about grammar, spelling, or punctuation—just put all your thoughts on paper. Write until you have nothing more to say. Then destroy the letter. Once you let go of your toxic feelings, you will be ready to deal constructively with whatever caused you to become upset.[41] Another approach is to express your feelings through daily journal entries. Studies indicate that a significant emotional uplift and healing effect can result from spending as little as 5 to 10 minutes a day writing about whatever issues or problems are getting you down.[42]

● Accommodating Your Emotions

At the beginning of this chapter we said an emotion can be thought of as a feeling that influences our thinking and behavior. Accommodation means you are willing to recognize, accept, and experience emotions and to attempt to react in ways appropriate to the situation. This style achieves an integration of one's feelings and the thinking process. People who display the accommodation style have adopted the "think before you act" point of view. Let's assume that as you are presenting a new project proposal at a team meeting, someone interrupts you and strongly criticizes your ideas. The criticism seems to be directed more at you than at your proposal. Anger starts building inside you, but before responding to the assailant, you pause and quickly engage in some rational thinking. During the few seconds of silence, you make a mental review of the merits of your proposal and consider the other person's motives for making a personal attack. You decide the person's comments do not warrant a response at this point. Then you continue with your presentation, without a

> **THINKING / LEARNING STARTERS**
>
> 1. Think about the last time someone expressed his or her anger to you. Were you able to respond in an appropriate way? Was the relationship between you and the angry person damaged?
> 2. Try to recall a situation where you either suppressed your feelings or overexpressed your feelings. How did your behavior affect the other person?

hint of frustration in your voice. If your proposal has merit, the other members of the group will probably speak on your behalf.

Do we always rely on just one of these four emotional styles? Of course not. Your response to news that a coworker is getting a divorce may be very different from your response to a demeaning comment made by your boss. You may have found appropriate ways to deal with your grief but have not yet learned to cope with the fear of making a presentation. Dealing with our emotions is a very complex process.

● Gender Differences in Emotional Style

Men often complain that women are too emotional. Women often complain that men are too rational and too insensitive to the emotions of others. Although these complaints are not valid in all cases, they can help us understand gender differences in emotional styles.[43] In many families, males are encouraged to hide their feelings, to appear strong and stable. Participation in team sports and work may reinforce this early conditioning. Many women say that men do not take their emotional needs seriously enough and do not respond with support and understanding. Joan Borysenko suggests that men take time to comfort a woman who wants to talk about an important problem and to validate her right to feel her emotions. An appropriate male response in this situation might be nothing more than a sincere acknowledgment of the problem: "Gee, Susan, I can see that you are really upset. Let's talk about the problem." Borysenko suggests that women keep in mind that many men find it difficult to talk about emotions and to display emotions. For example, many men still cling to the notion that crying is not a manly thing to do. A good relationship does not require both people to have the same emotional style, but it does require each person to respect the other person's style.[44]

Strategies for Achieving Emotional Control

Each day we wake up with a certain amount of mental, emotional, and physical energy that we can spend throughout the day. If we allow our "difficult" emotions to deplete our energy, we have no energy to change our life or to give to others.[45] The good news is that we can learn to discipline the mind and banish afflicting thoughts that create needless frustration and waste energy. In this, the final part of the chapter, we share with you some practical suggestions for achieving greater control of the emotions that affect your life.

● Identifying Your Emotional Patterns

We could often predict or anticipate our response to various emotions if we would take the time to study our emotional patterns—to take a running inventory of circumstances that touch off jealousy, fear, anger, or some other emotion. Tamra Reed, a graphic designer employed by a large newspaper, felt anger and frustration every time a coworker delivered material late. New to her position, Tamra was hesitant to discuss her feelings with the offending person, but she did record them in a journal. She recorded not only her conscious feelings, such as anxiety, but also other feelings in her body—a knot in her stomach and muscle tension when material arrived late. Tamra soon began to identify some patterns. The late arrival of the material meant she had less time to work on the final design, so her completed work often fell short of the high-quality standards she set for herself.

The journal entries helped Tamra become aware of ways to cope with her problem. She discovered that she had lost touch with the power of her own resources. Each time she accepted late material, she gave her power to the offending person. This was followed by feelings of anger toward herself and toward the person who turned in the material late. She finally resolved to stop accepting late material and made her intentions known to those who were missing deadlines.

Becoming a skilled observer of your own emotions is one of the best ways to achieve greater emotional control.

If you don't feel comfortable with journal writing, consider setting aside some quiet time to reflect on your emotional patterns. A period of quiet reflection will help you focus your thoughts and impressions. Becoming a skilled observer of your own emotions is one of the best ways to achieve greater emotional control.

In addition to journal writing and quiet reflection, there is one more way to discover emotional patterns. At the end of the day, construct a chart of your emotional landscape. Make a chart (see Table 9.1) of the range of emotions you experienced and expressed during the day.[46] Your first entry might be "I woke up at 6:00 A.M. and immediately felt _____." The final entry might be "I left the office at 5:30 P.M. with a feeling of _____." What emotions surfaced throughout your workday? Resentment? Creative joy? Anxiety? Boredom? Contentment? Anger? Reflect on the completed chart and try to determine which patterns need to be changed. For example, you might discover that driving in heavy traffic is a major energy drain. Repeat this process over a period of several days in order to identify your unique emotional patterns.

SALLY FORTH

TABLE 9.1	Charting Your Emotional Landscape	
Time	**Circumstance**	**Emotion**
6:00 A.M.	Alarm goes off. Mind is flooded by thoughts of all the things that must be done during the day.	Anxiety
7:10 A.M.	Depart for work. Heavy traffic interferes with plan to arrive at work early.	Anger and help-lessness
8:00 A.M.	Thirty-minute staff meeting scheduled by the boss lasts fifty minutes. No agenda is provided. Entire meeting seems a waste of time.	Anger and frustration
9:35 A.M.	Finally start work on creative project.	Contentment
10:15 A.M.	Progress on project interrupted when coworker enters office, sits down, and starts sharing gossip about another coworker.	Anger and resentment
11:20 A.M.	Progress is made on creative project.	Contentment
1:45 P.M.	Creative project is complete and ready for review.	Joy and contentment
2:50 P.M.	Give project to boss for review. She says she will not be able to provide any feedback until morning. This delay will cause scheduling problems.	Frustration
4:00 P.M.	Attend health insurance update seminar sponsored by human resources department. No major changes are discussed.	Boredom
5:40 P.M.	Give up on a search for a missing document, turn off computer, and walk to parking lot.	Relief and fatigue

● **Fine-Tuning Your Emotional Style**

Once you have completed the process of self-examination and have identified some emotional patterns you want to change, it is time to consider ways to fine-tune your emotional style. Bringing about discipline within your mind can help you live a fuller, more satisfying life. Here are four things you can begin doing today.

■ *Take responsibility for your emotions.* How you view your emotional difficulties will have a major influence on how you deal with them. If your frustration is triggered by thoughts such as "I can never make my boss happy" or "Things always go wrong in my life," you may never achieve a comfortable emotional state. By shifting the blame to other people and events, you cannot achieve emotional control.

■ *Put your problems into proper perspective.* Why do some people seem to be at peace with themselves most of the time while others seem to be in a perpetual state of anxiety? People who engage in unproductive obsessing are unable or unwilling to look at problems realistically and practically, and they view each disappointment as a major catastrophe. To avoid needless misery, anxiety, and emotional upsets, use an "emotional thermometer" with a scale of 0 to 100. Zero means that everything is going well, and 100 denotes something

TOTAL	**GERARD EGAN**
PERSON	AUTHOR, *YOU AND ME*
INSIGHT	"It's unfortunate that we're never really taught how to show emotion in ways that help our relationships. Instead, we're usually told what we should not do. However, too little emotion can make our lives seem empty and boring, while too much emotion, poorly expressed, fills our interpersonal lives with conflict and grief. Within reason, some kind of balance in the expression of emotion seems to be called for."

life-threatening or truly catastrophic. Whenever you feel upset, ask yourself to come up with a logical number on the emotional thermometer. If a problem surfaces that is merely troublesome but not terrible, and you give it 60 points, you are no doubt overreacting. This mental exercise will help you avoid mislabeling a problem and feeling upset as a result.[47]

■ *Take steps to move beyond negative emotions such as envy, anger, jealousy, or hatred.* Some people are upset about things that happened many years ago. Some even nurse grudges against people who have been dead for years. The sad thing is that the negative feelings remain long after we can achieve any positive learning from them.[48] Studies of divorce, for example, indicate that anger and bitterness can linger a long time. Distress seems to peak one year after the divorce, and many people report that it takes at least two years to move past the anger.[49] When negative emotions dominate one's life, whatever the reason, therapy or counseling may provide relief. Membership in a support group is often helpful.

■ *Give your feelings some exercise.* Several prominent authors in the field of human relations have emphasized the importance of giving our feelings some exercise. Leo Buscaglia, author of *Loving Each Other,* says, "Exercise feelings. Feelings have meaning only as they are expressed in action."[50] Sam Keen, author of *Fire in the Belly,* said, "Make a habit of identifying your feelings and expressing them in some appropriate way."[51] If you have offended someone, how about sending that person a note expressing regret? If someone you work with has given extra effort, why not praise that person's work? Make a decision to cultivate positive mental states like kindness and compassion. A sincere feeling of empathy, for example, will deepen your connection to others.

Every day of our personal and work life we face some difficult decisions. One option is to take only actions that feel good at the moment. In some cases, this means ignoring the feelings of customers, patients, coworkers, and supervisors. Another option is to behave in a manner that is acceptable to the people around you. If you choose this option, you will have to make some sacrifices. You may have to be warm and generous when the feelings inside you say, "Be cold and selfish." You may have to avoid an argument when your feelings are insisting, "I'm right and the other person is wrong!" To achieve a positive emotional state often requires restructuring our ways of feeling, thinking, and behaving.

■ Summary

business.college.hmco.com/students

We carry inside us a vast array of emotions that help us cope with our environment. An emotion can be thought of as a feeling that influences our thinking and behavior. We sometimes experience emotional imbalance because we learn to inhibit the expression of certain emotions and overemphasize the expression of others. Emotions play a critical role in the success of every organization. Emotional undercurrents are present in almost every area of the organization, and they influence employee morale, customer loyalty, and productivity.

Our emotional development is influenced by temperament (the biological shaper of personality), our unconscious mind, and cultural conditioning. These influences contribute to the development of our emotional intelligence. Throughout the long process of emotional development we learn different ways to express our anger and other emotions. Appropriate expressions of anger contribute to improved interpersonal relations, help us reduce anxiety, and give us an outlet for unhealthy stress. We must also learn how to handle other people's anger. It takes a great deal of effort to learn how to deal with our own anger and the anger of others.

In recent years we have seen an increase in workplace violence. Workplace violence encompasses a wide range of activities, including homicides, hostile remarks, physical assaults, and sabotage directed toward the employer or other workers. Although violence cannot be eliminated, steps can be taken to curb violent employee behavior.

To achieve emotional balance, we need to start with an examination of our current emotional style. When confronted by strong feelings, we are likely to display one of four different emotional styles: suppressing emotions, capitulating to them, overexpressing them, or accommodating them. Researchers suggest that there are gender differences in emotional style.

Emotional control is an important dimension of emotional style. The starting point in developing emotional control is to identify your current emotional patterns. One way to do this is to record your anger experiences in a diary or journal. Additional ways to identify emotional patterns include setting aside time for quiet reflection and developing a chart of your emotional landscape. Once you have completed the process of self-examination, you should consider appropriate ways to fine-tune your emotional style.

■ Career Corner

Q: When I started working for this company, I was never put in a situation where it was necessary to make presentations to others. After receiving a promotion to department head, I was expected to make monthly reports to my staff. I never feel comfortable in the role of group presenter. Hours before the monthly meeting I start feeling tense, and by the time the meeting begins I am gripped by fear. Two weeks ago, my boss asked me to make a presentation to senior management. Shortly before the meeting I started experiencing chest pain, sweating, and trembling. I told my boss I was sick and went home. Why am I so frightened of speaking to a group? Should I seek professional help?

A. It appears that you may have developed a social phobia. Social phobias are fears of situations in which the person can be watched by others. Phobias of various types are quite common—they currently afflict over 11 million Americans. Your problem could be serious, and you might consider seeking help from a qualified therapist. Psychotherapy can result in greater self-understanding and self-expression. Throughout the treatment you will learn new ways to cope with your problem. It is encouraging to note that about 80 percent of psychotherapy patients benefit from treatment.

■ Key Terms

emotion	Transactional Analysis
temperament	anger
unconscious mind	

■ Review Questions

1. What is the relationship between feelings and emotion? What role do feelings play in our life?

2. What is meant by the term *emotional balance?* What factors create an *emotional imbalance?*

3. List and briefly describe the three factors that influence our emotional development.

4. Emotions play a critical role in the success of every organization, yet many leaders seem unaware of this fact or choose to ignore emotions. Why?

5. Describe the human emotion we call anger, and explain why it is important to learn to control one's anger.

6. What four steps can improve the chances that another person will receive and respond to your feelings of anger?

7. During a recent performance review your boss said, "You lack kindness and compassion when dealing with coworkers and customers." What steps can you take to improve in this area?

8. Discuss what it means to accommodate your feelings. What are the positive aspects of this emotional style?

9. List and briefly describe four ways to fine-tune your emotional style.

10. Explain your understanding of the Gerard Egan Total Person Insight.

■ Application Exercises

1. Recall the last time you were angry at another person or were a victim of a situation that made you angry. For example, perhaps a housemate or roommate refused to pay her share of the grocery bill, or your manager accused you of wrongdoing without knowing all the facts. Then answer the following questions:

a. Did you express your anger verbally? Physically?

b. Did you suppress any of your anger? Explain.

c. What results did you experience from the way you handled this situation? Describe both positive and negative results.

d. If you could relive the situation, would you do anything differently? Explain.

2. To learn more about the way you handle anger, record your anger responses in a journal for a period of five days. When anger surfaces, record as many details as possible. What triggered your anger? How intense was the anger? How long did your angry feelings last? Did you express them to anyone? At the end of the five days, study your entries and try to determine whether any patterns exist. If you find this activity helpful, consider keeping a journal for a longer period of time.

3. To learn more about how emotions influence your thinking and behavior, complete each of the following sentences. Once you have completed them all, reflect on your written responses. Can you identify any changes you would like to make in your emotional style?

a. "When someone makes me angry, I usually . . ."

b. "The most common worry in my life is . . ."

c. "When I feel compassion for someone, my response is to . . ."

d. "My response to feelings of grief is . . ."

e. "When I am jealous of someone, my response is to . . ."

Internet Exercise

Many people have an anger management problem. Although anger is a natural human emotion, the mismanagement of anger can result in serious human relations problems. Help with anger management is as close as your computer. The American Psychological Association has a webpage on "Controlling Anger—Before It Controls You." The address is *www.apa.org/pubinfo/html.* Visit this site and prepare a written summary of the information presented. If you wish to study anger management in greater detail, visit *www.angermgmt .com* or *www.angermgt.com.*

Case 9.1 Coping with Grief

Grief over losing a loved one is one of the most difficult personal problems to discuss at work. Many of the estimated 4 million workers who are bereaved each year keep their grief a secret on the job. Bill Foote, CEO of USG Corporation, is an exception. Foote was promoted to the top position at USG one month before his wife, an accomplished attorney and the mother of three young daughters, died of breast cancer. Talking about his grief at work was not easy. He finally decided that hiding it would violate the leadership principles that guided him each day. He believes that building teamwork requires being open and honest about weaknesses as well as strengths.

Foote opened his first speech as CEO to 150 USG managers by talking about his loss and the spiritual lessons he had learned. Life is precious and fleeting, he told the group; live in the moment, and simplify your days to make time for what really matters. At one point he paused, struggling to contain his emotion. Some crusty USG veterans wiped away tears. The response to Foote's presentation was strengthened commitment to the new CEO and a renewed sense of the corporate value placed on family. One senior executive said the thinking among the managers after the presentation was clear: "If we have to go through a few walls for this guy, we're going to do it."

Dealing with grief at work can be very difficult, especially when the work environment is cold and indifferent to a grieving employee. Deborah DeVito met her brother's flight at the Albuquerque airport and walked with him to the baggage claim area. Suddenly he grew dizzy, then incoherent. A few hours later he was dead. The shock of his death was overwhelming, and DeVito struggled at work. She took five days off to arrange and attend her brother's funeral. When she requested an additional day to attend a memorial service for her brother, her boss denied her request. He then scolded her for missing an important teleconference. Once Ms. DeVito returned to work she felt "ready to explode" with grief.

Unsympathetic bosses often prolong the grieving process. An environmental specialist missed his father's funeral because he was working overseas. Depressed, he requested family leave to recover and set his mother's affairs in order. His boss refused to approve the request. His work soon deteriorated, and after a few months he was forced to resign.

Psychologists note that grieving is unpredictable and takes varying amounts of time. Unresolved grief can result in depression and lost productivity. Workplace grief, according to research conducted by the Grief Recovery Institute, costs U.S. businesses about $75 billion a year in reduced productivity, increased errors, and accidents. Sources of grief range from miscarriages to divorce. Managers and coworkers often do not know how to respond to grief. Workplace attitudes toward grief, in many organizations, seem to be stuck in the workplace practices common during the industrial age.[52]

■ Questions

1. Work/life specialists say that employers have much to gain from responding to grief with care and compassion. Do you agree?

2. Pitney Bowes provides its employees with a copy of a book entitled *One More Star in Heaven Now*. It describes how to help both bereaved employees and coworkers who may not know what to say to them. Is this a good use of company resources? Explain.

3. What information presented in this chapter would be helpful to someone who is trying to cope with the emotion of grief?

Case 9.2   Helping Employees Who Behave Badly

Organizations that want to survive in today's highly competitive global economy must learn how to deal with employees who behave badly. This includes the boss who frequently becomes angry and yells at employees. It also includes employees who treat customers with indifference and disrespect. Team members who cause friction and engage in infighting also need help. Many employees who behave badly are persons with valuable technical skills, so termination may not be an option. To salvage the career of an employee who possesses strong technical skills but lacks effective people skills is a challenge. Here is how some companies met this challenge.

- At Chemical Bank, based in New York City, some candidates for management positions have been encouraged to complete the Dale Carnegie human relations course. One enrollee was a 32-year-old employee who had a degree in accounting. He had good technical skills, but Chemical wanted him to develop his people skills.

- David Prosser, chief executive officer of RTW Inc., a worker's compensation management firm in Minneapolis, received complaints about one of his managers. This person would become angry and yell at other employees. Most of the targets of his wrath were lower-level employees who wouldn't dare fight back. Other managers met with him to discuss his behavior, but he denied he had done anything wrong. Prosser viewed the manager as a valued employee, so he sent him to Executive to Leader Institute, a local coaching firm. After several months of personal coaching, the manager learned to control his anger.

More serious cases include employees who have substance addictions or serious personality disorders such as depression. A potentially violent employee can present the greatest challenge because discharging an employee with a mental disability may be viewed as illegal by the courts. Antibias laws such as the Americans with Disabilities Act can make it difficult for employers to fire mentally unstable workers. Legal pitfalls exist because it is often difficult to distinguish between conduct that is the result of a mental disability and conduct that is the result of generally unacceptable behavior. Companies must also determine the best way to deal with domestic violence that spills over to the job. For example, many women who are victims of domestic abuse are threatened or abused while at work.[53]

■ Questions

1. At Chemical Bank some employees are encouraged to complete the Dale Carnegie human relations course. What are the advantages and disadvantages of this approach?

2. A manager at RTW Inc. was given help in the form of personal coaching. What are the advantages and disadvantages of this approach?

3. What would be your response if a fellow worker suddenly became moody and caused friction in your department? Would you attempt to offer assistance, or would you wait for someone else to deal with the problem?

10

BUILDING STRONGER RELATIONSHIPS WITH POSITIVE ENERGY

Chapter Preview

After studying this chapter, you will be able to

- Describe how positive energy contributes to improved interpersonal relationships.

- Create awareness of the strong need people have for encouragement and positive feedback.

- Understand how to use positive reinforcement to improve relationships and reward behavior.

- Describe the major barriers to the use of positive reinforcement.

- Explain how to reward individual and team performance.

When Jennifer Shroeger arrived at the Buffalo, New York, UPS distribution center, part-time workers were deserting at the rate of 50 percent a year. Shroeger, the newly assigned district manager, realized that attrition is both costly and disruptive. Yet loading and unloading boxes in a large warehouse can get old. Many new hires quit their job after a few weeks.

Shroeger started working for UPS as a temporary driver's helper while she was a college student, so she understands the needs and motives of part-time workers. She understands the thinking of new workers who feel overwhelmed at starting work in a noisy, cavernous building after only a brief training program. One of the first things she did was improve lighting throughout the building and in break rooms to make the environment feel more human. Some of her best part-time supervisors were given responsibility for training, and new hires were given performance feedback and additional training when needed. The supervisors offered encouragement and help in fixing small problems. Shroeger and her staff found ways to make work more fun with contests and after-hour outings.

Supervisors also began to demonstrate interest in their workers: What are his hobbies? Where does she go to school? What is this worker's career goal? Within a short period of time, the Buffalo district attrition rate dropped to 6 percent.[1] This dramatic change illustrates the economic benefits of a work environment characterized by good communications, respect, and positive feedback. Shroeger was able to create an energy force that transformed worker attitudes.

This chapter discusses the impact of positive energy on both individual and group behavior. **Energy** can be defined as the capacity for work, or the force that helps us do things with vitality and intensity. The chapter examines the importance of encouragement, the power of positive feedback, various types of positive reinforcement, and the reasons why many people have difficulty expressing positive thoughts and feelings. A section of the chapter is devoted to awards and incentive programs that a variety of organizations use.

How Positive Energy Contributes to Improved Interpersonal Relationships

Throughout periods of great uncertainty and turbulence, negative energy can become a powerful force. Many people go to work everyday wondering if they will be the next victim of a merger, buyout, downsizing effort, or business closing. Some wonder if they will be able to cope with rapid technological changes. Stressful working conditions caused by rising productivity demands and long hours can also be the source of negative energy. In a negative, stressful work climate, these pressures often result in physical fatigue, decreased optimism, and lower morale. A positive work climate is more likely to instill workers with positive energy, which results in greater strength of will, increased optimism, and higher employee productivity.

It is positive energy that helps us cope with disappointments, uncertainty, and work that is physically and mentally demanding.

It is positive energy that helps us cope with disappointments, uncertainty, and work that is physically and mentally demanding. In the presence of positive energy people feel uplifted, encouraged, and empowered. Positive energy helps us remain balanced in a work environment that is increasingly characterized by change and uncertainty.

Negative energy is created when good performance is ignored. Even the most confident, self-motivated employees eventually will feel taken for granted without occasional praise.[2] In the absence of encouragement and positive feedback, the organization becomes a negative force because employees feel their work is not appreciated, and they become progressively demoralized and defensive. Negative energy is also created when compensation is inadequate, when needed training is not provided, or when the employee's need for work/life balance is ignored.

● Actions and Events That Create Positive Energy

In the age of information, organizations need to discover creative ways to generate positive energy. Progressive companies find ways to frequently encourage, recognize, and reward employees. Consider the following examples:

■ Great Plains Software puts people first, and the result is a very low turnover rate of 5 percent—far below the information technology industry average, which ranges from 18 to 25 percent. The company gives employees ownership at every level and provides a wide range of personal development opportunities. Employees praise the company's commitment to work/life balance.[3]

Roy Snider, Director of Wow at Stew Leonard's supermarket, can often be seen dancing with customers and singing "Happy Birthday." He is also responsible for boosting employee morale and building team spirit. He understands the importance of building strong relationships with positive energy.

■ Stew Leonard's is a highly successful supermarket that offers groceries and an entertaining shopping experience. Roy Snider is the supermarket chain's official pep rally cheerleader. His title is Director of Wow, and he's responsible for boosting employee morale and building team spirit. Stop at Stew Leonard's and you might see Snider dancing with a customer or singing happy birthday to an employee.[4]

This is a very small sample of actions and events that can generate positive energy. Throughout the remainder of this chapter we will discuss how basic courtesy, positive written communication, encouragement, and various forms of positive reinforcement can be used to "accentuate the positive."

HUMAN RELATIONS IN ACTION

Most Important Pop Quiz Question

Justine Willis Toms, editor of *New Dimensions* magazine, feels we need to personalize the places where we live, work, study, and shop. One way to accomplish this is by getting to know the people who provide us with services. To make her point, she describes a student's experience in nursing school. The instructor gave the class a pop quiz, and the last question was "What is the first name of the woman who cleans our building?" The student didn't know, so she handed in the quiz with the last question unanswered.

Before the class ended, one student asked if the last question would count toward the quiz grade. The teacher said, "Absolutely," and then provided a rationale: "In your careers you will meet many people. All are significant. They deserve your attention and care, even if all you do is smile and say hello."

Our Need for Positive Experiences

Psychologist William James believed that the craving to be appreciated is a basic principle of human nature.

How strong is the need for positive experiences in our life? Psychologist William James believed that the craving to be appreciated is a basic principle of human nature. Mark Twain, the noted author, answered the question by saying he could live for three weeks on a compliment. Twain was willing to admit openly what most people feel inside. Many of us have a deep desire for personal recognition in one form or another but almost never verbalize these thoughts.

Few people have the strength of ego to maintain high self-esteem without encouragement and positive feedback from others. We often are not certain we have performed well until some other person tells us. Kenneth Blanchard and Spencer Johnson, authors of *The One Minute Manager*, stress the importance of "catching people doing things right" and engaging in "one minute praisings."[5] Without positive experiences, we often suffer from a sense of incompleteness.

● Support from Maslow

The hierarchy of needs developed by Abraham Maslow (discussed in Chapter 7) provides additional support for positive experiences. In part, the need for security (a second-level need) is satisfied by positive feedback from an approving supervisor, manager, coworker, or friend. You are likely to feel more secure when someone recognizes your accomplishments. A feeling of belonging (a third-level need) can be satisfied by actions that communicate, "You are part of the team." Maslow states that as each lower-level need is satisfied, the need at the next level demands attention. It would seem to be almost impossible to satisfy the esteem needs (fourth level) without positive feedback and reinforcement. A person's level of self-esteem may diminish in a work environment where accomplishments receive little or no recognition.

● Support from Skinner

The research of B. F. Skinner at Harvard University has contributed to our understanding of reinforcement as a factor influencing the behavior of people in a work setting. Skinner maintained that any living organism will tend to repeat a particular behavior if that behavior is accompanied or followed by a reinforcer. A **reinforcer** is any stimulus that follows a response and increases the probability that the response will occur again.[6] Skinner also demonstrated that the timing of reinforcement has an important effect on behavior change. He discovered that if the delay between a response (behavior) and its reinforcement is too great, a change in behavior is less likely to take place.

● Support from Berne

In Chapter 9, you were given a brief introduction to Transactional Analysis (TA), a theory of communication developed by Eric Berne. TA is a simplified explanation of how people communicate. Berne's research also provided evidence that most people have a strong need for recognition, or "strokes."

The word *stroking* is used to describe the various forms of recognition one person gives another. Strokes help satisfy the need to be appreciated. A **physical stroke** may be a pat on the back or a smile that communicates approval. **Verbal strokes** include words of praise and expressions of gratitude.

Berne said that stroking is necessary for physical and mental health. He believed, as do others, that infants who are deprived of physical strokes (hugs, caresses, and kisses) begin to lose their will to live. As people grow into adulthood, they are willing to substitute verbal stroking for physical stroking. Adults still need and want physical stroking, but they will settle for words of praise, positive feedback, awards, and other forms of recognition.

A stroke can be positive or negative. Positive strokes, called "warm fuzzies" in TA language, include such behaviors as listening with genuine attention, smiling, or simply saying "Thank you" sincerely to a customer who has just made a purchase. Negative strokes, sometimes called "cold pricklies," produce "I'm not OK" feelings inside people. A negative stroke may take the form of being sarcastic, failing to remember the name of a regular customer, or ignoring support personnel such as custodians or shipping clerks.

TOTAL	**TIM SANDERS**
PERSON	CHIEF SOLUTIONS OFFICER, YAHOO!
INSIGHT	"People are hungry for compassion. There's never enough of it. And the tougher the times are, the more important it becomes."

Positive Reinforcement—A Powerful Affirmation

When a behavior is followed by a positive outcome, we are more likely to want to engage in that behavior again. In a work setting, **positive reinforcement** can be described as the practice of preparing written thank-you notes, providing an award, giving praise, or providing some other form of recognition. We use the term to describe activities that not only increase productivity but also improve interpersonal relationships. Therefore, much of the information presented will have application in your personal as well as your professional life.

Do people need encouragement to do good work? A study conducted by the authors of *Encouraging the Heart* included this question: "When you get encouragement does it help you perform at a higher level?" About 98 percent of the participants said yes.[7] Encouragement has never been more important as it is now, when so many people encounter energy-draining experiences at work and in their personal lives. Positive energy is an important form of life enrichment.

Nearly all workers appreciate recognition for their accomplishments. They respond positively to notes, letters, gifts, and comments that express appreciation. Recognition can be even more powerful when it is given in front of coworkers.

THINKING / LEARNING STARTER

Recall a situation when you accomplished something important but no one seemed to notice. Try to remember the feelings that surfaced inside you. Did you experience disappointment? Hurt? Anger? Feelings of inadequacy? Why do you now think your accomplishments were ignored?

● Confirmation Behaviors

Evelyn Sieburg used the term **confirmation** to name a whole series of behaviors that have a positive, or "therapeutic," effect on the receiver.[8] In most cases, confirmation behaviors develop feelings of self-worth in the mind of the worker and may be reflected in increased productivity, less absenteeism, and greater interest in work. To understand the wide range of confirmation behaviors possible in a work setting, let's follow a new worker, Mary Harper, through her first year on the job.

Mary graduated from a local community college, where she had completed a legal assistant program, and then obtained a position with a large law firm. Upon arriving at work, she was greeted warmly by the office manager, given a tour of the office complex, and introduced to the people with whom she would be working. A highlight of the tour was a stop at the president's office, where she met the founder of the firm.

The orientation continued with a review of the firm's policies and procedures by the office manager as well as training that enabled Mary to use the firm's data retrieval system. As she demonstrated competence in using the equipment, the supervisor made comments such as "Well done . . . you're a quick learner," and "Good job . . . you're doing fine."

During the morning coffee break on her first day, she was surprised to see a notice on the bulletin board that said, "Please welcome Mary Harper to our office." This notice reminded other workers that a new person had joined the staff.

As the weeks passed, Mary was given positive reinforcement on several occasions. She received positive feedback from coworkers as well as her supervisor. When she had a problem, her supervisor proved to be a good listener. Every person Mary had contact with seemed to be instilled with positive energy. At the end of the first year, she received a letter from the president of the firm (see Figure 10.1).

Would you enjoy working in this organizational setting? Chances are your answer is yes. A host of confirming behaviors gave Mary encouragement and support during her first year on the job. Some of these confirmations follow.

Orientation and Training   The office manager realized that no orientation or poor orientation can reduce a new employee's effectiveness and contribute to dissatisfaction and turnover. She took time to give Mary Harper a thorough introduction to company policies and procedures and get her acquainted with other employees. A thorough orientation sends the message "You are important, and we want you to get off to a good start."

FIGURE 10.1	Letter Providing Positive Reinforcement

THOMAS, THOMAS, AND ROYAL
ATTORNEYS AND COUNSELORS AT LAW
DENVER, COLORADO

August 11, 2004

Ms. Mary Harper
Legal Assistant
Thomas, Thomas, and Royal
144 Walnut Street
Denver, CO 80204

Dear Mary:

You have now completed one year with our firm, and I want you to know we are very pleased with your work. Ms. Williams, your supervisor, has kept me posted: your performance to date is certainly praiseworthy.

I notice that you have not missed a single day of work in your first year. The enclosed gift certificate in the amount of $100 is an expression of our gratitude. We appreciate your dedication.

Best wishes for continued success with our firm.

Sincerely,

Stephanie Thomas
President

Praise Giving praise is one of the easiest and most powerful ways to make an employee feel important and needed. The person who receives the praise knows that his or her work is not being taken for granted. When handled correctly, praise can be an effective reinforcement strategy that ensures repetition of desired behaviors.

Courtesy The poet Alfred Tennyson once said, "The greater the man, the greater the courtesy." When Mary Harper reported to work, she was welcomed in a courteous manner and introduced to people throughout the office. Even the president of the firm was not too busy to greet her. Courtesy means being considerate of others in small ways, showing respect for what others revere, and treating everyone, regardless of position, with consideration.

Active Listening As discussed in Chapter 2, everyone feels a sense of personal value when speaking with a good listener. Active listening can be a powerful reinforcer. Active listening is the process of sending back to the speaker what you as a listener think the speaker meant in terms of both content and feelings.

Positive Written Communication   Most people respond positively to notes and letters that express appreciation. Unfortunately, this positive gesture is used all too infrequently. Mary Harper will probably keep the letter written to her by the president and may show it to friends and relatives. A letter of appreciation or a thank-you note can have considerable impact on employee morale and can improve interpersonal communication within the organization.

Barriers to Positive Reinforcement

The material in this chapter is based on two indisputable facts about human nature. First, people want to know how well they are doing and if their efforts are satisfactory. Second, they appreciate recognition for their accomplishments. Performance feedback, encouragement, and positive reinforcement can satisfy these important human needs. People often say they prefer negative feedback to no feedback at all. "Don't leave me in the dark" is a common plea (spoken or unspoken) of most people.

THINKING / LEARNING STARTER

Chances are you owe somebody a thank-you note. Think about the events of the past six months. Has someone given time and effort to assist you with a problem? Make a list of at least three people who deserve a thank-you note. Pick one, write that person a note of appreciation, and mail it today.

Barriers to positive reinforcement take many forms. When Jay Leno became host of *The Tonight Show,* his manager advised him not to say thank you to Johnny Carson, the person who had made the program an American institution. Leno later said that not thanking Carson was "the biggest mistake" he's ever made.[9] He had allowed someone else to talk him out of doing the right thing. Some additional reasons why we do not "do the right thing" are described in this section.

● Preoccupation with Self

If you want attention and appreciation, you must learn to give attention and appreciation.

One of the major obstacles to providing positive reinforcement is preoccupation with self. The term **narcissism** is often used to describe this human condition. Narcissism is a Freudian term alluding to the mythical youth who wore himself out trying to kiss his own reflection in a pool of water.

Deepak Chopra, author of *The Seven Spiritual Laws of Success,* encourages everyone to practice the "Law of Giving." This law states that you must give in order to receive. If you want attention and appreciation, you must learn to give attention and

TOTAL **PERSON** **INSIGHT**	**MALCOLM BOYD** EPISCOPAL PRIEST; AUTHOR, *"VOLUNTEERING THANKS"* "Feeling grateful is good for us. Gratitude is the opposite of the qualities of self-centeredness, indifference, and arrogance. Expressing gratitude affords each of us unique opportunities to reach out in love and share happiness. Saying thank you is a very positive thing to do."

appreciation. If you want joy in your life, give joy to others. He says the easiest way to get what you want is to help others get what they want.[10] Put another way, when you do good for another person, you do good for yourself.

The publication of *Random Acts of Kindness* and many people's acceptance of its central theme may have signaled a movement away from self-preoccupation. Random acts of kindness are those little things that we do for others that have no payback. They involve giving freely, purely, for no reason.[11] Here are some examples from the book:

- Send a letter to a teacher you once had letting him or her know about the difference he or she made in your life.

- Write a card thanking a service person for his or her care and leave it with your tip.

- Organize your friends and workmates to gather their old clothes and give them to homeless people.

● Misconceptions About Positive Reinforcement

Some people fail to use positive reinforcement because they have misconceptions about this human relations strategy. One misconception is that people will respond to positive feedback by demanding tangible evidence of appreciation.

"I've called you all here today for this meeting because I need a hug."

FIGURE 10.2	Congratulatory Letter Reinforcing Desirable Behavior

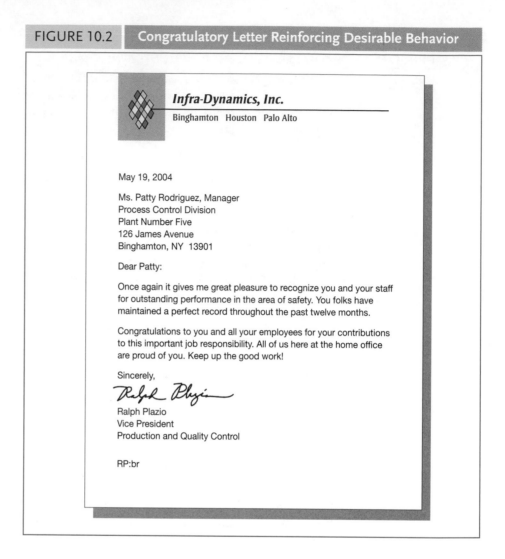

Infra-Dynamics, Inc.

Binghamton Houston Palo Alto

May 19, 2004

Ms. Patty Rodriguez, Manager
Process Control Division
Plant Number Five
126 James Avenue
Binghamton, NY 13901

Dear Patty:

Once again it gives me great pleasure to recognize you and your staff
for outstanding performance in the area of safety. You folks have
maintained a perfect record throughout the past twelve months.

Congratulations to you and all your employees for your contributions
to this important job responsibility. All of us here at the home office
are proud of you. Keep up the good work!

Sincerely,

Ralph Plazio
Vice President
Production and Quality Control

RP:br

"Tell people they are doing a good job and they will ask for a raise" seems to be the attitude of some managers. Actually, just the opposite response will surface more often than not. In the absence of intangible rewards (such as praise), workers may demand greater tangible rewards.

A few managers seem to feel they will lose some of their power or control if they praise workers. Yet if managers rely on power alone to get the job done, any success they achieve will no doubt be short-lived. When employees are doing a good job, why not reinforce that behavior with a little praise or a thank-you or congratulatory letter, like the one in Figure 10.2?

● The "Too Busy" Syndrome

Ken Blanchard, noted author and consultant, says, "We're often too busy or too stressed to remember that the recognition we crave, others crave as well."[12] When you are under a great deal of pressure to get your work done, and you

TABLE 10.1	One-Minute Praisings

The one-minute praising works well, say authors Kenneth Blanchard and Spencer Johnson, when you

1. Tell people up front that you are going to let them know how they are doing.
2. Praise people immediately.
3. Tell them what they did right—be specific.
4. Tell them how good you feel about what they did right and how it helps the organization and others who work there.
5. Stop for a moment of silence to let them feel how good you feel.
6. Encourage them to do more of the same.
7. Shake hands or touch people in a way that makes it clear that you support their success in the organization.

Source: The One Minute Manager by Kenneth Blanchard, Ph.D., and Spencer Johnson, M.D. Copyright © 1981, 1982 by the Blanchard Family Partnership and Candle Communications Corporation, Inc. Reprinted by permission of HarperCollins Publishers, Inc.

are struggling to achieve some degree of work/life balance, it's easy to postpone sending a thank-you note or contacting someone simply for the purpose of saying, "Thank you."

The key to solving this problem is planning. A consciously planned positive reinforcement program will ensure that recognition for work well done is not overlooked. One approach might be to set aside a few minutes each day to work on performance feedback and positive reinforcement activities. In *The One Minute Manager,* a book that has sold more than eleven million copies, the authors point out that positive feedback need not take long. They suggest using the simple plan that is outlined in Table 10.1.

Failing to Identify Commendable Actions

There are numerous opportunities to recognize the people you work with. By exercising just a little creativity, you can discover many actions that deserve to be commended.

Assume you are the manager of a large auto dealership. One of the key people within your organization is the service manager. This person schedules work to be performed on customers' cars, handles customer complaints, supervises the technicians, and performs a host of other duties. If you want to give your service manager performance feedback and positive recognition, what types of behavior can you praise? Table 10.2 (on p. 246) lists some examples.

Not Knowing What to Say or Do

Bob Nelson, author of *1001 Ways to Reward Employees,* reminds us that we can provide encouragement, praise, recognition, and rewards in a variety of ways. He encourages us to use thoughtful, personal kinds of recognition that signify

TABLE 10.2	Job Performance Behaviors to Be Reinforced

1. Performance Related to Interpersonal Relations
   a. Demonstrates empathy for customer needs and problems
   b. Is able to handle customer complaints effectively
   c. Is able to keep all employees well informed
   d. Cooperates with supervisory personnel in other departments
   e. Recognizes the accomplishments of employees
   f. Exhibits effective supervision of employees
2. Personal Characteristics
   a. Is honest in dealings with people throughout the organization
   b. Is punctual
   c. Does not violate policies and procedures
   d. Maintains emotional stability
   e. Maintains a neat appearance
   f. Is alert to new ways to do the job better
3. Management Skills
   a. Avoids waste in the use of supplies and materials
   b. Maintains accurate records
   c. Spends time on short- and long-range planning
   d. Takes steps to prevent accidents
   e. Delegates authority and responsibility
   f. Maintains quality-control standards

true appreciation.[13] Many words and phrases can communicate approval. Here are several examples (see also Table 10.3):

- "Good thinking!"
- "Excellent idea."
- "Thank you."
- "Keep up the good work."

TABLE 10.3	Six Phrases That Can Enrich Your Life

Six Phrases*

The following six phrases can be used every day to enrich your life and the lives of other people:

"I'm wrong."

"I'm sorry."

"I need you."

"Thank you."

"I'm proud of you."

"I love you."

*From a presentation by Rich DeVos, cofounder of Amway Corporation.

Source: "Rich DeVos Remarks—Delta Pi Epsilon Distinguished Lecturer," *Delta Pi Epsilon Journal* (Fall 1995), pp. 221–223.

Of course, you can express appreciation without using verbal communication. Nonverbal expressions of approval include:

- Making eye contact
- Nodding agreement
- Patting on the back
- Signaling okay with thumbs up
- Smiling
- Giving a firm handshake

And you can give recognition to others through some type of action. Here are some activities that show approval:

- Sending an employee to a workshop or seminar that covers a topic he or she is interested in

- Asking for advice

- Asking someone to demonstrate the correct performance or procedure for others

- Displaying another person's work, or discussing another person's ideas

- Recognizing someone's work at a staff meeting

It should not be surprising that some people view praise or recognition with some degree of apprehension. This is especially true in a work environment where the level of trust is low. Positive reinforcement must be sincere. Tim Sanders, one of America's most compassionate business leaders, says, "People hold you in the highest esteem when they realize you have no expectations that you will receive anything in return for what you are willing to give."[14]

Rewarding Individual and Team Performance

In recent years we have seen expanded use of positive reinforcement strategies in the workplace. In the past we viewed positive reinforcement as the responsibility of supervisors and managers. This view was much too narrow. As shown in Figure 10.3, everyone in the organization has opportunities to recognize the accomplishments of others. Persons in supervisory and

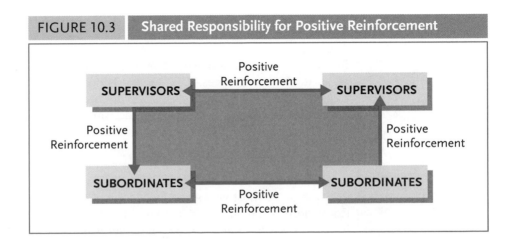

FIGURE 10.3 Shared Responsibility for Positive Reinforcement

Effective training can be a powerful confirmation behavior in the workplace. A well-designed training program sends the message "You are important and we want you to achieve success." This supervisor is helping a new employee learn the operation of the store's cash register system.

management positions can benefit from positive reinforcement initiated by subordinates.

Employees can also be encouraged to recognize the accomplishments of coworkers. In some cases, praise from a respected colleague is more important than praise from the boss. This is especially true when employees work together on a team.

The concept of teamwork and the growing popularity of various types of teams are changing the way companies structure their reward systems. If a work force is reorganized into self-directed work teams (discussed in Chapter 12), it makes sense to consider various types of team recognition plans. Such plans often emphasize the recognition of group performance rather than the recognition of individual performance.

● Incentive Programs

Every year organizations spend billions of dollars for incentives and awards given to their employees. This money is spent on color TVs, vacation trips, rings, plaques, pins, certificates, stock options, merit pay, cash bonuses, and a host of other items. An **incentive program** is a planned activity designed to motivate employees to achieve an organizational objective.[15] The objective may be increasing quality, improving sales, ensuring safety, decreasing absenteeism, fostering teamwork, rewarding participation in wellness programs, or improving customer service.

One of the most widespread developments in recent years has been the introduction of innovative incentive plans that reward increased productivity, improved quality, improved customer service, lower operating costs, or some

TABLE 10.4	Common Incentive Programs Involving Cash Payments
Type of Program	**Description**
Gain sharing	Managers and employees develop methods of increasing productivity, improving quality, and/or cutting costs. When a unit betters a predetermined performance objective, the resulting financial gains are divided according to a formula.
Profit sharing	Each employee receives a share of the company's profits, paid in cash or put in a retirement fund.
Production incentives	Employees receive payments based on how well they perform in relation to established standards. In a factory setting, for example, the rewards are often based on piecework. For each acceptable piece they produce, workers receive a specific payment.
Pay for knowledge	Workers are paid for the skills they master or tasks they perform. This plan is often used by companies that want employees to be able to perform more than one job.
Suggestion program	Employees who suggest ways to improve company operations receive a monetary award. The amount of the award is based on the estimated value of resulting increases in efficiency or cost cutting.

combination of these factors. These plans include cash and noncash awards. The most common noncash awards include merchandise, travel opportunities, and recognition in the form of a plaque, trophy, pin, or letter of commendation. Noncash awards offer some advantages over cash awards, particularly "memory value." A weekend at a luxury hotel, valued at $500, is likely to make a more lasting impression on the recipient than a $500 cash bonus. Noncash awards also have "trophy value." A high-quality gold pen or leather attaché case can be displayed and admired like a trophy.[16] Despite these advantages, many companies find that cash awards are needed to get employees to exert continuous effort. Table 10.4 provides a brief description of common incentive programs involving cash payments.

● Criticisms of Incentive Programs

There is no firm basis for the assumption that paying people more will encourage them to do better work or even, in the long run, more work.

Although the vast majority of U.S. companies use some type of incentive program based on cash or noncash rewards, the practice is not without its critics. One of the foremost critics of incentive programs is Alfie Kohn, author of *No Contest: The Case Against Competition* and *Punished by Rewards: The Trouble with Gold Stars, Incentive Plans, A's, Praise, and Other Bribes*. Kohn states that reward systems often fail for these reasons:

1. *Pay is not an effective motivator.* Citing research by Frederick Herzberg and others, Kohn argues, "There is no firm basis for the assumption that paying people more will encourage them to do better work or even, in the long run, more work."[17]

Wretched Excess?

Some employers are using expensive incentives such as automobiles and vacations in exotic places. NovaSoft Information Technology, a software consulting firm, has been giving Mercedes-Benz convertibles to star performers. During a two-year period, the company gave away sixteen of these cars. Peter Bruno, working 12-hour days, won a car after signing up fifty-two new customers. Neil Bhaskar, CEO of NovaSoft, is now raising the bar. Star performers will get the car, a Rolex watch, and some cash.

2. *Rewards can punish.* Employees may view the reward as a form of manipulation: "Do this and you will get that." Kohn further notes that, in the mind of the employee, failing to receive a reward one has expected is indistinguishable from being punished.[18]

3. *Rewards can damage relationships.* A reward system that forces people to compete for awards or recognition may undermine cooperation and teamwork. In addition to damaged interpersonal relationships, the reward plan may result in loss of self-esteem. Kohn says, "For each person who wins, there are many others who carry with them the feeling of having lost."[19]

4. *Rewards may mask real problems.* In some cases incentives treat the symptom, not the problem.[20] For example, a firm that gives merchandise awards or cash incentives may reduce absenteeism but fail to cure the real problem— which could be poor working conditions or poor supervision.

Although these criticisms have a great deal of merit, the fact remains that large numbers of organizations have achieved positive results with carefully developed incentive programs. It is possible to design programs that will have long-range benefits for both the organization and the individual employee. A well-designed program gives employees a specific, achievable goal and an adequate reward for reaching it. Also, incentive programs structured with employee input usually work best.[21]

● Reexamining Our Ideas About Productivity

We need to continuously reexamine our ideas about what actions and events increase employee productivity. Many firms take the position that if employees work more hours, they will be more productive. Therefore, overtime pay is used to reward some employees who work extra hours. Critics of this approach say that employees perform optimally for six or seven hours, but then the fatigue factor surfaces. Critics of overtime (voluntary and required) also point out the need for employees to have a life outside work.[22]

Will the employee who is rewarded for working faster be more productive? Critics of this approach note that slower, intuitive thinking is often more effective in solving problems. Also, they note that a greater number of complex, creative ideas result from a slower thought process.[23]

The idea that pay is the primary motivator for productivity is being challenged. Many research studies indicate that pay is not the primary factor in productivity. Looking into the future, we can anticipate that the value workers place on time versus money will shift in favor of time.[24]

● The Critical Importance of Environment

Positive energy flourishes in a supportive environment. Within the organization, there should be respect for each person, regardless of job title, duties performed, or earnings. The prevailing climate within the organization should also be positive. People must feel good about the organization, its leadership, and other employees. Positive energy comes naturally in a positive work environment. But positive energy will almost never flourish in a negative work environment.

■ Summary

business.college.hmco.com/students

ACE
Self-tests

Positive and negative energy can have a major influence on employee morale and productivity. We discussed the importance of encouragement, positive feedback, and various types of positive reinforcement.

People usually feel good when their accomplishments are recognized and become upset when they are ignored. Positive reinforcement, when used correctly to reward accomplishments, is a powerful motivator. Everyone needs to receive personal recognition and to feel appreciated.

Although many studies indicate that recognition is an important employee reward preference, often ranked higher than monetary rewards and job security, many people seem unable or unwilling to reward a job well done. Confirmation behaviors should be used in organizational settings more often. Praise, simple courtesy, active listening, written thank-you notes, incentives, and awards represent some of the ways we can instill positive energy.

Preoccupation with self is a major obstacle to providing reinforcement to others. Self-centered persons are likely to overlook the accomplishments of other people. Some people say a busy schedule does not allow time to give recognition to others. These and other barriers tend to minimize the use of positive reinforcement.

Common incentive programs were described, and criticism of incentive programs was discussed. Some of the most common incentive programs involving cash payments are gain sharing, profit sharing, production incentives, pay for knowledge, and suggestion programs. Employee stock options have also been popular in recent years.

■ Career Corner

Q: Is "kissing up" to the boss an acceptable behavior today? I have heard that this practice can make a difference in today's competitive workplace.

A: Performance is what matters most, but it would be a mistake to disregard the impact of flattery on your boss. Complimenting your supervisor on how he or she conducted a business meeting or solved a major problem may enhance your career. Employees with good people skills—which include building rapport with the boss—are the ones most likely to advance. The primary rule to follow when praising your boss is *Don't fake it*. Don't give a compliment unless you genuinely believe it is deserved. To offer endless, insincere flattery will backfire. And don't forget to praise the accomplishments of your coworkers. The people you work with can often help or hinder your move up the ladder.

Key Terms

energy	positive reinforcement
reinforcer	confirmation
physical stroke	narcissism
verbal strokes	incentive program

Review Questions

1. How does positive energy improve interpersonal relationships?

2. What evidence supports the contention that positive reinforcement is a major employee reward preference?

3. What are some of the common energy-draining forces in today's work environment?

4. How can a person's identity and self-worth be influenced by confirmation behaviors?

5. In a typical organizational setting, what confirmation behaviors might have a positive effect on employee performance?

6. What are some of the major criticisms of incentives and awards?

7. List and describe the most common incentive programs that involve the use of cash payments.

8. What are some common misconceptions about positive reinforcement?

9. What are some employee behaviors that might be recognized by a supervisor or manager? List at least five different performance-related behaviors.

10. Review the Total Person Insight by Malcolm Boyd. Do you agree? Explain your answer.

Application Exercises

1. Assume you are currently the owner of a small company with about one hundred employees. In recent years, rising premiums for employee health insurance have reduced profits. To encourage your employees to maintain a healthy lifestyle (which will reduce medical insurance claims), you are considering two options:

Option A: Add a $15 monthly surcharge to the health insurance premiums of employees who smoke. Establish healthy ranges for weight, cholesterol, and blood pressure, and assess small fines when employees fail to meet prescribed guidelines.

Option B: Provide a cash reward of $200 for any employee who quits smoking. Establish healthy ranges for weight, cholesterol, and blood pressure, and award small cash or merchandise incentives to employees who meet prescribed guidelines.

List the advantages and disadvantages of each proposal. Then select the proposal you feel will be most effective. Justify your choice.

2. Organizations are continually searching for ways to reward various employee behaviors. Pretend you are currently working at a retail clothing store and the manager asks you to help her design an incentive plan that would result in improved sales of clothing and accessories. She asks you to review and comment on the following options:

   a. Employee-of-the-month awards for highest sales. (A special plaque would be used to recognize each monthly winner.)

   b. Commission on sales. All employees would be given a 5 percent commission on all sales. Each salesperson would receive an hourly wage plus the commission.

   c. Time off. Employees who achieve sales goals established by management could earn up to four hours of paid time off each week.

   d. Prizes. Employees who achieve weekly sales goals established by management would be eligible for prizes such as sports or theater tickets, dinner at a nice restaurant, gift certificates, or merchandise sold by the store.

   Rank these four options by assigning "1" to your first choice, "2" to your second choice, "3" to your third choice, and "4" to your fourth choice. Provide a written rationale for your first choice.

3. The authors of *Random Acts of Kindness* tell us that the little things we do for others can have big payoffs. These acts give us an outward focus that helps us move away from self-preoccupation. Plan and initiate at least two acts of kindness during the next week, and then reflect on the experience. What impact did the act have on the other person? How did you feel about this experience?

Internet Exercise

Organizations spend billions of dollars on incentives and awards designed to motivate employees to achieve a specific objective. The Internet provides information on this topic. Using your search engine, type in the following keywords: *incentive programs, production incentives,* and *employee suggestion programs.* Review the resources (such as books, articles, and training programs) that are available, paying special attention to incentive programs that would appeal to you as a worker. Describe resources you would recommend to someone who would like to develop an effective incentive program. Also, visit the Society of Incentive and Travel Executives webpage (*www.SITE-intl.org*) for additional information. Prepare a written summary of your findings.

Case 10.1   Incentives: The Good, the Bad, and the Ugly

Frequent recognition of accomplishments ranks high as a worker preference in most industries. Thus recognition in the form of incentives can be an effective motivator. The Society of Incentive and Travel Executives has conducted research to determine the relationship among incentives, motivation, and performance in the workplace. The findings indicate that incentive programs aimed at individuals increased performance 27 percent and incentive programs aimed at teams increased performance by 45 percent.

Banks constitute one industry that has used incentives to achieve a variety of goals. Most of these programs are designed to improve customer service. Bank of America gives employees on-the-spot awards, such as small cash bonuses and gift certificates, when managers see them providing excellent service to customers. Bank One rewards good customer service with small cash bonuses and gives employees certificates and plaques they can display in their offices.

As health insurance costs increase, organizations are searching for better ways to help employees get healthy and stay healthy. L.L. Bean has given cash awards to employees whose families take prenatal classes, and Quad/Graphics printing company has given cash awards to employees who quit smoking. Other companies have given cash awards to families that adopt an exercise program, lower their cholesterol, or wear seat belts.

Of course, there is a dark side to some incentive programs. Competition for an award can sometimes undermine cooperation and teamwork. In some cases employees will abandon good work practices in order to "win" a contest. In the field of personal selling, for example, a salesperson might attempt to sell a product that the customer really does not need. And sometimes a reward will mask real problems. Cash rewards to reduce absenteeism may fail to solve the real problem, which is poor working conditions.

The ugly side of incentives surfaced during recent corporate scandals when stock options became the symbol of a compensation system gone haywire. Employees were given the opportunity to buy stock at a low price with the option to sell it later at a higher price. However, a parade of big companies, such as Enron, Xerox, Computer Associates, and Adelphia Communications, improperly inflated earnings (cooked the books) to achieve an increase in their stock price. Greed motivated many executives to engage in these unethical practices.[25]

■ Questions

1. Is money the best incentive to use when you want to encourage an employee to give better customer service or adopt a healthy habit? What other types of incentives might be just as effective or more effective?

2. Should employees at various levels of the organization be involved in the design and implementation of incentive programs?

3. Many of America's largest corporations are allocating shares to employee stock options, and experts expect this trend to continue. Do you support this practice? Would you like to work for a company that offers its employees stock options?

Case 10.2   Improving Quality with Suggestions

Employee suggestion programs are making a comeback. According to the Employee Involvement Association, over six thousand companies use suggestion programs, and these businesses save an average of $6,224 for each implemented suggestion. Suggestion programs offer the workers an easy way to submit whatever ideas they think up. The rationale is that employees are in the best position to identify something that can be improved. A well-designed system encourages the workers to think like managers. Many companies reward suggestions that are implemented with cash or with points that employees can exchange for gifts.

In most cases, the wooden suggestion box has been replaced with a high-tech system. Companies are now using e-mail and toll-free telephone numbers to solicit ideas. Charles Martin, a professor at Wichita State University in Kansas, says some companies that tried quality circles and total quality management (TQM) programs are now using suggestion programs. Employees see a direct link between a suggestion and the reward.

The United States Air Force provides an example of a successful employee suggestion system. The Innovative Development through Employee Awareness (IDEA) program replaced an old paper-driven system that was too complex. In recent years the Air Force has given out an average of $3 million a year for suggestions that have saved the service an average of about $2.2 million a year.[26]

■ Questions

1. Some companies have experimented with employee suggestion programs and have had great success. Other companies, however, say they receive very few ideas from employees. What factors might contribute to a successful employee suggestion program?

2. Would a well-designed suggestion system generate positive energy? Explain.

3. Some companies are seeking suggestions from their customers. Do you support this practice? Explain your answer.

11

DEVELOPING
A PROFESSIONAL
PRESENCE

Chapter Preview

After studying this chapter, you will be able to

- Explain the importance of professional presence.

- Discuss the factors that contribute to a favorable first impression.

- Define *image* and describe the factors that form the image you project to others.

- List and discuss factors that influence your choice of clothing for work.

- Understand how manners contribute to improved interpersonal relations in the workplace.

What do Craftsman tools, Lexus automobiles, and Starbucks coffee have in common? Each is a *brand* that receives the highest quality ratings and consistently lives up to expectations. A brand symbolizes a company's promise to deliver a good product to customers. In the age of mass marketing, brands can differentiate products and services.[1]

Why introduce the concept of brands in a book devoted to human relations? Because branding can play a crucial role in your career as well. Just like one sells a product, you can sell yourself. If you think you have a lot to offer, you will develop a unique way of "packaging" yourself. The authors of *Be Your Own Brand: A Breakthrough Formula for Standing Out from the Crowd* say branding can have a significant impact on your relationships, career, and life.[2] Developing a strong personal brand involves all the little ways in which you express your feelings about yourself and present yourself to others.

Dave Olsen, chief coffee guru with Starbucks, was once asked to describe the most important factor contributing to the company's success. Was it the coffee? The employees working behind the counter? The design of the stores? Olsen thought about the question for a while and then said, "Everything matters." When it comes to developing your own personal brand, everything matters.[3]

Professional Presence—An Introduction

There are many personal and professional benefits to be gained from a study of the concepts in this chapter. You will acquire new insights regarding ways to communicate positive impressions during job interviews, business contacts, and social contacts made away from work. You will also learn how to shape an image that will help you achieve your fullest potential in the career of your choice. Image is a major component of brand development.

This is not a chapter about ways to make positive impressions with superficial behavior and quick-fix techniques. We do not discuss the "power look" or the "power lunch." The material in this chapter will not help you become a more entertaining conversationalist or win new customers by pretending to be interested in their hobbies or families. Stephen Covey, author of *The 7 Habits of Highly Effective People,* says that the ability to build effective, long-term relationships is based on character strength, not quick-fix techniques. He notes that outward attitude and behavior changes do very little good in the long run *unless* they are based on solid principles governing human effectiveness. These principles include service (making a contribution), integrity and honesty (which serve as a foundation of trust), human dignity (every person has worth), and fairness.[4]

Few people can fake a sincere greeting or a caring attitude. If you really do not care about the other person's problem, that individual will probably sense your indifference. Your true feelings will be difficult to hide.

● Professional Presence—A Definition

We are indebted to Susan Bixler, president of Professional Image, Inc., and author of *Professional Presence,* for giving us a better understanding of what it means to possess professional presence. **Professional presence** is a dynamic blend of poise, self-confidence, control, and style that empowers us to be able to command respect in any situation.[5] Once acquired, it permits us to project a confidence that others can quickly perceive the first time they meet us. Obviously, to *project* this confidence, you need to *feel* confident.

Bixler points out that, in many cases, the credentials we present during a job interview or when we are being considered for a promotion are not very different from those of other persons being considered. It is our professional presence that permits us to rise above the crowd. Debra Benton, a career consultant, says, "Any boss with a choice of two people with equal qualifications will choose the one with style as well as substance."[6]

● The Importance of Making a Good First Impression

As organizations experience increased competition for clients, patients, or customers, they are giving new attention to the old adage "First impressions are lasting ones." Research indicates that initial impressions do indeed tend to linger. Therefore, a positive first impression can be thought of as the first step in building a long-term relationship.

Of course, it is not just first contacts with clients, patients, customers, and others that are important. Positive impressions should be the objective of every contact. Many organizations have learned that in the age of information, high tech without high touch is not a winning formula.

The Primacy Effect The development of professional presence begins with a full appreciation of the power of first impressions. The tendency to form and retain impressions quickly at the time of an initial meeting illustrates what social psychologists call a **primacy effect** in the way people perceive one another. The general principle is that initial information tends to carry more weight than information received later. First impressions establish the mental framework within which a person is viewed, and information acquired later is often ignored or reinterpreted to coincide with this framework.[7]

The development of professional presence begins with a full appreciation of the power of first impressions.

During his first term as president, Bill Clinton often appeared in brief jogging shorts and garish print shirts; his suits were loose fitting and in need of tailoring; and his military salute was viewed as halfhearted by many observers. Some observers felt that his appearance communicated a lack of respect for the office of president. Toby Fischer-Mirkin, fashion consultant and author of *Dress Code*, said the president did not communicate a very commanding image.[8] Early in his first term, Clinton appeared vulnerable to many people, and this image had a negative influence on his popularity. Later in his first term, he communicated a more "presidential" image and went on to be reelected to a second term. He discovered, or perhaps rediscovered, the power of the primacy effect.

The First Few Seconds When two people meet, their potential for building a relationship can be affected by many factors. Within a few moments, one person or the other may feel threatened, offended, or bored. Roger Ailes, communica-

HUMAN RELATIONS IN ACTION

Director of First Impressions

Cathleen Jivoin is Director of First Impressions at Teltronics, a company based in Sarasota, Florida. She has held this title for six years and loves her work. Her primary responsibility is to establish the right mood for everyone who visits the company. Jivoin says, "I see as many as thirty-five to forty people a day, and no one leaves unhappy." Customers and vendors tell her that they enjoy doing business with people who care about them and their lives. Jivoin says the best way to make a good first impression is "Smile! Then smile again."

tion adviser to three presidents and consultant to numerous *Fortune* 500 executives, says people begin forming an opinion of us in a matter of seconds. He believes that most people assess the other person very quickly and then settle on a general perception of that individual. Ailes says it is very difficult for us to reverse that first impression.[9] The following examples support his view of first impressions.

■ Paula rushed into a restaurant for a quick lunch—she had to get back to her office for a 1:30 P.M. appointment. At the entrance of the main dining area was a sign reading "Please Wait to Be Seated." A few feet away, the hostess was discussing a popular movie with one of the waitresses. The hostess made eye contact with Paula but continued to visit with the waitress.

■ When Sandy and Mike entered the showroom of a Mercedes-Benz dealer, they were approached by a salesperson wearing sport slacks (khaki color), a blue knit polo shirt (short sleeved), and casual gum-soled shoes. The salesperson smiled and said, "Are you looking or buying?"

In each of these examples, a negative first impression was created in a matter of seconds. The anxiety level of the restaurant customer increased because she was forced to wait while two employees talked about a personal matter.

THINKING / LEARNING STARTERS

To test the practical application of Roger Ailes's guideline in a real-life setting, examine it in the context of your past experiences. Review the following questions and then answer each with yes or no.

1. Have you ever entered a restaurant, hotel, or auto dealership and experienced an immediate feeling of being welcome after your first contact with an employee?

2. Have you ever met someone who immediately communicated to you the impression that he or she could be trusted and was interested in your welfare?

3. Have you ever placed a telephone call and known instinctively within seconds that the person did not welcome your call?

She concluded that they were inconsiderate. And the potential customers made judgments about the automobile salesperson based solely on his appearance and casual greeting. Unfortunately, these employees were probably not fully aware of the impression they communicated to customers.

TOTAL	**SUSAN BIXLER AND NANCY NIX-RICE**
PERSON	AUTHORS, *THE NEW PROFESSIONAL IMAGE*
INSIGHT	"Books are judged by their covers, houses are appraised by their curb appeal, and people are initially evaluated on how they choose to dress and behave. In a perfect world this is not fair, moral, or just. What's inside should count a great deal more. And eventually it usually does, but not right away. In the meantime, a lot of opportunities can be lost."

Assumptions Versus Facts   The impression you form of another person during the initial contact is made up of both assumptions and facts. Most people tend to rely more heavily on **assumptions** during the initial meeting. If a job applicant sits slumped in the chair, head bowed and shoulders slack, you might assume the person is not very interested in the position. If the postal clerk fails to make eye contact during the transaction and does not express appreciation for your purchase, you may assume this person treats everyone with indifference. Needless to say, the impression you form of another person during the initial contact can be misleading. The briefer the encounter with a new acquaintance, the greater the chance that misinformation will enter into your perception of the other person. The authors of a popular book on first impressions state that "depending on assumptions is a one-way ticket to big surprises and perhaps disappointments."[10] Nevertheless, we continue to assume many things during first encounters.

● Cultural Influence

Cultural influences, often formed during the early years of our life, lead us to have impressions of some people even before we meet them. People often develop stereotypes of entire groups. Although differences between cultures are often subtle, they can lead to uncomfortable situations. We need to realize that the Korean shopkeeper is being polite, not hostile, when he puts change on the counter and not in your hand. Some Asian students do not speak up in class out of respect for the teacher, not boredom.[11]

Many American companies are attempting to create a new kind of workplace where cultural and ethnic differences are treated as assets, not annoyances. Yet some employees feel pressure to conform to dress and grooming standards that their employer considers "mainstream." When LaToya Rivers, a black college student, applied for a position at the Boston Harbor Hotel, she asked whether braids were allowed. She was told, "Yes, as long as they are neat and professional in appearance." Once hired, the policy seemed to change. A manager told her to restyle her braided hair or leave.[12] Negative attitudes toward culturally inspired hairstyles are much less common today than in the past.

Negative attitudes toward ethnic hairstyles are less common today, but they do surface in the workplace. These views often stem from misconceptions about what the hairstyle represents. Terry Glover (left), associate editor for Playboy's website, and Cleo Wilson, a vice president at Playboy, prefer natural hairstyles. Both wear twists in their hair.

Norine Dresser, author of *Multiculture Manners—New Rules of Etiquette for a Changing Society,* notes that it is becoming more difficult for organizations to develop policies that do not offend one ethnic group or another. She argues that it is the collective duty of the mainstream to learn the customs and practices of established minority groups as well as the ways of the latest arrivals from other countries.[13]

The Image You Project

Image is a term used to describe how other people feel about you. In every business or social setting, your behaviors and appearance communicate a mental picture that others observe and remember. This picture determines how they react to you.

Think of image as a tool that can reveal your inherent qualities, your competence, your attitude, and your leadership potential. If you wish to communicate your professional capabilities and create your own brand, begin by scrutinizing your attitudes; only then can you invest the time and energy needed to refine and enhance your personal image.

In many respects, the image you project is very much like a picture puzzle, as illustrated in Figure 11.1 (on p. 262). It is formed by a variety of factors, including manners, self-confidence, voice quality, versatility (see Chapter 3), integrity (see Chapter 5), entrance and carriage, facial expression, surface language, competence, positive attitude, and handshake. Each of these image-shaping components is under your control, though some are harder to develop than others. As you reflect on the image you want to project, remember that a strong personal brand is built from the inside out.

FIGURE 11.1	Major Factors That Form Your Image

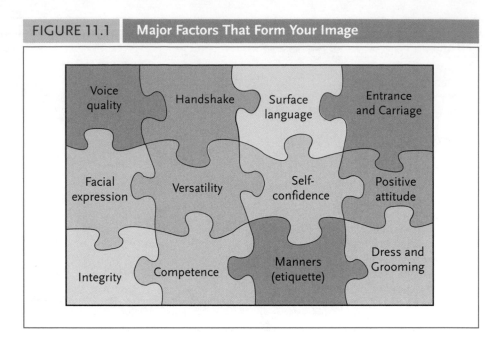

Surface Language

As noted earlier, we base opinions about other people on both facts and as-sumptions. Unfortunately, assumptions often carry a great deal of weight. Many of the assumptions we develop regarding other people are based on **sur-face language,** a pattern of immediate impressions conveyed by what we *see*—in other words, by appearance. The clothing you wear, your hairstyle, the fra-grances you use, and the jewelry you display all combine to make a statement about you to others. (We are not mind readers.)

According to many writers familiar with image formation, clothing is par-ticularly important. Although a more relaxed dress code has evolved in recent years, people judge your appearance long before they judge your talents. It would be a mistake not to take your career wardrobe seriously. Bixler suggests that those making career wardrobe decisions should keep in mind that three things haven't changed:[14]

> *A good rule to follow is to dress for the job you want, not the job you have.*

1. *If you want the job, you have to look the part.* Establish per-sonal dress and grooming standards appropriate for the organization where you wish to work. Before you apply for a job, try to find out what the workers there are wearing. If in doubt, dress conservatively. Casual dress can convey indifference.

2. *If you want the promotion, you have to look promotable.* A good rule to fol-low is to dress for the job you want, not the job you have. If you are cur-rently a bank teller and want to become a branch manager, identify the successful branch managers and emulate their manner of dress.

3. *If you want respect, you have to dress as well as or better than your industry standards.* One would expect to find conservative dress standards in banking, insurance, accounting, and law, and more casual dress standards in advertising, sports entertainment, and agriculture. Spend time researching the dress and grooming standards in the industry in which you hope to find a job.

THINKING / LEARNING STARTER

Do you recall a teacher, coworker, or supervisor whose surface language impressed you—either positively or negatively? What specific elements (such as dress or hairstyle) were evident in this person's surface language? What type of image do you think he or she was trying to project?

● Selecting Your Career Apparel

Millions of American workers wear a uniform especially designed for a particular job. The judges on the U.S. Supreme Court and the technicians at the local Midas Muffler and Brake shop have one thing in common—both groups wear a special uniform to work. Companies that have initiated extensive career apparel programs rely on uniforms to project an image of consistent quality, good service, and uniqueness.

Enterprise Rent-A-Car, the nation's largest recruiter of college students, requires its 52,000 workers to follow conservative dress and grooming policies. Men, for example, follow twenty-six rules that include no beards (unless medically necessary) and dress shirts with coordinated ties. Female employees follow thirty dress code guidelines, including one for skirt length (skirts must not

Special-design uniforms, like the one worn by this American Airlines flight attendant, represent a common form of career apparel. Organizations frequently rely on uniforms to project an image of consistent quality, good service, and uniqueness.

be shorter than two inches above the knee) and one for mandatory stockings. Why does Enterprise choreograph how its employees look? The company maintains that its personal appearance and grooming standards give it a marketing advantage.[15]

The uniforms worn by United Parcel Service employees, United Airlines reservation clerks, and the employees at your local restaurant might be classified as special-design **career apparel.** In addition to special-design uniforms, there is another type of career apparel, somewhat less predictable, worn by large numbers of people in the labor force. Here are some examples:

- A female lawyer representing a prestigious firm would be appropriately dressed in a gray or blue skirted suit. A dress with a suit jacket would also be acceptable. She should avoid clothing in brash colors or casual styles that might reduce her credibility.

- A male bank loan officer would be appropriately dressed in a tailored gray or blue suit, white shirt, and tie. This same person dressed in a colorful blazer, sport shirt, and plaid slacks would be seen as too casual in most bank settings.

- A technician employed by an auto dealership that sells new cars would be appropriately dressed in matching gray, tan, or blue shirt and pants. The technician would be inappropriately dressed in jeans and a T-shirt.

Many organizations seek advice about career apparel from image consultants. One source of image consultants is the Association of Image Consultants International.

● Wardrobe Engineering

The term **wardrobe engineering** was first used by John Molloy, author of *Dress for Success*, to describe how clothing and accessories can be used to create a certain image. This concept was later refined by several other noted image consultants in hundreds of books and articles on dress and grooming. Although these authors are not in complete agreement on every aspect of dress, they do agree on the four basic points presented in Table 11.1. Use this information as a guide. Although you should consider the dress and grooming standards of others in your field, don't give in to blind conformity. As noted by one consultant, "Effective packaging is an individual matter based on the person's circumstances, age, weight, height, coloring, and objectives."[16]

THINKING / LEARNING STARTER
Assume you are planning to purchase (1) a life insurance policy, (2) a Lexus automobile, and (3) eyeglasses. What types of career apparel would you expect persons selling these products to wear? What grooming standards would you recommend?

TABLE 11.1	Factors Influencing Your Choice of Clothing for Work

Dress codes are undergoing changes, and this complicates the selection of clothing for work. Use the four factors described here for guidance.

1. *Products and services offered.* In some cases the organization's products and services more or less dictate a certain type of dress. For example, a receptionist employed by a well-established law firm is likely to wear clothing that is conservative, modest, and in good taste. These same dress standards would apply to a pharmaceutical sales representative who calls on medical doctors.

2. *Type of person served.* Research indicates that first impressions created by dress and grooming are greatly influenced by unconscious expectations. Throughout life we become acquainted with real estate salespeople, nurses, police officers, and others employed in a wide range of occupations. We form mental images of the apparel common to each of these occupations. When we encounter someone whose appearance does not conform to our past experiences, we often feel uncomfortable.

3. *Desired image projected by the organization.* Some companies establish dress codes that help shape the image they project to the public. Walt Disney Company, for example, maintains a strict dress and grooming code for all its theme-park employees. They are considered "cast members" and must adhere to dress and grooming standards that complement the image projected by Disney theme parks.

4. *Geographic region.* Dress in the South and Southwest tends to be more casual than dress in the Northeast. Climate is another factor that influences the clothing people wear at work.

● The Business Casual Look

The term **business casual** is used to describe the movement toward dress standards that emphasize greater comfort and individuality. Business casual is clothing that allows you to feel comfortable at work but looks neat and professional. It usually means slacks, khaki pants, collared long-sleeved shirts and blouses, and shoes with socks or hosiery. It usually does not include jeans, T-shirts, shorts, sneakers, or sandals.[17]

Some companies are relaxing dress codes and allowing workers to dress casually. Although no precise definition of business casual exists, most companies have developed a casual dress code. The following casual-dress guidelines are typical.

1. *Wear dressier business clothing when meeting with customers or clients.* You should avoid creating inconsistencies between your message and your appearance. Workers at ProVox Technologies Corporation, based in Roanoke, Virginia, keep company-designed ProVox shirts and khakis in the office for client visits.[18]

2. *Respect the boundary between work and leisure clothing.* Victoria's Secret has sold body-hugging spandex tube tops as workplace wear, and Brooks Brothers has used tieless male models with shirts unbuttoned to reveal curly chest hair. Both companies are trying to make it big in the business casual market.[19] Anne Fisher of *Fortune* magazine's "Ask Annie" career advice column says, "As a rule, people should avoid wearing anything that shows so much skin that it distracts other people from their work." It is probably not a coincidence that the dress-down trend has been accompanied by an increase in flirtatious behavior.[20]

3. *Wear clothing that is clean and neat and that fits well.* Casual dress codes tend to emphasize the importance of this principle.

Do not let "dress-down" influences rob you of common sense. You don't get a second chance to make a good first impression, so select your casual clothing with care. If you have to ask yourself, "Is this clothing acceptable?" you probably shouldn't wear it to work.

● Your Facial Expression

After your overall appearance, your face is the most visible part of you. Facial expressions are the cues most people rely on in initial interactions. They provide the clues by which others read your mood and personality.

Facial expressions are the cues most people rely on in initial interactions.

Studies conducted in nonverbal communication show that facial expressions strongly influence people's reactions to each other. The expression on your face can quickly trigger a positive or negative reaction from those you meet. How you rate in the "good-looks" department is not nearly as important as your ability to communicate positive impressions with a pleasant smile and eye contact.

If you want to identify the inner feelings of another person, watch the individual's facial expressions closely. A frown may tell you "something is wrong." A smile generally communicates "things are OK." Everyone has encountered a "look of surprise" or a "look that could kill." These facial expressions usually reflect inner emotions more accurately than words. The smile is the most recognizable signal in the world. People everywhere tend to trust a smiling face.[21]

● Your Entrance and Carriage

The way you enter someone's office or a business meeting can influence the image you project, says Susan Bixler. She notes that "your entrance and the way you carry yourself will set the stage for everything that comes afterward."[22] A nervous or apologetic entrance may ruin your chances of getting a job, closing a sale, or getting the raise you have earned. If you feel apprehensive, try not to let it show in your body language. Hold your head up, avoid slumping forward, and try to project self-assurance. To get off to the right start and make a favorable impression, follow these words of advice from Bixler: "The person who has confidence in himself or herself indicates this by a strong stride, a friendly smile, good posture, and a genuine sense of energy. This is a very effective way to set the stage for a productive meeting. When you ask for respect visually, you get it."[23] Bixler says the key to making a successful entrance is simply believing—and projecting—that you have a reason to be there and have something important to present or discuss.

● Your Voice

The tone of your voice, the rate of speed at which you speak (tempo), the volume of your speech, and your ability to pronounce words clearly (diction) contribute greatly to the meaning attached to your verbal messages. Voice is a vital tool at work, but it is seldom used to full potential. Barbara Tannenbaum, a faculty member at Brown University, says that in a typical conversation, about 38 percent of our understanding comes from what we hear. It's much higher—70 percent—for telephone messages.[24]

A conscious effort to improve your voice can play an important role in your career. You can stop speaking in a monotone, talking too fast or too slow, or mumbling your words. You can even change your accent.

Although there is no ideal voice for all business contacts, your voice should reflect at least these four qualities: confidence, enthusiasm, optimism, and sincerity. Above all, try to avoid a speech pattern that is dull and colorless.

African Americans, Hispanics, Asians, Native Americans, and recent immigrants to America often face special challenges in verbal communication. New arrivals may have a unique accent because the phonetic habits of their native language are carried over to their new language. In addition, many people born and raised in America have a dialect that is unique. At age 22, Mike White learned that his east Tennessee accent and colorful backwoods syntax created problems at work. He admits that his southern drawl was a "turnoff" to many of the image-conscious people he worked with. One day his sales manager asked him if he had racquetball equipment, and White replied "Yeah, I brung it." Fortunately, White's supervisor had the courage to correct his grammatical problems and to help him communicate with greater clarity. Today, Mike White is CEO of a successful company and a regular speaker at trade shows.[25]

● Your Handshake

When two people first meet, a handshake is usually the only physical contact between them. A handshake is a friendly and professional way to greet someone or to take leave, regardless of gender. The handshake can communicate warmth, genuine concern for the other person, and strength. It can also communicate aloofness, indifference, and weakness. The message you send the other party through your handshake depends on a combination of the following factors:

1. *Degree of firmness.* Generally speaking, a firm (but not viselike) grip communicates a caring attitude, whereas a weak grip communicates indifference.

2. *Degree of dryness of hands.* A moist, clammy palm is unpleasant to feel and can communicate the impression that you are nervous. People who have this problem often remove the moisture with a clean handkerchief.

3. *Duration of grip.* There are no specific guidelines for the ideal duration of a grip. Nevertheless, by extending the handshake just a little, you can often communicate a greater degree of interest in and concern for the other person.

4. *Depth of interlock.* A full, deep grip is more likely to convey friendship to the other person.

5. *Eye contact during handshake.* Visual communication can increase the positive impact of your handshake. Maintaining eye contact throughout the handshaking process is important when two people greet each other.[26]

Most individuals have shaken hands with hundreds of people but have little idea whether they are creating positive or negative impressions. It is a good idea to obtain this information from those coworkers or friends who are willing to provide you with candid feedback. Like all other human relations skills, the handshake can be improved with practice.

● Etiquette for a Changing World

Why are so many etiquette guides crowding bookstore shelves? And why are many organizations hiring consultants to conduct classes on etiquette guidelines? Well, one reason is that we need advice on how to avoid annoying other people and what to do if they annoy us. In today's fast-paced, often tense, work environment, we have to work a little harder to maintain a climate of fairness, kindness, and mutual respect.[27]

Etiquette (sometimes called *manners* or *protocol*) is a set of traditions based on kindness, efficiency, and logic.[28] Letitia Baldrige, author and etiquette consultant, says, "It's consideration and kindness and thinking about somebody other than oneself."[29] Sometimes we need new etiquette guidelines to deal with our changing world. Today smoking at work is usually prohibited or restricted to a certain area. Meetings often begin with the announcement "Please silence your cell phones and beepers." And the nearly universal use of e-mail has spawned hundreds of articles on e-mail etiquette (see Chapter 2). A diverse work force has created many new challenges in the area of protocol.

Although it is not possible to do a complete review of the rules of etiquette, we will discuss those that are particularly important in an organizational setting.

Dining Etiquette   Business is frequently conducted at breakfast, lunch, or dinner, so be aware of your table manners. To illustrate decisions you might need to make during a business meal, let's eavesdrop on Tom Reed, a job can-

---

HUMAN RELATIONS IN ACTION | **Strategies for Building Global Relationships**

The authors of *Complete Business Etiquette Handbook* state that "The key to being successful in international business revolves around knowing where you've come from as well as where you are headed." Keep in mind these tips when hosting an international visitor or visiting another country.

■ Be respectful and non-judgmental about the cultural differences you encounter. Try to react positively to unusual experiences.

■ Understand your own viewpoint. International travel provides an opportunity to examine your own beliefs, values, and habits.

■ Be flexible and patient. If you are too rigid or set in your ways, international travel will be difficult.

■ Know enough about the etiquette in the country you plan to visit so you do not unwittingly offend its customs.

didate having a meal with several employees of the company he wants to work for. After introductions, the bread is passed to Tom. He places a roll on the small bread-and-butter plate to the right of his dinner plate. Soon, he picks up the roll, takes a bite, and returns it to the plate. Midway through the meal, Tom rises from his chair, places his napkin on the table, and says, "Excuse me; I need to make a potty run." So far, Tom has made four etiquette blunders: The bread-and-butter plate he used belongs to the person seated on his right; his own is to the left of his dinner plate. When eating a roll, he should break off one piece at a time and butter the piece as he is ready to eat it. The napkin should have been placed on his chair, indicating his plan to return. (When departing for good, leave it to the left of your plate.) And finally, the words *potty run* are too casual for a business meal. A simple statement such as, "Please excuse me; I'll be back in just a moment," would be adequate.

There are some additional table manners to keep in mind. Do not begin eating until the people around you have their plates. If you have not been served, however, encourage others to go ahead. To prevent awkward moments during the meal, avoid ordering food that is not easily controlled, such as ribs, spaghetti, chicken with bones, or lobster.

Meeting Etiquette   Business meetings should start and end on time. When you attend a meeting, arrive on time and don't feel obligated to comment on each item on the agenda. Yes, sometimes silence is golden. In most cases, you should not bring up a topic unless it is related to an agenda item. If you are in charge of the meeting, end it by summarizing key points, reviewing the decisions made, and recapping the responsibilities assigned to individuals during the meeting. Always start and end the meeting on a positive note.[30]

Cell Phone Etiquette   New technologies often bring new annoyances, and the cell phone is no exception. Cell phone contempt surfaces in offices, restaurants, houses of worship, and many other places. Cell phone etiquette is based on a few simple guidelines. First, it's not acceptable to use your cell phone at business meetings, in elevators, or at restaurants. If you receive a call at a restaurant, take the call outside the dining area. When making or receiving a call, talk in a normal speaking voice. Try to confine your calls to private areas; it's rude to inflict your conversation on people near you.[31] Finally, if a coworker or friend insists on "staying connected" at all times and you find this behavior annoying, confront the person. However, choose your words carefully. If a coworker takes a call at a meeting, for example, you might say, "When you answer your cell phone it makes the group feel that we don't have your full attention."[32]

> *Cell phone contempt surfaces in offices, restaurants, houses of worship, and many other places.*

Conversational Etiquette   When you establish new relationships, avoid calling people by their first name too soon. Never assume that work-related associates prefer to be addressed informally by their first names. Use titles of respect—Ms., Miss, Mrs., Mr., Professor, or Dr.—until the relationship is established. Too much familiarity will irritate some people. When the other person says, "Call me Ruth" or "Call me John," it is alright to begin using the person's first name.

"IF WE HAD HIS NUMBER, WE COULD CALL HIM AND PUT HIM ON HOLD."

©2001 WM. HOEST ENTERPRISES, INC.

A conversation that includes obscene language can create problems in the workplace. Although the rules about what constitutes profanity have changed over the years, inappropriate use of foul language in front of a customer, a client, or, in many cases, a coworker is a breach of etiquette. An obscenity implies lack of respect for your audience. Also, certain language taboos carry moral and spiritual significance in most cultures. Obscene language is often cited by persons who file sexual harassment charges.[33]

Networking Etiquette   Networking—making contact with people at meetings, social events, or other venues—is an effective job search method. Networking is also important to salespeople searching for prospects and to professionals (accountants, lawyers, consultants, etc.) who need to build a client base.

When you meet people at an event, tell them your name and what you do. Avoid talking negatively about any aspect of your current job or your life. In some cases you will need to make a date to call or meet with the new contact later. After the event, study your contacts and follow up.

Send a *written* thank-you note if someone has been helpful to you or generous with his or her time. You might also consider sending a newspaper or magazine article as an "information brief," since one goal of networking is information exchange.[34]

TOTAL	JUDITH MARTIN
PERSON	AUTHOR
INSIGHT	"In a society as ridden as ours with expensive status symbols, where every purchase is considered a social statement, there is no easier or cheaper way to distinguish oneself than by the practice of gentle manners."

We have given you a brief introduction to several areas of etiquette. This information will be extremely helpful as you develop a strong personal brand. Remember that good etiquette is based on consideration for the other person. If you genuinely respect other people, you will have an easier time developing your personal approach to business manners. You will probably also agree with most of the etiquette "rules" we have been discussing. Nancy Austin, coauthor of *A Passion for Excellence,* says, "Real manners—a keen interest in and a regard for somebody else, a certain kindness and at-ease quality that add real value—can't be faked or finessed."[35] Real manners come from the heart.

● Incivility—The Ultimate Career Killer

Civility in our society is under siege. In recent years we have witnessed an increase in coarse, rude, and obnoxious behavior. Unfortunately, some of the most outrageous behavior by athletes, coaches, politicians, and business leaders has been rewarded with wealth and influence.

As noted in Chapter 1, civility is the sum of the many sacrifices we are called upon to make for the sake of living together. At work, it may involve refilling the copier paper tray after using the machine or making a new pot of coffee after you take the last cup. It may mean turning down your radio so workers nearby are not disturbed or sending a thank-you note to someone who has helped you complete a difficult project. Small gestures, such as saying "Please" and "Thank you" or opening doors for others, make ourselves and others more content. Learning to discipline your passions so as to avoid obnoxious behavior will demonstrate also your maturity and self-control.

● Professional Presence at the Job Interview

Professional presence has special meaning when you are preparing for a job interview. In most cases you are competing against several other applicants, so you can't afford to make a mistake. A common mistake among job applicants is failure to acquire background information on the employer. Without this information, it's difficult to prepare questions to ask during the interview, and decisions about what to wear will be more difficult.

Keep in mind that regardless of the dress code of the organization, it's always appropriate to dress conservatively. If you arrive for an interview wearing torn jeans and a T-shirt, the person conducting the interview may think you are not serious about the job. The expectation of most employers is that the job applicant will be well groomed and dressed appropriately.

Professional presence has special meaning when you interview for a job. When you interview for a position, dress conservatively. Prior to the interview try to observe the people who work for the employer and then dress one step up in terms of professional appearance.

One of the most important objectives of a job interview is to communicate the image that you are someone who is conscientious, so be prepared. If possible, visit the place of business before your interview. Observe the people already working there; then dress one step up in terms of professional appearance. What's most important is that you show that you care enough to make a good impression.

■ Summary

business.college.hmco.com/students

Professional presence permits you to be perceived as self-assured and competent. These qualities are quickly perceived the first time someone meets you. People tend to form impressions of others quickly at the time they first meet them, and these first impressions tend to be preserved. In an organizational setting, the time interval for projecting a positive or negative first impression is often reduced to seconds. Positive impressions are important because they contribute to repeat business and customer referrals.

The impression you form of another person during the initial contact is made up of assumptions and facts. When meeting someone for the first time, people tend to rely heavily on assumptions. Many of your assumptions can be traced to early cultural influences. Assumptions are also based on perceptions of surface language—the pattern of immediate impressions conveyed by appearance. The clothing and jewelry you wear, your hairstyle, and the fragrances you use all combine to make a statement about you to others.

Image consultants contend that discrimination on the basis of appearance is a fact of life. Clothing is an important part of the image you communicate to others. Four factors tend to influence your choice of clothing for work: (1) the products or services offered by the organization, (2) the type of person served, (3) the desired image projected by the organization, and (4) the region where you work.

In addition to clothing, research indicates that facial expressions strongly influence people's reactions to each other. The expression on your face can quickly trigger a positive or negative reaction. Similarly, your entrance and carriage, voice, handshake, and manners also contribute to the image you project when meeting others. All the factors that form your image should be given attention prior to a job interview or any other situation where a positive first impression is important.

Also important are the little ways in which you behave—etiquette. Various forms of etiquette are discussed.

■ Career Corner

Q: In the near future I will begin my job search, and I want to work for a company that will respect my individuality. Some companies are enforcing strict dress and grooming codes and other policies that, in my opinion, infringe on the rights of their employees. How far can an employer go in dictating my lifestyle?

A: This is a good question, but one for which there is no easy answer. For example, most people feel they have a right to wear the fragrance of their choice, but many fragrances contain allergy-producing ingredients. In some employment settings, you will find "nonfragrance" zones. Secondhand smoke is another major issue in the workplace because some research indicates that it can be harmful to the health of workers. Rules regarding weight, hair length, and the type of clothing and jewelry that can be worn to work have also caused controversy. There is no doubt that many companies are trying to find a balance between their interests and the rights of workers. Enterprise Rent-A-Car has placed restrictions on the length of an employee's hair and established over twenty-five dress code guidelines for its employees. The company believes employee appearance is crucial to its success. The best advice I can give you is to become familiar with the employer's expectations *before* you accept a job. The company has a responsibility to explain its personnel policies to prospective employees, but sometimes this information is not covered until after a person is hired.

■ Key Terms

professional presence	surface language
primacy effect	career apparel
assumptions	wardrobe engineering
cultural influences	business casual
image	etiquette

■ Review Questions

1. Image has been described as "more than exterior qualities such as dress and grooming." What other factors shape the image we project?

2. Define the term *primacy effect*. How would knowledge of the primacy effect help someone who works in patient care or customer service?

3. Why do people tend to rely more heavily on assumptions than on facts during the initial meeting?

4. Why should career-minded people be concerned about the image they project? Do we have control over all of the factors that shape the image we project? Explain.

5. What are the four factors that influence your choice of clothing for work?

6. Let's assume you have decided to prepare for a nursing career. You want to develop a strong personal brand. What components of brand development should you focus on?

7. What is meant by the term *business casual?* What factors should you consider when selecting casual clothing for work?

8. Describe the type of speaking voice that increases a person's effectiveness in dealing with others.

9. Provide a basic definition of good manners. Why is the study of manners important?

10. Stephen Covey says that changing outward attitudes and behaviors does very little good in the long run unless we base such changes on solid principles that govern human effectiveness. Do you agree or disagree with his views? Explain your answer.

■ Application Exercises

1. Many people complain that interrupting has become a major annoyance. You begin speaking and someone finishes your sentence. Marilyn Vos Savant, author of the "Ask Marilyn" column, recommends a technique that can stop interrupters. When someone interrupts you, stop speaking abruptly and say "What?" This will highlight the interruption, and the person who interrupts you will be forced to repeat himself or herself too, which is an unpleasant experience. Repeat this method, if necessary, until the offender lets you complete your sentences. Marilyn Vos Savant says you should save this method for *chronic* interrupters.[36]

2. The first step toward improving your voice is to hear yourself as others do. Listen to several recordings of your voice on a dictation machine, tape recorder, or VCR, and then complete the following rating form. Place a checkmark in the appropriate space for each quality.

Quality	Major Strength	Strength	Weakness	Major Weakness
Projects confidence	_____	_____	_____	_____
Projects enthusiasm	_____	_____	_____	_____
Speaking rate is not too fast or too slow	_____	_____	_____	_____

Projects optimism	____	____	____	____
Voice is not too loud or too soft	____	____	____	____
Projects sincerity	____	____	____	____

3. To survive in today's competitive climate, organizations must provide good service. Employees who have direct contact with the customer, client, or patient play a key role in the area of service. Effective frontline employees are able to express a warm, sincere greeting, display a caring attitude, and provide competent service. During the next seven days keep a record of all contacts you have with frontline people. After each contact, record your impressions of the experience. Was it positive? Negative? Briefly describe what the person said or did that caused you to view the contact as either positive or negative.

 ### Internet Exercise

Throughout the past few years we have seen an increase in the number of etiquette consulting and training companies. These firms will help you develop and initiate dress codes and conduct etiquette-training programs for employees. Contact two of the companies listed below and review the services offered. Then prepare a written summary of your findings. Also, contact the Association of Image Consultants International (*www.aici.org*) to determine what services are offered to members.

Patricia Stephenson & Associates
West Palm Beach, FL
etiquettepro.com

The Protocol School of Washington
McLean, VA
psow.com

Brody Communications
Elkins Park, PA
brodycomm.com

Eticon Inc.
Columbia, SC
eticon.com

At Ease Inc.
Cincinnati
ateaseinc.com

Professional Image
Atlanta
theprofessionalimage.net

Case 11.1 The Importance of Class

The words *magnetism, charisma,* and *class* are used to describe persons who are admired and respected. These special individuals are also memorable. Some say class and charm are fading fast from the American scene, replaced by bad behavior displayed by professional athletes, movie stars, radio and TV commentators, and politicians. Many sports fans mourn the retirement of John Elway, Michael Jordan, and Wayne Gretzky, who were gracious in victory and gracious in defeat.

Arthur Ashe was the first African-American male to win the U.S. Open and Wimbledon tennis tournaments. He was also the first African-American male ranked number one in the tennis world. He displayed a unique combination of grace and class. His life was marked by personal modesty, civility, and generosity. Ashe led an exemplary family and professional life until his untimely death from AIDS contracted after heart bypass surgery. The late Payne Stewart, killed in the bizarre crash of a Learjet, is remembered as a vicious competitor and a classy hero to many golf fans.

The authors of *Make Yourself Memorable* say that memorable people have style. They describe the four interlocking elements of style as *look, conduct, speech,* and *presentation.* Ann Landers, the noted advice columnist, says that if you have class, success will follow. She has described some of the elements of class:[37]

- Class never tries to build itself up by tearing others down.

- Class never makes excuses.

- Class knows that good manners are nothing more than a series of small, inconsequential sacrifices.

- Class is comfortable in its own skin. It never puts on airs.

- Class is real. It can't be faked.

■ Questions

1. Some social critics say that too many people these days are rude, crude, and inconsiderate of others. Do you agree? Explain.

2. Make a list of prominent people who in your opinion have class. Also, make a list of friends or coworkers who have class. What personal qualities displayed by these individuals do you most admire?

3. Ann Landers says that if you have class, nothing else matters. Do you agree?

4. If you want to become a more memorable person—someone with class—what type of self-improvement program would you undertake? Explain. If you decided to develop a strong personal brand, would class be a major component of your brand?

Case 11.2 Do You Want to Be Your Own Brand?

About twenty years ago Toyota Motor Company decided to develop a line of luxury automobiles that would compete with Mercedes Benz, BMW, Cadillac, and Lincoln. After several years of research and development, the Lexus brand was born. Today, Lexus cars are recognized by automobile writers and consumers as the best mass-produced luxury cars. They stand for quality.

Branding, a concept that has been used in the field of marketing for over fifty years, has recently surfaced as a personal development strategy. Using the principles of successful brand development, many people are positioning themselves to stand for something—to say something important about themselves that will affect how others perceive them. The authors of *Be Your Own Brand* note that the concept of brand in business has a well-defined meaning: "A brand is a perception or emotion, maintained by a buyer or a prospective buyer, describing the experience related to doing business with an organization or consuming its products or services."[38] In a personal context, you can think of it this way: "Your brand is a perception or emotion, maintained by somebody other than you, that describes the total experience of having a relationship with you."[39]

The key to understanding the concept of personal and business branding is understanding the nature and needs of a relationship. L. L. Bean has become a major force in outdoor and casual clothing by implementing business practices that build customer loyalty and repeat business. In addition to selling quality products, this company works hard to build a trusting relationship with its customers.

Personal brand development begins with self-management practices that help you create and strengthen relationships with other people. Early in his career, Jerry Seinfeld decided he would never use profanity in his comedy routines. This personal decision forced him to use more creativity, and he became a stronger comedian. Jeff Bezos, founder of Amazon.com, recalls an early life experience that changed the way he viewed relationships. He made a comment to his grandmother that hurt her feelings. Later his grandfather met with him privately and said, "You'll learn one day that it's much harder to be kind than clever."[40] This insight has helped Bezos in his professional life.

To develop a distinctive brand that will help you in your interactions with others may require making some changes in your life. To become distinctive, you must stand for something. What you stand for relates to your values. Thus a strong personal brand is generally built from the inside out. But to some extent you can also decide what type of image you want these values to project. This may require changes in your manners, dress, voice quality, facial expression, posture or behaviors that reflect your integrity.

■ Questions

1. Given this brief introduction to brand development, would you consider taking steps to develop a distinctive personal brand? Explain your answer.

2. Experts in personal brand development say that employees should align their values with their employer's values. Do you agree with this recommendation?

3. The Association of Image Consultants International says its members help clients achieve authenticity, credibility, and self-confidence. Would you consider hiring a personal consultant to help you grow in these areas? Explain.

4. If you decide to develop a personal brand, what changes will you make in your life?

PART IV

IF WE ALL WORK TOGETHER . . .

12

TEAM BUILDING: A LEADERSHIP STRATEGY

Chapter Preview

After studying this chapter, you will be able to

- Explain the importance of teamwork in an organizational setting.

- Identify and explain common types of work teams.

- List the characteristics of an effective work team.

- Explain the behavioral science principles that support team building.

- Describe the team-building skills that leaders need.

- Describe the team-member skills that employees need.

Why do those New York Yankees win the World Series so often? This question has been asked many times by baseball fans from Detroit, Kansas City, Los Angeles, and other cities across the nation. Some say the answer is *money*. Yes, the owner of the Yankees does have deep pockets, but this is true of many other team owners. No, the credit for winning four World Series in five years must be given to Joe Torre, team manager.

Jerry Useem, senior writer for *Fortune* magazine, describes Joe Torre as a leader with outstanding team-building skills: "For five seasons he has taken a collection of rookies and retreads, recovering drug addicts and born-again Christians, Cuban defectors and defective throwers, and created a workplace that, were it not for its particular job requirements, would surely qualify for *Fortune's* list of the 100 best places to work."[1] What can we learn from Joe Torre about leadership and team building? Well, his list of management principles is not made up of complex theories or concepts that can only be understood by a Harvard graduate with a Ph.D. in management. For example, he says, "Be intense, but not tense" and "Don't punish failure."[2] As this chapter unfolds, you will learn more about the leadership practices of Joe Torre and other successful managers.

Leadership Challenges in a Changing Workplace

The New Economy is characterized by rapid change and demand for increased productivity. As the pace of change quickens and the pressure to work faster increases, the result is greater employee stress and tension. How can a

New York Yankees manager, Joe Torre, (left), puts his arm around pitcher Mariano Rivera as the team leaves the field following a victory. Player recognition is just one of the leadership strategies used by Torre.

supervisor motivate employees who are tired and frustrated? Some of the most important leadership strategies, such as building trust, empowering employees, and developing the spirit of teamwork, can take many months, even years, to implement. How do managers respond to leaders at the top of the organization who want changes implemented overnight?

Diversity has also become a more prominent characteristic of today's work force. We have seen increased participation in the labor force by women and minorities. Supervising a multicultural and multilingual work force can be very challenging. We have also seen greater use of part-time or temporary workers, who may have less commitment to the organization. Again, special managing skills may be needed.

Team Building: An Introduction

Managers at most progressive companies are being rewarded for their ability to develop a spirit of teamwork. In addition to reducing turnover, teamwork is often cited as the key to cost reduction, large production increases, gains in quality, and improved customer service. Almost every organization today is trying to develop the spirit of teamwork, and many organizations have organized their workers into teams. When a person assumes the duties of team supervision, the individual's title is likely to be "team leader" or "team facilitator." The changing role of this new breed of leader is discussed in this chapter. In addition, we discuss ways in which you can become an effective team member.

Can the element of teamwork make a difference between the successful and unsuccessful operation of an organization? Yes, there is evidence that a leadership style that emphasizes **team building** is positively associated with high productivity and profitability. Problems in interpersonal relations are also less common where teamwork is evident. Teamwork ensures not only that a job gets done but also that it gets done efficiently and harmoniously.

There is also evidence that team building can have a positive influence on the physical and psychological well-being of everyone involved. When employees are working together as a team, the leader and members often experience higher levels of job satisfaction and less stress.

Another positive outcome of teamwork is an increase in synergy. **Synergy** is the interaction of two or more parts to produce a greater result than the sum of the parts taken individually.[3] Mathematically speaking, synergy suggests that two plus two equals five. Teamwork synergy is especially important at a time when organizations need creative solutions to complex problems.

Teamwork Doesn't Come Naturally

Many organizations are working hard to get all employees to pull together as a team. Teamwork at a hospital, for example, may begin with acceptance of a common vision, such as providing outstanding health care services. The only way to make this vision a reality is to obtain the commitment and cooperation of every employee. This will require meaningful employee participation in planning, solving problems, and developing ways to improve health care.

Most jobs today require ongoing interaction between coworkers and managers. The spirit of teamwork helps cement these interpersonal relationships. However, working together as a team does not come naturally. Some people value individualism over teamwork. Conflict, in its many forms, can cause a breakdown in relationships. Heavy workloads and long hours often result in weary employees saying or doing things that damage relationships.[4] The good news is that teamwork does flourish under strong leadership.

THINKING / LEARNING STARTER

Reflect on your work experience and experiences in high school or college. Recall situations when you felt like a member of an effective team. What did the supervisor, manager, teacher, or coach do to develop the spirit of teamwork?

● The Transition to Team-Based Structures

One of the most popular workplace initiatives today is the development of organizations that are structured around teams. Over 40 percent of the organizations in America have adopted this approach.[5] Teams have become popular because they encourage **participative management,** the process of empowering employees to assume greater control of the workplace.[6] This section focuses on two of the most common types of teams: self-managed and cross-functional.

Self-Managed Teams   **Self-managed teams** assume responsibility for traditional management tasks as part of their regular work routine. Examples include decisions about production quotas, quality standards, and interviewing applicants for team positions. A typical self-managed team usually has five to fifteen members who are responsible for producing a well-defined product (such as an automobile) or service (such as processing an insurance claim). Team members usually rotate among the various jobs and acquire the knowledge and skills to perform each job. Each member eventually can perform every job required to complete the entire team task. Employees formerly concerned only with their own jobs suddenly become accountable for the work of the total team.[7] One advantage of this approach is that it reduces the amount of time workers spend on dull and repetitive duties.

> *Employees formerly concerned only with their own jobs suddenly become accountable for the work of the total team.*

The General Electric aircraft-engine assembly facility in Durham, North Carolina, has more than 170 employees but just one boss: the plant manager. Everyone reports to her. The jet engines, the size of a large automobile, are assembled by nine self-managed teams. Team members make a wide range of decisions, such as job assignments, how to improve the manufacturing process, vacation schedules, and the assignment of overtime. If a team member slacks off, members deal with the problem. Team members are also responsible for quality control.[8]

A growing number of organizations are structured around teams. In the medical field the spirit of teamwork not only builds strong interpersonal relationships, it can save lives!

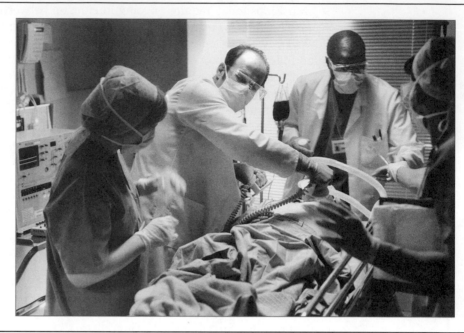

Cross-Functional Teams **Cross-functional teams** are task groups staffed with a mix of specialists focused on a common objective.[9] These teams are usually temporary units with members from different departments and job levels. The teams are often involved in developing new work procedures or products, devising work reforms, or introducing new technology in an organization. Team members often provide a link among separate functions, such as production, distribution, finance, and customer service. If the workers are represented by a union, then union representatives are usually part of the team. Cross-functional teams often make major decisions that directly influence quality and productivity improvements.

● Real Teams Are Rare

Although we are seeing greater use of teams, this approach to employee participation is by no means a quick fix. In the case of self-managed teams, it can sometimes take one or two years for members to learn all the tasks they will perform as they rotate from job to job. It also takes time for a team to mature to the point where it is comfortable making decisions in such areas as work scheduling, hiring, training, and problem solving.

Jon R. Katzenback, author of *Teams at the Top: Unleashing the Potential of Both Teams and Individual Leaders*, says teams like the ones at the General Electric aircraft-engine assembly facility are rare. He adds that most employee groups labeled "teams" are really single-leader work groups that rely on their leaders for purpose, goals, motivation, and assignments. A real team, by contrast, draws its motivation more from its mission and goals than from its leader. The members of self-managed teams in pure form hold one another accountable for the group's performance and results.[10]

Marine Corps Built upon Real Teams

U.S. Marines at all levels must be prepared to make decisions in response to fast-changing situations without consulting the chain of command. Even the lowly privates know they're expected to take whatever initiative is necessary to complete a mission. After Marines complete boot camp, they enter infantry school. Each Marine rotates through all the positions in a fire team—leader, machine gunner, assistant machine gunner, and rifleman. All the Marines learn when and how to shift the leadership role. By the time the team is ready for duty, it is truly a self-managed team. Each member is prepared to fill every position.

Basic Beliefs About Teamwork

One approach to the study of leadership is examining the careers of successful leaders who demonstrated their ability to develop teamwork. For instance, coach Dean Smith became a legend in college basketball. During his 36-year tenure at the University of North Carolina, his teams won 879 games. He recruited players from high schools all over the country—players accustomed to being the stars of their high school teams. He then worked hard to encourage this group of superstars to place "team before the individual."[11] Books such as *My American Journey* by Colin Powell and *Leadership* by Rudolph Giuliani provide us with gems of wisdom regarding effective leadership.

A second approach to the study of leadership is reviewing the findings of scholars who have identified the characteristics of successful leaders. What do successful leaders have in common? See, in the sections that follow, how Douglas McGregor, Robert Blake, Jane S. Mouton, and Jay Hall have answered this question.

● McGregor's Influence

In the late 1950s, a book by Douglas McGregor entitled *The Human Side of Enterprise* presented convincing arguments that management had been ignoring certain important facts about people. The author said that managers often failed to recognize the potential for growth of most workers and their desire for fulfillment. McGregor emphasized that "unity of purpose" is the main distinguishing characteristic of many productive work teams. When a work group shares common goals and a common commitment, it accomplishes more than it would without them.

In *The Human Side of Enterprise*, McGregor discusses several characteristics of an effective work team.[12]

1. The atmosphere of the workplace tends to be informal, comfortable, relaxed. There are no obvious tensions. It is a working environment in which people are involved and interested.

2. There is a lot of discussion about work-related issues. Virtually everyone participates, but contributions remain pertinent to the task of the group. The members listen to one another.

3. The tasks or objectives of the group are well understood and accepted by the members.

4. There is disagreement. The group is comfortable with this and shows no signs of having to avoid conflict.

5. People freely express their feelings as well as their ideas, both on the problem and on the group's operation. There is little avoidance, and there are few "hidden agendas."

McGregor's views on the characteristics of effective work teams represent "classic" thinking. His thoughts continue to have merit today.

TOTAL	**GENERAL COLIN POWELL (RET.)**
PERSON	UNITED STATES ARMY
INSIGHT	"The day soldiers stop bringing you their problems is the day you have stopped leading them. They have either lost confidence that you can help them or concluded that you do not care. Either case is a failure of leadership."

● The Leadership Grid®

In the early 1960s, Robert Blake and Jane Mouton authored a popular book entitled *The Managerial Grid.* The **Leadership Grid®** (formerly called the Managerial Grid®) is a model based on two important leadership-style dimensions: concern for people and concern for production.[13] Where work is physical, concern for production may take the form of number of units assembled per hour or time needed to meet a certain production schedule. In an office setting, concern for production may take the form of document preparation volume and accuracy. Concern for people can be reflected in the way a supervisor views work and safety conditions, compensation, recognition for a job well done, and awareness of employees' need to be treated with respect. The Grid helps clarify how these two dimensions are related and establishes a uniform language for communication about leadership styles and patterns. Although there are many possible leadership styles within the Grid, five encompass the most important differences among managers. Blake and Mouton developed descriptive names for each.[14]

■ *Impoverished management.* People with the **impoverished management** orientation might be classified as "inactive" managers. They display little concern for people or production.

■ *Country club management.* Low concern for production and high concern for people characterize the **country club management** orientation. These managers take steps to prevent unhappiness and dissension.

■ *Authority-compliance management.* The **authority-compliance management** style is task-oriented, placing much attention on getting the job done. Managers with this orientation display concern for production, not people.

■ *Middle-of-the-road management.* Managers with a **middle-of-the-road management** style display moderate concern for both people and production. They see a limited amount of participative management as practical.

■ *Team management.* The **team management** style is a proactive style of management. Persons with this orientation display a high concern for both people and production.

Blake and Mouton devoted more than thirty years to the study of the team-building leadership style. They maintain that this style is the one most positively associated with productivity and profitability, career success and satisfaction, and physical and mental health. The term *one best style* is used by the authors to describe this orientation. This style, they state, achieves production through a high degree of shared responsibility coupled with high participation, involvement, and commitment—all of which are hallmarks of teamwork.[15]

● Hall's Contributions

Jay Hall, founder of Teleometrics International Inc., a national consulting firm, completed a large-scale research project that supports the work of Blake and Mouton.[16] He studied several thousand managers—their personalities and management styles and patterns. In his book *The Competence Process,* he reports that high-achieving managers had a deep interest in both people and productivity and relied heavily on the participative approach. Low and moderate achievers, by contrast, avoided involving their subordinates in planning and decision making.

Hall says the values that supervisors and managers hold dear flow from their basic convictions about the worth of the people who perform the work in an organization.[17] Participative management practices are more likely to be fostered in an organization where supervisory-management personnel project confidence in the potentialities of subordinates than in organizations where they do not.

THINKING / LEARNING STARTER

Think about the supervisors and managers you have worked for or have observed. How much concern did each display toward people? Toward production? Assign each supervisor or manager one of the five leadership styles developed by Blake and Mouton.

● Behavioral Science Principles Supporting Team Building

In almost every field of study there are a few universal principles (sometimes called fundamentals) that are supported by research evidence. Principles can be thought of as general guidelines that are true regardless of time, place, or situation. In the field of human relations there are several principles—based on the behavioral sciences—that support the team-building leadership style. Blake and

Mouton have developed a list of these principles and have applied them to the art of leadership.[18]

1. *Shared participation in problem solving and decision making is basic to growth, development, and contribution.* When people are encouraged to participate in making decisions that affect them, they develop an identity and a sense of control over their destiny. Those employees who never get the opportunity to make such decisions may develop a feeling of powerlessness.

2. *Mutual trust and respect undergird productive human relationships.* Research consistently shows that employee commitment is directly linked to trust in the supervisor or manager. Trust is a catalyst. When trust exists within an organization, a spirit of teamwork is more likely to exist. As trust ebbs, people are less open with each other, less interdependent, and less willing to work as a team.

3. *Open communication supports mutual understanding.* Everyone has a need to communicate. People are naturally curious and interested in what is happening within the organization. Price Pritchett said it best: "Communication breathes the first spark of life into teamwork, and communication keeps teamwork alive."[19]

4. *Conflict resolution by direct problem-solving confrontation promotes personal health.* A primary goal of team building is to provide a natural forum for conflict resolution. Conflict can drain people of the energy they need to perform their regular duties.

5. *Responsibility for one's own actions stimulates initiative.* As humans grow and mature, they become less dependent on others and seek more control over their own lives. Generally adults tend to develop a deep psychological need to be viewed by others as self-directing.

Team-Building Skills for Leaders

Although many organizations are making the transition to a team-based structure, and some of these teams need little or no supervision, demand for leaders who possess team-building leadership skills will continue to be strong.[20] This section discusses ways that supervisory-management personnel can become team builders. Later in this chapter, you will see how employees can contribute to the team-building process.

TOTAL PERSON INSIGHT	**MICHAEL CROM**
	VICE PRESIDENT, DALE CARNEGIE & ASSOCIATES, INC.
	"Life is good when trust is present. Life hurts when trust disappears. We understand this at a level so deep it is indistinguishable from our very being."

The wide range of types of supervisory-management positions may cause you to ask, Do people in these positions have much in common? Will team-building strategies work in most situations? The answer to both questions is yes. A great majority of successful supervisory-management personnel share certain behavior characteristics. Two of the most important dimensions of supervisory leadership—consideration and structure—have been identified in research studies conducted by Edwin Fleishman at Ohio State University[21] and validated by several additional studies.

● Consideration

The dimension of **consideration** reflects the extent to which a supervisor's or manager's relationships with subordinates are characterized by mutual trust, respect for the employees, consideration of their feelings, and a certain warmth in interpersonal relationships. When consideration is present, the supervisor-subordinate relationship is characterized by a climate of good rapport and two-way communication. Consideration is the equivalent of "concern for people" on the Leadership Grid® and *social competence,* a concept introduced in Chapter 9.

● Structure

The dimension of **structure** reflects the extent to which a supervisor is likely to define and direct his or her role and the roles of subordinates toward goal attainment. Managers who incorporate structure into their leadership style actively direct group activities by planning, setting goals, communicating information, scheduling, and evaluating performance. People who work under the direction of a highly structured supervisor know what is expected of them. Structure is the equivalent of "concern for production" on the Leadership Grid®.

It is interesting to note that the dimensions of consideration and structure are independent of each other. A supervisor may be well qualified in one area but lack competence in the other. The good news is that anyone can consciously work to develop competence in both areas.

● Improving Consideration Skills

Brian Tracy says that effective leaders are guided by the *law of empathy*: "Leaders are sensitive to and aware of the needs, feelings, and motivations of those they lead."[22] This is good advice for anyone who wants to become an outstanding leader. To improve the dimension of consideration, one should adopt the following practices.

Recognize Accomplishments When individual achievements are overlooked, supervisors miss a valuable opportunity to boost employee self-confidence and build morale. As noted in Chapter 10, people need recognition for good work, regardless of the duties they perform or the positions they hold. Of course, recognition should be contingent on performance. When recognition is given for mediocre performance, the supervisor is reinforcing a behavior that is not desirable.

Provide for Early and Frequent Success   According to an old saying, "Nothing succeeds like success." A supervisor should provide each employee with as many opportunities to succeed as possible. The foundation for accomplishment begins with a carefully planned orientation and training program. Supervisors and managers should review job duties and responsibilities, organizational policies and procedures, and any other pertinent information with their employees early in the relationship. Successful leaders are successful teachers. No worker should have to rely on gossip or the advice of a perennially dissatisfied employee for answers to important questions.

> *A supervisor should provide each employee with as many opportunities to succeed as possible.*

Take a Personal Interest in Each Employee   Everyone likes to be treated as an individual. Taking a personal interest means learning the names of spouses and children, finding out what employees do during their leisure time, asking about their families, and acknowledging birthdays. The more you learn about the "whole person," the better you will be able to help employees balance their work lives with the rest of their lives. Some supervisors keep a record of significant information about each of their workers (see Figure 12.1). This record is especially helpful for supervisors who are in charge of a large number of employees and find it difficult to remember important facts about each person.

Establish a Climate of Open Communication   To establish a climate of open communication, the leader must be available and approachable. Employees should feel comfortable talking about their fears, frustrations, and aspirations. Communication is closely linked to employee morale—and morale is directly linked to productivity. Therefore, efforts to improve the communication process represent a good use of the supervisor's time and energy.

> *Therefore, efforts to improve the communication process represent a good use of the supervisor's time and energy.*

D. Michael Abrashoff, a commander in the U.S. Navy, took command of the USS *Benfold* at a time when the crew of 310 sailors were very unhappy. To improve morale and operations, he initiated a bold plan to improve communication. The starting point was a "get-to-know-you" session with every sailor. These one-on-one meetings provided an opportunity for sailors to recommend innovations and improvements. Commander Abrashoff asked a lot of questions and listened closely to the answers. Once crew members realized that the new commander was a good listener and would act on their suggestions, morale greatly improved. After several months of strong leadership and hard work by crew members, the USS *Benfold* was recognized as the pride of the Pacific fleet.[23]

Discover Individual Employee Values   Today's lean, flatter organizations offer employees fewer opportunities for promotion, smaller raises, and less job security. As a result, many workers no longer feel secure or identify with the company. Supervisors should encourage employees to explore their values and determine if there is a match between what matters most to them and the work they are doing. If a value conflict turns up, the supervisor may be able to re-

| FIGURE 12.1 | Employee Information Record |

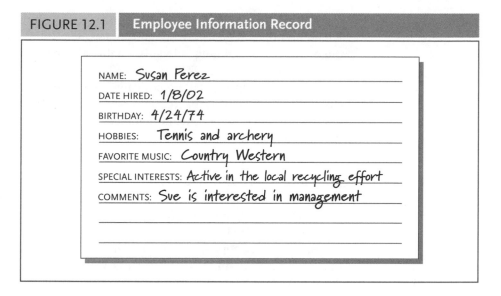

NAME: Susan Perez

DATE HIRED: 1/8/02

BIRTHDAY: 4/24/74

HOBBIES: Tennis and archery

FAVORITE MUSIC: Country Western

SPECIAL INTERESTS: Active in the local recycling effort

COMMENTS: Sue is interested in management

design the job or give an employee a new assignment.[24] Supervisors should also attempt to find out whether there are any conflicts between the employee's job and personal life. Many employees view their family and personal life as their primary source of satisfaction. The employee who feels pressured to work excessive overtime or travel a great deal may experience a major value conflict. Supervisors who are able to meet the needs of employees who have work/life conflicts embrace an important leadership fundamental: Live by your values, and encourage others to live by theirs.[25]

THINKING / LEARNING STARTER

Assume you are the manager of the record-keeping department at a small credit union. Three of your employees are responsible for sorting and listing checks and keeping personal and commercial accounts up-to-date. A fourth employee handles all inquiries concerning overdrafts and other problems related to customer accounts. List five specific behaviors you could develop that would contribute to the supervisory-management quality described as *consideration*.

● **Improving Structure Skills**

The supervisor who incorporates structure into his or her leadership style plays an active role in directing group activities. The team builder gives the group direction, establishes performance standards, and maintains individual and group accountability. The following practices can be used to develop the dimension of structure.

Communicate Your Expectations   Members of the group or team must possess a clear idea of what needs to be accomplished. Supervisors and managers who are successful in motivating employees usually provide an environment in which appropriate goals are set and understood. Bob Hughes, a consultant in the area of team building, suggests establishing baseline performance data so progress can be assessed.[26] In an office that processes lease applications, where accuracy and speed are critically important, the baseline data might include the number of error-free lease applications the team processes in one day. In an ideal situation, team members will be involved in setting goals and will help determine how best to achieve the goals.

Encourage Individual and Team Goal Setting   Setting and reaching goals can provide individuals and teams with a sense of accomplishment. Specific goals are more likely to motivate us than general goals. The goal-setting process is described in Chapter 4.

Some supervisors and managers are using a formal approach to goal setting called **management by objectives (MBO).** Management by objectives is an approach to planning and evaluation in which specific targets are established for a specific period of time. Ideally, the personal goals of the individual employee mesh with the overall goals of the organization. At a date set in advance, the supervisor meets with each employee, and together they agree on targets of performance. Depending on the type of organization, the targets might relate to improved accuracy, reduced absenteeism, increased sales, fewer accidents, or decreased expenses. At the end of the established time period, a review of accomplishments is conducted.

Provide Specific Feedback Often   Feedback should be relevant to the task performed by the employee and should be given soon after performance. Feedback is especially critical when an employee is just learning a new job. The supervisor should point out improvements in performance, no matter how small, and always reinforce the behavior she or he wants repeated. The most relevant feedback in a self-managed work team usually comes from coworkers because team members are accountable to one another. Some self-managed work teams design their own performance appraisal system.

Deal with Performance Problems Immediately   As a supervisor, you must also give feedback to the person who does not measure up to your standards of performance. When members of the group are not held accountable for doing their share of the work or for making mistakes, group morale may suffer. Other members of the group will quickly observe the poor performance and wonder why you are not taking corrective action. In this situation, criticism is better than saying nothing. To achieve the best results, focus feedback on the situation, issue, or behavior, not on the employee. A person can make a mistake and still be a valuable employee. Correct the person in a way that does not create anger and resentment. Avoid demoralizing the person or impairing his or her self-confidence.[27]

A person can make a mistake and still be a valuable employee.

> ### THINKING / LEARNING STARTER
>
> Assume the role of supervisor of a shipping department at a manufacturing plant. Your staff includes three dockworkers who load railcars and trucks, a forklift operator who assists with the movements of large portable platforms (pallets), and a dispatcher who maintains records of all products shipped. On a sheet of paper, list five specific behaviors that would help you develop the supervisory-management quality described as *structure* in this situation.

Situational Leadership

The **Situational Leadership Model,** developed by Paul Hersey and his colleagues at the Center for Leadership Studies *(www.situational.com),* offers an alternative to the Leadership Grid®. **Situational leadership** is based on the theory that the most successful leadership occurs when the leader's style matches the situation. Situational leadership theory emphasizes the need for flexibility.[28]

Before we discuss the differences between the Leadership Grid® and the Situational Leadership Model, let's look at the similarities between the two. Both models are based on two nearly identical dimensions. Paul Hersey says that the primary behaviors displayed by effective managers in the Situational Leadership Model can be described as *task behavior* and *relationship behavior.*

> Task behavior is defined as the extent to which the leader engages in spelling out the duties and responsibilities of an individual or group. The behaviors include telling people what to do, how to do it, when to do it, where to do it and who's to do it. Relationship behavior is defined as the extent to which the leader engages in two-way or multi-way communication if there is more than one person. The behaviors include listening, encouraging, facilitating, providing clarification, and giving socio-emotional support.[29]

Task behavior, concern for production, and structure really mean the same thing. And relationship behavior, concern for people, and consideration do not really differ. In essence, the situational leader and the person who uses the Leadership Grid® team management style rely on the same two dimensions of leadership. Both use task behavior (concern for production) and relationship behavior (concern for people) to influence their subordinates.

What is the major difference between these two leadership models? Hersey says that, when attempting to influence others, you must (1) diagnose the readiness level of the follower for a specific task and (2) provide the appropriate leadership style for that situation.[30] In other words, given the specific situation, you must decide how much task behavior and how much relationship behavior to display. Consider the situation when a rescue squad arrives at an accident scene. In this crisis-oriented situation, the leader of the squad may rely on a very structured leadership style because there is no time to talk things over or to seek feedback from squad members.

Effective leaders never stop learning. Programs offered by the Center for Creative Leadership help managers and executives learn how to work more effectively with people.

Space does not permit an in-depth comparison of situational leadership with the team manager style. But we can point out that it is not possible to become a situational leader without first developing task behavior (structure) and relationship behavior (consideration).

● Additional Leadership Qualities

In addition to consideration and structure skills, leaders need some additional qualities (see Figure 12.2). One of these is character. As noted in Chapter 5, character is composed of personal standards of behavior, including honesty, integrity, and moral strength. Effective leadership is characterized by honesty, truthfulness, and straight dealing with every person.[31] Without character it is impossible to build a trusting relationship with the people you lead.

A second important quality is emotional intelligence, a concept that was discussed in Chapter 9. Emotional intelligence is a much more powerful predictor of leadership success than IQ because it gives you the ability to monitor your own and others' emotions and deal with them effectively.[32] For example, a leader with high emotional intelligence is more likely to detect friction and

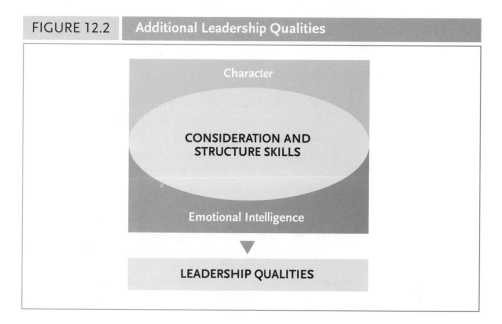

FIGURE 12.2 Additional Leadership Qualities

eliminate conflict among team members. This leader is also more flexible, and therefore better able to use situational leadership.

Character and emotional intelligence are leadership qualities that can be developed. Leaders create themselves—they are not born. One very important key to growth in both of these areas is self-awareness. Without self-awareness we may behave in ways that are potentially ineffective.[33]

Teamwork: The Employee's Role

Each member should assume an active part in helping the work unit achieve its mission. This means that every member of the work group can and should be a team member and a team builder. These dual roles are achieved when employees

---

HUMAN RELATIONS IN ACTION

Bosses Who Behave Badly

Bad bosses come in all shapes and sizes. There is the bully boss who seems to enjoy intimidating and publicly harassing employees. This behavior is often a false front displayed by a person filled with self-doubt and insecurity. Then there is the control freak who wants to micromanage everything. This person, usually lacking in confidence and trust, wants to make or influence every decision. The opposite of the controlling boss is the indifferent boss who no longer seems to care about anything. He or she may be burned out from 12-hour workdays, too much travel, and family pressures. And there are wimpy bosses, know-it-all bosses, and cruel bosses.

To avoid working for a boss who behaves badly, look for warning signs before accepting a job. Carefully question the interviewer to identify a culture that may be rigid or intolerant. Visit with employees and ask carefully worded questions. If no one can identify a top manager who has a life outside his or her work, you probably won't have an outside life either.

assume greater responsibility for the success of the work unit. Today's most valued employees are those who are willing to assume leadership responsibilities.

● Employees as Leaders

In traditional organizations there were leaders and followers, and the followers were not expected to develop leadership skills. Today, some of the most effective leaders are helping their work team members develop leadership skills so that the team's success will not ride on one person. At a time when most organizations are attempting to compete in a complex, ever changing global market, there is real merit in establishing a diversity of leadership within the work group. If we are willing to expand our definition of leadership, we can see leaders everywhere.[34]

- The quiet "worker bee" frequently serves as a leader when the issue is how to get the work done during a crisis situation.

- The "corporate counselor," who informally guides coworkers through stressful problems by merely listening, is an emotional leader.

- The rigid "rule follower" keeps our creativity from becoming irresponsible.

Will the "employees as leaders" approach catch on? J. Oliver Crom, CEO of Dale Carnegie & Associates, Inc., is optimistic. He says that leadership skills are needed at all levels of the organization and adds that "Every employee is a leader" might well be today's business slogan.[35]

● Becoming a Valued Team Member

Throughout your working life, your success is very likely to depend on your ability to be an effective team member. Here are some tips on how to become a respected team member in any organizational setting.[36]

1. *Avoid becoming part of a clique or subgroup within the team.* As a member of a clique you are very likely to lose the trust and respect of other team members.

2. *Avoid any action that might sabotage the team.* By engaging in frequent criticism of other team members, gossip, or other unconstructive behaviors, you undermine team efforts.

TOTAL PERSON INSIGHT	**JOHN C. MAXWELL**
	AUTHOR, *THE 17 ESSENTIAL QUALITIES OF A TEAM PLAYER*
	"Great challenges require great teamwork, and the quality most needed among teammates amid the pressure of a difficult challenge is collaboration. . . . Each person brings something to the table that adds value to the relationship and synergy to the team."

3. *Keep in mind that effective team membership depends on honest, open communication among team members.* Use the fundamentals of constructive self-disclosure discussed in Chapter 8.

4. *As a team member, do not feel the need to submerge your own strong beliefs, creative solutions, and ideas.* If the team members are about to make a decision that in your opinion is not "right," do not hesitate to speak up and express your views.

Teamwork can be a very satisfying experience. It can generate positive energy and contribute to a sense of optimism about the future. As a team member you have the opportunity to assume a very important leadership role.

● Managing the Relationship with Your Boss

The idea that you should manage the relationship with your boss may sound a little unusual at first. But it makes a lot of sense when you consider the advantages of assuming this responsibility. When the subordinate and the boss are both working to maintain a good relationship, conflict is less likely to surface. The boss-subordinate relationship is not like the one between parent and child—the burden for managing the relationship should not and cannot fall entirely on the one in authority.

When you take time to manage the relationship with your boss, he or she will become more effective in performing his or her job. In many cases, managers are no more effective than the combined competence of the people they supervise. Some employees do not realize how much their boss needs assistance and support from them.

How do you go about managing your boss? Here are some general considerations.

Assess Your Own Strengths The boss represents only one-half of the relationship. The development of an effective working relationship also requires reflecting on your own strengths, weaknesses, work habits, communication style, and needs. What personal characteristics might impede or facilitate working with your boss? The most effective team players assume the responsibility for self-assessment and adjustment. It is a burden they gladly accept.

Develop an Understanding of Your Boss Become familiar with this person's strengths, weaknesses, work habits, communication style, and needs. Spend time studying your boss. In some cases, the direct approach is best. Ask your boss, "How would you like me to work with you?" Try to determine his or her goals and expectations. What is the person trying to accomplish? Does your boss enjoy casual meetings to discuss business matters or formal meetings with written agendas?

Flex Your Communication Style In terms of communication style, is your boss supportive, emotive, reflective, or director? Once you have answered this question, begin thinking of how to flex your style in ways that will build rapport and avoid unnecessary stress. Remember, style flexing is a temporary

HUMAN RELATIONS IN ACTION

Tips for Young Managers

Wanted: A new breed of boss who can provide strong leadership, handle technology, inspire teamwork, and cope with uncertainty. The person who fits this description may be quite young and inexperienced. Many of today's leaders are no longer molded solely by seniority and experience. Here are some tips for the young manager:

■ Act as if you're the boss—even if you don't feel like one.

■ Establish your authority; make friends later. Err on the side of being formal.

■ Figure out where you fit in, in both formal and informal hierarchies.

■ Give before you take. Approach relationships (with subordinates, your boss, customers) with what you have to offer, not with what you want.

■ Reach out to people with more age and experience. They will be valuable allies.

effort to act in harmony with another person's dominant communication style (see Chapter 3).

Be Frank and Candid　Suppose that to avoid conflict you almost never disagree with your boss—even when the boss is obviously wrong. Are you making a contribution to his or her growth and development? Obviously not. At times you must be your own person and say what is on your mind. The information you share with your boss may in fact contribute to his or her success. Chapter 8 provides some excellent tips on how to effectively self-disclose your thoughts and feelings.

As organizations become flatter, with fewer layers of management and more projects carried out by teams, collaboration has become more important. Effective team members are those who collaborate actively with their leader and other members of the team.

■ Summary

business.college.hmco.com/students

Teamwork ensures not only that a job gets done but also that it gets done efficiently. Therefore, successful teamwork can often make the difference between the profitable and the unprofitable operation of an organization. The team-building leadership style is effective because it is suited to the needs of most of today's employees.

Many companies are forming specific types of teams. Two of the most common are self-managed teams and cross-functional teams.

Two ways to learn about teams is to study leaders who promote teamwork and scholars who discuss it; examples are McGregor, Blake and Mouton, and Hall.

An effective work team tends to be informal and relaxed, with no obvious tensions. People are involved, interested, and eager to participate in solving work-related problems. An effective work group also has clearly understood goals and objectives.

Two important dimensions of supervisory leadership contribute to team building. One of these dimensions, consideration, reflects the extent to which a supervisor maintains with employees relationships that are characterized by mutual trust, respect, and rapport. The other dimension, structure, reflects the extent to which a supervisor is likely to direct group activities through planning, goal setting, communication, scheduling, and evaluating. The Leadership Grid® and the Situational Leadership Model help clarify these two dimensions of leadership. Effective leaders must also develop the qualities of character and emotional intelligence.

Members of an effective work group should assume effective leadership and membership roles. Each helps the group achieve its mission. Everyone assumes the role of team member and team builder.

Employees are in a unique position to give guidance and support to their supervisor or manager. Most bosses need this assistance and support to achieve success. To manage the relationship with your boss, it is first necessary to understand him or her. Next, you must assess your own strengths and try to identify personal characteristics that might impede or facilitate a working relationship. And finally, you must be frank and candid. Sometimes you need to disagree with your boss.

■ Career Corner

Q: I work for a company that frequently uses cross-functional teams to complete certain projects. Whenever I serve on one of these teams, I feel frustrated. I want to get a promotion, but team assignments seem to hide my talents. How can I make the best of my next team assignment?

A: If your company is having success with these teams, the best way to get the attention of top management is to be an effective team member. When you get your next team assignment, make a quick study of how the group is working together and note any problems that could prevent the team from reaching its goals. Your visibility will increase if you find ways to enhance team performance. You might share important information with team members or offer to help team members develop some specific skills. In most cases it's possible to help your teammates grow while developing yourself.

■ Key Terms

team building	middle-of-the-road management
synergy	team management
participative management	consideration
self-managed teams	structure
cross-functional teams	management by objectives (MBO)
Leadership Grid®	Situational Leadership Model
impoverished management	situational leadership
country club management	
authority-compliance management	

■ Review Questions

1. Joe Torre says, "Be intense, but not tense" and "Don't punish failure." Do you agree with these leadership guidelines? Explain.

2. In *The Human Side of Enterprise,* Douglas McGregor discusses several characteristics of an effective work team. What was his view on disagreement?

3. Describe the two management-style dimensions of the Leadership Grid® developed by Blake and Mouton.

4. List and describe the two common types of teams that are currently used by organizations.

5. What are some of the behaviors displayed by supervisors who are strong in the area of consideration?

6. What are some of the behaviors displayed by supervisors who are strong in the area of structure?

7. Briefly describe the formal approach to goal setting called management by objectives. What targets of performance might be established jointly by the employee and supervisor?

8. Provide a brief description of situational leadership. What are the major similarities between the Situational Leadership Model and the Leadership Grid®?

9. Describe four major considerations that should guide you in any attempt to manage your boss.

10. Colin Powell says the day soldiers stop bringing you their problems is the day you have stopped leading them. Do you agree or disagree with his point of view? Explain.

■ Application Exercises

1. Business publications such as the *Wall Street Journal, Fortune, Business Week,* and *Fast Company* frequently feature articles describing problem bosses. Managers with high-tech backgrounds (computer science, electrical engineering, mathematics, etc.) sometimes create employee pain through insensitive or vindictive behavior. These so-called nerd managers are often more focused on technology than on people. They have high IQs but rank low in emotional intelligence, and they lack people skills. The result is often high employee turnover. Let's assume that you are working for a small business and the owner is often described by employees as the "nerd boss from hell." What steps might you take to influence your boss, who seems to spend all his time obsessing about technology and ignoring the needs of his employees? Review the material featured in this chapter, and then develop a plan that would help your boss develop a strong team-building leadership style.[37]

2. There is increasing pressure on organizations to allow employees' personal problems to be brought to the attention of the supervisor or manager. Personal problems that can disrupt people's lives include dealing with a teenager on drugs, coping with the needs of a sick parent, losing a babysitter, or getting a divorce. Schedule an interview with two persons who hold supervisory-management positions and ask these questions:
   a. Do you assume the role of mentor and counselor when an employee brings a personal problem to your attention?

b. Should you give the person with a serious problem some special consideration, such as time off, less demanding work, or professional help that is paid for by the company?

3. The skills needed to be an effective leader can be developed by anyone who is willing to invest the time and energy. It is possible to practice important leadership skills before you assume the duties of a supervisor or manager. Review the various ways to improve consideration and structure skills discussed in this chapter, and then begin searching for opportunities to practice these skills. Here are some opportunities for practice:
   a. Volunteer assignments in your community
   b. Group assignments at work, at college, or at place of worship
   c. Involvement in political, professional, or social activities

 Internet Exercise

Many companies provide Internet access for employees and allow them to work in virtual teams. Members may work at headquarters, in satellite offices, on the road, and from home. Virtual team members may never meet one another face to face because they communicate via e-mail, conference calls, and other methods. Web-based tools have been designed to help teams work together more effectively. Visit the following websites and review their services. Then prepare a brief written report on your findings.

Website	Purpose
GroupVine *www.groupvine.com*	Lets you create members-only discussion boards so that a team can post audio files, comments, documents, or pictures concerning a project.
Intranets.com *www.intranets.com*	An instant intranet. In less than 3 minutes, a company or department can have a central place for keeping everyone in a group up-to-date on work, reports, and so on.
ScheduleOnline *www.scheduleonline.com*	A group calendar that lets users schedule events, invite people to meetings, and reserve physical resources such as conference rooms or equipment.[38]

Case 12.1   Coaching to Improve Human Performance

Coaching has been defined as an interpersonal process between a manager and an employee; the purpose is to improve the employee's performance in a *specific* area. Coaching focuses on patterns of behavior such as arriving late for work after being told that tardiness is not acceptable, or violating safety rules after being reminded that safety is very important. The coaching process should help the employee recognize the need to improve performance and to make a commitment to improving performance. Coaching has become a very popular business initiative used to maximize employee productivity and morale.

Managers who develop a leadership style that combines structure and consideration behaviors possess the basic skills for being effective coaches. Coaching involves four steps.

Step One: Carefully document performance problems by collecting factual information. In some cases the best approach may be to observe and assess performance during actual job performance. A sales manager might accompany a salesperson during an actual sales call.

Step Two: Meet with the employee and try to get the person to recognize and agree that there is a need to improve performance in a specific area. Employees often do not see the problem in the same way as the manager views it.

Step Three: Involve the employee in the process of exploring solutions. The employee is often in the best position to suggest ways to improve performance.

Step Four: Get a commitment from the employee to take action. This step may involve development of a contract (verbal or written) that clarifies the coaching goals, approaches, and outcomes.

Throughout the coaching process the manager must use empathic listening (introduced in Chapter 2). This will ensure full understanding of the conditions and dynamics that led to the performance breakdown. At the conclusion of the coaching meeting, thank the employee briefly and describe his or her important role in the organization.[39]

■ Questions

1. Can the four-step coaching process be used with a group of employees? Explain.

2. Experts say the most critical aspect of coaching is getting an employee to recognize a need for performance improvement. Do you agree? Explain.

3. It has been said that through coaching we empower the employee—we allow the person to see and act on the capability and commitment that he or she already possesses. Do you believe this is true? Explain.

4. If you were preparing a manager to become a successful coach, what suggestions would you give this person? Can you think of some factors that would serve as barriers to effective coaching?

Case 12.2   Can You Become a Leader?

The number of career opportunities in supervision and management continues to be quite high. Persons working in the fields of health care, retailing, manufacturing, and many other employment areas will be given an opportunity to move up to a leadership position. What qualities do you need to achieve success? What sacrifices might be needed if you accept a promotion to the position of supervisor or manager? One way to prepare for a leadership position is to study the wisdom that can be gleaned from the writings of respected leaders. Consider these examples.

■ Rudolph Giuliani says he spent his entire life thinking about being a leader. This may explain how he became a successful federal prosecutor and an effective two-term mayor of New York City, a city many people thought ungovernable. In his book *Leadership* he describes what it was like to guide the recovery of New York City after the horror of the World Trade Center attack. The book also describes what he thinks it takes to be a leader during "normal" times. Giuliani feels that holding people accountable is very important. He scheduled morning meetings with top aides to keep them focused on specific problem areas. He recommends staying true to your core values, promising *only* what you can deliver, and not being a bully.[40]

■ Colin Powell, secretary of state in the George W. Bush administration, has been described as a leader who scores very high in emotional intelligence because he has the intuitive ability to connect with others. Powell has been guided by several "laws of power." Here are two of them.[41]

Dare to be the skunk. He says, "Every organization should tolerate rebels who tell the emperor he has no clothes." In other words, let your employees know it's OK to disagree with you.

Come up for air. Powell demands excellence from his staff, but he also insists they put balance in their life. He sets a good example by spending as much time as possible with his wife and children.

■ Joe Torre, manager of the New York Yankees, may be a model for today's corporate leaders. He will always be remembered as the leader of the team that won four World Series in five years. One of his management principles is "Every employee must feel useful." Today, every employee is important, or he or she wouldn't be on the payroll. The mailroom clerk and the person who cleans the hospital rooms should never feel they are not important. Another Torre management principle is "Manage against the cycle." When things get tense, Torre grows outwardly calmer.[42]

It's not difficult to find articles on bully bosses, supervisors who never give praise for work well done, or leaders who push too hard for increases in productivity. Yet there are many great leaders who can teach us a lot about effective leadership.

■ Questions

1. Select the two leadership qualities described above that you feel are most important. Provide a rationale for each selection.

2. If you needed a mentor to help you achieve success in a leadership position, which of these three persons would you select? Explain your choice.

13

RESOLVING CONFLICT AND DEALING WITH DIFFICULT PEOPLE

Chapter Preview

After studying this chapter, you will be able to

- ■ List and describe some of the major causes of conflict in the work setting.

- ■ Utilize assertiveness skills in conflict situations.

- ■ Implement specific strategies for handling difficult people.

- ■ Understand when and how to implement effective negotiation skills.

- ■ Identify key elements of the conflict resolution process.

- ■ Discuss contemporary challenges facing labor unions.

Conflict, in its many forms, tends to dominate the human experience. Television talk shows are often set up to be divisive, with opposing sides engaged in fierce debate. Politicians use combative rhetoric to weaken the position of their opponents. Marriages, parent-child relationships, and friendships all inherently involve conflict.

At work we may face conflicts over issues that did not exist fifteen or twenty years ago. A company wishing to integrate spirituality into the workplace establishes Christian Bible studies, causing employees who practice Judaism, Islam, or Buddhism to feel their needs are not being met. Some employees who are parents demand and receive benefits such as flextime, which allows working parents to tailor their arrival and departure times at work to fit their child-care arrangements. Conflicts can arise if single workers or married workers without children are not allowed to use the flextime schedule.

Problems can surface even when we try to avoid conflict. Fear of conflict can prevent us from offering timely help to a close friend or coworker. Fear of conflict might prevent a supervisor from taking corrective measures when an employee violates safety policies.

The fast pace of today's workplace provides less time for management personnel to resolve the day-to-day conflicts that wound your ego, hurt your feelings, or waste your time. This chapter will offer you and your organization guidelines for resolving a variety of conflicts.

A New View of Conflict

Most standard dictionaries define **conflict** as a clash between incompatible people, ideas, or interests. These conflicts are almost always perceived as negative experiences in our society. But when we view conflict as a negative experience, we may be hurting our chances of dealing with it effectively. In reality, conflicts can serve as opportunities for personal growth if we develop and use positive, constructive conflict resolution skills.[1]

Much of our growth and social progress comes from the opportunities we have to discover creative solutions to conflicts that surface in our lives. Dudley Weeks, professor of conflict resolution at American University, says conflict can provide additional ways of thinking about the *source* of conflict and open up possibilities for improving a relationship.[2] When people work together to resolve conflicts, their solutions are often far more creative than they would be if only one person addressed the problem. Creative conflict resolution can shake people out of their mental ruts and give them a new point of view.

Jerry Harvey, professor of management at George Washington University and author of *The Abilene Paradox and Other Meditations on Management,* says too much agreement is not always healthy in an organization. Members of a work team may be so anxious to be viewed as "team players" that they do not voice their concerns even when they have doubts about a decision being made. An example of this paradox comes from a large northeastern drug company. The management team never spoke

Much of our growth and social progress comes from the opportunities we have to discover creative solutions to conflicts that surface in our lives.

frankly in front of the company president because they knew they would be verbally abused, so everyone operated like "drones." Soon the president wanted to fire some of the drones because they had become useless yes men.[3]

TOTAL	**CHERYL SHAVERS**
PERSON	SENIOR MANAGER, INTEL CORPORATION
INSIGHT	"Companies pay a high price for conflict. Productivity drops, work relationships suffer and energy is wasted, as workers become increasingly angry, stressed and defensive."

● The Cost of Conflict

The amount of time and money invested in conflict resolution is surprisingly high. It is estimated that management personnel spend about 20 percent of their time resolving disputes among staff members.[4] The U.S. Postal Service is experiencing "grievance gridlock" because of about 126,000 postal employee grievances and pending arbitration cases. The acrimony prevents management and the postal workers from working together to tackle badly needed cost-saving strategies. A Postal Service executive asks, "How much effort are you going to get out of someone if [he or she has] a dispute that hasn't been dealt with?"[5]

In some cases, the revenue loss due to unresolved conflict can be extremely high. General Motors gave up $2 billion in lost production from two strikes that crippled its output across North America for more than seven weeks.[6] Comair's 1,300 pilots walked out over wage and quality-of-life issues, shutting down a regional airline that served ninety-five cities. The strike lasted eighty-nine days. Delta Air Lines, owner of Comair, estimates that it lost $5 million in revenue

---

HUMAN RELATIONS IN ACTION

Avoid Creating a No-Complaint Zone

Following the terrorist attacks on September 11, when so many people lost their lives while working, day-to-day problems seemed trivial. Some workers felt guilty about voicing complaints because they believed they should be grateful for just being alive and having a job. They resisted grumbling or griping because they feared they might be perceived as insensitive to someone with "real" problems. In reality, however, stifling complaints because they don't measure up to so-called real problems fails to recognize the importance of venting frustrations at work.

Telling your problems to someone at work often helps you deal with them instead of denying them. You may experience a sense of relief afterward. Perhaps the person you are complaining to has a creative solution to your problems or can help you see and cope with them in a new way. No one ever said you have to bear the burdens of life all alone. In some cases, sharing your problems with others helps build stronger relationships. There is a certain level at which complaints are the social lubricant of the workplace. Bonding at the water cooler rarely develops around how great things are!

each day from the strike.[7] In addition to dealing with this loss of revenue, GM and Comair had to find ways to rebuild employees' and customers' trust and loyalty after the conflicts were ended.

Finding the Root Causes of Conflict

Unless the root of the conflict is addressed, the conflict is likely to recur.

If left unattended, weeds can take over a garden and choke all the healthy plants. When inexperienced gardeners cut weeds off at the surface instead of digging down to find the roots, the weeds tend to come back twice as strong. Conflicts among people at work often follow the same pattern. Unless the root of the conflict is addressed, the conflict is likely to recur. If the root cause appears to stimulate *constructive* conflict, it can be allowed to continue. However, as soon as the symptoms of *destructive* conflict become apparent, steps need to be taken to correct the problem that is triggering it.[8] This segment of the chapter discusses the most common causes of conflicts in the workplace.

Ineffective Communication   A major source of personal conflict is the misunderstanding that results from ineffective communication. In Chapter 2 we discussed

*S*triking Comair pilots walk a picket line outside the Cincinnati/Northern Kentucky International Airport. Unresolved issues that cause conflict can result in massive economic losses as well as the loss of employees' trust and commitment.

the various filters that messages must pass through before effective communication can occur. In the work setting, where many different people work closely together, communication breakdowns are inevitable.

Often it is necessary to determine if the conflict is due to a misunderstanding or a true disagreement. If the cause is a *misunderstanding*, you may need to explain your position again or provide more details or examples to help the other person understand. If a *disagreement* exists, one or both parties have to be persuaded to change their position on the issue. Those involved in the conflict can attempt to explain their position over and over again, but until someone changes, the root problem will persist.[9] This issue is discussed in greater detail later in this chapter.

Value Clashes   In Chapter 5 you read that differences in values can cause conflicts between generations, among men and women, and among people with different value priorities. Consider the conflicts that might arise between "loyalists," who join their organization for life and make decisions for their own good as well as the good of the company, and "job-hoppers," who accept a job in order to position themselves for the next opportunity that might further their personal career advancement. The opportunities for value clashes are almost limitless in today's diverse organizations.

Culture Clashes   For generations, culture clashes have occurred between workers not only from other countries but also from different parts of the United States. Today's diverse work force reflects a kaleidoscope of cultures, each with its own unique qualities. The individual bearers of these different cultural traditions could easily come into conflict with one another. The issues may be as simple as one person's desire to dress in ethnic fashion and a supervisor's insistence on strict adherence to the company dress code, or as complex as work ethics.

Work Policies and Practices   Interpersonal conflicts can develop when an organization has unreasonable or confusing rules, regulations, and performance standards. The conflicts often surface when managers fail to tune in to employees' perceptions that various policies are unfair. Managers need to address the source of conflict rather than suppress it. Such matters can be handled through an appropriate structured conflict resolution process or grievance procedure, discussed in detail later in this chapter.

Adversarial Management   Under adversarial management, supervisors may view their employees and even other managers with suspicion and distrust and treat them as "the enemy." Employees usually lack respect for adversarial managers, resenting their authoritarian style and resisting their suggestions for change. This atmosphere makes cooperation and teamwork difficult.

Noncompliance   Conflict also surfaces when some workers refuse to comply with the rules and neglect their fair share of the workload. Coworkers get angry if they have to put forth extra effort to get the work done because others are taking two-hour lunch breaks, sleeping on the job, making personal phone calls during office hours, and wasting time. Now that so many organizations

Fire the Client?

Lisa Zwick knew that her client, the CEO of an Internet start-up company, was a problem. He was irritable and extremely hard to work with. When he called her California home at 5:00 A.M. one Monday morning from his New York City hotel room and asked her to order a limousine for him, she refused and took the issue to her boss. With his support, Lisa fired the client, telling him, "This isn't working out for several reasons; but most of all, you're a jerk!" Many firms are concluding that firing cantankerous clients can be a good business decision. One company fired a client who was bringing in $1 million a year, or 20 percent of the company's revenue, for making nasty, digging comments about employees. The owner of the company believed that if the irritating client was going to drive her employees crazy, the relationship wasn't worth it. Her respected employees replaced the lost business and have since doubled revenue to $10 million.

are organizing their work forces into teams, noncompliance has the potential for becoming a major source of conflict.

Competition for Scarce Resources It would be difficult to find an organization, public or private, that is not involved in downsizing or cost cutting. The result is often destructive competition for scarce resources such as updated computerized equipment, administrative support personnel, travel dollars, salary increases, or annual bonuses. When budgets and cost-cutting efforts are not clearly explained, workers often suspect coworkers of devious tactics.

Personality Clashes There is no doubt about it: Some people just don't like each other. They may have differing communication styles, temperaments, or attitudes. They may not be able to identify exactly what it is they dislike about the other person, but the bottom line is that conflicts will arise when these people have to work together. Even people who get along well with each other in the beginning stages of a work relationship may begin to clash after working together for many years.

● Resolving Conflict Assertively

Many times, coworkers, supervisors, and customers say or do something that irritates you. They get on your nerves. Your challenge is to deal professionally with these personal irritations before they overwhelm you and negatively affect *your* job performance. Many professionals advise going directly to the offending person and calmly discussing his or her irritating behavior, rather than complaining to others.[10] Figure 13.1 (on p. 310), "Dealing with People You Can't Stand," offers specific strategies you might use. By taking those steps to change *your* behavior, you might facilitate a powerful change in theirs. Keep in mind that some people are unaware of the impact of their behavior, and if you draw their attention to it, they may change it.

Whereas these strategies may be comfortable for some people, such a direct approach may be very uncomfortable for many others. This may be the time to reinforce your assertiveness skills. Assertiveness is based on rights. **Assertive**

FIGURE 13.1 Dealing with People You Can't Stand

THE BULLIES
Pushy and ruthless, loud and forceful, they assume that the end justifies the means.

STRATEGY: When under attack, hold your position, make direct eye contact, focus on breathing slowly and deeply. When they finish, say, "When you're ready to speak to me with respect, I'll be ready to discuss this matter."

THE SNIPERS
They identify your weaknesses and use them against you through sabotage behind your back or put-downs in front of the crowd.

STRATEGY: Stop in midsentence and focus your full attention on them. Ask them to clarify a grievance. If it is valid, take action; if invalid, express your appreciation and calmly offer new information.

THE KNOW-IT-ALLS
They will tell you what they know—for hours at a time—but they won't take a second to listen to your "clearly inferior" ideas.

STRATEGY: Acknowledge their expertise and be prepared with your facts. Use plural pronouns (*we, us*). Present your information as probing questions rather than statements so that you appear less threatening and willing to learn.

THE THINK-THEY-KNOW-IT-ALLS
They don't know much, but they don't let that get in the way. They exaggerate, brag, mislead, and distract.

STRATEGY: Acknowledge their input, but question their facts with "I" statements, such as "From what I've read and experienced. . ."

THE GRENADES
When they blow their tops, they are unable to stop. When the smoke clears and the dust settles, the cycle begins again.

STRATEGY: When their explosion begins, assertively repeat the individual's name to get his/her attention. Calmly address their first few sentences, usually the real problem. Suggest taking time out to cool down, then listen to their problem.

THE YES PERSONS
They are quick to agree but slow to deliver, leaving a trail of unkept commitments and broken promises.

STRATEGY: When they say yes, ask them to summarize their commitment and write it down. Arrange a deadline and describe the consequences that will result if they do not follow through.

THE MAYBE PERSONS
When faced with a crucial decision, they keep putting it off until it's too late and the decision makes itself.

STRATEGY: List advantages and disadvantages of the decision or option. Help them feel comfortable and safe, and stay in touch until the decision is implemented.

THE WHINERS
They wallow in their woe, whine incessantly, and carry the weight of the world on their shoulders.

STRATEGY: Listen and write down their main points. Interrupt and get specifics; identify and focus on possible solutions. If they remain in "it's hopeless" mode, walk away saying, "Let me know when you want to talk about a solution."

Source: Figure from *Dealing with People You Can't Stand* by Rick Brinkman and Rick Kirschner. Copyright © 1994 by McGraw-Hill, Inc. Reprinted by permission of The McGraw-Hill Companies.

behavior involves standing up for your rights and expressing your thoughts and feelings in a direct, appropriate way that does not violate the rights of others. It is a matter of getting the other person to understand your viewpoint.[11] People who exhibit assertive behavior skills are able to handle their conflicts with greater ease and assurance while maintaining good interpersonal relations. Use assertive behaviors when you sense someone is taking advantage of you, ignoring your needs, or disregarding your point of view.

Some people do not understand the distinction between being aggressive and being assertive. **Aggressive behavior** involves expressing your thoughts and feelings and defending your rights in a way that violates the rights of others. Aggressive people may interrupt, talk fast, ignore others, and use sarcasm or other forms of verbal abuse to maintain control. They do not view conflict resolution as a strategy for improving relationships. Aggressive behavior, of course, may bring out the worst in those on the receiving end. The receivers are likely to behave defensively, which just escalates the conflict.

People who attempt to avoid conflict by simply ignoring things that bother them are exhibiting **nonassertive behavior.** Nonassertive people often give in to the demands of others, and their passive approach makes them less likely to make their needs known. If you fail to take a firm position when such action is appropriate, colleagues may take advantage of you, and management may question your ability to lead.[12] Table 13.1 may give you a clearer understanding of how assertive, aggressive, and nonassertive individuals respond when confronted with conflict situations.

● How to Become More Assertive

If you are aggressive, nonassertive, or less assertive than you would like to be in certain situations, do not be discouraged. With practice, you can acquire the sense of well-being that comes with knowing that you can communicate your

TABLE 13.1	Behaviors Exhibited by Assertive, Aggressive, and Nonassertive Persons		
	Assertive Person	**Aggressive Person**	**Nonassertive Person**
In conflict situations	Communicates directly	Dominates	Avoids the conflict
In decision-making situations	Chooses for self	Chooses for self and others	Allows others to choose
In situations expressing feelings	Is open, direct, honest, while allowing others to express their feelings	Expresses feelings in a threatening manner; puts down, inhibits others	Holds true feelings inside
In group meeting situations	Uses direct, clear "I" statements: "I believe that . . ."	Uses clear but demeaning "you" statements: "You should have known better . . ."	Uses indirect, unclear statements: "Would you mind if . . . ?"

wants, dislikes, and feelings in a clear, direct manner without threatening or attacking others. Entire books are written describing assertiveness skills, so it is impossible to explain the various techniques within the context of this short chapter. Nevertheless, we can offer you three practical guidelines that will help you develop assertiveness skills.

In the beginning, take small steps.   Being assertive may be difficult at first, so start with something that is easy. You might decline the invitation to keep the minutes at the weekly staff meeting if you feel others should assume this duty from time to time. If you are tired of eating lunch at Joe's Diner (the choice of a coworker), suggest a restaurant that you would prefer. If someone insists on keeping the temperature at a cool 68 degrees and you are tired of being cold all the time, approach the person and voice your opinion. Asking that your desires be considered is not necessarily a bad thing.[13]

Use communication skills that enhance assertiveness.   A confident tone of voice, eye contact, firm gestures, and good posture create nonverbal messages that say, "I'm serious about this request." Using "I" messages can be especially helpful in cases where you want to assert yourself in a nonthreatening manner. If you approach the person who wants the thermostat set at 68 degrees and say, "You need to be more considerate of others," the person is likely to become defensive. However, if you say, "I feel uncomfortable when the temperature is so cool," you will start the conversation on a more positive note.

Be soft on people and hard on the problem.   The goal of conflict resolution is to solve the problem but avoid doing harm to the relationship. Of course, relationships tend to become entangled with the problem, so there is a tendency to treat the people and the problem as one. Your coworker Terry is turning in projects late every week, and you are feeling a great deal of frustration each time it happens. You must communicate to Terry that each missed deadline creates serious problems for you. Practice using tact, diplomacy, and patience as you keep the discussion focused on the problem, not on Terry's personality traits.

THINKING / LEARNING STARTERS

1. Identify some of the causes of conflict in an organization in which you worked as an employee or volunteer. What types of conflict seemed to cause the most trouble among people?
2. Have you ever experienced a conflict with a coworker? Explain. How did you handle the situation? Could you have handled the situation in a more assertive manner? Explain.

Learn to Negotiate Effectively

Danny Ertel, author and consultant in the area of negotiations, says, "Every company today exists in a complex web of relationships, and the shape of that web is formed, one thread at a time, through negotiations,"[14] Team assignments, compensation, promotions, and work assignments are just a few of the areas where you can apply negotiation skills.

● Think Win/Win

There are basically three ways to approach negotiations: win/lose, lose/lose, and win/win. When you use the **win/lose approach,** you are attempting to reach your goals at the expense of the other party's. For example, a manager can say, "Do as I say or find a job somewhere else!" The manager wins; the employee loses. Although this approach may end the conflict on a short-term basis, it doesn't usually address the underlying cause of the problem. It may simply sow the seeds of another conflict because the "losers" feel frustrated. (This strategy may be effective in those rare instances when it is more important to get the job done than it is to maintain good human relations among the work force.)

When the **lose/lose approach** is used to settle a dispute, each side must give in to the other. If the sacrifices are too great, both parties may feel that too much has been given. This strategy can be applied when there is little time to find a solution through effective negotiation techniques, or when negotiations are at a standstill and no progress is being made. Union-management disputes, for example, often fall into the lose/lose trap when neither side is willing to yield. In these cases an arbitrator, a neutral third party, may be called in to impose solutions on the disputing parties.

In general, the win/lose and lose/lose approaches to negotiating create a "we versus they" attitude among the people involved in the conflict, rather than a "we versus the problem" approach. "We versus they" (or "my way versus your way") means that participants focus on whose solution is superior, instead of working together to find a solution that is acceptable to all. Each person tends to see the issue from his or her viewpoint only and does not approach the negotiations in terms of reaching the goal.

The basic purpose of the **win/win approach** to negotiating is to fix the problem—not the blame! Don't think hurt; think help. Negotiating a win/win

> *The basic purpose of the win/win approach to negotiating is to fix the problem—not the blame!*

solution to a conflict is not a debate where you are attempting to prove the other side wrong; instead, you are engaging in a dialogue where each side attempts to get the other side to understand its concerns and both sides then work toward a mutually satisfying solution. Your negotiating skills are usually much better when you shift your emphasis from the tactical approach of how to counter your opponents' every comment to the more strategic one of how to solve the problem collaboratively with them.[15]

Perhaps the most vital skill in effective negotiations is listening. When you concentrate on learning common interests, not differences, the nature of the negotiations changes from a battle to win to a discussion of how to meet the objectives of everyone involved in the dispute.

● Beware of Defensive Behaviors

Effective negotiations are often slowed or sidetracked completely by defensive behaviors that surface when people are in conflict with each other. When one person in a conflict situation becomes defensive, others may mirror this behavior.

HUMAN RELATIONS
IN ACTION

"Win/Lose" Agreements Yield "Lose/Lose" Results

The owner of a large manufacturing company spoke with pride about his tough negotiation skills. When he needed a distribution network for a new product, he met with a large distributor and negotiated a "win/lose" agreement. He demanded an agreement that was very favorable to his company in terms of up-front payments and percentages of sales. It soon became apparent to the distributor that her company was on the losing side of the agreement. She and her staff had no incentive to fulfill the implied commitment to market the products. The "win/lose" agreement negotiated by the owner of the manufacturing firm turned out to be a "lose/lose" agreement. An agreement or settlement that leaves one party dissatisfied will usually come back to hurt you later.[16]

In a short time, progress is slowed because people stop listening and begin thinking about how they can defend themselves against the other person's comments.

We often become defensive when we feel our needs are being ignored. Kurt Salzinger, Executive Director for Science at the American Psychological Association, reminds us that conflicts are often caused by unfulfilled needs for things such as dignity, security, identity, recognition, or justice. He says, "Conflict is often exacerbated as much by the process of the relationship as it is by the issues."[17] Determining the other person's needs requires careful listening and respect for views that differ from your own. If you feel you are trapped in a win/lose negotiation and can hear yourself or the other person becoming defensive, do everything in your power to refocus the discussion toward fixing the problem rather than defending your position.

● Know That Negotiating Styles Vary

Depending on personality, assertiveness skills, and past experiences in dealing with conflict in the workplace, individuals naturally develop their own negotiating styles. But negotiating is a skill, and people can learn how and when to adapt their style to deal effectively with conflict situations.

Robert Maddux suggests that there are five different behavioral styles that can be used during a conflict situation. These styles are based on the combination of two factors: assertiveness and cooperation (see Figure 13.2). He takes the position that different styles may be appropriate in different situations.

TOTAL PERSON INSIGHT	**ROGER FISHER AND WILLIAM URY**
	AUTHORS, *GETTING TO YES*
	"Any method of negotiation may be fairly judged by three criteria: It should produce a wise agreement if agreement is possible. It should be efficient. And it should improve or at least not damage the relationship between the parties."

| FIGURE 13.2 | **Behavioral Styles for Conflict Situations** |

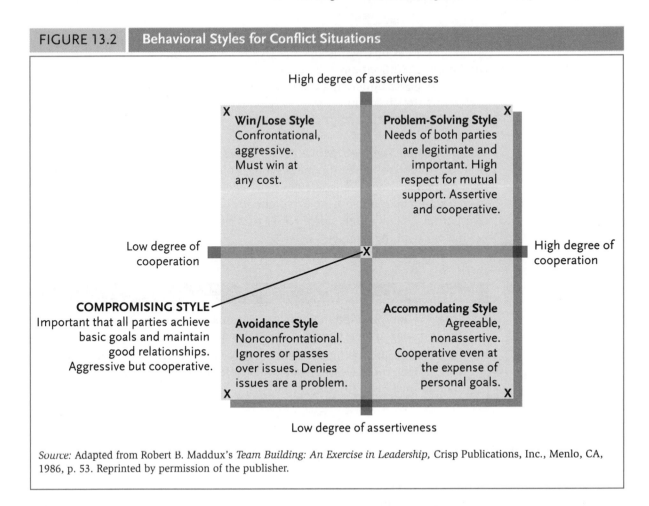

Source: Adapted from Robert B. Maddux's *Team Building: An Exercise in Leadership,* Crisp Publications, Inc., Menlo, CA, 1986, p. 53. Reprinted by permission of the publisher.

Avoidance Style (Uncooperative/Nonassertive)   This style is appropriate when the conflict is too minor or too great to resolve. Any attempt to resolve the conflict might result in damaging a relationship or simply wasting time and energy. Avoidance might take the form of diplomatically sidestepping an issue or postponing your response until a more appropriate time.

Accommodating Style (Cooperative/Nonassertive)   This style is appropriate when resolving the conflict is not worth risking damage to the relationship or general disharmony. Individuals who use this approach relinquish their own concerns to satisfy the concerns of someone else. Accommodating might take the form of selfless generosity or blind obedience to another's point of view.

Win/Lose Style (Uncooperative/Aggressive)   This style may be appropriate when the conflict involves "survival of the fittest," when you must prove your superior position, or when your opinion is the most ethically or professionally correct. This power-oriented position allows you to use whatever means seem appropriate when it is time to stand up for your rights.

Problem-Solving Style (Assertive/Cooperative) This style is appropriate when all parties openly discuss the issues and a mutually beneficial solution can be found without anyone making a major concession. Problem solvers attempt to uncover underlying issues that may be at the root of the problem and then focus the discussion toward achieving the most desirable outcome. They seek to replace conflict with collaboration.

Compromising Style (Moderately Aggressive/Moderately Cooperative) This style is appropriate when no one person or idea is perfect, when there is more than one good way to do something, or when you must give to get what you want. Compromise attempts to find mutually acceptable solutions to the conflict that partially satisfy both sides. Never use this style when unethical activities are the cause of the conflict.

THINKING / LEARNING STARTERS

1. Imagine and describe the human relations atmosphere in an organization where win/lose strategies are consistently applied.
2. Briefly describe the most recent conflict you had with another person. How might you have changed your conflict resolution style to better handle the situation?

Conflict Resolution Process

In the past, the responsibility for conflict resolution was often given to supervisors, department heads, team leaders, shop stewards, mediators, and other individuals with established authority and responsibility. Today, the picture is changing as more companies are organizing workers into teams. The trend toward increased worker participation in decision making and problem solving (employee empowerment) is also having an impact on conflict resolution practices. Many progressive organizations want employees to resolve their own conflicts whenever possible. This means that every employee needs to possess conflict resolution skills. The **conflict resolution process** consists of five steps that can be used at work and in your personal life.

To apply the five steps requires understanding and acceptance of everything we have discussed up to this point in the chapter: application of assertiveness skills, understanding how to deal with various types of difficult people, and support for the win/win approach to conflict resolution.

● **Step One: Decide Whether You Have a Misunderstanding
or a True Disagreement**

David Stiebel, author of *When Talking Makes Things Worse!*, says a misunderstanding is a failure to accurately understand the other person's point. A disagreement, in contrast, is a failure to agree that would persist despite the most

A misunderstanding is a failure to accurately understand the other person's point. A disagreement, in contrast, is a failure to agree that would persist despite the most accurate understanding.

accurate understanding. In a true disagreement, people want more than your explanation and further details; they want to change your mind.[18] When we fail to realize the distinction between these two possibilities, a great deal of time and energy may be wasted. Consider the following conflict situation.

As Sarah entered the driveway of her home, she could hardly wait to share the news with her husband Paul. Late that afternoon she had met with her boss and learned she was the number-one candidate for a newly created administrative position. Sarah entered the house and immediately told Paul about the promotion opportunity. In a matter of seconds, it became apparent that he was not happy about the promotion. He said, "We don't need the extra money, and you do not need the headaches that come with an administrative position." Expecting a positive response, Sarah was very disappointed. In the heat of anger, Sarah and Paul both said things they would later regret.

If Sarah and Paul had asked each other a few questions, this conflict might have been avoided. Prior to arriving home, Sarah had already weighed the pros and cons of the new position and decided it was not a good career move; however, she wanted her husband's input before making the final decision. This conflict was not a true disagreement, in which one person tries to change the other person's mind; it was a misunderstanding that was the result of incomplete information. If Sarah and Paul had fully understood each other's position, it would have become clear that a true disagreement did not exist.

"If you ask me what's wrong one more time, I'm going to tell you."

● Step Two: Define the Problem and Collect the Facts

The saying "A problem well defined is a problem half solved" is not far from the truth. It is surprising how difficult this step can be. Everyone involved needs to focus on the real cause of the conflict, not on what has happened as a result of it. At this stage, it is helpful to have everyone write a one- or two-sentence definition of the problem. When everyone is allowed to define the problem, the real cause of the conflict will often surface.

As you begin collecting information about the conflict, it may be necessary to separate facts from opinions or perceptions. Ask questions that focus on who is involved in the conflict, what happened, when, where, and why. What policies and procedures were involved?

Conflict resolution in the age of information offers us new challenges. As we are faced with information overload, we may be tempted to use the information we already have rather than search for the new information needed to guide a decision.[19]

● Step Three: Clarify Perceptions

Your perception is your interpretation of the facts surrounding the situations you encounter. Perceptions can have a tremendous influence on your behavior. In a conflict situation, it is therefore very important that you clarify all parties' perceptions of the problem. You can do this by attempting to see the situation as others see it. Take the case of Laura, a sales representative who was repeatedly passed over for a promotion even though her sales numbers were among the best in the department.

Over a period of time Laura became convinced that she was the victim of gender discrimination. She filed charges with the Equal Employment Opportunity Commission (EEOC), and a hearing was scheduled. When Laura's boss was given a chance to explain his actions, he described Laura as someone who was very dedicated to her family. He said, "It's my view that she would be unhappy in a sales management position because she would have to work longer hours and travel more." He did not see his actions as being discriminatory. Laura explained that she valued the time she spent with her husband and children but achieving a management position was an important career goal. Laura's and her boss's perceptions of the same situation were totally different.

Dudley Weeks says there are some important questions to be asked as you clarify perceptions of the conflict. What does each party think the conflict is about? Is the conflict over deeply held values or just preferences? Is the conflict over goals or methods? The answers to these questions can be important components of the conflict resolution process.[20]

● Step Four: Generate Options for Mutual Gain

Once the basic problem has been defined, the facts surrounding it have been brought out, and everyone is operating with the same perceptions, everyone involved in the conflict should focus on generating options that will fix the problem. Some people, however, do not consider generating options to be part of the conflict resolution process. Rather than broadening the options for mutual gain, some individuals want to quickly build support for a single solution. The authors of the best-selling book *Getting to Yes* say, "In a dispute, people usually believe that they know the right answer—their view should prevail. They become trapped in their own point of view."[21] This is where brainstorming comes in. **Brainstorming** is a process that encourages all those involved in the conflict to generate a wide variety of ideas and possibilities that will lead to the desired results. No one should be allowed to evaluate, judge, or rule out any proposed solution. Each person is encouraged to tap his or her creative energies without fear of ridicule or criticism. Once all options are on the table, you will need to eliminate those that will not lead to the desired results and settle on the most appropriate ones.

● Step Five: Implement Options with Integrity

The final step in the conflict resolution process involves finalizing an agreement that offers win/win benefits to those in conflict. Sometimes, as the conflict resolution process comes to a conclusion, one or more parties in the conflict may be tempted to win an advantage that weakens the relationship. This might involve hiding information or using pressure tactics that violate the win/win spirit and weaken the relationship. Even the best conflict solutions can fail unless all conflict partners serve as "caretakers" of the agreement and the relationship.[22]

Establish timetables for implementing the solutions, and provide a plan to evaluate their effectiveness. On a regular basis, make a point to discuss with others how things are going to be sure that old conflict patterns do not resurface. Conflict resolution agreements must be realistic and effective enough to survive as the challenges of the future confront them. Avoid the temptation to implement quick-fix solutions that may prove to be unsatisfactory in a few weeks.[23]

● Alternative Dispute Resolution

At times, you and your coworkers or employer may not be able to reach a satisfactory resolution to your conflicts. You may believe you have been fired without cause, sexually harassed, discriminated against, overlooked for a promotion, or unfairly disciplined. Your only recourse may be to ignore the situation or take your employer to court. Ignoring the situation does not make it go away, and court battles can take years and can be extremely expensive. In some instances, you may have a legitimate complaint but not a legal claim. To help keep valued employees content and out of court, many organizations such as Levi Strauss, Alcoa, and TRW have created formal Alternative Dispute Resolution programs, or ADRs. A recent Cornell University study discovered that over 80 percent of large employers nationwide operate internal ADRs, and all federal departments are required to offer ADR options.[24]

The International Centre for Dispute Resolution (ICDR) offers conflict resolution assistance to organizations that are doing business on a global scale. Cross-border disputes can sometimes be very complicated.

These programs usually involve any or all of the following: an open door policy that allows you to talk confidentially with upper management personnel, a toll-free hot line where employees can air grievances and get general advice, a peer review panel that investigates and attempts to resolve the problem, a third-party mediator who listens to arguments and attempts to forge a mutually acceptable solution, or an arbitrator who imposes a final and binding solution to the problem.[25] TRW's program offers an additional benefit. The ADR is mandatory for all employees with an unresolved grievance, but the arbitration option is *non*binding. If an employee is not pleased with the outcome, he or she is still able to take legal action. But if TRW is not pleased, the organization cannot appeal the arbitrator's decision but must abide by it.[26]

Fed Ex has a similar procedure, which it calls the Guaranteed Fair Treatment process (GFT). Employees who believe they have been treated unfairly can appeal a manager's decision through the GFT. Each week the CEO and two top officers of the company personally hear appeals that have worked their way through the system. Cases that have merit are turned over to a panel of five employees, three of whom are picked by the appealing employee, for a final and binding decision.[27]

The Role of Labor Unions in Conflict Resolution

Federal laws passed in the 1930s gave labor unions the legal right to organize and represent workers. Union membership grew steadily over the years, and in the early 1950s about 33 percent of all workers were union members. However, over the past half century union membership has declined steadily, partly because of international competition, deregulation, mergers, and automation. The percentage of workers who belong to unions is now about 13.5. The pervasive trend toward downsizing and outsourcing of work to foreign and nonunion firms continues to erode union membership.[28]

● Labor's Role in the New Economy

The work force has changed dramatically in recent years, and many workers are questioning the traditional roles of organized labor. Dual-income families, the growing use of temporary and contract workers, and telecommuters have changed the complexion of our labor force. In addition, the erosion of the traditional bonds between employee and employer has changed the way many employees view job security. When the economy is strong and jobs are plentiful, unhappy workers routinely quit when another job comes along. For these reasons, there is less incentive to form unions.

At the same time, some workers who would not have considered union representation in the past are now union members. Public school teachers have a long history of union involvement, but now graduate students on several campuses—including the University of Iowa, the University of Kansas, and the University of Massachusetts—have gained bargaining rights. About 17 percent of all registered nurses belong to a labor union, and the American Medical Association plans to organize resident physicians into "guilds" to improve their working conditions.

Most union leaders are working more closely with management to achieve common goals rather than perpetuating the traditional adversarial relationship.

Most union leaders are working more closely with management to achieve common goals rather than perpetuating the traditional adversarial relationship. Negotiations between major corporations and unions often set standards in the areas of wages and benefits that are followed in both union and nonunion sectors.[29]

● Collective Bargaining

Most management–labor union disputes escalate when the employment contracts that establish the workers' wages, benefits, and working conditions expire and need to be renegotiated. The overwhelming majority of employment contracts are settled through **collective bargaining,** a process that defines the rights and privileges of both sides involved in the conflict and establishes the terms of employment and length of the contract (usually from three to five years). However, if labor and management cannot settle their differences, they may submit their disputes to one of the following:

- **Mediation**—A neutral third party listens to both sides and suggests solutions. It carries no binding authority. Both parties are free to reject or accept the mediator's decision.

- **Voluntary arbitration**—Both sides willingly submit their disagreements to a neutral party. The arbitrator's decision must be accepted by both sides.

- **Compulsory arbitration**—When the government decides that the labor-management dispute threatens national health and safety or will damage an entire industry, it can appoint an arbitrator who dictates a solution that is binding on both sides and can be enforced in a court of law.

When collective bargaining, mediation, and arbitration are not enough to settle disputes, union leaders may recommend and members may vote to go on strike against their employers. A strike generally results in a lose/lose situation in which workers lose paychecks, employers lose sales, customers lose products or services, and communities lose economic stability.

● Contemporary Issues Facing Labor Unions

When the United States moved into a service economy (which is female dominated) from a manufacturing one (which was male dominated), unions were slow to wake up to the fact that women's needs must become a top priority. Karen Nussbaum, former head of the Women's Bureau of the U.S. Department

Some workers who would not have considered union representation in the past are now union members. These Yale University graduate students are waiting in line to vote on whether to unionize or not.

of Labor, is now director of the AFL-CIO's Working Women Department. Her task within the union is to "turn the labor movement into real advocates for women." Nussbaum plans to increase bargaining on work-and-family issues, expand family leave, and improve child and elder care.[30]

In addition to representation of women, there are other urgent issues. As labor unions strive for survival, they may thrive in the next millennium if they increase their awareness and take action to address the following needs of the current and future work force:

■ Workers are vitally concerned about the inequities between executives' million-dollar salaries and climbing corporate profits while employees' compensation (in real dollars) declines.

■ Health care continues to be a major concern for workers of all ages. It will be important to improve coverage of employees and try to find ways to provide coverage for all children. As the cost of Medicare goes up with the aging of the population, the probability of increased payroll taxes increases.[31]

■ Workers are desperate for "good" jobs that pay well. The low cost-of-living increases in recent years have created major challenges for low-income workers.

■ Economic conditions and labor laws make it far more feasible, and profitable, for some organizations to hire temporary and part-time workers rather than highly trained, qualified, and experienced workers.

Large-scale layoffs, recent corporate scandals, and the loss of many jobs to foreign countries have changed some workers' attitudes toward labor union membership. A recent study conducted by the AFL-CIO found that 50 percent of nonunion workers would vote to form a union. This change in sentiment offers a renewed opportunity for unions. However, strenuous anti-union efforts by management are, and will continue to be, a major barrier to labor gains.[32]

■ Summary

business.college.hmco.com/students

Conflicts among people in organizations happen every day and can arise because of poor communication, values and culture clashes, confusing work policies and practices, competition for scarce resources, or adversarial management. Often, however, conflicts come from coworkers who refuse to carry their fair share of the workload or have a difficult personality. While unresolved conflicts can have a negative effect on an organization's productivity, a difference of opinion sometimes has a positive effect by forcing team members toward creative and innovative solutions to the problem.

Assertiveness skills are necessary when you must continue to work with people you can't stand. One of the most effective strategies for handling personal conflicts with others is to determine the root of the problem and then negotiate toward a mutually satisfying solution. This win/win approach focuses on discussions that allow both sides to reach their goals. Both sides should learn to listen for what each side really needs and should respect each other's rights. You can vastly improve your skills for dealing with difficult people by knowing when and how to alter your negotiating style. Robert Maddux describes five different styles. When people cannot solve their conflicts in an informal manner, many organizations create solutions through a conflict resolution process. This five-step process is dependent on a clear outline of the steps that need to be taken to resolve the conflict. Often an Alternative Dispute Resolution program (ADR) can resolve conflicts that might otherwise lead to legal action.

Labor unions were established to help balance the power between labor and management. But organizations today face complex problems that did not exist when many of the labor laws were established following the Great Depression. Labor leaders and business owners are finding new ways to cooperate with each other rather than negotiating with an "us versus them" attitude. They are finding that flexibility and innovation are far more productive than old adversarial styles. However, if labor and management cannot settle their differences, they may submit their disputes to mediation, voluntary arbitration, or compulsory arbitration. Labor unions today must be more responsive to concerns of nontraditional union members such as women, graduate students, and resident physicians.

■ Career Corner

Q: I am in my mid-40s, have spent twenty-two years working my way up to be supervisor of my department in a major department store, and love my job. The new 31-year-old store manager has started to exclude me from memos and weekly management meetings, saying, "There's no reason for you to attend." Many of my coworkers are much younger than I, dress in jeans instead of professional suits, and seem to lack the traditional work ethic. To top it off, I just found out new managers are receiving "sign on" bonuses that bring their annual salaries near the amount I earn after 20+ years with the company. Those of us over 40 are finding it difficult to keep our mouths shut. Any suggestions?

A: It is obvious your conflict stems from a values clash that sometimes develops between older and younger workers. There also seems to be a breakdown in communication. Your younger coworkers and the store manager may be consciously or unconsciously building an "us versus them" scenario in relation to the more experienced members of the team. You need to establish more effective communication with your store manager. Openly discuss your concerns, and assertively seek an explanation for the changes that have taken place. When you allow others to ignore your needs and disregard your point of view, you display passive behaviors that will get you nowhere.

■ Key Terms

conflict	conflict resolution process
assertive behavior	brainstorming
aggressive behavior	collective bargaining
nonassertive behavior	mediation
win/lose approach	voluntary arbitration
lose/lose approach	compulsory arbitration
win/win approach	

■ Review Questions

1. Discuss the positive aspects of conflict in an organization.

2. What are some of the major causes of conflict between people in organizations?

3. What results might you expect when you implement the win/lose strategy? The lose/lose strategy? The win/win strategy?

4. Compare assertive behavior to nonassertive and aggressive behaviors.

5. What steps can you take to become more assertive?

6. What role does listening play when you are negotiating the resolution of a conflict with a coworker?

7. What specific behaviors can you use to improve your negotiation skills?

8. Describe the steps in the conflict resolution process. Briefly describe the impact each step might have on the final outcome.

9. Explain the difference between arbitration and mediation.

10. Do you think the labor union movement is dead? Why or why not?

■ Application Exercises

1. Has there been someone in your life (now or in the past) that you just can't (or couldn't) stand? Explain the behaviors this person exhibits that get on your nerves. Carefully examine Figure 13.1, determine which category fits the person best, and then describe what you might do to help this person change his or her behavior. Be specific.

2. Describe a conflict that is disrupting human relations at school, home, or work. It might involve academic requirements at school, distribution of responsibilities at home, or hurt feelings at work. Identify all the people involved in the conflict, and decide who should be involved in the conflict resolution process. Design a conflict resolution plan by following the steps given in this chapter. Implement your plan and report the results of this conflict resolution process to other class members.

3. To develop your assertiveness skills, find a partner who will join you for a practice session. The partner should assume the role of a friend, family member, or coworker who is doing something that causes you a great deal of frustration. (The problem can be real or imaginary.) Communicate your dislikes and feelings in a clear, direct manner without threatening or attacking. Then ask your partner to critique your assertiveness skills. Participate in several of these practice sessions until you feel confident that you have improved your assertiveness skills.

  Internet Exercise

Go to *www.adr.org* to view the website of the American Arbitration Association, the professional organization that offers support to some of the largest industries in the world during labor negotiations. Click on the Education link, discover the latest information about the organization's efforts, and report your findings to your class members.

Case 13.1   Couples Combat

According to a study conducted by the University of Denver, marital distress costs companies $6.8 billion in lost productivity. At any given time, one in every six employees has some sort of personal problem, including conflict with a significant other, that directly affects his or her productivity. These employees are three times more likely to think about quitting their job.

In an attempt to intercept this productivity hemorrhage, many organizations are taking a proactive approach to help their employees solve their marital conflicts before they happen. Managers are being taught how to help employees maintain healthy marriages and other personal relationships outside work by maintaining adequate staffing levels to avoid excessive overtime, discouraging workaholism, offering travel benefits for partners of employees who have to frequently travel on business, and encouraging vacations and occasional time off for personal reasons such as celebrating an anniversary.

Whether your employer is supportive or not, you as an individual need to take responsibility for maintaining your own marriage so that you can avoid the potentially negative effect a divorce might have on your personal life and your career track. In his book *Don't You Dare Get Married Until You Read This!*, Corey Donaldson says that the majority of issues that cause divorce already exist before the wedding because couples are not willing to ask or answer tough questions: Can physical violence by a mate be justified? What will we do if our child is born with a disability? Are you uncomfortable with women in high-paying jobs? If we both work, can we share the household duties? Daniel Caine, president of a financial planning firm for divorcing couples, says the most common causes for divorce are insecurity, money, communication, clash of values, and insufficient separation from family. He recommends asking such questions as: Are you comfortable with my religious observance? My family? My desire for wealth?[33]

Of course asking the right premarital questions does not guarantee a healthy relationship. Conflicts will and do occur in even the most solid marriages. Some experts suggest that bickering can be good for relationships. It may be one of the keys to a strong marriage because open conflict improves communication and allows each partner to vent his or her frustrations. But you need to learn how to argue effectively. Dr. Phil McGraw suggests several ways you can make your arguments as constructive as possible.[34]

■ Decide what you want before you even start the fight. Avoid simply complaining; ask for what you want.

■ Keep it relevant. Focus on what you are arguing about. If you stray, the argument will resurface again until the real issue is addressed.

■ Make it possible for your partner to retreat with dignity. Avoid calling each other names that linger beyond the argument. Show your partner courtesy and respect, even if he or she is wrong.

■ Know when to say when. If you have to give up too much of your life to maintain the relationship, maybe it's not worth it.

Keep in mind that if your objective in an argument is to win, the other person has to lose. This win/lose mind-set will only perpetuate the conflict.[35]

■ Questions

1. Have any of your coworkers experienced marital conflicts that affected their productivity at work? Did they have any impact on the organization and/or on you? Explain.

2. Have you had a conflict at home that had an effect on your work? Explain.

3. How might the premarital questions suggested in this case impact marital relations? What other questions need to be answered?

4. Recall your most recent conflict with your significant other. Did you follow Dr. Phil's suggestions? What was the outcome?

Case 13.2   Personal Assertiveness Pays Off

Jo Browning, a 5-foot-5-inch, 115-pound, soft-spoken daughter of an Air Force medic, never took up causes or ran for office in high school. In 1984 when she applied for a job building tires at Uniroyal-Goodrich, men in the plant took bets she wouldn't last and predicted, "That little skinny one ain't gonna be worth — ——." But for twelve years, she proved her worth, married a coworker, gave birth to Whitney, then worked back-to-back shifts with her husband so they could care for their daughter. The couple had little time together, and Jo learned to live on three hours of sleep a day.

The global economy forced Uniroyal to cancel stable weekday and weekend work schedules and convert to rotating shifts in order to lower costs and improve quality control. The new scheduling plan involved the rotation of four factory crews among four cycles that combined eight- and twelve-hour shifts. The delicate balance Jo had established for her family was shattered. None of the seventy-three child-care providers she called was willing to give weekend care.

Jo turned her bitterness and anger into action. She researched child care at the library, contacted advocacy groups, contacted management personnel about the problem when no one else in the plant would, and keynoted a union-hall child-care meeting. She encouraged Uniroyal's human resource managers to join a nineteen-employer child-care alliance studying the child-care needs of local workers. Child Care Systems of America saw the study and created a plan for an innovative 7-days-a-week child-care center. Jo took the plan to a city zoning meeting, and the center, funded by parent fees, is now open and available for use by all parents in the area.

Jo Browning's coworkers recognized her efforts and elected her secretary of her local 1,325-member steelworkers' union, the first woman to hold officer status. Getting what you want from the people you work with while respecting their rights is not always easy when you are young, diminutive, soft-spoken, and in a nontraditional work situation like Jo. However, her commitment and assertiveness at work effectively changed her world as well as others'. She discovered that those who speak up about well-thought-out ideas are often rewarded for their creativity. Those who rarely say a word rarely get rewarded. Madeleine Albright, the first female secretary of state in the history of the United States, suggests, "Timid workers, male or female, will always have it tough. . . . Sometimes you have to jump in first and ask questions later."[36]

■ Questions

1. What role did assertiveness play in Jo Browning's approach to this conflict resolution?

2. Which steps of the conflict resolution process detailed in this chapter did she follow?

3. Was the result of this personal approach to conflict resolution a lose/lose, win/lose, or win/win solution? Explain.

PART V

SPECIAL CHALLENGES IN HUMAN RELATIONS

14

RESPONDING TO PERSONAL AND WORK-RELATED STRESS

Chapter Preview

After studying this chapter, you will be able to

- Understand the stress factors in your life.

- Identify the major personal and work-related causes of stress.

- Learn how to assess the stress in your life.

- Recognize the warning signs of too much stress.

- Learn how to identify and implement effective stress management strategies.

- Identify stress-related psychological disorders.

Herman Lea recalls the day he accepted "the calling" from God to become a preacher. The Danville, Virginia, factory worker didn't realize that this life-changing event would put him on a collision course with a different sort of higher power: Goodyear Tire & Rubber Company. His employer announced that it would begin producing tires around the clock, 7 days a week, including Sunday. Lea's life became even more complicated when Goodyear moved to 12-hour shifts and his days off varied each week. The longer workday proved to be more grueling for the 50-year-old, and his dream of preaching on Sundays could not be realized because of work conflicts. He had a stroke, which he blames partly on the stress of juggling his schedule.[1]

Justine Fritz, leader of a twelve-member team overseeing a massive product launch at Medtronic, starts her day at 4:00 A.M. After an hour of quiet time at the computer, she heads for the club, where she completes an exercise routine. Back home, she takes a quick shower, gets dressed for work, and spends time with her son and husband. Once she arrives at work, there will be no quiet time. She will spend the day dashing from one meeting to the next, checking on the 100-plus projects her team is working on, and snacking on a cookie or popcorn when time permits. What drives Justine? Medtronic develops a variety of medical products that can help sick people. Reflecting on other jobs she has held, Fritz says, "I've just never worked on anything that so visibly, so dramatically changes the quality of somebody's life."[2]

Blue-collar and white-collar workers have one thing in common today—they are working harder and they are working longer hours. Most organizations are searching for ways to wring more productivity from a smaller number of employees. Job cuts are no longer a last resort in hard times, but an ongoing strategy to improve profits and stay competitive.[3] This downsizing often results in a work force that is insecure and more unsettled. Tensions build as people

Aquariums serve as cubicle dividers at Freshwater Software, Inc. Chris Anderson, vice president of creative direction, says the tanks create an atmosphere that is relaxing and fun. Freshwater Software, employer of sixty employees, is based in Boulder, Colorado.

work longer hours and then try to cram too many activities into their dwindling leisure time. In this chapter, we examine the most common sources of stress, help you assess your current stress load, and discover effective ways to respond to personal work-life stressors.

The Stress Factor in Your Life

Stress is the behavioral adjustment to change that affects you physically and psychologically. It is the process by which you mobilize energy for coping with change and challenges. Stress can come from your environment, your body, or your mind.[4] Environmental stress at work may be caused by noise, safety concerns, windowless settings, long hours, or unrealistic deadlines. Some bodily stress can be attributed to poorly designed workstations that produce eye strain, shoulder tension, or lower-back discomfort. But the stress that comes from our minds is the most common type of stress.

There can be positive aspects of mental stress. Stress *can* be a powerful stimulus for growth if it motivates you to do your best work. It can build within you the energy and desire needed to perform effectively. It can also promote greater awareness and help you focus on getting tasks completed quickly and efficiently. However, a great deal of the mental stress we encounter every day is caused by our negative thinking and faulty reasoning. For example, someone with large house payments and a great deal of personal debt may begin to worry excessively about the possibility of a layoff; the individual who lacks self-confidence may fear each technology change that is introduced at work; workers in organizations being merged may mentally anguish over who will be laid off next. Throughout the past decade we have seen mental stress levels rise to record highs. The American Institute of Stress estimates that problems related to stress (i.e., absenteeism, burnout, and mental health issues) now cost American businesses more than $300 billion a year.[5]

> *However, a great deal of the mental stress we encounter every day is caused by our negative thinking and faulty reasoning.*

● Responding to Stress

Stress consists of three elements: the event or thought (stressor) that triggers stress; your perception of it; and your response to it.[6] In his book *Stress for Success,* James Loehr suggests that as you are exposed to new stressors, you

TOTAL PERSON INSIGHT	**ROBERT EPSTEIN**
	EDITOR-IN-CHIEF, *PSYCHOLOGY TODAY*
	"We're all trained as children in the basics of reading and writing, but we're not taught about stress management. As adults, we flock to therapists, physicians, yoga classes and health clubs anxiously seeking magic cures, but relief rarely comes, and it's usually temporary."

should try to respond in ways that help you establish mental, physical, and emotional balance.[7] Unfortunately, most of us do not take the time to train our minds and bodies so that we build our capacity to handle the stress in our lives.

Our natural response to stress is as old as life itself—adapted by almost all species as a means of coping with threats to survival. When faced with an unexpected or possibly threatening situation, human beings—like animals—react with the **fight or flight syndrome:** Adrenaline pours into the bloodstream, heart rate and blood pressure increase, breathing accelerates, and muscles tighten. The body is poised to fight or run. Ironically, the same instincts that helped our ancestors survive are the ones causing us physical and mental health problems today.

Repeated or prolonged stress can trigger complex physiological reactions that may involve several hundred chemical changes in the brain and body.

The human response to stress is not easily explained. Repeated or prolonged stress can trigger complex physiological reactions that may involve several hundred chemical changes in the brain and body.[8] Everyone reacts differently to stress, so there is no single best way to manage it. Stress management methods must be tailored to individual needs.

As we discuss the major causes of stress, you will soon discover that it is virtually impossible to get rid of them and still function in today's society. Therefore, our approach is to help you train yourself to respond effectively to these stressors and thereby deepen your capacity to handle stress so that you will not only survive but thrive. The first step is to understand what might cause stress in your personal and professional life.

Major Causes of Stress

If you are searching for ways to combat stress and achieve a healthy balance between your personal life and your work life, join the crowd. A recent study by the National Institute for Occupational Safety and Health found that half the working people in the United States view job stress as a major problem in their lives.[9] If you listen closely, you will hear them saying, "Nothing seems simple anymore," or "We are working twice as hard for the same results." Some say the pace at work is so dizzying that it takes them hours to finally relax after the workday ends. Most of us can benefit from learning how to pinpoint the sources of stress in our life. If we can anticipate the stressors, we may be able to respond to them in a more effective manner.

● Change

Changes in the workplace come in many forms, including the need to do a job faster, to master advanced technology, or to take on a new work assignment. Consider employees who have been accustomed to working alone and now must work with a team, or employees who have held jobs that required little contact with the public and now must spend a great deal of time with clients, patients, or customers. When companies restructure in an attempt to meet demands of the marketplace, they often do not take into consideration the life demands of the employees. Many companies offer flexible work schedules, but many others do little or nothing to help employees balance jobs with personal and family life.

Many people have witnessed drastic layoffs in their organizations. These survivors have something in common with their former colleagues: Both remember what it was like to work in a stable and secure work environment, and both know they might never experience the same job security again. The survivor has a job but may no longer have peace of mind and, in some cases, may even experience as much stress as the unemployed worker.

HUMAN RELATIONS IN ACTION

Live Life Less Plugged In

As his career progressed from UPS package handler to production manager for telecommunications giant US West, 45-year-old Harvey Levitt became the ultimate plugged-in worker. He traveled most of the time, setting up mobile and remote offices for his employer; he carried a briefcase loaded with laptop, phone, pager, and other gadgetry. At home, he habitually worked after hours in a techno-gear-jammed bedroom that his wife called "the data center." Levitt's ability to work anywhere, anytime, through voice mail, e-mail, and the Internet, evolved into working everywhere, all the time.

One evening, Levitt experienced chest pains and, fearing a heart attack, was raced to a hospital emergency room. The trouble proved to be only indigestion brought on by stress. Instead

of resting, however, he frantically looked all over for his cell phone. The realization that he was more worried about his phone than about his health was a moment of truth. He began to "unplug" his life by throwing away his pager, tossing cables and batteries out of his briefcase, and resisting answering e-mails in the middle of the night and on weekends. Levitt travels less now and works from home. He turns off his three computers and two phones before dinner in the evenings, and then begins a similar shutdown process in his mind. He is gaining the mental discipline needed for drawing boundaries between work and personal life. The first time he opened the curtains in his home office, closed for years against the glare, he discovered a view of trees and sky. It gave a whole new perspective on the day.

● Technostress

After a decade of rapid advances in technology, today's plugged-in worker is trying to answer an important question: When is technology a help, and when does it become an intrusion on peace of mind and personal life?

There is no doubt that information technology, in its many forms, is now one of the great stressors in our lives. Craig Brod, a consultant specializing in stress reduction, was one of the first people to use the term *technostress* to describe this source of stress. **Technostress** is the inability to cope with computer and related technologies in a healthy manner. It may take several forms.[10]

Upgrade Anxiety As the processing speed of new computers increases, it is often necessary to acquire new equipment and new software every one or two years to keep up with the demands of customers, suppliers, and communications in general. With each upgrade, workers are forced to adapt to new technology just as they were adjusting to the previous system.

Tether Anxiety The authors of *Dot.Calm—The Search for Sanity in a Wired World* say the never-ending sea of information and our desire to access it result in a wireless tether. Our work is always with us through technology, and it is constantly demanding our immediate attention and response.[11] Many companies provide their employees with laptop computers, cell phones, pagers, and other types of wireless technology. These employees are often too accessible and are unable to create a balanced, sane personal life.

Monitoring Anxiety In order to assess employees' productivity, companies are developing new ways to monitor their work. Managers, in some cases, can track performance division by division, employee by employee, with startling precision.[12] Computer-based communications are being monitored at a growing number of companies. Software such as Investigator can track every keystroke and mouseclick. Video surveillance cameras, generally established for security purposes, monitor the worker's every movement. Many organizations have prerecorded telephone messages that warn incoming callers that their conversations may be monitored for quality assurance purposes. Even workers who travel outside the office may be tracked through global positioning satellite technology.

The information age has spawned many new technologies. Information technology, in its many forms, is now one of the major stressors in our lives. Duane Glover (left), NYCE Data Center technician, works with Monica Schwartzbach (center) and Mike Feingold to implement technical changes.

Computer Addiction   Many Internet users become addicted to computer use in the same way that some people become addicted to gambling or alcohol. Research indicates that from 2 to 5 million people may be addicted and that about 25 million may qualify as compulsive surfers.[13]

Another problem is that many computer users develop deep feelings of dependency on their machines and thereby lose the capacity to feel or relate to other people. Some workers adopt a machinelike mind-set that reflects the characteristics of the computer itself. Signs of the technocentered state include a high degree of factual thinking, poor access to feelings, and low tolerance for the ambiguities of human behavior and communication.[14]

> *Another problem is that many computer users develop deep feelings of dependency on their machines and thereby lose the capacity to feel or relate to other people. Some workers adopt a machinelike mind-set that reflects the characteristics of the computer itself.*

Information Overload   It is easy to experience sensory overload as you sort through the hundreds of messages that come to you daily by means of the Internet, e-mail, pagers, commercial advertising, and many other sources. *Data smog*, the term that David Shenk uses to describe the information-dense society we live in, is a problem because it crowds out quiet moments, obstructs much needed contemplation, and often leaves us feeling confused.[15] In an age where information is viewed as a valuable commodity, we have too much of it!

The Computer Workstation   Today's computer workstation is often housed in a drab 8-foot-by-10-foot prefabricated cubicle. Many employees spend their entire workday confined to a computer terminal. Carpal tunnel syndrome, a repetitive-stress wrist injury, is often caused by constant computer keyboarding and is one of the fastest-growing occupational hazards. Computer-related vision problems are also very common. These computer-related ailments have focused more attention on **ergonomics,** the study of optimal work area layout, lighting, furniture design, machine structure, and task limits. Figure 14.1 presents some pointers that might help alleviate some of the effects of workstation-related technostress.

● Noise Pollution

The human auditory system influences the frontal lobe of the brain, which plays a primary role in personality and intellectual functions. Loud noise (above 80 decibels) can produce harmful physical and mental effects.[16] *Noise* can be defined as unwanted sound. The roar of traffic, the neighbor's loud stereo music, or the loud voice of the person who occupies the cubicle nearby can increase your stress without your conscious awareness. About 30 million Americans have suffered a hearing loss. Loud workplaces remain the most common source of noise that causes such loss.[17] Research indicates that noise affects people more than any other work area pollutant (see Figure 14.2 on p. 338).

Many people experience hearing loss while working near loud machines, listening to loud music, or operating power equipment. About 36 million Americans have tinnitus in some form. Tinnitus is a persistent buzzing, ringing, or whistling sound that occurs in one or both ears. This very stressful hearing problem is usually worse when the tinnitus sufferer is around loud noises. Some

FIGURE 14.1	Suggestions for Alleviating Some of the Effects of Workstation-Related Technostress

WORKSTATION SPECIFICATIONS

Hard-copy holder close to the monitor to improve neck posture and reduce eye fatigue.

Gel-filled mouse platform positioned 20% higher than the elbows and in front of the body, not to the side.

Monitor positioned 26 inches from the eyes and slightly lower to avoid neck problems.

Seat back and positioned to provide lower-back support.

Space behind knees to improve leg circulation.

Ergonomically designed keyboard slightly inclined and placed at seated elbow height to encourage keying with straight wrists and relaxed shoulders.

90° angle or more between lower leg and thigh to improve leg circulation.

Feet on floor or footrest to improve stability.

Gel-filled and slightly curved wrist rest to keep wrists straight and reduce stress on shoulders and upper back.

Source: Gannett News Service. Used with permission.

companies are using sound-absorbing materials and sound-masking systems to help reduce noise levels. Many employers provide hearing protection devices.

● Long Hours/Irregular Schedules

Do Americans work longer hours today than in the past? Are more people addicted to work? Do more workers feel frazzled today? Finding answers to these questions is not easy because researchers often reach different conclusions. Some of the most important conclusions that do appear to have sufficient support follow.

■ Americans spend more time on the job than employees in any other developed nation. Workers in the United States take fewer and shorter vacations, and they are working more hours over the course of a year.[18]

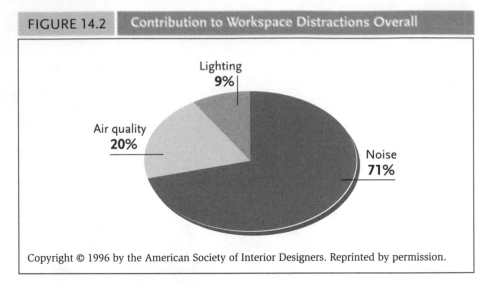

FIGURE 14.2 Contribution to Workspace Distractions Overall

Lighting **9%**

Air quality **20%**

Noise **71%**

Copyright © 1996 by the American Society of Interior Designers. Reprinted by permission.

■ In recent years, a growing number of workers call workloads excessive and say that they are bothered by increased pressure on the job. Many of the companies that have slashed their payroll now spread the same amount of work over fewer people.[19] Many workers are encouraged or required to add three to five hours of overtime to their workweek.

■ The New Economy, sometimes referred to as the 24/7 economy, is a non-stop "We never close" economy. Companies increasingly need employees who can work flexible schedules. Evening shifts, rotating shifts, 12-hour workdays, and weekend work often add stress to workers' lives.

In America, skilled and well-educated workers are especially likely to work long hours. Overtime in manufacturing is most prevalent among high-skilled employees.[20] Many of America's best and brightest workers are spending more time on the job and enjoying it less.

● **Incompetent Leaders**

Organizations often promote individuals into supervisory positions when they exhibit extraordinary talents in a specific technical field. The most talented electrician becomes maintenance supervisor. The most efficient surgical nurse

| TOTAL PERSON INSIGHT | **CAROL S. PEARSON**
EDITOR, *THE INNER EDGE*
"Our lives are complex, but we are not helpless to do something about the stress we feel. In fact, we often choose to intentionally overcrowd our schedules as a means of avoiding difficult feelings and choices. Then something forces us to slow down. We must listen to our hearts and bodies, and face a dawning awareness: My job, my spouse, my lifestyle—something—is not right for me." |

is promoted to nursing supervisor. The top salesperson is made sales manager. But technical superstars may be poor supervisors. And studies indicate that incompetent supervisors are a major source of stress in the workplace.[21] Incompetent leaders tend to ignore employee ideas and concerns, withhold information from employees, and fail to clarify roles and responsibilities. They may also set unrealistic deadlines and then blame employees for not meeting them.

Many supervisors are unable or unwilling to apply the leadership skills described in Chapter 12. Some of the reasons for incompetence include personality disorders, lack of training, and inability to learn from experience.

● Work and Family Transitions

In our fast-moving world, most of us have learned that certain transitions are inevitable. A **transition** can be defined as the experience of being forced to give up something and face a change. Author Edith Weiner states, "People are now in a constant state of transitioning. It is difficult for anyone to say with any degree of certainty where he or she will be maritally, professionally, financially or geographically five years from now."[22]

When a single person marries or a married couple divorces, the transition can be extremely stressful and can affect job performance. A new baby and the challenge of child care can cause stress in working mothers and fathers. As double-income parents attempt to meet the needs of the family, they often feel guilty about the time spent away from their children.

The twenty-something generation has produced a generation of concerned fathers, yet most organizations place little value on fathering as a workplace concern. A study conducted by Rosalind Burnett at Radcliffe College reinforced the results of many similar studies: Men are just as likely as women to worry about family problems while at work.[23] Yet many companies perpetuate the myth that men who want to be actively involved in the care and development of their children are not serious about their careers.

Assessing the Stress in Your Life

The Holmes-Rahe Social Readjustment Ratings Scale was developed to help people learn how much adjustment is needed to cope with various life events. The scale lists forty-two life events with numerical values ranging from 100 (death of a spouse) to 11 (minor violation of the law). The more stressful the event, the higher the number is. Although we usually think of marriage and retirement as positive events, both require considerable adjustment, according to the authors of the scale. Divorce and dismissal from work, both negative events, also require considerable adjustment. Research indicates that your chance of suffering a serious medical problem in the coming year is related to the number of stressful events you are experiencing now.[24]

To learn more about the sources of your stress, complete the NWNL Workplace Stress Test provided in the appendix and in the *Classroom Activities*

Manual that accompanies this textbook. It is typical of instruments designed to help employees become aware of stress sources on the job.

● **Warning Signals of Too Much Stress**

In today's stress-filled world, it makes sense to become familiar with the most common warning signals of stress. Physical signs might take the form of lower-back pain, headaches, loss of appetite, hypertension, coronary problems, or fatigue. Psychological symptoms might include anxiety, depression, irritability, paranoia, and reduced interest in personal relationships. Art Ulene, author of *Really Fit Really Fast,* says these unpleasant sensations may be your body's way of telling you that there is too much stress in your life.[25] The symptoms may be different for each person, but the message is the same: Listen to what your body is telling you.

Check the list of symptoms in Table 14.1 to see how many you are experiencing. As you review these stress signals, see if you circled the words *often* and *yes* many times. This pattern may indicate that stress is responsible for the way you are feeling. It may be time to begin using some type of stress management strategy.

THINKING / LEARNING STARTERS

As you begin to "manage" your stress, consider these questions:

1. What forms of exercise do you do? Would you like to add some form of exercise to your schedule? Which one? When will you start?
2. To what extent do you monitor the foods you eat? Give examples.

Stress Management Strategies

It is not possible to eliminate stress from your life, but you can determine when you have passed your limits and then do something about it. Stress can be harmful when you neglect to take control of your life and your body. Some people hold up well under stress for extended periods; others do not. The number of people who called in sick because of stress has tripled in the past few years. Stress that is not managed properly can weaken your immune system, disturb your sleep, and impair your mood and performance, thereby weakening your relationships with others.[26]

Everyone should make the effort to put stressful situations into proper perspective and deal with them accordingly. Once you become aware of what creates a stressful response in you (stress is very individualized), begin looking for stress management strategies that will help you cope with the stressful situations. Space does not permit an in-depth presentation of all stress management strategies, but we will describe those that are widely used today. You will be pleased to discover that many of these strategies require only a small investment of your time.

TABLE 14.1	Common Stress Signals				
		How Often You Have It **(Circle)**		**Occurs at Times of Stress** **(Circle)**	
Anger	Never	Sometimes	Often	Yes	No
Backache	Never	Sometimes	Often	Yes	No
Blurry vision	Never	Sometimes	Often	Yes	No
Cough	Never	Sometimes	Often	Yes	No
Dermatitis	Never	Sometimes	Often	Yes	No
Diarrhea	Never	Sometimes	Often	Yes	No
Dizziness	Never	Sometimes	Often	Yes	No
Excessive sweating	Never	Sometimes	Often	Yes	No
Fatigue	Never	Sometimes	Often	Yes	No
Feeling rushed	Never	Sometimes	Often	Yes	No
Frequent urination	Never	Sometimes	Often	Yes	No
Headache	Never	Sometimes	Often	Yes	No
High blood pressure	Never	Sometimes	Often	Yes	No
Hyperventilation	Never	Sometimes	Often	Yes	No
Impotence	Never	Sometimes	Often	Yes	No
Insomnia	Never	Sometimes	Often	Yes	No
Itching	Never	Sometimes	Often	Yes	No
Gnashing teeth	Never	Sometimes	Often	Yes	No
Late menstruation	Never	Sometimes	Often	Yes	No
Muscle spasms	Never	Sometimes	Often	Yes	No
Nail biting	Never	Sometimes	Often	Yes	No
Palpitations	Never	Sometimes	Often	Yes	No
Rapid heart rate	Never	Sometimes	Often	Yes	No
Stomachache	Never	Sometimes	Often	Yes	No
Vaginal discharge	Never	Sometimes	Often	Yes	No

Source: "Common Stress Signals," chart reprinted with permission from Feeling Fine Co., LLC.

● Sleep

Perhaps one of the most effective strategies for managing the negative aspects of stress is getting enough quality sleep. The amount of sleep your body requires is highly individualized and is based on several factors, including your age, fitness, amount of physical activity, diet, and chemical habits such as alcohol, nicotine, and caffeine consumption. Growth hormones and repair enzymes are released and various chemical restoration processes occur during sleep. (This explains why children need considerably more sleep than adults.) In order to train your body so that you can deepen your capacity to handle stress, follow these guidelines to improve your sleep recovery periods:

■ Develop a sleep ritual: Go to bed and get up at the same time as often as possible.

■ Avoid strenuous exercise within two hours of bedtime.

■ Avoid central nervous system stimulants near bedtime such as caffeine, chocolate, alcohol, or nicotine.

- Keep your bedroom cool, well ventilated, and dark.

- Get a half-hour of sunlight within thirty minutes of awakening. Light causes sleep hormones to be deactivated and replaced with hormones of arousal.[27]

Many workers get less than the recommended amount of sleep (7 to 8 hours) at night and therefore experience daytime drowsiness. This problem is so widespread that many employers encourage employees to take a short nap. Most employees are more productive and less apt to make fatigue-induced errors after waking from a short nap. If you don't feel comfortable taking a nap, lean back, breathe deeply, and close your eyes for several minutes. This activity will relax your body and change your perspective.[28]

● Exercise

Exercise can act as a buffer against stress, so stressful events have less of a negative impact on your health. Regular aerobic exercise—walking, swimming, low-impact aerobics, tennis, or jogging, for example—can increase your stress capacity. Exercise does not have to be strenuous to be helpful. Even gentle exercise like yoga or tai chi will help you manage your daily stress load.

Unfortunately, about 70 percent of Americans do not exercise regularly, and nearly 40 percent are not active at all. A study published recently in the *New England Journal of Medicine* indicates that by age 18 or 19, a majority of American females engage in virtually no regular exercise outside of their schools' physical education classes.[29] Too many people, men and women, fail to take advantage of

the physical and mental benefits of exercise. These benefits include lower cholesterol, weight loss, increased mental alertness, and a stronger heart.

Before you begin a strenuous physical exercise program, check with your doctor to be sure it is appropriate for you. Engage in a warm-up activity before any aerobic exercise. You want to prepare the muscles and joints for the activity that follows. Finally, choose an exercise program you enjoy; otherwise, you will probably abandon it after a few weeks.

● Nutrition

Health experts agree that the typical American diet—high in saturated fats, sodium, refined sugar, additives, and caffeine—is the wrong menu for coping with stress. The U.S. Senate Select Committee on Nutrition and Human Needs advises cutting down on fatty meats, dairy products, eggs, sweets, and salt. Fatty deposits can build up in the arteries, forming plaque. When stress increases the blood pressure, this plaque can tear away, damaging the arteries. Too much salt overstimulates the heart. Refined sugar acts first as a stimulant and then as a depressant to the central nervous system. The committee encourages greater consumption of fresh fruits, vegetables, whole grains, poultry, and fish. Eating the right foods in the proper amounts can replenish the vitamins and minerals the body loses when under stress and can also have a calming effect on your nervous system.

In recent years research into nutrition indicates that in many cases eating a carbohydrate-rich snack can actually help reduce feelings of impatience or distress. The best between-meal snacks are those that taste good to you but

---

HUMAN RELATIONS IN ACTION

Singing the Blues

Mitch Ditkoff was listening to a local blues band when the idea of singing the corporate blues first came to him. He realized that traditional blues is not about finding a solution to what's wrong; it's about stating what the feeling is. Joining forces with friend and fellow business consultant, Paul Kwiocinski, he formed Face the Music; a blues band that has been invited to perform at Consolidated Edison, General Electric, and other large companies. The following verse is part of a song entitled "Overcommitted Blues."

"My calendar's full,

My Day-Timer's frayed,

My voice mail's overloaded,

I'm way underpaid.

Got tons overdue,

Several deadlines to meet,

The only things working

Are my two left feet.

I'm a-fumblin'—got those overcommitted blues.

If you see me at the watercooler, please don't stop and schmooze."

Prior to each performance, Face the Music conducts extensive interviews. This "needs assessment" helps identify the client's prickly issues and problems, which then enables Face the Music to customize its intervention accordingly and write business blues songs tailored to their clients' needs. Employees often begin laughing when they realize that the band is singing about them.

also are high in complex carbohydrates and fiber and low in fat.[30] Complex carbohydrates are found primarily in foods from plant sources such as fruits, vegetables, pasta, cereals, and breads. The exception is milk, which is an animal source. Some snacks to consider include raisins, a whole-grain cracker with a thin slice of low-fat cheese, a handful of almonds, a cup of bean or lentil soup, or a small serving of nonfat pasta salad. As you develop the nutrition phase of your stress management plan, consider these basics:

- Always start your day with a healthy breakfast to stabilize your blood sugar and start your metabolism.

- Eat often and light. Small meals every two hours throughout the day raise your metabolic rate, stabilize your moods and energy levels, and reduce cravings for food.

- Reduce fat by baking, broiling, or grilling your foods instead of frying them.

- Drink eight glasses of water daily.

- Take a multivitamin supplement daily.[31]

● Meditation

Once the fight or flight syndrome was fully understood, researchers began searching for a way humans could respond to this condition. The stresses we face in today's world are likely to be psychological and interpersonal and not best handled by fighting or fleeing. A real breakthrough came with the discovery of the relaxation response by Herbert Benson at Harvard Medical School. The **relaxation response** is a simple meditation technique that can greatly reduce the damaging effects of stress. The technique slows your pulse, respiration, brain-wave activity, and blood pressure. It is especially helpful in cases where people suffer from chronic stress such as being under constant deadline pressure or having serious difficulties with their spouse. Benson says that a majority of all physician visits in the United States stem from stress-related conditions that can be helped through the relaxation response and similar meditation techniques now widely accepted in medicine.

The relaxation response is a simple meditation technique that can greatly reduce the damaging effects of stress. The technique slows your pulse, respiration, brain-wave activity, and blood pressure.

About 30 percent of the adult population in America uses some method to elicit the relaxation response.[32] Meditation, in one form or another, is probably the most common technique. Most meditation techniques involve these elements:[33]

1. Select a quiet place where you are not likely to be disturbed. Sit in a comfortable chair, or lie down on a couch or the floor.

2. Relax the muscles of your body from the top of your head to the tips of your toes. Let go of all the tension.

3. Focus on your breathing. Try to breathe naturally, letting the air come in through your nostrils and out of your mouth. Exhale slowly, letting all the air out of your lungs.

4. Every time you breathe out, repeat a word or phrase (mantra) that evokes the state you want to achieve. Your focus word might be *peace* or *relax*.

5. Assume a passive attitude, and when other thoughts come to mind, simply say to yourself, "Oh well," and gently return to the repetition. With practice, you will find it easy to turn back intruding thoughts, and you will have fewer of them.

Practicing these five elements each day will help to perfect your ability to meditate. Recent research indicates that meditating can bring about dramatic effects in as little as a 10-minute session.[34]

Why does this strategy work so well? As you inhale, you are bringing into your body fresh, clean air, and with it come sensations of peace, serenity, and regaining balance. With each exhalation, you imagine breathing out cynical thoughts and anxious feelings. With practice, the meditation technique will become effortless.

In addition to meditation, there are other stress management activities that can be used during brief pauses in your day. Table 14.2 provides some examples.

● Humor and Fun

Studies of the physiology of humor indicate that laughter is an invigorating tonic that heightens and brightens your mood and releases you from tensions. Laughter is a gentle exercise of the body, a form of "inner jogging." A good laugh involves many physiological changes, such as skin temperature, blood pressure, heart rate, brain-wave activity, and muscle tension.[35]

Laughter is a gentle exercise of the body, a form of "inner jogging."

Constantly work on improving your sense of humor. This has nothing to do with your ability to tell a joke or make others laugh. It's all about accessing the chemistry of humor through everyday happenings. Humor can come from many sources— cartoons, humorous stories, jokes, or ridiculous events that occur in your life. The average number of laughs per day for adults is 25. The average for children is 400![36] Just because you are an adult does not mean you have to give up fun things. Is there time in your life for a little fun? If not, you may be missing a wonderful opportunity to recover from the stress in your life.

TABLE 14.2	5-Minute Stress Busters

- Take 5 minutes to identify and challenge unreasonable or distorted ideas that precipitated your stress. Replace them with ideas that are more realistic and positive.
- Take a 5-minute stress-release walk outdoors: Contact with nature is especially beneficial.
- Relax your body and release tension with 5 minutes of deep breathing.
- Enjoy stress relief with a gentle 5-minute neck and shoulder massage.
- Spend 5 minutes visualizing yourself relaxing at your favorite vacation spot.
- Take a 5-minute nap after lunch.
- Spend 5 minutes listening to an audiotape featuring your favorite comedian.

TOTAL	**CHARLES L. PEIFER**
PERSON	PRESIDENT AND CEO, PRINCE SPORTS GROUP
INSIGHT	"I try to find a reason to laugh under high stress. It's an important part of everything I do. When things get rough, I actually look for funny things, particularly in myself. The more stress I have, the more I use humor to break me up and then refocus."

Some people have lost touch with what is fun for them. Ann McGee-Cooper, author of *You Don't Have to Go Home from Work Exhausted,* recommends making a list of things that are fun for you and then estimating the time they take.[37] This exercise may help you realize that there is plenty of time for fun things in your life. A walk in the park will require only 20 minutes, and reading the comics takes only 5 minutes out of your day.

● Solitude

Although some people feel uncomfortable when alone, many others feel "overconnected" because of the need to constantly respond to telephone calls, e-mail messages, and pager signals. Those who are constantly in touch with others can benefit from the therapeutic effect of solitude. Solitude can be viewed as an emotional breather, a restorer of energy, and a form of rest similar to sleep. Ester Buchholz, author of *The Call of Solitude,* says alone-time is a great protector of the self and the human spirit. She also notes that solitude is often required for the unconscious to process and unravel problems.[38] To experience the benefits of solitude, follow these suggestions:

■ Schedule a time for solitude each day. Consider getting up twenty minutes earlier in the morning.

■ Use this time for meditation, journal writing, or sitting in silence.

■ Consider this period of solitude a new experience of time, not dominated by current pressures and demands on your life.[39]

● Emotional Hardiness

At the beginning of this chapter, we noted that some stress can stimulate personal growth if you can develop the appropriate response to it. Some companies are helping employees build the stamina needed to cope with the stressors in their life. At 3M's headquarters in Maplewood, Minnesota, over seven thousand employees have completed the "Resilience at Work" training program. *Resilience* means being capable of bouncing back when you are confronted with stressful situations. The 3M program covers such diverse topics as financial planning, time management, parenting, and relaxation techniques.[40]

It is impossible to be in control of every event in your life, but you can take the necessary actions to *feel* in control. Ronald Nathan, an M.D. and coauthor

The special relationship between pets and people often benefits those who are experiencing excessive stress. The unconditional love and companionship of a loyal animal can have a calming effect on our lives.

of *The Doctors' Guide to Instant Stress Relief,* describes this quality as **emotional hardiness.** Those who possess it are in better control of their lives because they are committed to their goals, are challenged by change, and maintain their flexibility when their plans do not work as expected. Nathan says, "The key is to identify areas of your life where you do have control."[41]

In many cases, planning ahead is all that is needed to begin the process of taking control of your life. For example, if you have a deadline coming up, map out a plan that will prevent a crisis. You might schedule extra time between appointments to avoid feeling constantly under pressure to stay on schedule. Or you might take the last hour of every Friday to straighten up your workstation so that you can start your workweek under control. Getting up 15 minutes earlier in the morning will act as insurance that if anything does go wrong, you won't also have to deal with the stress of being late. Even little things like hanging a keyrack someplace in your home and forming the habit of always putting your keys there when you walk in can help. This will prevent the frantic search for them if you are running late.

Stress May Be Your Fault   One way to achieve emotional hardiness is by examining the expectations you have for yourself and others. Earlier in this chapter we discussed the stress people feel when they work long hours or irregular schedules. Yet many people do have choices when it comes to dividing their time between work and leisure. Many Americans work extra hours, or work a second job, in order to use the money for more consumer goods. Juliet Schor, author of *The Overspent American,* says the "sense of the necessary" has expanded too fast in recent years.[42] The desire for the latest big-screen TV or a larger sport utility vehicle often motivates people to work more.

Some people complain, "I'm so busy," but actually wear "busyness" as a badge of honor. We have created what might even be called a cult of busyness. So when people complain about the pressure they are under, they may actually be making a kind of boast: "I'm so busy, I must be important." In the modern workplace, busyness is often a measure of one's status.[43]

TOTAL	**JACOB NEEDLEMAN**
PERSON	AUTHOR, *TIME AND THE SOUL*
INSIGHT	"Culturally and individually, somewhere in our history, we chose to make material possessions important, not realizing that we would pay for all these things—consumer goods, improvements, technology—at the cost of our time."

Coping with Psychological Disorders

There is a difference between feeling stress because you are running late for an appointment and experiencing persistent anxiety. Feeling blue on Monday morning is not the same as deep-seated anxiety, depression, or burnout. Some people work 12-hour days because they love what they are doing, and others work the same schedule because they suffer from workaholism. In this final chapter segment, we briefly discuss some common psychological disorders and suggest ways to cope with them.

● Anxiety

Anxiety is a condition in which intense feelings of apprehension are long-standing and usually disruptive. Millions of Americans struggle with unwanted anxiety, and the cost in terms of suffering and lost productivity is very high. For most people, anxious feelings surface from time to time, but they are neither long-standing nor disruptive. If you have ever been tense before taking an exam or making an oral presentation, you have some idea of what anxiety feels like.[44]

Anxiety becomes a *disorder* only when it persists and prevents you from leading a normal life. Psychiatrists have found that there are several different anxiety disorders. A *phobia*, an irrational fear of a specific object or situation, represents one type of anxiety. Claustrophobia (fear of confined spaces) and agoraphobia (fear of crowds and public places) are two of the many phobias that can have a disruptive effect on a person's daily life.[45]

What is the best treatment for anxiety? Many anxious states are caused by stress, so consider using the stress management methods described in this chapter. Various methods of relaxation, for example, can lessen the severity of anxiety symptoms. However, when self-help methods do not bring the desired results, seek professional help. Your physician may recommend that you talk to a psychiatrist who can help you determine the causes of your anxiety.[46] You can get more information about anxiety and its treatments by contacting the Anxiety Disorders Association of America (*www.adaa.org*).

● Depression

Depression is a mood disorder. Nearly 19 million American adults suffer from it. This psychological disorder costs U.S. businesses nearly $70 billion annually in lost productivity, medical expenditures, and other related expenses. People of all ages can experience depression, but it primarily impacts workers in their most productive years: the 20s through 40s.[47]

When depression seriously affects a person's productivity on the job or interpersonal relationships, psychiatrists consider that individual to have a depression. Symptoms such as withdrawal, overwhelming sadness, or hopelessness may persist for weeks or months.[48] The exact cause of depression is not clear, but it can be triggered by a stressful event such as job loss or divorce.

In most cases depression is a treatable disorder, but it often requires a variety of approaches. Research shows that exercise can help improve mood and alleviate clinical depression.[49] Taking a short online quiz (*www.depression-screening.org*) can help you determine the severity of your condition. If you suffer from severe depression, don't self-medicate with drugs or alcohol. It is important that you get professional help.

● Burnout

Burnout is a gradually intensifying pattern of physical, psychological, and behavioral dysfunction that evolves in response to a continuous flow of stressors.[50] When you experience burnout, you feel that your energy fuel tank is operating on empty. Just as the engine of a car literally stops running without fuel and oil, a complete mental or physical breakdown can result from burnout. The most common symptoms of burnout include the following:

- Increased detachment from coworkers: irritability with coworkers along with less concern for them

- Increased detachment from customers or clients: failing to initiate contact with clients, labeling them as objects, and offering them short or rude answers to their questions

- Increased negative attitudes: constant complaining, cynicism, and moodiness

- Increased tardiness, absenteeism, clock watching, and carelessness

- Increased disorientation: forgetfulness, low concentration

- Increased physical problems: migraine headaches, backaches, ulcers, high blood pressure, sleep disorders

- Increased personal problems: drug or alcohol abuse, decreased social contacts, marital discord

All individuals experience one or two of these symptoms from time to time. But a person experiencing burnout exhibits these behaviors with increasing frequency and intensity. Those who burn out are usually successful, motivated, and committed to their work, but they often hold high-level positions in which there is little feedback from those who might offer a calming perspective to stressful events.

The report *Employee Burnout: America's Newest Epidemic* suggests that if you feel you are nearing burnout, take action immediately—at home *and* at work—before it's too late.[51]

1. Stop trying to do everything: When someone asks you to take on another task, always ask for its priority and a deadline. If necessary, explain that another task will have to be delayed if you accept this one.

2. If you must refuse a task, help devise an alternative solution so you do not alienate the people around you.

3. Clarify your value priorities. If you had just one year to live, what tasks would you stop doing? What would you do instead?

4. Make time to participate in as many stress management techniques as possible.

● Therapy Options

Sometimes psychological disorders can be addressed through self-help behavior modification and stress management strategies, but they often require participation in one-on-one or group therapy. Therefore, many organizations offer various **employee assistance programs** (EAPs) aimed at overcoming anxiety, depression, burnout, alcohol abuse, drug abuse, marital problems, and career and financial concerns. These programs are designed to address the negative effects of psychological disorders before employees become dysfunctional.

In addition to EAPs, millions of people choose to participate in one or more relevant **twelve-step programs** for help with various psychological disorders, including drug and alcohol addiction, eating disorders, and gambling addiction. All twelve-step programs rely on the same fundamentals:

- ■ *Working the steps.* This means admitting the problem, recognizing that life has become unmanageable, and turning life over to a higher power.

- ■ *Attending meetings.* Meetings of twelve-step programs are held in convenient locations throughout communities across the country. Members describe their own problems and listen to others who have experienced similar problems. In most cases, members form strong support groups.

Some critics say these programs simply replace one form of addiction with an addiction to group support. They advocate therapy programs that help people take control of their own life rather than turning it over to a higher power. Those who support twelve-step programs say that the emphasis on the connection to a higher power is a healthy alternative to the feelings of isolation and worthlessness generally found in those who enter the support groups.[52]

Web-based counseling is growing in popularity. Some licensed therapists give their clients a choice of face-to-face counseling or online counseling. In addition, there are thousands of support groups organized around various psychological disorders and moderated by therapists—some are licensed, some are not. Web-based therapy may be risky. There is often no guarantee that the

HUMAN RELATIONS IN ACTION

Modern-Day Walter Mittys

A growing number of workers are leading double lives to escape the extreme demands of today's jobs. They pursue extreme off-hours passions that provide experiences completely opposite from their daily working routines.

■ Stockbroker Ted Lipinski works around the clock. He takes work home from the office, reads global markets before he goes to sleep, and checks overseas activity when he wakes up in the morning. But every few months, he books a flight through Incredible Adventures in Sarasota, Florida, and blasts off in a fighter jet, breaks the sound barrier in a MIG-29 at 42,000 feet over Russian territory, streaks over the Arizona desert in a Thunderbird, or copilots a British-built jet over the Cape of Good Hope.

■ Bank credit officer Melissa Schuck gets a complete mental break as she bungee-jumps off a 180-foot bridge near Portland, Oregon. She claims the rush of hurtling earthward at 68 miles per hour provides a refreshing adrenaline rush that allows her to settle down and concentrate better at work.

■ Joanne Ambras, an internal consultant at Hewlett Packard, volunteers one day a week rescuing animals at a marine wildlife center. She recently taught orphaned seals to catch and eat fish. She confirms that seeing immediate results from her work at the center takes her mind off everything else.

self-proclaimed therapist is legitimate or licensed to practice in your state. In addition, critics say that no online therapist can promise confidentiality. To learn more about Internet therapy, visit *www.OnlineClinics.com,* an Internet therapy and referral service that connects clients with about four hundred *licensed* psychologists and social workers.[53]

■ Summary

When individuals cannot adequately respond or successfully adapt to a changing or unexpected set of circumstances, stress is usually the result. In some cases, stress may have a positive influence on behavior and spur a person on to achieving goals never thought possible. In other cases, however, stress may have a devastating effect on a person's personal and professional life.

Many of the stressors we experience are generated at work. Technostress, the inability to cope with computer technology in a healthy manner, is a significant contemporary threat to individuals and organizations. Some people feel the need to remain connected to their work at all times through electronic devices. Employers may demand this type of constant worker accessibility through technology and will often monitor employees' every move in and away from the workplace. The constant need to upgrade computer hardware and software, addiction to computers, the tremendous glut of information available through the Internet and e-mail, and poorly designed computer workstations are some of the elements that make technostress a negative force in the workplace. Noise pollution, irregular schedules, overtime mandates, and incompetent leaders add to the stress load of workers. In addition, transitions that occur in personal life, such as marriage, divorce, or relocation, may add more stressors that interfere with a person's effectiveness on the job.

Nevertheless, some stress in life is beneficial and helps keep a person motivated and excited. Therefore, the goal is not to eliminate stress but to learn how to assess the stressors in your life and increase your capacity to deal with them by participating in appropriate stress management strategies. You are more likely to handle the ever increasing stress of today's demands when you sleep, eat, and exercise regularly. Integrating meditation, time alone, and fun into a daily routine will help offset the negative effects of stress. Discovering the power available through emotional hardiness will also help.

When stress becomes persistent and overwhelming, it can lead to debilitating psychological disorders such as anxiety, depression, and burnout. While self-management techniques may sometimes help, there may come a time when one-on-one or group therapy with a licensed therapist is necessary. Employee assistance programs at work may help alleviate the problem. Some people turn to twelve-step programs; still others may benefit from online or face-to-face counseling.

■ Career Corner

Q: I work for a large company and have a terrific job. Because of downsizing, all of us in the office are working 60-hour weeks to get the work done. I take work home and do the work four people used to do. By the end of the week my mind is numb, my productivity is down, and I am exhausted. This not only is hard on my family but is bad for the company. It seems that if the work can't be handled during a normal workweek, then we need to hire more people to do the job. What do you suggest?

A: If you can get another job that is less stressful, then consider starting a job search. However, if you feel lucky to have your job, then let your boss know that you need help. Gather your colleagues together and present your case. Conduct your own research on the impact that unrelenting stress has on worker productivity. There is ample evidence that working on too many projects at one time reduces the brainpower available for each task. Explain that mental activity becomes sharper when you are able to shift your focus by going home, being with your family, or socializing. Set limits at work and quit taking work home. Perhaps this will allow you to be more productive at work. Don't accept an unreasonable amount of work because you are afraid you will be laid off. A job that is causing you to burn out is not worth it.

■ Key Terms

stress	emotional hardiness
fight or flight syndrome	anxiety
technostress	depression
ergonomics	burnout
transition	employee assistance programs
relaxation response	twelve-step programs

■ **Review Questions**

1. Are there any positive aspects to stress? Explain.

2. Identify the various forms of technostress, and explain how they affect workers' productivity.

3. Discuss the major work-related stressors and their impact on employee productivity.

4. Identify four stress management strategies you will use to help improve your response to stress in your life.

5. List some of the warning signals of too much stress.

6. Explain emotional hardiness. How will you know when you have achieved it?

7. What benefits can organizations and individuals derive from participating in physical fitness programs?

8. Why should organizations try to eliminate or minimize worker stress?

9. What role does humor play in managing the negative effects of stress?

10. Describe burnout and the steps that can be taken to avoid it.

■ **Application Exercises**

1. Determine what set of circumstances is causing the most stress in your life. For example, are you trying to work too many hours while going to school? Are you experiencing parental or peer pressure? Do you feel burdened with things you cannot control? Then answer the following questions:

   a. What aspects of the situation are under your control?

   b. Are there any aspects of the situation that are out of your control? Explain.

   c. What steps can you take to help eliminate the stress?

   d. What individual stress management strategies could you use to counteract the effects of this stress?

2. Consider the following company-sponsored stress management programs. List them in order from most beneficial to you to least beneficial. Explain your reasoning.

   a. Access to on-site exercise facilities or company-sponsored health club membership

   b. A workshop on stress management sponsored by the company

   c. A cafeteria where healthy, nutritionally balanced foods are served

   d. Access to a soundproof audiovisual room for viewing relaxing videotapes and listening to soothing music

3. Stress often increases as we struggle with time management. How well do you manage your time? Take a few minutes and answer each question

below. Then spend time developing a time management program that meets your individual needs.

a. Do you develop a daily "to do" list that indicates the activities you hope to work on?

b. Do you maintain a planning calendar—a single place to record daily appointments, deadlines, and tasks?

c. Do you have a series of personal and professional goals that guide you in setting priorities for use of your time?

d. Have you learned to say no to proliferating requests for your participation in team activities, projects, social activities, and so on, that may complicate your life?

 Internet Exercise

Go to *Monster.com*, the online jobs database, and enter *fun* or *humor* into the search box. Are there any organizations in your area that promote a "fun" working environment? Search East Coast (example: New York City), West Coast (example: San Diego), and Midwest (example: Kansas City) locations. Which region exhibits more fun opportunities than the others? What semantics are used to describe the fun working environment?

Case 14.1　Work/Life Balance in a Chaotic World

Today's high-tech work environment often functions with the basic premise that long hours and tunnel vision translate into higher productivity. The dot.com industry, for example, must focus on making fast money because tomorrow's business may go to the newest dot.com company. The resulting philosophy of "Get it now; enjoy it later" has become the dot.com world's guiding principle. But building instant fortunes often means treating people like machines: Run them around the clock until they burn out, and then bring in the new model. Barbara Johnson, founding CEO of Streetmail.com, with offices in New York City and North Adams, Massachusetts, explains that the idea that you have to be obsessed and work around the clock in order to make a good business proposition successful is absurd. In her experience, the opposite is true: "The biggest mistakes that I've ever made have occurred when I was exhausted."[54]

This level of intensity simply cannot be sustained as the information age workers begin to age and transfer their priorities to their families' needs. Dan Miller, CEO of BuyingDecisions.com and father of six children, states, "I could just dedicate myself completely to work. But if I do that, what happens is that my marriage suffers, my kids suffer, and I suffer. I've learned that when you don't have balance in your life, then you end up getting stressed out. You bring that burden and conflict to work with you, and then you can't be as productive. A lot of guys my age just don't get that yet. They think constantly about accumulating wealth, but they don't think much at all about the consequences of what they're doing—and not doing—in the rest of their lives."[55]

Some organizations believe that employees who feel overwhelmed by the requirements of their jobs combined with those at home reflect an attitude problem. Statistical analysis of the Maslach Burnout Inventory, however, reveals that burnout occurs when the workplace does not recognize the human side of work or demands superhuman efforts. Many organizations are catching on and are doing something about it.

- Jeff Reese, a 34-year-old Intel advertising manager, was commuting forty-five miles each way from his San Francisco home to his office in Santa Clara. After trying the train and carpooling with other Bay Area employees to no avail, Jeff and his colleagues convinced Intel's management to open a pilot program using a satellite office in downtown San Francisco. It was such a raging success that the trial program became a full-fledged satellite office where 103 workstations occupy an entire floor of a high-rent financial district skyscraper. The company plans to add three more Bay Area satellite facilities near high-traffic suburbs. Reese, whose commute is down to 12 minutes, says, "Now I can wake up an hour after I normally would and I don't have to listen to traffic reports. . . . It really removes the stress."[56]

- Calico Commerce Inc. has a strong telecommuting policy, plans to add more satellite offices for people with long commutes, and offers paid time off and leaves of absence for employees who need a break. Lynn Corsiglia, vice president of Calico's human resources department, traded her quarterly bonus for extra vacation time so that she could travel with her daughter, a high school junior, to visit colleges.

- Hewlett Packard encourages employees to take advantage of its company's virtual office program, as well as part-time and job-sharing programs.

- Liquid Price.com pays for second phone lines and high-speed Internet access at home so that employees can efficiently telecommute.

- Purchases of desktop and laptop personal computers for their telecommuters are subsidized by respond.com.

- 3Com Corporation offers concierge service that sends valets directly to employees' desks to pick up laundry and drycleaning and performs personal administrative tasks such as shopping for and delivering birthday gifts.

- Cisco Systems Inc. opened a $10 million childcare center at its San José headquarters, complete with Internet cameras so that parents can log on and check on their children.[57]

■ Questions

1. How has technology added to workers' work/life stress? How has it eased the stress of balancing work and home life?

2. What work/life qualities will you expect from your employer to enable you to maintain a healthy balance?

3. Some human resource managers believe that the highest risk of burnout comes from those workers who do *not* have obligations outside their workplace. Do you believe this is true or false? Explain.

Case 14.2 Drugs on Campus

It is estimated that 1.6 million incoming college freshmen experience episodes of depression and that approximately 20 percent of the nation's student population take antidepressants at some point in their college years. College health officials know that students, some on their own without parental guidance for the first time in their lives, live with academic pressure, experience frequent romantic rollercoasters, eat too much junk food, and get too little sleep. To help students cope with the pressures associated with college life, many campuses conduct screenings for depression, eating disorders, anxiety, and alcohol abuse. They create public service ads and posters aimed at increasing students' awareness of these potentially debilitating psychological disorders.

To help defray the costs of these on-campus programs, some college administrators are accepting the financial sponsorship of drug companies that offer programs meant to raise students' awareness of depression and the drugs that can treat it. Wyeth (maker of the antidepressant Effexor) created a 90-minute forum called "Depression in College: Real World, Real Life, Real Issues." Wyeth joined with Pfizer Inc. (maker of the antidepressant Zoloft), Glaxo (maker of the antidepressant Paxil), and Eli Lilly & Co. (maker of the antidepressant Prozac) to help underwrite the National Depression Screening Day.

Glaxo offered an online self-test to raise awareness of *general anxiety disorder.* Some of the questions on the self-test were: "Do you worry excessively?" "Are you anxious a lot of the time?" "Do you have trouble sleeping?" "Does anxiety ever interfere with your family or social life?" "Do you avoid giving speeches?" "Does criticism frighten you?" If participants answered yes to any or all of these questions, they were advised that they might be candidates for antidepressant drugs and encouraged to contact their physicians.

While drugs like Paxil, Prozac, Zoloft, and Effexor are helping millions of people live more productive lives, critics believe that there is an inherent problem in having the producers of such drugs presenting on-campus forums and issuing online diagnoses of depression or anxiety. They believe these programs run the risk of misdiagnosis and unnecessary prescriptions. While they agree that it is important to recognize the danger signs of psychological disorders, they encourage those who participate in these programs to question: Who doesn't feel tense, tired, or irritable at some time? They suggest better self-test questions might be: "Is there something wrong with me, or is there something wrong with my academic or career choices?" "Do my efforts give me satisfaction?" "Do I feel valued by my friends and colleagues?" "Do I receive recognition for a task well done?" If the answer to these is no, maybe the self-test participants should take action, not drugs.

In defense of events sponsored by drug companies, Karen Milo, professor of psychiatry at the University of South Florida's College of Medicine, said, "As long as the presentation is very balanced and the marketing isn't happening at all, then we have not found it to be a problem thus far." Laurie Reitman, director of the student health and counseling center at Washington University, says, "I don't see anything wrong with utilizing every available resource to publicize education resources for our students."[58]

■ Questions

1. Does it bother you that drug companies have a role in educating college students about the warning signs and possible medicinal solutions to psychological disorders? Explain your reasoning.

2. What is meant by the statement that "maybe self-test participants should take action, not drugs"?

3. Are there alternatives to drug therapy for psychological disorders that college students might implement to help them with the stress of college life? What are they?

15

VALUING WORK FORCE DIVERSITY

Chapter Preview

After studying this chapter, you will be able to

- Define the primary and secondary dimensions of diversity.

- Discuss how prejudiced attitudes are formed.

- Develop an awareness of the various forms of discrimination in the workplace.

- Understand why organizations are striving to develop organizational cultures that value diversity.

- Identify ways in which individuals and organizations can enhance work force diversity.

- Discuss the current status of affirmative action programs.

The Polo Ralph Lauren flagship store in New York City is a place where dreams can take shape. Soon after Sikita Smith began working at the store as a sales associate, she dreamed of one day moving to headquarters as an executive. The recent college graduate, who is black, felt comfortable working with the store's fashion-conscious customers. When her client list and commissions grew, she began to anticipate a promotion. As the months passed, however, she began to believe that promotions would more likely be awarded to her white coworkers. She quit her job after only one year.[1]

Although nearly all major companies have made a commitment to diversity, including Polo Ralph Lauren, most have not achieved racial balance at the management level. According to the U.S. Bureau of Labor Statistics, Latinos and African Americans together hold only 12 percent of all executive, managerial, and administrative jobs. Many companies have a revolving door for talented minorities. They recruit the best and the brightest but cannot keep them. Even those companies that make *Fortune* magazine's "America's 50 Best Companies for Minorities" list must work hard to achieve diversity in upper ranks.[2]

Organizations are discovering the waste of valuable human resources that occurs when employees face barriers to advancement not only because of race, but also because of gender, age, ethnicity, religion, sexual orientation, or physical or mental disabilities. This chapter can help you understand the detrimental effects of prejudice and discrimination in the workplace and help you handle such behaviors if or when you are the victim.

Work Force Diversity—A Definition

E Pluribus Unum: "Out of many, one." No other country on earth is as multiracial and multicultural as the United States of America. The strength of some nations lies in their homogeneity. Japan is made up mostly of people of Japanese descent, and their economy and business transactions reflect this common heritage. The People's Republic of China is populated mostly with people of Chinese ancestry, and their values and culture are a major part of their global economic strength. But America has always served as host to a kaleidoscope of the world's cultures, and the diversity movement is likely to continue. The foreign-born population in America now numbers 32.5 million people and is projected to increase exponentially (see Figure 15.1 on p. 360).[3] Therefore, business practices must adjust accordingly.

> *In the past, most U.S. organizations attempted to assimilate everyone into one "American" way of doing things.*

In the past, most U.S. organizations attempted to assimilate everyone into one "American" way of doing things. Labor unions were formed so that everyone would be treated the same. The women's rights movement began when women wanted to be treated just like men in the workplace. The emphasis now, however, is on **valuing diversity,** which means appreciating everyone's uniqueness, respecting differences, and encouraging every worker to make his or her full contribution to the organization. Organizations that foster the full participation of all workers will enjoy the sharpest competitive edge in the expanding global marketplace.

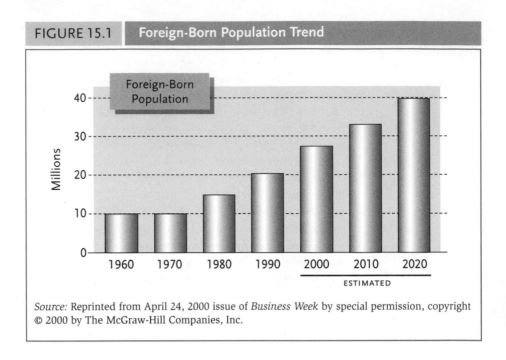

| FIGURE 15.1 | Foreign-Born Population Trend |

Source: Reprinted from April 24, 2000 issue of *Business Week* by special permission, copyright © 2000 by The McGraw-Hill Companies, Inc.

TOTAL	**J.T. "TED" CHILDS, JR.**
PERSON	VICE PRESIDENT, IBM GLOBAL WORKFORCE DIVERSITY
INSIGHT	"No matter who you are, you're going to have to work with people who are different from you. You're going to have to sell to people who are different from you, and buy from people who are different from you, and manage people who are different from you."

● Dimensions of Diversity

There are primary and secondary dimensions of diversity. The **primary dimensions** are core characteristics of each individual that cannot be changed: age, race, gender, physical and mental abilities, and sexual orientation (see Figure 15.2). Together they form an individual's self-image and the filters through which each person views the rest of the world. These inborn elements are interdependent; no one dimension stands alone. Each exerts an important influence throughout life. Marilyn Loden and Judy Rosener describe individual primary dimensions in their book *Workforce America!* They say, "Like the interlocking segments of a sphere, they represent the core of our individual identities."[4]

The greater the number of primary differences between people, the more difficult it is to establish trust and mutual respect. When we add the secondary dimensions of diversity to the mix, effective human relations become even more difficult. The **secondary dimensions** of diversity are elements that can be changed or at least modified. They include a person's health habits, religious beliefs, education and training, general appearance, relationship status,

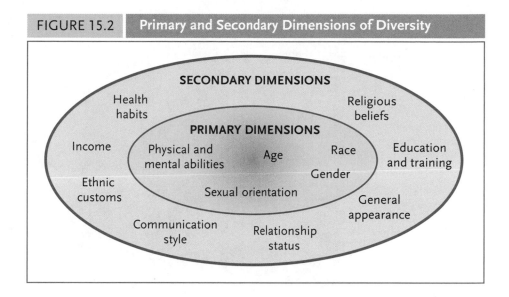

FIGURE 15.2 | Primary and Secondary Dimensions of Diversity

ethnic customs, communication style, and income (see Figure 15.2). These factors all add a layer of complexity to the way we see ourselves and others. The blend of secondary and primary dimensions adds depth to each person and helps shape his or her values, priorities, and perceptions throughout life.[5]

Each of us enters the work force with a unique perspective shaped by these dimensions and our own past experiences. Building effective human relationships is possible only when we learn to accept and value the differences in others. Without this acceptance, both primary and secondary dimensions of diversity can become roadblocks to further cooperation and understanding.

Prejudiced Attitudes

Prejudice is a premature judgment or opinion that is formed without examination of the facts. Throughout life we often prejudge people in light of their primary and secondary dimensions. Rather than treat others as unique individuals, prejudiced people tend to think in terms of **stereotypes**—perceptions, beliefs, and expectations about members of some group. In most cases, a stereotype involves the false assumption that all members of a group share the same characteristics. The most common and powerful stereotypes focus on observable personal attributes such as age, gender, and ethnicity.[6]

TOTAL	**VERNON E. JORDAN, JR.**
PERSON	ATTORNEY AND CIVIL RIGHTS LEADER
INSIGHT	"So long as black and white Americans see each other as stereotypes and not as people with the same dreams, ambitions and values, this nation will be frozen in suspicion and hate."

Fannie Mae, the Washington D.C. based mortgage company, ranks very high on *Fortune* magazine's list of 50 Best Companies for Minorities. The company employs a high percentage of minorities at all levels of management. Fannie Mae is also a leader in workforce mentoring, with 12 percent of minority employees participating.

In some cases a stereotype can evolve into an anxiety disorder. Fear of foreigners or other strange-seeming people is known as **xenophobia.** Researchers are discovering that xenophobia can develop quickly, even among people who claim to have no cultural biases. For many Arab and Muslim Americans, the months after the 9/11 terrorist attacks were very trying. Many were harassed at work, and some had their property vandalized. When it comes to whom we fear and how we react, we can choose not to give in to our xenophobic tendencies.[7]

Prejudiced attitudes and the resulting stereotypes are more likely to change when we take time to learn more about specific members of a particular group. For example, twenty years ago, women were often viewed as indecisive, passive, and too emotional to succeed in leadership positions. As the work force became increasingly female, men and women began working together and learning that leadership ability might *not* be gender-related. Now that women

HUMAN RELATIONS IN ACTION

Tools for Tolerance: Personal

- Attend a play, listen to music, or go to a dance performance by artists whose race or ethnicity is different from your own.
- Visit a local senior citizens center and collect oral histories. Donate large-print reading materials and books on tape. Offer to help with a craft project.

- Take a conversation course in another language that is spoken in your community.
- Sign the Declaration of Tolerance (see Figure 15.3).
- Speak up when you hear slurs. Let people know that biased speech is always unacceptable.

occupy a greater proportion of management and executive positions, stereotypes formed by prejudiced attitudes are contradicted by facts.

● How Prejudicial Attitudes Are Formed and Retained

Three major factors contribute to the development of prejudice: childhood experiences, ethnocentrism, and economic conditions.

Childhood Experiences   Today's views toward others are filtered through the experiences and feelings of childhood. Children watch how their family members, friends, teachers, and other authority figures respond to different racial, ethnic, and religious groups. As a result, they form attitudes that may last a lifetime, unless new information replaces the old perceptions. Prejudicial attitudes are not unalterable. Whatever prejudice is learned during childhood can be unlearned later in life.[8]

FIGURE 15.3	Declaration of Tolerance

Declaration of Tolerance

Tolerance is a personal decision that comes from a belief that every person is a treasure. I believe that America's diversity is its strength. I also recognize that ignorance, insensitivity, and bigotry can turn that diversity into a source of prejudice and discrimination.

To help keep diversity a well-spring of strength and make this country a better place for all, I pledge to have respect for people whose abilities, beliefs, cultures, race, sexual identity or other characteristics are different from my own.

To fulfill this pledge, I will. . .
- examine my own biases and work to overcome them,
- set a positive example for my family and friends,
- work for tolerance in my own community, and
- speak out against hate and injustice.

_____
Signature

Please sign and mail a copy to:
National Campaign for Tolerance,
400 Washington Avenue
Montgomery, AL 36104.

Source: Adapted from "101 Tools For Tolerance: Simple Ideas for Promoting Equity and Celebrating Diversity." Copyright © 2000, Southern Poverty Law Center, Montgomery, AL. *101 Tools for Tolerance* is available free from the SPLC. For more information, visit *www.splcenter.org* or send a fax to (334) 264-7310. Reprinted by permission of Southern Poverty Law Center.

Ethnocentrism   The tendency to regard our own culture or nation as better or more "correct" than others is called **ethnocentrism.** The word is derived from *ethnic,* meaning a group united by similar customs, characteristics, race, or other common factors, and *center.* **Ethnicity** refers to the condition of being culturally rather than physically distinctive.[9] When ethnocentrism is present, the standards and values of our own culture are being used as a yardstick to measure the worth of other cultures.

In their book *Valuing Diversity,* Lewis Brown Griggs and Lente-Louise Louw compare ethnocentrism in an organization to icebergs floating in an ocean. We can see the tips of icebergs above the water level, just as we can see our diverse coworkers' skin color, gender, mannerisms, and job-related talents and hear the words they use and their accents. These are basically "surface" aspects of a person that others can easily learn through observation. However, just as the enormous breadth of an iceberg's base lies beneath the water's surface, so does the childhood conditioning of people from different cultures. As icebergs increase in number and drift too close together, they are likely to clash at their base even though there is no visible contact at the water's surface.[10] As organizations increase the diversity of their work force, the potential for clashes resulting from deep-seated cultural conditioning and prejudiced attitudes also increases.

Economic Factors   When the economy goes through a recession or depression, and housing, jobs, and other necessities become scarce, people's prejudices against other groups often increase. If enough prejudice is built up against a particular group, members of that group may be barred from competing for jobs. The recent backlash against immigrants can be traced, in part, to a fear that the new arrivals will take jobs that would otherwise be available to American workers. Prejudice based on economic factors has its roots in people's basic survival needs, and, as a result, it is very hard to eliminate.

Rising income and wealth inequality in America is viewed by many as a serious barrier to racial harmony. Ronald Walters, University of Maryland political scientist, says, "You can only have meaningful racial reconciliation when people of roughly equal socioeconomic status can reach across the divide of race."[11] The gap in well-being between whites and nonwhites barely changed throughout the booming 1990s and remains huge. The racial divide in wealth (value of all assets) and income shows no sign of narrowing.[12]

THINKING / LEARNING STARTERS

1. Have you ever been the object of prejudice? What were the circumstances? How did this behavior affect your self-esteem?

2. Do you carry any prejudices that are obvious carryovers from your childhood? Explain.

3. Are you doing anything to overcome these prejudices? What would the benefits be if you could overcome them?

The Many Forms of Discrimination

Discrimination is behavior based on prejudiced attitudes. If, as an employer, you believe that overweight people tend to be lazy, that is a prejudiced attitude. If you refuse to hire someone simply because that person is overweight, you are engaging in discrimination.

> *Discrimination is behavior based on prejudiced attitudes.*

Individuals or groups that are discriminated against are denied equal treatment and opportunities afforded to the dominant group. They may be denied employment, promotion, training, or other job-related privileges on the basis of race, lifestyle, gender, or other characteristics that have little or nothing to do with their qualifications for a job.

● Gender

Discrimination based on gender has been, and continues to be, the focus of much attention. The traditional roles women have held in society have undergone tremendous changes in the past few decades. More and more women are entering the work force not only to supplement family income but also to

This 40-year old electrician returned to college to meet certification requirements. Older workers must take personal responsibility for their own career development.

TABLE 15.1	Age-Related Discriminatory Practices

Many organizations have fostered cultures of age bias. This bias is expressed in a variety of age-related discriminatory practices:

■ Cutting off older workers from job-related training and career development opportunities

■ Excluding older workers from important activities

■ Favoring younger job applicants over older, better-qualified candidates

■ Forcing older workers out of the work force with negative performance evaluations

■ Pressuring older workers to accept financial incentives and retire early

Source: Sheldon Steinhauser, "Age Bias: Is Your Corporate Culture in Need of an Overhaul?" *HR Magazine,* July 1998.

pursue careers in previously all-male professions. Men have also been examining the roles assigned them by society and are discovering new options for themselves. Most companies have recognized that discrimination based on gender is a reality and are taking steps to deal with the problem. Chapter 16 is devoted to an in-depth discussion of overcoming gender bias in organizations.

● Age

Discrimination based on age can apply to workers in the 40-to-70 age range and to younger workers from 18 to 25. Youth can be a disadvantage when potential employers show a reluctance to hire young people because of their lack of practical experience in the workplace. Generally speaking, young adults—even those who are older but simply *look* young—can overcome age bias when they seek out and accept difficult job assignments. This process of "paying your dues" will help prove to coworkers that age does not necessarily determine intelligence or competence.

Older workers face different employment problems. There is the widespread perception that older workers are unable or unwilling to adapt to accelerating change.[13] This stereotypical notion exists in spite of studies indicating that workers 55 and over are productive, cost-effective employees who can be trained in new technologies as easily as younger people. Because of prejudice, workers over 50 take nearly twice as long to find a new job as do younger people.[14] Many must accept positions that pay considerably less than their previous job.

According to recent reports from the Equal Employment Opportunity Commission (EEOC), age discrimination is on the rise. As companies search for ways to cut costs, they often find creative ways to get rid of older workers (see Table 15.1) and replace them with younger workers who earn less. The rise in age discrimination complaints is also due to our aging work force. By 2015, workers 55 and older will make up nearly 20 percent of the work force.[15]

In some cases companies are unwilling to make a commitment to skill upgrading and new technology training needed by older workers. In these cases, older workers must take personal responsibility for their own career development by keeping up with what is going on within their company, accepting change, taking the initiative to learn and use new technologies, and keeping fit so that they can stay energized and competitive.

● Race

Few areas are more sensitive and engender more passion than issues surrounding race. **Race** denotes a category of people who are perceived as distinctive on the basis of certain biologically inherited traits such as skin color or hair texture.[16] Because people cannot change these inherited traits, they can easily become victims of discrimination.

Throughout American history we have seen attempts to place people in racial categories and judge them as racial symbols rather than as unique individuals. During World War II, many Japanese Americans of Japanese ancestry were confined in concentration camps because they were considered a security threat, merely because of their racial heritage. Until the mid-1960s, some African Americans were not allowed to drink from public water fountains, to sit anywhere but in the rear of public transportation, or to attend public schools established for white children only. Because of the war on terrorism, today's "racial" targets often include immigrants from Pakistan, Iraq, and other Arabic countries, as well as their American-born children.

There is as much genetic variability between two people from the same "racial group" as there is between two people from any two different "racial" groups.

The Myth of Race Critics of racial categories view them as social inventions that intensify and reinforce racist beliefs and actions. They believe that one way to break down racial barriers and promote a race-free consciousness is to get rid of traditional racial categories (see Table 15.2). A growing number of geneticists and social scientists reject the view that "racial" differences have an objective or scientific foundation.[17] The American Anthropological Association (AAA) has taken the official position that "race" has no scientific justification in human biology. The AAA position is that "There is as much genetic variability between two people from the same 'racial group' as

TABLE 15.2	Traditional Nonwhite Race Categories
Black	Persons who descended from peoples of African origin. Many blacks have a preference for the name *African American*.
Hispanic	This is the broadest term used to encompass Spanish-speaking peoples in both American hemispheres. The widely used term *Latino* is generally restricted to persons of Latin American descent.
Asian	The term *Asian* is preferred over *Oriental* for persons of East, Southeast, and South Asian ancestry, such as Chinese, Koreans, Japanese, Indonesians, and Filipinos.
Native American	This term refers to peoples indigenous to America. However, the term *Indian* is sometimes used as a term of pride and respect by Native Americans.

Source: American Heritage Dictionary, 4th ed. (Boston: Houghton Mifflin, 2000), pp. 189–190, 105, 832, 1171.

there is between two people from any two different 'racial' groups."[18] Put another way, individual differences are much greater than group differences, regardless of how the group is defined.[19]

It is important to keep in mind that individual differences are much greater than group differences, regardless of how the group is defined. The Asian label includes a wide range of groups, such as Vietnamese, Filipinos, Chinese and Koreans, with distinct histories and languages. The label "African American" does not take into consideration the enormous linguistic, physical, and cultural diversity of the peoples of Africa.[20]

The rise in interracial marriages has created millions of Americans who have mixed-race identity and who are likely to resist attempts to be shoehorned into racial categories that seem meaningless to them. Golf champion Tiger Woods (his father is African American and his mother is from Thailand) is proud of his multiracial background. He joins a growing number of Americans who believe that identities can evolve, that people needn't be locked into the identities bestowed on them at birth. As a result, respondents to the 2000 U.S. census had the opportunity to check one or more boxes from sixty-three racial options.[21]

Race as Social Identity   Although races are not scientifically defensible, they are "real" socially, politically and psychologically. Race and racism affect our own self-perception and how we are treated by others. Groups that are working to build ethnic pride, such as Native Americans, oppose efforts to get rid of the traditional racial categories. They view racial labels as part of a positive identity. They believe that the only way to ensure that individuals of all races and national origins are treated fairly is to maintain the traditional racial categories. They say that this system is needed to create minority voting districts and to administer an array of federal laws and programs designed to ensure that minorities get equal housing, education, health care, and employment opportunities.[22] That is why the federal government has assured the public that the agencies responsible for enforcement of nondiscriminatory housing laws, employment laws, and so forth will break down the many census report categories in ways that allow them to enforce the current laws.

● Religion

Discrimination based on a person's religious preference has been an issue throughout history. Even though Christians represent the dominant religion in the United States, members of various denominations often lack tolerance for beliefs that differ from their own. When John F. Kennedy ran for president of the United States, a strong faction campaigned against having a Catholic in the White House. Mormons, Jehovah's Witnesses, and Southern Baptists often experience subtle discrimination and rude comments from their fellow Christians. Even members of the same denomination, such as Lutherans, will sometimes lack tolerance for members of a similar but separate church in the same town.

Christianity is the most commonly practiced religion in the United States, and Judaism is the second.[23] However, during the 1930s, many Christian Americans considered Jews a separate "race" and treated them accordingly.

Even during the 1940s and World War II, when Americans were in a battle against the Nazis and their persecution of the Jews, anti-Semitic (anti-Jewish) sentiment in the United States ran deep, and help wanted ads sometimes specified, "Christians only."[24] When the new millennium began and Joseph Lieberman, a Jew, ran for vice president of the United States, anti-Semites campaigned against him.

Today the headlines document the pervasive discrimination of Muslims in the workplace. They are often ridiculed for their daily prayer routine. Misunderstandings seem to occur frequently over relatively minor issues such as Muslim women's right to wear head scarves and Muslim men's right to maintain facial hair. With more than 5 million Muslims in America, Islam is expected to soon surpass Judaism and become the second most practiced religion in the United States. The EEOC has reported an increase in discrimination complaints brought by Muslims, Arabs, Middle Easterners, South Asians, and Sikhs. Even those who are American born but are "perceived to be" members of these groups can become victims of this type of discrimination. Recently the EEOC announced a $1.11 million settlement against Stockton Steel, a California-based company that was accused of job bias against Muslims. In this case, four Pakistani machine operators said they were routinely given the worst jobs, ridiculed during their daily prayers, and called derogatory names.[25]

● Disability

Wilfredo "Freddy" Laboy is described by his coworkers at Gap Inc. as the "wild man in a wheelchair." Freddy practically dances across the store, popping wheelies and spinning himself around to the beat of the ever-present pop music. The fast-talking, goateed 36-year-old, who lost both legs when he fell off a freight train at age 9, never hesitates to hop off his chair to retrieve an item that has fallen on the floor. Freddy loves working at the Gap, and the Gap loves Freddy.[26]

Freddy Laboy is one of the country's 15 million disabled persons of working age. Despite the Americans with Disabilities Act (ADA) passed over a decade ago, many of the disabled people who are of working age are currently unemployed. The ADA sets forth requirements for businesses with fifteen or more employees. It bans discrimination against workers and customers with disabilities and requires employers to make "reasonable accommodations" so that the disabled can access and work in the workplace. It covers a wide range of disabilities, including mental impairments, AIDS, alcoholism, visual impairments, and physical impairments that require use of a wheelchair.

With this legal protection in place, why are so many disabled people victims of discrimination? Some business owners are unable, or unwilling, to bear the expense of costly accommodations such as ramps, power doors, and voice-activated technology. They fail to see that these adjustments might serve as a gateway to valuable, hard-working employees, a new customer base, and an economic opportunity. Some employers are simply unwilling to hire the person who is blind or uses a wheelchair. The good news is that several companies are setting a good example with major programs to accommodate both employees and customers

TABLE 15.3	Enabling Those with Disabilities
Company	**Type of Assistance**
Crestar Bank	Provides voice-activated technology for disabled customer service representatives. Makes special services available to customers with disabilities.
Honeywell	Participates in Able to Work program, a consortium of 22 companies that find ways to employ disabled persons. Uses its high-tech innovations to assist employees with disabilities.
Johnson & Johnson	Has established a comprehensive disability management program that tailors work assignments to employees returning to work after an injury.
Caterpillar	Serves as a model of high-tech accessibility for the disabled; sponsors Special Olympics.

Sources: John Williams, "The List—Enabling Those with Disabilities," *Business Week,* March 6, 2000, p. 8; and "The New Work Force," *Business Week,* March 20, 2000, pp. 64–74.

with disabilities (see Table 15.3). In addition, many corporate diversity training programs include sessions on disability awareness and employment.

● **Sexual Orientation**

Discrimination based on a person's sexual orientation is motivated by *homophobia,* an aversion to homosexuals. Not long ago, gays and lesbians went to great lengths to keep their sexuality a secret. But today many gays and lesbians are "coming out of the closet" to demand their rights as members of society. Indeed, many young people entering the work force who are used to the relative tolerance of college campuses refuse to hide their orientation once they are in the workplace.

Gay rights activists are working hard to create awareness that discrimination based on sexual orientation is no less serious than discrimination based on age, gender, race, or disability. Activists are also working to rid the

HUMAN RELATIONS IN ACTION | **Meeting Someone with a Disability**

Here are a few suggestions for making a good impression. If the person . . .

. . . is in a wheelchair. Sit down, if possible. Try to chat eye to eye. Don't touch the wheelchair. It is considered within the boundaries of an individual's personal space.

. . . has a speech impediment. Be patient, actively listen, and resist the urge to finish his or her sentences.

. . . is accompanied by a guide dog. Never pet or play with a guide dog; you will distract the animal from its job.

. . . has a hearing loss. People who are deaf depend on facial expressions and gestures for communication cues. Speak clearly and slowly. Speak directly to the person, not to an interpreter or assistant if one is present.

This cartoon reminds us that some people strongly oppose homosexual orientation. These beliefs are often based on religious convictions that are supported by church theology. Today, tolerance for homosexuals varies greatly among the many religious denominations. Some denominations encourage members to concentrate on the person, not on the homosexual orientation itself.

© Lynn Johnston Productions, Inc. Distributed by United Feature Syndicate, Inc.

workplace of antigay behaviors such as offensive jokes, derogatory names, or remarks about gays. An atmosphere in which gays and lesbians are comfortable about being themselves is usually more productive than an atmosphere in which they waste their time and energy maintaining alternate, and false, personalities.

The authors of *Straight Talk About Gays in the Workplace* describe what Walt Disney Company, Polaroid, Lotus, Xerox, and other companies are doing to combat homophobia.[27] Some companies have established lesbian and gay employee associations that provide a point of contact for previously invisible employees. More than half of *Fortune* 500 companies have added sexual orientation to their nondiscrimination policies, and nationwide over two hundred major public and private employers have extended medical benefits to same-sex partners. Some major companies such as American Express and J.P. Morgan & Company are targeting recruiting efforts at gay and lesbian college students.[28]

Many state and local governments have passed laws that help protect gays and lesbians from discrimination and violence. Policies aimed at preventing verbal and physical harassment of homosexual students have been adopted by many public schools. In some cases, these initiatives have generated considerable controversy. Some religious and conservative groups have actively opposed these violence-prevention efforts, believing that they promote homosexuality.[29]

● **Subtle Forms of Discrimination**

A person who feels he or she has been the victim of discrimination based on gender, age, race, abilities, or sexual orientation can take legal action by filing a complaint with his or her state's office of the Equal Employment Opportunity

Tools for Tolerance: Workplace

- Hold a "diversity potluck" lunch. Invite coworkers to bring foods that reflect their cultural heritage.
- Suggest ways to overcome any barriers that might prevent people of color and women from succeeding.
- Value the input of every employee. Reward managers who do.
- Push for equitable leave policies. Provide paid maternity and paternity leave.

- Start a mentoring program that pairs employees of different ages, such as seniors with entry-level workers.
- Vary your lunch partners. Seek out coworkers of different backgrounds, from different departments, and at different levels in the company.

Commission. However, while state and federal laws protect individuals from discrimination based on these issues, they do not specifically protect workers from the more subtle forms of discrimination. For example, those who graduated from an Ivy League college may treat coworkers who graduated from state-funded colleges as inferior. Overweight employees might experience degrading remarks from coworkers. Those who speak with a distinct regional accent may hear snickers behind their back at work. People who do not value differences often equate a difference with a deficiency.

In its valuing diversity training program, Kaiser Permanente identifies twenty concrete examples of human differences that might cause discrimination among its workers. The list includes the standard diversity issues, but it also identifies characteristics such as education, politics, personal history, and socioeconomic status.[30] Since there are no laws regarding these issues, employees need to understand the negative impact these subtle forms of discrimination can have on the organization and take responsibility for creating an atmosphere where they are not tolerated.

● What Can You Do?

What should you do if you discover you are the target of some form of subtle, unprotected discrimination because you are different from others at work? If you want to stay in the organization, you will need to determine whether the "difference" is something you can change—your weight, the way you dress, your manner of speaking. If the difference is something you cannot or choose not to change, you may need to address the situation directly. Review the assertiveness skills you studied in Chapter 13. Your assertiveness may help change other people's attitudes and in turn alter their discriminatory behaviors. Another powerful method of eliminating subtle discrimination is to compensate for it by excelling in your work. Become an expert on the job, and work to increase your skills and your value to the organization. As your colleagues gain respect for your talents, they will change their attitudes toward you. But if your future appears blocked, investigate other workplaces where management may be more open to diversity. The important point is that you should refuse to allow discrimination to limit your personal and professional success.

THINKING / LEARNING STARTERS

1. Describe your own primary and secondary dimensions of diversity.
2. Do you hold any prejudices that might create problems for you in your career? In your personal life?

The Issue of Valuing Diversity

As we look back through the previous decades, we see a pattern of workers continually struggling to be treated alike. As we have seen, however, the new millennium has brought a strong shift away from treating everyone the same and toward valuing diversity. In a work setting, this means that a company intends to make full use of the ideas, talents, experiences, and perspectives of all employees at all levels of the organization. To remain competitive in the new economy, organizations are being forced to recognize and hire the best talent available in the labor pool, regardless of skin color, gender, and cultural background. Once on board, these talented individuals will choose to stay only if they are appreciated and valued.

● ## The Economics of Valuing Diversity

Valuing diversity is not only a legal, social, and moral issue; it is also an economic issue, because an organization's most valuable resource is its people. The

Valuing diversity is not only a legal, social, and moral issue; it is also an economic issue, because an organization's most valuable resource is its people.

price tag for *not* helping employees learn to respect and value each other is enormous in terms of lost time, wasted energy, delayed production, and increased conflict among employees.

■ Highly skilled and talented employees will leave an organization that does not value diversity.

■ Substantial dollars will be spent on recruiting and retraining because of high employee turnover.

■ Costly discrimination complaints will result from mismanagement of diverse employees (see Table 15.4 on p. 374).

■ A comment, gesture, or joke delivered without malice but received as an insult will create tension between coworkers.

■ Absenteeism associated with stress and low morale in the workplace is likely to occur.

■ Time will be wasted because of miscommunication and misunderstanding between diverse employees.[31]

TOTAL PERSON INSIGHT	LEWIS BROWN GRIGGS AND LENTE-LOUISE LOUW
	AUTHORS, *VALUING DIVERSITY: NEW TOOLS FOR A NEW REALITY*
	"More and more, organizations can remain competitive only if they can recognize and obtain the best talent; value the diverse perspectives that come with talent born of different cultures, races, and genders; nurture and train that talent; and create an atmosphere that values its workforce."

Recognizing the value of diversity and managing it as an asset can help eliminate these negative effects and exert a positive influence on productivity and cooperation within the work force. Companies that pursue diversity and make it part of their culture usually outperform companies that are less committed to diversity.

| TABLE 15.4 | The High Cost of Discrimination and Harassment |

Company	Award	Complaint
Coca-Cola Company	$192.5 million	Race discrimination class action lawsuit involving approximately 2,000 current and former employees
American Express	$31 million	Sex and age discrimination lawsuit involving over 4,000 women
Smith Barney	$40 million	Sexual harassment and discrimination lawsuit by thousands of women employees
Wal-Mart	$6.8 million	U.S. Equal Employment Opportunity Commission lawsuit alleging illegal screening of prospective employees with disabilities
Texaco	$175 million	Racial discrimination lawsuit filed by African American employees
Denny's	$54.4 million	Two class action lawsuits brought by black customers who were refused seating and service
Adams Mark Hotels	$8 million	Racial discrimination suit by the Justice Department (Florida) and black guests at a college reunion
American General Corporation	$215 million	Civil lawsuit alleging that African Americans were charged higher premiums
First Union Corporation	$58.5 million	Age discrimination suit by former employees

Sources: Betsy McKay, "Coke Settles Bias Suit for $192.5 Million," *Wall Street Journal,* November 17, 2000, p. A3; Jerry Markon and Jill Carroll, "Financial Firm Agrees to Settle Bias Lawsuit," *Wall Street Journal,* February 21, 2002, p. A3; "Deal Reached with EEOS over Hiring-Bias Charges," *Wall Street Journal,* December 17, 2001, p. B3; Kenneth Labich, "No More Crude at Texaco," *Fortune,* September 6, 1999, p. 205; Theodore Kinni, "Book Reviews," *Training,* August 2000, pp. 74–76 (includes a review of *The Denny's Story,* published by John Wiley & Sons); "Race-Discrimination Suits Cost Hotel Chain $8 Million," *Wall Street Journal,* March 22, 2000, p. B9; Greg Jaffe and Rochelle Sharpe, "First Union to Pay $58.5 Million to Settle Age-Discrimination Suit by Ex-Workers," *Wall Street Journal,* October 23, 1997, p. B4; Scot J. Paltrow, "Insurer to Settle Race Suit," *Wall Street Journal,* June 22, 2000, p. C1; Tom Lowry, "Judge Approves Smith Barney Bias Settlement," *USA Today,* July 27, 1998, p. 5B.

Managing Diversity

Managing diversity is the process of creating an organizational culture where the primary and secondary dimensions of diversity are respected. This process can be a challenge now that the work force is composed of so many different nationalities. Managers at some Marriott Hotels work with employees from thirty different countries. The employees who are part of the Toyota Formula 1 race team represent twenty-seven nationalities. Even some small retail stores have become a kind of United Nations. The Kroger supermarket in Durham, North Carolina, has employees from ten countries.[32]

● What Individuals Can Do

People tend to hang on to their prejudices and stereotypes. If certain white people believe people of color are inferior, they are likely to notice any incident in which a person of color makes a mistake. But when a person of color exhibits competence and sound decision-making abilities, these same white people may not notice, or they may attribute the positive results to other circumstances. You cannot totally eliminate prejudices that have been deeply held and developed over a long time. But you can take steps to change those attitudes and behaviors that may have a negative impact on your employer's efforts to enhance diversity.

Learn to look critically and honestly at the particular myths and preconceived ideas you have been conditioned to believe about others.

1. *Learn to look critically and honestly at the particular myths and preconceived ideas you have been conditioned to believe about others.* Contact among people of different races, cultures, and lifestyles can break down prejudice when people join together for a common task. The more contact there is among culturally diverse individuals, the more likely it will be that stereotypes based on myths and inaccurate generalizations will not survive.

2. *Develop a sensitivity to differences.* Do not allow gender-based, racist, or antigay jokes or comments in your presence. If English is not a person's native language, be aware that this person might interpret your messages differently from what you intended. When in doubt as to the appropriate behavior, ask questions. "I would like to open the door for you because you are in a wheelchair, but

I'm not sure whether that would offend you. What would you like me to do?"

3. *Develop your own diversity awareness program.* The starting point might be creation of a "diversity profile" of your friends, coworkers, and acquaintances. How much diversity do these individuals have in terms of race? Ethnicity? Religion? Assess the cultural diversity reflected in the music you listen to and the books you read. Visit an ethnic restaurant and try to learn about more than the food. Study Islam, Buddhism, and other faiths that may be different from your own.[33]

● What Organizations Can Do

A well-planned and well-executed diversity program can promote understanding and defuse tensions between employees who differ in age, race, gender, religious beliefs, and other characteristics. Programs that are poorly developed and poorly executed often backfire, especially in organizations where bias and distrust have festered for years.[34] Most of the programs that fail are not comprehensive and do not have the full support of top management. A comprehensive diversity program has three pillars:[35] organizational commitment, employment practices, and training and development (see Figure 15.4).

Organizational Commitment What are the major goals of today's diversity programs? Catalyst, a research and advisory group, recently conducted a survey of 106 global companies to determine why these companies use diversity strategies as part of their overall business plan. Nearly 90 percent said their diversity program was designed to help them gain a competitive advantage.[36]

What can individuals do to enhance diversity? Katie Cramer, (left), Hajirah Saeed, (center), and Sarah Syed applaud during a gathering of Muslims and non-Muslims at a day of solidarity and understanding held in Chicago.

| FIGURE 15.4 | Three Pillars of Diversity |

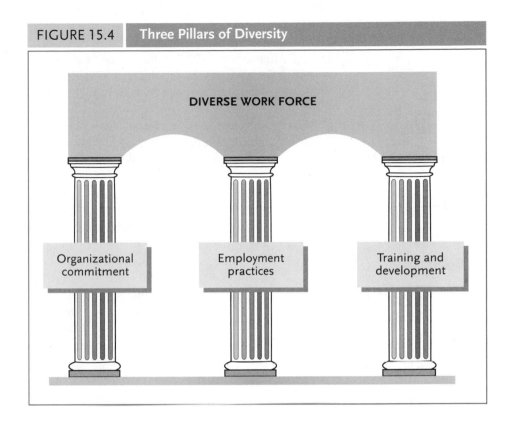

When the objective of the diversity initiative is to achieve a stronger competitive position, the commitment is usually quite strong.

Do diversity programs make a difference? Companies that see diversity programs as an *event*—a one-day workshop that promotes the advantages of a diverse work force—are very likely to answer no to this question. In fact, some of these quick-fix programs create greater, not less, divisiveness among workers. Companies that see diversity programs as a *process* are more likely to answer this question in the affirmative. The key to a successful diversity program is long-term commitment.

Diversity programs need clear objectives and standards that will permit the organization to assess program outcomes. At Consolidated Edison, responsibility for diversity extends to the entire management team. Each of the 2,100 officers and managers is reviewed and compensated in part for their success in hiring, promoting, and retaining minorities. Pepsico, the soft drink maker, links bonuses to diversity performance. Both of these companies made "America's 50 Best Companies for Minorities" list published by *Fortune*.[37]

The quest for diversity is difficult, and some companies struggle for years to achieve success in this area. Publicly, Coca-Cola Company has been a strong backer of civil rights, but it has not always been a model for diversity in corporate America. Former black employees sued the company, alleging vast discrepancies in pay, promotions, and performance evaluations. Reporting on the lawsuit, *Business Week* said, "The cola giant needs a cultural overhaul. Just as

Texaco needed to scrub its 'oil rig' culture clean of racism, Coke needs to scrap the insular environment that ex-employees say is dominated by good ol' boys. . . ." After paying $192.5 million to settle a race discrimination class action lawsuit in 2000, the company took steps to strengthen its diversity program. In 2002, Coca-Cola made the *Fortune* list of best companies for minorities.[38]

> *To achieve work force diversity, organizations need to design a plan that actively recruits men and women of different ethnicity, family situations, disabilities, and sexual orientation. Diversity should not be limited to race and gender.*

Employment Practices To achieve work force diversity, organizations need to design a plan that actively recruits men and women of different ethnicity, family situations, disabilities, and sexual orientation. Diversity should not be limited to race and gender. One approach is to make a special effort to plug into networks that are often ignored by corporate recruiters. Many communities have established groups such as the Center for Independent Living for those with limited abilities, the Family Service League for displaced homemakers and single parents, and Parents, Families, and Friends of Lesbians and Gays. All of these groups can help supply employees.

Organizations must also foster a climate for retention. Newly hired people who are different from the majority must often contend with an atmosphere of tension, instability, and distrust and may soon lose the desire to do their best work. Subtle biases often alienate these employees and create unnecessary stress. An organization that makes every effort to make *all* employees comfortable will reduce this stress and thus benefit from low turnover and high individual and team performance levels. Research indicates that minorities who advance the furthest all have had a strong network of mentors who have nurtured their development and served as coaches, advocates, and counselors to them.[39]

Training and Development To develop a culture that values and enhances diversity, organizations need training programs that give managers and employees the tools they need to work more effectively with one another regardless of their backgrounds. These programs can also reduce an organization's liability for discrimination.

Dallas-based Texas Instruments is often cited as a company that has distinguished itself through effective diversity training initiatives. The starting point is a one-day seminar to learn to value diversity and uncover unconscious behavioral patterns that could impede the progress of women and minority employees. Senior managers attend a two-day session. Follow-up courses focus on ways to foster inclusiveness and respect for the individual.[40]

Done well, diversity training programs can promote harmony and reduce conflict. Training courses that are poorly designed and delivered by incompetent trainers, however, can end up alienating and offending employees. These programs need to clearly describe unacceptable conduct and explain that the organization will not condone it. The basic rules of civil behavior should be clearly spelled out. Most people want concrete examples of behavior that will not be tolerated. For example, employees would learn that humor that contains degrading racial or cultural content is unacceptable. We cannot stop people from bringing prejudices to work, but we can explain that they must learn to act as though they have none.[41]

Affirmative Action: Yesterday and Today

Although the first civil rights legislation was passed in 1866, the Civil Rights Act of 1964 marked the beginning of antidiscrimination employment legislation. In an attempt to make up for past discrimination in the workplace, organizations that received federal funds were required to take affirmative (positive) action to include women and racial minorities in the work force. Title VII, the portion of the Civil Rights Act that deals with employment, was amended in 1972 to go beyond federal contractors, and now the rules and regulations affect most employers in the United States (see Table 15.5). Various laws have been passed to expand the list of *protected* individuals beyond women and racial minorities. The updated list includes those who share the following characteristics:

- Sex/gender (women, including those who are pregnant)
- Racial or ethnic origin (not limited to those of color)
- Religion (special beliefs and practices: e.g., attire, holidays)
- Age (individuals over 40)
- Individuals with disabilities (physical or mental)
- Sexual orientation (some state and city laws, not federal laws)
- Military experience (Vietnam-era veterans)
- Marital status (same-gender couples; some state laws, not federal laws)

Affirmative action plans (AAPs) are the formal documents that employers compile annually for submission to various enforcement agencies, including the EEOC. The documents clarify the organizations' efforts to actively seek out,

TABLE 15.5	Organizations Subject to Affirmative Action Rules and Regulations
■ All private employers of 15 or more people who are employed 20 or more weeks per year	
■ All educational institutions public and private	
■ State and local governments	
■ Public and private employment agencies	
■ Labor unions with 15 or more members	
■ Joint labor/management committees for apprenticeships and training	

Source: From *Human Resource Management* with West Group Product Booklet 10th edition by Mathis/Jackson, © 2003. Reprinted with permissions of South-Western, a division of Thomson Learning: www.thomsonrights.com, fax 800-730-2215.

Tools for Tolerance: Community

- Frequent minority-owned businesses and get to know the proprietors.
- Start a language bank of volunteer interpreters for all foreign languages used in your community.
- Host a "multicultural extravaganza" such as a food fair or an art, fashion, and talent show.

- Bring people of diverse faiths together for retreats, workshops, or potluck dinners. Be welcoming to agnostics and atheists, too.
- Participate in a blood drive or clean up a local stream. Identify issues that reach across racial, ethnic, and other divisions and forge alliances for tackling them.

employ, and develop the talents of individuals from the various protected classes. The affirmative action programs that fulfill the AAPs of many organizations include the following:[42]

1. Active recruitment of women and minorities

2. Elimination of prejudicial questions on employment application forms

3. Establishment of specific goals and timetables for minority hiring

4. Validation of employment testing procedures

Affirmative action allowed a tremendous influx of diverse individuals through the front door of thousands of schools and organizations. Many were able to work their way into advanced, top-level positions. At the same time, however, affirmative action reinforced the historical view that the members of protected groups are not qualified for various positions and therefore need assistance just to get a job.

The Affirmative Action Debate   Many people say it is time to rethink affirmative action or even eliminate it. Recent political and legal interpretations of affirmative action have stimulated a nationwide debate over the merits of any program that grants preferential treatment to specific groups. The following are common arguments voiced by those who want to end preferential policies:[43]

- *Preferences are discriminatory.* They tend to discriminate against those who are not members of the "right" race or gender, such as white men. Preferential policies often give a leg up to those who have suffered no harm, while holding back those who have done no wrong.

- *Preferences do not make sense, given changing demographics.* The population eligible for affirmative action continues to grow several times faster than the "unprotected" population. Hugh Davis Graham, author of *Collision Course,* believes the future of affirmative action programs is threatened because of the explosive growth in the number of people immigrating to the United States. Recent immigrants are eligible for affirmative action programs originally designed to empower minorities.[44]

Secretary of State Colin Powell, a distinguished African American military leader and diplomat, takes a more moderate position on affirmative action. He says, "If affirmative action means programs that provide equal opportunity, then I am all for it. If it leads to preferential treatment or helps those who no longer need help, I am opposed."[45] Barbara Bergmann, professor at American University and author of *In Defense of Affirmative Action,* presents the view that affirmative action is the only practical way to rectify discrimination in hiring. She states that many companies and government agencies will not embrace fairness in hiring and promotion as long as guidelines are voluntary.[46] Arthur A. Fletcher, considered by many the father of affirmative action, believes that a great deal of progress has been made but that achieving diversity in the workplace will take many more years. He encourages the business community to invest in training and education for underprivileged minorities. Fletcher says that hiring women and minorities can be done without compromising work performance.[47]

The debate about affirmative action will continue for many years. The concept and the means for implementing it will continue to be challenged in the courts. The most recent Supreme court ruling (*Grutter v. Bollinger*) states that affirmative action programs designed to achieve diversity goals are acceptable. An employer can consider race on the grounds that it is seeking to obtain a diverse workplace environment. However, if the hiring process resembles a quota system, it will likely be considered illegal. This 2003 landmark ruling was welcomed by employers who believe that diversity is not just a nice idea, but a business imperative.[48]

■ Summary

ACE

business.college.hmco.com/students

Work force diversity has become an important issue for organizations that want to remain competitive in a global economy. These organizations are beginning to move away from focusing on prejudice and discrimination and toward valuing diversity. Two dimensions, or sets of characteristics, are the basis of every individual's diversity. Primary dimensions include gender, age, race, physical and mental abilities, and sexual orientation. Secondary dimensions include health habits, religious beliefs, ethnic customs, communication style, relationship status, income, general appearance, and education and training.

Prejudice and discrimination are major barriers to effective human relations. Prejudice is an attitude based partly on observation of others' differences and partly on ignorance, fear, and cultural conditioning. Prejudiced people tend to see others as stereotypes rather than as unique individuals. Prejudicial attitudes are formed through the effects of childhood experiences, ethnocentrism, and economic factors. Discrimination is behavior based on prejudicial attitudes. Groups protected by law from discrimination in the workplace include people who share characteristics such as gender, age, race, abilities, religion, and sexual orientation. More subtle discrimination can arise when individuals have different appearances or educational backgrounds. These subtle forms of discrimination may not be classified as illegal, but they are disruptive to a productive work force.

The issue of valuing diversity is an economic one for most organizations. The changing demographics of American society mean that the work force will soon be made up of a minority of white men and a majority of women, people of color, and immigrants. Companies cannot afford to ignore this change in the pool of human resources.

Individuals can enhance diversity by letting go of their stereotypes and learning to critically and honestly evaluate their prejudiced attitudes as they work and socialize with people who are different. They will need to develop a sensitivity to differences and develop their personal diversity awareness programs. Organizations must develop a commitment to valuing individual differences and implementing effective employment practices that respect and enhance diversity. Their diversity training programs should become an internal process rather than an event. They need to seek out, employ, and develop people from diverse backgrounds.

Affirmative action guidelines have helped bring fairness in hiring and promotion to many organizations. Today, however, some people believe these guidelines are discriminatory because they allow preferential treatment for the people they were designed to protect. These preferences may no longer make sense, critics say, given the changing demographics of today's work force.

■ Career Corner

Q: I receive phone calls at work from customers located all over the world. Most of them speak English, but because of their accents, I often have difficulty understanding what they are trying to say to me. How can I handle these calls more effectively?

A: The fact that your customers can speak two languages indicates that they are probably well educated and intelligent, so treat them with respect. Statements like "I can't understand you," or "What did you say?" are rude and should be avoided. Instead, take personal responsibility for improving the communications and gently say, "I am having a little difficulty understanding you, but if you will be patient with me I am sure I will be able to help." Ask them to slow down so that you can hear all the information correctly. Listen for key words and repeat them back to the caller. Identify coworkers who are fluent in a particular language, and ask them to help when calls come in from customers who share the same ethnic identity. Remember, people with foreign accents are not necessarily hard of hearing, so don't shout.

■ Key Terms

valuing diversity	ethnocentrism
primary dimensions	ethnicity
secondary dimensions	discrimination
prejudice	race
stereotypes	managing diversity
xenophobia	affirmative action plans

■ Review Questions

1. Distinguish between the primary and secondary dimensions of diversity, and give examples of each.

2. Why should organizations be concerned about valuing diversity?

3. How do the changing demographics of American culture affect the human resources pool of the future? Be specific.

4. Define *prejudice* and *discrimination*. How do these two terms differ in meaning?

5. What are some of the ways in which people acquire prejudices?

6. Who is protected from discrimination in the workplace by federal, state, or local laws?

7. How can subtle forms of discrimination hurt the victim's chances to succeed in his or her career?

8. What role does affirmative action play in today's organizations? What are some of the arguments for and against affirmative action?

9. What steps can individuals take to avoid discriminating against others? What can they do if they are victims of discriminatory behavior?

10. What flaws in diversity training programs can cause a negative backlash among participants?

■ Application Exercises

1. The "managing diversity" movement has raised the discussion of equal employment opportunity and affirmative action to a higher level. Consider the following comments by R. Roosevelt Thomas, Jr., which appeared in a *Harvard Business Review* article entitled "From Affirmative Action to Affirming Diversity":

   Managers usually see affirmative action and equal employment opportunity as centering on minorities and women, with very little to offer white males. The diversity I'm talking about includes race, gender, creed, and ethnicity but also age, background, education, function, and personality differences. The objective is not to assimilate minorities and women into a dominant white male culture but to create a dominant heterogeneous culture.[49]

   Do you agree or disagree with this author's views? Would his views on diversity be acceptable in corporate America? Explain.

2. For one week, keep a diary that records every instance in which you see actions or hear comments that reflect outmoded, negative stereotypes. For instance, watch a movie, and observe whether the villains are all of a particular race or ethnic group. As you read textbooks from other courses you are taking, notice whether the pictures and examples reflect any stereotypes.

Listen to your friends' conversations, and notice any time they make unfair judgments about others based on stereotypes. Finally, reflect on your own attitudes and perceptions. Do you engage in stereotyping?

Share your experiences with class members, and discuss what steps you can take to help rid the environment of negative stereotyping.

3. John Hope Franklin, professor of history at Duke University, was selected to lead former President Clinton's advisory board on race. In an interview conducted shortly after he accepted the assignment, he noted that there are constant reminders of the deep racial divide that exists in America and that cannot easily be bridged unless people from different ethnic or racial groups begin to establish a dialogue.

Meet with someone who is a member of a racial or ethnic group different from your own, and attempt to build a relationship by discussing the things that are important to each of you. As you get to know this person, become aware of his or her beliefs and attitudes. Try not to be diverted by accent, grammar, or personal appearance; rather, really listen to the person's thoughts and ideas. Search for things you and your new acquaintance have in common, and do not dwell on your differences.

 Internet Exercise

Before, during, and after the terrorist attacks and the war in Iraq, Muslims became victims of discrimination throughout the world merely because of their religious beliefs and stereotyped physical appearance. Some people from other cultures and religions were afraid to be in their presence, and some Muslims were verbally, if not physically, abused by those who could not see beyond the terrorist stereotype. Just as Americans discriminated against the Japanese before, during, and after World War II, Muslims will probably face the same behaviors in the years to come—unless individuals take the responsibility to learn more about their culture. Visit the Muslim Public Affairs Council website at *www.mpac.org,* the Muslim American Society at *www.masnet.org,* or *Islam101.com,* an introductory guide for non-Muslims. What did you learn that would help you visit with someone who displays a bias against Muslims in your presence?

Case 15.1   Quality Education Through Enhanced Diversity

For decades universities have sought to admit students from different cultures and social backgrounds. Educators contend that academic discussion is most beneficial and has the most lasting social benefits when it draws on different experiences and perspectives. Various affirmative action programs have been developed to assure such diversity through admissions policies that create preferential treatment of minority applicants. But they are not the only preferences operating in higher education. Some schools use "legacy preferences," which favor children of alumni. At some colleges and universities, preference is given to students whose parents are wealthy—sometimes called "development admits." Of course, most schools extend preferences to athletes.

In an effort to create a diverse undergraduate student body at the University of Michigan, admissions standards were revised so that black, Hispanic, and Native American applicants could effectively compete with white students, including Asian and Arab applicants, who often had the advantages of better schools and supportive social structures that the protected groups were historically denied. The protected students automatically received 20 points on the 150-point "selection index" that assigned a numerical value to each of several factors of an applicants' history, including 110 points for academic achievement. As a result, a minority student with a GPA of 3.0 and an ACT score of 18 would be accepted into undergraduate programs, but a white student with a GPA of 3.6 and an ACT score of 21 would be rejected. The University of Michigan said it did not have a quota system (reserving a specific number of openings for protected class members) but did have admission policies designed to ensure that each class included a "critical mass" of minorities. Two white applicants with outstanding GPAs and ACT scores were denied admission, and they filed a lawsuit (*Gratz v. Bollinger*) charging reverse discrimination. In a companion case (*Grutter v. Bollinger*), the university was sued by a white student who was denied admission to its law school.

After a variety of appeals in the Michigan courts, the Supreme Court agreed to hear both cases at the same time and thereby attempt to clarify the confusion regarding affirmative action legislation which began following the landmark 1978 *Bakke v. Regents of the University of California* Supreme Court case. That case involved Allan Bakke, who had been denied admission to medical school in favor of minority candidates who were considered less qualified. In the 2003 decision, the Supreme Court voted to uphold the *Bakke* ruling and thereby endorsed the use of race in choosing students for the University of Michigan law school. However, it decided in favor of the two white undergraduate University of Michigan students. The Court ruled that the university's undergraduate admissions process resembled a quota system because it unfairly rewarded or penalized an applicant because of their race. The Court said that schools can implement affirmative action programs that consider an applicant's race for the purpose of creating a diverse student body but prohibits them from using a strict formulaic approach that leads to racial quotas. The Court agreed that the law school has a right as well as responsibility to use race as a factor among many in order to pursue the educational benefit of diversity while training the nation's future lawyers. In her opinion, Justice Sandra Day O'Connor wrote that attaining a diverse student body is "at the heart of the law school's proper institutional mission.[50]

■ Questions

1. Most people agree that a diverse classroom population can create a rich learning environment that will enhance the education of all students. The lingering question seems to be how a university can establish a diverse student population without developing admissions quotas for various races? List your suggestions.

2. Will *any* black, Hispanic, or Native American student in a college class bring their culture's perspective to the discussion? Does it matter if these students attended an impoverished inner-city high school or a chic prep school? Should this issue be incorporated into an admissions policy at a university?

3. Studies show that university affirmative action policies have improved racial diversity not only in the classrooms but also later in life, in business and in the professions.[51] In what ways might affirmative action programs at the university level affect the dynamics of interracial interactions in the work force?

Case 15.2   Xenophobia: Fear of Foreigners

The unknown is almost always frightening. Perhaps, when you were a child, you were afraid of the dark because you did not know what was in there. As you were exposed to more and more experiences in the dark, you learned that there was little reason to be afraid. The elimination of this fear brought with it new opportunities to work and play in your world, even though it might be dark. When you examine other phobias, such as the fear of spiders or snakes, you soon discover that the more you know, the less you fear.

It would seem logical that xenophobia, the fear of foreigners or strangers, could be overcome in much the same way. If America prides itself on being a melting pot of cultures, why do so many Americans react to those who are different with xenophobic tendencies? After all, these differences tend to enrich American society. Could it be that many of us have too little contact with foreigners?

It appears that there is an unconscious desire to divide the world into "us" and "them." We split people into the "in" group and the "out" group using criteria such as nationality, religion, race, language, lifestyle, or age. However, research shows that such prejudices are fluid and that when we become conscious of our biases, we can take active and successful steps to combat them. In experiments, researchers have discovered that as people become consciously aware of their prejudices, they feel guilty and try harder to rid themselves of them.

Once you are aware of your xenophobic tendencies, feel guilty about them, and have the desire to overcome them, the cure is meaningful contact and knowledge about the different culture. Jordan's Queen Rania attended an English school in her native Kuwait that had children from Europe, Africa, the Far East, and the United States. She acknowledges that her interactions with the children from various cultures helped her realize that those things that make everyone similar far outweigh those things that make them different. At the end of the day, everyone wants the same thing out of life. Abdul-Hafeez Waheed of the Muslim American Society in Durham, North Carolina, shares the same belief. He states that Christians and Muslims may have their differences, but they have more things in common.

Today it is easy to obtain information about different countries and cultures through the Internet, TV news, and journalists' reports from various regions of the world. As neighborhoods are integrated with various cultures from around the world, people learn to live with and respect their neighbors' traditions. Biases change when members of racially mixed groups cooperate to accomplish shared goals. Simple steps such as integrating a basketball or football team can reset xenophobic tendencies, rendering race and ethnicity less important.[52]

■ Questions

1. Do any of your family members exhibit xenophobic tendencies? If so, where do you believe those attitudes originated? Do you share the same beliefs? Why or why not?

2. Many people favor careful examination of people in airports who appear to be of Arab descent, even though they may actually be Greek, Italian, Indian, Latino, or South Asian. Is this practice a form of discrimination? If so, is it illegal? Do you favor or oppose such "racial profiling" in airports? Explain your reasoning. If some people favor this practice in airports, does this indicate that they are prejudiced?

16

THE CHANGING ROLES OF MEN AND WOMEN

Chapter Preview

After studying this chapter, you will be able to

- Describe how the traditional roles of men and women are changing.

- Understand problems facing women and men as a result of gender bias in organizations.

- Discuss ways to cope with gender-biased behaviors.

- Identify ways to achieve work/life balance.

- Explain the forms of sexual harassment and learn how to avoid being a victim or perpetrator of them.

Pick up a copy of *Fortune*, the *Wall Street Journal, Business Week, Working Women,* or any other business publication and you will likely find articles that describe one or more workplace gender issues.

■ A recent issue of *Fortune* described the fifty most powerful women in business, and the cover story focused on the "trophy husband." We learn that many of these fast-track wives have stay-at-home husbands who mind the kids, manage the home, and provide support.[1]

■ Sue Shellenbarger, author of the Work & Family column in the *Wall Street Journal,* frequently writes about the downside of taking family leave. Taking time off to care for your ailing mother or a sick child might cost you a promotion or, in extreme cases, the loss of your job. Shellenbarger says today's precarious job market heightens the risk of taking family leave.[2]

■ *Business Week* recently featured an article entitled "No Way to Treat a Lady." A very large sex discrimination suit has been filed against Wal-Mart, the nation's largest retailer. The focus of this legal action is pay and promotion disparities. If the suit is granted class action status, it could cover several thousand women.[3]

Throughout this chapter we will examine these and other gender issues that create human relations problems in the workplace. Women and men continue to face injustices due to gender stereotypes and misunderstanding of gender roles in the work force. Gender inequity is rooted in our cultural patterns, and therefore it surfaces in organizations.

Traditional Roles Are Changing

All cultures promote one set of behaviors for boys and a separate set for girls. Children generally learn their socially acceptable roles by the time they are 5 years old, but these roles are often continually reinforced throughout the life cycle by teachers, parents, authority figures, and the media. These traditional roles can be harmful to both men and women. For instance, the expectation that men should be aggressive and unemotional stifles their sensitivity and creativity. The assumption that women are emotional and weak hinders them in reaching leadership positions. Although men and women will always be different, their roles can and should be more nearly equal.

Gender bias (also known as **sexism**), which is discrimination on the basis of gender, persists today. The women's movement that began in the 1960s with Betty Friedan's book *The Feminine Mystique* has helped women make tremendous strides toward equality with men in the workplace.[4] Only recently, however, have men begun to realize that they have been shortchanged when it comes to enjoying the options women have experienced for generations. Men have traditionally been the breadwinners while women had the option of staying home and caring for the children or choosing to work.

When employers base employment, promotion, job-assignment, and compensation decisions on a person's gender, human relations and productivity suffer.

Gender bias is no longer a female-only issue, and many organizations are making the necessary adjustments.

● Changes in the Role of Women

In the past, children were more likely to see their mothers as homemakers and their fathers as breadwinners. This has dramatically changed, with women joining the work force in record numbers. In the mid-1960s, about 40 percent of women worked outside the home. Today, over 60 percent of all women work, and 76 percent of the women between 25 and 44 work. The number of dual-income families has doubled since 1950. In addition, women receive more than 55 percent of both the bachelor's and the master's degrees awarded by U.S. colleges.[5] Research conducted by Claudia Goldin and Lawrence Katz, authors of the academic study *The Power of the Pill: Oral Contraceptives and Women's Career and Marriage Decisions*, indicates that the birth control pill (approved by the FDA in 1960) had a major impact on women's ascent into corporate America. The rise in affirmative action in the mid-1960s and the liberalizing of state abortion laws in the early 1970s gave additional support for women's desire to plan their futures.[6]

The impact of women in the workplace has been described as the "revolution that won't quit." As more and more women spend time and money on their education and postpone marriage and motherhood, we will no doubt see women's participation in the work force increase even more. Many women receive important financial and intrinsic rewards from their work, but they also

Ebay Chief Executive Officer, Meg Whitman, opens the front doors of ebay headquarters. The Internet auction site has been highly successful, thanks to her strong leadership.

face many challenges. Those who choose to have children must decide if and when to leave the work force and for how long. Women who leave their jobs to start a family wonder if their education and skills will be obsolete by the time they return to work. There is the very real possibility that during these women's absence, the types of jobs they were trained for will disappear.

When new mothers return to work, they often find it difficult to find jobs with schedules that are flexible enough to allow for the demands of a family. They actively seek out organizations that are not only female-friendly in hiring and promotion, but also family-friendly in their employment practices. It has been more than thirty years since the National Organization for Women (NOW) was formed to fight business policies and behaviors that discriminate against women, and there is reason for women to celebrate their progress. They have made significant gains in a wide range of traditionally male-dominated areas such as finance, marketing, law, medicine, and computer technology. However, some problem areas persist. Studies indicate that men continue to dominate craft, repair, and construction jobs, whereas women hold only 2 percent of these skilled trade jobs. Although nearly half of all managers and professionals are women, they hold only 12 percent of the top-level jobs at the five hundred largest U.S. companies (see Figure 16.1).[7]

Achieving success in the new millennium will require women to take risks that could lead to failure in their personal as well as their professional lives. Yet many women today are impelled by fearless confidence that they can achieve anything they choose. They embrace these risks as opportunities for success, recognition, and financial security.

FIGURE 16.1	Women in the U.S. Labor Force

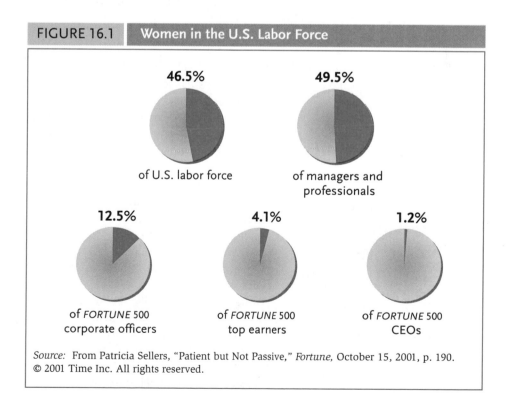

46.5% of U.S. labor force

49.5% of managers and professionals

12.5% of *FORTUNE* 500 corporate officers

4.1% of *FORTUNE* 500 top earners

1.2% of *FORTUNE* 500 CEOs

Source: From Patricia Sellers, "Patient but Not Passive," *Fortune,* October 15, 2001, p. 190. © 2001 Time Inc. All rights reserved.

● Changes in the Role of Men

Many boys have been conditioned from their early years to be competitors and to win. They have been urged to be aggressive, to learn teamwork, to select traditional male pastimes such as sports and cars, and to enter a masculine profession such as sales, automotive repair, management, engineering, or law. A boy was taught to withstand physical pain and to push his body to the limits. Above all, he was not to act like a girl, to take up interests that were considered feminine, or to show any tendencies that could be considered homosexual. A girl could be a tomboy, but a boy could not be a "sissy." Whereas a woman's worth was measured in terms of her physical attractiveness, a man's was measured by his ability to compete and achieve his goals. This man's world attaches great value to independence and autonomy and less value to relationships and connection. If women have been viewed as "sex objects," perhaps men have been seen as "success objects." A man is under constant pressure to prove himself and keep moving up the ladder. Even though men have learned the value of teamwork, they have also had to learn to look over their shoulders for whoever might be gaining on them.

TOTAL PERSON INSIGHT	**ROBERT BLY** AUTHOR, *IRON JOHN* "We are living at an important and fruitful moment now, for it is clear to men that the images of adult manhood given by the popular culture are worn out; a man can no longer depend on them. By the time a man is thirty-five he knows that the images of the right man, the tough man, the true man which he received in high school do not work in life."

The Burden of Stress Psychologists have become increasingly aware that we have neglected the stress associated with being male throughout the generations. The 1950s "organization man" assumed the role of breadwinner—a role accompanied by a great deal of self-imposed as well as societal stress. The pressure to achieve in the workplace was intense, but he was still expected to be the head of the household at home. His male identity often revolved around being the sole provider of the family's income because the woman's place was in the home. Men would be reluctant to leave a bad job because they feared losing their family's only paycheck. The 1980s baby boomer men were likely to equate success with high income, movement up the career ladder, and the accumulation of material things such as a nice home and a nice car. Long hours at work often meant that men were emotionally and physically absent from friends and family members, which resulted in a great deal of guilt.[8]

> *The men of the twenty-first century are discovering that the strong, unemotional, in-control image supported by previous generations is not healthy or realistic.*

The men of the twenty-first century are discovering that the strong, unemotional, in-control image supported by previous generations is not healthy or even realistic. Many have learned to define the kind of life they want to lead, rather than being restricted to traditional gender-role stereo-

Many men are reexamining their professional and personal lives. Keith Lussier enjoys spending time with his two-year-old adopted Korean daughter.

types. Andy Ayers, a 29-year-old account manager for a pharmaceutical company, used to work 80-hour weeks. When he and his wife had a baby, he decided to cut back on his work hours and spend more time with his family. He discovered that this adjustment produced an upward spiral in the quality of both his professional life and his personal life. Ayers's decision came after observing how older coworkers' immersion in their work resulted in a decline in their home lives.[9]

Where Is the Balance?   As men reexamine their role in society, they face conflicting role messages, even as women entering the work force do. Both men and women often discover that the joy of parenting can be just as satisfying as the achievement of career goals. But such feelings are confusing. Men and women alike are often expected to maintain aggressive attitudes toward their careers while being attentive husbands or wives and fathers or mothers. Those who were brought up in homes with a single parent who struggled to make ends meet have had few role models from whom to learn how to balance career and family life. Is it any wonder they feel frustrated?

TOTAL PERSON INSIGHT	**DEBRA E. MEYERSON AND JOYCE K. FLETCHER**
	PROFESSORS, CENTER FOR GENDER IN ORGANIZATIONS, SIMMONS GRADUATE SCHOOL OF MANAGEMENT
	"It took a revolution to get women where they are in business today. But now, to push hard-won gains wider and deeper, a different approach is necessary. It is a strategy based on small wins—incremental changes that have the power to transform organizations positively for both men and women."

Problems Facing Women in Organizations

When women pursue careers, they often face three major challenges: the wage gap, the glass ceiling, and balancing career and family. Many employers are making changes that will accommodate the needs of the growing number of working women and mothers, but more needs to be done.

● The Wage Gap

The gap between women's and men's earnings has been shrinking since the 1980s, yet wage inequality continues. (See Figure 16.2.) The Bureau of Labor Statistics (BLS) reports that women earn about 76 cents for every dollar men earn. The inequity is even more serious for minorities: 63 cents for black women and 53 cents for Hispanic women.[10] These figures are somewhat misleading because the bureau does not compare similar jobs held by men and women; it lumps together all jobs that women hold and all jobs that men hold.

Although discrimination is partly to blame for wage disparities, other factors also contribute to this problem. Today, women are more committed to building a career, but many still take time off to have children. This works against them, since continuous work experience tends to increase both productivity and pay in many employment settings.[11]

Research indicates that some women are willing to accept lower pay than men, and women are less apt to haggle when offered a starting salary or a pay raise. Women, as well as men, need to acquire as much information as possible about their value in the open market and use their negotiation skills to achieve equity in compensation.[12]

● The Glass Ceiling

There is a condition in the workplace that gives women a view of top management jobs but blocks their ascent. It is often referred to as the **glass ceiling.** Catalyst, a women's advocacy group that has studied women in business since 1962, has documented widespread limits on career advancement to the highest levels of our nation's largest corporations. Only 4.1 percent of the *Fortune* 500

FIGURE 16.2	Income Disparity

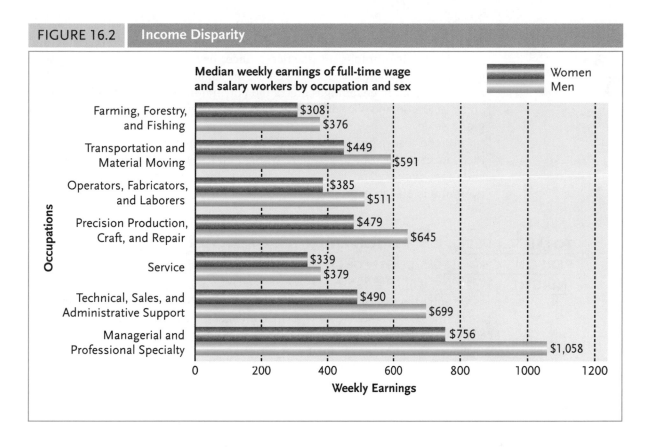

Median weekly earnings of full-time wage and salary workers by occupation and sex

Legend: Women, Men

Occupations (Weekly Earnings):

- Farming, Forestry, and Fishing — Women $308, Men $376
- Transportation and Material Moving — Women $449, Men $591
- Operators, Fabricators, and Laborers — Women $385, Men $511
- Precision Production, Craft, and Repair — Women $479, Men $645
- Service — Women $339, Men $379
- Technical, Sales, and Administrative Support — Women $490, Men $699
- Managerial and Professional Specialty — Women $756, Men $1,058

X-axis: Weekly Earnings (0, 200, 400, 600, 800, 1000, 1200)

top earners are women, and only 1.2 percent of the *Fortune* 500 companies have a female CEO (see Figure 16.1).[13] Although we are seeing some positive change, especially among the middle-management ranks, women are still being held back by some widely held misconceptions. Top male executives say the major barrier for women is a lack of significant general management and line experience and less time in the "pipeline." Women in senior management positions say the *real* problems are (1) preconceptions of women held by men and (2) exclusion of women from informal networks of communication.[14]

Many companies are helping women break through the glass ceiling. Officials at Deloitte & Touche LLP, a large Wilton, Connecticut, accounting firm, were disappointed that too few women advanced to the level of partner and that many talented women were leaving the company. Officials had mistakenly assumed that women were leaving only to start families. When they discovered that the majority of women who quit working for large companies moved on to other companies that were more female-friendly, they launched the "Advancement of Women" initiative. All of the organization's 4,700 managers and partners were sent to a 2-day workshop where they could explore work-related gender differences. The company also set up a mentoring program, made sure women received career-advancing experience, and developed more family-friendly policies. The result after three years was a 30 percent increase in women partners and reduced turnover among women.[15]

Why should we be concerned about the dominance of men in top leadership positions? Cultures that are totally masculine often lack compassion and give rise to rigid, intolerant practices, since they lack the intuitive, empathic qualities more common among women. In some cases, a highly competitive masculine culture encourages greed and corruption. The male-dominated hierarchy at Enron and WorldCom, for example, fostered unethical practices on a grand scale.

Macho leadership styles can also alienate women. The idea is not to push men off the stage, but to get more women on the stage with them. In an ideal situation, women and men will share the stage and create a culture where everyone is able to express the full range of his or her talents.[16]

TOTAL PERSON INSIGHT	**DEBRA E. MEYERSON AND JOYCE K. FLETCHER** PROFESSORS, CENTER FOR GENDER IN ORGANIZATIONS, SIMMONS GRADUATE SCHOOL OF MANAGEMENT "As we enter the new millennium, we believe that it is time for new metaphors to capture the subtle, systemic forms of discrimination that still linger. It's not the ceiling that's holding women back; it's the whole structure of the organizations in which we work: the foundation, the beams, the walls, the very air."

● Balancing Career and Family Choices

Women today know that they will probably be working for pay for part or all of their adult lives. This expectation is quite a departure from previous generations, when most women assumed the responsibilities of wife and mother. The challenge of performing multiple roles, however, can be stressful and tiring. A majority of the women in two-income families not only contribute significantly to their family's income, but also do most of their family's household chores. Lily Tomlin once said, "If I'd known what it was like to have it all, I would have settled for a lot less."[17] Many women in America no doubt share this thought.

When women began entering the work force in large numbers, they often did it on men's terms. Employers did not make an effort to meet the needs of women who wanted to balance career and family responsibilities. Although the demographics of work have changed dramatically over the past forty years, some observers say the workplace has not changed enough. In a world that requires long hours and "face time" to achieve recognition and advancement, women often find themselves neglecting the personal and family lives they hold so dear.

As we look for ways to help women balance career and family, we should not overlook the rewards that are experienced by women who work. Many women who hold both work and family roles treasure the friendships they develop at work and enjoy the intellectual challenges that work provides. Yet a large number of women who try to balance work and family roles say "work is no haven." They feel frustrated because many long-standing work and family problems remain unresolved. These include a lack of quality, affordable child care, inflexible work schedules, and time management problems.[18]

Discovering the Hidden Barriers

In the past, the women's movement used strong rhetoric and legal action to drive out overt discrimination. Today most of the barriers that exist are hidden—or at least not fully understood. One author said, "Even the women who feel its impact are often hard-pressed to know what hit them." And even companies that sincerely want to increase the number of women managers and executives create barriers unintentionally.

A large retail company based in Europe could not figure out why it had so few women in senior positions and had such a high turnover rate among women in its middle-management ranks. A consultant hired to study the problem quickly identified an important inequity for women. The company culture emphasized an informal approach to conducting business. People were casual about setting deadlines. Meetings were routinely canceled and often ran late. Managers were expected to be available at all times to attend delayed or emergency meetings. This way of conducting business created problems for women, who typically had to bear a disproportionate amount of responsibility for home and family; they had more demands on their time outside the office.

The "Mommy Track" and Other Options   Over a decade ago, Felice Schwartz, founder of Catalyst, wrote an essay entitled "Management Women and the New Facts of Life." She stated that companies needed to provide women with more flexibility, not force them to choose between work and family. She believed that women are far more inclined than men to give a high priority to raising children. Critics of the essay said Schwartz was encouraging companies to create a "mommy track" for women who wanted a career *and* children. Schwartz responded that women who opted to make raising children their highest priority had to accept the fact that this emphasis would have some impact on their careers, at least temporarily.[19]

Many women want to expand their life choices but are uncertain about the options available. If you are a woman who wants both career and family, then consider the following:[20]

- Choose a career that will give you the gift of time. Some careers provide more flexibility and are more forgiving of interruptions such as parental leave.

- Choose a partner who supports your goal of having a career and family.

- Choose an employer who has given work/life balance a high priority. Be prepared for some disappointments, because many corporate leaders are still unwilling to respond to work/life issues.

- Be prepared to use your negotiation skills to push for policies and practices that are favorable to employees with children. If your employer does not provide job-protected leave or flexible work schedules, use your assertiveness skills to press for policy changes.

Problems Facing Men in Organizations

Many men are beginning to realize that they have been as rigidly stereotyped in their role as women have been in theirs. Men encounter resistance from their family, coworkers, and friends when they attempt to break out of their stereotypes. The changes a man makes to alter traditional masculine role characteristics can be threatening to others and can cause serious problems in his relationships. Yet the stress men are under today to conform to the expectations of society often leads to heart disease and other health problems. Many wonder if upholding the male image is worth the price.

● Men Working with Women

Male attitudes toward female ambitions have changed over the years. One reason for this change is the dramatic increase of female college classmates. Men have learned that they will be competing with these smart and ambitious women in the workplace. They are also learning that women can be excellent coworkers, team members, and leaders. Those men who are secure in their talents and abilities welcome the opportunity to work beside equally self-assured women. Those men who are threatened by powerful, talented women need an attitude adjustment.

● Balancing Career and Family Choices

Henry David Thoreau observed that "the mass of men lead lives of quiet desperation." Does this dire observation apply to men who are pursuing careers and assuming family roles today? The answer is a qualified yes. Men, like women, now have more choices regarding marriage and family life and face many barriers to achieving work/life balance.

- The long-term trend toward wage equality gives families more choices regarding who should assume the roles of breadwinner, child-care provider, and housekeeper. Because of their upbringing, most men are often ill suited to staying at home with their children while their wives become the breadwinners.[21]

- Men often seek a "package deal" in life that includes four elements: marriage, fatherhood, employment, and homeownership—not necessarily in that order. Yet these goals often conflict. Many men express the desire to be closer to their children than their traditional fathers were to them, but they get caught in the traditional cycle of working long hours to pay for a nice home for the wife and kids.[22] Unfortunately, men are often reluctant to talk openly about personal pressures created by these work/family conflicts, and the cycle continues.

- Working fathers who want to take paternity leave, or time off to help raise their children, often suffer discrimination in the workplace. Women who choose these options are generally seen in a more positive light. Many men still feel that taking parental leave will unofficially penalize them.[23] Just as women struggle with this issue, men must also step forward and encourage employers to commit to family-friendly workplace policies and practices.

■ Men are less likely than women to adopt a healthy lifestyle and seek health care when it is needed. As a result, they lead in each of the ten leading causes of death and have a life span that is 5.8 years shorter than that of their female counterparts.[24]

> *During life's most stressful transitions, such as divorce or loss of a job, men often spend more time reflecting on things they value in life.*

During life's most stressful transitions, such as divorce or loss of a job, men often spend more time reflecting on things they value in life. Those who feel that their male identity is dependent on what is accomplished at work and that success is measured by the size of their paycheck sometimes reestablish their priorities. In a *Wall Street Journal* article entitled "Who's the New Guy at Dinner? It's Dad . . . ," one dad explains his transition following the loss of his managerial job at AOL. He says he told his young twin daughters, "I'm going to find a new job doing something I love that makes people happy." When he was hired as a fifth-grade teacher, his children were thrilled, and so was he. He can now spend more time with his children.[25]

Challenges and Opportunities for Working Men and Women

As men and women struggle with their career and family choices, progressive organizations are gearing up to meet the needs of their employees in the twenty-first century. They are recognizing the demands placed on working parents and are attempting to address the problems associated with quality child care. At the same time, they realize they must provide flexible work schedules that adjust to the changing roles of men and women.

● The Challenge of Child Care

The need for affordable, quality child care has never been greater. Mothers and fathers alike face forced overtime and unpredictable hours as their employers attempt to cut costs while improving productivity. At the same time, many day-care providers shut their doors at 6 P.M. and on weekends. Workers who cannot balance the demands of work with available child care are often disciplined or fired.

Some companies provide on-site day-care centers and find this fringe benefit a strong factor in retaining valuable employees who are also parents. The subsidized on-site day-care center at Genentech, a San Francisco biotech firm, offers classrooms, outdoor playgrounds, and a staff of seventy who care for employees' children 6 weeks to 5 years old. Judy Heyboer, senior vice

HUMAN RELATIONS
IN ACTION

The Family and Medical Leave Act

The 1993 Family and Medical Leave Act (FMLA) guarantees continuation of any paid health benefits, plus a return to the same or an equivalent job, for employees (men as well as women) who take up to twelve weeks' unpaid time off—all at once or intermittently—so that they can care for themselves or an ailing family member such as a parent, child, or spouse during a serious health condition, or for childbirth or adoption. (Some states are considering providing financial compensation during part or all of the employee's time off.)

To qualify, you must work for an employer with fifty or more employees and at a location with at least fifty employees within seventy-five miles.

Your employer can deny leave if you haven't worked there for at least twelve months and for at least 1,250 hours during the past year. You also may be ineligible for protection if you are among your employer's top 10 percent of employees, based on pay.

The FLMA also prohibits employers' retaliation against leave takers; however, some employers are attempting to get around the intent of the law. For example, they provide unfavorable performance appraisals because work was not completed in a timely manner. Some attempt to reduce or refuse to award year-end bonuses or annual raises because the person was absent due to a family medical emergency.

To protect yourself against this subtle discrimination, train your temporary replacement before you leave so that your responsibilities are covered; if it's feasible, establish a telecommuting arrangement; and invite coworkers to in-home meetings to stay on top of changing events at work. If all else fails and you feel you have a legitimate family leave dispute, contact the Wage and Hour Division of the United States Department of Labor (*www.wageandhour.dol.gov*).

THINKING / LEARNING STARTERS

1. Identify an organization in your area that is known for its family-friendly atmosphere. Describe the benefits working mothers receive as a result. Do these benefits apply to working fathers also?

2. Think of three men whom you know and admire. What roles do they play in their families? Have you observed any changes in these roles in recent years? Explain.

president of human resources, explains, "Our employees work really hard when they are here because they don't have to worry that their home life is out of control." Once every three months, the center stays open until 10:00 P.M. for "Date Night." Employees of the company are encouraged to take their spouses out for the evening while their children enjoy a slumber-party atmosphere complete with pajamas, pizza, and games.[26]

Parents who face forced overtime and unpredictable hours place a high value on affordable, quality child care. This employee is visiting his children at the day-care center provided by Corning, Inc.

Keep in mind, however, the resentment that builds among child-free employees who see employees with children receiving special treatment. These other workers are often expected to work overtime, the night shift, or weekends while their coworkers who are parents arrive late or leave early to manage child-care demands. During the workday, these workers frequently must absorb extra work to cover for parents called away for child-related emergencies.

● Flexible Work Schedule Opportunities

Men and women who are concerned about balancing personal and work lives say that flexible work schedules rank very high on the list of desired benefits. As a result, many organizations allow various scheduling options so that they can recruit and retain the top talent in the labor market.

Flextime **Flextime** typically includes a core time when all employees work, usually between 9:00 A.M. and 3:30 P.M. Employees can determine their own arrival and departure times within certain limits, which may mean arriving at 7 A.M. or leaving at 5:30 P.M. (see Figure 16.3 on p. 402). Today about 30 percent of all workers enjoy flexible schedules, compared to 15 percent in 1991.[27]

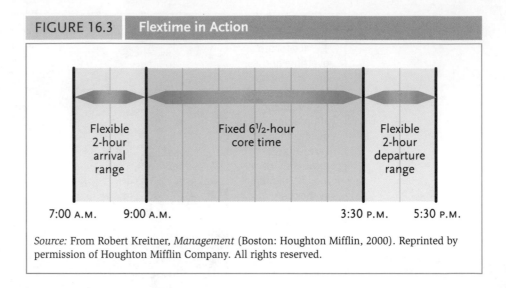

FIGURE 16.3 | **Flextime in Action**

| Flexible 2-hour arrival range | Fixed 6½-hour core time | Flexible 2-hour departure range |

7:00 A.M.   9:00 A.M.   3:30 P.M.   5:30 P.M.

Source: From Robert Kreitner, *Management* (Boston: Houghton Mifflin, 2000). Reprinted by permission of Houghton Mifflin Company. All rights reserved.

Compressed Workweek   Typically, a **compressed workweek** consists of four 10-hour days—for example, Monday through Thursday, or Thursday through Sunday. Employees may be given the opportunity to adjust their work schedules to fit their lifestyle. One of the newest compressed workweek schedules, often called the 9/80, is growing in popularity. Employees work one extra hour each day for nine days, a total of eighty hours in two weeks, and receive a three-day weekend every other week.[28]

Job Sharing   With **job sharing,** two employees share the responsibilities of one job. For example, one employee might work the mornings and the other works the afternoons. In some cases, each job sharer works two days alone and one day overlapping with the other person. This means the job is fully covered and each job sharer knows what the other is doing.[29]

Telecommuting   The availability of powerful home-office computer and communication technologies, large-scale use of temporary workers due to massive downsizing, and the demands of workers who want to blend work and family have fueled an increase in **telecommuting**—employees working at home at a personal computer linked to their employer's computer.

How to Cope with Gender-Biased Behavior

Traditional attitudes, beliefs, and practices are not changed easily. If you are a man or woman breaking into a nontraditional role, you may encounter resistance. In addition, you may be confused about how to act or may be overly sensitive about the way others treat you. As a result, if you are choosing a new role for yourself, you will need to learn new skills to control your own behavior as well as to confront some of the very real obstacles you will encounter.

● Sexual Harassment in the Workplace

One of the most sensitive problems between men and women in organizations is **sexual harassment,** unwelcome verbal or physical behavior that affects a person's job performance or work environment. Employers have a legal and moral responsibility to prevent sexual harassment, which can occur from men harassing women, women harassing men, or same-sex harassment. As men and women work together on teams, more employers are becoming acutely aware of the increased potential for misinterpreted comments and actions between the genders. When sexual harassment is present in the workplace, the cost of increased absenteeism, staff turnover, low morale, and low productivity can be high.

One of the most sensitive problems between men and women in organizations is sexual harassment, unwelcome verbal or physical behavior that affects a person's job performance or work environment.

Forms of Sexual Harassment   Under the law, sexual harassment may take one of two forms. The first is **quid pro quo** (something for something), which occurs when a person in a supervisory or managerial position threatens the job security or a potential promotion of a subordinate worker who refuses to submit to sexual advances. These kinds of threats are absolutely prohibited, and employers are liable for damages under the Fair Employment Practices section of the Civil Rights Act. These behaviors can take the form of comments of a personal or sexual nature, unwanted touching and feeling, or demands for sexual favors.

The second form of sexual harassment involves the existence of a **hostile work environment.** Supreme Court decisions have held that sexual harassment exists if a "reasonable person" believes that the behavior is sufficiently severe or pervasive to create an abusive working environment, even if the victim does not get fired or held back from a promotion. A hostile work environment exists when supervisors, coworkers, vendors, or customers use sexual innuendo, tell sexually oriented jokes, display sexually explicit photos in the work area, discuss sexual exploits, and so on. Unlike quid pro quo harassment, hostile work environment claims tend to fall in a gray area: What is offensive to one person may not be offensive to another. The bottom line is that most kinds of sexually explicit language, conduct, and behavior are inappropriate in the workplace, regardless of whether such conduct constitutes sexual harassment within the legal meaning of the term.

● How to Deal with Sexual Harassment

Ever since Professor Anita Hill accused Supreme Court nominee Judge Clarence Thomas of lewd and overbearing conduct toward her, the country has been trying to determine the difference between innocent comments and sexual harassment. The key word is *unwelcome.* Victims of sexual harassment need to tell the harasser, in no uncertain terms, that his or her behavior is inappropriate. Meanwhile, victims should record the occurrence in a journal that includes the date and details of the incident. They should also talk with coworkers, who can provide emotional support and help verify instances of harassment. Chances are, if one person is being harassed, others are as well. If the harasser continues the behavior, the victim should go to a higher authority, such as the harasser's supervisor or the organization's human resources division. Under the law, companies are legally liable if they do not immediately investigate the situation and take action to eliminate the offensive behaviors. These actions can include reprimand, suspension, or dismissal of the harasser.

The Supreme Court has recently given employees and employers help in understanding the legal aspects of sexual harassment. The court handed down two landmark rulings that included the following guidelines.[30]

- Companies can be held liable for a supervisor's sexually harassing behavior, even if the offense was never reported to management.

- An employer can be liable when a supervisor threatens to punish a worker for resisting sexual demands—even if such threats aren't carried out.

The court also offered employers advice on how to avoid costly legal fees. A company can deflect sexual harassment charges by developing a zero-tolerance policy on harassment, communicating it to employees, and making sure victims can report abuses without fear of retaliation. If the employer can show that an employee failed to use internal procedures for reporting abusive behavior, the company will be protected in a court of law.

Although the courtroom doors are open for individuals to protect themselves from unwanted behavior, pressing a sexual harassment charge is a lengthy, expensive, and psychologically draining experience. Before you file charges, be sure you have used all the remedies available to you through your employer.

Learn to Understand and Respect Gender Differences

As mentioned in Chapter 2, gender bias often acts as a filter that interferes with effective communication between men and women. In recent years, popular books such as *You Just Don't Understand: Women and Men in Conversation* by Deborah Tannen and *Men Are from Mars, Women Are from Venus* by John Gray have heightened awareness of the differences between women's and men's communication styles. These differences, according to Tannen, are due to linguistic style. **Linguistic style** refers to a person's speaking pattern and includes such characteristics as directness or indirectness, pacing and pausing, word choice, and the use of such elements as jokes, figures of speech, stories, questions, and apologies. Linguistic style is a series of culturally learned signals that we use to communicate what we mean.[31] Communication experts and psychologists have made the following generalizations concerning gender-specific communication patterns:

- Men tend to be more direct in their conversation, whereas women are more apt to emphasize politeness.

- Men tend to dominate discussions during meetings and are more likely to interrupt.

- Women prefer to work out solutions with another person; men prefer to work out their problems by themselves.

- Men tend to speak in a steady flow, free of pauses, interrupting each other to take turns. Women tend to speak with frequent pauses, which are used for turn taking.

- Male-style humor tends to focus on banter, the exchange of witty, often teasing remarks. A woman's style is often based on anecdotes in which the speaker is more likely to mock herself than she is to make fun of another person.

- Women are likely to downplay their certainty; men are likely to minimize their doubts.[32]

Does linguistic style really make a difference? Let's assume that two employees, Mary and John, are being considered for promotion to a management position. The person who must make the decision wants someone who displays a high degree of self-confidence. If John is regularly displaying the "male" communication patterns described above, he may be viewed as the more confident candidate. But if the person making the promotion decision is searching for someone who is sensitive, an attentive listener, and a consensus builder, Mary may win the promotion. We know that people in positions of power tend to reward linguistic styles similar to their own, so the candidate (male or female) with the greatest versatility may get the promotion.[33] You will recall that in Chapter 3 we defined *versatility* as acting in ways that earn social acceptance.

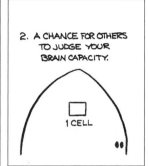

● A Few Words of Caution

Differences do exist: Men are somewhat more competitive, assertive, and task-focused, and most women are more sensitive, cooperative, and people-focused than most men. However, our stereotypes about men and women are often too strong and too inflexible.[34] When we place too much emphasis on the ways in which women and men differ, we stop viewing them as individuals. As noted in Chapter 3, it is tempting to put a label on someone and then assume the label tells you everything you need to know about that person.

Once you understand the concept that men and women communicate in different ways, you can begin to flex your style. Refer to Table 16.1 for more specific suggestions on how to communicate better with the opposite gender. Keep in mind, however, that an overextension of a strength *can* become a weakness. It is interesting to note that some men who have worked with women on a regular basis for many years and have successfully adjusted their communication style accordingly may find it difficult to communicate in a male environment. The same may be true for women who have worked for years in a male environment. They may find it difficult to transfer into a new work setting that is dominated by women.

TABLE 16.1	Workplace Tips for Avoiding Gender-Specific Language Barriers

Men can . . .

■ think about women as fellow employees rather than sexual objects.

■ recognize that, within their gender group, women are as unique as men.

■ communicate with women based on their individuality, rather than on the characteristics of a stereo-typed group.

■ use general humor, not sexual humor.

■ remember that even when intentions are good, the impact of your communication may be bad.

■ follow this rule: When in doubt, do not make the statement or act out the thought.

Women can . . .

■ stay calm when expressing feelings to avoid being labeled as overemotional.

■ express feelings verbally rather than nonverbally. Men are not always good at reading behavior.

■ avoid male bashing.

■ use general humor, not self-effacing humor.

■ say what needs to be said concisely, without excessive apologies or disclaimers.

■ recognize that a man may not understand the impact of his sexually related comment. When something is offensive, say something right away.

Source: From "Working Toward a Truce in the Battle of the Sexes." Anita Bruzzese, *Gannett News Service*, August 9, 1994, p. B1.

TOTAL	**ALICE SARGEANT**
PERSON	AUTHOR, *THE ANDROGYNOUS MANAGER*
INSIGHT	"Men and women should learn from one another without abandoning successful traits they already possess. Men can learn to be more collaborative and intuitive, yet remain result-oriented. Women need not give up being nurturing in order to learn to be comfortable with power and conflict."

Men and women have so much to learn from each other. Harvard psychologist Carol Gilligan offers this metaphor: "One can think of the oboe and the clarinet as different, yet when they play together, there is a sound that's not either one of them, but it doesn't dissolve the identity of either instrument."[35]

● **Learn New Organization Etiquette**

As women enter into upper levels of management and men begin to work in support positions, the ways in which men and women deal with each other change subtly. Does this change require new rules of etiquette? In some cases, yes. The following guidelines may help you understand how to act in these new situations:

1. When a woman visits a man's office, he should rise from his desk to greet her. When a man enters a woman's office, she should rise from her desk.

2. Whoever has a free hand (could be a small woman) should help anyone carrying too heavy a load (could be a large man).

3. Women resent being "go-fers." Meeting participants should not expect a woman to take notes, answer the phone, or type material. Men and women should rotate such clerical duties. A woman should not leap to serve coffee when it is time for a break.

4. Whoever arrives first at a door should open it, and whoever stands in the front row in the elevator should get off first.

5. Whoever extends an invitation to lunch or dinner should in most cases pay the tab.

6. Training materials, memos, and so on should be written in gender-free language. Clerical and secretarial personnel should not be referred to only as "she" or "her" and management personnel only as "he" or "him."

The new etiquette provides a means to overcome old stereotypes and traditional ways of setting men and women apart solely on the basis of gender. By practicing these points of etiquette and adopting a positive, helpful attitude toward each other, men and women can help ease the transition from traditional to nontraditional roles. Women and men both will be winners.

■ Summary

Gender bias is discrimination based on widely held beliefs about the abilities, characteristics, and behavior of men and women. The traditional roles assigned to both genders limit their opportunities to choose careers and lifestyles best suited to their abilities and true interests.

Many men and women are breaking out of these traditional roles. Over the past few decades, women have entered the job world in increasing numbers and in professions previously considered all-male. As a result, men and women have a wider range of choices regarding marriage and children than ever before. Organizations are beginning to offer their employees options such as job sharing, flextime, and home-based work so that they can better handle the demands of work and family.

Women are still subject to a wage gap, earning less than the wages men receive for similar work, but the gap is narrowing. Moreover, the Department of Labor has confirmed that the glass ceiling does exist and is holding women back from achieving high-level positions in organizations.

Men are also choosing new roles for themselves. They are working to dispel the myth that men must always be in control, emotionally unexpressive, logical, and achievement oriented. They realize that the rigid male role has had adverse effects on men's health and on their relationships with women and other men. Men are learning to make conscious choices about marriage, children, and career emphasis that better fit their values systems. Men are choosing more personally rewarding careers that allow time for family responsibilities, even if they must sacrifice some material gain to do so.

Sexual harassment may be a problem for some men as well as women. It may take one of two forms: quid pro quo, the threat to job security or promotion if sexual favors are not granted, or sexually explicit language, photos, or innuendo that creates a hostile work environment. Most organizations have developed guidelines to help employees avoid harassment or fight it when it occurs.

Methods of coping with gender-biased behavior include learning how to effectively communicate with the opposite gender and observing the new rules of etiquette in the workplace.

■ Career Corner

Q: I am a middle-aged man working in an organization that used to be dominated by men. Now almost half of my colleagues are women, most of whom I respect a great deal. But I have heard horror stories about sexual harassment charges, and I am scared to death that I will say or do something wrong around my female colleagues. Help!

A: You are not alone in your fears about potential sexual harassment charges. There are, however, a few rules that might be helpful for both men and women.

1. Use the "same-gender" standard: If you are not sure whether a comment is appropriate, determine whether you would make the comment if your colleague were of your own gender.

2. Try the "candid-camera" test: Would you be embarrassed if someone videotaped your behavior or comment? If your answer is yes, don't do it or say it!

3. Compliment on merit, not appearance: Be sure to praise a person's job skills, not what the individual is wearing or how he or she looks. This puts the person's status as a coworker above that of gender or appearance.

■ **Key Terms**

gender bias (sexism)   telecommuting
glass ceiling   sexual harassment
flextime   quid pro quo
compressed workweek   hostile work environment
job sharing   linguistic style

■ **Review Questions**

1. List some of the qualities men and women traditionally have been encouraged to develop.

2. List some of the characteristics of traditional roles that men and women are changing as a result of the men's and women's movements.

3. Describe the flexible work schedules that many organizations now offer.

4. What are some of the nontraditional choices regarding marriage and children open to men and women today?

5. What are some of the problems women still face as a result of discrimination in organizations?

6. Describe some of the difficulties men encounter when they attempt to make changes in their traditional role.

7. Explain the benefits and drawbacks to the careers of men and women who choose to take time off from work to raise their children.

8. Explain the two illegal forms of sexual discrimination in the workplace, and give an example of each.

9. What steps can individuals take to eliminate sexual harassment? What do organizations need to do to help reduce sexual harassment litigation?

10. List some reasons why men and women tend to have problems communicating. What adjustments can be made to remove these barriers to effective human relations?

■ **Application Exercises**

1. The following situations represent either quid pro quo or hostile environment forms of sexual harassment in the workplace. Identify the form represented by each situation, and explain your reasoning. Describe the actions you might take if you were the potential victim in each incident.

   a. Julie thinks David is very handsome. She often stares at him when she thinks he is not looking. David is aware of Julie's staring and is very uncomfortable but is too shy and embarrassed to say anything to her.

   b. While sitting at her desk, Karen receives the following electronic message from her boss on her computer screen: "Can we discuss your possible promotion over dinner this evening?"

   c. At a convention reception, one of Joan's most important clients invites her out for cocktails and dinner. She politely declines. He announces loudly, "She won't go out to dinner with me, and I'm her best customer!" Under his breath he says, "Honey, if you want my business, you'd better cooperate." Joan's boss insists she go to dinner with the client.

2. On a sheet of paper, list and explain the various choices you would make when attempting to balance your career and family responsibilities. For example, will marriage be a part of your future? Will you have children? When? How will you provide care for these children while you and your spouse are at work? Would you prefer home-based work? Which flextime options would you consider valuable? Do you want to work for someone else or own your own business?

3. Over a period of one week analyze your verbal and nonverbal communications with people who are of the opposite gender. Try to determine if any linguistic style differences are apparent during conversations. If you discover style differences, try to determine if they serve as a barrier to effective communication.

 Internet Exercise

As men and women struggle with interpreting their changing roles at work and at home, they need all the information and support they can find. Websites created by professional organizations like the National Association of Female Executives (*www.nafe.com*), the Families and Work Institute (*www.familiesand work.org*), and At-Home Dad (*www.athomedad.com*) offer tremendous support. Those who would like to examine the various flexible work schedule options can visit *www.att.com* and click on Telework Guide, then Getting Started, *www.workoptions.com*, *www.workfamily.com*, or *www.gilgordon.com*. Visit the site of your choice and write an analysis of how it might help individuals make an educated decision about their personal and professional life choices. Share your findings with your classmates.

Case 16.1　Salomon Smith Barney Learns the Hard Way

In her book *Tales from the Boom-Boom Room, Women vs. Wall Street,* author Susan Antilla detailed the landmark sexual harassment and discrimination lawsuit against the brokerage firm Salomon Smith Barney (recently re-named Citigroup Global Markets). Before the lawsuit was settled, women working at a Smith Barney brokerage office in Garden City, New York, were exposed to triple-X-rated sexual harassment, including strippers brought into the office to celebrate male brokers' birthdays, pornographic videotapes played in the office, simulated phone sex on speaker phones during work hours, and lewd, threatening, and humiliating comments. In addition to this hostile work environment, women were paid lower base salaries than their male equivalents, had clients and commissions taken away, and were often demoted following maternity leave. They were refused access to the study materials that helped their male brokers earn their licenses and, as a result, were eight times less likely to make broker status than the men in the firm.

Traditionally, brokerage firms have required all professionals to agree never to sue their employers and to submit to an industry-sponsored arbitration instead. Under the system, the complainants do not have the opportunity to present their case in a court of law and therefore receive few of the protections of legal precedent or due process. They have a diminished opportunity for a generous award, little explanation of the arbitrators' decision, and almost no chance to appeal. Since arbitration treats each case individually, there is little evidence against serial harassers. All of the details of the proceedings are kept secret, which protects the victims' privacy but also nullifies the civic value of their complaints. However, when the women of Smith Barney banded together and filed a class action suit, they were able to sue in regular court and won the right for each of the 1,950 complainants to appear before an internal forum and have her individual claim heard. As a stipulation to this agreement, none of the accused harassers would ever be deposed or held liable. If a woman accepted one of Smith Barney's offers, she signed an agreement to keep the entire affair confidential. To this day, no one but the firm knows how much cash the women received, but it is estimated that Smith Barney paid in the hundreds of millions of dollars.

Tameron Keyes, a broker in the Los Angeles branch of Shearson Lehman Brothers (now owned by Smith Barney), complained about her hostile work environment and was granted a transfer to their Beverly Hills office. There, she was forced to sit in a broker "bullpen" for five years even though empty offices were available. The firm interfered with her attempts to collaborate with other brokers, refused to provide financial assistance for marketing, held her to a higher production standard than her male counterparts, and gave her no accounts from departing brokers. Her complaints to the firm's human resources officials failed to produce any remedy.

The arbitration panel agreed that Keyes was subjected to a sexually hostile work environment. They further ruled that the firm was guilty of retaliatory actions by failing to undertake any meaningful investigation of her complaints, refusing to interview witnesses to learn whether the allegations were true, and failing to impose any sanctions on those responsible. As a result, she was entitled to compensation because of the "disruption of her career by the work environment" and was awarded $3.2 million for economic losses, emotional distress, and punitive damages.[36]

■ Questions

1. Have you witnessed similar sexual harassment or discrimination in your professional life? Explain. Were remedies implemented to prevent the perpetuation of the hostile work environment, or is it still going on?

2. Conditions have changed at Salomon Smith Barney. As part of the settlement, the firm allocated $15 million to design and implement a diversity plan and agreed to:

   ■ hire and retain qualified women and minorities as brokers, analysts, and investment bankers

   ■ link managers' compensation to women's success at the firm

   ■ dramatically increase the percentage of female branch managers, brokers, and broker trainees

   ■ put all employees on notice that the firm would not tolerate sexual harassment of any kind

   It took more than six years and millions of dollars in legal fees—let alone cash settlements—to reach these workplace adjustments. Was it worth it? Would you have the personal fortitude to pursue legal action if you were a victim of sexual harassment or discrimination? Explain.

3. Are there viable alternatives to legal action? Explain.

Case 16.2   Creating a Balance

A new, young generation of baby boomers, the "40-somethings," are taking over the leadership of many of the nation's companies. Most of them have survived heavy travel requirements, round-the-clock shifts, and forced overtime that allowed little time or energy for their families. Because they have suffered work/family conflicts throughout their climb to the top, they often serve as role models and sounding boards for their employees going through the same struggles. They have had to conscientiously juggle their own work and family duties and are taking steps to help their employees do the same. This is producing a subtle yet profound change in the way organizations are run in this country.

■ Charter Communications CEO Jerald Kent says, "The biggest way to illustrate the importance of balancing work and family is to believe in it and do it yourself."

■ When asked about his company's work/life policies, Jonathan Spiller, CEO of Armour Holdings, says, "Nobody has to make excuses for wanting to be involved with their families. Life's too short."

- Michael Critelli, CEO of Pitney Bowes and father of three, conducted a dozen focus groups on life-balance issues among the company's thirty thousand employees.

- Eddie Bauer Inc. offers an annual "Balance Day" to all of its 5,500 full-time employees nationwide. The extra day off each year allows workers time to find balance in their lives and do whatever they want.

- BP–Amoco provides $1,500 a year for expenses related to employees' unscheduled business trips—even if it means flying Grandma in to take care of the children.

Though many organizations are making adjustments to accommodate their workers' desire for balance between their personal and professional lives, many are not. Therefore, individuals must be creative in learning ways to make these adjustments themselves. Arthur Emlen, professor emeritus at Portland State University and a researcher for the Oregon Child Care Research Partnership, offers a somewhat analytical approach to the problem. He says that the lives of working parents are interdependent triangles of support: work, family, and child care. Those who reach a successful balance have discovered that they must create flexibility in at least one of these areas to make up for the rigidity in the others—for example, a flexible work environment such as those just listed, a supportive partner or stay-at-home spouse, or flexible child-care facilities or extended-family caregivers such as grandparents. One family found a unique solution when they enrolled their children in a school that operates until 6:00 P.M. year round and allows students to learn at their own pace, so that they can take vacations at their families' convenience. Dr. Emlen's succinct approach to finding work/life balance offers a variety of options if you really think it through: Be creative and open-minded and then go for it![37]

■ Questions

1. As you strive to keep a healthy balance between your professional and personal life, which of the three dimensions of support—work, family, or child care—do you project will be the most flexible? Explain your answer.

2. Most experts agree that the creation of work/life employee benefits will, in the long run, benefit the organizations that participate as well as the children of the future. Do you agree? Why?

3. From the foregoing list of organizations that are making work/life adjustments, which benefits would apply to only those workers who have children? Do you believe these benefits would cause resentment among workers who do not have children? Explain.

PART VI

YOU CAN PLAN FOR SUCCESS

17 A LIFE PLAN FOR EFFECTIVE HUMAN RELATIONS

415

17

A LIFE PLAN FOR EFFECTIVE HUMAN RELATIONS

Chapter Preview

After studying this chapter, you will be able to

- ■ Define success by standards that are compatible with your needs and values.

- ■ Learn how to cope with the forces that influence work/life balance.

- ■ Discuss the meaning of *right livelihood*.

- ■ Describe four nonfinancial resources that can enrich your life.

- ■ Provide guidelines for developing a healthy lifestyle.

- ■ Develop a plan for making needed changes in your life.

Andrew Johnston recalls the day his life took a fateful turn. He and his bride were on their Hawaiian honeymoon when they visited a small art gallery on the Big Island. Johnston was mesmerized by a series of landscape paintings on display. He immediately began making plans to begin painting. The well-paid financial analyst with an MBA degree returned to his job in Denver, but life would never be the same again. He began immediately to devote every free moment to painting. Later he took art classes from a well-known artist. The motivation to become an artist was strong because, in his words, "I wanted out of my job." Today, at age 31, he is a full-time artist and his work is represented by four galleries.[1]

Kathy Rogg was a partner at a Washington, D.C., law firm when she made a radical career change. The life-changing event was an 18-day rafting trip through the Grand Canyon. The following year she returned for a second rafting trip and her fondness for the Southwest grew stronger. She then decided to move to Denver and practice law. But after just one ski trip that fall, she decided to leave her law practice and work for a ski resort. For over ten years she has spent her winters working at the ski resort and her summers working as a rafting guide in Utah.[2]

Andrew Johnston and Kathy Rogg have discovered that radical career changes can prove satisfying. They both walked away from secure, well-paying jobs to find greater fulfillment elsewhere.

Many observers of the American scene say you can have a good job or a life, but not both. Workers who are struggling with long hours and unrewarding working conditions say life is work and work is life. But this is not necessarily so, as these two stories make clear.

Achieving Balance in a Chaotic World

We are being told to envision a future filled with sharp detours and many re-definitions of our work lives. Tom Peters, noted author and consultant, talks about the disappearing career ladder:

> A typical career path today isn't linear or even always upward. It's more like a maze, full of hidden turns, zigs, and zags that go in all sorts of directions—even backward sometimes, when that makes sense. The satisfaction that you derive from the job is what should matter most, not the directions [in which] you appear to be going.[3]

The dream of finding job security and knowing that we have "arrived" seems sadly obsolete. As we change jobs eight or more times during our working lives, we will need to reshape our work identity.[4]

In this chapter we help you construct a life plan that will enhance your relationships with people in your personal life and in your work life. This plan will also help you better manage the relationship you have with yourself. We discuss the meaning of success and suggest ways to cope with major disappointments that will surface in your work life. You will learn how to avoid being trapped by a lifestyle that offers financial rewards but little else. This chapter also helps you define your relationship with money and describes four nonfinancial resources that give meaning to life. Finally, you will learn how to develop the mental and physical fitness needed to keep up in today's frantic, fast-paced world.

Toward a New Definition of Success

Most of us have been conditioned to define success in narrow terms. Too frequently we judge our own success, and the success of others, by what is accomplished at work. Successful people are described as those who have a "good job" or have "reached the top" in their field. We sometimes describe the person who has held the same job for many years as successful. We do not stop to consider that such a person may find work boring and completely devoid of personal rewards.

From early childhood on we are taught to equate success with pay increases and promotions. Amy Saltzman, author of *Downshifting,* notes that many people tend to set goals and measure success along a vertical career path that is often described as the "career ladder" or the "fast track." Saltzman says, "One is not successful, according to this school of thought, unless one is consistently moving up the ladder in some clearly quantifiable way."[5] Too often the person who is striving to achieve an immediate career goal (one more rung on the career ladder, for example) is forced to give up everything else that gives purpose and meaning to life. This may mean spending less time with family members and friends, spending less time keeping physically fit, abandoning vacation plans, and spending weekends at work.

> *From early childhood on we are taught to equate success with pay increases and promotions.*

TOTAL	**RALPH FIENNES**
PERSON	ACTOR
INSIGHT	"I call people successful not because they have money or their business is doing well but because, as human beings, they have a fully developed sense of being alive and engaged in a lifetime task of collaboration with other human beings—their mothers and fathers, their family, their friends, their loved ones, the friends who are dying, the friends who are being born."

● The Need for New Models of Success

In recent years, a growing number of people are angry, disillusioned, and frustrated because they have had to abruptly change their career plans. They gave their best efforts to an employer for ten, fifteen, or twenty years, and then the company eliminated their jobs. For years the firm said, "Take care of business and we'll take care of you," but then the situation changed. Under pressure from new global competition, hostile takeovers, and the need to restructure, companies started getting rid of experienced workers. The unwritten and unspoken contract between the company and the employee was broken. Many of the people who lost their jobs during the past decade were once told that if

When Maggie Melanson (center) was laid off from her job in advertising, she was forced to rethink her career goals. After a lot of soul searching she decided to start Gimme the Skinny, a catering firm that specialized in a lighter, lower-fat cooking style.

they had ambition and worked tirelessly to achieve their career goals, success would be their reward. But the "reward" for many people has been loss of a job, loss of self-esteem, and increased anxiety about the future.

We should certainly feel sympathy for persons who have lost their jobs and watched their dreams dissolve. But there is another group of people who also merit our concern. These are the persons who put in long hours, climbed the ladder of success, and still have a job but have discovered that something important is missing from their lives. They invested ten, fifteen, or twenty years in a job, gave up all or most of their leisure time, gave up quality time with friends and family, climbed the career ladder, and then discovered that life was empty and unfulfilling.

It is inspiring to look at a different way of living. When Jeff Soderberg founded Software Technology Group, a technology consulting business based in Salt Lake City, he created a new model of success. His company provides employees with plenty of time to have a life. He doesn't believe there is a correlation between time spent at work and success. He refuses to hire workaholics, and in an industry where 80-hour workweeks are common, he tells new hires, "We expect a 40-hour workweek." Soderberg sets a good example by frequently taking time off during the week to enjoy rock climbing in the nearby canyons.[6]

One-Dimensional Model The traditional success model defined success almost exclusively in terms of work life. The model emphasized working long hours, reaching work-related goals, and meeting standards often set by others.

"I see you have no life.
We like that in an employee."

The old model of success required us to be "one-dimensional" people for whom work is the single dimension. In the life of such a person, everything that has meaning seems to be connected to the job. When a person defines himself or herself by a job and then loses that job, what does that person have left? Of course, the loss of a job encourages some people to search for meaning beyond their work. People who are able to broaden their perspectives, develop interests beyond their jobs, and put balance in their lives not only usually achieve more self-fulfillment but also are more valuable as employees.[7]

TOTAL	**CHERYL SHAVERS**
PERSON	SENIOR MANAGER, INTEL CORPORATION
INSIGHT	"We don't like to think of ourselves as slaves to money, prestige or power, but in fact many only feel worthy by attaining these things. When we allow 'things' to have power over us to the extent that we lose ourselves, our values, our ability to choose, we become slaves."

● Loss of Leisure Time

Throughout history Americans have burdened themselves with a very demanding work ethic. They spend more time on the job than employees in any other industrialized nation. What's more, downsizing efforts have left fewer people to do the same amount of work, so many people are working even harder. Most of these workers yearn for more leisure time.

U.S. workers not only work long hours, but they spend less time on vacation than do workers in most other industrialized countries. A typical American worker averages about 13 vacation days a year, *including* public holidays. By comparison, workers in Germany, France, and Italy take 35 and 40 vacation days each year.[8] In addition, American workers, equipped with cell phones, pagers, and PalmPilots, are often too accessible during their vacations. There is a growing sense, matched by growing reality, that our work is always with us, demanding our attention.[9]

Some of America's best-managed companies are beginning to realize the negative consequences of long hours on the job and loss of leisure time. The director of human resource strategy and planning for Merck and Company says, "You can't build an effective company on a foundation of broken homes and strained personal relationships." A senior executive at Price Waterhouse says, "We want the people who work for our firm to have lives outside Price Waterhouse—people with real lives are well rounded, and well-rounded people are creative thinkers."[10]

● Developing Your Own Life Plan

The goal of this chapter is to help you develop a life plan for effective relationships with yourself and others. The information presented thus far has, we hope, stimulated your thinking about the need for a life plan. We have noted that personal life can seldom be separated from work life. The two are very much intertwined. We have also suggested that it is important for you to develop your own definition of success. Too frequently people allow others (parents, teachers, counselors, a spouse) to define success for them. Judging your success by the standards established by someone else may lead to a life of frustration.

HUMAN RELATIONS IN ACTION

The Gospel According to Sullivan

Seminars conducted by a company called the Strategic Coach resemble an Alcoholics Anonymous meeting. Those who attend are entrepreneurs who are reformed workaholics. People who start their own business often feel the need to work long hours in order to achieve success. Dan Sullivan, who founded Strategic Coach, says long hours with little time off are counterproductive. He strongly encourages seminar participants to take Free Days, time when they are totally disconnected from their business. They must go cold turkey—no cell phones, no pagers, no contact with their employees. The goal of Free Days is the rejuvenation of the mind and body. Nearly all attendees say the Free Days contribute significantly to the success of their business.

Many people today are discovering that true success is a combination of achievements. Becoming too focused on one narrow goal may not provide the self-satisfaction you are seeking. One author makes this observation: "Everyone wants to be successful. But each person must have a personal definition of what success will feel like, and understand that true success rarely means having just one goal."[11] A narrow definition of success may actually prove to be counterproductive if it means giving up everything else that adds meaning to life.

Because work is such an important part of life, we now move to a discussion of items that will help you in your career planning. We discuss the concept of "right livelihood."

Toward Right Livelihood

At age 45 Vera Shanley closed her lucrative medical practice in Atlanta and moved to a small farm near Hillsborough, North Carolina. She had a busy practice and good friends, but she was working sixty to eighty hours a week and thinking about passions that needed to be explored. Now she travels to Third World countries as a volunteer with Interplast, a nonprofit agency that performs free facial reconstructive surgeries on needy people. When she is back home, she works several hours a day as a potter.[12]

Vera Shanley, like many other people, has been searching for "right livelihood." The concept of right livelihood is described in the core teachings of Buddhism. In recent years, the concept has been described by Michael Phillips in his book *The Seven Laws of Money* and by Marsha Sinetar in her book *Do What You Love . . . The Money Will Follow*. **Right livelihood** is work consciously chosen, done with full awareness and care, and leading to enlightenment. Barbara Sher, contributor to *New Age* magazine, says right livelihood means that you wake up in the morning and spend all day working at something you really want to do.[13] Ronald Sheade, once a vice president at a *Fortune*

The search for right livelihood motivated Dr. Vera Shanley to think about interests that needed to be explored. Today she travels the world as a volunteer with Interplast, a nonprofit group that performs free facial reconstructive surgeries on people in Third World Countries. When she is home, Shanley works as a potter.

1,000 company, now teaches eighth-grade science in a suburb of Chicago. He doesn't make big money anymore, but he loves teaching and now gets to spend more time with his family.[14]

There are three characteristics to right livelihood: choice, emphasis on more than money, and personal growth.

● Right Livelihood Is Based on Conscious Choice

Marsha Sinetar says, "When the powerful quality of conscious choice is present in our work, we can be enormously productive."[15] She points out that many people have learned to act on what others say, value, and expect and thus find conscious choice very difficult:

> It takes courage to act on what we value and to willingly accept the consequences of our choices. Being able to choose means not allowing fear to inhibit or control us, even though our choices may require us to act against our fears or against the wishes of those we love and admire.[16]

To make the best choices, you must first figure out what you like to do, as well as what you are good at doing. What you like doing most is often not obvious. It may take some real effort to discover what really motivates you. Students often get help from career counselors or explore a career option during a summer internship. If you are employed, consider joining a temporary project team. A team assignment provides an opportunity to work with persons who perform very different types of duties. You might also consider reassignment within your organization.

● Right Livelihood Places Money in a Secondary Position

People who embrace this concept accept that money and security are not the primary rewards in life. Michael Phillips explains that "right livelihood has within itself its own rewards; it deepens the person who practices it."[17] For example, people who work in the social services usually do not earn large amounts of money, but many receive a great deal of personal satisfaction from their work. Vera Shanley may not make much money as a potter, but the work provides enormous personal satisfaction.

Many people who once viewed success in terms of wealth, material possessions, and status are realizing that something is missing from their lives. They do not *feel* successful. They once felt pressured to "have it all" but now feel disappointed that their achievements have not brought them real happiness.

● Right Livelihood Recognizes That Work Is a Vehicle for Personal Growth

Most of us spend from 40 to 60 hours each week at work. Ideally, we should not have to squelch our real abilities, ignore our personal goals, and forget our need for stimulation and personal growth during the time we spend at work.[18] Most employees know intuitively that work should fulfill their need for self-expression and personal growth, but this message has not been embraced by many leaders. Too few organizations truly empower workers and give them a sense of purpose. When employees feel that the company's success is their own success, they will be more enthusiastic about their work.

> *Most employees know intuitively that work should fulfill their need for self-expression and personal growth, but this message has not been embraced by many leaders.*

The search for right livelihood should begin with a thoughtful review of your values. The values clarification process (see Table 5.1) should be completed *before* you interview for a job. Mark Buzek, a graduate of Ohio State University, decided not to take a job that would require frequent relocation and excessive travel. Although he is not married, he has strong ties with his parents, two sisters, and a brother in Ohio. Staying close to family members is an important value in his life. Sarah Schroeder, another college graduate, says she cut off interviews with several employers who expect continuous sixty-hour-plus workweeks.[19]

When a job fails to fulfill your expectations, consider changing jobs, changing assignments, or changing careers. If the job isn't right for you, your body and your mind will begin sending you messages. When you begin feeling that something is lacking, try to answer these basic questions: What is making me feel this way? What, exactly, about my current position is unpleasant? Choosing a satisfying career and lifestyle requires understanding what contributes to your job satisfaction. Self-exploration and continual evaluation of your needs, goals, and job satisfaction are important. Don't wait for a crisis (layoff) to clear your vision.[20]

THINKING / LEARNING STARTERS

1. Do you agree that many people define success in terms that are too narrow? Reflect on your personal knowledge of friends and family members before answering this question.

2. In your opinion, does the concept of right livelihood seem realistic? Is right livelihood an option for everyone, or only a select few? Explain.

● Defining Your Relationship with Money

Money is a compelling force in the lives of most people. It often influences the selection of a career and the commitment we make to achieve success in that career. Sometimes we struggle to achieve a certain economic goal only to discover that once we got what we wanted it didn't fulfill us in the way we had hoped.

Many people struggle with money management decisions and seem unable to plan for the future. The personal savings rate in America is at a record low, and the household debt burden is at a record high. Losing one's job can result in a relentless financial drain as we search for a new job, but many people are ill prepared for this eventuality.[21]

According to Juliet Schor, author of *The Overspent American,* Americans spend a great deal of time and money keeping up with the Joneses. Schor argues that people compete for status within "reference groups," persons they work with at the office or factory, members of their professions, and friends or relatives. When we strive to keep up, but fall short, we often feel anxious and poorer.[22]

True Prosperity   The way we choose to earn, save, and spend our money determines, in large measure, the quality of our lives. For example, if you think that having *more* money is going to produce happiness or peace of mind, will you ever earn enough? Shakti Gawain, author of *Creating True Prosperity,* says that more money does not necessarily bring greater freedom, fewer problems, or security. Rather, "prosperity is the experience of having plenty of what we truly need and want in life, material and otherwise." Gawain says, "The key point to understand is that prosperity is an *internal* experience, not an *external* state, and it is an experience that is not tied to having a certain amount of money."[23] Many of us go through life unconscious of our own real needs and desires. Gawain advises that we begin to think about what we "truly want."[24] How do we do this? Steven Reiss (see Chapter 7) says that nearly everything we experience as meaningful can be traced to one of sixteen basic desires or to some combination of those desires (see Figure 7.1). Now would be a good time to revisit this list of basic desires and identify the five or six that seem most important to you. This review may help you understand your relationship with money.

Mature Money Management   Some people do not have a mature relationship with money. They spend everything they earn and more, and then have bouts of financial anxiety. People who are deep in debt often experience symptoms of depression. Money issues continue to be the number one cause of divorce in the United States. Space does not permit a comprehensive examination of money management, but here are some important tips on how to manage your personal finances:

■ *Develop a personal financial plan.* With a financial plan, you are more likely to achieve your financial goals. Without a plan, you are likely to follow a haphazard approach to management of your finances. A key element of your plan is determining where your income is going. With a simple record-keeping system, you can determine how much you spend each month on food, housing, clothing, transportation, and other things. Search for spending patterns you may want to change.

■ *Spend less than you earn.* Stacy Johnson, author of *Life or Debt: A One-Week Plan for a Lifetime of Financial Freedom,* reminds us that the only way to save money is to not spend it. Most people who spend more than they earn are buying things they do not really need. Johnson also believes that getting rid of credit cards is an important step to financial freedom.[25]

■ *Maintain a cash cushion.* If you lost your job today, how long could you live on your current cash reserves? Financial consultants suggest that cash reserves should be equal to the amount you earn during a two-month period.

Plan to Win the Lottery?

Chances are, you won't win the lottery anytime soon. You can, however, build a large fund with a regular savings plan. A mixture of the following three things can produce amazing results:

- A small amount of money
- An average rate of return
- A period of time for your investment to grow

Steve Moore of the Cato Institute and Tom Kelly of the Savers and Investors Foundation provide a simple illustration of the stunning results that can be achieved. If your parents placed $1,000 in a mutual fund in 1950, and the money was allowed to grow at the stock market's average rate of return, they would now have $217,630. This is a reminder that fortunes can be made even by low-wage earners who save regularly during their working years.

- *Discuss financial matters with your significant other.* Many people do not think about financial compatibility before or after marriage. When couples talk about financial issues and problems, the result is usually less conflict and smarter financial decisions. David Bach, author of several books on financial planning, helps couples achieve financial compatibility. He has the partners start by writing down what's most important to each of them— their five top values. They are also instructed to write down what the purpose of money is. He says, "Smart financial planning is more than a matter of numbers; it involves values first and stuff second."[26]

Com-Corp Industries, a manufacturing plant based in Cleveland, Ohio, sees personal money management skills as one key to reducing conflict in the workplace. Employees who cannot live within their means are often under great stress and are more likely to experience interpersonal problems at work and at home. The company provides employees with classes on such subjects as developing a household budget and wise use of credit.[27]

TOTAL PERSON INSIGHT	**JULIE CONNELLY**
	CONTRIBUTING EDITOR, *FORTUNE*
	"Keep in mind that there is no harder work than thinking—really thinking—about who you are and what you want out of life. Figuring out where your goals and your skills match up is a painful, time-consuming process."

● Defining Your Nonfinancial Resources

If you become totally focused on your financial resources, then chances are you have ignored your **nonfinancial resources.** And it is often the nonfinancial resources that make the biggest contribution to a happy and fulfilling life. A strong argument can be made that the real wealth in life comes in the form of good health, peace of mind, time spent with family and friends, learning (which develops the mind), and healthy spirituality. Paul Hwoschinsky, author

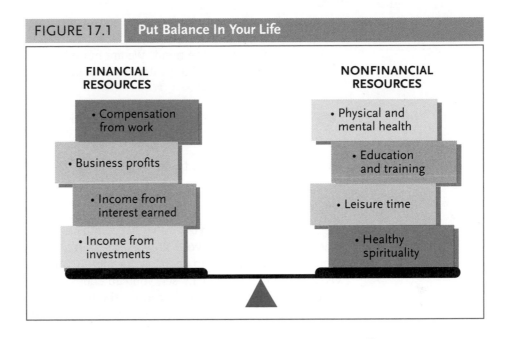

FIGURE 17.1　Put Balance In Your Life

FINANCIAL RESOURCES
- Compensation from work
- Business profits
- Income from interest earned
- Income from investments

NONFINANCIAL RESOURCES
- Physical and mental health
- Education and training
- Leisure time
- Healthy spirituality

of *True Wealth,* makes this observation about nonfinancial resources: "If you are clear about who you are, and clear about what you want to do, and bring your financial and nonfinancial resources together, it's extraordinary what can happen. I encourage people to really honor their total resources, and magical things happen. New options occur."[28]

If you focus most or all of your attention on work and you suffer a major work-related disappointment, then the result is likely to be feelings of depression and despair. Thoughts such as "Now I have lost everything" can surface when you fail to get a promotion, find out that you were not selected to be a member of a special project team, or learn that your job has been eliminated. But if you fully understand the power of your nonfinancial resources, then work-related disappointments are easier to cope with. The starting point is to realize that *most* of your resources are nonfinancial. During periods of great uncertainty, it is especially important that you think about your nonfinancial assets and consider ways to enhance them. We briefly discuss four nonfinancial resources that can enrich your life: physical and mental health, education and training (intellectual growth), leisure time (time for family, socializing, recreation), and healthy spirituality (see Figure 17.1).

Physical and Mental Health　Is the statement "Health means wealth" just a worn-out cliché, or is this slogan a message of inspiration for people who want to get more out of life? If good health is such an important nonfinancial asset, then why are so many people flirting with self-destruction by eating the wrong foods, drinking too much, exercising too little, and generally choosing unhealthy lifestyles? The answer to the second question may be lack of awareness of the benefits of physical fitness. Susan Smith Jones, a fitness instructor at UCLA and author of *Choose to Be Healthy,* offers these benefits of good health:

■ There is an interrelationship between health and outlook on life. For example, when the physical body is fit, toned, and strong, this condition has a positive effect on the mind. We are more likely to experience higher levels of self-esteem, feel a greater sense of self-confidence, and have a more positive outlook on life.

■ Poor health tends to interfere with everything else in life: family harmony, work schedules, and relationships.

■ Regular exercise and a healthy diet produce greater mental clarity, a higher energy level, and a more youthful appearance.[29]

Jones states that good health is something you must *choose* to have. She says, "Regardless of the lifestyle you've lived until now, you can, at any moment, choose differently."[30] If your breakfast is currently five cups of coffee and a danish, you can choose to change your diet. If you are spending thirty hours a week sitting in front of a TV set, you can choose to spend that time in a different way. Your current level of health is the result of many choices you made in the past. Later in this chapter we discuss ways to form new habits that will help you achieve vibrant health.

Education and Training (Intellectual Growth)   The New Economy thrives on a well-educated and well-trained work force. It rewards workers who take personal responsibility for their learning. The need to continually update, train, and develop yourself has never been greater. Here are some tips on how to acquire the skills and abilities you need:

■ *Think of yourself as a unique brand.* In Chapter 11 we noted that branding can play a crucial role in your career success. Developing a strong personal brand requires giving attention to several things, one of which is staying competent. To do this you must build your strengths and try to overcome your weaknesses. The authors of *What Every Successful Woman Knows* say, "Build your brand and toot your own horn—a lot."[31]

■ *Be selective in what you learn.* Learning often requires large amounts of time and energy, so consider carefully what knowledge or skill will generate the most improvement.

■ *Take advantage of various learning pathways.* It helps to think of your job as a learning resource. Take full advantage of instructional programs offered by your employer. Volunteer for team assignments that will provide new learning opportunities. Peter Senge, author of *The Fifth Discipline,* says the fundamental learning unit in any organization is a team.[32] And look outside the company at community college classes or programs offered by Toastmasters, Dale Carnegie, or other organizations.

In his best-selling book *The Art of Happiness*, the Dalai Lama says the role of learning and education in achieving happiness is widely overlooked. He notes that numerous surveys have conclusively found that higher levels of education

Denise, a volunteer at Raptor Recovery Nebraska, releases a young bald eagle that has been treated for its injuries. The eagle, when found, was suffering from a shoulder injury and lead poisoning. Volunteer work provides an excellent way to increase your social connections and improve your health.

have a positive correlation with better health and a longer life, and even protect us from feelings of depression.[33]

Leisure Time   Leisure time can provide an opportunity to relax, get rid of work-related stress, get some exercise, spend time with family and friends, or simply read a good book. Many people think they want more leisure time, but when it is available, they do not know what to do. Some people even feel guilty when they are not working.

If you are working for someone who is on the fast track, someone who may have given up all or most of his or her leisure time, you may be pressured to work at the same pace. If your boss is constantly trying to meet impossible deadlines and deal with last-minute rushes, you may feel the need to give up time for recreation or family. If this happens, try to identify the consequences of being overworked. Look at the situation from all points of view. If you refuse to work longer hours, what will be the consequences for your relationship with the boss, your relationship with other employees, your future with the organization?[34] You have choices, but they may be difficult ones. If it looks as though the pressure to work longer hours will never end, you may want to begin searching for another job.

Is it worth taking some risks to protect the leisure time you now have? Should you increase the amount of leisure time available in your life? Consider the following benefits of leisure time:

■ As we noted previously in this text, maintaining social connections with friends and family can be good for your health. A growing number of studies show that if you have strong and fulfilling relationships, you may live longer, decrease your chances of becoming sick, and cope more successfully when illness strikes.[35] Time spent with friends and family can be a powerful source of mental and physical renewal. An excellent way to increase your social connections and improve your own health is to become a volunteer. Research indicates that volunteers experience pleasurable physical sensations such as feelings of warmth, well-being, and calmness, and increased energy levels.[36]

■ One of the best ways to feel satisfied about your work is to get away from it when you begin to feel worn out. People who take time off from work often return with new ideas, a stronger focus, and increased energy. When you discover that end-of-the-week exhaustion is still hanging around Monday morning, it's time to take some vacation or personal days.[37]

■ A growing body of research indicates that the American trend toward skipping vacations is hazardous. People who skip vacations have a higher risk of death from heart disease and other serious health problems.[38] You need time away from work to relax, renew your creative powers, and reduce your level of stress.

■ Find some quiet time for yourself each day. You might use it to meditate, take the dog for a walk, or just sit quietly. Use this time to nourish yourself and bring balance to your life.

If you want more leisure time, then you must establish your priorities and set your goals. This may mean saying no to endless requests to work overtime or rejecting a promotion. Sometimes you must pull back from the endless demands of work and "get a life."

Healthy Spirituality   A discussion of nonfinancial resources would not be complete without an introduction to healthy spirituality. To become a "whole" or "total" person requires movement beyond the concrete, material aspects of life to the spiritual side of the human experience. Healthy spirituality can bring a higher degree of harmony and wholeness to our lives and move us beyond self-centeredness.

Spirituality can be defined as an inner attitude that emphasizes energy, creative choice, and a powerful force for living. It involves opening our hearts and cultivating our capacity to experience reverence and gratitude. It frees us to become positive, caring human beings.[39]

Spirituality encompasses faith, which can be described as what your heart tells you is true when your mind cannot prove it. For some people, faith exists within the framework of a formal religion; for others it rests on a series

An understanding of the many aspects of spirituality can give us an expanded vision of what it means to be human.

of personal beliefs such as "Give others the same consideration, regard, kindness, and gentleness that you would like them to accord you."[40]

An understanding of the many aspects of spirituality can give us an expanded vision of what it means to be human. Although spirituality is often associated with religion, it should be viewed in broader terms. Robert Coles, of Harvard Medical School, likes a definition of spirituality given to him by an eleven-year-old girl:

I think you're spiritual if you can escape from yourself a little and think of what's good for everyone, not just you, and if you can reach out and be a good person—I mean live like a good person. You're not spiritual if you just talk spiritual and there's no action. You're a fake if that's what you do.[41]

The words of this young girl remind us that one dimension of spirituality involves showing concern and compassion for others. It means turning away from rigid individualism and investing some time and energy in helping others.

A number of books and articles report on the growing interest in spirituality at work. Linda Ferguson, author of *The Path for Greatness—Work as Spiritual Service,* says, "Often it is in our work that we find the best opportunities for spiritual growth to take place." Through encounters with coworkers and customers we have the opportunity to be understanding, compassionate, accepting, and forgiving.[42]

TOTAL PERSON INSIGHT	**ROBERT WUTHNOW**
	AUTHOR, *AFTER HEAVEN—SPIRITUALITY IN AMERICA SINCE THE 1950s*
	"Faced with growing uncertainties and with ample opportunities for choice, people will need to spend more time than ever before reflecting on the deep values that make life worth living and the sources of those values, including spirituality."

In many ways, large and small, work can be made more spiritual. The philosophy of Worthington Industries is expressed in a single sentence: "We treat our customers, employees, investors and suppliers as we would like to be treated."[43] Allied Holdings Inc., Herr Foods Inc., and many other campanies have hired chaplains to provide needed support and counseling to their employees.[44] Lotus Development Corporation formed a "soul" committee to examine the company's management practices and values. The company wants to find ways to make the work environment as humane as possible.[45] Edward Bednar teaches Zen Buddhist meditation techniques to employees working in the Wall Street area. He is attempting to help them live a more contemplative life.[46] The American Stock Exchange has a Torah study group; Boeing has Jewish, Christian, and Muslim prayer groups; and Microsoft has an online prayer service.[47]

Many activities can be considered spiritual. Visiting an art gallery, listening to a concert, or walking near the ocean can stimulate healthy spirituality. Table 17.1 (on p. 432) describes some ways to begin your journey to healthy spirituality.

Healthy spirituality can often serve as a stabilizing force in our lives. As noted in Chapter 14, the various twelve-step programs (Alcoholics Anonymous

TABLE 17.1	Ways to Achieve Healthy Spirituality

As interest in healthy spirituality grows, people are searching for ways to become more spiritual. The following spiritual practices draw our focus away from ourselves and the anxieties in our lives.

■ **Meditation**   Oprah Winfrey described the powerful influence of meditation this way: "There is no greater source of strength and power for me in my life now than going still, being quiet and recognizing what real power is." (See Chapter 14 for a step-by-step guide to meditation.)

■ **Prayer**   Dr. Larry Dossey, physician and author of numerous books on the role of spirituality in medicine, says prayer can be a powerful force in our lives. Prayer groups have been established at many organizations.

■ **Spiritual Reading**   In addition to sacred readings, consider *Healing and the Mind* by Bill Moyers, *The Soul of a Business* by Tom Chappell, and *The Hungry Spirit* by Charles Handy.

■ **Time with Nature**   Spiritual contemplation during a walk in the woods or a visit to a quiet lake can help us balance mind, body, and spirit.

Sources: David Elkins and Amanda Druckman, "Four Great Ways to Begin Your Spiritual Journey," *Psychology Today,* September/October 1999, p. 46; Larry Dossey, M.D., "Can We Change the World?" *The Inner Edge,* June/July 2000, pp. 22–23.

is one example) emphasize the need for a spiritual connection. "Working the steps" means, among other things, turning life over to a higher power. This spiritual connection seems to give hope to persons who feel a sense of loneliness and isolation.

For many people, a commitment to a specific religion is an important dimension of spirituality. Active membership in a religious group provides an opportunity to clarify spiritual values and achieve spiritual direction. It also provides social connections—an extended family that you can depend on for social support.[48]

As more organizations accept the whole person in the workplace, healthy spirituality will grow in importance. Hyler Bracey, consultant and author of *Managing from the Heart,* said, "We used to check our feelings, health, sexuality, spirituality and family problems at the door of the workplace. We've matured enough to get beyond that. The unspeakable is now acceptable."[49]

TOTAL PERSON INSIGHT	**AUTHOR, UNKNOWN**
	"Don't get crispy fried in business. The insidious suction of achievement could leave you with no soul."

Developing a Healthy Lifestyle

Earlier in this chapter we noted that a healthy lifestyle can provide a higher energy level, a greater sense of self-confidence, and generally a more positive outlook on life. People who maintain good health usually have more endurance, spend less time feeling tired or ill, and miss less work than persons who are not healthy. Good health is receiving greater attention today because many

Americans are investing more time and energy in their work. They are being asked to work longer hours and do more in less time. Good health can help combat stress and tension at work and at home.

The first step toward adopting a healthy lifestyle is to become well-informed—to read, study, and learn what can be done to maintain your current level of health or improve your health. In this section we offer guidelines that form the framework for a good diet and a good exercise program.

● Guidelines for a Healthy Diet

Eating the right foods can improve your health, boost your energy level, and in some cases extend your life. The link between health and diet is quite clear. We will review several important dietary guidelines.

Maintain a Diet That Is Balanced and Varied Several years ago the U.S. Department of Agriculture (USDA) published the Food Pyramid. Recently, critics of the Food Pyramid have said the recommendations are outdated and based on shaky science. One of the strongest critics, Dr. Walter Willett of Harvard University, proposed a new "Healthy Eating Pyramid." The Willett Pyramid (see Figure 17.2) conveys a few general principles to follow when you make food choices.[50]

FIGURE 17.2	Recommended Food Groups and Amounts Necessary for a Healthy Diet

WILLETT PYRAMID

Red meat, butter
Use sparingly

White bread, white rice, potatoes, pasta, sweets
Use sparingly

Dairy or calcium supplement
1-2 times a day

Fish, poultry, eggs
0-2 times a day

Nuts, legumes
1-3 times a day

Vegetables
In abundance

Fruits
2-3 times a day

Whole grains
Most meals

Plant oils

Daily exercise

Weight control

Multivitamins for most people

Alcohol in moderation (unless contraindicated)

Eating a variety of foods is important because you need more than forty different nutrients for good health: vitamins and minerals, amino acids (from proteins), essential fatty acids (from fats and oils), and sources of energy (calories from carbohydrates, fats, and proteins). The number of servings you need each day depends on your total calorie intake. Keep in mind that servings are small—just one slice of bread or piece of fruit; half a cup of cooked rice, pasta, or vegetables; three ounces of cooked lean meat, poultry, or fish.

Reduce Calorie Intake   Over 60 percent of Americans are overweight or obese. One major cause of this problem is increased calorie intake because of larger portions. In general, people are eating more and exercising less. If you want to lose weight, you must reduce the number of calories you consume, burn more calories through exercise, or do both.[51]

Cut Down on Fatty Foods   The foods that are popular with many Americans are relatively high in fat, especially saturated fat, which contributes to high blood cholesterol levels. Many restaurant foods are high in fat because it gives menu items the flavor people often seek when eating out (see Table 17.2). Heart disease and certain kinds of cancer are byproducts of foods that contain highly saturated fats. Although diet is the most important factor in lowering cholesterol, exercise can help.

TABLE 17.2	Food Choices High in Fat, Sodium, and Calories—Followed by Healthy Alternate Choices		
	Fat (grams)	Sodium (milligrams)	Calories
McDonald's Big Breakfast	51	1580	760
Burger King Biscuit (with sausage egg, and cheese)	43	1650	620
Denny's Grand Slam	50	2240	800
Dunkin' Donuts Bagel (plain)	1	710	340
Eggo Nutri-Grain Whole Wheat Waffles	3	430	140
Scrambled Egg Substitute (2 eggs' worth)	6	190	130

Source: Excerpt from "The Breakfast Breakdown." Copyright 1999, CSPI. Reprinted/adapted from *Nutrition Action Healthletter,* published by the Center for Science in the Public Interest (CSPI), 1875 Connecticut Avenue, NW, Suite 300, Washington, DC 20009-5728. $24.00 for 10 issues.

Eat Foods with Adequate Starch and Fiber   Foods high in starch, such as breads made with whole grains, dry beans and peas, and potatoes, contain many essential nutrients. Many starches also add dietary fiber to your diet. A growing number of scientists believe that high-fiber diets can help reduce the odds of getting cancer of the colon. Some cereals and most fruits and vegetables are good sources of fiber.

Avoid Too Much Sodium   A common byproduct of excess sodium is high blood pressure. In the United States, where sodium-rich diets are very common, the average person consumes about 5,000 milligrams of sodium each day, more than twice the amount the American Dietetic Association recommends.[52] Table 17.2 includes some examples of foods that are high in sodium.

If You Drink Alcohol, Do So in Moderation   Alcoholic beverages are high in calories and low in nutrients and cause serious health risks when used in excess. Excessive alcohol consumption has been linked to liver damage, certain types of cancer, and high blood pressure.

With the help of these healthy diet guidelines, you can develop your own plan for achieving a healthful diet. Keep in mind that good nutrition is a balancing act. You want to select foods with enough vitamins, minerals, protein, and fiber but avoid too much fat and sodium. You want to consume enough calories to maintain the energy level required in your life but avoid weight gain.

● Improving Your Physical Fitness

With regard to exercise, people often choose one of two extreme positions. Some adopt the point of view that only high-intensity activities (marathon running, high-impact aerobics) increase physical fitness. These people believe in the "no-pain, no-gain" fitness approach. The other extreme position is to become a "couch potato" and avoid all forms of exercise. Both positions should be avoided.

Physical fitness can be defined as the ability to perform daily tasks vigorously and have enough energy left over to enjoy leisure activities. It is the ability to endure difficult and stressful experiences and still carry on. Physical fitness, which involves the performance of the lungs, heart, and muscles, can also have a positive influence on mental alertness and emotional stability. Research indicates that even a moderate level of physical activity can have a surprisingly broad array of health benefits on virtually every major organ system in the body.[53] For most people, a program that involves regular physical activity at least three or four times a week and includes sustained physical exertion for twenty to thirty minutes during each activity period is adequate.[54] This modest investment of time and energy will give you a longer and healthier life.

You do not need to become an obsessive fitness fanatic to achieve lifesaving benefits from exercise. Start slowly with an aerobic fitness activity you feel you will enjoy. Walking, swimming, running, low-impact aerobics, and jogging are aerobic exercise. When we engage in aerobic exercise, the body is required to improve its ability to handle oxygen.[55] These exercises strengthen the heart, burn up calories, increase stamina, and help release tension.

Dare to Change!

In the New Economy there are no rules about how young or how old you should be to relaunch your career. Melissa is the director of training and development for a large retail outlet, and she loves the job. She spent many years searching for a meaningful and fulfilling career. She was first a flight attendant, then a high school teacher, and then a manager of a retail store. Today Melissa feels content because she feels she is doing something worthwhile. Her advice to those who feel their current position is lacking something important? Dare to change!

If you are younger than 35 and in good health, you probably do not need to see a doctor before beginning an exercise program. If you are older than 35 and have been inactive for several years, consult your doctor before engaging in vigorous exercise.[56]

Planning for Changes in Your Life

Throughout this book we have emphasized the concept that you can control your own behavior. In fact, during these turbulent times changes in your behavior may be one of the few things under your control. If making changes in your life seems to be a logical course of action at this point, then it is time to do some planning. The starting point is to clearly identify the personal growth goals that can make a difference in your life. What are some behaviors you can adopt (or alter) that will make an important positive change in your life? Once you have identified these behaviors, you can set goals and do what is necessary to achieve them.

At the end of Chapter 1 you were encouraged to complete the Human Relations Abilities Assessment (HRAA) Form that is in the appendix of this book (see Application Exercise 1 in Chapter 1) and in the Classroom Activities Manual. If you completed this instrument, then you no doubt gained awareness of your strengths and a better understanding of the abilities you want to improve. Now would be a good time to complete the instrument a second time and determine if your *X*s have moved to the right on the various scales. Completion of the HRAA Form will help you identify the behaviors you want to change.

● The Power of Habits

Before we discuss specific goal-setting methods, let us take a look at the powerful influence of habits. Some habits, like taking a long walk three or four times a week, can have a positive influence on our well-being. Simply saying "Thank you" when someone does a favor or pays a compliment can be a habit. Other habits, such as smoking, never saying no to requests for your time, feeling jealousy, or constantly engaging in self-criticism, are negative forces in our lives. Stephen Covey, author of *The 7 Habits of Highly Effective People,* makes this observation: "Habits are powerful factors in our lives. Because they are consistent, often unconscious patterns, they constantly, daily, express our character and produce our effectiveness . . . or ineffectiveness."[57]

Breaking deeply embedded habits, such as impatience, procrastination, or criticism of others, can take a tremendous amount of effort. The influences supporting the habit, the actual root causes, are often repressed in the subconscious mind and forgotten.[58] How do you break a negative habit or form a positive habit? The process involves five steps.

Motivation   Once you are aware of the need to change, you must develop the willingness or desire to change. After making a major commitment to change, you must find ways to maintain your motivation. The key to staying motivated is to develop a mind-set powerful enough that you feel compelled to act on your desire to change. You must continuously remind yourself why you want to change a bad habit or form a new habit. Only when the activity (exercise, weight loss, etc.) becomes personally meaningful will you be motivated to do it regularly.

Knowledge   Once you clearly understand the benefits of breaking a habit or forming a new one, you must acquire the knowledge you need to change. Seek information, ask for advice, or learn from the experiences of others. This may involve finding a mentor, joining a group, or gathering sufficient material and teaching yourself. For example, suppose you decide you need to lose weight. Your first step might be to visit a bookstore or the Internet. Your next step might be to talk with others who share the same goal. You might consider joining a support group or talking to a counselor or an expert in nutrition. In the process of acquiring information, you are actually gaining a better understanding of the habit you want to learn or unlearn.

Practice   Information is only as useful as you make it. This means that to change your behavior you must *practice* what you have learned. If you are a shy person, does this mean you need to volunteer to make a speech in front of several hundred people? The answer is no. Although there is always the rare individual who makes a major change seemingly overnight, most people find that the best and surest way to develop a new behavior is to do so gradually. This is particularly true if you feel a lot of anxiety about changing. Take your time. Allow yourself to ease into your new behavior until you feel comfortable with it.

Feedback   Whenever you can, seek feedback as you attempt to change a habit. Dieters lose more weight if they attend counseling sessions and weigh-ins. People who want to improve their public speaking skills benefit from practice followed by feedback from a teacher or coach. Everyone has blind spots, particularly when trying something new. You will often need to rely on the feedback of others to tell you when you are off course or when you have really changed—sometimes you are too close to the process to tell.

Reinforcement   When you see yourself exhibiting the type of behavior you have been working to develop—or when someone mentions that you have changed—reward yourself! The rewards can be simple, inexpensive ones—

treating yourself to a movie, a bouquet of flowers, a favorite meal, or a special event. This type of reinforcement is vital when you are trying to improve old behaviors or develop new ones. Do not postpone rewarding yourself until the goal is reached. Intermediate success is just as important as the final result.

● The Goal-Setting Process

Goals should be an integral part of your plan to break old habits or form new ones. You will need an assortment of goals that address the different needs of your life. After a period of serious reflection, you may be facing many goal-setting possibilities. Where do you begin? We hope that reading the previous chapters in this book, completing the HRAA Form, and reviewing the material in this chapter will help you narrow the possibilities.

The goal-setting process was described in Chapter 4. The major principles of goal setting are outlined in Table 4.1. These time-tested principles can help you achieve any realistic goal.

The Choice Is Yours

Are you ready to develop a life plan for effective human relations? We hope the answer is yes. One of the positive aspects of personal planning is that you are making your own choices. You decide what kind of person you want to be and then set your own standards and goals. The results can mean not only career advancement and financial benefits, but also the development of strong, satisfying relationships with others. These relationships may be the key to future opportunities, and you in turn may be able to help others reach their goals.

In the opening chapter of this text, we talked about the total person approach to human relations. By now, we hope you realize that you are someone special! You have a unique combination of talents, attitudes, values, goals, needs, and motivation—all in a state of development. You can decide to tap your potential to become a successful, productive human being, however *you* understand those terms. We hope this book helps you to develop your human relations skills and to become what you want to be. You can turn the theories, concepts, and guidelines presented here into a plan of action for your own life and career. We wish you the best!

■ Summary

The traditional definitions of success that most of us know are too confining. They view success almost entirely in terms of measurable job achievements. These definitions leave out the intangible successes to be had in private and in professional life.

Many people today are discovering that true success is a combination of achievements. Achieving right livelihood is one important dimension of success. Right livelihood is work consciously chosen, done with full awareness and care, and leading to enlightenment. Right livelihood is based on conscious

business.college.hmco.com/students

ACE

Self-tests

choice. Although right livelihood recognizes that work is a vehicle for self-expression, it is a concept that places money in a secondary position. People who choose right livelihood are more likely to be self-disciplined and have established meaningful goals.

A person's nonfinancial resources make one of the biggest contributions to a happy and fulfilling life. Each of us has four nonfinancial resources that can enrich our lives: physical and mental health, education and training (intellectual growth), leisure time (time for family, socializing, recreation), and healthy spirituality. These nonfinancial resources can be acquired throughout our lives.

Many Americans are working to achieve healthy lifestyles. Healthy lifestyles can give us a higher energy level, a greater sense of self-confidence, and generally a more positive outlook. People who maintain good health usually have more endurance, spend less time feeling tired or ill, and miss less work than persons who are not physically fit.

Planning for changes in your life often requires breaking negative habits or forming positive habits. The process of breaking habits and forming new ones involves five steps: motivation, knowledge, practice, feedback, and reinforcement. Goal setting is also an integral part of a successful plan to make changes. Chapter 4 deals with goal setting in detail.

■ Key Terms

right livelihood	spirituality
nonfinancial resources	physical fitness

■ Review Questions

1. What have been the traditional criteria used to measure success? What are some of the reasons we need a new model for success in our society?

2. Explain the reasons many Americans have experienced a decline in leisure time. What can be done to reverse this trend?

3. What does the term *right livelihood* mean? What are the common characteristics of right livelihood?

4. Critics say Americans live in a commercial culture that encourages spending. They say too many people have adopted a work-and-spend cycle. Do you agree? Explain.

5. List and describe the four nonfinancial resources.

6. Julie Connelly in the Total Person Insight says there is no harder work than thinking about who you are and what you want out of life. Do you agree or disagree with her point of view? Explain.

7. What are the major reasons we should embrace healthy spirituality?

8. List and describe the guidelines for a healthy diet.

9. Provide a brief description of physical fitness. Why is physical fitness so important in the life of a typical worker?

10. What are the five steps involved in breaking a negative habit or forming a positive habit?

■ Application Exercises

1. In recent years, it has become popular for organizations to develop a mission statement that reflects their philosophy and objectives. The Gear for Sports vision statement provides one example (see Chapter 5). Prepare a personal mission statement that reflects your goals and aspirations for a successful life. Your mission statement should cover the roles of financial and nonfinancial resources in your life.

2. Throughout this chapter you were encouraged to take control of your life and establish your own definition of success. This chapter has a strong "all development is self-development" theme. Can we really control our own destinies? Can we always make our own choices? Mike Hernacki, author of the book *The Ultimate Secret of Getting Absolutely Everything You Want,* says yes:

> To get what you want, you must recognize something that at first may be difficult, even painful to look at. You must recognize that *you alone* are the source of all the conditions and situations in your life. You must recognize that whatever your world looks like right now, you alone have caused it to look that way. The state of your health, your finances, your personal relationships, your professional life—all of it is *your* doing, yours and no one else's.[59]

Do you agree with this viewpoint? Take a position in favor of or in opposition to Hernacki's statement. Prepare a short one- or two-paragraph statement that expresses your views.

3. There are many ways to deepen and extend your spirituality. One way is to begin placing a higher value on silence, tranquillity, and reflection. If your life is extremely busy, you may not be taking time for thought or reflection. If you are accustomed to living in the presence of noise throughout the day, quiet times may make you feel uncomfortable at first. Over a period of one week, set aside a few minutes each day for your own choice of meditation, prayer, contemplation, or reflection. Try to find a quiet place for this activity. At the end of the week, assess the benefits of this activity, and consider the merits of making it part of your daily routine.[60]

 ### Internet Exercise

At some point in your life, full-time employment will become less appealing. You will begin thinking about part-time work that will give you time to pursue a personal interest, start a family, become an independent consultant, earn a degree, or simply enjoy more leisure time. Several Internet sites can help you acquire information:

Name	URL	Services
Resources Connection Associates	*www.connectionassociates.com*	Helps find work for legal, technical, and marketing professionals
Aquent	*www.aquentpartners.com*	Helps find work for print, technical, and Web multimedia professionals
Manpower	*www.manpower.com*	Finds assignments in a wide variety of fields
Monster	*www.monster.com*	Lists several contract jobs and includes a ten-question quiz on whether "flex work" is right for you

Visit two of these websites and study the job opportunities. Prepare a written summary of your findings.

Case 17.1 Friendships as a Source of Positive Energy

Friendships formed on the job and off the job can be an important source of positive energy. Edward M. Hallowell, author of *Connect,* says, "To thrive, indeed just to survive, we need warm-hearted contact with other people." He believes that a human-contact deficiency weakens the body, the mind, and the spirit.

Research indicates that the ability to form friendships at work is an important characteristic of a productive workplace. Information age jobs tend to create a work environment where people draw close very fast and rely on one another for support. Diana Freeland, a former manager with a large energy company, says that enjoying friends at work went hand in hand with doing her best work. However, layoffs, reorganizations, and the movement of headquarters resulted in the loss of several good friends. In addition to various job upheavals, the struggle to balance career and family often leaves little room for time with friends.

The Dalai Lama, in his book *The Art of Happiness,* discusses the value of connecting with others through volunteer work. In addition to helping others, volunteer activities can bring us some significant health benefits. Research indicates that interacting in a warm and compassionate way increases life expectancy. He says showing compassion for others is "emotionally nourishing."

Making friends and staying connected with them takes effort and some degree of risk. Some people avoid developing new friendships because they fear being hurt or rejected, or they feel life is too busy to make room for a friendship. Yet when we hold back too often, it becomes a habit. We *need* those human moments—time spent with a friend—in order to thrive in life.[61]

■ Questions

1. Many employees report that some of their closest friends are also their colleagues. Can you think of any problems that might surface if your closest friends were colleagues on the job?

2. Interacting with others in a warm and compassionate way seems to offer us improved health and vitality. What would explain these beneficial effects?

APPENDIX

Human Relations Abilities Assessment Form

The purpose of this instrument is to help you assess those attitudes and skills that contribute to effective human relations. An honest response to each item will help you determine your areas of strength and those abilities that need improvement. Completion of this self-assessment form will provide you with information needed to develop a plan for improved human relations.

Directions: Circle the number from 1 to 5 that best represents your response to each statement. Review the following information before you complete the form: (1) Strongly disagree (*never do this*); (2) Disagree (*rarely do this*); (3) Moderately agree (*sometimes do this*); (4) Agree (*frequently do this*); (5) Strongly agree (*almost always do this*).

1. I am an effective communicator who sends clear, concise oral and written messages. 1 2 3 4 5

2. When people talk, I listen attentively and frequently use active listening skills. 1 2 3 4 5

3. I am conscious of how I express nonverbal messages (facial expression, tone of voice, body language, etc.) when communicating with others. 1 2 3 4 5

4. When forming attitudes about important matters I maintain an open mind, listen to the views of others, but think for myself. 1 2 3 4 5

5. I make every effort to maintain a positive mental attitude toward other people and the events in my life. 1 2 3 4 5

6. I seek feedback and clarification on the influence of my attitudes and behaviors on others. 1 2 3 4 5

7. I am willing to change my attitudes and behaviors in response to constructive feedback from others. 1 2 3 4 5

8. I monitor my self-talk in order to maintain high self-esteem. 1 2 3 4 5

9. I tend to be future oriented and not overly concerned with past mistakes or failures. 1 2 3 4 5

10. I have developed and maintained high expectations for myself.   1 2 3 4 5

11. I accept myself as a changing, growing person capable of improvement.   1 2 3 4 5

12. My goals are clearly defined, attainable, and supported by positive self-talk.   1 2 3 4 5

13. I accept the fact that each communication style has its unique strong points and that there is no "best" communication style.   1 2 3 4 5

14. I make a deliberate attempt to change or alter my communication style (style flexing) in order to meet the needs of other persons.   1 2 3 4 5

15. I have identified my internal motivations and continue to seek opportunities to fulfill these motivations.   1 2 3 4 5

16. I base my personal and professional decisions on clearly defined personal values.   1 2 3 4 5

17. I accept the fact that others' values may differ from mine, and I respect their right to maintain a value system different from my own.   1 2 3 4 5

18. I have a clear sense of what is right and wrong, and my character reflects the fundamental strengths of honesty, fairness, service, humility, and modesty.   1 2 3 4 5

19. I maintain my integrity by practicing what I believe in and keeping my commitments.   1 2 3 4 5

20. I am able to share information about myself in appropriate ways, avoiding the extremes of complete concealment and complete openness.   1 2 3 4 5

21. I engage in appropriate self-disclosure in order to achieve improved communication and increased self-awareness and to build stronger relationships.   1 2 3 4 5

22. I am able to solve problems and make decisions in a logical manner without allowing my emotions to interfere.   1 2 3 4 5

23. My relationships with people at home, school, and work do not suffer because of my expressions of anger or impatience.   1 2 3 4 5

24. I have developed effective ways to cope with my own anger and the anger of others.   1 2 3 4 5

25. I am familiar with and can apply several strategies for achieving emotional control.   1 2 3 4 5

26. I make every effort to recognize the accomplishments of others and celebrate my own successes.　　1　2　3　4　5

27. I understand and can apply several forms of positive reinforcement.　　1　2　3　4　5

28. I project to others an image that matches my talents and aspirations.　　1　2　3　4　5

29. The factors that form my image (career apparel, manners, facial expression, etc.) are appropriate and do not detract from the image I project to others.　　1　2　3　4　5

30. In the role of team member, I listen carefully to the views of others and speak frankly about the issues that are uppermost in my mind.　　1　2　3　4　5

31. I make every effort to screen out negative thoughts and accentuate positive thinking.　　1　2　3　4　5

32. As a team member, I help create an atmosphere of mutual trust and respect.　　1　2　3　4　5

33. When people disagree with me, I listen closely to what they have to say and do not try to respond immediately.　　1　2　3　4　5

34. I do not hang on to grudges or resentments because these behaviors limit my personal growth and my effectiveness in the area of human relations.　　1　2　3　4　5

35. When I experience conflict with others, I strive to be cooperative yet assertive.　　1　2　3　4　5

36. In my attempts to resolve conflict I strive for a solution that all parties can accept.　　1　2　3　4　5

37. I have developed good habits of diet, sleep, and exercise in order to cope more effectively with the negative stressors in my life.　　1　2　3　4　5

38. I accept change as an ongoing process in my life and realize the need to establish new goals.　　1　2　3　4　5

39. I manage stress and tension so I am not over-whelmed by the negative stressors in my life.　　1　2　3　4　5

40. I refuse to perpetuate negative stereotypes and accept each person as a unique individual worthy of my respect.　　1　2　3　4　5

41. I make every effort to identify my own prejudiced attitudes and avoid stereotypical attitudes toward people of color, older people, people with disabili-ties, and others who are different from me.　　1　2　3　4　5

42. I work hard to combat prejudice because it has a negative impact on my self-esteem and the self-esteem of the victim. 1 2 3 4 5

43. I stay connected with family and friends and network with professional and business associates. 1 2 3 4 5

44. I try to maintain balance in my life by avoiding addiction to work and by engaging in leisure time activities. 1 2 3 4 5

45. I envision my existence in a larger context and view healthy spirituality as a positive, enlightening force in my life. 1 2 3 4 5

46. I avoid rigid individualism (self-centered behavior) by investing time and energy in helping others. 1 2 3 4 5

47. I seek advice and counsel from friends, coworkers, and professionals in order to cope with life's problems. 1 2 3 4 5

48. I constantly strive to improve my knowledge, skills, and sense of purpose in my life's work. 1 2 3 4 5

49. I have established well-thought-out, realistic goals for my life, and these goals are tied to my values. 1 2 3 4 5

50. I take responsibility for my actions and do not rely on others to plan my future. 1 2 3 4 5

The NWNL Workplace Stress Test

The issue of increased stress, especially in the workplace, is a growing concern today. The following material is part of a package prepared by Northwestern National Life Insurance Company. It is intended for both employees and employers to assess the levels of stress in their work environment. Read the sample letter to employees and complete the questionnaire that follows, keeping in mind a current or previous work environment.

Sample letter to employees

Date

Dear Employee:

Stress has become a serious problem in the workplace. Four in 10 American workers say they feel their job is very or extremely stressful, according to a study by Northwestern National Life. Employees who feel their job is highly stressful are twice as likely to burn out on the job.

Job stress can cause employee turnover, absenteeism and health problems, as well as lower productivity and job satisfaction. We at _____ are concerned about the effect of job stress on our workforce. We would like to find out how serious stress is at our company and identify ways we can reduce job stress and burnout.

To help us evaluate job stress levels, we would like you to fill out the enclosed questionnaire by _____. It will take 10 minutes or less to complete.

Return it to _____ in the attached envelope. Confidentiality is guaranteed. Do not sign your name to the questionnaire.

Thank you for your cooperation. We value your opinion and will share the results of this survey with you.

Sincerely,

CEO or Human Resources Manager

The NWNL Workplace Stress Test

Instructions

Thinking about your work site, how strongly do you agree or disagree with the following statements? For each statement, fill in the circle with a pencil under the response that best describes your work site.

Response

	Disagree Strongly	Disagree Somewhat	Neutral or Don't Know	Agree Somewhat	Agree Strongly
SECTION A					
1. Management is supportive of employee's efforts.	○	○	○	○	○
2. Management encourages work and personal support groups.	○	○	○	○	○
3. Management and employees talk openly.	○	○	○	○	○
4. Employees receive training when assigned new tasks.	○	○	○	○	○
5. Employees are recognized and rewarded for their contributions.	○	○	○	○	○
6. Work rules are published and are the same for everyone.	○	○	○	○	○
7. Employees have current and understandable job descriptions.	○	○	○	○	○
8. Management appreciates humor in the workplace.	○	○	○	○	○
9. Employees and management are trained in how to resolve conflicts.	○	○	○	○	○
10. Employees are free to talk with one another.	○	○	○	○	○

Response

	Disagree Strongly	Disagree Somewhat	Neutral or Don't Know	Agree Somewhat	Agree Strongly
SECTION B					
11. Workloads vary greatly for individuals or between individuals.	○	○	○	○	○
12. Employees have work spaces that are not crowded.	○	○	○	○	○
13. Employees have access to technology they need.	○	○	○	○	○
14. Few opportunities for advancement are available.	○	○	○	○	○
15. Employees are given little control in how they do their work.	○	○	○	○	○
16. Employees generally are physically isolated.	○	○	○	○	○
17. Mandatory overtime is frequently required.	○	○	○	○	○
18. Employees have little or no privacy.	○	○	○	○	○
19. Performance of work units generally is below average.	○	○	○	○	○
20. Personal conflicts on the job are common.	○	○	○	○	○
21. Consequences of making a mistake on the job are severe.	○	○	○	○	○

Response

	Disagree Strongly	Disagree Somewhat	Neutral or Don't Know	Agree Somewhat	Agree Strongly
SECTION C					
22. Employees expect the organization will be sold or relocated.	○	○	○	○	○
23. There has been a major reorganization in the past 12 months.	○	○	○	○	○

Response

	Disagree Strongly	Disagree Somewhat	Neutral or Don't Know	Agree Somewhat	Agree Strongly
SECTION D					
24. Meal breaks are unpredictable.	○	○	○	○	○
25. Medical and mental health benefits are provided by the employer.	○	○	○	○	○
26. Employees are given information regularly on how to cope with stress.	○	○	○	○	○
27. Sickness and vacation benefits are below that of similar organizations.	○	○	○	○	○
28. Employee benefits were significantly cut in the past 12 months.	○	○	○	○	○
29. An employee assistance program (EAP) is offered.	○	○	○	○	○
30. Pay is below the going rate.	○	○	○	○	○
31. Employees can work flexible hours.	○	○	○	○	○
32. Employees have a place and time to relax during the workday.	○	○	○	○	○
33. Employer has a formal employee communications program.	○	○	○	○	○

Response

	Disagree Strongly	Disagree Somewhat	Neutral or Don't Know	Agree Somewhat	Agree Strongly
SECTION E					
34. Child-care programs or referral services are available.	○	○	○	○	○
35. Referral programs or day care for elderly relatives are offered.	○	○	○	○	○
36. Special privileges are granted fairly based on an employee's level.	○	○	○	○	○
37. New machines or ways of working were introduced in the past year.	○	○	○	○	○
38. Employer offers exercise or other stress-reduction programs.	○	○	○	○	○

Response

	Disagree Strongly	Disagree Somewhat	Neutral or Don't Know	Agree Somewhat	Agree Strongly

SECTION F

	Disagree Strongly	Disagree Somewhat	Neutral or Don't Know	Agree Somewhat	Agree Strongly
39. Work is primarily sedentary or physically exhausting.	○	○	○	○	○
40. Most work is machine-paced or fast-paced.	○	○	○	○	○
41. Staffing or expense budgets are inadequate.	○	○	○	○	○
42. Noise or vibration is high, or temperatures are extreme or fluctuating.	○	○	○	○	○
43. Employees deal with a lot of red tape to get things done.	○	○	○	○	○
44. Downsizing or layoffs have occurred in the past 12 months.	○	○	○	○	○
45. Employees can put up personal items in their work area.	○	○	○	○	○
46. Employees must react quickly and accurately to rapidly changing conditions.	○	○	○	○	○

Please check that you have filled in one response for each statement. Thank you for completing the questionnaire.

Reprinted by permission from Northwestern National Life Insurance Company, "Employess Burnout: Causes and Cures," 1992.

NOTES

Chapter 1

1. Kip Tindell, "Who Says a Trash Can Can't Make You Smile? Transcending Value at The Container Store," *Retailing Issues Letter*, January 2000, pp. 1–6; Daniel Roth, "My Job at The Container Store," *Fortune*, January 10, 2000, pp. 74–78; Robert Levering and Milton Moskowitz, "The 100 Best Companies to Work For," *Fortune*, January 20, 2003, p. 128.

2. Edward M. Hallowell, *Connect* (New York: Pantheon Books, 1999), pp. 1–14.

3. John Seely Brown and Paul Duguid, *The Social Life of Information* (Boston: Harvard Business School Press, 2000), pp. 2–13.

4. Joann S. Lublin, "Mergers Often Trigger Anxiety, Lower Morale," *Wall Street Journal*, January 16, 2001, pp. B1, B4; Daniel Roth, "How to Cut Pay, Lay Off 8,000 People, and Still Have Workers Who Love You," *Fortune*, February 4, 2002, pp. 63–68.

5. Sabrina Jones, "How We'll Work," *The News & Observer*, January 2, 2000, p. 3E; Ron Zemke, "Free Agent Nation," *Training*, January 2002, p. 18.

6. Jeffrey Pfeffer, *The Human Equation* (Boston: Harvard Business School Press, 1998), pp. 293.

7. Chris Lee, "The Death of Civility," *Training*, July 1999, pp. 24–30.

8. Stephen L. Carter, *Civility* (New York: Basic Books, 1998), p. 11.

9. Jeff Pettit, "Team Communication: It's in the Cards," *Training & Development*, January 1997, p. 12.

10. Jon Hilsenrath, "Income Gap Narrowed at End of '90s," *Wall Street Journal*, April 24, 2002, p. A2; Kelly K. Spors and Sarah Lueck, "More People Lack Health Insurance," *Wall Street Journal*, September 30, 2002, p. A2; Lauren Storck, "The Rich Make Us Sick," *Psychology Today*, September/October 1999, p. 2; "Helping America's Working Poor," *Business Week*, July 17, 2000, p. 164.

11. Kevin Dobbs, "Tires Plus—Taking the Training High Road," *Training*, April 2000, pp. 57–63; Casey Selix, "Employers Push Resilience as a Key Skill for Workers," *San Jose Mercury News*, March 4, 2001, p. 1PC.

12. Tammy Galvin, "A Culture of the Heart," *Training*, March 2001, pp. 80–81.

13. Robert Kreitner, *Management*, 8th ed. (Boston: Houghton Mifflin, 2001), p. 282.

14. Allan A. Kennedy, interview by, in "The Culture Wars," *Inc.*, 20th Anniversary Issue, 1999, pp. 107–108.

15. Anita Raghavan, Kathryn Kranhold, and Alexei Barrionuevo, "How Enron Bosses Created a Culture of Pushing Limits," *Wall Street Journal*, August 26, 2002, p. B1.

16. Suein L. Hwang, "Workers' Slogans Find New Home This Side of the Great Wall," *Wall Street Journal*, October 16, 2002, p. B1.

17. William W. Arnold and Jeanne M. Plas, *The Human Touch* (New York: Wiley, 1993), pp. 1 and 2.

18. Sue Shellenbarger, "Along with Benefits and Pay, Employees Seek Friends on the Job, "*Wall Street Journal*, February 20, 2002, p. B1.

19. "Great Expectations," *Fast Company*, November 1999, p. 224.

20. Betsy Jacobson and Beverly Kaye, "Balancing Act," *Training & Development*, February 1993, p. 26.

21. Sue Shellenbarger, "Job Candidates Prepare to Sacrifice Some Frills and Balance—For Now," *Wall Street Journal*, November 21, 2001, p. B1; Stephanie Armour, "Workers Put Family First Despite Slow Economy, Jobless Fears," *USA Today*, June 6, 2002, p. 38.

22. Haidee E. Allerton, "How To," *Training & Development*, April 1998, p. 10.

23. Rochelle Sharpe, "Labor Letter," *Wall Street Journal*, September 13, 1994, p. 1.

24. Alan Farnham, "The Man Who Changed Work Forever," *Fortune*, July 21, 1997, p. 114.

25. George F. Will, "A Faster Mousetrap," *New York Times Book Review*, June 15, 1997, p. 8; "Scientific Management," *Training*, December 1999, p. 33.

26. Bradley J. Rieger, "Lessons in Productivity and People," *Training & Development*, October 1995, pp. 56–58.

27. For a detailed examination of the Hawthorne criticisms and the legacy of the Hawthorne research, see David A. Whitsett and Lyle Yorks, *From Management Theory to Business Sense* (New York: American Management Association, 1983).

28. Jim Collins, "The Classics," *Inc.*, December 1996, p. 55.

29. Thomas J. Peters and Robert H. Waterman, Jr., *In Search of Excellence: Lessons from America's Best-Run Companies* (New York: Harper & Row, 1982), p. 14; Tom Peters, "Tom Peters' True Confessions," *Fast Company*, December 2001, p. 80.

30. *Human Connections* (Englewood Cliffs, N.J.: Prentice-Hall, 1982), p. xii.

31. Stephen R. Covey, *The Seven Habits of Highly Effective People* (New York: Simon & Schuster, 1989), pp. 66–67.

32. Richard Koonce, "Emotional IQ, A New Secret of Success," *Training & Development*, February 1996, p. 19; Cary Cherniss and Daniel Goleman, eds., *The Emotionally Intelligent Workplace* (San Francisco: Jossey-Bass, 2001), pp. 13–26.

33. Denis Waitley, *Empires of the Mind* (New York: Morrow, 1995), p. 133.

34. Michael Crom, "Building Trust in the Workplace," *The Leader*, October 1998, p. 6; Ron Zemke, "Can You Manage Trust?" *Training*, February 2000, pp. 76–83.

35. Harold H. Bloomfield and Robert K. Cooper, *The Power of 5* (Emmaus, Pa.: Rodale Press, 1995), p. 61.

36. Thomas Petzinger, Jr., "The Front Lines," *Wall Street Journal*, May 21, 1999, p. B1.

37. Thomas Petzinger, Jr., "The Front Lines," *Wall Street Journal*, May 21, 1999, p. B1; Lucy McCauley, "Relaunch!" *Fast Company*, July 2000, pp. 97–108; Liz Stevens, "In the Race, America Has the Most Rats," *The News and Observer*, November 21, 1999, p. E3; Julie Gordon, "Teaching Selling Skills to the Financial World," *Denver Business Journal*, November 3, 2000, p. 10B.

38. Stephanie Armour, "Workers Put Family First Despite Slow Economy, Jobless Fears," *USA Today*, June 6, 2002, p. 3B; "The 100 Best Companies for Working Mothers List 2002." [cited 28 October 2002]. Available from workingmother.com; INTERNET.

Chapter 2

1. Lin Grensing-Pophal, "Follow Me," *HR Magazine*, February 2000, p. 41.

2. Ginger L. Graham, "If You Want Honesty, Break Some Rules," *Harvard Business Review*, April 2002, pp. 4–6.

3. Grensing-Pophal, "Follow Me," p. 41.

4. Don Clark, "Managing the Mountain," *Wall Street Journal*, June 21, 1999, p. R4.

5. John Stewart and Gary D'Angelo, *Together—Communicating Interpersonally* (New York: Random House, 1988), p. 5.

6. David Shenk, *Data Smog—Surviving the Information Glut* (San Francisco: Harper Edge, 1997), p. 54.

7. Sy Lazarus, *Loud and Clear* (New York: AMACOM, 1974), p. 3.

8. Ronald G. Shafer, "Government Bureaucrats to Learn a New Language: Simple English," *Wall Street Journal*, June 2, 1998, p. B1.

9. Suein L. Hwang, "It Was a Wombat for the Meatware, But It Was a Good Sell," *Wall Street Journal*, May 15, 2002, p. B1.

10. "Memos from Hell," *Fortune*, February 3, 1997, p. 120.

11. Matthew McKay, Martha Davis, and Patrick Fanning, *Messages: The Communication Skills Book* (Oakland, Calif.: New Harbinger, 1995), p. 108.

12. Ibid.

13. Sharon Begley, "In Love and Jealousy, Men Are from Earth, and So Are Women," *Wall Street Journal*, October 4, 2002, p. B1; Roy M. Berko, Andrew D. Wolvin, and Darlyn R. Wolvin, *Communicating*, 8th ed. (Boston: Houghton Mifflin, 2001), pp. 122–126.

14. Berko, Wolvin, and Wolvin, *Communicating*, pp. 124–125.

15. Peter F. Drucker, quoted by Bill Moyers in *A World of Ideas* (Garden City, N.Y.: Doubleday, 1990).

16. Phyllis Mindell, "The Body Language of Power," *Executive Female*, May/June 1996, p. 48.

17. Roger E. Axtell, ed., *Do's and Taboos Around the World*, compiled by Parker Pen Company, 3d ed. (New York: Wiley, 1993), p. 46.

18. Ibid, p. 47.

19. Ibid, p. 49.

20. William B. Gudykunst, Stella Ting-Toomey, Sandra Sudweeks, and Lea Stewart, *Building Bridges: Interpersonal Skills for a Changing World* (Boston: Houghton Mifflin, 1995), pp. 315–316.

21. C. Glenn Pearce, "How Effective Are We as Listeners?" *Training & Development*, April 1993, pp. 79–80.

22. Cheryl Shavers, "Stopping Your Chatty Boss Calls for Sensitivity, Insight," *San Jose Mercury News*, October 26, 1997, p. 3E.

23. John Chaffee, *Thinking Critically*, 5th ed. (Boston: Houghton Mifflin, 1996), pp. 40, 72.

24. Michael Toms, "Dialogue—the Art of Thinking Together—Sparks Spirit of 'Aliveness' in Organizations," *The Inner Edge*, August/September 1998, p. 462.

25. Stephen R. Covey, *The Seven Habits of Highly Effective People* (New York: Simon & Schuster, 1989), pp. 240–241.

26. C. Glenn Pearce, "Learning How to Listen Empathically," *Supervisory Management*, September 1991, p. 11.

27. Robert Epstein, "Waiting," *Psychology Today*, September/October 2001, p. 5.

28. Robert Kreitner, *Management*, 8th ed. (Boston: Houghton Mifflin, 2001), pp. 446–447.

29. Michael Warshaw, "They Hear It Through the Grapevine," *Fast Company*, April 1998, p. 160.

30. Ibid.

31. Robert Kreitner, *Management*, pp. 373–375.

32. Karen Carney, "How to Keep Staff in a Boom Economy," *Inc.*, November 1998, p. 110.

33. Toms, "Dialogue—the Art of Thinking Together," p. 11.

34. Suzy Wetlaufer, "The Business Case Against Revolution," *Harvard Business Review*, February 2001, p. 119.

35. Winston Wood, "Work Week," *Wall Street Journal*, February 6, 2001, p. A1.

36. "Etiquette with Office Gadgets," *Training*, January 1999, p. 24.

37. Michael Barlett, "Good E-Mail Communication Requires Hard Work—Study." [cited 31 July 2001]. Available from www.bcentral.com/resource/articles/isyndicate/tech/3b6774a3.7531.1.asp; INTERNET.

38. Ibid.

39. Matthew Boyle, "What We Learned," *Fortune*, December 24, 2001, p. 179.

40. "Etiquette with Office Gadgets," p. 24.

41. Matthew Holohan, "How to Use E-mail Responsibly at Work." [cited 21 June 2000]. Available from ehow.com/Center/catIndex/o,1004,1016,00.html; INTERNET.

42. Sabrina Jones, "Employees Using E-Mail to Gossip, Kill Time or Swap Jokes Seem Blithely Unaware That They Have No Right to Privacy," *Wall Street Journal*, July 24, 1999, p. D1; Michael J. McCarthy, "Virtual Morality: A New Workplace Quandary," *Wall Street Journal*, October 21, 2000, p. B1; Michael R. McCarthy, "Your Manager's Policy on Employees' E-Mail May Have a Weak Spot," *Wall Street Journal*, April 25, 2000, p. B1; Julia Angwin, "A Plan to Track Web Use Stirs Privacy Concern," *Wall Street Journal*, May 1, 2000, p. B1; Douglas Dahlbert, "Web Surfers Beware: The Company Tech May Be a Secret Agent," *Wall Street Journal*, January 10, 2000, p. A1; Stephen D. Lewis and Linda

G. McGrew, "Teaching the Perils of E-Mail," *Business Education Forum*, February 2000, pp. 26–27; Michelle Conlin, "Workers, Surf at Your Own Risk," *Business Week*, June 12, 2000, p. 105; Michael Schrage, "E-Mail or E-Sting? Your Boss Knows, but He's Not Telling," *Fortune*, March 20, 2000, p. 240; Dale Buss, "Spies like Us," *Training*, December 2001, pp. 45–48; "Big Bro Is Eyeing Your E-mail," *Business Week*, June 4, 2001, p. 30; Nick Wingfield, "The Rise and Fall of Web Shopping at Work," *Wall Street Journal*, September 27, 2002, p. B1; "Workers, Surf at Your Own Risk," *Business Week*, June 11, 2001, p. 14.

43. Kara Swisher, "Bill Gates Got an Education; So Should We," *Wall Street Journal*, June 8, 2000, p. B1.

44. Ann David, Joseph Pereira, and William M. Bulkeley, "Security Concerns Bring New Focus on Body Language," *Wall Street Journal*, August 15, 2002, p. A1, A6; Robert Kreitner, *Management*, pp. 369–372; "The Power of Body Language," Course Archive. [cited 6 January 2003]. Available from www.presentersuniveristy.com/courses/show_archive.cfm?RecordID =39; INTERNET.

Chapter 3

1. Mike McNamee and Christopher Schmitt, "The Chainsaw Al Massacre," *Business Week*, May 28, 2001, p. 48; Dennis K. Berman and Joann S. Lublin, "Restructuring, Personality Clashes Led to Lucent Executive's Exit," *Wall Street Journal*, May 17, 2001, p. B1.

2. Charles Fishmann, "Jeff Bezos," *Fast Company*, February 2001, pp. 80–82; Betsy Morris, "Replacing a Legend," *Fortune*, November 18, 2002, p. 57.

3. Douglas A. Bernstein, Louis A. Penner, Alison Clarke-Stewart, and Edward J. Roy, *Personality*, 6th ed. (Boston: Houghton Mifflin, 2003), p. 518.

4. Robert Bolton and Dorothy Grover Bolton, *People Styles at Work* (New York: AMACOM, 1996), p. 10.

5. Tony Alessandra, *Behavioral Profiles: Participant Workbook* (San Diego: Pfeiffer & Company, 1994), p. 12.

6. Bolton and Bolton, *People Styles at Work*, pp. ix–x.

7. Karen Waner and Lonnie Echternacht, "Using the Myers-Briggs Type Indicator to Compare Personality Types of Business Teachers Who Teach Office Occupations with Personality Types of Office Professionals," *The Delta Pi Epsilon Journal*, Spring 1993, pp. 56, 58.

8. Bolton and Bolton, *People Styles at Work*, p. x.

9. Robert J. Sternberg, *Thinking Styles* (New York: Cambridge University Press, 1997), p. 8.

10. Bolton and Bolton, *People Styles at Work*, p. x.

11. Susan Foster, "What's Your Client's Style?" *Selling*, December 1998.

12. David W. Johnson, *Reaching Out—Interpersonal Effectiveness and Self-Actualization* (Englewood Cliffs, N.J.: Prentice-Hall, 1981), pp. 43–44. The dominance factor was described in an early book by William M. Marston, *The Emotions of Normal People* (New York: Harcourt, 1928). Research conducted by Rolfe La Forge and Robert F. Suczek resulted in the development of the Interpersonal Check List (ICL), which features a domi-

nant-submissive scale. A person who receives a high score on the ICL tends to lead, persuade, and control others. The Interpersonal Identity Profile, developed by David W. Merrill and James W. Taylor, features a factor called "assertiveness." Persons classified as high in assertiveness tend to have strong opinions, make quick decisions, and be directive when dealing with people. Persons classified as low in assertiveness tend to voice moderate opinions, make thoughtful decisions, and be supportive when dealing with others.

13. Christopher Caggiano, "Psychopath," *Inc.*, July 1998, pp. 77–85.

14. American Management Association, *Catalog of Seminars* (New York: American Management Association, 2002), p. 33.

15. The research conducted by La Forge and Suczek resulted in identification of the hostile/loving continuum, which is similar to the sociability continuum. Their Interpersonal Check List features this scale. L. L. Thurstone and T. G. Thurstone developed the Thurstone Temperament Schedule, which provides an assessment of a "sociable" factor. Persons with high scores in this area enjoy the company of others and make friends easily. The Interpersonal Identity Profile developed by Merrill and Taylor contains an objectivity continuum. A person with low objectivity is seen as attention seeking, involved with the feelings of others, informal, and casual in social relationships. A person who is high in objectivity tends to be indifferent toward the feelings of others. This person is formal in social relationships.

16. "On the Human Side," *Time*, February 19, 1979, p. 75.

17. Bolton and Bolton, *People Styles at Work*, p. 87.

18. Ibid.

19. "Ask Dr. E," *Psychology Today*, January/February 2000, p. 28.

20. David W. Merrill and Roger H. Reid, *Personality Styles and Effective Performance*, Radnor, PA: Chilton Book, 1981, p. 88.

21. Wilson Learning Corporation, *Growth Through Versatility* (Eden Prairie, Minn.: Wilson Learning Corporation), p. 4.

22. Bob Reeves, "It Takes All Types," *Lincoln Star*, May 24, 1994, p. 11.

23. "People Skills Still a Sales Basic," *Training & Development*, December 1994, pp. 7–8.

24. Tony Alessandra and Michael J. O'Connor, *People Smart* (La Jolla, Calif.: Keynote Publishing, 1990), p. 10.

25. Gary A. Williams and Robert B. Miller, "Changing the Way You Persuade," *Harvard Business Review*, May 2002, pp. 65–67.

26. Stuart Atkins, *The Name of Your Game* (Beverly Hills, Calif.: Ellis & Stewart, 1981), pp. 49–50.

27. Ibid., p. 51.

28. Chris Lee, "What's Your Style?" *Training*, May 1991, p. 28.

29. Michael Kaplan, "How to Overcome Your Strengths," *Fast Company*, May 1999, p. 225.

30. Robert Kreitner, *Management*, 8th ed. (Boston: Houghton Mifflin, 2001), p. 293; "The Best Managers," *Business Week*, January 13, 2003, p. 72.

31. "The New Corporate World Is Flat," *LIFO Training News*, vol. 7, no. 1 (Beverly Hills, Calif.: Stuart Atkins, Inc.).

Chapter 4

1. Gerhard Gschwandtner, "Rendezvous with a Rainmaker," *Selling Power*, May 2001, pp. 98–102.

2. Dan Rather, "They Live the Dream," *Parade Magazine*, May 6, 2001, pp. 6–8.

3. Brian Tracy, *The 100 Absolutely Unbreakable Laws of Business Success* (San Francisco: Berrett-Koehler Publishers, 2000), pp. 23–24.

4. Nathaniel Branden, *The Six Pillars of Self-Esteem* (New York: Bantam, 1994), p. 7.

5. Nathaniel Branden, *Self-Esteem at Work* (San Francisco: Jossey-Bass, 1998), p. xii.

6. Kate Berry, "Starbucks Opens First Stores in Miami, Hoping to Woo Lovers of Cuban Coffee," *Wall Street Journal*, March 31, 1997, p. A9; Jennifer Reese, "Starbucks—Inside the Coffee Cult," *Fortune*, December 9, 1996, pp. 190–198.

7. David E. Shapiro, "Pumping Up Your Attitude," *Psychology Today*, May/June 1997, p. 14.

8. Douglas A. Bernstein, Louis A. Penner, Alison Clarke-Stewart, and Edward J. Roy, *Psychology*, 6th ed. (Boston: Houghton Mifflin, 2003), pp. 534–535; Richard Laliberte, "Self-Esteem Workshop," *Self*, May 1994, p. 201.

9. Branden, *The Six Pillars of Self-Esteem*, p. 39.

10. Robert Reasoner, "The True Meaning of Self-Esteem," National Association for Self-Esteem, Normal, Il. [cited April 30, 2003]. Available from INTERNET.

11. Phillip C. McGraw, *Self Matters* (New York: Simon & Schuster, 2001), pp. 69–70.

12. Sharon Begley, "Follow Your Intuition: The Unconscious You May Be the Wiser Half," *Wall Street Journal*, August 30, 2002, p. B1; Sharon Begley, "How Do I Love Thee? Let Me Count the Ways—and Other Bad Ideas," *Wall Street Journal*, September 6, 2002, p. B1.

13. Margaret Henning and Ann Jardim, *The Managerial Woman* (New York: Anchor Books, 1977), pp. 106–107.

14. Ellen Graham, "Leah: Life Is All Sweetness and Insecurity," *Wall Street Journal*, February 9, 1995, p. B16.

15. Emmett Miller, *The Healing Power of Happiness* (Emmaus, Pa.: Rodale Press, 1989), pp. 12–13.

16. Lacey Beckmann, "One More Thing Money Can't Buy," *Psychology Today*, November/December, 2002, p. 16.

17. Amy Saltzman, *Downshifting* (New York: Harper-Collins, 1990), pp. 15–16.

18. Miller, *The Healing Power of Happiness*, pp. 12–13.

19. McGraw, *Self Matters*, p. 73.

20. Reasoner, "The True Meaning."

21. Arthur H. Goldsmith, Jonathan R. Veum, and William Darity, Jr., "The Impact of Psychological and Human Capital on Wages," *Economic Inquiry*, October 1997, p. 817.

22. Hyrum W. Smith, *The 10 Natural Laws of Successful Time and Life Management* (New York: Warner Books, 1994), p. 178.

23. Roy F. Baumeister, Jennifer D. Campbell, Joachim I. Krueger, and Kathleen D. Vohe, "Does High Self-Esteem Cause Better Performance, Interpersonal Success, Happiness, or Healthier Lifestyles?" *Psychological Science in the Public Interest*, May 2003, p. 1.

24. Don Miguel Ruiz, *The Four Agreements* (San Rafael, Calif.: Amber-Allen Publishing, 1997), pp. 47–61.

25. Branden, *The Six Pillars of Self-Esteem*, p. 33.

26. Matthew McKay and Patrick Fanning, *Self-Esteem*, 2d ed. (Oakland, Calif.: New Harbinger, 1992), p. 42.

27. McGraw, *Self Matters*, pp. 209–212.

28. Annie Gottlieb, "The Radical Road to Self-Esteem," *O The Oprah Magazine*, March 2001, pp. 101–102.

29. Arnold A. Lazarus and Clifford N. Lazarus, *The 60-Second Shrink* (San Luis Obispo, Calif.: Impact Publishers, 1997), p. 40.

30. Chip R. Bell, "Making Mentoring a Way of Life," *Training*, October 1996, p. 138; Lin Standke, review of *Managers as Mentors: Building Partnerships for Learning*, by Chip R. Bell, *Training*, April 1997, pp. 64–65.

31. Matt Murray, "GE Mentoring Program Turns Underlings into Teachers of the Web," *Wall Street Journal*, February 15, 2000, p. B1.

32. Fara Warner, "Inside Intel's Mentoring Movement," *Fast Company*, April 2002, pp. 116–120.

33. Hal Lancaster, "It's Harder, but You Still Can Rise Up from the Mail Room," *Wall Street Journal*, June 18, 1996, p. B1.

34. Ibid.

35. Gottlieb, "The Radical Road to Self-Esteem," p. 101.

36. Stan Goldberg, "The 10 Rules of Change," *Psychology Today*, September/October 2002, pp. 38–44.

37. Annie Murphy Paul, "Self-Help: Shattering the Myths," *Psychology Today*, March/April 2001, p. 64; Lazarus and Lazarus, *The 60-Second Shrink*, pp. 3, 4.

38. James Bauman, "The Gold Medal," *Psychology Today*, May/June 2000, pp. 62–68.

39. See McGraw, *Self Matters*, for comprehensive coverage of how internal dialogue influences our self-concept.

40. McKay and Fanning, *Self-Esteem*, pp. 18, 19.

41. Ibid., pp. 33–34.

42. Herb Kindler, "Working to Change Old Habits," *Working Smart*, May 1992, p. 8.

43. McGraw, *Self Matters*, pp. 204–205.

44. Roy J. Blitzer, Colleen Petersen, and Linda Rogers, "How to Build Self-Esteem," *Training & Development*, February 1993, pp. 58–60.

45. Dave Longaberger, *Longaberger: An American Success Story* (New York: Harper Business, 2001), p. 8.

46. "David Longaberger Sets the Standard for Success," *Selling*, May 2000, p. 8; Steve Williford and Dave Longaberger, *The Longaberger Story: And How We Did It* (Lincoln-Bradley Publishing, 1991); *Dave Longaberger: An American Success Story* (New York: Harper Business, 2001); P. Kelly Smith, "Entrepreneurial Expert Tami Longaberger: What She Learned from Her Father About Business and Life," April 16, 2001. [cited

8 January 2003]. Available from www.entrepreneur.com/Your_Business/YB_SegArticle/0,4621,288626,00.html; INTERNET.

47. Frank Jossi, "Mentoring in Changing Times," *Training*, August 1997, p. 52.

48. Jennifer Reingold, "Want to Grow as a Leader? Get a Mentor!" *Fast Company*, January 2001, p. 58.

49. Fara Warner, "Inside Intel's Mentoring Movement," *Fast Company*, April 2000, p. 119.

50. Cheryl Hall, "Mentoring as Critical as Ever, but Companies Are Ignoring It," *San Jose Mercury News*, February 11, 2001, p. 1PC.

51. Amy Joyce, "May the Workforce Be with You," *Washington Post*, April 21, 2002, p. H4; Jeff Barbian, "The Road Best Traveled," *Training*, May 2002, pp. 38–42; Reingold, "Want to Grow as a Leader?" pp. 58–60; Warner, "Inside Intel's Mentoring Movement," pp. 116–120; Hall, "Mentoring as Critical as Ever," p. 1PC.

Chapter 5

1. Sarah Saliven, "Honor Committee Progresses Quickly with Bloomfield Cases," *The Cavalier Daily Online.* [cited 21 November 2002]. Available from cavalierdaily.com; INTERNET

2. Carolyn Kleiner and Mary Lord, "The Cheating Game," *U.S. News & World Report*, November 22, 1999, p. 56.

3. Jeff Barbian, "A Cheater's Paradise," *Training*, November 2002, p. 92.

4. *2002 Report Card: The Ethics of American Youth*, press release and data summary. [cited 8 January 2003]. Available from www.josephsoninstitute.org/Survey 2002/survey2002-pressrelease.htm; INTERNET.

5. David Gergen, "Candidates with Character," *U.S. News & World Report*, September 27, 1999, p. 68.

6. Patrick Smith, "You Have a Job, but How About a Life?" *Business Week*, November 16, 1998, p. 30.

7. Nathaniel Branden, *Self-Esteem at Work* (San Francisco: Jossey-Bass, 1998), p. 35.

8. Stephen R. Covey, *The Seven Habits of Highly Effective People* (New York: Simon & Schuster, 1989), p. 92.

9. CHARACTER COUNTS! National Office. [cited 12 January 2003]. Available from www.charactercounts.org; INTERNET.

10. "Where to Learn More About Character Education," *Techniques*, May 1999, p. 29.

11. Hyrum W. Smith, *The 10 Natural Laws of Successful Time and Life Management* (New York: Warner Books, 1994), pp. 14–15.

12. J. David McCracken and Ana E. Falcon-Emmanuelli, "A Theoretical Basis for Work Values Research in Vocational Education" *Journal of Vocational and Technical Education*, April 1994, p. 4.

13. Sue Shellenbarger, "Some Top Executives Are Finding a Balance Between Job and Home," *Wall Street Journal*, April 23, 1997, p. B1.

14. Katharine Mieszkowski, "FitzGerald Family Values," *Fast Company*, April 1998, p. 194.

15. Rebecca Ganzel, "Book Reviews," *Training*, June 2000, pp. 76–77.

16. Robin Toner, "Those Were the Days," *New York Times Book Review*, October 28, 2001, p. 7.

17. Ron Zemke, "Here Come the Millennials," *Training*, July 2001, pp. 44–49.

18. Katherine Paterson, "Family Values," *New York Times Book Review*, October 15, 1995, p. 32.

19. Toms, "Investing in Character," *The Inner Edge*, June/July 2000, pp. 5–8.

20. Chris Lee and Ron Zemke, "The Search for Spirit in the Workplace," *Training*, June 1993, p. 21.

21. Stanley M. Elam, Lowell C. Rose, and Alec M. Gallup, "The 26th Annual Phi Delta Kappa/Gallup Poll of the Public's Attitudes Toward the Public Schools," *Phi Delta Kappan*, September 1994, p. 49.

22. Sonia L. Nazario, "School Teachers Say It's Wrongheaded to Try to Teach Students What's Right," *Wall Street Journal*, April 6, 1990, p. B1; Steve Rosen, "Battle Against Corporate Swindlers Hits the Classroom," *Springfield Newsleader*, January 21, 2003. p. C1.

23. Sanford N. McDonnell, "A Virtuous Agenda for Education Reform," *Wall Street Journal*, February 18, 1997, p. A22.

24. Linda Formichelli, "Programming Behavior," *Psychology Today*, January/February 2001, p. 10.

25. Morris Massey, *The People Puzzle* (Reston, Va.: Reston Publishing, 1979).

26. O. C. Ferrell, John Fraedrich, and Linda Ferrell, *Business Ethics*, 5th ed. (Boston: Houghton Mifflin, 2002), pp. 123–135.

27. Neal Donald Walsch, *Conversations with God, Book 1 Guidebook* (Charlottesville, Va.: Hampton Roads, 1997), p. 71.

28. Sue Shellenbarger, "In Cataclysmic Times, Workers Need Room to Rethink Priorities," *Wall Street Journal*, September 19, 2001, p. B1.

29. Toddi Gutner, "A Balancing Act for GenX Women," *Business Week*, January 21, 2002, p. 82.

30. John Beebe, "Conscience, Integrity and Character," *The Inner Edge*, June/July 2000, pp. 9–11.

31. "Making Sense of Ethics." [cited 13 January 2003]. Available from www.josephsoninstitute.org/ MED/MED-1makingsense.htm; INTERNET.

32. "Workers Cut Ethical Corners, Survey Finds," *Wall Street Journal*, March 10, 1995, p. A2.

33. Price Pritchett, *The Ethics of Excellence* (Dallas, Tx.: Pritchett & Associates, n.d.), p. 28.

34. "CyberSource® Joins with Association of Certified Fraud Examiners to Support 2002 National Fraud Awareness Week," July 29, 2002. [cited 13 January 2003]. Available from www.cybersource.com/news_and_events/view.xml?page_id=949; INTERNET.

35. "Making Sense of Ethics."

36. Jerry Useem, "Welcome to the New Company Town," *Fortune*, January 10, 2000, pp. 62–70.

37. Jeffrey Ball, "Religious Investors Press GM, Ford to Cut Emissions," *Wall Street Journal*, December 12, 2002, p. D3.

38. Betsy Weisendanger, "Doing the Right Thing," *Sales & Marketing Management*, March 1991, p. 82.

39. Jerry Useem, "New Ethics . . . or No Ethics," *Fortune*, March 2000, pp. 81–86.

40. Susan Scherreik, "A Conscience Doesn't Have to Make You Poor," *Business Week*, May 1, 2000, pp. 204–206.

41. "A Different Kind of Andreas at ADM," *Business Week*, July 9, 2001, p. 62.

42. James Bandler and Mark Maremont, "Xerox to Pay $10 million in SEC Case," *Wall Street Journal*, April 2, 2002, p. A3.

43. Gregory L. White and Amy Merrick, "Exide Unit Pleads Guilty to Charges over Battery Flaws," *Wall Street Journal*, March 26, 2001, p. B9.

44. Mary Ellen Egan, "Old Enough to Know Better," *Business Ethics*, January/February 1995, p. 19.

45. Bob Filipczak, "The Soul of the Hog," *Training*, February 1996, pp. 38–42.

46. Kathryn Cates Moore, "Taking the High Road," *Journal Star*, April 28, 2001, p. 1B.

47. Andrew Stark, "What's the Matter with Business Ethics?" *Harvard Business Review*, May/June 1993, p. 38.

48. "Tom Chappell—Minister of Commerce," *Business Ethics*, January/February 1994, p. 17.

49. Ferrell, Fraedrich, and Ferrell, *Business Ethics*, pp. 182–183.

50. Patrick M. Lencioni, "Make Your Values Mean Something," *Harvard Business Review*, July 2002, pp. 5–9.

51. Joshua Hyatt, "How to Hire Employees," *Inc.*, March 1990, p. 2.

52. Richard Lacayo and Amanda Ripley, "Persons of the Year," *Time*, December 31, 2002, pp. 32–33.

53. Paula Swyer and Dan Carney, with Amy Brrus and Lorraine Woellert in Washington and Christopher Palmeri in Los Angeles, "Year of the Whistleblower," *Business Week*, December 16, 2002, pp. 107–108; Michael Orey, "WorldCom-Inspired 'Whistle-Blower' Law Has Weaknesses," *Wall Street Journal*, October 1, 2002, p. B1.

54. Swyer and Carney, "Year of the Whistleblower," p. 107.

55. Ibid., p. 108.

56. Jan Yager, *Business Protocol—How to Survive and Succeed in Business*, 2d ed. (Stanford Conn.: Hannacroix Creek Books, 2001), pp. 109–119.

57. Chris Hill and Toby Hanlon, "26 Simple Ways to Change How You Feel," *Prevention*, August 1993, p. 126.

58. Anne Fisher, "I Got Caught Smoking Pot. Who's Going to Hire Me Now?" *Fortune*, September 16, 2002, p. 224.

59. M. Corey Goldman, "The Liars Index," *ABC NEWS.com*, July 25, 2001. [cited 20 January 2003]. Available from http://abcnews.go.com/sections/business/DailyNews/resumelying_index_010725.html; INTERNET.

60. "Little Infractions Can Lead to Big Ones," *News & Observer*, December 1, 2002, p. 14E; Fisher, "I Got Caught Smoking Pot," p. 224; Goodell, "Liar, Liar," *O The Oprah Magazine*, January 2002, pp. 146–147 and 166–167; Kenneth Bredemeier, "Boss's Resume Inflated," *ANG Newspapers*, July 21, 2002, p. 1C; Jeff Meredeith, "Checking Educational Credentials Gets Easier," *News & Observer*, October 7, 2001, p. 5E; "O'Leary Leaves Irish After Lies Are Exposed," *Des Moines Register*, December 15, 2001, p. C1; Goldman, "Liars Index."

61. "SLC Olympics Rings Up $101 Million Profit," *Seattle Times*, September 23, 2002. [cited 22 January 2003]. Available from www.Seattletimes.nwsource.com; INTERNET.

62. Stefan Fatsis, "Olympic Scandal Is Result of Culture of Corruption, US Panel Concludes," *Wall Street Journal*, March 2, 1999, p. A4.

63. Jo Thomas and Kirk Johnson, "Money Big Part of Bid," *New York Times*, January 30, 1999, p. C1; Peter Waldman, "A Scandal Revisited," *Wall Street Journal*, February 24, 2002, p. A6; Gerry Brown, "Olympics: Five Ring Circus." [cited 22 January 2003]. Available from www.factmonster.com/spot/olympicscandal1.html; INTERNET; "Italians Get Olympics in Upset." [cited 22 January 2003]. Available from www.cbsnews.com/stories/1999/06/19/world/printable33860.shtml; INTERNET; SportsLine.com wire reports, "Italian City Prepares for Next Winter Olympics," February 24, 2002. [cited 22 January 2003]. Available from www.cbs.sportsline.com/olympics/story/5055393; INTERNET.

Chapter 6

1. Rob Walker, "Hook, Line, & Sinker," *Inc.*, August 2002, p. 86.

2. Ibid., p. 88.

3. Ibid., p. 87.

4. Douglas A. Bernstein, Louis A. Penner, Alison Clarke-Stewart, and Edward J. Roy, *Psychology*, 6th ed. (Boston: Houghton Mifflin, 2003), p. 660.

5. Harry E. Chambers, *The Bad Attitude Survival Guide* (Reading, Mass.: Addison-Wesley, 1998), pp. 17–37.

6. Bill Breen, "Full House," *Fast Company*, January 2001, pp. 111–121.

7. Jerome Kagan, *Psychology: An Introduction* (New York: Harcourt Brace Jovanovich, 1984), p. 548.

8. William F. Schoell and Joseph P. Guiltinan, *Marketing*, 5th ed. (Boston: Allyn & Bacon, 1992), pp. 166–167; William M. Pride and O. C. Ferrell, *Marketing* (Boston: Houghton Mifflin, 2000), p. 211.

9. Joan Hamilton, "Net Work: At Icarian, It's All Work and Some Play," *Business Week E.BIZ*, April 3, 2000, p. EB116.

10. Nicholas Varchaver, "Who's the King of Delaware?" *Fortune*, May 13, 2002, pp. 124–128.

11. Thomas E. Ricks, "New Marines Illustrate Growing Gap Between Military and Society," *Wall Street Journal*, July 27, 1995, p. A1.

12. "Up Front," *Business Week*, December 30, 2002, p. 16.

13. Nathaniel Branden, *Self-Esteem at Work* (San Francisco: Jossey-Bass, 1998), pp. 94–97; "Adjusting an Attitude," *San Jose Mercury News*, August 20, 1997, p. G6.

14. His Holiness the Dalai Lama and Howard C. Cutler, *The Art of Happiness* (New York: Riverhead Books, 1998), pp. 16–17.
15. Michael Crom, "Live Enthusiastically and You'll Live Successfully," *Training*, April 1999, p. 6.
16. Dalai Lama and Cutler, *The Art of Happiness*, p. 22.
17. Ibid., p. 23.
18. Patricia Sellers, "Now Bounce Back!" *Fortune*, May 1, 1995, p. 57.
19. Martin Seligman, *Learned Optimism* (New York: Knopf, 2001), p. 4.
20. Redford Williams and Virginia Williams, *Anger Kills* (New York: Harper Perennial, 1993), p. 12.
21. Bob Wall, *Working Relationships* (Palo Alto, Calif.: Davies-Black, 1999), pp. 11–12.
22. Ibid., p. 17.
23. Brian Tracy, *The 100 Absolutely Unbreakable Laws of Business Success* (San Francisco: Berrett-Koehler Publishers, Inc., 2000), pp. 67–70.
24. Branden, *Self-Esteem at Work*, pp. 111–112.
25. Harry E. Chambers, *The Bad Attitude Survival Guide* (Reading, Mass.: Addison-Wesley, 1998), pp. 6–7.
26. Hamilton, "Net Work," p. EB117.
27. Quoted in Nancy W. Collins, Susan K. Gilbert, and Susan Nycum, *Women Leading: Making Tough Choices on the Fast Track* (Lexington, Mass.: Stephen Greene Press, 1988), p. 1.
28. "100 Best Companies to Work For," *Fortune*, January 20, 2003, pp. 128–152.
29. Timothy Aeppel, "Not All Workers Find Idea of Empowerment as Neat as It Sounds," *Wall Street Journal*, September 8, 1997, p. A1; Barbara Moses, *Career Intelligence* (San Francisco: Berrett-Koehler, 1998). Available from www.go.com/workingwounded /SoLongStability—[cited 14 July 2000]; INTERNET.
30. Walker, "Hook, Line, & Sinker," p. 88.
31. Dave Murphy, "Going to School with 'FISH,' Happy Employees Can Save Companies More than a Few Fins," *San Francisco Chronicle*, April 21, 2002, pp. J1–2; Stephen C. Lundin, Harry Paul, and John Christensen, *Fish!* (Hyperion, 2000); Stephen C. Lundin, John Christensen, Harry Paul, with Philip Strand, *Fish! Tales* (Hyperion, 2001); Walker, "Hook, Line, & Sinker," pp. 85–88.

Chapter 7

1. Claudia Rosett, "TV: Some Like it Cold," *Wall Street Journal*, March 25, 2002, p. A16.
2. Kate Laird, "Icebergs, Blazing Heat and One Tough Woman," *Wall Street Journal*, February 21, 2001, p. A24.
3. Anne Bruce and James S. Pepitone, *Motivating Employees* (New York: McGraw-Hill, 1999), pp. 11–12.
4. Douglas A. Bernstein, Louis A. Penner, Alison Clarke-Stewart, and Edward J. Roy, *Psychology*, 6th ed. (Boston: Houghton Mifflin, 2003), pp. 381–382.
5. M. G. Lord, "Raison McÊtre," *New York Times Book Review*, August 18, 2002, p. 13.
6. Jim Carlton, "Wild Horses, Couldn't Drag Them Away from Stones Shows," *Wall Street Journal*, November 22, 2002, p. A1.
7. Robert Kreitner, *Management*, 7th ed. (Boston: Houghton Mifflin, 1998), pp. 156–157.
8. Data were collected by use of the Reiss Profile, a standardized psychological test used to measure sixteen desires.
9. Steven Reiss, "Secrets of Happiness," *Psychology Today*, January/February 2001, pp. 50–56. To learn more about the Reiss Profile, see *Who Am I: The 16 Basic Desires That Motivate Our Happiness and Define Our Personalities* (New York: Berkley Books, 2000).
10. Cynthia Berryman-Fink, *The Managers' Desk Reference* (New York: AMACOM, 1989), pp. 156–157.
11. Robert Kreitner, *Management*, 8th ed. (Boston: Houghton Mifflin, 2001), pp. 395–396.
12. "Belonging Satisfies Basic Human Need," *The Menninger Letter*, August 1995, p. 6.
13. "Maslow's Term and Themes," *Training*, March 1977, p. 48.
14. Kreitner, *Management*, 8th ed., p. 399.
15. Caela Farren, "Sailing the Good Ship Career," *Training & Development*, February 1998, pp. 43–44.
16. Kreitner, *Management*, 8th ed., p. 399.
17. The book *Eupsychian Management* by Abraham H. Maslow has been republished as *Maslow on Management* (New York: Wiley).
18. Frederick Herzberg, Bernard Mausner, and Barbara Black Snyderman, *The Motivation to Work* (New York: Wiley, 1959).
19. C. R. Snyder, "Hope Helps," *Psychology Today*, November/December 1999, p. 20.
20. Richard Barrett, "The Power of Purpose," *The Inner Edge*, August/September 1999, p. 20.
21. Kreitner, *Management*, 8th ed., p. 403.
22. Ibid., p. 403; Ron Zemke, "Toxic Energy Dumps," *Training*, January 2001, p. 18.
23. Berryman-Fink, *The Manager's Desk Reference*, pp. 156–157.
24. Clare Ansberry, "In the New Workplace, Jobs Morph to Suit Rapid Pace of Change," *Wall Street Journal*, March 22, 2002, p. A1.
25. David Stamps, "Relaxed Fit," *Training*, October 1996, p. 96.
26. Brigitte Blobel, "If You Have Class, Then You Are Just as Good as Your Guests," *Audi Magazine*, December 2001, pp. 72–75.
27. Ron Zemke, "Here Come the Millennials," *Training*, July 2001, p. 47.
28. Michelle Conlin, "Now It's Getting Personal," *Business Week*, December 16, 2002, pp. 90–92.
29. Rosabeth Moss Kanter, "The New Managerial Work," *Harvard Business Review*, November/December 1989, p. 91.
30. Leslie Overmyer-Day and George Benson, "Training Success Stories," *Training & Development*, June 1996, p. 27.

31. "Great Expectations," *Fast Company*, November 1999, pp. 212–224.
32. "Creativity, Productivity Rise When Workers Have More Say," *San Jose Mercury News*, March 12, 1997, p. 6G.
33. Richard Pascale, "Their Grassroots Leadership Agenda," *Fast Company*, April 1998, pp. 110, 115.
34. Jill Rosenfeld, "MTW Puts People First," *Fast Company*, December 1999, pp. 86–88.
35. "Living Down to Expectations," *Training*, July 1998, p. 15.
36. Sherri Eng, "Are You Scared of Success?" *San Jose Mercury News*, January 17, 1996, pp. 6G, 7G; Douglas A. Bernstein, Edward J. Roy, Thomas K. Srull, and Christopher D. Wickens, *Psychology*, 4th ed. (Boston: Houghton Mifflin, 1997), pp. 357–359.
37. G. Pascal Zachary, "The New Search for Meaning in 'Meaningless' Work," *Wall Street Journal*, January 9, 1997, p. B1.
38. Robin A. Sheerer, *No More Blue Mondays* (Palo Alto, Calif.: Davies-Black Publishing, 1999).
39. Ron Zemke, "Unconventional Wisdom," *Training*, January 2001, p. 18.
40. Ibid.; Leigh Buchanan, "Managing One-to-One," *Inc.*, October 2001, p. 88; Liz Thach and Chuck McPherson, "Motivating Employees During Down Times," *Training*, April 2002, pp. 44–48; Jeff Barbian, "C'mon, Get Happy," *Training*, January 2001, pp. 92–95.
41. Jack Stack's *The Great Game of Business* (New York: Currency Books, 1992) has become the industry's leading resource for open-book management.
42. Ibid., p. 124.
43. Ilan Mochari, "The Talking Cure," *The Whole New Business Catalog*, November 2001, pp. 121–123; Michael Schrage, "More Power to Whom?" *Fortune*, July 23, 2001, p. 270; Seth Silver, "Power to the People," *Training*, October 2001, p. 88; Marjorie Kelly, "A Tale of Two Employee-Owned Companies," *Business Ethics*, September/October 2001, pp. 12 and 17; Stack, *The Great Game of Business*.

Chapter 8

1. Jeffrey Zaslow, "How to Tell People You've been Laid Off (and How to Cope with Their Sympathy)," *Wall Street Journal*, May 2, 2002, p. D1.
2. Sue Shellenbarger, "Parents of Teenagers Demand, and get More Outside Support," *Wall Street Journal*, June 28, 2000, p. B1.
3. Martha Beck, "True Confessions," *O The Oprah Magazine*, June 2002, pp. 183–184.
4. Daniel Goleman, "What Makes a Leader?" *Harvard Business Review*, November/December 1998, p. 95.
5. Cary Cherniss and Daniel Goleman, *The Emotionally Intelligent Workplace* (San Francisco: Jossey-Bass, 2001), p. 258.
6. John Powell, *Why Am I Afraid to Tell You Who I Am?* (Chicago: Argus Communications, 1969), p. 77.
7. Roy M. Berko, Andrew D. Wolvin, and Darlyn R. Wolvin, *Communicating* (Boston: Houghton Mifflin, 1995), p. 46.
8. *Communication Concepts—The Johari Window* (New York: J. C. Penney Company, Consumer Affairs Department, 1979).
9. Parker J. Palmer, "Life on the Mobius Strip," *Inner Edge*, August/September 2000, pp. 22–23.
10. Michael Ryan, "A Hidden Talent," *Parade Magazine*, May 28, 1989, p. 30.
11. Dennis E. Coates, "Don't Tie 360-Degree Feedback to Pay," *Training*, September 1998, pp. 68–78; Maury A. Peiper, "Getting 360 Feedback Right," *Harvard Business Review*, January 2001, pp. 3–7.
12. Beverly Engel, "Making Amends," *Psychology Today*, July/August 2002, pp. 40–42.
13. Sharon Nelton, "The Power of Forgiveness," *Nation's Business*, June 1995, p. 41.
14. Lazarus and Lazarus, *The 60-Second Shrink* (San Luis Obispo, Calif.: Impact Publishers, 1997), pp. 76–79.
15. John R. Diekman, *Human Connections* (Englewood Cliffs, N.J.: Prentice-Hall, 1985), p. 63.
16. Bob Wall, *Working Relationships* (Palo Alto, Calif.: Davies-Black, 1999), p. 166.
17. Hendrie Weisinger and Norman Lobsenz, *Nobody's Perfect—How to Give Criticism and Get Results* (Los Angeles: Stratford Press, 1981), p. 39.
18. Joyce Brothers, "The Most Important People We Know . . . Our Friends," *Parade Magazine*, February 16, 1997, pp. 4–6.
19. Mark Matousek, "The Cat Is on the Roof," *Common Boundary*, January/February 1997, p. 64.
20. *The American Heritage Dictionary of the English Language*, 3d ed. (Boston: Houghton Mifflin, 1992), p. 1920.
21. Blaine Hartford, "Trust Your Surgeon? Mate? Friends? Colleagues? What Makes Up a Feeling of Trust?" *Health & Healing*, June 2000, p. 36.
22. Ron Zemke, "Can You Manage Trust?" *Training*, February 2000, p. 78; Ron Zemke, "A Matter of Trust," *Training*, December 2002, p. 12.
23. Aubrey C. Daniels, *Bringing Out the Best in People* (New York: McGraw-Hill, 1994), p. 41.
24. Jack R. Gibb, *Trust: A New View of Personal and Organizational Development* (Los Angeles: Guild of Tutors Press, 1978), p. 29.
25. Ibid., p. 192.
26. Derek Reveron, "Employee Criticism: Do It with Sensitivity," *San Jose Mercury News*, July 12, 1992, p. 1PC; "How to Sidestep Verbal Pitfalls," *San Jose Mercury News*, January 31, 1993, p. 2PC; "Speaking Out Counts at Work," *San Jose Mercury News*, December 20, 1992, p. 1PC.
27. Mary Scott, "Interview with Howard Schultz," *Business Ethics*, November/December 1995, p. 28; Kate Berry, "Starbucks Opens First Stores in Miami, Hoping to Woo Lovers of Cuban Coffee," *Wall Street Journal*, March 31, 1997, p. A9; Jennifer Reese, "Starbucks—Inside the Coffee Cult," *Fortune*, December 9, 1996, pp. 190–198; Coates, "Don't Tie 360-Degree Feedback to Pay," pp. 68–78; "Work Week," *Wall Street Journal*, March 7, 2000, p. A1.

Chapter 9

1. Chip Cummins, "Workers Wear Feelings on Their Hard Hats and Show True Colors," *Wall Street Journal*, November 11, 2000, p. A1.
2. Jane Cys, "Foam Blocks Turn Cubicles into Castles," *Washington Business Journal*. [cited 19 January 2003]. Available from bizjournals.com; INTERNET.
3. Douglas A. Bernstein, Louis A. Penner, Alison Clarke-Stewart, and Edward J. Roy, *Psychology*, 6th ed. (Boston: Houghton Mifflin, 2003), pp. 412–413.
4. Carol S. Pearson, "The Emotional Side of Workplace Success," *The Inner Edge*, December 1998/January 1999, p. 3.
5. Daniel Goleman, *Emotional Intelligence* (New York: Bantam Books, 1995), p. 34.
6. Daniel Goleman, *Working with Emotional Intelligence* (New York: Bantam Books, 1998), pp. 24–28.
7. Jeff Barbian, "Heart Smarts," *Training*, February 2001, p. 24.
8. John Selby, *Conscious Healing* (New York: Bantam Books, 1989), p. 32.
9. Ibid.
10. James Georges, "The Not-So-Stupid Americans," *Training*, July 1994, p. 90.
11. Tim Sanders, *Love Is the Killer App* (New York: Crown Business, 2002), pp. 17–18.
12. Ibid., p. 23.
13. Ron Zemke, "Contact! Training Employees to Meet the Public," *Service Solutions* (Minneapolis: Lakewood Books, 1990), pp. 20–23.
14. Bernstein et al., *Psychology*, 6th ed., p. 454.
15. Ibid.
16. William C. Menninger and Harry Levinson, *Human Understanding in Industry* (Chicago: Science Research Associates, 1956), p. 29.
17. Joan Borysenko, *Guilt Is the Teacher, Love Is the Lesson* (New York: Warner Books, 1990), p. 70.
18. Donella H. Meadows, "We Are, to Our Harm, What We Watch," *Roanoke Times & World-News*, October 16, 1994, p. G3.
19. Bernstein et al., *Psychology*, p. 22.
20. Rachel Zimmerman, "Study Finds Violence Takes 1.6 Million Lives a Year," *Wall Street Journal*, October 3, 2002, p. D5; Kimberley Shearer Palmer, "Young Women Turn Wrong Way to Escape Abusive Boyfriends," *USA Today*, September 10, 2001, p. 17A.
21. Shakti Gawain, *The Path of Transformation* (Mill Valley, Calif.: Nataraj Publishing, 1993), p. 96.
22. Ibid.
23. Harold H. Bloomfield and Robert K. Cooper, *The Power of 5* (Emmaus, Pa.: Rodale Press, 1995), p. 334.
24. Redford Williams and Virginia Williams, *Anger Kills* (New York: HarperCollins, 1993), p. 3.
25. Kimes Gustin, *Anger, Rage, and Resentment* (West Caldwell, N.J.: St. Ives' Press, 1994), p. 1.
26. Art Ulene, *Really Fit Really Fast* (Encino, Calif.: HealthPoints, 1996), pp. 170–174.
27. Al Pearce, "Strange Year," *Autoweek*, December 16, 2002, pp. 29–30.
28. Susan Bixler, *Professional Presence* (New York: G. P. Putnam's Sons, 1991), pp. 190–191.
29. Rolland S. Parker, *Emotional Common Sense* (New York: Barnes & Noble Books, 1973), pp. 80–81.
30. Pamela Kruger, "Betrayed by Work," *Fast Company*, November 1999, p. 186.
31. Gustin, *Anger, Rage, and Resentment*, p. 37.
32. Les Giblin, *How to Have Confidence and Power in Dealing with People* (Englewood Cliffs, N.J.: Prentice-Hall 1956), p. 37.
33. Mike France and Michael Arndt, "After the Shooting Stops," *Business Week*, March 12, 2001, pp. 98–100.
34. Kevin Dobbs, "The Lucrative Menace of Workplace Violence," *Training*, March 2000, p. 55; Albert R. Karr, "Work Week," *Wall Street Journal*, April 4, 2000, p. A1.
35. Kenneth Labich, "Psycho Bosses from Hell," *Fortune*, March 18, 1996, p. 123.
36. Jennifer J. Laabs, "Employee Sabotage: Don't Be the Target," *Workforce*, July 1999, pp. 32–42; Michelle Conlin and Alex Salkever, "Revenge of the Downsized Nerds," *Business Weeek*, July 30, 2001, p. 40.
37. Laabs, "Employee Sabotage," pp. 32–42.
38. "Preventing On-the-Job Violence," *Inc.*, June 1996, p. 116.
39. Arnold A. Lazarus and Clifford N. Lazarus, *The 60 Second Shrink* (San Luis Obispo, Calif.: Impact Publishers, 1997), pp. 54–55.
40. Walton C. Boshear and Karl G. Albrecht, *Understanding People: Models and Concepts* (San Diego: University Associates, 1977), pp. 41–46.
41. Chris Hill and Toby Hanlon, "Twenty-Six Simple Ways to Change How You Feel," *Prevention*, August 1993, p. 63.
42. Bloomfield and Cooper, *The Power of 5*, p. 368.
43. Joan Borysenko, *Minding the Body, Mending the Mind*, pp. 164–165. New York: Bantam Books, 1987.
44. Ibid.
45. Don Miguel Ruiz, *The Four Agreements* (San Rafael, Calif.: Amber-Allen Publishing, 1997), p. 111.
46. Sam Keen, *Fire in the Belly—On Being a Man* (New York: Bantam Books, 1991), p. 242.
47. Lazarus and Lazarus, *The 60-Second Shrink*, pp. 10–11.
48. Borysenko, *Minding the Body, Mending the Mind*, p. 169.
49. Ellen Safier, "Our Experts Answer Your Questions," *Menninger Letter*, May 1993, p. 8.
50. Leo F. Buscaglia, *Loving Each Other* (Thorofare, N.J.: Slack, 1984), p. 160.
51. Keen, *Fire in the Belly*, p. 242.
52. Jeffrey Zaslow, "Putting a Price Tag on Grief," *Wall Street Journal*, November 20, 2002, p. D1; Sue Shellenbarger, "A Workplace Can Seem Cold and Indifferent to a Grieving Employee," *Wall Street Journal*, January 12, 1999, p. B1; Sue Shellenbarger, "An Anguishing Flaw in Many Benefit Plans: Bereavement Leaves," *Wall Street Journal*, February 23, 2000, p. B1.
53. Perri Capell, "Salvaging the Careers of Talented Managers Who Behave Badly," *Wall Street Journal*, December 24, 1996, p. B1; Thomas A. Stewart, "Looking

Out for Number 1," *Fortune*, January 15, 1996, p. 36; Edward Felsenthal, "Potentially Violent Employees Present Bosses with a Catch-22," *Wall Street Journal*, April 5, 1995, p. B1.

Chapter 10

1. Keith H. Hammonds, "Handle with Care," *Fast Company*, August 2002, pp. 103–107.
2. Roger L. Hale and Rita F. Maehling, *Recognition Redefined* (Exeter, N.H.: Monochrome Press, 1993), p. 8.
3. Sarah Boehle, "From Humble Roots," *Training*, October 2000, pp. 106–113.
4. Robert Levering and Milton Moskowitz, "100 Best Companies to Work For," *Fortune*, January 20, 2003, p. 152.
5. Kenneth Blanchard and Spencer Johnson, *The One Minute Manager* (New York: Morrow, 1982), p. 43.
6. Douglas A. Bernstein, Louis A. Penner, Alison Clarke-Stewart, and Edward J. Roy, *Psychology*, 6th ed. (Boston: Houghton Mifflin, 2003), p. 197.
7. James M. Kouzes and Barry Z. Posner, *Encouraging the Heart* (San Francisco: Jossey-Bass, 1999), pp. 3–4.
8. Evelyn Sieburg, "Confirming and Disconfirming Organizational Communication," in *Communication in Organizations*, ed. James L. Owen, Paul A. Page, and Gordon I. Zimmerman (St. Paul, Minn.: West, 1976), p. 130.
9. "Leno Regrets Not Thanking Johnny," *San Francisco Examiner*, September 8, 1995, p. C17.
10. Deepak Chopra, *The Seven Spiritual Laws of Success* (San Rafael, Calif.: Amber-Allen, 1994), pp. 30–31.
11. *Random Acts of Kindness* (Berkeley, Calif.: Conari Press, 1993), pp. 1, 54, 68, 91.
12. Bob Nelson, *1001 Ways to Reward Employees* (New York: Workman, 1994), p. ix.
13. Ibid., p. xv.
14. Tim Sanders, *Love Is The Killer App* (New York: Crown Business, 2002), p. 39.
15. "How to Run an Incentive Program," *Incentive*, July 1990, p. 2.
16. Susan Sonnesyn Brooks, "Noncash Ways to Compensate Employees," *HR Magazine*, April 1994, p. 39.
17. Alfie Kohn, "Why Incentive Plans Cannot Work," *Harvard Business Review*, September/October 1993, p. 58.
18. Ibid.
19. Ibid., pp. 58–59.
20. Ibid., pp. 61–62.
21. Dave Murphy, "If You Want Gold, Give Them a Goal," *San Francisco Chronicle*, April 14, p. J1; Jeff Barbian, "Golden Carrots," *Training*, July 2002, p. 18.
22. Cedric B. Johnson, "When Working Harder Is Not Smarter," *The Inner Edge*, April/May 2000, p. 18–21.
23. Ibid., p. 19.
24. Ibid; Sue Shellenbarger, "Work & Family," *Wall Street Journal*, December 29, 1999, p. B1.
25. David Wessel, "Why the Bad Guys of the Boardroom Emerged en Masse," *Wall Street Journal*, June 20, 2002, pp. A1 and A6; Crayton Harrison, "Happy Customers Are Loyal, Banks Find," *San Jose Mercury*

News, January 29, 2001, p. PC1; Barbian, "Golden Carrots," p. 18.
26. Steven Ginsberg, "Companies Look for a Little Help Out of the Box," *San Jose Mercury News*, March 17, 1998, p. 13C; "If We Might Make a Suggestion . . . ," *Training*, July 1999, p. 20.

Chapter 11

1. Don Peppers, Martha Rogers, and Bob Dorf, *The One to One Fieldbook* (New York: Currency Doubleday, 1999), pp. 329–330.
2. Heather Johnson, "A Brand-New You," *Training*, August 2002, p. 14.
3. Gerry Khermouch, "What Makes a Boffo Brand," *The Business Week*, Spring 2002, p. 20.
4. Stephen R. Covey, *The 7 Habits of Highly Effective People* (New York: Simon & Schuster, 1989), pp. 22, 34.
5. Susan Bixler, *Professional Presence* (New York: G. P. Putnam's Sons, 1991), p. 16.
6. "Author: Success Pivots on First Impressions," *San Jose Mercury News*, November 8, 1992, p. 2PC.
7. Douglas A. Bernstein, Alison Clarke-Stewart, Louis A. Pence, Edward J. Roy, and Christopher D. Wickens, *Psychology*, 5th ed. (Boston: Houghton Mifflin, 2000), pp. 226–227.
8. "Dress Codes for Presidential Candidates," *Parade Magazine*, November 5, 1995, p. 17.
9. Malcolm Fleschner, with Gerhard Gschwandtner, "Power Talk," *Personal Selling Power*, July/August 1995, p. 14.
10. Leonard Zunin and Natalie Zunin, *Contact—The First Four Minutes* (New York: Ballantine Books, 1972), p. 17.
11. Clyde Haberman, "No Offense," *New York Times Book Review*, February 18, 1996, p. 11.
12. Diane E. Lewis, "Some Firms in a Twist over Braids," *San Jose Mercury News*, May 25, 1997, p. 1PC. For an update on this hairstyle issue, see Ray A. Smith, "Cornrows for Men Built Momentum, Exploded into Mainstream This Year," *Wall Street Journal*, July 31, 2000, p. B11; T. Shawn Taylor, "Hairstyles at Work Get More Diverse," *News & Observer*, August 12, 2001, pp. 1E and 12E.
13. Haberman, "No Offense," p. 11.
14. Bixler, *Professional Presence*, p. 141.
15. Suein L. Hwang, "Enterprise Takes Idea of Dressed for Success to a New Extreme," *Wall Street Journal*, November 20, 2002, p. B1.
16. Dave Knesel, "Image Consulting—A Well-Dressed Step up the Corporate Ladder," *Pace*, July/August 1981, p. 74.
17. Cora Daniels, "The Man in the Tan Khaki Pants," *Fortune*, May 1, 2000, p. 338.
18. Megan Schnabel and Amy Kane, "Toss the Tie, Lose the Suit—The Casual Look Is In," *The Roanoke Times*, September 5, 1999, pp. B1, B2; Gene Bedell, *3 Steps to Yes* (New York: Crown Business, 2000), p. 143.

19. Wendy Bounds, Rebecca Quick, and Emily Nelson, "In the Office, It's Anything Goes," *Wall Street Journal*, August 26, 1999, pp. B1, B4.

20. Anne Fisher, "Ask Annie," *Fortune*, May 15, 2000, p. 504; Frederic M. Biddle, "Work Week," *Wall Street Journal*, February 15, 2000.

21. Deborah Blum, "Face It!" *Psychology Today*, September/October 1998, pp. 34 and 69.

22. Susan Bixler, *The Professional Image* (New York: Perigee Books, 1984), p. 217.

23. Ibid., p. 219.

24. John P. Mello, Jr., "Voice Rarely Used to Its Full Potential," *Boston Globe*, January 19, 2003, p. G7.

25. David E. Weliver, "My Fair CEO," *Inc.*, October 30, 2001, p. 112.

26. Adapted from Zunin and Zunin, *Contact*, pp. 102–108; "Handshake 101," *Training & Development*, November 1995, p. 71.

27. Cynthia Crossen, "Etiquette for Americans Today," *Wall Street Journal*, December 28, 2001, p. W13.

28. Barbara Pachter and Mary Brody, *Complete Business Etiquette Handbook* (Englewood Cliffs, N.J.: Prentice-Hall, 1995), p. 3.

29. Amy Gamerman, "Lunch with Letitia: Our Reporter Minds Her Manners," *Wall Street Journal*, March 3, 1994, p. A14.

30. Ann Marie Sabath, "Meeting Etiquette: Agendas and More," *DECA Dimensions*, January/February 1994, p. 8.

31. Leila Jason, "Are There Rules of Etiquette for Cellphone Use?" *Wall Street Journal*, September 10, 2001, p. R16.

32. Dana May Casperson, "Break Those Bad Cellphone Habits," *Selling*, January 2002, p. 9.

33. Gene Veith, "Curse of the Foul Mouth," *Wall Street Journal*, January 24, 2003, p. D1; Tara Parker-Pope and Kyle Pope, "When #@%&@ Is—and Isn't—Appropriate," *Wall Street Journal Sunday*, featured in *News & Observer*, January 21, 2001, p. D4.

34. Barbara Moses, *Career Intelligence* (San Francisco: Berrett-Koehler Publishers, 1997), p. 175.

35. Nancy K. Austin, "What Do America Online and Dennis Rodman Have in Common?" *Inc.*, July 1997, p. 54.

36. Marilyn Vos Savant, "Ask Marilyn," *Parade*, May 30, 2002, p. 19.

37. Stephanie G. Sherman, *Make Yourself Memorable* (New York: American Management Association, 1996), pp. 3–4; Michael J. McCarthy, "America Saw Itself in DiMaggio, and It Liked What It Saw," *Wall Street Journal*, March 9, 1999, pp. A1 and A8; "People in the News," *U.S. News & World Report*, November 8, 1999, p. 12; Ann Landers, "If You've Got Class, Nothing Else Matters," *The News & Observer*, July 11, 1998, p. 2E.

38. David McNally and Karl D. Speak, *Be Your Own Brand* (San Francisco: Berrett-Koehler Publishers, 2002), p.4.

39. Ibid.

40. "The Right Words at the Right Time," *O The Oprah Magazine*, May 2002, p. 202.

Chapter 12

1. Jerry Useem, "A Manager for all Seasons," *Fortune*, April 30, 2001, pp. 66–72.

2. Ibid., p. 72.

3. "Synergy: Or, We're All in This Together," *Training*, September 1985, pp. 64, 65.

4. Bob Wall, *Working Relationships* (Palo Alto, Calif.: Davies-Black, 1999), pp. 28–29.

5. "Industry Report—1997," *Training*, October 1997, p. 62.

6. Robert Kreitner, *Management*, 8th ed. (Boston: Houghton Mifflin, 2001), p. 414.

7. Ibid., pp. 415–416.

8. Paul Roberts, "Live from Your Office! It's . . . ," *Fast Company*, October 1999, p. 180.

9. Kreitner, *Management*, pp. 446–447.

10. Jon R. Katzenbach and Jason A. Santamaria, "Firing Up the Front Line," *Harvard Business Review*, May/June 1999, pp. 107–117.

11. Gene Hoffman, "Beware the Superstars Syndrome," *San Jose Mercury News*, April 2, 2000, p. 2E.

12. Adapted from a list in Douglas McGregor, *The Human Side of Enterprise* (New York: McGraw-Hill, 1960), pp. 232–235.

13. The Leadership Grid® from *Leadership Dilemmas—Grid Solutions* by Robert R. Blake and Anne Adams McCanse (formerly of the Manager Grid Figure by Robert R. Blake and Jane S. Mouton.) Gulf Publishing Company, p. 29. Copyright ©1991 by Scientific Methods, Inc. Reprinted by permission.

14. Text list of Blake/Mouton descriptive names for leadership styles in grid. From *The New Managerial Grid*, by Robert R. Blake and Jane Srygley Mouton. Houston: Gulf Publishing Company. Copyright ©1978, p. 11. Reprinted by permission of Scientific Methods.

15. Robert R. Blake and Jane Srygley Mouton, "How to Choose a Leadership Style," *Training & Development*, February 1982, pp. 41–42.

16. Reported in Ron Zemke, "What Are High-Achieving Managers Really Like?" *Training/HRD*, February 1979, pp. 35–36.

17. Jay Hall, *The Competence Connection* (The Woodlands, Tex.: Woodstead Press, 1988), p. 77.

18. Material by *Training Magazine*. Copyright 1998 Bill Communications. Reproduced with permission of Bill Communications, via Copyright Clearance Center.

19. Price Pritchett, *Teamwork—The Team Member Handbook* (Dallas, Tex.: Pritchett & Associates Inc., 1992), p. 2.

20. "An Interview with Warren Bennis," *Training*, August 1997, p. 33.

21. These two dimensions can be measured by the *Leadership Opinion Questionnaire* developed by Edwin A. Fleishman and available from Pearson Reid London House (www.reidlondonhouse@pearson.com).

22. Brian Tracy, *The 100 Absolutely Unbreakable Laws of Business Success* (San Francisco: Berrett-Koehler Publishers, Inc., 2000), pp. 138–139.

23. D. Michael Abrashoff "Retention Through Redemption," *Harvard Business Review*, February 2001, pp. 1–7 (Reprint RO102L).

24. "Making a Nickel Do a Dime's Work," *Training*, April 1994, p. 12.

25. Sue Shellenbarger, "Enter the New Hero: A Boss Who Knows You Have a Life," *Wall Street Journal*, May 8, 1996, p. B1.

26. "Tips for Teams," *Training*, February 1994, p. 14.

27. David G. Baldwin, "How to Win the Blame Game," *Harvard Business Review*, July/August 2001, pp. 1–7 (Reprint RO107C).

28. Kreitner, *Management*, p. 470.

29. Paul Hersey, *The Situational Leader* (Escondido, Calif.: Center for Leadership Studies, 1984), pp. 29, 30. To obtain current information on the Situational Leadership Model, visit www.situational.com.

30. Ibid., p. 57.

31. Tracy, *The 100 Absolutely Unbreakable Laws of Business Success*, p. 121.

32. Cary Cherniss and Daniel Goleman, *The Emotionally Intelligent Workplace* (San Francisco: Jossey-Bass, 2001), pp. 22–23.

33. Will Schutz, *The Human Element* (San Francisco: Jossey-Bass, 1994), pp. 237–238.

34. Margaret Kaeter, "The Leaders Among Us," *Business Ethics*, July/August 1994, p. 46.

35. J. Oliver Crom, "Every Employee a Leader: Part One," *The Leader*, April 1997, p. 6.

36. Peter Koestenbaum, *Leadership—The Inner Side of Greatness* (San Francisco: Jossey-Bass, 1991), pp. 179–183.

37. Michaele Weissman, "Nerd Alert!" *Wall Street Journal*, May 14, 2001, p. R14; Peter Frost and Sandra Robinson, "The Toxic Handler: Organizational Hero—and Casualty," *Harvard Business Review*, July/August 1999, pp. 97–106.

38. Eleena de Lisser, "Firms with Virtual Environments Appeal to Workers," *Wall Street Journal*, October 5, 1999, p. B2; Gina Imperato, "Real Tools for Virtual Teams," *Fast Company*, July 2000, p. 382.

39. Kenneth R. Phillips, "The Achilles' Heel of Coaching," *Training & Development*, March 1998, pp. 41–44.

40. Clyde Haberman, "Kinder and Gentler, but Still Rudy," *New York Times Book Review*, Sunday, October 13, 2002, p. 11.

41. Oren Harari, "Open Doors Behind," *Modern Maturity*, January/February 2002, pp. 49–50.

42. Jerry Useem, "A Manager for All Seasons," *Fortune*, April 30, 2001, pp. 66–72.

Chapter 13

1. Dudley Weeks, *The Eight Essential Steps to Conflict Resolution* (New York: G. P. Putnam's Sons, 1992), p. 7.

2. Ibid., pp. 7–8.

3. Beth Fitzgerald, "No Hard Feelings," *San Jose Mercury News*, April 15, 2000, p. 15C.

4. Anne Fisher, "Which One Should I Fire? . . . Is My Voice Mail Monitored? . . . and Other Queries," *Fortune*, November 25, 1996, p. 173.

5. Rick Brooks, "Blizzard of Grievances Joins a Sack of Woes at U.S. Postal Service," *Wall Street Journal*, June 21, 2001, p. A1.

6. Rebecca Blumenstein and Gregory L. White, "The $2 Billion Tag May Seem a Rather High Price for Some Labor Peace," *Wall Street Journal*, July 30, 1998, p. 31.

7. Martha Brannigan, "Comair to Resume Limited Flights After Strike," *Wall Street Journal*, June 25, 2001, p. A4.

8. Robert Kreitner, *Management*, 8th ed. (Boston: Houghton Mifflin, 2001), p. 506.

9. David Stiebel, "The Myth of Hidden Harmony," *Training*, March 1997, p. 114.

10. Carol Kleiman, "How to Deal with a Co-worker Who's Getting on Your Nerves," *San Jose Mercury News*, October 3, 1999, p. PC1.

11. "Assertiveness: More Than a Forceful Attitude," *Supervisory Management*, February 1994, p. 3.

12. Stephen Ash, "How to Make Assertiveness Work for You," *Supervisory Management*, p. 8.

13. Albert Ellis, *Effective Self-Assertion*, Psychology Today audiotape, 1985.

14. Danny Ertel, "Turning Negotiation into a Corporate Capability," *Harvard Business Review*, May/June 1999, p. 3.

15. Cheryl Shavers, "Strategy, Not Tactics, Is the Better Approach for a Winning Negotiator," *San Jose Mercury News*, January 24, 1999, p. 5E.

16. Adapted from Brian Tracy, *The 100 Absolutely Unbreakable Laws of Business Success* (San Francisco: Berrett-Koehler Publishers, Inc., 2000), pp. 235–236.

17. Kurt Salzinger, "Psychology on the Front Lines," *Psychology Today*, May/June 2002, p. 34.

18. David Stiebel, *When Talking Makes Things Worse!* (Dallas: Whitehall & Nolton, 1997), p. 17.

19. Roger Fisher and Alan Sharp, *Getting It Done* (New York: Harper Business, 1998), pp. 81–83.

20. Ibid., pp. 90–101.

21. Roger Fisher and William Ury, *Getting to Yes* (New York: Penguin Books, 1981), p. 59.

22. Weeks, *The Eight Essential Steps to Conflict Resolution*, p. 228.

23. Ibid., p. 223.

24. University of North Texas-Dallas: Alternative Dispute Resolution Certificate Brochure, updated 25 March 2002 [cited 22 February 2003]. Available from www.unt.edu/unt-dallas/brochures/adresd.htm; INTERNET.

25. Toddi Gutner, "When It's Time to Do Battle with Your Company," *Business Week*, February 10, 1997, pp. 130–131.

26. Ibid., p. 131.

27. Interview with Robert Wehrman, vice president, Fed Ex Services, August 19, 2000.

28. Aaron Bernstein, "Grad Students vs. California," *Business Week*, December 14, 1998, p. 6; De'Ann Weimer, "The Doctor Is In—A Union Meeting," *Business Week*, February 8, 1999, p. 6; Arthur B. Shostak, "Unions Best with Backs to Wall," *USA Today*, September 29, 2001; Adam Geller, "State of the Unions: Weakest in

Decades," *The News & Observer*, September 31, 2002, p. D1.

29. Kathy Chen, "Nurses Group Is Expected to Vote to Join AFL-CIO," *Wall Street Journal*, June 14, 2001, p. A2; Jill Rosenfeld, "Are Guilds the Future of Unions?" *Fast Company*, May 2001, p. 140.

30. Carol Kleiman, "More Than Just a 'Brotherhood,'" *San Jose Mercury News*, May 11, 1997, p. 1PC; Sue Shellenbarger, "Karen Nussbaum Plans to Focus Unions on Family Issues," *Wall Street Journal*, February 19, 1997, p. B1.

31. "Labor's Modest Quid Pro Quo," *Business Week*, November 11, 1996, p. 38.

32. Sheridan Prasso, "Will CEO Pain Lead to Labor Gains?" *Business Week*, September 16, 2002, p. 6.

33. Jeffrey, Zaslow, "Ready to Pop the Question? Hold Off Until You've Done the Interrogation," *Wall Street Journal*, February 6, 2003, p. D1.

34. Phillip C. McGraw, "Couples Combat: The Great American Pastime," *O*, August 2002, p. 43.

35. Ibid.; "How To," *Training & Development*, April 1998, p. 10; Jeffrey Zaslow, "Divorce Makes a Comeback," *Wall Street Journal*, January 14, 2003, pp. D1, D10; Zaslow, "Ready to Pop the Question?" p. D1.

36. Sue Shellenbarger, "Jo Browning Built a Child-Care Agenda into a Factory's Plan," *Wall Street Journal*, August 6, 1997, p. B1; Dave Murphy, "In the Business World, the Meek Inherit Nothing," *The News & Observer*, April 28, 2002, p. 12E; Amy Joyce, "Author's Advice: No Wimping Out in the Workplace War," *San Jose Mercury News*, September 3, 2000, p. 2PC.

Chapter 14

1. Timothy Aeppel, "More Plants Go 24/7, and Workers Are Left at Sixes and Sevens," *Wall Street Journal*, July 24, 2001, p. A1.

2. David Whitford, "A Human Place to Work," *Fortune*, January 8, 2001, pp. 109–110.

3. Michelle Conlin, "The Big Squeeze on Workers," *Business Week*, May 13, 2002, pp. 96–97.

4. Arnold A. Lazarus and Clifford N. Lazarus, *The 60-Second Shrink* (San Luis Obispo, Calif.: Impact Publishers, 1997), p. 86–87; Howard I. Glazer, *Getting in Touch with Stress Management* (American Telephone and Telegraph, 1988), p. 2.

5. Cora Daniels, "The Last Taboo," *Fortune*, October 28, 2002, pp. 137–144.

6. Richard Laliberte, "Lighten Up," "*New Choices*, June 2001, p. 65.

7. James E. Loehr, *Stress for Success* (New York: Times Books, 1997), p. 4.

8. Harold H. Bloomfield and Robert K. Cooper, *The Power of 5* (Emmaus, Pa.: Rodale Press, 1995), p. 18.

9. Daniels, "The Last Taboo," p. 138.

10. Craig Brod, *Technostress: The Human Cost of the Computer Revolution* (Reading, Mass.: Addison-Wesley, 1984), p. 16.

11. Jane Bozarth, "In Print," *Training*, August 2001, p. 60.

12. Carol Hymowitz, "Can Workplace Strees Get Worse?" *Wall Street Journal*, January 16, 2001, p. B1.

13. Heather Holliday, "Hooked on the Net," *Psychology Today*, July/August 2000, p. 10; Carol Potera "Trapped in the Web," *Psychology Today*, March/April 1998, pp. 66–72.

14. Brod, *Technostress*, p. 17.

15. David Shenk, *Data Smog—Surviving the Information Glut* (San Francisco: HarperEdge, 1997), p. 31.

16. Bloomfield and Cooper, *The Power of 5*, p. 299.

17. John Carey, "Heading Off Hearing Loss at the Passage," *Business Week*, August 17, 1998, p. 56.

18. Sue Shellenbarger, "The American Way of Work (More!) May Be Easing Up," *Wall Street Journal*, January 19, 2000, p. B1.

19. Sue Shellenbarger, "Are Saner Workloads the Unexpected Key to More Productivity?" *Wall Street Journal*, March 10, 2000, p. B1.

20. Paul Raeburn, "The Perils of Part-Time for Professionals," *Business Week*, March 6, 2000, p. 125; "Higher Skills, Longer Hours," *Business Week*, April 24, 2000, p. 8.

21. Kenneth Labich, "Psycho Bosses from Hell," *Fortune*, March 18, 1996, p. 123; Vanessa Ho, "Companies Get the Message That Happy Workers Help Bottom Line," *Roanoke Times & WorldNews*, November 13, 1995, p. E6.

22. Edith Weiner, "The Fast Approaching Future," *Retail Issues Letter*, July 1994, p. 3.

23. Sue Shellenbarger, "Work and Family," *Wall Street Journal*, November 2, 1994, p. B1.

24. Art Ulene, *Really Fit Really Fast* (Encino, Calif.: HealthPoints, 1996), p. 59.

25. Ibid., pp. 56–58.

26. Daniels, "The Last Taboo," p. 138.

27. Loehr, *Stress for Success*, pp. 179, 183.

28. "Nappers of the World, Lie Down and Be Counted," *Training*, May 2000, p. 24; Donald D. Hensrud, "The Mayo Clinic Doctor," *Fortune*, April 2, 2001, p. 202.

29. Robert Tomsho, "Exercise Levels Drop for Teenage Women," *Wall Street Journal*, September 5, 2002, p. D3; "What's News," *Wall Street Journal*, April 8, 2002, p. A1.

30. Bloomfield and Cooper, *The Power of 5*, pp. 25–26.

31. Loehr, *Stress for Success*, pp. 185–186.

32. Beth Baker, "The Faith Factor," *Common Boundary*, July/August 1997, pp. 20–26.

33. Adapted from Herbert Benson, *The Relaxation Response* (New York: Morrow, 1975), p. 19; Redford Williams and Virginia Williams, *Anger Kills* (New York: Harper Perennial, 1993), pp. 86–89; Bloomfield and Cooper, *The Power of 5*, pp. 34–35.

34. Cary Barbor, "The Science of Meditation," *Psychology Today*, May/June 2001, p. 54.

35. Robert Ornstein and David Sobel, *Healthy Pleasures* (Reading, Mass.: Addison-Wesley, 1989), pp. 215–217; Norman Cousins, *Anatomy of an Illness: Reflections on Healing and Regeneration* (New York: Bantam Books, 1981).

36. Loehr, *Stress for Success*, p. 191.

37. Ann McGee-Cooper, *You Don't Have to Go Home from Work Exhausted* (New York: Bantam Books, 1992), pp. 52–53.

38. Ester Buchholz, "The Call of Solitude," *Psychology Today*, January/February 1998, pp. 50–54.

39. Adapted from material prepared by Barry Heermann, "Being Accountable to Others and Self," *The Inner Edge*, June/July 2000, pp. 18–19.

40. Casey Selix, "Employers Push Resilience as a Key Skill for Workers," *San Jose Mercury News*, March 4, 2001, p. PC1.

41. "Stress," *Men's Health*, November 1993, pp. 61–63.

42. Sue Shellenbarger, "Do We Work More or Not? Either Way, We Feel Frazzled," *Wall Street Journal*, July 30, 1997, p. 1.

43. Barbara Moses, "The Busyness Trap," *Training*, November 1998, p. 38.

44. Douglas A. Bernstein, Louis A. Penner, Alison Clark-Stewart, and Edward J. Roy, *Psychology*, 6th ed. (Boston: Houghton Mifflin, 2003), pp. 565–569.

45. Charles B. Clayman, *Family Medical Guide* (New York: Random House, 1994), p. 325.

46. Ibid., p. 325.

47. Paul Raeburn, "Mental Health: Better Benefits Won't Break the Bank," *Business Week*, December 17, 2001, p. 100; Elyse Tanouye, "Mental Illness: A Rising Workplace Cost," *Wall Street Journal*, June 13, 2001 p. B1.

48. Clayman, *Family Medical Guide*, pp. 321–322.

49. John Swartzberg, "Speaking of Wellness," *U.C. Berkeley Wellness Letter*, November 2002, p. 3.

50. Douglas A. Bernstein, Louis A. Penner, Alison Clark-Stewart, and Edward J. Roy, *Psychology*, 6th ed. (Boston: Houghton Mifflin, 2003), p. 495.

51. *Employee Burnout: America's Newest Epidemic* (Minneapolis, Minn.: Northwestern National Life Insurance Co., 1991), p. 17.

52. Joan Borysenko, "Ridden with Guilt," *Health*, March 1990, p. 78.

53. Rebecca Segall, "Online Shrinks: The Inside Story," *Psychology Today*, May/June 2000, pp. 38–43; Joshua Rosenbaum, "The Typing Cure," *Wall Street Journal*, September 16, 2002, p. R10.

54. Tony Schwartz, "What Happens Next Is That People—Especially Women—Burn Out and End Up Leaving," *Fast Company*, May 2000, p. 334.

55. Ibid.

56. Pui-Wing Tam, "Silicon Valley Belatedly Boots Up Programs to Ease Employees' Lives," *Wall Street Journal*, August 29, 2000, p. B1.

57. Christina Maslach and Michael P. Leiter, "Take This Job and . . . Love It," *Psychology Today*, September/October 1999, pp. 50–53, 78–80; Tam, "Silicon Valley Belatedly Boots Up Programs," pp. B1, B16; Tony Schwartz, "What Happens Next," pp. 330–336.

58. Paul Glader, "From the Maker of Effexor: Campus Forums on Depression," *Wall Street Journal*, October 10, 2002, pp. B1–B3; Suein L. Hwang, "Feeling Blah at Work? It May Be Your Job, Not Your Prescription," *Wall Street Journal*, September 18, 2002, p. B1; Rosen-baum, "The Typing Cure," p. R10; Raeburn, "Mental Health," p. 110.

Chapter 15

1. Teri Agins, "A Fashion House with an Elite Aura Wrestles with Race," *Wall Street Journal*, August 19, 2002, pp. 1 and 9.

2. Julie Bennett, "Corporate Commitment to Diversity Boosts Long-Term Competitive Advantage," *Wall Street Journal*, October 22, 2002, p. B11.

3. Eduardo Porter, "Immigrants' Population Gains Maintain Speedy 1990s Pace," *Wall Street Journal*, March 10, 2003, p. 82.

4. Marilyn Loden and Judy B. Rosener, *Workforce America!* (Homewood, Ill.: Business One Irwin, 1991), pp. 114–115.

5. Ibid., p. 21.

6. Douglas A. Bernstein, Louis A. Penner, Alison Clarke-Stewart, and Edward J. Roy, *Psychology*, 6th ed. (Boston: Houghton Mifflin, 2003), p. 666.

7. Margo Monteith and Jeffrey Winters, "Why We Hate," *Psychology Today*, May/June 2002, pp. 4–48.

8. D. Stanley Eitzen and Maxine Baca Zinn, *In Conflict and Order* (Boston: Allyn & Bacon, 2001), p. 237.

9. Ibid.

10. Lewis Brown Griggs and Lente-Louise Louw, *Valuing Diversity* (New York: McGraw-Hill, 1995), pp. 3–4, 150–151.

11. Ibid., p. 151.

12. Yochi J. Dreazen, "U.S. Racial Wealth Gap Remains Huge," *Wall Street Journal*, March 14, 2000, p. A2.

13. Sue Shellenbarger, "Baby Boomers Already Are Getting Agitated over Age-Bias Issues," *Wall Street Journal*, May 30, 2001, p. B1.

14. Anne Fisher, "Finally! A Ray of Hope for Job Seekers over 50," *Fortune*, December 10, 2001, p. 278.

15. Kathy Chen, "Age-Discrimination Complaints Rose 8.7% in 2001 amid Overall Increase in Claims," *Wall Street Journal*, February 25, 2002, p. B13.

16. Craig Calhoun, Donald Light, and Suzanne Keller, *Sociology*, 6th ed. (New York: McGraw-Hill, 1994), p. 241.

17. Robert S. Boynton, "Color Us Invisible," *New York Times Book Review*, August 17, 1997, p. 13.

18. Stephen Magagini, "A Race Free Consciousness," *The News & Observer*, November 23, 1997, pp. 25a–26a.

19. James Q. Wilson, "A Long Way from the Back of the Bus," *New York Times Book Review*, November 16, 1997, p. 10.

20. Carol Mukhopadhyay and Rosemary C. Henze, "How Real Is Race? Using Anthropology to Make Sense of Human Diversity," *Phi Delta Kappan*, May 2003, p. 675.

21. John McWhorter, "We're Not Ready to Think Outside the Box on Race," *Wall Street Journal*, March 28, 2002, p. A20; G. Pascal Zachary, "A Mixed Future," *Wall Street Journal*, January 1, 2000, p. R43. A recent book entitled *One Drop of Blood—The American Misadventure of Race* by Scott L. Malcomson provides an excellent review of America's separatist history.

22. Carol Mukhopadhyay and Rosemary C. Henze, "How Real Is Race? Using Anthropology to Make Sense of Human Diversity," *Phi Delta Kappan*, May 2003, pp. 673–676.
23. Robert Kreitner, *Management*, 8th ed. (Boston: Houghton Mifflin, 2001), p. 117.
24. Roger Ebert, "'Focus' Stares Down Anti-Semitism in American Culture," *Des Moines Register*, December 14, 2001, p. G6.
25. Marjorie Valbrun, "More Muslims Claim They Suffer Job Bias," *Wall Street Journal*, April 15, 2003, p. B1.
26. John Williams, "The New Workforce," *Business Week*, March 20, 2000, p. 65.
27. "Gays in the Workplace," *Inc.*, January 1996, p. 86.
28. Rachel Emma Silverman, "Wall Street, a New Push to Recruit Gay Students," *Wall Street Journal*, February 9, 2000, p. B1.
29. Robert Tomsho, "School & Efforts to Protect Gays Face Opposition," *Wall Street Journal*, February 20, 2003, p. B1.
30. Michael L. Wheeler, *Diversity: Business Rationale and Strategies* (New York: The Conference Board, 1995), p. 9.
31. Loden and Rosener, *Workforce America!* p. 12.
32. Kreitner, *Management*, p. 80; "Toyota's Charge Toward the Pinnacle of the Sport," *Canadian Grand Prix Program 2002*, p. 54; Robin Townsley Arcus, "World Market," *The Urban Hiker*, October 2000, p. 34.
33. *101 Tools for Tolerance* (Montgomery, Ala.: Southern Poverty Law Center), pp. 4–7.
34. Alex Markels, "A Diversity Program Can Prove Divisive," *Wall Street Journal*, December 4, 1996, p. B1.
35. Adapted from Leone E. Wynter, "Do Diversity Programs Make a Difference?" *Wall Street Journal*, December 4, 1996, p. B1.
36 "Time to Diversify," *Sales & Marketing Management*, May 2002, p. 62.
37. Jonathan Hickman, "America's 50 Best Companies for Minorities," *Fortune*, July 8, 2002, pp. 110–120.
38. Ibid., p. 118; Dean Foust, "Coke: Say Good-Bye to the Good Ol' Boy Culture," *Business Week*, May 29, 2000, p. 58.
39. Keith A. Caver and Ancella B. Livers, "Dear White Boss," *Harvard Business Review*, November 2002, pp. 1–7 (Reprint RO211E); David A. Thomas, "The Truth About Mentoring Minorities: Race Matters," *Harvard Business Review*, April 2001, pp. 99–107 (Reprint R0104F).
40. Stephen M. Paskoff, "Ending the Workplace Diversity Wars," *Training*, August 1996, p. 44.
41. Ibid., pp. 46–47.
42. Kreitner, *Management*, pp. 334–335.
43. Terry Eastland, "Endgame for Affirmative Action," *Wall Street Journal*, March 28, 1996, p. A15; John J. Miller, "Out of One Set of Preferences, Many . . . and Many New Debates," *New York Times Book Review*, March 27, 2002, p. A16; Roger Pilon, "The Complexities of Unfair Discrimination," *Wall Street Journal*, December 13, 2002, p. A17.
44. John J. Miller, "Out of One Set of Preferences, Many . . . and Many New Debates," *New York Times Book Review*, March 27, 2002, p. A16.
45. Michael K. Frisby, "Powell Reshapes Debate on Affirmative Action, Deepening Divisions Among Black Republicans," *Wall Street Journal*, August 13, 1996, p. A14.
46. Paul Berman, "Redefining Fairness," *New York Times Book Review*, April 14, 1996, p. A14.
47. Arthur A. Fletcher, "Business and Race: Only Halfway There," *Fortune*, March 6, 2000, pp. F75–F78; Gene Koretz, "Does Hiring Minorities Hurt?" *Business Week*, September 14, 1998, p. 26; June Kronholz, Robert Tomsho, and Robert S. Greenberger, "Court Preserves Affirmative Action," *Wall Street Journal*, June 24, 2003, p. A1.
48. Geoffrey Brewer, "Why We Can't All Get Along," *Sales & Marketing Management*, December 1995, p. 32.
49. R. Roosevelt Thomas, Jr., "From Affirmative Action to Affirming Diversity," *Harvard Business Review*, March/April 1990, p. 114.
50. "The Court's Social Agenda," *Wall Street Journal*, "December 3, 2002, p. A22; Ward Connerly and Edward Blum, "Do the Right Thing," *Wall Street Journal*, December 4, 2002, p. A18; Ronald Dworkin, "Keeping on Course with Affirmative Action," *The News & Observer*, April 22, 2001, p. 31A; Robert L. Mathis and John H. Jackson, *Human Resource Management*, 10th ed. (Thomson South-Western), Manson, OH, 2003, pp. 144–146; Daniel Golden, "Buying Your Way into College," *Wall Street Journal*, March 12, 2003, p. D1; Adam Wolfsen, "What Makes a Difference," *Wall Street Journal*, Februay 26, 2003, p. D10.
51. Dworkin, "Keeping on Course with Affirmative Action," p. 31A.
52. Monteith and Winters, "Why We Hate," pp. 44–50, 87; and Robert Epstein, "In Her Own Words," *Psychology Today*, May/June 2002, pp. 40–42; Patrick O'Neill, "Some Pastors Put Off by Attacks on Muslims," *The Chapel Hill News*, June 19, 2002, p. B6; Suein L. Hwang and Pui-Wing Tam, "In High-Tech World, Attack Reverberates for Indians, Pakistanis," *Wall Street Journal*, October 3, 2001, p. A1.

Chapter 16

1. Betsy Morris, "Trophy Husbands," *Fortune*, October 14, 2002, pp. 79–98.
2. Sue Shellenbarger, "A Downside of Taking Family Leave: Getting Fired While You're Gone," *Wall Street Journal*, January 23, 2003, p. D1; Sue Shellenbarger, "The Incredible Shrinking Family Leave: Pressed Bosses Are Cutting into Time Off," *Wall Street Journal*, October 17, 2002, p. D1.
3. Wendy Zellner, "No Way to Treat a Lady," *Business Week*, March 3, 2003, p. 63.
4. Wendy Kaminer, "Sexual Politics, Continued," *New York Times Book Review*, March 23, 1997, p. 12.
5. Gene Koretz, "My Daughter the Ph.D.," *Business Week*, March 27, 2000, p. 30; "When Saying Good-Bye Is Easy," *Business Week*, September 28, 1998, p. 8;

Carol Kleiman, "Women in the Workplace: A Revolution That Won't Quit," *San Jose Mercury News*, April 26, 1998, p. PC1.

6. Rob Norton, "Not So Fast: Sex, Drugs, and Career Choices," *Fortune*, April 3, 2000, p. 68.

7. "No Easy Path for Women in Non-Traditional Careers," *Techniques*, April 1997, p. 17; Patricia Sellers, "Patient but Not Passive," *Fortune*, October 15, 2001, pp. 188–190.

8. Sue Shellenbarger, "For Harried Workers in the 21st Century, Six Trends to Watch," *Wall Street Journal*, December 29, 1999, p. B1.

9. Ibid.

10. Bonnie Erbe, "Pay Equity, Corporate Style," *Working Woman*, February 2000, p. 22.

11. "A Salary Gap Remains Between Genders, Census Results Indicate," *Wall Street Journal*, March 25, 2003, p. D1; Charles J. Whalen, "Closing the Pay Gap," *Business Week*, August 28, 2000, p. 38.

12. Gene Koretz, "She's a Woman, Offer Her Less," *Business Week*, May 7, 2001, p. 34.

13. Sabrina Jones, "Cracking the Glass," *The News & Observer*, January 16, 2000, pp. 1E and 4E; Sellers, "Patient but Not Passive," pp. 188–190.

14. Gale Duff-Bloom, "Women in Retailing—Is There a Glass Ceiling?" *Retailing Issues Letter*, Center for Retailing Studies, Texas A&M University, May 1996, pp. 1–4; Margaret Heffernan, "The Female CEO," *Fast Company*, August 2002, pp. 60–61.

15. "How to Crack the Glass Ceiling," *Training*, February 1995, pp. 19–21.

16. "The Emancipated Organization," *Harvard Business Review*, September 2002, pp. 1–3 (Reprint F0209B). (This article features an interview with Kim Campbell, Canada's first female prime minister.)

17. "Women Taking Care of Business," *Roanoke Times & World-News*, May 13, 1995, p. 16A.

18. Sally Harris, "Research Finds Work Not 'Haven' from Home," *Spectrum*, February 21, 2003, p. 1.

19. Tony Schwartz, "While the Balance of Power Has Already Begun to Shift, Most Male CEOs Still Don't Fully Get It," *Fast Company*, December 1999, pp. 362–366.

20. Sylvia Ann Hewlett, "Executive Women and the Myth of Having It All," *Harvard Business Review*, April 2002, pp. 5–11; Margaret Heffernan, "The Female CEO," *Fast Company*, August 2002, pp. 58–66.

21. Sue Shellenbarger, "As Moms Earn More, More Dads Stay Home: How to Make the Switch Work," *Wall Street Journal*, February 20, 2003, p. D1.

22. "Today's Dads: Same Old Parenting Trap," *Business Week*, October 14, 2002, p. 167. (This article summarizes the views of Nicholas Townsend, author of *The Package Deal*, a book about the many life/work conflicts men face.)

23. Jeffrey Winters, "The Daddy Track," *Psychology Today*, September/October 2001, p. 17.

24. David Gremillion, "Men's Health Needs a Heartfelt Change," *The News & Observer*, June 17, 2001, p. 31A.

25. Jeffrey Zaslow, "Who's the New Guy at Dinner? It's Dad; Laid-Off Fathers Face Tough Job at Home," *Wall Street Journal*, October 2, 2002, p. D1.

26. "Corporate Lullaby: You Two Go Out: The Boss Will Babysit," *Fortune*, January 24, 2000, p. 152.

27. Sue Shellenbarger, "Bob's Mobile Office and Day-Care Center," *Wall Street Journal*, December 26, 2002, p. D1.

28. Kathy Bergen, "Compressed Workweek Pays Off—On 10th Day," *Roanoke Times & World-News*, March 30, 1997, p. B2.

29. Carol Kleiman, "Get Two Workers for the Price of One!" *The News & Observer*, February 26, 2003, p. 14E.

30. Susan B. Garland, "Finally, a Corporate Tip Sheet on Sexual Harassment," *Business Week*, July 13, 1998, p. 39.

31. Deborah Tannen, "The Power of Talk: Who Gets Heard and Why," *Harvard Business Review*, September/October 1995, pp. 129–140.

32. Jayne Tear, "They Just Don't Understand Gender Dynamics," *Wall Street Journal*, November 20, 1995, p. A14; Dianna Booker, "The Gender Gap in Communication," *Training Dimensions* (West Des Moines, Ia.: American Media Incorporated, Fall 1994), p. 1; Jennifer J. Laabs, "Kinney Narrows the Gender Gap," *Personnel Journal*, August 1994, pp. 83–85; Scot Ober, *Contemporary Business Communication*, 5th ed. (Boston: Houghton Mifflin, 2003), pp. 58–59.

33. Tannen, "The Power of Talk," p. 146.

34. Sharon S. Brehm, Saul M. Kassin, and Steven Fein, *Social Psychology*, 5th ed. (Boston: Houghton Mifflin, 2002), pp. 154–156.

35. Anastasi Toufexis, "Coming from a Different Place," *Time*, Fall 1990, p. 66.

36. Randall Smith, "Salomon Is Told to Pay Broker $3.2 Million," *Wall Street Journal*, December 17, 2002, p. C1; Jodi Kantor, "Tales from the Boom-Boom Room," *New York Times Book Review*, December 22, 2002, p. 7; Mary Stowell and Linda Friedman, "What Women Gained at Salomon Smith Barney," *Business Week*, December 23, 2002, p. 15.

37. Carol Kleiman, "More Companies Are Recognizing That Single Workers Have Lives, Too," *San Jose Mercury News*, May 3, 1998, p. PC1; Sue Shellenbarger, "New Research Helps Families to Assess Flaws in Work Plans," *Wall Street Journal*, May 12, 1999, p. B1; Sue Shellenbarger, "Family-Friendly CEOs Are Changing Cultures at More Workplaces," *Wall Street Journal*, September 15, 1999, p. B1; Sue Shellenbarger, "Taking On Employers over Family Issues Can Scare Even Victors," *Wall Street Journal*, October 14, 1998, p. B1.

Chapter 17

1. Bonnie Gangelhoff, "Andrew Johnston—Following His Passion for Painting," *Southwest Art*, February 2001, pp. 108–111.

2. Kelly Greene, "Travel Tales," *Wall Street Journal*, June 24, 2002, p. R5.

3. Robert M. Strozier, "The Job of Your Dreams," *New Choices*, April 1998, p. 25.

4. Richard Simon, "From the Editor," *Network*, January/February 1998, p. 2.

5. Amy Saltzman, *Downshifting* (New York: Harper-Collins, 1991), p. 16.

6. Ethan Watters, "Come Here, Work, and Get Out of Here, You Don't Live Here. You Live Someplace Else," *Inc.*, October 30, 2001, pp. 56–61.

7. Robert McGarvey, "Softening the Blow," *U.S. Air*, September 1991, p. 18.

8. Diane Brady, "Rethinking the Rat Race, "*Business Week*, August 26, 2002, pp. 142–143.

9. Jane Bozarth, "In Print," *Training*, August 2001, p. 60. (This article reviews *Dot. Calm—The Search for Sanity in a Wired World*, a book written by Debra A. Dinnocenzo and Richard B. Swegan.)

10. Sue Shellenbarger, "Keeping Your Career a Manageable Part of Your Life," *Wall Street Journal*, April 12, 1995, p. B1; "Career vs. Family: Companies Respond," *Fortune*, April 28, 1997, p. 22.

11. "When Success Fails to Make You Happy," *Working Smart*, September 1991, p. 1.

12. Mary E. Miller, "The Best Use of Her Time," *The News & Observer*, March 9, 2003, p. 1D.

13. Yvonne V. Chabrier, "Focus on Work," *New Age*, 1998, p. 95.

14. Ronald Henkoff, "So You Want to Change Your Job," *Fortune*, January 15, 1996, p. 52.

15. Marsha Sinetar, *Do What You Love . . . The Money Will Follow* (New York: Dell, 1987), p. 11.

16. Ibid., pp. 11–12.

17. Michael Phillips, *The Seven Laws of Money* (Menlo Park, Calif.: Word Wheel and Random House, 1997), p. 9.

18. Sinetar, *Do What You Love*, pp. 14–15.

19. Sue Shellenbarger, "New Job Hunters Ask Recruiters, Is There a Life After Work?" *Wall Street Journal*, January 29, 1997, p. B1.

20. Carole Kanchier, "Dare to Change Your Job and Your Life in 7 Steps" *Psychology Today*, March/April 2000, pp. 64–67.

21. Glenn Ruffenach, "Fewer Americans Save for Their Retirement," *Wall Street Journal*, May 10, 2001, p. A2; Marilyn Vos Savant, "Ask Marilyn," *Parade*, December 23, 2001, p. 14.

22. Peter T. Kilborn, "Splurge," *New York Times Book Review*, June 21, 1998, p. 34.

23. Shakti Gawain, *Creating True Prosperity* (Novato, Calif.: New World Library, 1997), p. 7.

24. Ibid., pp. 9, 10, and 25.

25. "Business Book Reviews," *The News & Observer*, February 3, 2002, p. D3.

26. Toddi Gutner, "Talk Now, Retire Happily Later," *Business Week*, April 2, 2001, p. 92.

27. Teri Lammers Prior, "If I Were President . . . ," *Inc.*, April 1995, pp. 56–60.

28. Michael Toms, "Money: The Third Side of the Coin" (interview with Joe Dominguez and Vicki Robin), *New Dimensions*, May/June 1991, p. 7.

29. Susan Smith Jones, "Choose to Be Healthy and Celebrate Life," *New Realities*, September/October 1988, pp. 17–19.

30. Ibid., p. 18.

31. Toddi Gutner, "A 12-Step Program to Gaining Power," *Business Week*, December 24, 2001, p. 88.

32. Ron Zemke, "Why Organizations Still Aren't Learning," *Training*, September 1999, p. 43.

33. His Holiness the Dalai Lama and Howard C. Cutler, *The Art of Happiness* (New York: Riverhead Books, 1998), pp. 227–228.

34. Jay T. Knippen, Thad B. Green, and Kurt Sutton, "Asking Not to Be Overworked," *Supervisory Management*, February 1992, p. 6.

35. Art Ulene, *Really Fit Really Fast* (Encino, Calif.: HealthPoints, 1996), pp. 198–199.

36. Ibid., p. 199.

37. Marilyn Chase, "Weighing the Benefits of Mental-Health Days Against Guilt Feelings," *Wall Street Journal*, September 9, 1996, B1.

38. Sue Shellenbarger, "Slackers, Rejoice: Research Touts the Benefits of Skipping Out on Work," *Wall Street Journal*, March 27, 2003, p. D1.

39. Leo Booth, "When God Becomes a Drug," *Common Boundary*, September/October 1991, p. 30; David N. Elkins, "Spirituality," *Psychology Today*, September/October, 1999, pp. 45–48.

40. Harold H. Bloomfield and Robert K. Cooper, *The Power of 5* (Emmaus, Pa.: Rodale Press, 1995), p. 484.

41. "Making the Spiritual Connection," *Lears*, December 1989, p. 72.

42. Linda J. Ferguson, *The Path for Greatness—Work as Spiritual Service* (Victoria, B.C.: Trafford Publishing, 2000), pp. 1–3.

43. Robert Bolton and Dorothy Grover Bolton, *People Styles at Work* (New York: AMACOM, 1996), pp. 110–111.

44. Rachel Emma Silverman, "More Chaplains Take Ministering into the Workplace," *Wall Street Journal*, November 27, 2001, p. B1.

45. G. Paul Zachary, "The New Search for Meaning in Meaningless Work," *Wall Street Journal*, January 9, 1997, p. B1.

46. Judith Valente, "Some Employ Faith to Get the Job Done," *USA Today*, June 16, 1995, p. B1.

47. Corinne McLaughlin, "Workplace Spirituality Transforming Organizations from the Inside Out," *The Inner Edge,* August/September 1998, pp. 25–28.

48. Redford Williams and Virginia Williams, *Anger Kills* (New York: HarperCollins, 1993), pp. 181–182.

49. Chris Lee and Ron Zemke, "The Search for Spirit in the Workplace," *Training*, June 1993, p. 25.

50. "Building a Better Pyramid," *UC Berkeley Wellness Letter*, December 2001, p. 4.

51. Paul Raeburn, "Why We're So Fat," *Business Week*, October 21, 2002, pp. 112–114.

52. Cassandra Wrightson, "Snacks Worth Their Salt," *Health*, June 2001, p. 52.

53. Ulene, *Really Fit Really Fast*, pp. 20–21; Robert Langreth, "Every Little Bit Helps," *Wall Street Journal*, May 1, 2000, p. R5.

54. John Swartzberg, "Exercise: It's Not Just Physical," *UC Berkeley Wellness Letter*, November 2002, p. 3.

55. Robert A. Gleser, *The Healthmark Program for Life* (New York: McGraw-Hill, 1988), p. 147.

56. *Fitness Fundamentals* (Washington, D.C.: Department of Health and Human Services, 1988), p. 2.

57. Stephen R. Covey, *The Seven Habits of Highly Effective People* (New York: Simon & Schuster, 1989), p. 46.

58. James Fadiman, *Be All That You Are* (Seattle: Westlake Press, 1986), p. 25.

59. Mike Hernacki, *The Ultimate Secret of Getting Absolutely Everything You Want* (New York: Berkley Books, 1988), p. 35.

60. Adapted from Bloomfield and Cooper, *The Power of 5*, pp. 492–493.

61. Sue Shellenbarger, "Work & Family," *Wall Street Journal*, January 12, 2000, p. B1; Edward M. Hallowell, *Connect* (New York: Pantheon Books, 1999), p. 3; His Holiness the Dalai Lama and Howard C. Cutler, *The Art of Happiness*, pp. 126–127.

CREDITS

Career Corner Credits

Chapter 1: Louis S. Richman, "How to get Ahead in America," *Fortune,* May 16, 1994, pp. 46-54; Ronald Henkoff, "Winning the New Career Game,: *Fortune,* July 12, 1993, pp. 46-49.

Chapter 2: Joann S. Lublin, " You Blew the Interview, but You Can Correct Some of the Blunders," *Wall Street Journal,* December 5, 2000, p. B1; Anne Faircloth, "How to Recover from a Firing," *Fortune*, December 7, 1998, p. 239; Chris Serres, "They Want to Get Inside Your Head," *News & Observer,* May 6, 2001, p 1E; "Ask Annie; Knowing When It's Time to Quit, and False Promises," *Fortune*, February 7, 2000, p.210.

Chapter 3: Barry L. Reece and Gerald L. Manning, *Supervision and Leadership in Action* (New York: Glencoe, 1990); Camille Wright Miller, "Working It Out," *Roanoke Times & World-News,* July 17, 1994, p. F-3.

Chapter 4: Maxwell Maltz, *Psycho Cybernetics* (New York: Pocket Books, 1972) pp. 6-7.

Chapter 5: Hal Lancaster, "You Have Your Values, How Do You Identify Your Employer's?" *Wall Street Journal,* April 8, 1997. p.B1. Sue Shellenbarger, "How to Find Out if You're going to Hate A New Job Before You Agree to Take It," *Wall Street Journal,* June 13, 2002, p.D1.

Chapter 6: Joann S. Lublin, " Getting Your Company to Take You Back After a Dot-Com fling," *Wall Street Journal,* June 5, 2001. p. BI.

Chapter 7: Carol Kleiman, "The Move to Telecommuting," *San Jose Mercury News,* April 16, 2000, p. PC1; Carol Kleiman, "Work/Life Programs Now Essential, Not a Frill, Consulting Firm Says," *San Jose Mercury News,* April 2, 2000, p. PC1.

Chapter 8: Joan E. Rigdon, "Even When They Ask, Bosses Don't Want Your Complaints," *Wall Street Journal,* August 10, 1994, p. B1.

Chapter 9: Glen O. Gabbard, "Are All Psychotherapies Equally Effective?" *Menninger Letter,* January 1995, pp. 1-2; "Fact About: Anxiety Disorders," published by Carrier Foundation, Belle Mead, N. J.

Chapter 10: Mitchell Schnurman, "Kissing Up: It Works. . . . But Only If You Mean It," *Roanoke Times & World-News,* September 28, 1993, p. E1.

Chapter 11: "How Much Can Employer Dictate Your Lifestyle?" *San Jose Mercury News,* May 2, 1993, pp. 1 PC and 2 PC; Susan Barciela, "Looks and Dress Still Count, Though the Lawyers Might Argue," *Roanoke Times & World-News,* June 19, 1993, p. D2; Susan Bixler, "Your Professional Presence," *Training Dimensions,* Vol. 9, No. 1, 1994, p.1.

Chapter 12: Timothy D. Schellhardt, "To Be a Star Among Equals, Be a Team Player," *Wall Street Journal,* April 20, 1994, p. B1.

Chapter 13: Sue Schellenbarger and Carol Hymowitz, "As Population Ages, Older Workers Clash with Younger Bosses," *Wall Street Journal,* June 3, 1994, pp. A1 and A5.

Chapter 14: Based on Ann Landers, "Maybe It's Time to Change Jobs," *Roanoke Times & World-News,* September 1994; Camille Wright Miller, "'Prime' Is Performance, Attitude Issue," *The Roanoke Times,* September 22, 1996, p. B2.

Chapter 15: "Good Customer Phone Form," *Training & Development,* December 1992, p. 9.

Chapter 16: Based on Dianne Hales and Robert Hales, "Can Men and Women Work Together? Yes, If . . .," *Parade Magazine,* March 20, 1994, pp. 10-11.

Total Person Insight Credits

Chapter 1
p. 6: Harry E. Chambers, *The Bad Attitude Survival Guide* (Reading, Mass.: Addison-Wesley, 1998), p.1; p. 10: Anne Fisher, "Success Secret: A High Emotional IQ," *Fortune,* October 26, 1998, p. 293; p. 13: William Raspberry, "Topmost Priority: Jobs," *Washington Post,* (n.d.), 1977; p. 15: James Baughman quote from Frank Rose, "A New Age for Business?" *Fortune,* October 8, 1990, p. 162.

Chapter 2
p. 30: Eric Maisel, *20 Communication Tips @ Work,* Novato, CA: New World Library, 2001, pp. 12-13; p. 40: Harriet Lerner, *The Dance of Connection: How to Talk to Someone When You're Mad, Hurt, Scared, Frustrated, Insulted, Betrayed, or Desperate,* Harper Collins, 2001.

Chapter 3
p. 60: Paul Mok and Dudley Lynch, "Easy New Way to Get Your Way," *Reader's Digest,* November 1982, p. 73; p. 81: David W. Merrill and Roger H. Reid, *Personal Styles and Effective Performance* (Radnor, Penn.: Chilton Book Company, 1980), p.2.

Chapter 4
p. 89: Oprah Winfrey, "You Are the Dream," *O, The Oprah Magazine,* March 2001, p. 39; p. 92: Don Miguel Ruiz, *The Four Agreements,* San Rafael, CA: Amber-Allen Publishing, 1997, p. 12; p. 96: Fran Cox and Louis Cox, *A Conscious Life* (Berkeley, Calif.: Conari Press, 1996), p. 12.

Chapter 5
p. 113: Peter Senge quote from Brian Dumaine, "Mr. Learning Organization," *Fortune,* October 17, 1994, p. 147; p. 119: William J. Bennet, "Educating for National Leadership: A 20 Year Anniversary Seminar," *Imprimis,* November 2002, p.4; p. 123: Dan Rice and Craig Dreilinger, "Rights and Wrongs of Ethics Training,"

Training & Development, May 1990, p. 105; p. 126: www.josephsoninstitute.org, 7/12/01.

Chapter 6
p. 138: Price Pritchett, *New Work Habits for the Next Millennium* (Dallas, Tex.: EPS Solutions, 1999), p. 2; p. 148: His Holiness The Dalai Lama and Howard C. Cutler, *The Art of Happiness* (New York: Riverhead Books, 1998), p. 37.

Chapter 7
p. 162: Stephen R. Covey, *The 7 Habits of Highly Effective People,* Franklin Covey Company, Salt Lake City, Utah, August 1990, p. 185; p. 177: Joan Borysenko, *Minding the Body, Mending the Mind*, New York: Bantam New Age Books, 1987, p.22.

Chapter 8
p. 189: Albert J. Bernstein and Sydney Craft Rozen, "Why Don't They Get It?" *Executive Female,* March/April 1995, p. 33; p. 198: Beverly Engel, " Making Amends" *Psychology Today*, July/August 2002, p. 40; p. 201: Terry Mizrahi, President, National Association of Social Workers, "How Can you Learn to Trust Again?" *Psychology Today*.

Chapter 9
p. 214: James Georges, The Not-So-Stupid Americans," *Training*, July 1994, p. 90; p. 220: Robert Rosell, "The Respectful Workplace," *Training*, November 2001, p. 80; p. 228: Gerard Egan, *You and Me* (Monterey, Calif.: Brooks/Cole, 1977), p. 73.

Chapter 10
p. 239: Tim Sanders, *Love Is the Killer App,* New York: Crown Business 2002, pp. 20-21; p. 243: Malcolm Boyd, "Volunteering Thanks," *Modern Maturity,* May/June 1997, p. 72.

Chapter 11
p. 260: Susan Bixler and Nancy Nix-Rice, *The New Professional Image* (Holbrook, Mass.: Adams Media Corporation , 1997), p. 3; p. 271: Judith Martin, "Low Income Is Not Low-Class," *Roanoke Times & World-News,* March 13, 1988, p. E 10.

Chapter 12
p. 236: Oren Harari, *The Leadership Secrets of Colin Powell,* New York: McGraw-Hill, 2002, p. 256; p. 288: Michael Crom, "Building Trust in the Workplace," *The Leader,* October 1998, p.6; p. 296: John C. Maxwell, *The 17 Essential Qualities of a Team Player,* Nashville, TN: Thomas Nelson Publishers 2002, pp. 13-14.

Chapter 13
p. 306: Cheryl Shavers, "Some Positive Steps That You Can Take to Resolve Conflicts," *San Jose Mercury News,* March 21, 1999, p. 3E; p. 314: Roger Fisher and William Ury, *Getting to Yes* (New York: Penguin Books, 1981), p.4.

Chapter 14
p. 332: Robert Epstein, "Stress Busters," *Psychology Today,* March/April 2000, p. 30; p. 338: Carol S. Pearson, "Breaking Out of the Time Bind," *The Inner Edge,* December 1999/January 2000, p.3; p. 346: Charles L. Peifer quote from James E. Loehr, *Stress for Success* (New York: Times Books, 1997), p. 191; p. 348: Michael Toms, "In

Search of Time: An Interview with Jacob Needleman," *The Inner Edge,* December 1999/January 2000, p. 7.

Chapter 15
p. 360: Keith H. Hammonds, "Difference Is Power," *Fast Company,* July 2000, p. 260; p. 361: Vernon E. Jordan, Jr., "Look Outward, Black America," *Wall Street Journal,* October 27, 1995, p. A14; p. 374: Lewis Brown Griggs and Lente-Louise Louw, *Valuing Diversity: New Tools for a New Reality* (New York: McGraw-Hill, Inc., 1995), p.9.

Chapter 16
p. 392: Robert Bly, *Iron John* (Reading, Mass.: Addison-Wesley, 1990), p. iv; p. 393: Debra E. Meyerson and Joyce K. Fletcher, "A Modest Manifesto for Shattering the Glass Ceiling," *Harvard Business Review,* January/February 2000, p. 127; p. 396: Debra E. Meyerson and Joyce K. Fletcher, "A Modest Manifesto for Shattering the Glass Ceiling," *Harvard Business Review,* January/February 2000, p. 136; p. Alice Sargeant, *The Androgynous Manager,* New York American Management Association, 1983, p. 37.

Chapter 17
p. 418: Ralph Fiennes, "Success – An Owner's Guide," *O, the Oprah Magazine,* September 2001, p. 51; p. 420: Cheryl Shavers, "Set a Pace That Lets You Enjoy the Fruits of Your Labor," *San Jose Mercury News,* October 19, 1997, p. 30; p. 426: Julie Connelly, "How to Choose Your Next Career," *Fortune,* February 6, 1995, p. 45; p. 431: Robert Wuthnow, "Roots & Wings," *Common Boundary,* January/February 1999, pp. 24-31; p. 432: Patricia Sellers, "Don't Call Me Slacker!" *Fortune,* December 12, 1994, p. 196.

Human Relations in Action
Chapter 1
p. 8: Chris Lee, "The Death of Civility," *Training,* July 1999, p. 25; p. 12: George Gendron, "That Magic Moment," *Inc.,* June 2000, p. 11; Shelly Branch, "The 100 Best Companies to Work For in America," *Fortune,* January 11, 1999, p. 123; p. 19: "Business Bulletin," *Wall Street Journal,* September 30, 1999; "Job-Turnover Tab," *Business Week,* April 20, 1998.

Chapter 2
p. 32: Suein L. Hwang, "It Was a Wombat for the Meatware, But It Was a Good Sell," *Wall Street Journal,* May 15, 2002, p. B1; p. 39: Excerpt adapted from "Ask Annie," *Fortune,* July 19, 1999. Copyright © 1999 Time Inc. All rights reserved.; p. 47: Adapted from "The 10 Commandments of E-MAIL," *Harvard Communications Update,* Vol. 2, No. 3, March 1999, pp. 7-8; Carolyn Kleiner, "Online Buffs Hit or Miss on Manners," *U. S. News and World Report,* March 22, 1999, p. 60; "Etiquette with Office Gadgets," *Training,* January 1999, p. 24; p. 49: "Telephone Tips," *The Office Professional,* see www.hardatwork.com; INTERNET.

Chapter 3
p. 72: Christopher Caggiano, "Psychopath," *Inc.,* July 1998, p. 83; p.78: Patricia Sellers, "Yep, He's Gone," *Fortune,* July 20, 1998, p. 32.

Chapter 4
p. 87: www.es.emory.edu/mfp/efficacynotgiveup.html Accessed November 17, 2000; p. 97: Anne Fisher, "Ask Annie," *Fortune,* October 12, 1998, p. 208.

Chapter 5
p. 120: Dennis T. Jaffe and Cynthia P. Scott, "How to Link Personal Values with Team Values," *Training & Development,* March 1998, pp. 24-26; p. 129: Adapted from Kris Maher, "Wanted: Ethical Employer," *Wall Street Journal,* July 9, 2002, p. B1. (This article includes "A Job Seeker's Ethics Audit," by Linda K. Trevino.)

Chapter 6
p. 141: Ellen Joan Pollack, "The Selling of a Golden Speech," *Wall Street Journal,* March 31, 1999, p. B-1; p. 142: Phaedra Hise, "Avoid the Stuff That Sucks," *Inc. 500,* 1999, pp. 195-196; p. 147: Mikhail V. Gratchev, "Making the Most of Cultural Differences," *Harvard Business Review,* October 2001, pp. 2-3.

Chapter 7
p. 164: Michael Specter, "The Long Ride," *The New Yorker,* July 15, 2002, pp. 48-58; p. 172: "Management Theory? Management Madness," *Psychology Today,* March/April 1997, pp. 58-62.

Chapter 8
p. 197: James Prichard, "Knight Apologizes, Sort Of," *The News & Observer,* May 14, 2000, p. C-16; "The President's Comments," *The News & Obrserver,* December 12, 1998, p. A-19; p. 200: Cynthia Crossen, "In This Tell-All Era. Secrets, Secrets Just Aren't What They Used to Be," *Wall Street Journal,* March 31, 1998, p. A-1; Bob Wall, *Working Relationships* (Palo Alto, Calif.: Davies-Black Publishing, 1999), pp. 166-167.

Chapter 9
p. 214: Daniel Goleman, *Working with Emotional Intelligence* (New York: Bantam Books, 1998), p. 23; p. 218: Ira Poddell, "Caught in the Act," *The Herald Sun,* February 23, 2000, p. D-1; "Detail of Sprewell Hearing Revealed," *The News & Observer,* March 7, 1998, p. 9-C; Jason Silverman, "The Art of Trash Talk," *Psychology Today,* September/October 1999, p. 10; p. 223: David Tarrant, "Crying Shame," *The News & Observer,* January 31, 1999, p. 1-C.

Chapter 10
p. 237: Justine Willis Toms, "A Baby Step Toward Better Community," *New Dimensions,* May/June 1999, p. 2; p. 250: Stefani Eads, "The Carrot-and-Rolex Approach," *Business Week,* July 3, 2000, p. 10.

Chapter 11
p. 259: "Job Titles of the Future," *Fast Company,* June 1999, p. 82; p. 268: Barbara Pachter & Majorie Brody, *Complete Business Etiquette Handbook,* Englewood Cliffs, NJ: Prentice Hall 1995, pp. 279-280.

Chapter 12
p. 285: David H. Freeman, "Corps Value," *Inc.,* April 1998, pp. 54-65; Jon R. Katzenback and Jason A. Santamaria, "Firing Up the Front Line," *Harvard Business Review,* May/June 1999, pp. 107-117. p. 295: Sherri Eng, "Bad Bosses," *San Jose Mercury News,* February 10, 1998, p. C14; Sue Shellenberger, "Spotting Bad Bosses Before You Get Stuck Working for Them," *Wall Street Journal,* p. B-1; p. 298: Dimitry Elias Legger, "Help! I'm the New Boss," *Fortune,* May 29, 2000, p. 281.

Chapter 13
p. 306: Tara Parker-Pope and Kyle Pope, "Work Shouldn't Be a No-Complaint Zone," *Wall Street Journal Sunday,* Printed in the *News and Observer,* November 18, 2001; p. 309: Excerpt abridged from "More Firms, Siding with Employees, Bid Bad Clients Farewell" *Wall Street Journal* (1889–1959) [STAFF PRODUCED COPY ONLY] by Sue Shellenbarger. Copyright 2000 by Dow Jones & Co. Inc. Reproduced with permission of Dow Jones & Co. Inc. in the format Textbook via Copyright Clearance Center, p. B1; p. 314: Adapted from Brian Tacy, *The 100 Absolutely Unbreakable Laws of Business Success,* San Francisco, CA. Berret-Koehler Publishers Inc. 2000. pp. 235-236.

Chapter 14
p. 334: Excerpts abridged from "A Technology Junkie Learns to Live Life a Little Less Plugged In" *Wall Street Journal* (1889–1959) [STAFF PRODUCED COPY ONLY] by Sue Shellenbarger. Copyright 2000 by Dow Jones & Co. Inc. Reproduced with permission of Dow Jones & Co. Inc. in the format Textbook via Copyright Clearance Center, p. B-1; p. 343: Excerpt abridged from "The Change Agent Blues" by Anna Muois, as appeared in the May 2000 issue of *Fast Company.* Copyright 2000 by Bus Innovator Group Resources/Inc. Reproduced with permission of Bus Innovator Group Resources/Inc. via Copyright Clearance Center; Lyrics from "Overcommitted Blues." Copyright © 1999 Face the Music Publishing, Paul Duffy (aka Deaf Lemon Meringue). Reprinted by permission of Face The Music; p. 351: Excerpt abridged from "For Harried Workers, Time Off Is Not Just for Family Affairs," *Wall Street Journal* (1889–1959) [STAFF PRODUCED COPY ONLY] by Sue Shellenbarger. Copyright 2000 by Dow Jones & Co. Inc. Reproduced with permission of Dow Jones & Co. Inc. in the format Textbook via Copyright Clearance Center.

Chapter 15
p. 362: "Tools for Tolerance: Personal," adapted from *101 Tools for Tolerance: Simple Ideas for Promoting Equity and Celebrating Diversity.* Copyright © 2000, Southern Poverty Law Center, Montgomery, AL. Reprinted by permission of Southern Poverty Law Center. *101 Tools for Tolerance* is available free from the SPLC. For more information, visit www.splcenter.org or send a fax to (334) 264-7310.; p. 370: "When Meeting Someone with a Disability." Adapted from "Communication Solutions." Used by permission of Progressive Business Publications. p. 372: "Tools for Tolerance: Workplace," adapted from *101 Tools for Tolerance: Simple Ideas for Promoting Equity and Celebrating Diversity.* Copyright © 2000, Southern Poverty Law Center, Montgomery, AL. Reprinted by permission of Southern Poverty Law Center. *101 Tools for Tolerance* is available free from the SPLC. For more information, visit www.splcenter.org or send a fax to (334) 264-7310.; p. 380: "Tools for Tolerance: Community," adapted from *101 Tools for Tolerance: Simple Ideas for Promoting Equity and Celebrating Diversity.* Copyright © 2000, Southern

Poverty Law Center, Montgomery, AL. Reprinted by permission of Southern Poverty Law Center. *101 Tools for Tolerance* is available free from the SPLC. For more information, visit www.splccenter.org or send a fax to (334) 264-7310.

Chapter 16
p. 397: Debra E. Meyerson and Joyce K. Fletcher, "A Modest Manifesto for Shattering the Glass Ceiling," *Harvard Business Review,* January/February 2000, p. 127; p. 400: Aaron Bernstein, Ronald Grover, and Cliff Edwards, "Making Family Leave Family Friendly," *Business Week,* September 30, 2002, p. 44; Sue Shellenbarger, "Shaky Job Market Makes Family Leave Riskier Business," *Wall Street Journal,* August 22, 2001, p. D1; Sue Shellenbarger "A Downside of Taking Family Leave: Getting Fired While You Are Gone," *Wall Street Journal,* January 25, 2003, p. D1; and "The Incredible Shrinking Family Leave: Pressed Bosses Are Cutting Into Time Off," *Wall Street Journal,* October 17, 2002, p. D1.

Chapter 17
p. 421: Gay Jervey, "Workaholics Anonymous," *Fortune,* March 3, 2003, p. 150[A] to 150 to 150[D]; p. 426: "Who Wants to Be a Millionaire?" *San Jose Mercury News,* Weekly Tip; p. 436: Carole Kanchier, "Dare to Change Your Job and Your Life in 7 Steps," *Psychology Today,* March/April 2000, pp. 64-67.

Photo and Cartoon Credits
Chapter 1
p. 3: © Billy E. Barnes/PhotoEdit; p. 5: Don Wright/*The Palm Beach Post;* p. 7: © Tony Freeman/PhotoEdit; p. 20: © AP/Wide World Photos.

Chapter 2
p. 33: © Michael Newman/PhotoEdit; p. 39: © Larry Kolvoord/The Image Works; p. 42: Reprinted with Special Permission of King Features Syndicate; p. © David Burnett (Contact Press Images).

Chapter 3
p. 57: © AP/Wide World Photos; p. 66: © AP/Wide World Photos; p. 70: © Mark Richards/PhotoEdit; p. 75: Bonn Sequenz/Imapress/The Image Works.

Chapter 4
p. 88: © Hulton Archive/Getty Images; p. 90: © Dorothy Littell Greco/The Image Works; p. 91: © The Stuttering Foundation www.stutteringhelp.org; p. 92: © *The New Yorker Collection* 2002 David Sipress from cartoonbank.com. All Rights Reserved; p. 98: © Spencer Grant/PhotoEdit.

Chapter 5
p. 111: © AP/Wide World Photos; p. 116: © Rommel Pecson/The Image Works; p. 117 © The New Yorker Collection 2002 Alex Gregory from cartoonbank.com. All Rights Reserved.; p. 126: From *The Wall Street Journal* – Permission, Cartoon Features Syndicate; p. 127: © Reuters NewsMedia Inc./CORBIS.

Chapter 6
p. 136: © AP/Wide World Photos; p. 139: © AP/Wide World Photos; p. 144: © Peter Hvizdak/The Image Works;

p. 146: From The Wall Street Journal – Permission, Cartoon Features Syndicate; p. 152: Courtesy of Baptist Health Care.

Chapter 7
p. 160: © AP/Wide World Photos; p. 165: © AP/Wide World Photos; p. 169: © Lee Snider/The Image Works; p. 176: From The Wall Street Journal – Permission, Cartoon Features Syndicate.

Chapter 8
p. 187: © Steve Kagan/Getty Images; p. 189: Copyright P. C. Vey, originally appeared in *Harvard Business Review;* p. 193: © Bill Aron/PhotoEdit; p. 196: © Jane Wexler.

Chapter 9
p. 213: © AP/Wide World Photos; p. 215: © Arnold Gold/*New Haven Register*/The Image Works; p. 219: © AP/Wide World Photos; p. 226: Reprinted with Special Permission of King Features Syndicate.

Chapter 10
p. 236: © Greg Betz; p. 239: © Digital Vision/Getty Images; p. 243: From The Wall Street Journal – Permission, Cartoon Features Syndicate; p. 248: David Young-Wolff/PhotoEdit.

Chapter 11
p. 261: Knight Ridder/Tribune Media Services; p. 263: © Dana White/PhotoEdit; p. 270: Wm. Hoest Enterprises, Inc.; p. 272: © Michael Newman/PhotoEdit.

Chapter 12
p. 281: © AP/Wide World Photos; p. 284: © Digital Vision/ Getty Images; p. 294: Center for Creative Leadership.

Chapter 13
p. 307: © AP/Wide World Photos; p. 317: © The New Yorker Collection 2002 David Sipress from cartoonbank.com. All Rights Reserved; p. 320: Photo Courtesy of American Arbitration Association; p. 322: © AP/Wide World Photos.

Chapter 14
p. 331: © Diane Huntress Photography; p. 335: © Jim Sulley/WirePix/The Image Works; p. 342: © The New Yorker Collection 2002 Sam Gross from cartoonbank.com. All Rights Reserved; p. 347: John Kelly/The Image Bank/Getty Images.

Chapter 15
p. 362: © Adam Friedberg; p. 365: © Sonda Dawes/The Image Works; p. 376: © AP/Wide World Photos.

Chapter 16
p. 390: © AP/Wide World Photos; p. 393: © Michael Greenlar/The Image Works; p. 401: © Michael Greenlar/The Image Works.

Chapter 17
p. 419: © The Boston Globe via www.Merlin-Net.com; p. 420 From *The Wall Street Journal*—Permission, Cartoon Features Syndicate; p. 422: Staff photo by Chris Seward/The News & Observer; p. 429: © AP/Wide World Photos.

NAME INDEX

SUBJECT INDEX

SUPPLEMENTS DESIGNED TO AID INSTRUCTORS AND STUDENTS

For Students

Classroom Activities Manual. More than just a study guide, this manual includes practice test questions, self-assessment instruments, role-playing situations, and small group discussion exercises. Each chapter concludes with a journal entry page.

Student Website. This site provides additional tools and links to information that help enhance the concepts presented in the text. Included are:

- the Internet exercises from the text (with updates as necessary)
- links to the companies highlighted in each chapter
- links to sites of general human relations interest
- ACE self-tests

For Instructors

Instructor Website. This password-protected site provides tools to help prepare and deliver lectures. It includes downloadable files from the *Instructor's Resource Manual* and *PowerPoint® slides* that can be edited or used as is.

Instructor's Resource Manual with Test Bank. This manual opens with an overview of teaching and learning methods and principles that facilitate human relations training and includes a description of suggested term projects. *Chapter Teaching Resources* include for every chapter a preview, purpose and perspective, presentation outline, and suggested responses to the questions. *Additional Application Exercises* are included so that the instructor can choose from over 100 exercises in the text and this manual. The *Test Bank* includes true/false, multiple-choice, completion, short answer, essay, and mini-case items for every chapter. Answers and teaching tips for using the *Classroom Activities Manual* are also included. A final section provides a list of *Video Resources* that instructors may use to supplement their course.

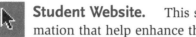